Economic Anthropology

The International Library of Critical Writings in Economics

Series Editor: Mark Blaug

Professor Emeritus, University of London
Professor Emeritus, University of Buckingham
Visiting Professor, University of Exeter

This series is an essential reference source for students, researchers and lecturers in economics. It presents by theme a selection of the most important articles across the entire spectrum of economics. Each volume has been prepared by a leading specialist who has written an authoritative introduction to the literature included.

A full list of published and future titles in this series is printed at the end of this volume.

Wherever possible, the articles in these volumes have been reproduced as originally published using facsimile reproduction, inclusive of footnotes and pagination to facilitate ease of reference.

For a list of all Edward Elgar published titles visit our site on the World Wide Web at
http://www.e-elgar.co.uk

Economic Anthropology

Edited by
Stephen Gudeman
Professor of Anthropology
University of Minnesota, USA

THE INTERNATIONAL LIBRARY OF CRITICAL WRITINGS IN ECONOMICS

An Elgar Reference Collection
Cheltenham, UK • Northampton, MA, USA

Published by
Edward Elgar Publishing Limited
Glensanda House
Montpellier Parade
Cheltenham
Glos GL50 1UA
UK

Edward Elgar Publishing, Inc.
6 Market Street
Northampton
Massachusetts 01060
USA

A catalogue record for this book
is available from the British Library.

Library of Congress Cataloguing in Publication Data

Economic anthropology / edited by Stephen Gudeman.
(The international library of critical writings in economics : 99)
Includes bibliographical references and index.
1. Economic anthropology. I. Gudeman, Stephen. II. Series.
III. Series: An Elgar reference collection.
GN488.E26 1999
306.3—dc21 98–42878
CIP

ISBN 1 85898 759 8

Printed and bound in Great Britain by MPG Books Ltd, Bodmin, Cornwall

Contents

PART II PROCESSES: PRODUCTION

PART III PROCESSES: EXCHANGE

PART IV PROCESSES: SPHERES OF EXCHANGE

Acknowledgements

The editor and publishers wish to thank the authors and the following publishers who have kindly given permission for the use of copyright material.

Academic Press Inc. for excerpt: Allen Johnson (1980), 'The Limits of Formalism in Agricultural Decision Research', in Peggy F. Barlett (ed.), *Agricultural Decision Making: Anthropological Contributions to Rural Development*, Chapter 2, 19–43.

Allen & Unwin, Routledge for excerpt: Fredrik Barth (1964), 'Capital, Investment and the Social Structure of a Pastoral Nomad Group in South Persia', in Raymond Firth and B.S. Yamey (eds), *Capital, Saving and Credit in Peasant Societies*, Chapter 4, 69–81, bibliography.

American Anthropological Association for articles and excerpt: Paul Bohannan (1955), 'Some Principles of Exchange and Investment among the Tiv', *American Anthropologist*, **57**, 60–70; Sidney W. Mintz (1961), 'Pratik: Haitian Personal Economic Relationships', in Viola E. Garfield (ed.), *Symposium: Patterns of Land Utilization and Other Papers: Proceedings of the 1961 Annual Spring Meeting of the American Ethnological Society*, 54–63; Mary Beth Mills (1997), 'Contesting the Margins of Modernity: Women, Migration, and Consumption in Thailand', *American Ethnologist*, **24** (1), 37–61.

Basic Books, a division of HarperCollins Publishers, Inc. for excerpt: Mary Douglas and Baron Isherwood (1978), 'Separate Economic Spheres in Ethnography', in *The World of Goods: Towards an Anthropology of Consumption*, Chapter 7, 131–46, 213.

Paul Bohannan for excerpts: Paul and Laura Bohannan (1968), 'Farms and Produce (*Yiagh*)', in *Tiv Economy*, Chapter 4, 39–64, bibliography; Paul and Laura Bohannan (1968), 'Land Rights: Social Relations in Terrestrial Space', in *Tiv Economy*, Chapter 6, 77–92, bibliography.

Cambridge University Press for article and excerpts: Maurice Godelier (1977), '"Salt Money" and the Circulation of Commodities among the Baruya of New Guinea', in *Perspectives in Marxist Anthropology* (trans. Robert Brain), Chapter 5, 127–51, 233–5; Michael Taussig (1977), 'The Genesis of Capitalism Amongst a South American Peasantry: Devil's Labor and the Baptism of Money', *Comparative Studies in Society and History*, **19** (2), April, 130–55; Igor Kopytoff (1986), 'The Cultural Biography of Things: Commoditization as Process', in Arjun Appadurai (ed.), *The Social Life of Things: Commodities in Cultural Perspective*, Chapter 2, 64–91; Stephen Gudeman and Alberto Rivera (1990), 'The House', in *Conversations in Colombia: The Domestic Economy in Life and Text*, Chapter 3, 39–53, references.

Plenum Publishing Corporation for article: Clifford Geertz (1972), 'The Wet and the Dry: Traditional Irrigation in Bali and Morocco', *Human Ecology*, **1** (1), 23–39.

Routledge for excerpts: Bronislaw Malinowski (1922/1961), 'The Essentials of the Kula', in *Argonauts of the Western Pacific*, Chapter III, 81–104; Mary Douglas and Baron Isherwood (1978), 'Separate Economic Spheres in Ethnography', in *The World of Goods: Towards an Anthropology of Consumption*, Chapter 7, 131–46, 213; Stephen Gudeman (1986), 'Rice and Sugar: Local Models of Change', in *Economics as Culture*, Chapter 1, 1–27, 158, references; Stephen Gudeman (1986), 'Physiocracy: a Natural Economics', in *Economics as Culture*, Chapter 4, 71–89, 159–60, bibliography.

Royal Anthropological Institute of Great Britain and Northern Ireland for articles: Manning Nash (1961), 'The Social Context of Economic Choice in a Small Society', *Man*, **LXI** (219), November, 186–91; Alfred Gell (1982), 'The Market Wheel: Symbolic Aspects of an Indian Tribal Market', *Man* (N.S.), **17** (3), September, 470–91; Caroline Humphrey (1985), 'Barter and Economic Disintegration', *Man* (N.S.), **20** (1), March, 48–72; Jonathan Parry (1986), '*The Gift*, the Indian Gift and the "Indian Gift"', *Man* (N.S.), **21**, 453–73; Keith Hart (1986), 'Heads or Tails? Two Sides of the Coin', *Man* (N.S.), **21** (4), December, 637–56.

Tavistock Publications for excerpts: Marshall D. Sahlins (1965), 'On the Sociology of Primitive Exchange', in Michael Banton (ed.), *The Relevance of Models for Social Anthropology, ASA Monographs I*, 139–86, 225–36; Fredrik Barth (1967), 'Economic Spheres in Darfur', in Raymond Firth (ed.), *Themes in Economic Anthropology*, 149–74.

Stanford University Press and the Board of Trustees of the Leland Stanford Junior University for excerpt: Stuart Plattner (1989), 'Economic Behavior in Markets', in Stuart Plattner (ed.), *Economic Anthropology*, Chapter 8, 209–21, 448–9.

University of Chicago Press for articles: Maurice Godelier (1978), 'Infrastructures, Societies, and History', *Current Anthropology*, **19** (4), December, 763–8, 771; Nurit Bird-David (1992), 'Beyond "The Original Affluent Society": A Culturalist Reformulation', *Current Anthropology*, **33** (1), February, 25–34, 45–7.

Wenner-Gren Foundation for Anthropological Research, Inc. for excerpt: E.R. Leach (1960), 'The Sinhalese of the Dry Zone of Northern Ceylon', in George Peter Murdock (ed.), *Social Structure in Southeast Asia*, (29) Chapter 7, 116–26, bibliography.

Every effort has been made to trace all the copyright holders but if any have been inadvertently overlooked the publishers will be pleased to make the necessary arrangement at the first opportunity.

In addition the publishers wish to thank the Library of the London School of Economics and Political Science, the Marshall Library of Economics, Cambridge University and B&N Microfilm, London for their assistance in obtaining these articles.

Introduction

Stephen Gudeman

Economic anthropologists carry out research in all parts of the globe, producing ethnographic studies, cross-cultural comparisons, and theoretical works. In the earlier part of this century, they focused on 'exotic' groups and rural folk; today they may study how growing markets, new technologies, and expanding capital affect marginalized people or the gender control of wealth. The field has fuzzy edges, however, because economic anthropologists also explore links between material processes and the environment, community maintenance, and cultural values.

The empirical studies of economic anthropology, based on the method of participation and observation, provide an information bank for testing formal theories. These findings often challenge prevailing concepts of modern economics, because much of the collected ethnography falls outside accepted paradigms or schemes. Economists may assume they work within a world whose features are specified by a shared language; disagreements arise about the connections and modeling of variables, and sometimes about their definition or the inclusion of new ones. Anthropologists observe material practices that are very different from their own and often find that these behaviors cannot be directly 'mapped' onto familiar ones. They do presume that the form and meaning of other ways of life can be learned through intensive fieldwork, but the 'translations' also vary, depending on the interpretive scheme, the ethnographer, the context of the study, and the field techniques.

Given the difference in empirical findings and methodologies between the two fields, anthropologists often conclude that the standard assumptions and tools of modern economics are not cross-culturally applicable. For example, ethnographers frequently find that the material values of others cannot be reduced to a singe dimension or measure. As a result, they are cautious about presuming the existence of utility or preference scales, and may not emphasize the centrality of rational choice in material life. Because these and other differences separate ethnographers from economists, anthropology's critical perspective on Western material life and its wisdom is not always well accepted by economists. Yet both fields are enlivened by the other.

For this collection, I have chosen a range of studies that display points of difference and convergence between anthropology and economics. The selections also provide a glimpse of developments in economic anthropology from Malinowski's 1922 study, (Chapter 17), of the Kula exchange in the Trobriand Islands of the Western Pacific – where males pass highly valued armshells and necklaces between groups – to contemporary work on rural to urban migration, consumption, and gender power – as exemplified by Mill's 1997 study, (Chapter 27), of young women in Thailand. In the 75 years separating these two studies, anthropologists have focused on economic *processes*, such as production, exchange, and consumption, and have applied *theories*, such as Marxist, institutionalist, and rational actor or neoclassical explanations. I have arranged the selections by these large categories. But the reader will find that the essays overlap, and they often present contextual information that economists would consider extraneous.

For anthropologists, attention to context is a central part of fieldwork, because the meaning of the verbal categories and actions of a people is tied to their uses. But the content and 'edges' of a context are never predictable, and so field research, marked by exploration and discovery, in many respects is about defining a context and finding an appropriate language to describe it. When anthropologists report their findings, they present a sufficient amount of context so that readers may come to share a common ground with them and the people studied. Anthropologists rarely present deductive works in the style of economists, and most of their studies, while overlapping, do not precisely duplicate, confirm, or disconfirm one another. These differences between the fields – in methods, data, and 'outcomes' – suggest something about the explanatory powers and limits of both. The essay by Johnson, (Chapter 3), discusses these issues, and illustrates why anthropologists sometimes think that formal modeling has limits when applied to real behavior.

Economic anthropology boasts many fine results and insights, and much progress theoretically and in the understanding of economic processes. Its principal discovery is the difference between – what I term – the community and market dimensions of economy. In the market or trading sphere of material life, exchanges are anonymous and socially disarticulated. In the community sphere, material exchanges are connected to social relationships. In the first case, relationships of production or exchange are contractual; in the second, they are carried out through lasting bonds. In one, self-interest and aggrandizement rule exchange; in the other, the morality of shared values guides transactions. The distinction resonates with the difference between use and exchange, embedded and disembedded economies, and incommensurate and commensurate value realms. But I postulate that all economies feature both realms, although their importance varies, and that these two spheres of material life are intertwined in practices and institutions, and as economic sectors. I further presume that the two have a dialectic relationship or a lasting tension with one another. At the individual level, the two sides represent the search for material and social certainty, and the desire for context transcendence and serendipity. One is achieved by sharing communal norms, the other through encountering anonymous others and innovating. Both sides – context stability and context transcendence – infuse material life.

Not all economic anthropologists, and certainly not all economists, agree with this depiction of material life. Theorists who see economy as undergirded by communal norms – the list extends from Aristotle, to Marx, to Polanyi – often elide the market side of the dialectic. For them, anonymous market transactions are a mystification of underlying relationships, a realm of ideology, or a moral degradation. Contemporary market economics in its many forms takes the other side, by presuming that material life and behavior that occurs outside real markets falls outside 'economy' or constitutes an externality that must be priced. For such theorists, carrying out material life by using communal forms that allot resources and allocate products is inefficient, suboptimal or nonrational, and a curtailment of human freedom. My two-sided model, which is supported by nearly a century of ethnographic studies, contests both extreme discourses. Real economies and material practices are a shifting mix of two realms. The essays in this volume, though not explicitly discussing this model of material life, illustrate it one way or another.

Theories

To explain material processes in society, anthropologists use three schools of thought from outside the field – Marxism, substantivism, neoclassical – and have developed one of their own cultural economics. Because the external theories will be known to readers, I have not devoted space to their description, but the reader should know how they inform the studies and have provoked controversies in anthropology.

Many economic anthropologists – consciously and unconsciously – draw on principles of market theory to interpret ethnography. Three selections apply this wisdom. The article by Manning Nash, (Chapter 1), now over 35 years old, presents an exemplary case in which general and shared concepts of modern economics are applied to an ethnographic situation. Examining a small Mayan community in southern Mexico, Nash focuses on the output of pottery by individual households. He assumes that economic units are rational and attempt to maximize returns. But output throughout the year is irregular, for it varies with the communal festal cycle and the season, both of which determine demand. Pottery output per household also varies by the unpaid labor the unit commands (workers are never paid a wage; all returns flow to the household). Finally, output varies by a household's cash needs which have an inverse relationship to the amount of land and size of cattle herd it controls; households that 'maximize' pottery output are principally ones who command fewer resources.

At a larger level, shared values hold together the households of the village, and all are subject to leveling mechanisms that drain large increments of wealth differentiating one from another.

Nash offers a picture with micro- and macro-dimensions. Households attempt to maximize returns given the resources they control. But this drive is constrained by the macro-order made up of religious and social values. Nash does not explain why or how the larger macro-order persists, and so the macro- and micro-orders seem to contradict each other. If actors are rational, as Nash claims, then the normative order should dissolve through rational choice; but if the macro-order is an outcome of individual preferences, then how explain these preferences that do not fit the desire to maximize output and returns? None the less, the analysis implies that economic development depends on ridding the culture of impinging social forms or frictions, such as religious offices that drain accumulated wealth or witchcraft beliefs and practices that enforce the leveling mechanisms, and establishing a free market so that labor may efficiently move between households.

The selection by Stuart Plattner, (Chapter 2), written nearly 30 years after Nash, employs the same premises of rational actors and maximization. But Plattner also looks at personal connections within market transactions. Nash considered social norms and values to be external constraints on the expression of rationality, whereas Plattner – following recent developments in economics – argues that lasting social bonds in trading relationships reduce risk (and are rational). Drawing on contemporary ideas about limited information and undeveloped legal mechanisms, Plattner embraces the 'new institutionalism' in which rational choice is extended to explain features of the social realm.

For many anthropologists, however, this type of analysis is reductionistic and represents a form of methodological individualism. They would argue that such a perspective cannot account for cultural variation, that social relationships are being seen as calculated contracts rather than moral commitments, and that the social realm escapes discussion. As in the example from Nash, a hiatus separates the macro and the micro, or community and market spheres, and the explanation is limited to one dimension.

A critique and discussion of standard economics is offered by Allen Johnson, (Chapter 3), who provides a sophisticated example of formal modeling in economic anthropology. He contrasts this modeling, largely of a deductive sort, with empirical results from fieldwork. Sympathetic to both sides, Johnson implicitly suggests that the value of formal modeling is limited in ethnographic situations due to uncertainty or lack of knowledge so that the limits of modeling are set by the limits of a knowledge system. Going beyond this knowledge frontier is partly what field anthropology is all about.

In the 1960s and 1970s, Marxism influenced economic anthropology in a variety of ways. One influential Marxist writer has been Maurice Godelier who, in the selection provided, (Chapter 4), summarizes many years of his thought. Aware of the problem of applying concepts, such as 'forces of production' to complex ethnographic forms, Godelier uses Marxist ideas in a supple way. Drawing together both an anthropological and Marxist approach, he also relies on the (often criticized) notion of social function.

Michael Taussig, (Chapter 5), uses Marxist thought in a very different way when he considers the development of ideology, ritual and fetishism among Latin American peasants. He suggests that peasants emerging from a communal formation develop ritual forms and 'money fetishism' in response to their initial encounter with market capitalism. Though cast in a Marxist vein, the argument hinges on the division between community and market to which I draw attention. Taussig's observations raise the question whether the dialectic of community and market occurs only in Western discourse, in ethnography, or both. (See also Taussig's later discussion in *Comparative Studies in Society and History*, 1995, **37** (2), April.)

Many anthropologists have been influenced by the work of Karl Polanyi, the economic historian. Polanyi tried to develop what he called 'substantivist' economics (as opposed to 'formalist' economics of the market). In fact, he offered a form of institutionalism, though it differed from Veblen's. Polanyi argued that in some economies, material life is 'embedded' in social relationships rather than 'disembedded' and carried out by market transactions. He further proposed that in embedded economies, relationships of reciprocity and redistribution – rather than contract and anonymous trade – are the principal ways of circulating goods. The influence of Polanyi may be seen in many of the essays, especially the studies by Paul Bohannan on 'spheres of exchange', (Chapter 22) and Marshall Sahlins on 'primitive exchange', (Chapter 6). Both show how exchange is embedded in social relationships, as Polanyi argued.

Like most anthropologists, Polanyi was deeply influenced by Malinowski's study of the Kula exchange, which is the classic example of reciprocity; anthropologists also have been swayed by Marcel Mauss's slim volume, *The Gift* (1990 [1950]) that was first published shortly after Malinowski's study. In his essay, Jonathan Parry, (Chapter 7), provides a sophisticated review and critique of Mauss's work and of its theoretical impact in the last fifty years.

A fourth approach in economic anthropology recently emerged, when ethnographers, influenced by Clifford Geertz and Sahlins, applied the concept of culture to material life. What would it mean, they asked, to develop a cultural economics? What if material life is culturally constituted and not governed by natural laws? I apply this idea, (Chapter 8), that the economy is culturally constructed to the written work of an early Western school of economists, the Physiocrats, to suggest that a cultural approach may be brought to bear on Western models as well as others. In a different selection, (Chapter 9), Alberto Rivera and I analyze household economies in the highlands of Colombia as functioning cultural models. Nurit Bird-David, (Chapter 10), subsequently shows how the material life of hunters and foragers is best understood through a cultural perspective; she also applies this understanding to an influential theoretical statement by Sahlins (1972) who had argued that hunters and foragers are 'affluent' not because they have high output but because their wants are limited and they need to work only a short time to satisfy them. Finally, the comparative study on irrigation by Clifford Geertz, (Chapter 14), and the essay on consumption by Mary Douglas and Baron Isherwood, (Chapter 26), also show how material practices can be analysed in terms of local culture.

Processes

I have divided the processes of material life into the categories of production, exchange, spheres of exchange, market, and consumption. But the studies in each overlap and illustrate the complex interlocking of the community and trade realms in material life.

Production

In his fine study of nomads in Persia (Iran), Fredrik Barth, (Chapter 11), uses categories of analysis familiar to economists; stocks and flows, technological constraints, saving, and the impact of the life cycle on capital accumulation. He shows as well how sedentary and pastoral ways of life are connected. At the theoretical level, readers may wish to note how Barth distinguishes between economy and social structure to show how they interact; but for Barth, social structure is not a realm for carrying out material life apart from real economic or market processes.

The two selections from Paul Bohannan and Laura Bohannan, (Chapters 12 and 13), provide a picture of traditional farming in West Africa and show how agricultural land is allocated as a community possession. Access to the productive resource is a right of lineage membership, and though rent is never paid, lineage duties must be fulfilled to secure rights of usufruct. These articles show how a community economy controls resources, yet the resources are separately used, and individuals may build up differential accumulations of wealth. Displaying a substantivist or institutionalist influence, the studies also show how the two realms of economy are brought into play at local levels.

In his comparative study of irrigation in Bali and Morocco, Geertz, (Chapter 14), illustrates how water rights can be very differently managed in community and market systems. In one case (Bali), communities control irrigation systems through ritual regulations while allowing individual use of water; in the other (Morocco), market control and private ownership of water rights are regulated through a communal or shared legal and contractual system. (The two systems are linked to very different ecological settings as well.)

Edmund Leach's detailed study, (Chapter 15), of irrigation in Northern Ceylon (Sri Lanka) provides a picture of the way a community (in this case a subcaste) controls joint water and land rights, yet individuals within the subcaste manipulate their holdings through strategic marriages and use of the inheritance system. Within the community framework, there is room for aggrandizement and self-interest, a kind of contained market.

Finally, my study of rice and sugar-cane in Panama, (Chapter 16), shows how a peasantry moved from raising a domestic crop by shifting (or slash-and-burn) agriculture to planting a semi-permanent market crop. The people's changing ideas about private property, rent, value, commensuration, and profit illustrate how forces of modernization are experienced at the local level, changing a community to a market economy.

Exchange

No topic has so engaged economic anthropologists as exchange. In an important reconsideration of Bronislaw Malinowski's Trobriand ethnography, (Chapter 17), Keith Hart (Chapter 18), argues that money is two-sided. Issued and secured by a state (the community), money can be exchanged with anyone for anything (in the market). He applies this dialectical notion to fish transactions in the Trobriands, for fish can be exchanged through the Kula or by individual barter. The form used depends on whether or not an encompassing political order is present. Individual barter takes place only within larger, existing social relationships, whereas Kula transactions make or construct these ties. Trobriand Islanders, he argues, shift between the two modes as political and material conditions change.

The study of barter by Caroline Humphrey, (Chapter 19), offers a critique of the standard idea that barter historically precedes the use of money. She shows that barter arises when confidence in the monetary system fails: there is a breakdown of community. Barter also may or may not take place in the context of a larger measurement system or numeraire; it seems to straddle the frontier between a system in which values of goods and services are commensurate (the market) and one in which they are incommensurate (community), and cannot be reduced to a single scale or ranking. On this view, barter is both a community and market exchange.

These same issues are taken up by Godelier, (Chapter 20), in his study of salt money among the Baruya of New Guinea. Within the Baruya community, salt is produced, then shared and distributed according to need. Baruya also trade with neighboring groups, and in this realm the value of salt is a function of supply and demand. Both community and market theory seem to apply. The contradiction is dissolved when it is seen that community economy principles apply within the group, whereas market principles obtain between groups, and the two are set in a delicate, if not dialectical, balance. This distinction between in-group (community) and out-group (market) transactions, and their dissonant if not dialectical connection, has been encountered by other ethnographers in New Guinea and elsewhere, and was long ago discussed by Aristotle, which suggests its generality across cultures. (For an earlier and more complete version of this article see Godelier, (1971), '"Salt Currency" and the Circulation of Commodities among the Baruya of New Guinea' in George Dalton (ed.), *Studies in Economic Anthropology*, Chapter 4, Washington: American Anthropological Association.)

Igor Kopytoff's essay, (Chapter 21), on the way that goods can serve as both commodities and noncommodities rounds out this section. He develops the distinction between use and exchange by suggesting it be seen as a continuum, and that goods may serve both as noncommodities and commodities. In fact, material things often have a life cycle with commodity and noncommodity periods. At one time, they may be 'singularities' – or components of a plural value system – at another they may be commodities measured against an agreed value scale. Social contexts determine their shifting meanings.

Spheres of Exchange

In his study of exchange and investment among the Tiv, Bohannan, (Chapter 22), provides the classic description of *spheres of exchange* by which an economy is divided into distinct exchange circuits: goods circulate against one another within a sphere and infrequently cross between them. The spheres are socially ranked so that when exchanges do occur between them, they are morally charged with one party gaining and the other losing social position. The existence of spheres of exchange belies the view that an economy consists of a seamless market in which all things are considered to be commensurate and may be exchanged against one another. It shows how community morality structures markets, and raises the possibility that similar spheres may exist in industrial society (body parts, blood, kinship relationships). Again, the interplay between market (trade within spheres) and community (transactions between them) provides the implicit theoretical framework.

Barth, (Chapter 23), uses the idea of spheres of value to examine the relation between subsistence and market production among the Fur of the Sudan. In recent years, the possibilities for raising and selling crops have expanded. Barth shows how a few entrepreneurs have taken advantage of the differences in value between the communal and trade spheres, and reaped profits through arbitrage. By joining the two spheres in new ways, entrepreneurs can draw on the resources of the community realm of economy – depleting some of its ability to sustain itself – in order to secure a monetary gain. As in the case of the Tiv, sustained market expansion leads to the collapse of the spheres of value.

Markets

Anthropologists have long been interested in market practices and systems – from the micro-behavior of trading to the macro-framework of regional and world markets. Sidney Mintz' early study, (Chapter 24), of women's marketing in Haiti presents one of the important themes and puzzles: the presence of enduring bonds between buyers and sellers within large, anonymous, competitive markets. Such arrangements, often termed 'trade partnerships', have been found in many societies, and are akin to trading diasporas and ethnic monopolies. What anthropologists term 'ceremonial exchange' – in which normal trade is carried out at the same time as elaborate non-utilitarian exchanges (such as the Kula) – constitutes a similar form, and poses a similar theoretical problem. How are we to understand and model these cases that mix sociality and competitive price-making? From a market perspective, or drawing on the new institutionalism (as in the case of the Plattner reading), the social bond can be seen as a rational response when there is heightened risk due to lack of product information, contract laws, shared values, or a developed infrastructure. A more dialectical understanding is presented by Hart who argues that ceremonial exchange and regular trade, as alternatives, depend on the emergence or withering of a larger political structure. My view is that all exchanges are two-sided and that the social bond – whether expressed by ties of a common language, shared values and laws, common identity, or an enduring personal relationship such as Mintz reports – cannot be reduced to, or explained as, the result of a risk calculation. Markets are never *sui generis* but in complex ways – not yet fully explored – implicate, generate and draw on ties of human sociality in order to function.

In his study of a rural market in India, Alfred Gell (Chapter 25), provides both a sociological and cultural analysis, combines a community and market perspective, and draws on findings from many earlier market studies. He shows how the spatial layout of the marketplace reproduces social categories; how higher valued transactions occur at its center; how wealth, ethnicity and caste are implicated in the physical arrangements; and how within this welter of social forms, self-interested and anonymous trade also takes place. At the same time, outside the physical marketplace, individual traders make use of pre-existing social relationships when they trade and decide whether to offer credit to buyers. This study again suggests that anonymous trade and markets always require the structure and certainty afforded by community or sociality, as represented by the way space is arranged in the marketplace or by the social relationships that allow trade relations to occur outside it.

Consumption

In recent years, anthropologists have increasingly turned to processes of *consumption* in industrialized and nonindustrialized societies. Douglas and Isherwood, (Chapter 26), use the idea of economic spheres to argue that consumption provides information about social position and power. High valued goods, such as paintings, are exchanged infrequently but in a public context involving large social units. Low value goods, such as ordinary foods, are exchanged frequently and in the context of small social units. In the view of Douglas and Isherwood, goods convey information about status and power so that consumption has to do with controlling commodities and sending messages to others.

Finally, in a recent article, Mary Beth Mills, (Chapter 27), examines connections among modernization, consumption, gender, migration, and the expansion of the transglobal market in Thailand. She shows how women are not simply low paid laborers who produce goods for international markets but active and conflicted participants in struggles over identity. For example, traditional religious ceremonies and processions may become consumption displays as women are pulled between ties linking them to local communities and to the city. This article suggests some of the ethnographic contexts and theoretical problems that economic anthropologists will face in the years to come just as all the studies represent a small sample of a vibrant, challenging and growing field.

References

Mauss, Marcel, ((1990)[1923–1924]) *The Gift: the form and reason for exchange in archaic societies*, trans. W.D. Halls. London: Routledge.

Sahlins, Marshall, (1972) *Stone Age Economics*. Chicago: Aldine.

Part I
Theories

[1]

THE SOCIAL CONTEXT OF ECONOMIC CHOICE IN A SMALL SOCIETY*

by

DR. MANNING NASH

University of Chicago

219 The distinctions between complex, monetized and civilized societies and the small-scale, non- or partially monetized peasant and primitive societies in economic life are startling, deeply rooted and easily apparent. These distinctions have frequently been laid to a special rationale of economic choice in small-scale non-Western societies. Boeke (1947, p. 2) finds a cleavage so deep between the small-scale economy and the capitalistic organization of economic life that a new name is needed, and he suggests 'oriental economics' to account for the workings of non-Western economies. Polanyi (1957, pp. 46f.) sees the essential difference in the 'absence of a motive of gain' from peasant and primitive societies, and of course from Maine onward there is a literature which claims that peasant values subordinate economic activity to social ends. It is the contention of this paper that the rationale of economic choice in peasant society follows the same general rule of maximization as economic activity does anywhere, at any time. What is distinctive about peasant and primitive societies are not the habits of mind about advantage, nor an inability to calculate costs and benefits of a course of action, nor even an absence of a motive of gain; but rather the possession of a set of concrete social organizations which directly channel economic choice, on the one hand, and a set of sanctions which operate to keep economic deviants in physical as well as moral jeopardy on the other. A corollary of this contention is that debate of rules of choice or abstract principles of economic organization will be barren and lead only to a 'spectral dance of bloodless categories,' to the profusion of empty boxes of theory; while the emphasis on the stipulation of the economic consequences of concrete social structures will generate an empirically powerful body of middle-range theory.

By an examination of the economy of peasant Indians in the state of Chiapas, Mexico,[1] I hope to show how the structure and membership criteria of production units limit maximization; how the level and rhythm of output are consequences of the ceremonial cycle; and how notions of witchcraft and the supernatural combine to keep wealth from being used for economic ends and thus contribute to the steady state of small, reduplicative, productive units with little interest in, or incentive for, technological or social innovation.

In south-eastern Chiapas, Tzeltal- and Tzotzil-speaking Indians are the predominant population. These Indians live in communities whose general characteristics are familiar from work done with neighbouring highland Maya in Guatemala (Tax, 1937). One Tzeltal community is that of Amatenango de Valle. Amatenango is a *municipio* (the administrative unit of Mexico, like a township, but tending to coincide with an Indian society in highland Chiapas and Guatemala) situated just off the Pan-American Highway some 44 kilometres south of the region's largest Mexican city. Amatenango, for an Indian community, has a reputation for wealth and independence. Its people call themselves *Tzontajal*; they wear a distinct costume; their mode of speech is dialectically distinct from neighbouring Tzeltal-speaking communities; they are nearly endogamous; they have economic skills not shared by neighbours; a local civil administration; a local set of sacred officials, and a particular calendar of sacred and secular festivals. They are a corporate community (Wolf, 1954), united by blood and custom, living on their own territory, with an ethnic distinctiveness which sets them apart in their minds, and in fact, from their Indian neighbours and the superordinate communities of Mexicans which surround them.

Amatenango makes its living by cultivating the soil, by cattle-raising, and by producing pottery. The technology of agriculture is on a relatively low level. The ox-drawn plough, the machete, the digging stick, the sickle and a net bag make up the tool kit. A simple irrigation system of ditching serves some of the land, and the watered lands are rotated between milpa crops (corn beans, squash) and a wheat cash crop. Fertilizer is not used. Soil-nutrient is added only by the burning of corn or wheat stubble and leaving the ash, or by turning animals loose in the fields after harvest. Seed-selection is not rigorous. And as in most peasant agriculture the vicissitudes of wind, rain, frost and sun make for wide swings in the annual harvest. Famine, or even real hunger, however, is not part of Amatenango experience, except in the days when the warring factions of the Mexican revolution swept through the region and disrupted life and devastated agriculture. The agricultural complex also includes garden plots near house sites, as distinct from field lands. Garden plots are used for some milpa, but their chief economic significance lies in the growing of *chayote*, a squash-like plant, and its root which are sold to other communities. The maguey plants, lima and avocado tree and some fruit trees supply domestically used produce. The agricultural complex is part of a system of regional interdependence based on ecological and traditional differences. Nearby communities specialize in other products, and there is a lively exchange of agricultural products between Amatenango, its neighbours and the nearby coastal 'hot' lands. The interpretation of the agricultural complex seems simple enough: ecological specialization on the base of natural resources combined

* *With three text figures*

with special agricultural skills and knowledge. The actual distribution of agricultural specialities results from the operation of comparative advantage over a long stretch of time.

Insight into the economic dynamics of the community and of the region may be had more clearly through the industrial rather than the agricultural organization of Amatenango. Agriculture does not, by itself, maintain Amatenango at its expected level of living. The making and selling of pottery is an important component in the meeting of the customary standard of life. Of the 280 households in the town centre of Amatenango (the peripheries of the community were recently settled either by Indians uprooted from other communities, or by poor Mexicans, and pose a special problem for social analysis) only two or three are not engaged in the production of pottery for sale. Pottery-making is a community specialization, not an individual skill. It is part of the socialization process for women in Amatenango. All women who are born and grow up in Amatenango know how to, and do, make pots. The striking nature of the community specialization comes home forcibly when it is observed that an adjoining community with virtually the same natural resources as Amatenango does not produce one single pot, and that in a region nearly 40 miles long and 30 across, there is no other Indian pottery-making community, although a few pottery-makers are scattered elsewhere in the region. In short, in a regionally diversified marketing area, only the people of Amatenango produce salable pottery, and all of the women produce it. The technique does not spread to other Indian communities, whatever the abstract profitability of such diffusion might be, because making pottery is part of a way of life, learned in the informal, intimate setting in which the basic parts of culture are acquired, and not a technique of production to be acquired by whoever sees the main chance.

Although women are the makers of pottery in Amatenango, pottery is not considered, and is not, strictly a woman's product. Men bring most of the firewood necessary for the firing of the pottery, and men take the pottery to the points of sale (now by bus and truck passage, but formerly on horseback), but the packing of pots in grass-padded net bags is still an arduous task. Pottery requires male and female co-operation, and single women make pots only if they live in a household with male members, or have male relatives who are willing to aid in the work.

The technology of pottery-making is simple and inexpensive. As the skills come to the women potters in the process of being socialized (there are, however, some women who do not know how to make the more specialized pottery like incense-burners and perforated pots, and 'on order' pottery sold exclusively to *Ladinos*, as the non-Indians are called, is made by very few families) and so provide every household with the art, so the technology, in terms of skill and materials, is within the reach of even the poorest household in the community. Pottery is a hand industry. No wheel, no mould, no oven are required. The shaping hand of the female potter, the open street firing of the ware, the slipping and decorating are ingenious skills, but technologically simple. Not even purchased, non-indigenous materials are necessary in pottery-production. The clay, the temper, the pigment, the scraping stone, the wood used in firing, the net bags used in packing, all come from communal resources and are open to every member of Amatenango equally. No payment or special permission is needed to use these resources. Community membership gives free (but not costless, since labour is involved) access to the materials of pottery-making. If one purchases part of the equipment (a steel blade for scraping, a smooth board for resting pot bases, a burlap bag or skirt under the potter's knees, nets, bags) the cost is under three dollars, and every household has that at its disposal.

There exists wide variations in the output of different pottery-making households. Estimating the range of variation in output and finding the reasons for output differences is, in a preliterate culture, a difficult task. In one household a daily record covering the entire annual production was obtained, and in three other households lesser periods, ranging from one to four months, were recorded. This information is supplemented by observations on pottery-making in several dozen households, and was checked against the complete field census of the community, so that the typicality of the sample can be judged. At any rate, the problem of measuring the gross community output of pottery was not the major research interest (though a reasoned and plausible estimate could be constructed from the data in hand). The problem was to assess the limits of output variability and to pin these down to a set of factors which were the determinants of production. The determinants of production would, when checked by micro-comparison between households in the community, indicate the 'controlling mechanism' regulating the pottery industry, and by extension the economic life of the community.

Fig. 1 is a composite of the production of one of the most intensive pottery-producing households in the community. An inspection of this figure (the special ware represents pottery made only in a few households, the dash line is commonly but not universally made ware, and the solid is pottery made in all households) shows that pottery-making tends to reach its peak just before the major festive occasions in the community and in surrounding communities. This is explicable in terms of the nature of the ecological market situation. Pottery-making is a cash-raising activity. Ware is sold in an impersonal, free market with prices set by the interaction of supply and demand. The festal occasions are the times when Amatenangueros need money; they are also the periods when the largest demand from visitors to a local fiesta may be expected, so producers reach a maximum of output just prior to the festal times of heavy buying and selling. Production is maximized not at the time of highest prices on the market, but rather in time with the rhythm of sacred and secular celebration which require cash outlay and provide opportunities for disposal without storage problems.

The peaks reached for fiestas are not of the same height. Two things operate here: the size or local importance of

No. 219 *MAN* November, 1961

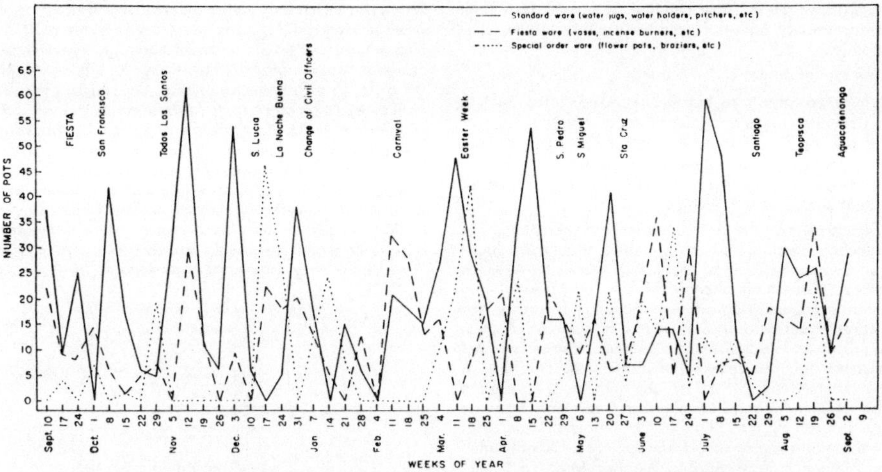

Fig. 1. Annual production in household 13 (4 women producers, no children)

the given fiesta and whether it falls in the rainy or dry seasons. In the rainy months (from June to September, but heaviest from late July to mid September) less pottery is made than in the dry sunny times of the year. However, in January and February, dry sunny months, there is high wind which complicates the drying of pottery (because the pottery must be kept under leaves to keep moisture in it until it is ready for firing) and hence output is reduced. The general pattern of seasonal flux is common to all households, and so is the peak and trough pattern of production along with fiestas.

While fig. 1 establishes the rhythm of pottery-production common to the society by virtue of its technology and annual cycle, fig. 2 compares the differences in level of production among three households. Household No. 6 outproduces No. 4, and No. 13 outproduces both No. 6 and No. 14 (the numbers refer to a genealogical map and census of the community which is not here included). Each of the households is differently constituted in numbers of potters in it. Household No. 13 has four potters (two young women, one middle-aged and one old). Household No. 6 has two potters (one young and one middle-aged woman) and No. 14 has two potters (one young and one middle-aged). Therefore the sheer number of hands which can be mustered in No. 13 is greater and helps explain its greater output. Furthermore No. 14 and No. 6 have small children under three years of age in the household, and No. 13 does not. Child care and household maintenance compete with pottery-making for a woman's time, so the small child is a further brake on production in these two households.

Inspection of fig. 2 shows that four women produce more than twice as much as do two women (even adjusting for children). Part of this is an 'economy of scale.' Pottery-production has some assembly-line aspects. Women work on a part of a pot, making bases, then they turn to making bodies, then to making necks, and finally to putting handles on the pot. Between these operations the pots are partially dried. If there are four women, the division of labour is better, and relative efficiency of the producing unit rises. Beyond four, not much increase occurs. But the differences in output between No. 6 and No. 14 are such that sheer numbers of hands will not serve as an explanation, and the factors of relative efficiency, or of skill, are so nearly matched in these households, that it does not really enter as a factor in the account of output differences. Explanation must be sought in the wider economic setting of the productive unit.

If all of the households in the community were ranked in terms of the major source of wealth—land at the disposal of the household—an immediate connexion would be noted between the wealth of the household and its level of output. The motivation to work at the top of the bent is stronger in poorer households, because alternative sources of income are less, and more of the family's subsistence must come from pottery-making. Land, of course, needs men to work it, and household No. 13 has but one old man, and he cannot work much land, nor lay claim to government-grant lands (*ejido*) of any considerable size. In richer households (in terms of land and cattle owned) there is sufficient milpa raised to ensure that corn need not be bought, and the need for continuous cash income is not so pressing. This also has a circular effect: richer households tend to be able to keep more children alive; with more children to care for, women devote less time to pottery. Conversely poorer households depend upon pottery income, have fewer living children, and hence have both the opportunity and the need to produce almost continuously.

The rate of output is determined on two levels:

(1) that common to the whole society (technology, resources, seasons and ceremonial cycle);

(2) the organization and wealth differences among producing units (number of women, number of children under three, number of men, and amount of land and cattle owned).

To understand why the second level of determinants of production continues to be operative, involves a move from the micro-structural analysis of producing units, to the macro-structural analysis of the whole social and economic organization of Amatenango. It moves the question from that of incentives and motivations of actors and producers to the plane of the structural sources of and constraints upon incentives and motivation. The units of production are households, and the households are kinship units. As a kinship unit, membership comes only by being born or marrying into the unit. The household unit, with its kinship of recruitment, sets the size of the 'labour force' available for pottery-making. No one hires out to do pottery for wages, since pottery-making is only part of a woman's job as a member of a household (and even if a wage were paid it could not cover all activities and still yield anything to an employer). Amatenango's kinship system is one of nearly perfectly balanced bilateralism. A combination of personal tastes and wealth of the household determines whether a married couple will live with his or her parents. Wealthier households can attract either sons-in-law or daughters-in-law to live with them, and have a slightly larger labour force potential. But the absence of wage labour in a household production system limits any given unit's ability to expand pottery activities. Expected, and, of course observed, is the common feature of peasant economic organization, a multiplicity of small reduplicative, productive units, with no tendency toward agglomeration or centralization. Furthermore, since pottery-production is household-organized, many activities compete with it for the time of the same set of personnel. Economic activities are but one field in which maintenance needs are met. Internal family social relations, the socialization of members, sickness and curing, religious activity, social status, and dispute settlement are tasks partly centred in the family, and in household organization. Economic activity, be it in the market, field, or handicraft, is a means to implement and provide facilities for other aspects of household activity. It is not an instance of conflicting standards when a woman with small children stops pottery-making, but rather a case of clear priorities.

This bears on an analogy sometimes used by anthropologists when a household is compared to a firm (Tax, 1952). A household may be conceived of as a unit trying to maximize, given its resources and personnel. The analogy is misleading, not on the grounds of the kind of *rules* of allocation, but on the nature of the social structures involved. Firms are special organizations for economic activity in societies of highly differentiated structure based on complex technology, extensive social division of labour, large numbers of people, and deliberate, continual technical and economic innovation. Firms may or may not follow the rule of income-maximization depending upon the larger social structure (*viz.* the firm in the Soviet economy and the firm in the United States economy). But in peasant and primitive societies like Amatenango the context of economic choice is a multi-purposed social organization, which, unlike a firm, cannot liquidate if it makes poor calculations. Households, or more precisely the members of them, in Amatenango are as acutely aware as we are of relative costs and are keenly sensitive to economic gain. When marketing their pottery they go to Las Casas, or

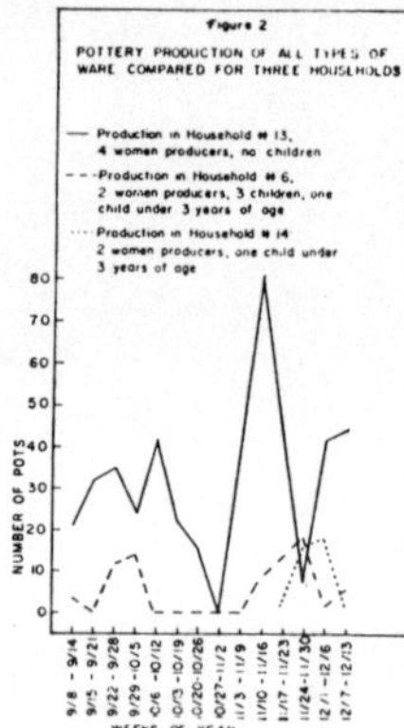

FIG. 2. POTTERY-PRODUCTION OF THREE HOUSEHOLDS

Comitán, or Las Rosas, or other points of sale in accord with price differentials. They closely question men returning from the various places as to prevailing prices and act accordingly. Price is on every tongue and is a topic of unending interest. Amatenangueros are 'rational' economic actors in the sense of bringing means and ends together, only their ends are values other than (or in addition to) maximization of a given single magnitude. The formal convergence of rules of choice in a household and in a firm does not lead to similar social arrangements or similar social consequences simply because the organization of personnel, resources and methods of role-recruitment form a different social structure.

The households, of course, form a social system. And the social system operates so that households orient to the prevailing value system, on the one hand, and remain fairly equivalent in wealth, on the other. Fig. 3 gives a land-distribution chart based upon the informant's self-reported wealth (it does not include the two *tablones* of government land which most family heads have granted to them). This suffers from underestimation and deliberate concealment of assets, but serves to approximate the *shape* of the real distribution of land. Land is the best index to wealth. The features of social life which account for the shape of the curve, and the position of any given family at a point on the curve can be conceptualized as a levelling mechanism (Nash, 1958, 1959). Levelling mechanisms are ubiquitous devices in peasant economies in this region (Wolf, 1954). Not only do they ensure a 'democracy of poverty' but they serve to inhibit economic expansion of any given unit within the society under the threat of expulsion or sacral retribution. The levelling mechanism rests first on the absolute level of wealth in the community. Amatenango's low-level technology and its restricted land base impose severe limits on the wealth of the society as a whole, and for households and individuals

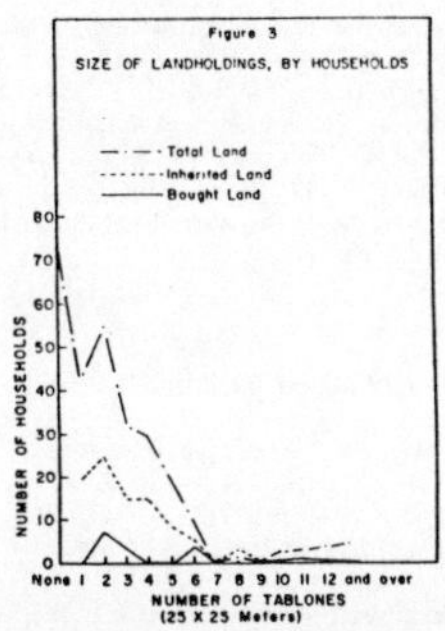

FIG. 3. SIZE OF LANDHOLDINGS

a correspondingly low level. No household is so rich that the sceptre of poverty is not a real possibility in the wake of long illness or a sustained run of bad luck. Given a relatively low level of absolute wealth, the inheritance mechanism tends to fracture such estates as are accumulated. In Amatenango inheritance is bilateral, with equal inheritance for all the offspring (although there are prerogatives of women in inheriting houses and house sites, and of men in receiving horses and cattle). The process of inheritance scrambles land-holdings among sons and daughters even before death of the head of a household. However, fig. 3 shows a skewed land-distribution, and this is a necessary part of Amatenango's social organization. The important point is that the rich, or large land-holders, change from generation to generation, and if the technical and economic levelling factors do not inhibit accumulation of wealth or capital, there are social means for ensuring that wealth does not adhere to family lines. There are a series of offices in which a man (as a representative of a family) must serve. This hierarchy of civil and religious offices is a drain on work time and uses up some of the resources of the household. Its offices are unpaid, and since a man must serve in 12 such offices before he is relieved of communal service, they are a continuing cost all through his adult, productive life.

Another social mechanism reducing accumulation is the institution of the *Alférez*. The Alférez office, of which there are four to be filled every year, is a ritual and sacred office filled by a younger man. The cost of this office is, in terms of Amatenango's wealth, exorbitant. An Alférez expends more than the annual income of even the richest Amatenanguero in feasting a group of neighbours, relatives and officers of the hierarchy, in the great consumption of liquor and the renting of the special costumes. Before the Alférez feasts weeks of preparation for it occupy the household. Woman make pottery to use for the cooking of the larger amounts of special food, as well as pottery for sale. Men of the household spend their time making liquor in the hills near Amatenango, and chopping wood for the firing of pits and cooking of foods. They also make extra trips to sell pottery. Members of the bilateral kindred come in to aid in the pottery-making and liquor-distilling. Undertaking the post of Alférez leaves the family in reduced straits and with depleted assets.

Alfereces are selected by the officials of the civil and religious hierarchy, and the selection is almost strictly on ability to pay. The eligible households are few in number, and are those on the right-hand side of fig. 3. Richer households have a levy placed against them in consequence of their prosperity. In a community like Amatenango it is nearly impossible to conceal one's wealth—the cows and horses owned are visible, and the land cultivated is public knowledge, and the health of one's children is a reliable index of it. Strong negative sanctions—witchcraft, gossip and envy—would be consequent on a refusal to accept the post of Alférez when it was proferred. These things together—(1) low level of technology and limited land, (2) fracture of estate by bilateral inheritance, (3) expenditure of time and resources in communal office, (4) forced expenditure in ritual by the wealthy—combine to keep the fortunes of the various households nearly equivalent, and to maintain the shift of family fortunes throughout time. In addition, the business of marrying is expensive and uses household resources. Nobody gains goods in exchanges like marriage payment, or Alférez feasts or payments for dispute-settlement. The use of liquor as the medium of payment—the completely consumable good—precludes accumulation.

Not only are households in a situation where maximization of an output or income dimension is unfeasible because of their social structure, but should a given household decide on the course of maximization or be lucky or exceedingly skilled in its economic operations, the 'levelling mechanism' comes into play to minimize differences. In short, Amatenango presents a socio-economy where wealth is not easily turned to technical and economic uses, but is drained by the social and religious constitution of the culture.

Behind, and sanctioning, the social and religious organization of Amatenango is a pervasive system of belief in witchcraft. Witchcraft befalls those who violate the norms of familial and household harmony, who do not get along with neighbours, who are rich but not generous, who refuse communal obligations, who become outstanding in

NOVEMBER, 1961 MAN Nos. 219, 220

some dimension which violates the corporate nature of the community or upsets its tendency to economic homogeneity. Amatenangueros do not formulate the principles of witchcraft in this manner, but they behave as if their actions were governed by these premises. Witchcraft as a working means of sanctioning behaviour is not an easy thing to live with, and at least one man is killed every two months for being a practitioner of witchcraft. But the tension between economic expansion and social coercion is apparently not so strong that the system appears in immediate or even remote danger of falling under its own weight.

The economy of Amatenango, like the rest of the social structure, shows little dynamism, and change and innovation are not by-products of economic activity, as they are in the 'developed' industrial societies. The simple technology, the absence of literary skills, the shortage of capital, the lack of credit all help to explain this fact. But the social and cultural basis of Amatenango's indifference to finding means to economic change depends upon the twin facts of household organization of production and the social and religious system of witchcraft which inhibits accumulation and prevents the discovery or utilization of economic opportunity. No one can run the risks of wide economic differentials, and even if the risks were taken, membership in the community would require investment in social relations, not economic ones. Amatenango presents the paradox of a community whose market economy makes it aware of economic calculation and relative costs and benefits, but a social structure and value system which channels economic choice toward economic stability and social continuity. Communities like Amatenango develop in the face of great economic pressure from the superordinate society, or *via* the extension of economic links with persons and social systems in which the rules of choice and values, and organizations are congruent with sustained ability to seize or make economic opportunity.

In small-scale societies like Amatenango, the facts of interconnexion of economy and society and their reciprocal interaction are open to inspection. They need not be bracketed away in the abstract language of formal economic analysis. Anthropologists do not have to lose the advantages of small scale by following the trend to principle-construction at the level of the skeletal model, universal, beyond time and space, for the dubious benefits of elegance and easy manipulation. The task of understanding a representative series of social structures and their economic consequences and correlates is still to be done. With this intellectual task pursued, the making of 'principles' or the fashioning of 'models' will be only the happy task of summary and extrapolation.

Note

[1] I am indebted to the National Institute of Mental Health, the Department of Anthropology and the Graduate School of Business of the University of Chicago for financing the field work on which this paper is based. June Nash covers in detail the social structure of Amatenango in Social Relations in Amatenango: An Activity Analysis, unpublished Ph.D. thesis, University of Chicago. Miss Joan Ablon aided in some of the data here reported during her field work in the community.

References

Boeke, J. H., *Oriental Economics*, Institute of Pacific Relations, New York, 1947.

Nash, Manning, *Machine Age Maya*, Free Press, and Memoir 87 American Anthropological Association, 1958.

——, 'Some Social and Cultural Aspects of Economic Development,' *Economic Development and Cultural Change*, Vol. VII (1959), pp. 137–50.

Polanyi, K., C. Arnesberg and H. Pearson (eds.), *Trade and Market in the Early Empires*, Free Press and Falcon's Wing Press, 1957.

Tax, Sol, 'The Municipios of the Midwestern Highlands of Guatemala,' *Amer. Anthrop.*, Vol. XXXIX, No. 3, 1937, pp. 423–44.

——, *Penny Capitalism: A Guatemalan Indian Economy*, Smithsonian Institution, Institute of Social Anthropology, No. 16, Washington, 1953.

Wolf, Eric R., 'Types of Latin American Peasantry,' *Amer. Anthrop.*, Vol. LVII (1955), pp. 452–69.

[2]

Economic Behavior in Markets

Stuart Plattner

The previous chapter deals with economic behavior in settlements, towns, and systems of markets but does not focus explicitly upon individuals. This chapter explores individual economic behavior in markets. It analyzes the conditions that lead people to establish personalized economic relationships, which seem as much "social" as "economic." Why does a buyer or a seller in a market sometimes search for the best short-run deal available at one time, and at other times establish a personalized, long-run reciprocal relationship with a customer?[1] The answer is that reciprocal economic relationships reduce risk in transactions that would otherwise be too uncertain or expensive to undertake.

The *transaction* is a key concept here. It refers to any change in the status of a good or service between persons, such as a sale. Transactions have costs. Some costs are obvious: If I use a credit card, I will probably pay interest on the amount; if the store I prefer is across town, I might spend hours accomplishing my purchase. Some costs are not obvious and relate to the risk of making a "bad" purchase. A well-known example in the used car market (to be analyzed below) is the risk of buying a "lemon." These risks will be analyzed here.

I will first define differences between personalized, long-run and impersonal, short-run economic relationships. The importance of information in economic relationships is then examined by analyzing problems in the separate elements of an exchange: the type of goods, the nature of the transaction, and the identity of the actors. Then the causes of informational problems are analyzed by looking at market infrastructure, consisting of systems of communications, political inte-

[1] The scientific strategy of analyzing social situations as caused by choice does not imply that every actor actively thinks about each strategy every day. But this approach forces the social scientist to consider the rationality of behavior that otherwise could be merely labeled as "habit," "custom," or "tradition."

gration, and transportation and storage. These causes are finally set in the context of the basic relationship between labor and capital in the society.

This abstract analysis can be set in a context by describing the problems in collecting a debt that two Mexican long-distance traders told me about in the 1970's. They had sold a horse to a resident of a distant town while on a peddling trip. (See the case study in Chapter 7.)*The buyer paid them a small amount and said he would gather the rest of the money while they continued their peddling trip, and would deliver the cash to them when they passed through his town on their return. Ten days later they returned, traveling by horseback in this region of few paved roads, to find him not at home. They pastured their horses (for a fee) and put up in a hotel, "suffering," as they put it, "the cost of feeding ourselves in restaurants." There were no telephones, so they had to periodically visit his home to see if he was there. He finally arrived and said he would gather the money in a few days, since his own business was going poorly. They pleaded with him to pay them, but he refused. They finally appealed to the man's father for help. After another day they got their payment in the form of sacks of coffee. They considered themselves lucky to have gotten paid at all.

The peddlers' problems were typical and were caused in large part by faulty information due to a poor economic environment. This chapter will analyze the effects of such problems on economic transactions. The first step in the analysis is to define two opposite types, or modes, of exchange.

Modes of Exchange: Impersonal Versus Personal

There are basically two diametrically opposite ways to engage in transactions: They can be impersonal or *atomized*, or else personal or *embedded* (Granovetter 1985). Impersonal transactors have no relationship with each other beyond the short term of the exchange; thus in the aggregate they are *atomized*, or not organized into groups or social structures. Personalized transactions are between people who have a relationship that endures past the exchange; they are *embedded* in networks of social relations. The hypothetical "perfectly competitive market" of classical economic theory is built upon an assumption of atomized actors engaging in impersonal transactions. These buyers and sellers have no interest in a long-term relationship but consider only the specifics of each transaction with an eye toward maximal profit. In the real world, academics as well as businessmen have noted that people do not act that way. In most circumstances they establish long-run

* not reproduced here

relationships with economic partners. Is this irrational? Are such transactors losing money, or trading off economic goals for social approval, status, or power? This chapter argues that a long-term personalized relationship is economically superior in certain environments.

The most important attribute of long-run exchanges is that they tend to be personalized, meaning that knowledge of the other's personality, family, history, church, and so on is relevant to the trust one has that the exchange will be satisfactorily completed. The riskier the economic environment, the more traders need additional information about a partner over and above the specific facts of the proposed deal. The Mexican peddlers in the story above might have known about their debtor's tendency to avoid paying his bills, but they needed to make the deal; and in any case they also knew enough to find and convince his father to help them.

The impersonal mode of exchange refers to short-run exchanges where each transaction has few implications for the future. These transactions can be said to be closed-ended, as opposed to the open-ended personal mode of exchange. The relationship between the buyer and seller in a department store is a good example. The transactions usually have no meaning aside from the specific things exchanged, and the dominant goal for each actor is to protect and maximize self-interest. The fact that the relationship is openly instrumental is appropriate, within the bounds of social norms. We understand that diners in roadside restaurants, where they do not expect to see the waiter again, feel free to leave little or no tip.[2] The relationship exists to support and facilitate the exchange, rather than the other way around.[3]

Economic exchanges within families are extreme examples of personalized market exchange. Consider the hiring of dependent children by family firms. A parent who searches for the best worker to hand over the family business to, rather than encouraging a child to work in the firm, would be seen as odd. A family worker should not attempt to bargain with a family boss about working hours or vacation time in the same way that a nonrelative could. The work relationship is in the context of a long-term flow of resources and obligations. Continuing the relationship is the dominant goal. A child who attempted to decompose the transactions and negotiate each element separately—for example, by asking for extra money for work to be done extra carefully and extra fast—would be morally criticized. In fact, the group (espe-

[2] Granovetter (1985) discusses why they would leave a tip at all in his consideration of "embeddedness" and the concepts of "oversocialized" and "undersocialized" actors.

[3] Frank Cancian (1966) discusses maximization as a behavioral norm in comparison with other uses of the maximization strategy.

cially the family) is often the basic actor whose interest governs those of each individual. If an extrafamilial authority is called in, it is usually a sign that the family structure has lost its integrity. We can categorize these relationships as long-term, open-ended, and generalized with a strong affective, noninstrumental component.

In reality, impersonal and personal market modes are not so neatly separated. Corporations often want their employees to feel a "family" loyalty toward the firm.[4] This normally means they should place the corporation's interests above their own in the short run, in return for the expectation of sharing the firm's long-run success. Family farmers often exchange services and goods in the name of "neighboring" and friendship, while they secretly record a count of the economic values exchanged "to keep things straight" (Bennett 1968).

Long-term trading partnerships, in which elements of impersonal and of personal modes intermingle, are often found in peasant marketplaces. The goal of each actor is his or her economic self-interest, yet the maintainance of the relationship is valued over an immediate short-run profit. Transactions are contracted in specific commercial terms, but a parallel relationship of generalized reciprocity seems to support the strictly commercial relationship.[5] The key element is that exchanges do not have to be balanced in the short run, since past or future shortfalls are adjusted in the continuing stream of exchanges. In developed societies, these relationships have been reported for situations where the quality of the goods is hard to assess. For example, consider fishermen and fish dealers. The cost of unloading a shipload of fish (or any variable, perishable, low central-place level good) is too great to do so without a commitment to buy, and the price fluctuates at the wholesale market. A price is usually negotiated before the ship is unloaded. If later events show that price to have been unfair to either party, future prices are adjusted to make up for these past imbalances (Wilson 1980). For example, an average price may have been negotiated at dockside, but the fish later resold for a very high price. The fisherman can expect the broker to share the windfall profits. In the same way, a dealer who

[4] One organizational theorist talks about "clan" industrial organization, where firms achieve high productivity through kinship-type role expectations (Ouchi 1980).

[5] Generalized reciprocity is defined as an exchange relationship balanced only in the long run, where the maintenance of the relationship is more important than any short-run gain and where the norm of the relationship is altruism (the parent-child relationship is exemplary). It is contrasted with balanced reciprocity, where the balance is calculated (but not too overtly) and where fair exchange is the norm (the relationship between business partners is an example). The other extreme is negative reciprocity, where selfishness with no attention to balance is the norm of the relationship. Exchanges between strangers —who will never meet again and whose behavior is not governed by altruistic goals— would be expected to fit in this category (Sahlins 1972).

pays a relatively high price at the shore but who can sell the fish for only very low prices will argue for a low price the next time to make up the shortfall. The possibilities for cheating and the need for trust in this situation are clear. (See Acheson 1985 for a case study of these issues in the Maine lobster market.)

I name this latter class of economic relationships "equilibrating" to call attention to these key features: the predominance of long- over short-run goals and the flexible, continuing process of reciprocating value in a relationship that is explicitly instrumental.[6] In some circumstances equilibrating relationships become so strong and regular (that is, formalized) that they are described as "trading partnerships." One of the most significant contributions of the economic anthropology of markets has been the analysis of such relationships in the markets of underdeveloped societies. Mintz provided the seminal description of these partnerships in Haiti, where they are known as *pratik*:[7]

> A buying pratik who knows her selling pratik is coming will wait at the proper place and time, refusing to buy stock from others that she is sure her pratik is carrying. . . . [T]o the extent that her stock is committed in such arrangements a selling pratik will refuse to sell to others until she has met her pratik buyer. [Mintz 1961: 61]

This sort of behavior gives rise to the famous (probably apocryphal) story of the female market trader trudging to market on a dusty road with a heavy sack of produce on her head. A foreigner met her and offered a relatively enormous amount of money for the entire sack. She refused and continued on her way. Frustrated, the foreigner complained about the lack of economic sense in her behavior (and by extension, the behavior of all petty market traders): "They are more interested in socializing with their friends at market than they are in making a profit." The truth is that it would have been foolish for a trader to sacrifice a long-run business relationship (by disappointing a regular customer) for a one-time killing—assuming that in fact such a partner were waiting at the market.

Long-term trading partnerships are important mechanisms for reducing trading risks, and as such they are advantageous to both parties. Traders report many reasons for these relationships. The sellers' desire to stabilize and regularize their incomes and the buyers' wish to do the

[6] I use the term "equilibrating" rather than "reciprocal" for these intermediary modes to point to the balancing procedure that the back-and-forth transactions are aimed at. The term does not imply equilibrium in the conventional economic sense.

[7] Several economic anthropologists have studied similar trading relationships: of higglers in Jamaica (Katzin 1960), *Onibara* in Nigeria (Trager 1981), *Suki* in the Philippines (Szanton 1972; Davis 1973), and *clientes* in Guatemala (Swetnam 1978).

same for their value over the long run are fundamental. As Mintz concludes, "Those middlemen who make pratik state that they trade some part of their gain in return for long-range security, and some protection from the vagaries of the market" (1964: 262).

Elements of Exchange: Goods, Transactions, Actors

Why do some traders concentrate on security before income? Basically, because some exchanges are too risky to engage in without the extra security of personalized relationships. Risk exists because of faulty information in the three major components of exchanges: goods, meaning the things exchanged (including services for simplicity); transactions, referring to the rules, understandings, and procedures that pertain; and actors, meaning the people engaging in the exchange. The classic model of perfect competition is predicated on full information about goods, transactions, and actors. In the real world the information necessary for safe and sensible decisions is always imperfect and incomplete.

Goods

Goods possess multiple attributes, or qualities, about which a buyer must learn. It is important to distinguish two aspects of goods: "search" and "experience quality" (Nelson 1970). The former denotes obvious attributes—the style, size, or color in clothing, for example. The consumer's problem is to locate the preferred bundle of attributes in the market. "Experience quality" refers to those attributes revealed only through use, such as durability in clothing. The buyer's information problem is to find out any particular good's "experience quality" *before* purchase, when that quality is not apparent.

For example, a new car is high in "search" quality, since it is standardized. A buyer may assume that any given car of a particular make and model is the same as any other, and devote his or her time to searching out the best deal. But a used car is an "experience quality" good. It may be a normal specimen, or it may be a lemon. How is an average buyer to know?

Consider the plight of the seller of a used car in perfect condition. The seller knows that his car is worth more than most similar cars, but how does the buyer? Unless the seller can give accurate information about his unique automobile to the buyer, the latter will normally only offer an average price. (Because used cars are not standardized like new cars, the original equivalence of model and price no longer holds.)

The situation becomes worse as the used car market is flooded with lemons, or below-average cars, as Akerloff's influential work shows (1970). Because buyers cannot evaluate the cars as well as sellers, lemons can be sold as average cars for profit. The reasonable buyer who becomes familiar with the market will not offer more than the value of a lemon if he cannot evaluate each car. A seller of an average or superior car will be faced with accepting less than fair value or of not selling his car at all.

The problem is that the buyer and the vendor do not have the same information about the value of the good. Because the buyer cannot rely upon a standardized rule to assess value (as he can with new cars), he and the vendor must somehow agree upon a fair, accurate measure of the value of unique and variable goods.[8] Equilibrating relationships resolve this problem by extending the payment schedule (the quid pro quo) of each transaction in time so that problems can be adjusted. When the buyer discovers that the deal is not what he or she thought it was, the existence of the long-run relationship allows a renegotiation of the price. Others must rely on the seller's reputation in the community, spend the resources to evaluate the car on their own, take the risk of buying a lemon, or stay out of the market.

In more general terms, market performance is impaired; in fact, a market may cease to function without government intervention, in conditions of "asymmetrical imperfect information" (Spence 1976). This issue is relevant to the developing world, which much of economic anthropology studies, since most goods traded in traditional market systems are unstandardized and highly variable. Hence the problem of establishing value is crucial. Akerloff's contribution is to show that unequal information about variable goods is at the heart of the market problem. The solution chosen in most situations of cheap labor is to personalize the trade relationship so that equilibration can reduce the risks created by imperfect information.

Transactions

The information most relevant to a transaction is the price, the conditions of payment, and the probability that the transaction will be successfully completed. Knowledge of the price alone is not enough, since one must also know the context. Exchanges that occur under short-run profiteering conditions are obviously different from those where the terms of the transaction are in line with a long-run pattern. For example, the unreliable distribution of commodities to an underdevel-

[8] Note that the individual's problem of not having enough information to make a sensible decision translates into society's problem of the useless market, which brings sellers and buyers together who cannot agree upon a price.

oped area allows local monopolists to exploit the situation. When a delivery of sugar (or cooking oil, or some other good) fails to arrive at a hinterland town, the store owners may withdraw old stock from their shelves in order to mark it up or sell it "under the counter." Consumers with long-term relationships may buy at the normal price or may be assured of a supply in this circumstance. Automobile drivers in the United States learned this lesson in the gasoline shortages of the mid-1970's, when some drivers found it convenient to make off-hours appointments with their gasoline dealer to buy a tank of gas.

The rules that define payment include the specification of what things may be exchanged (cash, other valuables, services) and the time frame (immediate or deferred payment, credit charges, and so on). For example, long-distance itinerant traders I studied in Chiapas, Mexico, would sell their goods cheaply to hinterland Indian customers, from whom they would buy food and lodging. In the traders' minds, the lower income received for goods was worth the assurance of hospitality; for the Indians, the sowing of hospitality reaped cheaper manufactured goods and cultural brokerage (see the case study in Chapter 7).

These issues may seem irrelevant to transactions in the developed world. People in rich economies tend to assume that transactions will probably be completed as specified. Communities in the United States have small claims courts, Better Business Bureaus, and consumer protection agencies as support systems. Businessmen have all the legal protection they can buy. Compare that to the situation of the Mexican peddlers described above.

I found a similar example in a study of buyers of fresh produce on wholesale spot markets. The conditions under which they transact their business make it impossible to examine the entire lot of apples or oranges. They buy produce in the middle of the night, with strong social pressures to buy large quantities of boxed produce that cannot be inspected until unpacked at the point of retail sale. The best buyers are those who have efficient personal relationships with wholesalers. The wholesale vendors will not cheat them (or will cheat them less) because they know they will be relying upon each other for future deals (Plattner 1982, 1983).

In summary, problematic information about prices, payments, and probabilities increases risk in transactions. Some interpret this risk as a heavy cost to producers and assume that it is the major variable explaining the very existence of firms. This approach asks why firms choose to incorporate the production of intermediate goods rather than purchase them on a spot market. (Williamson 1981 has been very influential.) Consider the example of a restaurant deciding whether to bake its own bread or buy from a baker. The higher the cost of the transactions with the independent baker, the more attractive the employed baker becomes. Is the price of the bread seriously unpredictable? Will the baker sometimes insist upon cash payment and other times deliver on credit? (That is, are the conditions of payment not specifiable in advance?) And, perhaps worst of all, is the delivery not reliable? Imagine the problem of running a restaurant and not being sure of the price, quality, and quantity of bread available to you each day.[9]

Actors

Economists from Adam Smith to Milton Friedman have dreamed of a market where the smooth workings of competition ensure economic efficiency between faceless traders. But problems of information create incentives for people to know more than the nature of the goods and the transaction.

A well-known example of troublesome personal information concerns "adverse selection" in an insurance market. A vendor of dental insurance, for example, can set his rates by calculating the cost of fixing an average person's teeth. People with bad teeth will have incentives to sign up, since they expect heavy dental bills. The insurance, being predicated on the average need, will cost less than they expect to spend. People with good teeth may or may not sign up, depending upon their preference for insurance. But if the people with dental problems are overrepresented in the insurance company's clientele, then the insurer must raise the rates to cover the higher-than-average costs. The higher the rates, the less likely the healthy folks are to join, and the higher the proportion of expensive clients, bringing about even higher costs, and so on.

This is a problem of information, as Akerloff points out (1970: 493). The vendor of insurance does not know the likelihood that his insured population will claim benefits as well as the buyers do. Without accurate information about the personal characteristics of each client or some institutional support (like group rates or Medicare), the market will fail. This will leave people who want to buy insurance unable to deal with people who want to sell.

In circumstances of pervasive market ignorance, the most significant piece of information to know about a trader is what social category he

[9] Ouchi (1980) extends Williamson's analysis to discuss "clan" industrial organizations. His use of the term "clan" is loose, however. Oberschall and Leifer (1986) take a broad look at this sort of analysis, which they identify as the "new institutional economics." They doubt that "efficiency" is adequate as an explanation of social institutions, without analysis of power and goal ambiguities.

or she belongs to. In the extreme this may be a caste identity; otherwise, it may be a class, kinship, or social network affiliation. Knowing *who* a trader is may sometimes be the best way to know *what* he is buying or selling. Ben-Porath argues that specialization in identity can also create savings (1980). He generalizes Adam Smith's argument that specialization lowers costs because of returns to scale in production. The scale benefits exist when a significant part of the costs are "set-up" as opposed to production flow costs (the difference between a license to trade and a tax on sales). The Mexican peddlers' experience, described in Chapter 7,* is an example of such costs. Once they learned who the trustworthy people were in that distant town, their next visits would be much more productive.

To summarize the argument so far, I have characterized economic exchanges on a continuum whose polar extremes are impersonal and personal modes of behavior. When information about important elements of exchanges is lacking, the impersonal mode of behavior (implying faceless traders and transactions without past or future) involves excessive risk and cost. Impersonality may not allow economic exchange if traders deal in goods high in experience quality, which can create a restricted, "lemons" market, if prices are variable and transactions are risky; or if traders are ignorant about important attributes of trading partners so that adverse selection is a problem. In such conditions, traders choose to invest their resources in establishing long-term relations with partners whose identity becomes a factor of economic value (if the government does not intervene to support the market).

The frequency of exchange (the Central Place order of the good, in terms defined in Chapter 7)* is an important cause of equilibration. Exchanges that take place rarely may not be important enough to merit equilibration, whereas frequent exchanges allow the ongoing adjustment of values. The more significant the transaction costs, the larger the share of set-up over production flow costs; the more frequent the transaction, the more likely are traders to seek equilibrating relationships.[10]

In the next section I discuss how infrastructural poverty increases risks and costs.

[10] Oberschall and Leifer (1986) look at transactional efficiency as a cause of social institutions in general. They discuss the importance of *uncertainty*, meaning the costliness of knowledge about the goods; *frequency*, referring to the central place order of the goods (see Chapter 7),* and *asset specificity*, meaning the investment necessary to engage in specialized transactions. High levels of uncertainty, frequency, and asset specificity motivate decision makers to invest in equilibrating relationships.

* not reproduced here

Market Infrastructure

One of the main differences between the developing and the developed world is in the wealth invested in the institutions that support economic exchange. Institutional poverty in communications, political control, transportation, and storage creates problems for buyers and sellers.

If there is no efficient communication network for news of the availability of goods to flow between producing, distributing, and consuming areas, then buyers and sellers must seek out those who have the relevant information and judge for themselves whether their sources are truthful or not. This process is obviously riskier the further one gets from a personal network.

If society is poorly integrated under one legal authority, so that contracts made between strangers in one area are not easily enforceable elsewhere, then anyone attempting to trade with someone outside his personal network will face some risk of loss.

For example, in 1968 I studied rural Ladino (non-Indian) traders in the Mayan Indian town of Bachajon, Chiapas, Mexico. They obtained their dry goods from the stores in the regional center of San Cristóbal, a three-day walk. The rural retailers were born in San Cristóbal, and the personal contacts that they had were the only reason they were provisioned from San Cristóbal rather than from other sources in the region. They knew that prices were lower in the state capital. But they could not afford to pay cash, and since they did not live in the capital, they had no credit with wholesalers there (Plattner 1975). Retailers also knew that factories in Mexico City sold merchandise more cheaply, but they could not afford the trip (by mule to the regional center and by bus to the capital, a one-way total of four travel days) and did not have the contacts needed to place their orders.[11]

If the state of roads, railways, and other avenues of transportation makes costs extraordinarily high, then poorer people will be priced out of the market. Likewise, if processing or storage facilities are not available to prolong the life of perishable items, then the variability of goods will be increased, as will the problems discussed above concerning being able to experience goods. The factors mentioned here heighten seasonal variation in agricultural goods and cause sporadic fluctuations in the supply of all goods not produced in a local area. Mintz describes the effects of this in Haiti, where

[11] By 1982, the economic development of the region had advanced such that goods were available by telegraph order from central Mexico or from large warehouses in the state capital.

distribution is likely to have a markedly irregular character. This unevenness is magnified when seasonal variation in the supply of various goods, and income, is often sharp. . . . Under such circumstances, pratik relationships stabilize sequences of dyadic economic transactions. Taken together, they afford greater order to the distributing system as a whole. [1961: 55]

Factors of Production: Cheap Labor and Scarce Capital

In markets where capital is expensive and labor cheap, the style of economic relationships requires a heavy input of time. Barbara Ward's seminal work has shown how the credit market in traditional societies is instituted on the need for personal relationships between creditors and debtors (1960). Ward shows that asymmetrical information about credit causes adverse selection, which is avoided by knowledge from personal relationships. Her work is important because she showed that a non-Western style of relationships was based upon familiar economic constraints.

In summary, the infrastructural problems that give rise to the need for equilibrating relationships also maintain a low value of labor and facilitate the process of specialization by identity. The "old-fashioned" style of business in many developing countries, where personal conversation and sociability circumscribe business relationships, has a clear basis in economic structure of (cf. Dannhaeuser 1979).

Conclusion

In socioeconomic environments rich in information, impersonal market relationships are suitable for goods high in "search" quality. The poorer the information, the higher the "experience" quality of the goods; the higher the transaction costs, the riskier the exchange and the more valuable an investment in personalized relationships.

This discussion has dealt with market societies, but the principles generalize to any economic exchange. A New Guinea tribesman seeking to barter feather plumes for shells must also be concerned with the risk that his transaction will fail. Healey (1984) studied exchanges among the Kundagai Maring of Papua New Guinea. This central highland tribe raised pigs and cultivated swidden gardens (see Chapter 3, this volume). They distinguished trade in material objects from "prestations" (Healey's term), which were explicitly concerned with human relationships. Bride wealth and death payments were the major forms of prestations. Trade took place between related or unrelated people and always took the form of barter, an exchange of object for object. How-

TABLE 8.1
Kundagai Maring Trading Patterns

	Relations between traders	
	Not related	Related
Exchange delayed	35	697
Exchange immediate	483	71
Total	518	768

SOURCE: Healey (1984).

ever, some trades were reciprocated immediately, while others were paid back later. Healey studied the trading histories of 58 adult men and hypothesized that whether the exchange was delayed or immediate was a function of the personal relationship between the traders. The data is reproduced in Table 8.1. Trade between nonrelatives was most often immediate, whereas the increased trust between relatives allowed trades to be delayed. The additional support of a kinship tie is relied upon to reduce the risk of default.

In many cases tribesmen seeking to exchange goods call unrelated persons by kin terms. This extension of kinship expectations to nonkin is built on relationships such as the fact that the traders' mothers were born in the same village. Healey notes that "the search for kinship ties between erstwhile strangers introduces moral principles that should obtain between the parties" (1984: 55). In other words, the lack of political integration between local communities increases the risk that traders will default, so individuals personalize their exchange relationships. Embedding such relationships in a kinship matrix lowers the risk because of the added moral sanction.

In this chapter I have shown how individuals struggle to get around problems of risky transactions by creating and using the personal networks available to them. The issues discussed here are part of a broad movement in social science called "socio-economics" (Etzioni 1988). Similar issues are discussed in legal studies, where the contract, instead of the transaction, is the focus (Macneil 1981). The approach taken here is to analyze the difference in economic behavior between societies as due to economic constraint and rational choice rather than to differences of cultural or economic values and goals. This is not meant to deny the importance of such differences, but to put them into perspective.

Plattner: Economic Behavior in Markets

Acheson, James
1985 "Social Organization of the Maine Lobster Market." In *Markets and Marketing*, edited by S. Plattner. Lanham, Md.: University Press of America for the Society for Economic Anthropology.

Akerloff, George
1970 "The Market for 'Lemons': Quality Uncertainty and the Market Mechanism." *Quarterly Journal of Economics* 84: 488–500.

Bennett, John
1968 "Reciprocal Economic Exchanges Among North American Agricultural Operators." *Southwestern Journal of Anthropology* 24: 276–309.

Ben-Porath, Yoram
1980 "The F-Connection: Families, Friends, and Firms and the Organization of Exchange." *Population and Development Review* 6: 1–30.

Cancian, Frank
1966 "Maximization as Norm, Strategy and Theory." *American Anthropologist* 68: 465–70.

Dannhaeuser, Norbert
1979 "Development of a Distribution Channel in the Philippines: From Channel Integration to Channel Fragmentation." *Human Organization* 38: 74–78.

Davis, William
1973 *Social Relations in a Philippine Market*. Berkeley: University of California Press.

Etzioni, Amitai
1988 *The Moral Dimension*. New York: Free Press.

Granovetter, Mark
1985 "Economic Action and Social Structure: The Problem of Embeddedness." *American Journal of Sociology* 91: 481–510.

Healey, Christopher
1984 "Trade and Sociability: Balanced Reciprocity as Generosity in the New Guinea Highlands." *American Ethnologist* 11: 42–60.

Katzin, Margret
1960 "The Business of Higglering in Jamaica." *Social and Economic Studies* 9: 297–331.

Macneil, Ian
1981 "Economic Analysis of Contractual Relations: Its Shortfalls and the

Need for a 'Rich Classificatory Apparatus.'" *Northwestern University Law Review* 75: 1018–63.
Mintz, Sidney
1961 "Pratik: Haitian Personal Economic Relationships." *Proceedings of the 1961 Annual Spring Meeting of the American Ethnological Society*.
1964 "The Employment of Capital by Market Women in Haiti." In *Capital, Saving and Credit*, edited by R. Firth and B. Yamey. Chicago: Aldine.
Nelson, Paul
1970 "Information and Consumer Behavior." *Journal of Political Economy* 78: 311–29.
Oberschall, Anthony, & Eric Leifer
1986 "Efficiency and Social Institutions: Uses and Misuses of Economic Reasoning in Sociology." *Annual Review of Sociology* 12: 233–53.
Ouchi, William
1980 "Markets, Bureaucracies and Clans." *Administrative Science Quarterly* 25: 129–42.
Plattner, Stuart
1975 "The Economics of Peddling." In *Formal Methods in Economic Anthropology*, edited by S. Plattner. Washington, D.C.: American Anthropological Association.
1980 "Economic Development and Occupational Change in a Developing Area of Mexico." *Journal of Developing Areas* 14: 469–82.
1982 "Economic Custom in a Public Marketplace." *American Ethnologist* 9: 399–420.
1983 "Economic Custom in a Competitive Marketplace." *American Anthropologist* 85: 848–58.
Sahlins, Marshall
1972 "On the Sociology of Primitive Exchange." *Stone Age Economics*. Chicago: Aldine.
Spence, Michael
1976 "Information Aspects of Market Structure: An Introduction." *Quarterly Journal of Economics* 90: 591–97.
Swetnam, John
1978 "Interaction Between Urban and Rural Residents in a Guatemalan Marketplace." *Urban Anthropology* 7: 137–53.
Szanton, Maria
1972 *Right to Survive*. University Park: Pennsylvania State University Press.
Trager, Lillian
1981 "Customers and Creditors: Variations in Economic Personalism in a Nigerian Marketing System." *Ethnology* 20: 133–46.
Ward, Barbara
1960 "Cash or Credit Crops?" *Economic Development and Cultural Change* 8: 148–63.
Williamson, Oliver
1981 "The Economics of Organization: The Transaction Cost Approach." *American Journal of Sociology* 87: 548–77.
Wilson, James
1980 "Adaptation to Uncertainty and Small Numbers Exchange: The New England Fish Market." *Bell Journal of Economics* 11: 491–504.

[3]

The Limits of Formalism in Agricultural Decision Research

ALLEN JOHNSON

An often noted difference between economics and anthropology is the preference of the economist for formal prescriptive models and the anthropologist for broad-ranging ethnographic descriptions. A review of the major journals in each field bears this out. Economists' journals are dominated by arguments in mathematical–deductive form that usually are neither tested nor even exemplified by empirical data, whereas anthropologists' journals are dominated by ethnographic descriptions of individual cases strung together by loosely phrased theoretical commentaries. However, there is also a substantial minority of the opposite preference in each field: Economists have their ethnographers and historians, and anthropologists have their mathematicians.

Rarest of all, in both fields, is the presentation of formal arguments or models tested by empirical data. Even though most scholars know that an ideal of scientific method is the use of rigorous theory to develop expectations (predictions, retrodictions) about the world that can be compared with directly observed events so that discrepancies between model and data can be used to improve the model and to gather new and better data, the tendency to polarize to one extreme or the other—the formal–prescriptive or the empirical–descriptive—apparently remains too powerful to resist.

In both camps, there is a certain lack of understanding about what formal models can and can not accomplish. Those who favor formalism

AGRICULTURAL DECISION MAKING:
Anthropological Contributions to
Rural Development

ISBN 0-12-078882-9

tend to overlook the consistent failures of their models to predict interesting real-world events, holding instead to a kind of "persistent optimism" (Dreyfus 1972) that the failure is due either to a temporary imperfection in the model or to shortcomings in the data. Those who favor ethnography, on the other hand, overlook the benefits that the rigor of formal models brings to our reasoning, and may in practice overemphasize the chaos and mystery of human economic behavior. The middle ground between these extremes may be avoided in part because it is an uncomfortable place to be: For the formalist, because it exposes the inevitable empirical narrowness of the model, and for the ethnographer, because it exposes confusion in the theory that lies behind the description.

I take it for granted that formal model building based on rigorous deductive reasoning is a powerful aid in the analysis of economic behavior, in nonindustrial as well as in industrial settings. But I am concerned about the tendency of model builders to become absorbed in the interiors of their models and to lose apparent interest in their outward, empirical usefulness. In Simon's (1977) terms, formalists show a marked preference for "well-structured problems" over "ill-structured problems," even though it is the "ill-structured" form of a theoretical problem that is closest to the real-world problem we are trying to solve.

In this chapter, I will explore the implications of the well-structured–ill-structured dichotomy by applying a formal model to an aspect of agricultural decision making in a subsistence economy, and then examining discrepancies between the model and observed behavior. I will argue that the formal model is by itself virtually uninterpretable without reference to an ethnographic context that can be provided only by participant observation over a long term of field research. This is no momentary obstacle to complete formalization of a problem but is, rather, an inherent limitation on the extent to which formal models can account for observed outcomes of agricultural decisions.

The polarization into two camps has turned the middle ground into a sort of depopulated buffer zone across which opponents regard one another with a palpable antipathy. For example, Georgescu–Roegen (1979:318–325), whose "institutional" economics, with its holistic breadth and dialectical mode of reasoning, has been criticized by formalists as "vague and impressionistic," responds by criticizing his critics for their "arithmomania." Spirited debate is always welcome: Still, we should bear in mind that this is not a contest one side is likely to win. And the atmosphere is such that those who choose to occupy the middle ground are apt to be regarded by both groups as having "left camp," either to be disregarded or else treated as part of the opposition.

Another form of avoiding the middle ground is to deny that opposing positions exist. Simon (1977:137–153), for example, argues that there is no essential difference between normative and descriptive economics. He sees normative economics as a set of descriptive statements transformed into imperatives. Thus, if descriptive economics asserts "firms behave so as to maximize profits, normative theory asserts maximize profit! [p. 138]." But Simon leaves out altogether the descriptive issue of whether and under what circumstances real firms maximize profits or otherwise behave according to formal models.

To the degree that this middle ground remains barren, the study of agricultural decision making suffers. Agricultural decision research has substantive practical relevance owing to the precarious state of the world's food supply and the major dislocations wrought by modern changes in technology and markets. Even if it is true that the majority of these changes are impersonal, historical, and beyond the control of any group or agency, there still remain arenas in which governments and international firms and foundations exert powerful influences on local agrarian populations. The quality of the understanding on which these agencies act has a direct bearing on the well-being of the people on whom they act, and on the "success" of their programs. It is of particular importance whether or not our understanding includes the ability to anticipate the reactions of local farmers to new opportunities and constraints.

The polarization of agricultural decision studies creates two traditions that are each weaker in isolation than they are together. In the next section, I briefly review the success of formal models in predicting food-related decisions in non-Western economies. This is followed by a formal analysis (linear programing) of food-production decisions in a subsistence economy that just is beginning to experience economic modernization. Next I explore discrepancies between the predictions of the model and the observed economic behavior, in some detail, to illuminate what the formal model accomplishes and what it does not, and why. Finally, I return to the formal–descriptive polarization to argue the need for research and policies specifically aimed at combining both approaches in full partnership.

Predicting Observed Outcomes from Formal Models in Economic Anthropology

The capacity of formal decision models to predict or retrodict observed economic behavior in nonindustrial economies, although undeniable, has been limited severely, especially when contrasted with optimistic forecasts of success by enthusiasts (e.g., Buchler and Nutini 1969:2–7; White 1973:386–387). Anthropologists have had no success, for example, with the theory of games, which attempts to formalize optimizing strategies for situations of competition between two or more "players." Early game-theory papers by anthropologists (Buchler and Nutini 1969; Moore 1957) were programmatic, speculative, and presented no quantitative data, either in the cells of a game matrix or as empirical tests of game-theory solutions.

Other game-theory studies, where quantitative data were presented, were fundamentally flawed. Gould (1963) presented a quantitative game matrix from which he calculated an optimizing strategy in Tanzanian farmers' choice of crops, but then he notes, almost in passing (p. 294), that he manufactured the data matrix only for the purpose of illustrating his argument about the *potential* uses of game theory. Davenport's (1960) analysis of Jamaican fishing strategies was based on the unacceptable assumption that the opponent, Nature, was purposely and strategically shifting ocean currents to minimize the fishermen's catch. Thus, although the model does predict fishermen's actual behavior, this result is meaningless. When the model is restated correctly with the reasonable assumption that nature is indifferent rather than malevolent, the game collapses into a simple cost–benefits analysis that utterly fails to predict actual fishermen's behavior (Read and Read 1970).

Elsewhere (Johnson 1978:141–157), I have reviewed a number of cases where economic anthropologists have compared quantitative predictions with empirical data. The formal models from which predictions are derived include (among others) a computer simulation of decision processes, a profit function based on input–output analysis of production, and a "central place" analysis of a peasant marketing system. In most of these cases, a small but significant portion of the data is accounted for by the model. But in each of these cases it becomes necessary to draw on qualitative ethnographic considerations to explain why the majority of the data fail to conform to predictions of the model (cf. Boyd 1975:253–254).

Of special relevance to the example I will give is a quantified linear-programing model that predicts agricultural behavior in a nonindustrial economy. White (1973:395–399) analyzes agricultural strategies among the Kapauku Papuans, using data collected by Pospisil (1963). White's linear-programing model predicts the amounts of labor and land that the Kapauku should use to maximize their calorie food production;

observed Kapauku behavior conforms *exactly* to White's prediction. This result, however, is partially a logical outcome of how the model was constructed, rather than an empirical verification. White (1973) set the constraints on the model so that the allowable solutions could either be equal to or less than the empirically observed amounts of labor and land the Kapauku use, *but they could not exceed either amount*. When a solution was sought in the form of a strategy that would maximize food production (calories), logically it employed the maximum amounts of land and labor available to it (i.e., those that the Kapauku actually use).

White's model did allow for the possibility that calories could be maximized with less than the observed labor and land, and consequently the formal analysis suggests that there is no way for the Kapauku to achieve the same level of calorie production by using less land or labor than they do. But the model does not account for the observed fact that the Kapauku actually use less land and labor than they have available.

An interesting prediction of White's model concerns the mix of three crops (sweet potatoes, sugar cane, and root crops) the Kapauku should plant. This prediction is quite different from observed behavior: The Kapauku actually plant 49% of the land in sweet potatoes, 32% in sugar cane, and 19% in root crops, whereas the linear-programing solution is to plant 85% in sweet potatoes, none in sugar cane, and 15% in root crops. White explains the discrepancy as due to a "balance of different crops [being] sought [p. 398]," but this, of course, is one of those qualitative, post hoc explanations I identified as the rule when formal models fall short of predicting observed behavior. Still, as in other cases, White's model is close enough to the mark that it predicts some of the data (e.g., the low proportion of root crops) and can be used as a springboard for further, more informed exploration of the data.

In short, it is fair to say that rigorous deductive models have not yet been accurate in predicting or otherwise accounting for observed economic behavior in nonindustrial settings. Formal model builders would agree, no doubt, that this is to be expected: Deductive models rarely predict all the observed cases (and even when they do, we still allow that nature may present us with an exception tomorrow). In an area of knowledge as fragmentary and uneven as non-Western economies, we probably should be delighted at even the partial success of a model. But I am not concerned here simply with the models' failures to predict. Rather, I am concerned with the discernable tendency of model-builders to go only as far as their models permit and to stop there. This reflects an implicit stance that everything of interest in the universe of economic decision making ultimately is formalizable, and that other modes of understanding are inferior or unimportant and should be eliminated. We turn now to an examination of this assumption, in the context of a specific example.

Example: A "Well-Structured Problem"

The formal economist has a preference for "well-structured problems." In Simon's (1977:238–239; 305–307) terms, a well-structured problem is tied intimately to a developed system of deductive reasoning, and has the following properties:

1. A set of axioms or previously proved theorems.
2. A sequence of expressions derived mechanically from the axioms or theorems in Property 1 by means of legitimate operations.
3. A solution, which can be the last expression in the sequence 2, if the problem is purely formal; or else, if the solution involves acting upon the world in some way, there must also be a body of knowledge that will "reflect with complete accuracy . . . the laws (laws of nature) that govern the external world [p. 306; parentheses in original]."

Linear programing is generally conceded to be a well-structured problem-solving technique of proven usefulness, both by the proponents (e.g., Simon 1977:143) and the opponents (e.g., Georgescu-Roegen 1979:320) of formal analysis. The present example is a variety of the "optimum diet" problem, which in its general form asks what combination of available foods provides an adequate diet at the lowest cost. Because specific foods differ in both nutritional value and price, the task of linear programing is to find the amounts of each food that, taken together, will meet the nutritional requirements of a population while minimizing cost. Obviously, cheaper foods will be substituted for more expensive foods whenever possible, and expensive foods will be included only in the smallest amounts necessary to meet the minimum requirements for scarce nutrients.

This problem-solving technique seems especially promising in regard to subsistence farmers, who could be expected to allocate their scarce labor supplies with the goal of providing a good diet for the least cost. If we can operationalize "good diet" to mean "fully nutritious" and "least cost" to mean "least caloric energy [work] expended in food production," then linear programing will provide a solution that predicts the optimum strategy for achieving these ends.

Data for the present example were collected in a community of horticultural Indians in the tropical rainforest of the Peruvian Amazon.[1] The Machiguenga are a recently contacted group of Arawakan-speaking Indians who traditionally live in single-family houses, or in clusters of two or three houses, separated from each other by large expanses of tropical forest. Recently, such clusters have been attracted into the sphere of influence of small "school communities," where they settle within about an hour's walk of the school to obtain medicines, small quantities of trade goods (e.g., machetes, aluminum pots), and an opportunity for their children to attend primary school taught in their native language. Ethno-historical evidence indicates that the gradually increasing local population densities (average density is .8 persons per square mile), in interaction with the greater availability of steel tools, have led the Machiguenga to plant bigger gardens and to spend less time obtaining wild foods such as game and fish than they used to (Johnson 1977). Keeping in mind these changes in the conditions of food production, what mix of production strategies would provide a nutritious diet for the least work?

In seeking a solution to a problem like this with a formal technique, usually it is necessary to try different formulations of the problem. The linear-programing routine (here, in the form of a computer program) requires input of an array of foods and their nutritional contents, a cost vector (the labor cost in calories of work expended per kilogram of each food), and a vector of nutritional requirements (see Tables 2.1 and 2.2, and Footnote 4). The computer then searches through the available foods for combinations that meet the nutritional requirements, minimizing for cost. But the required input may be presented to the problem-solving routine in a variety of forms, each of which will lead to a unique solution.

The simplest form of the present problem groups Machiguenga foods under three production strategies:

1. Game and other wild foods obtained by hunting and gathering along forest trails.
2. Fish obtained by various techniques from local rivers and streams.
3. Domesticated crops cultivated in slash-and-burn gardens.

These are the three main categories of food production acknowledged by the Machiguenga, and each is regarded as a distinct strategy with no significant overlaps between them. Each provides a "food basket" or aggregate of foods, and each basket differs from the other two in cost

[1] For discussion of methods see Johnson 1975, Johnson and Behrens 1980, and Montgomery and Johnson 1976.

TABLE 2.1
Labor Costs and Nutrient Content of Machiguenga Food Strategies

	Hunting–gathering	Fishing	Gardening	Total required per house[a] per year
Labor cost per kilogram (kcal)	1151	739	80	
Nutrient content per kilogram				
Calories	880	1010	1330	4,540,965
Protein (gm)	55	179	15	60,980
Calcium (mg)	590	200	360	2,044,000
Phosphorous (mg)	730	1800	490	2,044,000
Iron (mg)	15	7	13	37,230
Vitamin A (r.e.)	1050	0	190	1,700,900
Thiamine (mg)	.9	.3	.7	2,190
Riboflavin (mg)	.8	.8	.4	2,590
Niacin (mg)	15	30	6	28,760
Vitamin C (mg)	350	0	210	124,100

Source: Johnson and Behrens (1980).
[a] Average household = 7.4 persons.

and nutritional value. The nutritional value of a particular basket can be calculated by averaging the quantities of a given nutrient provided by each food in the basket, in proportion to its share by weight, in the whole basket. Inspecting Table 2.1, we can see that the garden basket is clearly the least expensive, but of somewhat limited nutritional value compared to the expensive hunting and gathering basket, which is the most balanced source of nutrients. Fish are intermediate in cost, but relatively unbalanced in nutrients.

The first run of the computer was set to find a solution that met minimum requirements of nutrients without further constraints. It is not surprising, given the great cost differentials between strategies, that the solution given in this run was to devote 100% of labor time to gardens. Since the garden basket in aggregate has the typical nutritional value of a root crop, this would be analogous to telling an American family to eat nothing but inexpensive potatoes, since, if they were to eat plenty, they would get enough of every required nutrient at a low cost. Obviously, this solution is unacceptable because the human body is unable simply to sift through the nutrients in potatoes, discarding the overabundant calories while retaining the scarce other nutrients.

Hence, the first solution presented here (Solution 1 in Table 2.2) is

TABLE 2.2
Observed Behavior and Linear Programming Solutions[a] Compared

	Percentage of minimum requirement provided by strategy									
	Calories	Protein	Calcium	Phos-phorus	Iron	Vitamin A	Thiamine	Ribo-flavin	Niacin	Vitamin C
Solution 1 (Labor = 2,816,600 kcal/household/year)										
hunting–gathering 95%										
fishing 0%										
gardening 5%	100	232	100	128	159	164	155	101	160	972
Solution 2 (Labor = 278,100 kcal/household/year)										
hunting–gathering 0%										
fishing 0%										
gardening 100%										
maize 10%										
arrowroot 53%										
plantain 20%										
pigeon peas 17%	100	166	100	177	125	100	247	100	125	357
Observed behavior (Labor = 990,000 kcal/household/year)										
hunting–gathering 23%										
fishing 22%										
gardening 55%	210	248	128	196	251	88	230	120	183	1208

[a] Solutions 1 and 2 were computed by the L–P routine of the SOUPAC library of statistical computer programs.

under the constraint not to exceed the food energy requirement (calories), although all other nutrients in the model are free to exceed the minimum requirements. This constraint literally reversed the solution by calling for 95% of labor to be invested in hunting and gathering and only 5% in gardens; fish, again, are excluded altogether. This solution is about as far from observed behavior as it can be: In fact, the Machiguenga devote about one-fourth of their labor to hunting and gathering, another one-fourth to fishing, and the remaining one-half to gardens.

This extreme and unrealistic solution reflects the rigidity of the model in this form: The solution is forced to the hunting–gathering strategy by the poor nutritional balance of the garden and fish food-baskets. Although it fails to predict actual behavior, Solution 1 does help us to understand why the hunting–gathering strategy, despite its great cost, might be attractive to subsistence cultivators because of the nutritional diversity it offers.

The rigidity in the model to this point comes from considering the diet problem for subsistence farmers as one of production, not consumption. Simply because the Machiguenga produce food in certain quantities, it does not follow that they consume everything they produce, or that they consume everything in proportion as it is produced. Field observations show that the Machiguenga are exceedingly careful not to waste foods obtained in the forest or the rivers, but this is not the case for garden foods, where some foods are indeed "wasted." In particular, manioc, which is rich in calories but poor in other nutrients, is produced in great quantities. It is *the* staple food of the Machiguenga, and its overproduction is understood best as a security mechanism in a society where links of interdependence among households are comparatively weak and fragmentary. The food energy stored in the manioc roots in the garden acts as a kind of reserve fund in case of emergency. The Machiguenga eat foods selectively from their gardens, so that when a garden is abandoned manioc and occasionally other root crops are left over. In fact, one of the Machiguenga expressions for an abandoned garden is *ashi shintori*, meaning 'it [the manioc] belongs to peccary.'[2]

The only obstacle to treating each food separately is that a unique cost

[2] I often am asked whether this could be a deliberate strategy to attract peccary with manioc "bait." There is no doubt that it does work out this way in fact, for peccary (and other game) are bagged in gardens from time to time. But, when I put this question to a Machiguenga informant, he laughed and said, "Oh no, it is too much work for too little return. The peccaries are just pests in the gardens that we have to live with." I conclude that "extra" manioc is intended primarily as a security hedge, although it certainly does no harm to the meat supply.

cannot be assigned in the same way as prices are set for foods in a market place. A Machiguenga hunting trip, for example, is not labor expended in obtaining a single food but is completely opportunistic. The hunter usually has a single species of game in mind, depending on the season and information from neighbors about sightings of game, but he takes a variety of arrows intended for different categories of game; in short, he will hunt whatever he encounters. The hunting trip is also an occasion for opportunistic gathering of fruits, nuts, palm hearts, and insect foods. Thus the labor of a hunting–gathering trip produces an average of several foods, just as garden labor produces an aggregate of food crops. Still, there is nothing to prevent the Machiguenga from varying the proportions of crops in their gardens, and evidence is clear that they do.[3]

Hence, another form of the problem treats each food as separate, assigning to it an average cost proportional to its share of its particular basket, but allowing the linear-programing routine to sort through 18 foods and to select any combination.[4] The solution to this second form of the problem is to devote 100% of labor to garden foods, divided as follows among specific crops: 10% to maize, 53% to cocoyam, 20% to plantains, and 17% to pigeon peas (Solution 2, Table 2.2). With just these four garden foods, a balanced diet is obtained without need for hunting and gathering, or fishing.

Comparing Solutions 1 and 2 to the observed behavior of the Machiguenga (Table 2.2), we see that the observed behavior falls between the two solutions. The first solution is much more expensive than the observed pattern and is roughly analogous to a gourmet diet of exotic foods. The second solution is much less expensive than the observed pattern and is analogous to "good plain fare," nutritious but monotonous. Neither solution is close to predicting the observed pattern of Machiguenga food production. The two solutions do, however, effectively bracket the observed pattern and help us to understand it. The first solution may be said to establish the plausibility of expending

[3] That the Machiguenga do experiment with crops is clear. They plant experimental gardens (as do subsistence farmers typically—see Johnson 1972) where they cultivate new crop varieties obtained from neighbors as well as from distant regions.

[4] The 18 foods are, hunting and gathering (5): game, grubs and other insects, palm hearts, fruits, and nuts; fishing (1): various fresh-water fish, averaged; gardening (12): maize, manioc, cocoyam, sweet potato, sugar cane, papaya, pineapple, plantain, guava, beans, pigeon peas, banana.

Actually, if we count separate species of game, insects, fruits, nuts, and fish, the number of foods surely exceeds 100, and this does not take into account the many varieties of each garden crop distinguished by the Machiguenga.

effort in the expensive hunting and gathering strategy. The second helps us to understand how the garden can provide a substantially balanced diet despite the heavy emphasis on raising poorly balanced root crops. In fact, the actual balance of the 12 foods in the garden complex is not unrelated to the predictions of the model. If we group manioc and yams together with cocoyam into a category, "root crops," group plantains with bananas, and group beans with pigeon peas as "legumes," the comparison between model and observed behavior looks like this:

	Crop proportions by weight (Solution 2)	
Crop category	Model	Observed
maize	10%	5%
root crops	53% (cocoyam)	76% (cocoyam, manioc, yams)
banana/plantain	20% (plantain)	7% (banana, plantain)
legumes	17% (pigeon peas)	0.2% (pigeon peas, beans)
other	—	12% (sugar cane, papaya, pineapple, guava)

The main discrepancies here are the "overproduction" of roots (previously explained in terms of "security"), and the "underproduction" of legumes (protein foods with which the model would replace Machiguenga fish and game). We also may note that Solution 2 leaves sugar cane and fruits out of the picture, neglecting their possible role as sources of sugar for quick energy (an important function of these crops among the Machiguenga). Apart from this, there is an approximate fit between model and observed reality that is quite suggestive.

Neither solution has anything to say about fish, however. In order to explore and interpret the various inconsistencies between formal model and empirical reality, and to examine the role formal models can play in our understanding of this and other problems in agricultural decision making, we now turn to Simon's (1977) concept of the "ill-structured problem."

The Linear-Programing Example as an "Ill-Structured Problem"

> In general, the problems presented to problem solvers by the world are best regarded as Ill-Structured Problems. They become Well-Structured Problems only in the process of being *prepared* for problem solvers. It is not exaggerating much to say that there are no Well-

> Structured Problems, only Ill-Structured Problems that have been formalized for problem solvers [Simon 1977:309; emphasis added].

Behind the linear-programing diet problem lies an original form of the problem that, though general and imprecise, is nonetheless the essence of the question we are really asking: Given that the Machiguenga produce their own food through their own efforts, what is the most satisfying diet they can obtain, taking into account the dissatisfaction entailed in producing it?

Preparing this problem for a well-structured problem solver like linear programing requires two steps:

1. *Reduction* of the original problem to a small subset of attributes permitted by the formal problem-solving routine.
2. *Assumptions* about the data needed to fill the gaps between our imperfect knowledge of the real world and the perfect knowledge demanded by the routine. Actually, these are simply successive stages in moving the problem from an intuitive to an objective form.

Reduction of the problem is necessary because any formal problem-solving routine is highly restricted in the kinds of information it can use. I (like any ethnographer after long-term fieldwork among one people), can list readily many factors that play a role in the Machiguengas' calculations about food production. Nutrition is certainly one of these. The Machiguenga recognize that different foods have different properties, and that a balance must be struck between them. The late afternoon meal—their main meal of the day—ideally includes a starchy staple (manioc, cocoyam), a vegetable (palm heart, leafy garden vegetables), and a small portion of meat (fish, game; red meats are regarded as potent, to be eaten in small quantities).

Also relevant to their nutritional attitudes is a strong emphasis on food diversity, seen both in their conversations about food and in the large variety of foods we observed in their homes. The Machiguenga, however, are more likely to discuss this matter in terms of "taste," an area in which they have an ample vocabulary for describing the flavors and textures of food. Many of the foods in their diet are of excellent quality; the fish, in particular, are equal in flavor and texture to our salmon or trout, and when roasted or smoked are without peer. But the Michiguenga also show a high regard for all the foods in their diet, and rarely express distaste for any particular food (except in the case of personal food taboos, a subject too complex to be taken up here). Thus, they would eat with apparent relish not only sweet ripe fruits, but also green ones that to me seemed dry and tasteless.

The dissatisfaction entailed in productive work is also complicated. Participant observation has convinced me that the Machiguenga enjoy a certain amount of work, and if they were somehow forced not to work they would feel impoverished. But they also prefer certain kinds of work over others. Garden work, on the whole, is least preferred; the monotonous routines in the tropical sun wear them down. Fishing is the most sociable kind of work; usually, it is undertaken by whole families or groups of families, and is characterized throughout by a spirit of joviality and ribaldry. Hunting and gathering, although in terms of pure energy expenditure by far the most demanding labor, is clearly the most preferred. Forest trails are steep and difficult, but the forest is cool, attractive, and continuously surprising, and the foods obtained there are among the most desired. Sometimes the trip into the forest has the quality of a picnic, and it would be difficult for the anthropologist to see it as work at all, were not detailed advance planning and animated discussion of alternative routes evidence of an underlying seriousness.

In this light, the linear-programing form of the problem appears almost absurd in its simplicity: a labor cost vector (measured in calories of energy expended), a vector of minimum nutritional requirements, and an array of foods and their nutrient contents. It must be stressed that this is not by choice but by necessity: There simply exist no methods for including all the considerations that we have good reason to believe enter into people's efforts to balance the satisfaction from food with the cost of obtaining it.

But even in this reduced form, we still do not have a well-structured problem. The main features of a well-structured problem are met in this example by linear programing itself: that is, axioms and mechanical procedures for producing a solution. It is the caveat that Simon adds, almost as an afterthought, that really opens Pandora's box: the need to reflect "with complete accuracy" the relevant attributes of the external world. For our knowledge of that world is far from perfect and recedes in quality with our distance from the scene we are trying to understand. In preparing the data for a well-structured solution, we make innumerable assumptions that in effect "gloss over" the incompleteness of the data. How rare it is to see the presentation of a formal model compared to an empirical data set, then followed by a detailed list of all the assumptions and small "fudgings" that were needed to complete the data analysis! If this were required (as something approximating it is in the laboratory sciences), the list would take up more space than the analysis. Instead, we find a certain impatience with these data questions, that just "get in the way" of clear thinking and lead to "vague and impressionistic" analyses.

To illustrate, I choose three of the numerous questions that can be asked about the present data; and give examples of the kinds of assumptions that are inevitable if a formal model is to be tested by empirical data.

1. What is a nutritious diet? As our knowledge of human needs goes, we have a rather good body of reliable knowledge on diet and nutrition. For the model, recommendations made by respected international panels of nutritionists were followed (FAO 1970, 1973; NAS 1974). Yet these recommendations are open to many criticisms. For example:

(*a*) The minimum requirements are set high enough that persons with very unusual needs for particular nutrients can be satisfied. The National Academy of Sciences notes that its estimate of calcium requirements could probably be halved without serious health consequences. Inflated values are given for certain other nutrients as well. That this inflation is by 100%, rather than by some more precise figure like 82% or 117%, indicates the level of accuracy that is available to us. Also, apropos the discussion, a political aspect of the high intake recommendations has been identified by some observers (Clark 1970:10–15).

(*b*) There are complex interaction effects between particular nutrients. A well-known example is that both maize and beans contain incomplete proteins, but in combination each complements the other to constitute a good source of protein. As it happens, the second linear-programing solution, combining maize and pigeon peas, might accidentally lead to a similar complementarity, but the food composition data do not contain this information (INCAP 1961) and this complementarity of proteins is in no way taken into account by the linear-programing procedure in seeking a solution. There are many other, even less well-understood, interaction effects (e.g., that high rates of protein consumption also require higher rates of calcium) that cannot be included in the well-structured form of the problem.

2. What is the true picture of Machiguenga food production? The data reported here are reliable data, in terms of the state of the art in this kind of research; all are based on representative sampling and have been quantified according to generally accepted procedures. But other questions remain. For example, most of the data were collected over a 13-month period of fieldwork in 1972–1973. How can those data claim to

be representative of an average year? I can report that the Machiguenga considered it an unexceptional year, but this is certainly "soft" data. Furthermore, the data were collected on a sample of only 105 adults and children, because these were the only people accessible in reasonable walking time from our field residence. What of the isolated forest settlements inaccessible except for short visits after difficult treks, or other communities living at different elevations and under different ecological circumstances? Again, we are at the limits of present knowledge, for either our tool kit of methods is inadequate, or research funds and personnel are insufficient ever to answer these questions satisfactorily.[5]

3. Another set of uncertainties enters when we try to mesh our knowledge of specific populations with our knowledge of food and nutrition in general. For example, the analysis of the nutritional content of Machiguenga foods is based on published analyses of typical foods from Latin America. There is no guarantee that the maize or plantain samples analyzed in published studies are identical to the local varieties grown by the Machiguenga. Likewise, we have no way of knowing if our nutritional theory concerning a healthy diet, which is based largely on studies of populations in industrialized societies, is applicable to an Amazon Indian population.

"Persistent Optimism" and the Limits of Formalism

Given these two transformations from an ill-structured into a well-structured problem—that the problem must be reduced to a fraction of its original form, and that the empirical data are far from meeting the formal requirements for perfect information—it is not reasonable to expect formal decision models to predict more than certain limited features of any relatively comprehensive description of economic behavior. This does not mean that the *idea* that people make decisions in terms of their own perceived self-interest, is wrong. We cannot follow Dalton (1969:67–68) in denying that traditional agriculturalists make choices. But it is not enough to say that decision theory *in principle* applies to all human behavior, because *in practice* it cannot; or rather, for the majority of cross-cultural instances, formal decision analyses do

[5] These data shortcomings are not simply true of anthropology. Economic data are also full of lacunae and sampling problems. For example, despite the current energy "crisis," there is no reliable knowledge concerning how much petroleum is now in storage in the United States. Yet model builders in both fields tend to gloss over these *inherent* problems rather than confront them and accept the implications.

not account for the data without the ad hoc, intuitive, soft considerations that formal models are explicitly supposed to avoid.

At this point I am sure that objections will have begun to mount in many readers' minds. Is not this simply a temporary situation owing to the newness of our efforts? Does not the great success of formal economics at predicting economic behavior in western economies imply that success in other areas is likely as soon as we catch up to economists in sophistication? What is the point of these discouraging words if we have nothing better to offer? I would reply that the situation is more fundamental than temporary, that the success of economics is limited even in western economies, and that we do have something better to offer.

The idea that failure to predict is a temporary situation, to be expected in a new field, reflects the persistent optimism that is common among model builders. Simon, for example, despite his inventive excursions outside the most narrow formalisms of economics, in the end returns repeatedly to this optimistic position (Simon 1977:151–152, 174, 241, 319, 324). He is consistent in arguing that there is no fundamental difference between mathematical–deductive decision theory and the adjustments required by his concepts of the "good enough solution" and the "ill-structured problem." His view is that every ill-structured problem can be resolved into a finite set of well-structured problems, each of which separately can lead through suitably mechanical procedures to unambiguous solutions. These rigorous solutions, then, *somehow* will add up to a sort of macrosolution to the ill-structured problem. He walks repeatedly to the edge of the known world, so to speak, looks down into the chasm beyond, and then hurries back to the touchstone of formal economics. In my view, this form of belief falls in the domain of faith rather than science (Johnson 1978:12–21).

There is nothing wrong with this per se, as long as it is recognized for what it is. But this particular belief may be questioned on two counts. First, there is the troublesome inability of formal models to predict observed outcomes, as noted earlier in this chapter. Model builders typically do not test their models with new empirical research, tending rather to illustrate them with simplified, or even imaginary, examples. This has led Dreyfus (1972:188) to suspect many formalists of choosing highly simplified areas of experience where problems *can* be solved with formal procedures, rather than letting prior theoretical commitments determine which problems should be attempted. Buchler and Nutini (1969:2–3), in fact, explicitly favor this selective approach: "If it is unrealistic to assume that the universe conforms to mathematical principles, then we must search for those aspects of the universe which admit of mathematical formulations." This seems to put the cart before the horse, to say that we are to be mathematicians first and problem-oriented social scientists only when the mathematical conditions permit.[6]

Second, behind this persistent optimism lies a highly dubious psychological assumption that "The mind can be viewed as a device operating on bits of information according to formal rules. . . . [It is] a third-person process in which the involvement of the "processor" plays no essential role [Dreyfus 1972:68]." The assumption is that when people anywhere make decisions, their problem-solving procedures are identical in all the significant ways to the mathematico–deductive routines we program computers to follow. Specifically, holistic processes of pattern recognition and evaluation by integrated "selves" that bear traditions and have emotions as well as logic are effectively eliminated from the theory.

There is a natural tendency for devotees of a unified theoretical framework like that of formal economics to exaggerate the scope and power of the theory. Homans (1967) docs this when he treats the principles of rational choice as the unique general theory for all the social sciences—all others being regarded as special-purpose theories for limited problem areas. In the present case, Homans would say that the optimizing decision model in the form of linear programing is the embodiment of the general theory, whereas the specific model of ecological adaptation in the form of nutritional requirements and energy costs reflects a special purpose theory useful for applying this particular case of the general theory.

But this can be easily turned around to make adaptation the general theory: Human beings must survive to be able to make decisions, just as they must make decisions to survive. It really makes no sense, for example, to ask whether the Machiguenga are primarily decision makers seeking satisfaction or organisms adapting to an environment, since both are equally true and in no way contradictory. And if an adaptation perspective leads us to consider decision processes that cannot be formalized in the foreseeable future, like the desire for dietary diversity

[6] At this point, in an earlier draft of this chapter, two readers wondered why Behrens and I had not tried to bring the model and data closer together by "guestimating" more parameters, like the "security value" of manioc, or the "negative utility" of agricultural work versus hunting–gathering work. The point is precisely this: Such guestimates are not the genuine quantification demanded by the model. To present such a "fudged" correspondence between model and data would be misleading at best and at worst would violate the strict canons of science concerning what it means to test a model.

or the subjective enjoyment of work, then these processes should not be ignored, but treated qualitatively and, in a word, ethnographically.

The Irreducible Need for Ethnography: Political Considerations

But, can our plea for a middle ground between formalist and holistic–qualitative approaches be justified in view of the demonstrated success of formalist principles via constant testing of economic theory in daily practice in Western economies? First, we must note that doubts about the adequacy of formalist theory even in Western economies are crystallizing as old models fail to account for recent behavior affecting unemployment, inflation, and energy: "The malaise of which economists now suffer is not imaginary . . . ; the respect that economists inspire among business circles is not what it used to be [Paul Samuelson, quoted in Georgescu–Roegen 1979:319]." Second, when our interest shifts to behavior during economic change in non-Western societies, the balance has to shift in favor of holistic ethnographic research, because economic circumstances in these societies are too unfamiliar for existing theories to be expected to apply without modification.[7]

The decision whether to rely on our ready-made formal theories or to turn to new empirical descriptions for guidance is not simply a scientific question, but also a political one. The implicit perspective of formal economic theory is that all the necessary information concerning the economic motivation of the actors already exists fully in the theory. The rigorous deductive form of the theory ensures us accurate and reliable solutions to such problems as resource allocation, factor mix, marketing strategy, and so on. The ability to predict the actual behavior of real farmers, storekeepers, and middlemen can be defined as a nonissue; if observed behavior does not conform to the models, this is just taken as evidence that the behavior falls short of "optimum" (or, perhaps, that our empirical descriptions are faulty).

What makes this a political assumption is that it joins formal economists with change agents as allies convinced of their superior

[7] Most readers will be familiar with Burling's (1962) article, "Maximization Theories and the Study of Economic Anthropology," but I would urge a fresh look at the section (pp. 805–809) where he discusses the limitation of economics in practice to items and processes that carry a price tag.

knowledge and engaged in an effort to bring enlightenment to the less informed. It is also a political fact that "ignorant" populations are often poorly controlled by the central governments trying to change them, and that the likely outcome of "successful" change is increased central political and economic control. The assumption that our models are more correct than those of the actors they refer to can be taken as a license to introduce economic change even against the wishes of local populations, on the grounds that the people "do not know what is good for them."

The criticisms of formal modeling at this level are equally political. One asserts the right of local populations to self-determination, without undue external pressure or misleading claims about the benefits of change (Bodley 1975:168–169). Another stresses the existence of great local variation in environmental and social circumstances that make it impossible for outsiders to have a sufficient understanding of the situation to safeguard their theoretically reasonable models against prescribing empirically absurd strategies (Cancian 1977). In either case, the political message is that the people whose lives are directly affected by the change should determine its course.

How this issue is viewed by governments and other agencies of economic development determines how the role of the anthropologist is evaluated. For example, a colleague of mine, a physician and specialist in health-care delivery, was asked to visit hospitals and clinics in several developing countries as a consultant to a firm of economists evaluating government health-care programs. At the end of his 2-week tour of duty, the physician asked why they had not included an anthropologist, since there were many cultural and social factors to be taken into account in planning health-care improvements. They answered that they would have liked to, but that they needed to complete such a study in about six weeks, from initial research to final report and recommendations; they said that an anthropologist would need a year or two, and then still might not have the information they wanted.

This last comment is an exaggeration, since anthropologists who are familiar with a region can draw upon previous experience in conjunction with a relatively short term of additional research to offer unique and valuable insights. The experienced ethnographer can visit a new community in a region with which he or she is already familiar, and in a rather short time develop reliable forecasts or "anticipations" on specific questions like "What form of credit do the people want?" "Will they accept cooperatives?" "Will they try high-yield hybrid seed?" The answers often will be imprecise compared to quantitative predictions derived from profit-maximization models, but they will stand a greater chance of being plausible and leading to feasible policy; and that also is a kind of precision.

At a deeper level, what seems to be at stake is a fundamental difference in approach to evaluating the effectiveness of research on economic change. The economist, confronted by practical realities in the form of limited budgets and political pressure to reach decisions rapidly and to keep the "facts" simple and numerical, naturally prefers to operate within the framework of clear-cut models of decision making under certainty, rather than deal with the ambiguities of how people perceive their own needs, the complicated and "folksy" notions they have about their environment, and a more humanized, qualitative sense of what is "good for them." It is in these last two senses that anthropologists evaluate the effectiveness of their research on economic change.

The machine-like procedures of formal decision theory assume machine-like people making decisions in the real world. But the fact that people are not machine-like is a major reason that formal models have trouble predicting their behavior. The ethnographer, however, is not a machine. In the course of ethnographic fieldwork, there develop not mere impressions, but solidly based intuitions drawing upon the same ability to weigh large numbers of factors and arrive at good enough solutions as the people being studied. I want to stress that these intuitions are neither "vague" nor "impressionistic," but reflect the experience and accumulated cultural wisdom of the people themselves.

In our present example, Solution 2 misleadingly suggests that the Machiguenga could provide a suitable diet by farming about half as much land as they now do; they need neither forests nor streams. This could be said to justify the current government's plans to legalize Indian control over small plots of land, opening up the remainder of their common habitat to legal settlement by impoverished farmers from the overpopulated highlands. But the Machiguenga now obtain most of their materials for tools, houses, matting, utensils, and their prized diversity of diet, in the forest. To obtain these under the proposed changes, they would have to work for wages and raise cash crops. This would integrate them into the Peruvian economy, and increase the flow of cash (which in government statistics will count as economic development).

Questions about whether this is "fair" to the Machiguenga (who, incidentally, control their own population quite effectively and do not need to expand their territory), or about how to evaluate the change in "quality of life" that accompanies a rise in "standard of living," are generally neglected and may even appear naive in the light of political reality. The scientist and the moralist may have little to do with what actually happens in economic change, which is often enough an implacable process of historical change that sweeps everyone before it. But in those areas of economic change where there is some control, in the form of public policy decisions and the expenditure of development funds, and where there is a commitment to local participation in the change process, there is no alternative but to include, as an equal partner to the formal theoretical analysis, an ethnographic investigation capable of fleshing out the analysis and rooting it in the local soil.[8]

Conclusion

In his review of mathematical "optimization" studies in anthropology, White (1973) writes: "Anthropology to date has contributed only in a limited degree to the empirical refining of the theories of optimization, even though anthropological fieldwork provides the best possible natural laboratories for such work [p. 387]." Both parts are true: The contribution has been limited, and the possibilities are great. It may be, however, that more than "refining" is needed. The formalism and effectiveness of economics are not due to power inhering in the theory as such, but to a particular operationalization in the form of "price theory," that is culturally and historically limited in its application.

In this chapter I have deliberately understated the benefits of formalist model-building for an understanding of problems in agricultural decision making. Anyone who has done formal modeling will see no paradox when I say it is at once a highly organizing experience and an imaginatively stimulating one. It promotes clarity of thought, detailed attention to measurement, and orderly exploration of alternative possibilities. I have emphasized instead the reasons for avoiding a reductionistic adherence to formalism and the associated tendency to depreciate alternative approaches, particularly when this reductionism becomes an implicit part of the political decision process.

The unique powers of a formal analysis are purchased at the expense of flexibility, particularly in the ability to anticipate the creativity, or "novelty" (Georgescu–Roegen 1979:321) of human solutions to eco-

[8] Cancian (1978) has pointed out that the professional anthropologist is too expensive for local agricultural communities. But anthropologists can take a regional approach, gaining direct experience in a few specific communities and generalizing through briefer visits to numerous other communities in a region.

nomic problems. Agricultural decision making is full of surprising behavior. Several of the chapters in this volume attest to the mystification (and frustration) of economists or government officials when confronted with the behavior of particular farmers. In fact, what is actually surprising is that anyone would think that an abstract theory, operationalized with reference to an industrial firm or similar limited frame, could prescribe behavior for farmers who have lived in an environment their entire lives, observed countless details about its soils, crops, weather, labor supply, market prices, and government intervention, and have integrated these experiences with cultural "rules of thumb" into a total understanding that all our research methods in combination can hardly fathom.

But if the formal and abstract technology of our discipline cannot by itself generate the understanding we seek, we have another aid of inestimable value in the person of the ethnographer, who develops the ability to apprehend the whole context of decision making by living in the locale long enough to overcome ethnocentric bias and sense the rationality by which decisions are made locally. This understanding can be made more careful and rigorous by being formalized wherever possible in models of proven effectiveness, but it can never fully be reduced to or comprehended by them.

Acknowledgement

I thank Peggy Barlett, Frank Cancian, Michael Chibnik, Nicholas Georgescu-Roegen, Daniel Gross, Orna Johnson, David Richards, and Douglas White for their helpful comments.

References

Bodley, John
1975 Victims of Progress. Menlo Park, CA: Cummings.
Boyd, David
1975 Crops, Kiaps, & Currency: Flexible Behavioral Strategies Among the Ilakia Awa of Papua New Guinea. Ph.D. Dissertation, Anthropology. UCLA.
Buchler, Ira, and Hugo Nutini, Eds.
1969 Game Theory in the Behavioral Sciences. Pittsburgh: University of Pittsburgh Press.
Burling, Robbins
1962 Maximization Theories and the Study of Economic Anthropology. American Anthropologist 64:802–821.

Cancian, Frank
1977 Can Anthropology Help Agricultural Development? Culture and Agriculture, No. 2 (March 1977).
1978 Practical Generalizations in Development Anthropology. Paper presented at the Tenth International Congress of Anthropological and Ethnological Sciences, New Delhi.

Clark, Colin
1970 *Starvation or Plenty?* London: Secker and Warburg.

Dalton, George
1969 Theoretical Issues in Economic Anthropology. Current Anthropology 10:63–101.

Davenport, William
1960 Jamaican Fishing: A Game Theory Analysis. Yale University Publications in Anthropology 59:3–11.

Dreyfus, Hubert
1972 What Computers Can't Do: A Critique of Artificial Reason. New York: Harper.

FAO
1970 Requirements of Ascorbic Acid, Vitamin D, Vitamin B_{12}, Folate, and Iron. Food and Agriculture Organization, Nutrition Meetings Report No. 47. Rome.
1973 Energy and Protein Requirements. Food and Agriculture Organization, Nutrition Meetings Report No. 52. Rome.

Georgescu–Roegen, Nicholas
1979 Methods in Economic Science. Journal of Economic Issues 13:317–328.

Gould, Peter
1963 Man Against His Environment: A Game Theoretic Framework. Annals of the Association of American Geographers 53:290–297.

Homans, George
1967 The Nature of Social Science. New York: Harcourt Brace, and World.

INCAP
1961 Tabla de Composición de Alimentos para Uso en América Latina. Guatemala: Instituto de Nutrición de Centro América y Panama.

Johnson, Allen
1972 Individuality and Experimentation in Traditional Agriculture. Human Ecology 1:149–159.
1975 Time Allocation in a Machiguenga Community. Ethnology 14:301–310
1977 The Energy Costs of Technology in a Changing Environment: A Machiguenga Case. *In* Material Culture. H. Lechtman and R. Merrill, Eds. pp. 155–157. St. Paul: West.
1978 Quantification in Cultural Anthropology. Stanford: Stanford University Press.

Johnson, Allen, and Clifford Behrens
1980 Machiguenga Food Production Decisions: A Linear Programming Analysis. Unpublished Manuscript, University of California, Los Angeles.

Montgomery, Edward, and Allen Johnson
1976 Machiguenga Energy Expenditure. Ecology of Food and Nutrition 6:97–105.

Moore, Omar Khayam
1957 Divination: A New Perspective. American Anthropologist 59:69–74.

NAS
1974 Recommended Dietary Allowances. Washington, D.C.: Food and Nutrition Board, National Academy of Sciences.

Pospisil, Leopold
1963 Kapauku Papuan Economy. New Haven: Yale University Publications in Anthropology.

Read, Dwight, and Katherine Read
1970 Critique of Davenport's Game Theory Analysis. American Anthropologist 72:351–355.
Simon, Herbert
1977 Models of Discovery. Boston: Reidel.
White, Douglas
1973 Mathematical Anthropology. *In* Handbook of Social and Cultural Anthropology. J. Honigmann, ed. pp. 369–446. Chicago: Rand McNally.

[4]

CURRENT ANTHROPOLOGY Vol. 19, No. 4, December 1978

Infrastructures, Societies, and History[1]

by Maurice Godelier

THIS ARTICLE is a translation of my response to a request from the review *Dialectiques* for my opinion on two points fundamental to the social sciences, namely, ideology and class. For want of space, I shall merely outline some provisional conclusions that I have reached as briefly and as clearly as possible. I shall be dealing with four topics in turn: (1) the distinction between infrastructure and superstructure; (2) the relationship between the determinant role of the economy in the last analysis and the dominant role of any given superstructure; (3) the *idéel*[2] aspect of social reality and the distinction between ideological and nonideological when dealing with *idéel* realities; (4) the role of violence and consent in the workings of the power of domination of an order or a class, etc. (can we speak of a paradox of "legitimacy" regarding the emergence of classes and the state?).

Before going any farther, I should like to emphasize my debt to the ever-growing—and already immense—body of fresh material being thrown up by anthropological and historical research. As far as history is concerned, I am a mere amateur. My reading has centered mainly on problems of state formation and the transformation of class relations. I am afraid I shall probably disappoint those of my readers who would have liked me to spell out more precisely the connections between my general, abstract positions and this wealth of anthropological material.

[1] This article summarizes the main themes of a book due to be published by Gallimard under the title *Infrastructures, Sociétés, Histoire*. It is a translation of the paper "Infrastructures, Sociétés, Histoire," which appeared in the journal *Dialectiques* no. 21, pp. 41–53. The translation, by Rupert Swyers, is by permission of the editor of *Dialectiques*.

[2] The word *idéel* is a neologism used rarely and almost exclusively by modern French philosophers influenced by German phenomenology. Rather than coin a fresh English neologism, the translation remains with the original.

MAURICE GODELIER is Professor of Anthropology and Economics and Director of Studies at the Ecole des Hautes Etudes en Sciences Sociales (54, Boulevard Raspail, 75270 Paris Cedex 06, France). Born in 1934, he was educated at the Ecole Normale Supérieure in Paris (Agrégé de Philosophie, 1959). He has done fieldwork among the Baruya of New Guinea (1967–69) under the auspices of the Centre Nationale de Recherche Scientifique. His research interests are Melanesia, economic systems, Marxist analysis, processes of class formation, and ideology. His publications include *Rationalité et irrationalité en économie* (Paris: Maspero, 1966; English translation, London, 1973), *Sur les sociétés précapitalistes* (Paris: Editions Sociales, 1970), *Horizon, trajets marxistes en anthropologie* (Paris: Maspero, 1973; English translation, Cambridge, 1977), and the edited volume *Un domaine contesté: L'anthropologie économique* (Paris: Mouton, 1974).

The present paper, submitted in final form 10 III 78, was sent for comment to 40 scholars. The responses are printed below and are followed by a reply by the author.

THE DISTINCTION BETWEEN INFRASTRUCTURE AND SUPERSTRUCTURE

For a Marxist, surely, any examination of the role of ideology, of the conditions governing its formation and its transformation, or of its impact upon the evolution of societies must involve investigation into the relations between infrastructure, superstructure, and ideology. Ought we, with Althusser, Balibar, and Establet (1965), to call these different things "instances"? Ought we to regard them as "levels" of social reality? as somehow substantive distinctions between different kinds of social reality? as institutional slices or cross-sections of its substance? I don't think so. To my mind, a society does not have a top and a bottom, or even levels. This is because the distinction between infrastructure and superstructure is not a distinction between institutions. Its principle, rather, is one of a distinction between functions. What, then, does the notion of infrastructure really cover?

It designates a combination—which exists in all societies—of at least three series of social and material conditions that enable a society's members to produce and to reproduce the material conditions of their social existence. These sets are:

1. The specific ecological and geographical conditions within which a society exists and from which it extracts its material means of existence.

2. The productive forces, i.e., the material and *intellectual* means that the members of a society implement, within the different "labour" processes, in order to work upon nature and to extract from it their means of existence, thereby transforming it into a "socialized" nature.

3. Social relations of production, that is, relations of any kind that assume one or another (or all) of the following three functions: (*a*) determining the social form of access to resources and to control of the means of production; (*b*) allocating the labour force of a society's members among the different labour processes which produce its material base, and organizing these different processes; (*c*) determining the social form of redistribution of the product of individual or collective labour and, consequently, the forms of circulation or noncirculation of these products.

We should bear in mind that, strictly speaking, what Marx (1958:13) called the economic structure of a society was merely the social relations of production: "These relations of production taken together form the economic structure of society."[3] We should also bear in mind that, although productive forces and relations of production are distinct phenomena, they never exist separately; they always exist together in some specific combination. What Marx calls "mode of

[3] "Der Gesamtheit dieser Produktions verhältnisse bildet die Ökonomische Struktur des Gesellschaft."

production" or "social form of production" are in fact the various specific forms of these combinations. These definitions call for a certain number of remarks.

First, among the different productive forces I include what I have referred to as "intellectual" means of acting upon nature. By this I mean all the "knowledge" that a given society may have of nature, but also its body of technical processes, of rules governing the manufacture of tools, of rules governing the use of the body in work, etc. It will be observed, then, that right at the heart of man's most material relationship with the material nature surrounding him lies a complex body of representations, ideas, patterns, etc., which I call *idéel* realities; their presence and their action are essential for any kind of material activity to be able to occur. Contemporary anthropology has started to take stock of the *idéel* realities which form part of the different material processes in the societies investigated. It is this that constitutes the vast field of *ethnoscience*, collecting native taxonomies of plants, animals, soils, climates, rules for the manufacture of tools, etc. This is also the purpose of Needham's (1954–76) studies of Chinese technology and science or of the work of Haudricourt (1962; Haudricourt and Brunhes-Delamarre 1955, Haudricourt and Hedin 1943).

Now, these *idéel* realities may be grasped, in the first place, in the speech of the peoples and social groups that use them. They thus exist as *linguistic* realities, as facts that are indissociable from language and thought, and it is through these that they may be communicated throughout the social body and transmitted from one generation to the next.

Clearly, then, the distinction between infrastructure, superstructure, and ideology may be seen as a distinction between functions and not between institutions. As we have just seen, thought and language may function as components of the infrastructure, as part of a society's forces of production. The distinction, then, is not between material and immaterial, for I fail to see in what way thought could be less material than the rest of social life. Nor is it a distinction between tangible and intangible. It is a distinction of position within those activities necessary to the reproduction of social life.

The second point on which I should like to comment is the notion of the *labour process*. First of all, it should be noted that the concept of work is not common to all societies. Ancient Greek has two words, *poiein* and *prattein*, neither of which means to work: respectively they mean making and doing. In Latin, the word *labor* is used for any kind of heavy activity, like the word *ponos* in Greek, and the word *negotium* designates an activity that interrupts or counteracts the *otium*, or leisure, that is the mark of a free man as well as being the condition permitting him to conduct his political and cultural activities. It is extremely rare, furthermore, that the word labour, where used, is used to connote and contain the idea of a "transformation" of nature and of man. All these representations form part of the labour process, and they are joined by other representations which legitimize the presence or absence of a given social group in a given labour process. These representations may, for example, serve to justify the fact that it is the women that are sent out to gather wild plants, or to carry firewood, and they may moreover present such activities as being unworthy of men, to whom are reserved—as of right, we may say—nobler activities such as hunting, war, or the mastery of rituals. But in touching on this question we are in fact touching on the *points of contact* between relations of production and the division of labour.

It is important to bear in mind, on the question of relations of production, that, depending on the society and the historical epoch under consideration, relations of production do not occupy the same *locus*, nor do they take the same form; consequently, they do not have the same effects upon the evolution of societies. I shall offer two examples of what might be termed the topology of economics—the comparative topology of relations of production. In hunter-gatherer societies such as that of the Australian Aborigines, it has been observed that the social relations that govern the hunting and gathering territories, determine the composition of the groups doing the hunting and gathering, and decide how the product of these activities is shared out are relations of kinship, i.e., relations of descent, marriage, and residence. To be more precise, we may observe that the (somewhat) *abstract* condition of appropriation of nature is membership in a *descent* group, which inherits common (though "nonexclusive") rights over the undomesticated resources of different territories from generation to generation. In the everyday process of *concrete* appropriation, what happens is that consanguineal *and* affinal relations form the cooperative framework for hunting and gathering and for the distribution of produce. But we need to go farther still, for in practice an Australian band—a unit of direct, everyday appropriation of nature—is composite in structure. It is composed of a central core of men descended patrilineally from a number of common ancestors and heirs to rights over a given portion of territory; around this core is a cluster of allies, i.e., representatives of different groups that have either given or received wives in the course of earlier generations. This provides the group with the possibility of using several different territories should the need arise. The chief feature of the system, then, is the fact of *shared* ownership of resources by a number of kinship groups; these kinship groups, moreover, are not exclusive owners of these rights, since, in certain critical circumstances, allied groups also have rights to the same territory.

Here we arrive at a fundamental point, namely, the relationship between the nature of the forces of production and the nature of social relations of production. Underlying this system of shared, though nonexclusive, ownership of resources, we find not only that the individual is unable to reproduce himself except in groups, but also that groups cannot reproduce themselves if they are alone and require other groups in order to be able to do so. This is where productive forces mesh with social forms of relations of production. We shall be coming back to this point later, but already it is difficult to escape the conclusion that, here, *relations of kinship function as relations of production* and that they do so *internally*. The distinction between infrastructure and superstructure is not a distinction between institutions, but a *distinction between different functions within a single institution*.

My second example—based on the work of Frankfort (1948), Oppenheim (1964), Adams (1966), and others—deals with ancient Sumerian organization. It would seem that, in the city-states of Mesopotamia, the land was originally regarded as belonging to a god, the god whose temple stood in the middle of the city. The economy worked as a vast centralized system within which the communities of the city and the surrounding countryside were subject to the authority of the priests of the god who owned the land, and these communities owed a portion of their labour and their produce to these priests. Here, it will be observed, it was religious relations that functioned internally as relations of production. The example of a Greek city-state, on the other hand, would show that membership—by birth—in a *polis* gave the free citizen both private and public rights over the city's land. Here, politics, in the Greek sense of the word, functioned internally as a relation of production.

Before drawing any general conclusions from this analysis, I should like to return to one essential point, one that has given rise to a good deal of confusion among Marxists: the distinction between labour process and process of production. Certain anthropologists, such as Terray (1969) and Rey (1971, 1973), have dubbed the different forms of labour process that they have discovered in the description of a particular society—in this case, Meillassoux's (1964) description of the different forms of hunting, farming, and crafts to be found among the Ivory

Coast Guro—"mode of production." Hence, we have hunting, farming, pastoral, etc., modes of production. This, however, is to confuse *forms of the division of labour* with *modes of production*. The practice, within the *same* relations of production, of, for example, farming combined with animal husbandry and small-scale domestic handicrafts does not imply the existence of several different modes of production with interconnections that need to be found. It is at this point that some people invoke the concept of "economic and social formation." In fact, what basically defines a mode of production are the different forms of appropriation of resources, of means of production, and of the product itself. There may, therefore, be several different forms of labour process and cooperation which combine on the basis of a single form of property. One can imagine just how profitable a rigorous review of the vast mass of anthropological and historical material now available would be. But one can also see that by no means everything that ought to be said has been said regarding abstract notions such as force of production, and that even within these notions there remain vast unexplored regions waiting to be opened up by theoretical analysis.

We may already draw one general conclusion, at any rate. This is that the distinction between infrastructure and superstructure is not a distinction between institutions, or instances, but between functions. *It is only in certain societies, and particularly in capitalist society, that this distinction between functions happens to coincide with a distinction between institutions.* This, in my view, is the real reason for the "epistemological break" brought about by Marx's work; the prime reasons for this break are to be sought not in Marx's thought itself, but in the nature of the capitalist mode of production, which, far more than many others, separated economics, politics, religion, kinship, art, etc., into so many distinct institutions.

Once this has been grasped, a vast new field of investigation opens up, namely, the search for the reasons and the conditions which, in history, have brought about shifts in the locus—and hence changes in the forms—of relations of production. To carry out this investigation, though, it is first necessary to eschew attempts to deduce the locus and form of a society's economy from some dubious abstract theory. For a Marxist—as for anyone else—the main thing is to go and take a close look for oneself. This is not to say that Marxism is a kind of empiricism, but of all theoretical approaches it is assuredly the one that is obliged to submit itself most thoroughly to the concrete diversity of experience.

Marxists are not entirely unarmed in this respect; after all, Marx did suggest that there might be some "correspondence" between the nature of the forces of production and the nature of relations of production. Nature here means locus, form, and effect. But I shall make no secret of the fact that I find this hypothesis tricky to handle, for several reasons. The term "correspondence" is unclear. Does it refer to a relation of causality or a relation of compatibility? Furthermore, we lack reliable analyses of forces of production and their evolution. Only this kind of investigation could allow us to break out of the current impasse, in which all one can do is say that while we have no difficulty seeing what specific productive forces *prevent*, it is impossible to see exactly what they *permit*, still less what they impose. While there is no question of our being able to deduce social forms from forces of production, we must nevertheless seek to identify the limits of their range of possibilities and the mechanisms whereby one of these possibilities is in fact selected. I shall be returning to these problems at the end of the second section, in which I shall attempt to discuss the controversy between Marxists and non-Marxists (and among Marxists themselves) concerning the bases for the domination, in any society, of what Marxists see as a superstructure: kinship in certain primitive societies, the politico-religious sphere in Pharaonic Egypt, etc. I shall be discussing this controversy, moreover, in terms of what has already been said here about the notion of infrastructure. How can Marxists reconcile the hypothesis that it is the infrastructure which is determinant in the last analysis with the fact that in certain historical societies one finds a superstructure occupying a dominant position?

ECONOMIC DETERMINATION AND SUPERSTRUCTURAL DOMINATION

One not infrequently comes across anthropologists and historians claiming that the facts falling within their speciality refute Marxism. For Radcliffe-Brown (1930–31), it was enough to show that kinship was the dominant factor among Australian Aborigines to conclude this refutation. Dumont (1966) sees this refutation as furnished by the blatant domination of religion in India and by the fact that the caste system takes the form of an ideological opposition between pure and impure. For the historian Will (1972), the domination of politics in ancient Greece shows clearly that economics did not play the determining role and did not even amount to a system. What are we to make of this?

Reviewing these examples in the light of our definition of relations of production, we find that in each case the dominant "superstructure" functions simultaneously as a relation of production. In each of the three societies dealt with above, descent and marriage are regulated by kinship, as in all societies; yet kinship is dominant in one case only, that of the Australian Aborigines. In all three, man's relations with the supernatural are regulated by religion, but only in one, Hindu society, does religion predominate. We may thus put forward the hypothesis that the *explicit* functions of kinship and religion, which are to regulate socially respectively the reproduction of life itself through the regulation of marriage and descent and the relations with the invisible powers supposed to control the reproduction of the universe, are *not in themselves enough* to allow one or the other of these "superstructures" to attain a dominant position where it in fact does so. I should therefore like to put forward an alternative working hypothesis:

For a social activity—and with it its corresponding and organizing ideas and institutions—to play a dominant role in the functioning and evolution of a society, and hence in the thought and action of the groups and individuals composing it, *it is not enough* for this activity to fulfill several functions; it must necessarily, in addition to its own ostensible purpose and its explicit functions, function *directly and internally as a relation of production*.

This hypothesis makes no assumptions regarding the nature of social relations eligible to function as relations of production. It merely assumes something about the reasons for the *relative* weight and the *unequal* importance of the various forms of social activity in the functioning and evolution of societies; it assumes that this relative weight depends less upon what social relations *are* (kinship, religion, etc.) than on what they *do* or, better, make people do. If we managed to verify that social relations dominate when they function as relations of production, then we should have worked our way back to Marx's hypothesis regarding the determinant role, in the last analysis, of infrastructure. This hypothesis should be construed in the sense of the universal existence of a *hierarchy of functions* to be assumed by social relations in order for a society to be able to exist *as such* and to carry on reproducing; but this hypothesis does not permit us to jump to any conclusions regarding the nature and the form of relations of production in any given society. It thus becomes impossible to attempt to refute Marxism by pointing to the dominance of a superstructure.

This view contrasts with the way Marxists such as Althusser,

Balibar (1965), and their followers in anthropology and history have conceived the causality of economics in the last analysis. They view the economy as *selecting* from among the different instances the one that is to occupy the dominant position and then *placing* it in that position. This twofold action is regarded as constituting the infrastructure's causal mechanism. Unfortunately, this view is incapable of explaining how a *single* institution—kinship, for example—can act both as a relation of production *and* as a superstructure. Whatever the answer to this question may be, we must seek to explain how it is that kinship (or religion) comes to function as a relation of production and hence to dominate. Concerning kinship, we may imagine that in primitive societies *living* labour force counts for more than labour accumulated in the form of tools, domesticated resources, etc. We know that in all societies the reproduction of life is governed by different forms of kinship. It may be, then, that we should look for the ultimate reasons for kinship relations' functioning as relations of production, and hence for kinship's dominance, in some given state of the productive forces, i.e., in some *relation* between "living" (present) labour and "dead" (past) labour.

Perhaps, on the basis of the foregoing, we can now take a look at the question of the distinction between the ideological and the nonideological spheres.

THE IDÉEL IN REALITY AND THE PROBLEM OF THE IDEOLOGICAL SPHERE

Does the foregoing suggest a new approach to the problem of differentiating, among all the different *idéel* realities that any society contains, which are ideological and which are not? Apparently, we have done nothing to alter the view, generally held to be Marxist, of ideologies and their domination. We may, indeed, on the basis of the idea advanced above—namely, that the dominant social relations within a society are those which (regardless of which they are) function as relations of production—suggest that the ideas that represent and legitimize these dominant social relations ought to play a dominant role almost automatically. Or, if we take social relations for what they are, namely, concrete relations between distinct social groups occupying different positions in relations (functioning as relations) of production—whether these be relations of men's domination over women in classless societies or relations of one caste's or class's domination over the others—we may guess that the ideas that legitimize this domination of a sex, caste, or class will virtually or almost automatically be the dominant ideas in the society in question. In the same vein, we may also anticipate that the development of the *specific contradictions* contained in different types of relations of production and social relations will bring about changes in the relations between dominant and dominated and in power relations and ideological relations; we may equally anticipate that this will lead to the transformation of the dominated person's consciousness of the reality dominating him.

Once we have taken these customary Marxist propositions into account, the difficulties begin. First, they lack any precise criterion of what turns an idea into an "ideological" representation. It would appear that what is ideological is any idea that *legitimizes* an existing social order, along with the relations of domination and oppression that it contains within it. One might even go so far as to say that the idea's content, the fact that it is true or false, or more or less true, is irrelevant, and that any idea can become ideological the moment it enters the service of a dominant social group and presents this domination as a natural phenomenon. At the same time, though, surely an idea automatically becomes partly *false* the moment its presents *a* social order as the *only* possible, immutable, social order? An historic lie thus turns into a theoretical error.

Further, if we assume the existence of dominant ideas in the service of dominant classes, do we automatically thereby have to assume the existence of dominated ideas for the dominated classes? But then, are not dominant ideas dominant precisely because they are widely *shared* by the dominated classes themselves? Of course, experience shows that in any social system members of the dominated group entertain ideas that oppose them and that they themselves oppose to those of the dominant group. Are we then to conclude, in reference to the foregoing demonstration, that these dominated people's ideas are what might be termed ideas "against," a sort of counter-ideology, and hence a different ideology? Or are we to say that they cannot be called an ideology since they do not legitimize the existing order and do not participate in its mendacity? But are all legitimizing ideas illusory? If so, illusory for whom? Not for those—dominant and dominated—who share them. Therefore it must be for those who reject this social order and want to change it, or for us outside observers. As can be seen, then, it is impossible to define an idea as ideological either in terms of a single criterion—truth or falsehood, legitimization or non-legitimization—or in terms of a combination of the two. The reasoning breaks down in each case. In fact, if we are to escape this dilemma of formal or functional definitions of the ideological sphere, we are going to have to develop a theory of the components of the power of domination and oppression, a theory of relations between violence and consent.

We cannot develop such a theory, however, if we continue to consider ideas merely as a passive reflection, in the mind, of social relations that are themselves regarded as being born outside the mind, independently of it and prior to it. This brings us to a fundamental problem—a strategic crossroads in the interpretation of social facts and history and also in practice. Indeed, we find ourselves at a parting of the ways, at a point where various ways of being *materialist* diverge. Here we shall return to our earlier analysis of the *idéel* element contained in every material relationship with the material nature surrounding us. As we have seen, any material productive force contains in it, right from the outset, a complex *idéel* element which is not a passive, a posteriori, representation of this productive force in the mind, but, from the very beginning, an active ingredient, an internal condition of its very emergence. We should have no difficulty in showing, moreover, that this analysis can be extended to all social relations. For example, it is impossible for kinship relations to emerge and to reproduce down the generations without definition of the rules and the terms of descent, marriage, and residence and the notions of kinship and nonkinship; these rules, terms, and notions are not a posteriori reflections of kinship relations, but an integral component that has to exist right from the word go. Needless to say, kinship relations cannot be reduced to these different *idéel* components, but they cannot exist without them. And we can generalize from this and advance the idea that all social relations *arise and exist simultaneously both in thought and outside of it*—that all social relations contain, from the outset, an *idéel* element which is not an a posteriori reflection of it, but a condition for its emergence and ultimately an essential component. The *idéel* element exists not only in the form of the content of consciousness, but in the form of all those aspects of social relations that make them relations of signification and make their *meaning* or *meanings* manifest.

A certain type of Marxism has all too often neglected the fact that thought does not passively "reflect" reality, but rather interprets it actively. But this is not the most serious point, for people have also tended to forget that thought not only interprets reality, but actually *organizes* every kind of social *practice* on the basis of this reality, thereby contributing to the production of new social realities. It is this which makes all the difference between the several different ways of being materialist in scientific and political practice. The differences become even more marked if we start confusing man's relationship with nature with his relationship with history, for while nature exists, always has existed, and always will continue to exist independently of man and his thought and—where its nondomesticated portion is concerned—without man's intervention, a social relation can only lead a double life, both outside of man's thought and within it. Social relations, therefore, are simultaneously a material and an *idéel* reality.

To conclude, I shall attempt to apply this analysis to the problems of the origins of class and of the state. I would take this opportunity to remind the reader that, as Bonte (1975) has shown for the Kel Gress Tuareg of Niger, class societies can exist without their having to have a state as well—without requiring a distinct, centralized institution through which the dominant class may wield its power.

VIOLENCE AND CONSENT: PARADOXES UNDERLYING THE ORIGINS OF CLASSES AND THE STATE

The power of domination consists of two indissoluble elements whose combination constitutes its strength: violence and consent. At the risk of shocking a certain number of readers, I would go so far as to say that, of these two components of power, the stronger is not the violence of the dominant, but the consent of the dominated to their domination. I am perfectly aware of the differences between consent obtained under duress, passive acceptance, lukewarm adherence, and shared conviction. I realize that in any society, even a classless one, not all individuals or groups are equally consenting in their acceptance of the social order. Even when active, their consent is not always given without reservations or contradictions. The reason lies beyond the realm of thought, in the fact that all societies, including the most egalitarian classless ones, contain a mixture of common and particular interests that are constantly conflicting and compromising. Without this, we would never have had any history. But although it is enormously important to the evolution of a society—and to the individual or collective fate of its members—whether the dominated persons or groups are deeply convinced, half-convinced, or submissively convinced of the legitimacy of their system or latently opposed or even overtly hostile to this system, the fact is that all these are particular configurations of a major historical force in the preservation or transformation of societies, namely, the force of ideas, of ideologies, and this force is born not merely of the content of these ideas, but also of the fact that they are *shared*.

This poses a theoretical problem: under what conditions do dominated groups come to share interpretations of the world that legitimize the existing social order not only in the eyes of the dominant group, but also in their own eyes? Certain philosophers and anthropologists, such as Deleuze and Guattari (1972) in *L'Anti-OEdipe* and Clastres and Lefort (1977) in their analysis of La Boétie's *Discours sur la servitude volontaire*, refer to a certain number of savage tribes—selected arbitrarily but carefully reinterpreted—in order to argue that classes and the state (although these are by no means the same thing) were born out of some people's reprehensible wish to be served and the remainder's reprehensible wish to be enslaved. On this view, the emergence of the State, of the Despot, of the One above all others, within the internal evolutionary process of primitive societies remains unaccountable. It doesn't seem to me that classes could be an avatar of desire, although I do not for a moment wish to deny the power to desire, feelings, or emotional forces in the lives of individuals or of societies. I am becoming increasingly persuaded that we are in fact dealing with a paradox that is diametrically opposed to the views of Deleuze and Guattari, Lefort and Clastres, et al., namely, that classes could only have grown up in classless societies *legitimately*—or, at least, that the process of transformation must have been slow and the legitimacy of their formation must long have weighed more heavily in the balance than such factors as violence, usurpation, betrayals, etc.

For example, among the So, a farming tribe of 5,000 in Uganda (Laughlin and Laughlin 1972), political and religious power was concentrated in the hands of roughly 50 elders, who were old men representing the different patrilineal clans. These elders belonged to an initiatory society called the Kenisan. They alone had the power to communicate with the ancestors and, through them, with God, the master of the rain and of health and prosperity. When we examine their activities, we find them involved in all the rituals required for rainmaking, for blessing the sorghum, for driving away sickness, for halting enemies at the frontiers—in a word, in everything required to preserve peace, justice, and prosperity. There was no police force, but each noninitiate lived under the permanent threat of going mad and eating his own excrement should he seek to communicate with the ancestors himself and to infringe the elders' monopoly. As we can see, here, *consent is always backed by the threat of violence*, even though the latter remains on the horizon, keeping a low profile. But it would be equally vain to try to imagine a durable power of domination and oppression based solely either on naked violence and terror or on the total consent of every member of society. These would be extreme cases, highly ephemeral and transitory in the evolution of history. Even societies founded upon conquest, such as the Yatenga Mossi, so admirably described by Izard (1975), end up, after a time, adopting an institutional pattern that demands at least some consent on the part of the dominated to their domination. We can see this in the enthronement ritual of the new king, with his famous *ringu* journey: the new king, selected by the dominant group, sets out dressed in rags to visit the villages of the dominated and to be recognized as king by them. At the end of his journey, he reenters his capital, but this time as king, clothed in the ornaments of his function and riding on a white horse.

I should now like to formulate the following hypothesis: for relations of domination and exploitation to have arisen and reproduced themselves durably in formerly classless societies, such relations must have presented themselves *as an exchange* and as an exchange of *services*. This was how they managed to get themselves accepted, and this was how they managed to obtain the consent—passive or active—of the dominated. I should further be inclined to hypothesize that, among the factors leading to internal differentiation of social status and to the more or less gradual formation of new hierarchies based on the division of society into orders, castes, or classes, the services rendered by the dominant individuals or group must have involved, in the first place, invisible realities and forces controlling (in the thought of these societies) the reproduction of the universe and of life, and that this fact must have played a vital role.

To my way of thinking, the monopoly of the means (to us imaginary) of reproduction of the universe and of life must have preceded the monopoly of the visible material means of production, i.e., of those means which everyone could and had to produce in order to reproduce, given their relative simplicity. In the balance that emerged between services exchanged, however, those rendered by the dominant group appeared to be all the more fundamental inasmuch as they touched upon the invisible part of the world; the more material and visible the tasks performed by the dominated groups, the more their services were regarded as trivial. We may even suggest that the formation of classes may have taken the form of an *unequal* exchange, one that looked more advantageous to the dominated than to the dominant, and it is perhaps this that we call an extreme case of alienation. The dominant were obliged, however, to provide "proof" that the lives of the dominated depended upon them. For example, certain kings in Africa were put to death when they grew old or fell sick, as it was feared that their condition placed their kingdom under the threat of bad harvests, epidemics, or some other catastrophe.

I am prepared to suggest, moreover, that these transformations occurred under very precise circumstances, namely, the late sedentarization of hunter-gatherer populations and, later, the development of farming and animal husbandry. A new kind of dependence grew up during the latter phase: here, we are no longer dealing with savage man existing in savage nature but, gradually, with a domesticated nature and with "civilized" man, whose task it was to reproduce this domesticated nature. It was perhaps in this context that the religious sphere developed in such a way as to bring about the establishment of stabilized social hierarchies, of aristocracies, thus creating the conditions for the extraction of supplementary labour from the common people. Firth's (1965) study of the Tikopia contains an important example that merits consideration. He shows that the aristocracy possessed a monopoly of communication with the gods and the ancestors, but that it enjoyed—where material rewards and place in the production process were concerned—only minor advantages.

In conclusion, I should like to draw attention to one final problem: Ought we really to be using words such as class and state when referring to hierarchized precapitalist ancient or exotic societies?

First of all, I should point out that Marxists ought to reread Marx's *German Ideology* very carefully, because he takes the utmost pains to distinguish between order, or estate (as in the expression "Third Estate"), and class, a social group *exclusively* defined by its place in relation to the means of production. Such definition was not the case, for example, for hierarchies of status or rank in exotic aristocratic societies or for the ruling orders in the ancient Roman or Greek city. Capitalism has simplified social relations to the point where the status of the individual is defined, first and foremost, by economic criteria. So what did Marx mean when he used the term class for what he knew to be orders in antiquity or in the Middle Ages? Certainly not that we ought to start hunting for classes hiding behind the orders—classes that Marxists alone would be able to discover and that the Greeks or the Romans, history's actors, could never have seen for themselves. What Marx was really saying was that we ought to interpret these social differences by seeking the reasons for them in material factors and in relations of production and by shedding light on the oppressive character of relations of exploitation of men by men.

Now, how does this tie in with the first two sections of my analysis? In other words, how does this relate to my definition of relations of production and to my explanation of the domination of superstructures? In the example of Athens, we find that the fact that political relations in the city functioned as relations of production and that they dominated the thought and actions of members of society (both free men and slaves) prevented contradictions between free men and slaves from *directly* making their appearance in the *political* arena. We may say that the locus and the form of relations of production, and their intimate links with politics, made it unthinkable and impossible for the slaves themselves to acquire political consciousness of their situation and thus to wage *directly* political struggles to put an end to their slavery and their oppression. Even so, little by little the slave system piled up internal blockages which, in the long run, were to weaken it and slowly to reduce it to stagnation. But it was to take a good deal more than that, and barbarian invasions in particular, before these slave relations ultimately gave way to other forms of domination. The thinkable and the do-able thus reach out beyond thought, but they cannot escape the nature of the relations of production and the productive forces existing in a given society. It is perhaps this that is meant by "historical necessity."[4]

[4] On the subject of the thinkable and the do-able, I should like to make one important point clear. The fact that kinship, for example, is dominant in a given society means that every problem or event is going to take the form of a problem of kinship; where politics dominates, every problem will inevitably assume a "political" form in order to become thinkable. Thus, depending on the locus and the form of relations of production, history's actors, on each occasion, develop a *specific form of illusion* regarding their own conditions of existence. Each mode of production thus spontaneously engenders a specific mode of screening, of occultation—in the *spontaneous* consciousness of the members of a society—of the content and foundations of their social relations. Far from taking a society's own illusions about itself for reality, my theoretical approach seeks to lay these bare and to explain their existence.

References Cited

ADAMS, R. McC. 1966. *The evolution of urban society*. London: Weidenfeld and Nicolson.
ALTHUSSER, L., E. BALIBAR, and R. ESTABLET. 1965. *Lire le Capital*. Vol. 2. Paris: Maspero.
BALIBAR, E. 1965. "Sur les concepts fondamentaux du matérialisme historique," in *Lire le Capital*. Edited by L. Althusser, E. Balibar, and R. Establet, vol. 2, p. 221. Paris: Maspero.
BLOCH, M. 1977. The past and the present in the present. *Man* 12(2). [MB]
BONTE, P. 1975. "L'organisation économique des Touareg Kell Gress," in *Eléments d'ethnologie*. Edited by R. Cresswell, pp. 166–215. Paris: A. Colin.
CLAESSEN, HENRI J. M., and PETER SKALNÍK. Editors. 1978. *The early state*. The Hague: Mouton. [HJMC]
CLASTRES, P., and C. LEFORT. 1977. "Introduction," in *Discours sur la servitude volontaire*, by E. de la Boétie. Paris: Payot.
DELEUZE, G., and F. GUATTARI. 1972. *L'Anti-Oedipe*. Paris: Editions de Minuit.
DUMONT, L. 1966. *Homo hierarchicus*. Paris: Gallimard.
ETZIONI, AMITAI. 1964. *Modern organizations*. Englewood Cliffs: Prentice-Hall. [ZT]
FIRTH, RAYMOND. 1965. 2d edition. *Primitive Polynesian economy*. London: Routledge and Kegan.
FRANKFORT, H. 1948. *Kingship and the gods*. Chicago: University of Chicago Press.
GANS, HERBERT J. 1967. *The urban villagers: Group and class in the life of Italian Americans*. New York: Free Press; London: Collier Macmillan. [ZT]
GEERTZ, CLIFFORD. 1973. *The interpretation of cultures*. New York: Basic Books. [OPS]
GODELIER, MAURICE. 1977. *Perspectives in Marxist anthropology*. Cambridge: Cambridge University Press. [OPS]
HARRIS, MARVIN. 1971. *Culture, man, and nature*. New York: Crowell. [OPS]
HAUDRICOURT, ANDRÉ. 1962. Domestication des animaux, culture des plantes et traitement d'autrui. *L'Homme* 2(1):40–50.
HAUDRICOURT, A., and M. JEAN BRUNHES-DELAMARRE. 1955. *L'homme et la charrue*. Paris: Gallimard.
HAUDRICOURT, A., and L. HEDIN. 1943. *L'homme et les plantes cultivées*. Paris: Gallimard.
IZARD, M. 1975. "Le royaume du Yatenga," in *Eléments d'ethnologie*. Edited by R. Cresswell, pp. 207–48. Paris: A. Colin.
LAUGHLIN, CHARLES, and ELIZABETH LAUGHLIN. 1972. Kenisan: Economic and social ramifications of the Ghost Cult among the So of north-eastern Uganda. *Africa* 42:9–20.
LÉVI-STRAUSS, CLAUDE. 1952. *Race et histoire*. Paris: UNESCO. [ZT]
MARX, KARL. 1956. *Karl Marx: Selected writings in sociology and social philosophy*. Edited and translated by T. B. Bottomore. New York: McGraw-Hill. [DDG]
———. 1958. 3d edition. *Zur Kritik der politischen Ökonomie*. Berlin: Dietz.
MEILLASSOUX, C. 1964. *Anthropologie économique des Gouro de Côte d'Ivoire*. Paris/La Haye: Mouton.
NEEDHAM, J. 1954–76. *Science and civilization in China*. 5 vols. Cambridge: Cambridge University Press.
OPPENHEIM, L. 1964. *Ancient Mesopotamia: Portrait of a dead civilization*. Chicago: University of Chicago Press.
ORWELL, GEORGE. 1961. *The road to Wigan Pier*. New York: Berkley. [OPS]
RADCLIFFE-BROWN, A. R. 1930–31. The social organization of Australian tribes. *Oceania* 1(1–4).
REY, P.-P. 1971. *Colonialisme, néo-colonialisme et transition au capitalisme*. Paris: Maspero.
———. 1973. *Les alliances de classe*. Paris: Maspero.
TERRAY, E. 1969. *Le marxisme devant les sociétés primitives*. Paris: Maspero.
———. 1975. "Classes and class consciousness in the Abron kingdom of Gyaman," in *Marxist analysis and social anthropology*. Edited by Maurice Bloch, pp. 85–135. London: Malaby. [HJMC]
WERTHEIM, W. F. 1970. *Evolutie en revolutie*. Amsterdam: Van Gennep. [HJMC]
WHYTE, MARTIN KING. 1978. Cross-cultural codes dealing with the relative status of women. *Ethnology* 17:211–37. [OPS]
WILL, E. 1972. *Le monde grec et l'Orient*. Paris: Presses Universitaires de France.

[5]

The Genesis of Capitalism Amongst a South American Peasantry: Devil's Labor and the Baptism of Money

MICHAEL TAUSSIG
The University of Michigan

What does wage labor and capital mean to a peasantry that is subjected to rapid rural proletarianization and what is the basis of that meaning?

I wish to discuss an aspect of this question in the light of certain ideological reactions manifested by a South American lowland peasantry as expanding sugar plantations absorb their lands and peasants are converted into landless wage laborers. In the southern extremities of the Cauca Valley, Colombia, it is commonly thought that male plantation workers can increase their output, and hence their wage, through entering into a secret contract with the devil. However, the local peasants, no matter how needy they may be, never make such a contract when working their own plots or those of their peasant neighbors for wages. It is also thought that by illicitly baptizing money instead of a child in the Catholic church, that money can become interest bearing capital, while the child will be deprived of its rightful chance of entering heaven.

Analysis of these beliefs in their social and historical context indicates that the lower classes' implicit understanding of the new mode of production is inherently critical and antagonistic and that the axiomatic basis of this antagonism rests on their conscious opposition of "use values" to "exchange values"—the opposition of the satisfaction of natural wants, on the one side, to the limitless search for profits and capital accumulation on the other. In making this distinction these people share a close affinity with the economic theorizing of the Schoolmen of the European Middle Ages, and with the economic philosophy of Aristotle, whose insights on this matter were often quoted favorably by Karl Marx himself, since the opposition of use value to exchange value was basic to his entire system of analysis.

I would like to thank Elinor Melville, Tony Skillen and Karen Shedlowe for their criticisms of an earlier version of this essay. Anthropological fieldwork was done by the author in the area between 1969 and 1972.

Further elucidation of this distinction leads to a discussion of the metaphysical and moral bases underlying the lower classes' understanding of capitalist relations of production and exchange, in which their folk mysticism is contrasted with that form of capitalist mystification to which Marx gave the name of "commodity fetishism." Evaluation of this contrast is enhanced by an analysis of the mode of reasoning utilized by the supporters of the use value economy. This reasoning appears to derive from a concept of the universe as an interrelated organism which is understood through the conscious application of animistic analogies, rather than by means of the atomistic causal paradigm which has gained ascendancy in the social sciences since the rise of Newtonian mechanics and the birth of the industrial revolution in the West.

ATTITUDES TOWARDS WAGE LABOR

A theme of constant interest to historians of the industrial revolution in Europe, as well as to sociologists concerned with socio-economic development in the Third World, is the attitude of workers who are new to the modern wage labor situations. The first reaction of peasants and artisans who become wage workers in modern business enterprises is frequently if not universally one of indifference to wage incentives. Regarded as a failure to maximize market opportunities, a lack of labor commitment, or a peculiar irrationality about complying with the postulates embodied in *homo oeconomicus*, this response has persistently frustrated capitalist entrepreneurs the world over.

Max Weber referred to this response as "primitive traditionalism," and much of his research was an attempt to explain its transcendence by the capitalist spirit and the capitalist work ethic.

> This traditionalism survives far down into the present; only a human lifetime in the past it was futile to double the wages of an agricultural laborer in Silesia who mowed a certain tract of land on a contract, in the hope of inducing him to increase his exertion. He would simply have reduced by half the work expended because with this half he would have been able to earn as much as before (Weber, 1927: 335).

In a recent work, an anthropologist sums up some of his findings on this subject in terms of the persistence of use value practices rather than in terms of "primitive traditionalism":

> Recruited as plantation hands, they frequently showed themselves unwilling to work steadily. Induced to raise a cash crop, they would not react "appropriately" to market changes: as they were interested mainly in acquiring specific items of consumption, they produced that much less when crop prices rose, and that much more when prices fell off. And the introduction of new tools or plants that increased the productivity of indigenous labor might only then shorten the period of necessary work, the gains absorbed rather by an expansion of rest than of output. All these and similar responses express an enduring

quality of traditional domestic production, that it is production of use values, definite in its aim, so discontinuous in its activity (Sahlins, 1972: 86).

The exotic attitudes and beliefs which so-called traditional cultures exhibit towards the early stages of penetration by the modern capitalist economy often seem bizarre and irrational to Western eyes. Luther's identification of the devil with capitalism (Brown, 1959: 218–9; Tawney, 1954: 72–91), some Melanesian cargo cults, certain messianic movements, Weber's examples of "primitive traditionalism," as well as the beliefs we consider below, are but some of the numerous instances of such attitudes and concepts. Rather than dismissing these responses as "traditional" or irrational, the approach adopted in this essay is that it would seem to be more true to the facts as well as more enlightening to consider these reactions as outcomes of a clash between a use value orientation and an exchange value orientation, thus viewing them as the beginning of a potential critique of capitalism. They provide us with insights into the irrational basis of our own economy and stereotype of *homo oeconomicus,* and can be usefully considered as illustrative of a form of "primitive Marxism."

This "primitive Marxism" was undoubtedly inherent in the outlook of the European proletariat in the early stages of the birth of the capitalist system, but has since been largely superseded by a new world view which regards the wage contract system, market pricing, and the institutionalization of profit and greed as natural and ethically commendable.[1] In the light of this historical amnesia, which afflicts all social classes in a developed market economy, it is all the more important to dwell on the critique offered us by those neophytic proletarians in the Third World today, who are just entering the capitalist system with their goods and labor and who often appear to regard that system as anything but natural and good.[2] In the Cauca Valley the sense given to the devil and his role in contracting wage labor is like the definition of the early Christian fathers as "he who resists the cosmic process," which in this context comes close to the idea of forcing things in the interest of private gain without regard to what are seen as their intrinsic principles (cf. Needham: 69–71).

The destruction of the pre-capitalist metaphysics of production and exchange was considered by at least two influential social theorists as mandatory for the successful establishment of modern capitalism. Max

[1] Research on this subject is pitifully inadequate. While it is obviously true that the theory and ideology of capitalism in the West is based on such a perspective, it has yet to be documented to what degree working class people, from the beginning of the industrial revolution till today, see and act on the world in this manner.

[2] Peasant "superstitions" regarding money, labor, and raw materials, form an exceedingly fruitful body of information and insights from this perspective. Hence the rather neglected field of 'folklore' deserves much more scrutiny than it has hitherto received.

Weber regarded the magical superstitions associated with production and trade to be one of the greatest obstacles to the rationalization of economic life (1927: 355), and in his essay on *The Protestant Ethic and the Spirit of Capitalism* often reiterated the point that

> Labor must . . . be performed as if it were an absolute end in itself, a calling. But such an attitude is *by no means a product of nature*. It cannot be evoked by low wages or high ones alone, but can only be the product of a long and arduous process of education. To-day, capitalism once in the saddle, can recruit its laboring force in all industrial countries with comparative ease. In the past this was in every case an extremely difficult problem (Weber, 1958: 62, my emphasis).

And as Karl Marx observed, the transition to the capitalist mode of production is only completed when direct force and external economic conditions, although still used, are only employed exceptionally. An entirely new set of traditions and habits have to be developed among the working class, to the point where common sense regards the new conditions as natural.

> It is not enough that the conditions of labor are concentrated in a mass, in the shape of capital, at the one pole of society, while at the other are grouped masses of men who have nothing to sell but their labor power. Neither is it enough that they are compelled to sell it voluntarily. The advance of capitalist production develops a working class, which by education, tradition, habit, looks upon the conditions of that mode of production *as self-evident laws of Nature* (Marx, 1967, I:737, my emphasis).

However, the behavior and certain beliefs of the lower classes on whom this article focuses suggest strongly that the characteristics of the capitalist mode of production are there viewed neither as good nor as self-evident laws of Nature; in fact they are regarded as unnatural and even evil.

The lower classes are of Afro-American stock, and until 1955 or thereabouts most of them were smallholders owning parcels of land without legal title in the southern extremities of the Cauca Valley, an extremely fertile region in the southwest of Colombia. Since about 1955 the majority of these peasants have had little choice but to work full or part-time as wage laborers for the surrounding sugar plantations which have expropriated much of the peasant's land, often through direct physical force.

Historical sources amply demonstrate that ever since the abolition of slavery in 1851 the peasants have shown a marked aversion towards wage labor on the large estates of the rural elite.[3] Until the early

[3] The historical sources referred to are derived from local oral history, private and Colombian Government archives, and secondary works in Spanish and English. An important source of information lies in the private correspondence of the largest of the old landowning families in the region. The interested reader is advised to consult my unpublished doctoral thesis, "Rural Proletarianization: A Social and Historical Enquiry

decades of the twentieth century they were able to retain their position as independent smallholders and formed a powerful political group capable of thwarting their previous owners who desperately needed labor to maintain the flagging estates and gold mines. However, with the opening of the valley to the international sea lanes in 1914, the influx of vast amounts of foreign capital at about the same time, and a sharp natural increase in local population, the large estate owners have been able to appropriate peasant lands and establish a flourishing plantation economy, a process accelerated by the *Violencia* of the early 1950s.[4]

Today no more than one-fifth of the population in the south of the valley lives in the countryside, while the remainder live in the rural slum towns, little more than impoverished barracks for plantation workers, bereft of clean drinking water and adequate sewerage. Few of the townspeople own land, and many of the peasants who still occupy farm land also work on the plantations. By any standards the bulk of the population is poor, and malnutrition is rife.[5]

In the opinion of the estate managers, the plantation workers, despite the spur of poverty, do not work hard, and fail to respond to wage incentives in a positive or predictable manner. Although official statistics indicate very high levels of unemployment throughout the region, the managers state that it is very difficult to find sufficient numbers of reliable workers. The chief research worker of "Asocaña" (the Sugar Growers' Association), for example, says this about the workers in the cane fields of the Puerto Tejada region in the south of the Valley.

into the Commercialization of the Southern Cauca Valley, Colombia," University of London, 1974.

[4] Production of sugar in metric tons by plantations located south of the Desbaratado River in the southern region of the Cauca Valley, 1938–1969 was as follows:

Year	*Metric Tons*
1938	2,000
1963	13,220
1969	91,750

Source: Asocaña, Cali, Colombia (nd).

In the rural area of the southern Cauca Valley, the ratio of smallholders to landless day laborers was on the order of 53:10 in the year 1912 according to official census materials. By 1938 the ratio was around 9:10. Following the outbreak in 1948 of the so-called civil war, the *Violencia,* cash crops of the peasants were sprayed with herbicides by the plantations, reducing peasant production of cocoa by some 80 percent between 1950 and 1958, further accelerating the removal of peasants from the land.

[5] A recent study of malnutrition in the *municipio* (municipality) of Candelaria which adjoins the southern *municipios,* the region of concern in this article, and to which it is very similar sociologically, found that 40 percent of pre-school children were suffering from protein-calorie malnutrition. As regards the life prospects of the adult males in this region, the report says: "They can anticipate that as they get older their income will not increase, while the number of mouths to feed will; they are able to provide less adequately for their families; more and more of their children will become malnourished" (Wray & Aguirre, 1969).

The workers there sabotage the machinery. This happens whenever there are Blacks. They slash the tires of the tractors and drain the oil from the motors. Yes, the workers there have a lot of resentment. They are very resentful. They are also very cunning and very lazy. Despite the great unemployment it is hard to find cane cutters. The other day, for example, the Ingenio Rio Paila needed 250 cane cutters. From their usual sources they only managed to obtain 25! So they had to send trucks into Nariño to bring back Indios to cut the cane. The Indios from there take to the discipline better and don't steal, but the Blacks are stronger. The fact is that cane cutting is terribly hard work and people simply don't like doing it. Even when the wages are increased a man doesn't cut more. What happens is that they just cut until they have made enough money for the day and then they leave. Or else they work more slowly. So we don't know what to do. What is more, they hate working to orders and hate discipline.

So we, the cane growers, are slowly getting into the position where we are going to use cane cutting machines because of the scarcity of willing labor. I say, with confidence, that in 10 years there will be cane cutting machinery throughout the Valle del Cauca. And already we are starting to use mechanical loaders. You can see them all around the Palmira area.

The workers themselves by and large confirm these statements. At the same time they feel that they are being constantly cheated, underpaid, and humiliated. They distrust and hate the plantations and generally resent the fact that the crops produced on the large estates are destined for export and not for local consumption. With their trade unions in ruin since the early 1960s, sabotage of mill machinery and tractors is common, and the plantation owners and managers travel the area in constant fear of assault and kidnapping.[6] Police and soldiers are continually stationed in the mill compounds, and workers have been shot during scuffles on paydays. The mill owners always travel with an escort of armed guards, and all high-ranking personnel are equipped with two-way radios in communication with the *Defensa Civil* and army located in the nearest city.

THE DEVIL AND PROLETARIAN LABOR

In the southern Cauca Valley today, it is commonly believed by local people—townspeople and country people, proletarians and peas-

[6] The militant plantation workers' trade unions were severely weakened in the early 1960s through the development of the labor contractor system by means of which work is subcontracted by the plantations to small-scale private contractors living in the rural towns and hamlets adjoining the cane fields. The contractors mobilize their kin and neighbors to form ephemeral and small work gangs. Being outside the trade union structure these workers lack legal rights to strike or to claim higher wages or better working conditions. Such gangs are usually of a short life-span, are recruited for specific tasks, and their membership is highly unstable—all of which serves to atomize the work force. Today something like 30 percent or more of the total plantation work force is constituted by these contracted workers often referred to as *iguazos* (migratory ducks) or *piratas* (pirates). In parallel with this development, the plantations have decreased their rate of land acquisition and have turned increasingly to large landholders (*colonos*) with whom they make contracts to grow sugar cane or from whom they rent land. Some two-thirds of the sugar cane milled in the valley now comes from *colonos* or rented land (cf., Knight; C.I.M.; Asocaña).

ants—that the male plantation workers sometimes make individual and secret contracts with the devil in order to increase individual output and hence their wage. Generally speaking, it is felt that output can be increased greatly by the individual worker only if he does make such a contract. The landless wage workers are widely supposed to sell their souls to the devil in order to maintain, or more commonly increase, productivity. Indian tin miners in highland Bolivia show similar patterns of behavior (Nash, 1972). But both groups of people do *not* do this as *peasants* working their own land. It is only when they become proletarianized that the devil enters the scene in this way. While the imagery of God and good, or the spirits of Nature and of ancestors, dominate the ethos of labor in the peasant mode of production, the devil and evil permeate the local metaphysics associated with the capitalist mode of production.

It is commonly thought that such a contract can increase a plantation worker's yield by two to three times. As a result of such a contract, however, the individual concerned will die prematurely and in agony, and while alive is souless and a mere puppet in the hands of the devil. Furthermore, certain conditions attach to the money thus gained. This money cannot serve as productive "capital" but has to be spent immediately on what are considered to be luxury consumer items such as fine clothes, liquor, butter, and so on. To invest this money so as to produce more money—i.e., to use it as capital—is to invite ruin. For example, if one buys or rents land, that land will not produce, and if one buys a piglet to fatten for market, the animal will sicken or die. It is also believed that plantation sugar cane thus cut will not regrow. The ratoon or root will die, and the plantation land will not produce until plowed over and replanted.

It is crucial to realize that the local *peasantry* do *not* make contracts with the devil in order to augment or maintain productivity levels on their own plots. Neither do they make such a contract when working for wages on the plots of other peasants. People point out that such a practice would damage the peasant plot and that the money gained could not be used to maintain equipment or land. Despite the poverty that afflicts the majority of the local peasants, they are not therefore tempted by the monetary rewards that result from the devil contract, since those rewards are thought to diminish or curtail natural fertility. The notion of extracting more money from nature in the above way applies only to proletarians.[7]

[7] The belief does not apply to all proletarians, but is restricted to *male* proletarians. Like peasants of both sexes, *female* wage laborers are *not* supposed to make a devil contract to increase their wages. The reason given for this is that since the "wages of the devil" are inherently destructive and barren, and since women assume almost all the

The only magic allegedly used on the peasant plots is "good" magic worked through the Catholic saints and the *ánimas*—the souls of the ancestors—and such magic is aimed at curing the plot of malign influences in general and as a prophylaxis against thieving in particular. Petty retailers and middlemen also use magic to ensure success, but once again this is considered to be "good" magic and is worked through the medium of the Saints and the *ánimas*.[8]

BAPTISM OF MONEY AND THE SECRET OF INTEREST-BEARING CAPITAL

According to the belief in *el bautizo del billete* (baptism of the bill), the Godparent-to-be conceals a peso note in his or her hand during the baptism of the child by the Catholic priest. The peso bill is thus believed to receive baptism instead of the child. When such a baptized bill enters into general monetary circulation it is believed that it will continually return to its owner with interest, enriching the owner and impoverishing the other parties to the deals transacted by the owner of the bill. The owner is now the Godparent of the peso bill. The child remains unbaptized, a cause of great concern since the child's soul is denied supernatural legitimacy and has no chance of escaping from Limbo or Purgatory, depending on when it dies. This practice is heavily penalized by the Church.

The baptized bill receives the name—the "Christian name" as we say in English—that the baptismal ritual was meant to bestow on the child and is now referred to by that name. It is then set to work as follows. The Godparent pays the bill over as part of a routine monetary transaction, as when one pays for goods in a store. The Godparent mutters the following type of refrain:

José	José
¿te vas o te quedas?	Are you going or staying?
¿te vas o te quedas?	Are you going or staying?
¿te vas o te quedas?	Are you going or staying?

obligation of raising children, it would be devastatingly counter-productive for them to try to raise a family with such money. An additional reason could be that short matrilines form the basis of the social structure, and that the souls of the deceased maternal ancestors are a very critical link to the rest of the supernatural world. Therefore, if a mother sells her soul to the devil, she deprives her descendants of their most crucial link with the spirit world of good ancestors, the Saints, and God.

[8] These observations serve to emphasize that it is neither money per se, inequality, nor involvement in buying and selling activities which leads to the opprobrium of devil's work. The peasants spend most of their time in the cultivation of cash crops (cocoa and coffee) on their own plots or the plots of their neighbors, and of course retailers are almost exclusively involved in buying and selling. Furthermore, material inequalities abound within these social groups. The critical fact is that none of these activities is directly organized by capitalist relations of production, and that money is used only as a means of facilitating exchange, not as something to be maximized as an end in itself.

The bill, referred to by its name, is asked three times whether it is going to return to its Godparent or not. If everything works as it should, then it will soon return to its Godparent, bringing a large amount of money with it. This transfer is accomplished invisibly.

A black middle-class family owned a corner store in the village. Halfway through the morning, when the wife was alone, she went out the back and then quickly returned because she thought she heard a noise in the till. Opening it she found all the cash gone. She then remembered that one of the customers had behaved peculiarly earlier that morning, and realized that someone had passed her a baptized bill. As soon as her back was turned, this bill had made off with all the money in the cash register.

In a busy supermarket in the large city nearby, a shop detective was startled to hear a woman standing near a cash register chanting under her breath: "Guillermo! ¿Te vas o te quedas? ¿Te vas o te quedas? ¿Te vas o te quedas?" He promptly concluded that she had passed a baptized bill and was waiting for it to return to her with the contents of the register, and he immediately arrested her. She was taken away and nobody knows what happened thereafter.

One of the few successful black store owners in the village was saved from a great loss only by a most unusual coincidence. Serving in his shop he was startled to hear a strange noise in his cash register. Peering in he saw two bills fighting with each other for possession of the contents, and he realized that two customers, each with their own baptized bills, must have just paid them over and were awaiting their return. This strange coincidence allowed him to prevent the spiriting away of his cash.

INTERPRETATION

Let us examine these beliefs with two questions in mind. What is the natural character attributed to monetary exchange and the productive process? What is the system of reasoning used to explain the exchange economy in a society geared to the production of use values? We will discuss the former in terms of commodity fetishism, and the latter in terms of analogical reasoning.

Commodity Fetishism. Bizarre as the aforementioned beliefs may appear, in what way do they differ from our own? If we look at popular conceptions of capital in a developed capitalist society, we may note that elaborate metaphorical identifications of capital with the animate world are pervasive.

Take the financial section of the *New York Times* (April, 1974) for example. We read of the "economic climate," the "sagging dollar," of "earnings booming ahead," of "cash flows," of treasury bills "backing up," of runaway and galloping inflation, of "climbing interest rates," of "bear markets" and "bull markets," of factories referred to as "plants," of "money growing" in accordance with investment, of how "your investments can go to work for you," and so on. The active mood predominates: "Weakness in the market was widespread and reflected the performance of the 15 most active issues" and "Despite gasoline shortages and uncertain supplies, 10 of the 15 most active issues traded on Monday could be classed as travel-oriented." "Can the individual investor still find happiness in the market?" asks the muse, who on reflection answers, "today there are dozens of ways to put your capital to work." A Chicago banker is reported as saying, "A general feeling seems to persist that something had definitely gone wrong with what had come to be regarded as the natural order of economic, financial and commercial life." The price of copper bears no proportion to the value of the coins in which it is minted; one spokesman for an important producer said, "While our selling price is killing us, we do have contractual and other obligations to deliver, whether we like to or not." "Splitting his time between New York and his plant in Italy, Joe can't afford to waste time when he's dealing with his bank. That's where Bob comes in. 'As far as I'm concerned,' Joe says, 'Bob *is* Chemical Bank.' " Hence, "Our Man is your bank—Chemical Bank. The businessman, when his needs are financial, his reaction is chemical."

These are but commonplace manifestations of what Marx referred to as *commodity fetishism* occurring in a developed capitalist culture wherein capital and workers' products are spoken of in terms that are used for people and animate beings. It is money as interest-bearing capital that lends itself most readily to this type of fetishism. Capital appears to have an *innate* property of self-expansion, and this property diffuses into all economic life since in capitalism money is the universal equivalent and mediator between persons and all objects. Everything has to be paid for and everything has its price. "Cast in this role, money is said to have changed into a true God, for the intermediary reigns in real power over the things it mediates for me. Its cult becomes an end in itself" (Marx, cited in Ollman, 1971: 203).

The concept of commodity fetishism is meant to draw attention to the fact that capitalist society presents itself to consciousness as something other than it basically is, even though that consciousness does reflect the more or less superficial and hypostatized configuration of society. Fetishism denotes the attribution of life, autonomy, power, and even dominance to otherwise inanimate objects and presupposes the draining of these qualities from the human actors who bestow the attribution. Thus in the case of commodity fetishism, social relationships are dismembered and appear to dissolve into relationships between things—the products of labor exchanged on the market—so that the sociology of exploitation masquerades as a natural relationship between systemic artifacts. Definite social relationships are reduced to the magical matrix of things. An ether of naturalness—fate and physicality—conceals and enshrouds human social organization and the historical human significance of the market and the development of a propertyless wage-earning class. Rather than man being the aim of production, production has become the aim of man and wealth the aim of production; rather than tools and the productive mechanism in general having liberated man from the slavery of toil, man has become the slave of tools and the instituted processes of production.

In surveying the opinions of eighteenth and nineteenth century British economists and statesmen on the question of capital and interest, Marx sarcastically pointed out that in their eyes it becomes "a property of money to generate value and yield interest, much as it is an attribute of pear trees to bear pears . . . Thus we get the fetish form of capital and the conception of fetish capital . . . a mystification of capital in its most flagrant form" (Marx, 1967, III:392). Elsewhere in the same chapter in *Capital* Marx quotes at length from economists like Price and Joshiah Child, and from economic journals of the mid-nineteenth century. He makes lavish use of the biological metaphors that their views of money so strongly suggest. "Money is now pregnant." "As the growing process is to trees, so generating money appears as innate in capital in its form as money-capital." In reference to remarks on the geometrical progression involved in lending money at compound interest, in which the conception of capital as self-reproducing and self-expanding were at their most extreme, Marx wrote of ". . . the fabulous fancies of Dr. Price, which outdo by far the fantasies of the alchemists; fancies in which Pitt believed in all earnest, and which he used as pillars of his financial administration in his laws concerning the sinking fund" (Marx, 1967, III:394). Dr. Price regarded "capital as a self-regulating automaton, as a mere number that increases itself (just as Malthus did with respect to population in his geometrical progression . . .)."

Benjamin Franklin in his *Advice to a Young Tradesman* (1748) could just as well have been the target of Marx's irony.

> Remember, that money is of the prolific, generating nature. Money can beget money, and its offspring can beget more, and so on. Five shillings turned is six, turned again it is seven and threepence, and so on, till it becomes a hundred pounds. The more there is of it, the more it produces every turning, so that the profits rise quicker and quicker. He that kills a breeding-sow, destroys all her offspring to the thousandth generation (Franklin, cited in Weber, 1958:49).

At the same time these "fabulous fancies which outdid by far the fantasies of the alchemists" were systematically interwoven with the Weltanschauung of *homo oeconomicus*—the supposed epitome of rationality. How could such an odd combination of rationality and fantasy so systematically coexist? What gave conviction to these biological metaphors? The answer lies in the peculiar and unique character of the social relations embodied both in capital and the commodities produced in the capitalist mode of production.

At great length and from a variety of viewpoints Marx argued that these social relations of production impressed themselves on everyday consciousness in such a way that the entire process of production and of the generation of surplus value is overlooked or slighted so that the social process of capital reproduction and expansion may easily appear as a property inherent in the thing itself, rather than the process of which it is part. This socially conditioned appearance is a mystification in which the entire social context conspires, so to speak, to mask itself. In this process of decontextualization, profit no longer appears to be the result of a social *relation,* but of a *thing*; i.e. reification.

Marx made his views on this clear when he compared the formula for interest bearing capital with what he called merchant's capital.

> The relations of capital assume their most externalised and most fetish-like form in interest bearing capital. We have here M-M′, money creating more money, self-expanding value, without the process that effectuates these two extremes. In merchant's capital, M-C-M′, there is at least the general form of the capitalist movement, although it confines itself solely to the sphere of circulation, so that profit appears merely as profit derived from alienation; but it is at least seen to be the product of a social *relation,* not the product of a mere *thing* (Marx, 1967, III:391).

The same point is made by Marx in many of his writings. For instance in the *Grundrisse*, in a passage where his antipathy to what he calls crude materialism is explained in terms of fetishism, he says:

> The crude materialism of the economists who regard as the *natural properties* of things what are social relations of production among people, and qualities which things obtain because they are subsumed under these relations, is at the same time just as crude an idealism, even fetishism, since it imputes social relations to things as inherent characteristics, and thus mystifies them (Marx, 1973: 687).

Appealing to nature, to the paradoxical extreme wherein certain lifeless things are seen as animated, is merely one historically specific manifestation of that probably universal tendency whereby any culture externalizes its social categories onto nature, and then turns to nature in order to validate its social norms as "natural". Durkheim saw this attempt to invoke the principle of biological determinism in the ideology of "primitive" society, and Marx spotted the same phenomenon in the genesis, acceptance, and use of Darwinism.

The whole Darwinist teaching of the struggle for existence is simply a transference from society to living nature of Hobbes' doctrine of 'bellum omnium contra omnes' and of the bourgeois-economic doctrine of competition together with Malthus' theory of population. When this conjuror's trick has been performed . . . the same theories are transferred back again from organic nature into history and it is now claimed that their validity as eternal laws of human society has been proved (cited in Schmidt:47).

The same point can perhaps be made with regard to Newtonian physics and the role of human beings subordinated to the impersonal controls of the self-regulating market, the central institution if not the "solar system" of capitalist economy.[9] E.A. Burtt draws our attention to the following characteristics of Newtonian metaphysics which have direct implications for our discussion of commodity fetishism and the philosophical roots of the ideology to be found in a market society.

Here were those residual souls of men, irregularly scattered among the atoms of mass that swam mechanically among the etheral vapors in time and space, and still retaining vestiges of the Cartesian *res cogitans*. They too must be reduced to mechanical products and parts of the self-regulating cosmic clock . . . Wherever it [the universal formula of gravitation], was taught as truth there was also insinuated as a nimbus of surrounding belief that man is but the puny and local spectator, nay irrelevant product of an infinite self-moving engine . . . which consists of raw masses wandering to no purpose in an undiscoverable time and space, and is in general wholly devoid of any qualities that might spell satisfaction for the major interests of human nature . . . (Burtt: 300–1).[10]

Thus, in the fetishism of commodities we encounter a more general formula guiding social awareness which can apply to capitalist culture as a whole. This formula, following Marx, is rooted in the relations of production and exchange as they impress themselves on consciousness in the workaday world. Briefly, this formula is none other than that the social relation is consummated in the relationship of a thing to itself, and that ontology lies not in a relational gestalt but squarely within the thing itself. Atomized, self-encapsulated things—what Burtt refers to as "raw masses"—become the prime object of analysis because their meaning and properties appear to lie within themselves alone. True

[9] Unlike other societies' unconscious or conscious appeal to nature, the West has had the singular advantage since the seventeenth century of viewing the relationships that exist between natural phenomena as "*laws*," and not merely as "reason," "ratios," "principles," "harmonies," etc. (Cf. Needham: 540).

[10] Newton's scheme earned the undying admiration of Adam Smith, the foremost theoretician of the capitalist market. To Adam Smith, Newton's system was ". . . everywhere the most precise and particular that can be imagined, and ascertains the time, the place, the quantity, the duration of each individual phenomenon . . .", and it seemed to him to intuitively fit with the world of everyday experience. "Neither are the principles of union which it employs, such as the imagination can find any difficulty in going along with." The Newtonian principles were not only applicable to gravity and the inertness of matter, but were "the same which takes place in all other qualities which are propagated in rays from a center . . ." It all amounted to "the discovery of an immense chain of the most important and sublime truths, all closely connected together, by *one capital fact, of the reality of which we have daily experience* (Smith, 1967:107–8; my emphasis).

explanation and understanding now seek to reduce whole phenomena to their simplest parts, and ultimate causality is to be found in the unchanging movement of elementary physical atoms. This dominance of "thinghood" (together with the logical conventions of identity and noncontradiction) tends to obliterate peoples' awareness and efface their capacity for moral evaluation of the bio-logic and socio-logic of relationships and process, particularly as regards their awareness of socio-economic activities and relationships. This is not to say that in this view things as such cannot be related to other such things and harmoniously related at that. Newton's scheme of the planets and Adam Smith's view of the self-regulating market are the outstanding examples of corpuscular interrelatedness forming an harmonious totality, much as modern Systems Theory is today. However, the relations that bind the things are viewed as *external* to the individuated things-in-themselves, whose identity and power is given in themselves alone.

But from another perspective this view is a gross deception since these apparently self-bounded and potent "things" are but the embodiments and concretizations of relationships which bind them to a larger whole. Their identity, existence, and natural properties spring from their *position* in an all-encompassing organic *pattern* of organization in which things are understood as but partial expressions of a self-organizing totality. The properties and activities of things will then be explained holistically and "structurally" in terms of their reticulate intelligibility as parts of an organic whole, and not in terms of mechanical causation and corpuscular collisions as separate bits of matter. If attention focuses on a single thing, as it must at some point in any analysis, then the thing is to be seen as containing its relational network and surrounding context within itself; the "thing" is a system of relationships.

On the other hand, if the atomistic view prevails, as it does in our culture, then the isolated thing-in-itself must inevitably tend to appear as animated because in reality it is part of an active process. If we "thingify" parts of a living system, close our eyes to the context of which they are part, and then observe that the things move, so to speak, it logically follows that the things may well be regarded or spoken of as though they were alive with their own autonomous powers. If regarded as mere things, they will appear as though they are indeed *animate* things—fetishes—so that capital, for instance, is regarded as analogous to a tree that bears fruit, and the thing itself is the source of its own increase. Hence, reification leads to fetishism.

Fetishism: Pre-Capitalist versus Capitalist. In pre-capitalist societies, where commodity exchange and the market are absent, animism, magic, and various forms of fetishism flourish. But is this fetishism similar to the fetishism of commodities to be found in a capitalist mode of production, and is there anything to be gained by asking such a question? Marx, for one, was clearly of the opinion that there was a world of difference, and that in posing the question one was well on the way towards demystifying the illusions induced by the commodity form of exchange. "The whole mystery of commodities, all the magic and necromancy that surrounds the products of labor as long as they take the form of commodities," he wrote, "vanishes therefore so soon as we come to other forms of production" (1967:76).

Following this suggestion, we return to the belief in the baptism of money in the southern Cauca Valley. The belief is that through this illicit religious mechanism—illicit in that it deceives the parents, the child, and the priest, and spiritually mutilates the child, annihilating its acceptance into the citizenry of God—money shall breed money, or that money will grow. In other words, it is an exotic expression of the standard Marxist formula for capitalist circulation, M-C-M′ (money-commodity-more money) or simply M-M′, as opposed to the circulation associated with use value and the peasant mode of production, C-M-C (commodity A-money-Commodity B; selling in order to buy). The problem that Marx set himself, the mystery of capitalist economic growth and accumulation of capital whereby capital appeared to breed more of itself, is in this situation seen to occur as a result of the supernatural forces incurred by the Christian baptism of the money bill. Once activated in this way money becomes interest-bearing capital. An inert medium of exchange becomes a self-breeding quantity, and in this sense becomes a fetish, a thing with lifelike powers.

If this is a bizarre belief, then one has to consider that the system against which it is levelled is surely no less bizarre. We who have been accustomed to the laws of capitalist economics for several centuries have come to accept the manifestation of these laws as utterly natural and commonplace. The early prophets and analysts of capitalism, such as Benjamin Franklin, regarded the operations of the economy as completely natural to the degree that they could casually refer to interest as an inherent property of capital itself. The peasantry of the southern Cauca Valley, however, regard this as utterly unreal and supernatural, and their belief in the baptism of money expresses this unreality.

Not only is it unreal, but it is done at the terrible cost of denying the child a legitimate place in rites of the life cycle and in the cosmological order, and hence bears the same profound stigma as does the wage workers' contract with the devil. This, in the second place, is what makes the difference with "pure" or capitalist commodity fetishism, because the baptism is seen as *immoral*.

Third, and, quite apart from this powerful value judgment, the sacrilegious baptism is still seen as the outcome of a chain of events *initiated by man.* It is true that the relationship is still "mystified," since *super*natural power is seen as necessary for the money to bear interest, yet it is clearly understood that the money would *not* do this *on its own.* The multiplication of money as capital is not seen as a power inherent in money. It is not *commodity* fetishism since these people do not consider it a *natural* property of money to reproduce more of itself. Indeed, it is so unnatural that supernatural power has to be obtained by devious and destructive means. And while the true relationship of capital to labor is mystified, there still remains the fact that Man is seen as necessary to trigger off the magical cycles, and this is in keeping with the fact that in a use value economy the regulations that men enter into in their work appear to them as direct, reciprocal, personal relations, and not as activities controlled by the relationships of their products. Indeed, it is precisely due to this consciousness of human interdependence and reciprocity in which both persons and their products are seen as forming a unity, that the specific forms of pre-capitalist fetishism that here concern us arise. When people are confronted by the early stages of penetration of the commodity market, it is the warping and imbalancing of that interdependence which casts the fetish into the realm of the unnatural and evil—the illicit baptism of money and the proletarians' devil contract. Until the spread of capitalist institutions has permeated most aspects of social life, the lower classes continue to perceive the bonds that unite people with their employers and with the fruits of their labor as mutual personal relations, albeit relations which are distorted, evil, and destructive, and not as the result of forces naturally inherent in things.

Analogical Reason and the Philosophy of Use Value. The principles underlying the belief in the baptized bill bear a striking resemblance to those concerning money and exchange in Aristotle's *Politics* and the economic theory of the late Middle Ages. Basic to this outlook was the distinction Aristotle drew between what are today called *use* value and *exchange* value, a distinction that occupies a central place in Marxist theory as well. In Book I of *The Politics* Aristotle writes:

> Every article or property has a double use; both uses are uses of the thing itself, but they are not similar uses; for one is the proper use of the article in question, the other is not. For example a shoe may be used either to put on your foot or to offer in exchange. Both are uses of the shoe; for even he that gives a shoe to someone who requires a shoe, and receives in exchange cash or food, is making use of the shoe as shoe, but not the use proper to it, for a shoe is not expressly made for exchange purposes. The same is the case with other articles of property . . .

While the exchange function of any article could be utilized legitimately within a householding or subsistence economy, it was from this exchange function that money-making or capitalism arose to the detriment of the householding or "natural economy."

In accordance with the distinction between use value and exchange value, Aristotle distinguished between the natural and unnatural uses of money. As Eric Roll points out, this distinction between the two arts of money making,

> was not just an attempt to drive home an ethical distinction. It was also a true analysis of two different forms in which money acts in the economic process: as a medium of exchange whose function is completed by the acquisition of the good required for the satisfaction of a want; and in the shape of money capital leading men to the desire for limitless accumulation (1973:33).

Roll gives emphasis in his discussion of Aristotle to the idea that money as used in the circulation of use values—Aristotle's householding, the natural economy—is *barren*. "Money is intended to be used in exchange, but not to increase at interest; it is by nature barren; through usury it breeds, and this must be the most unnatural of all the ways of making money" (1973:33). Table I shows this in tabular form.

TABLE I

Types of Value	*Use Value*	*Exchange Value*
Aim of Circulation	To satisfy natural wants	To gain money as an end in itself
Characteristics of Money	Means of exchange (C-M-C) Natural Barren	Means to make more money (means as ends; capital) (M-C-M′) Unnatural Fertile

From this set of contrasts several analogies clearly emerge. For instance:

Use Value of Money (money)		Exchange Value of Money (capital)
natural / barren	:	unnatural / fertile

But in nature, in the biological world for example, things are naturally fertile, and Aristotle says on this score, "Money was intended to be a means of exchange, interest represents an increase in the money itself. We speak of it as a yield, as of a crop or a litter; for each animal produces its like, and interest is money produced out of money. Hence of all ways of getting wealth this is the most contrary to nature."

Following the method propounded by Hesse in her discussion of analogy (1963); this can be expressed as a set of positive and negative analogies, in which there is explicit recognition of *both* similarity and difference between the paired terms that constitute the analogy (see Table II).

TABLE II
Positive and Negative Analogies

[biological realm] (natural)		[use value of money] (natural)		[exchange value of money] (unnatural)
$\frac{\text{animal}}{\text{litter}}$	:	$\frac{M}{M}$	:	$\frac{M}{M'}$

(Where M = Money, and M' = Money plus interest on that money; i.e. capital.)

The analogy between animals and money as use value expresses a relationship of both similarity and of difference: they are similar because both are part of the natural world, and their properties function so as to ensure the original purpose of the ideal society ("to reestablish nature's own equilibrium of self-sufficiency," as Aristotle phrases it); and different because it is the natural property of animals to breed more of themselves, while money is by nature barren.

The analogy between animals and capital, or between money and capital, is also based on a set of similarities and differences. For instance capital exhibits the same properties as animals with regard to multiplication, but while one is natural, the other is unnatural. Similarly, money in the use value paradigm is similar to money as capital, but while the former is barren, the latter is fertile.

The task facing the inhabitants of the plantation zones in the southern Cauca Valley is how to explain and in some cases actually effect the transfer of properties of similarity into those of difference and those of difference into relationships of similarity. How to transmute the properties of animals, for example, into those of money, whose natural property is to remain barren? How to explain the transformation of money into interest-bearing capital? How to convert use values into exchange values?

This is done through the illicit rite of baptizing money. Unbaptized or natural money is not and should not be capital; it cannot and should not yield interest in the way capital or animals are seen to breed more of themselves. Money can achieve this unnatural property if it is acted on ritually through means of baptism. Barren money can become unnaturally fertile when transferred to God's domain and stamped with His life-giving properties.

The efficacy and rationality of the magical act would seem to be understood by means of a comparison between observed relationships of similarity and difference in separate spheres of existence, and the rite is utilized to manipulate and transmute relationships of difference into relationships of similarity.

NATURAL		UNNATURAL
$\frac{\text{animal}}{\text{litter}}$	:	$\frac{M}{M'}$

The litter is the natural yield of the animal, whereas the increase of capital (M') is unnatural. The negative analogy (the comparison of difference) can be overcome and harnessed to the comparison of similarity (positive analogy) by means of the baptismal rite. Thus:

$$\frac{\text{baptism of child}}{\text{legitimation and growth}} : \frac{\text{illicit baptism of money}}{\text{delegitimation and growth}}$$

Nevertheless, that transfer is achieved by an *illicit* rite when applied to money, and is a sacrilege which deprives a human child of salvation and the endorsement necessary to the fulfillment of human potential. Thus although money can be converted into interest-bearing capital, this is seen as both supernatural and anti-natural. Capital is thus explained in terms which reveal it to be unnatural and immoral. The analogical paradigms based on a use value orientation can be restructured through supernatural means, but for all the restructuring, the original meaning of use-value economics is still upheld.

The Devil Contract and the Magic of Capitalist Production. In the case of the devil contract made by the plantation wage laborers in order to increase production, the money earned is understood to be barren. Thus, while the proletarian's production can increase, the money is not fertile; in fact it is redolent with infertility—the antithesis of baptized money. What is the meaning of this?

At one level this could be explained by the fact that as opposed to God, the contract is made with His antithesis—the devil. But one can dig deeper behind the symbols and explore Aristotle's and Marx's distinctions further. Aristotle makes the connection between production and the different forms of money in the following way:

> Hence we seek to define wealth and money-making in different ways; and we are right in doing so, for they *are* different; on the one hand true wealth, in accordance with nature, belonging to household management, productive; on the other money-making, with no place in nature, belonging to trade and not productive of goods in the full sense.

Here the antithesis between money as a mere means of exchange, and money as capital, is paralleled by the contrast between productive and non-productive goods and activities. Indeed, for Aristotle the contrast is even more stark than this, since "money-making" or capitalism is inherently *destructive* of the natural or householding economy, destructive of the reciprocal interplay of natural forces responsible for production and growth.

Thus the initial frame of reference which referred to the barren and fertile characteristics of money as a medium of *exchange,* is placed in the wider and more determinate context of *production* and a more profound sense of fertility. The analogy between animals and their offspring on the one side and money breeding money on the other is a totally unnatural one in Aristotle's eyes; unnatural especially in the sense that the naturally barren form of money is grounded in productive activity—"in the full sense"—while the fertile form of money is not. Only in its naturally barren form does "money keep to its original purpose; to reestablish nature's own equilibrium of self-sufficiency." Hence use-values, money as a neutral mediator of exchange, nature's equilibrium of self-sufficiency, and productivity in the full sense, are all intrinsically related and necessary to one another.

A basic set of positive and negative analogies derived from this view is as follows:

$$\frac{\text{money}}{\text{capital}} \quad : \quad \frac{\text{productive capacity}}{\text{destructive}}$$

The problem facing the people in this culture is, therefore, how to explain and effect the inversion of these natural analogies, since it is empirically true that production can be maintained and increased within the sphere of capitalist production. On inversion:

$$\frac{\text{money}}{\text{capital}} \quad : \quad \frac{\text{destructive}}{\text{productive}}$$

This inversion is effected and explained in terms of the devil contract. Through the agency of this evil and destructive force, production within capitalist relations on the sugar plantations can be increased, and at the same time, as the analogy so neatly displays, the money wage gained is non-productive; it kills whatever it buys except for luxury articles consumed immediately. The natural set of relationships that should obtain according to the use-value paradigm can be transformed into capitalist relationships which defy the use-value analogies. But these capitalist relationships are viewed neither as natural nor as good since they necessitate the agency of the devil.

CONCLUSION

The "superstitions" we encountered in the Cauca Valley are thus revealed to be beliefs which systematically endorse the logic of the contradiction between use values and exchange values. In doing so, these beliefs are identical with the basic tenets of Aristotelian economics, the dominant doctrine of economics as postulated by Aquinas and others in the late Middle Ages, and one of the basic premises of Marxism. (Not for nothing did R.H. Tawney call Marx the last of the Schoolmen.) These "superstitions" are not confused vestiges deriving from a prior era when peasant life or Church influence was more intact, but are precise formulations which entail a systematic critique of the encroachment of the capitalist mode of production.

The sensitivity to the distinction between use values and exchange values as manifested by these beliefs is not merely the result of mummified ideals retained from the days when the peasant mode of production was flourishing. Nor would it seem solely due to the fact that some peasant production still coexists with the developing capitalist mode of production. It is also due to the fact that the "slum economy" of the recently urbanized peasants is similarly one based to a major degree on use value practices.

The paradigm of rationality entailed in these formulations is heavily dependent on analogical reason, examples of which are given above. Analogical explanations involve an account of the unfamiliar in terms of the familiar, and the analogical mode of reasoning at issue here is inherently holistic and dependent on identifying things in terms of their relationships to larger wholes. On the other hand, the causal paradigm which so thoroughly permeates modern Western social science and the mainstream of what is loosely called "Western thought" since the seventeenth century, is inherently atomistic and reductionist, defining identity in terms of the thing itself and not in relation to the context of which the thing is part. In light of this enormous epistemological difference it is obvious that the categories of contemporary sociology and classical economics tend to mystify peasant economics and to deny that peasant economic theory and behavior could be relevant to a critique of classical economics.

The mode of analogical reason outlined above would appear to be most prolific and consciously used in cultures which are guided by use value economics. As Tambiah has so elegantly shown in his interpretation of Zande magic, an awareness of its logic and systematization dispels the pejorative confusions entailed when such beliefs are subjected to the cannons of validity embodied in modern positivist methodology. Where Tambiah falls short, however, is in his failure to consider the underlying system of metaphysics from which the terms in such analogies draw their meaning. While it is a great service to have demonstrated how apparently weird connections and influences between phenomena can be postulated and upheld in terms of the purely *formal* properties of an analogical set, the indigenous ontology has to be considered as well. Placing the emphasis on the formal characteristics of analogical rationality gives us an understanding of the systematic precision entailed in modes of explanation which are not based on the cause-effect paradigm alone. Nevertheless, one still has to ask why certain properties and co-occurences are considered to be analogically related, and why those properties are thought to exist in the first place. While we can point to the analogical relationship between money and capital, for instance, and demonstrate the problem and solution such an analogy conveys, we are still doing no more than pointing to a set of givens whose meaning ultimately lies in a basis other than that given in the formal reasoning rules themselves. This basis is to be found in the metaphysics of nature and the indigenous social philosophy of the group concerned, and in this specific case a large aspect of that philosophy is conveyed by the paradigm of use value economics.

In a culture where Nature is regarded as animate, things which we consider as inert seem to be credited with mind, intelligence, and volition, in the same manner as we reserve those characteristics for the human being exclusively. Nature is seen as permeated with Mind, regulating some Grand Design. The human understanding of things in nature thus proceeds as much through a reckoning of the *meaning* and *intent* established by these things, as through their observable empirical characteristics. Furthermore, given this metaphysical scheme, the meaning and power of things depends on the *relational network* of which the thing is part, which is precisely what makes the analogical mode of reason so compelling.

The types of analogies considered in the examples taken from the Cauca Valley are exceedingly interesting in that the relationships of cause and similarity between the separate terms that make up any analogy depend upon the total set and are not given in the terms themselves. The concept of "cause" herein entailed is not that of mechanical causation, but rather that of "pattern," association, and purpose. In subjecting the latter to the mechanical paradigm of interacting forces akin to the percussion of rebounding billiard balls or interlocking cog wheels,[11] nothing but confusion can result; hence the misguided attribution of irrationality by Western observers when presented with such forms of reason. In describing the properties of the following type of analogy, which is the same type as those considered above, Mary Hesse points out that the relations of similarity at the horizontal level are contingent upon the particular meaning established by the vertical relationships.

[11] Of course the mechanical paradigm can be viewed as an analogical form of reasoning too! However, like commodity fetishism it is the analogy which de-analogizes, for it directs attention from relationships to forces supposedly inherent in things.

$$\frac{\text{father}}{\text{child}} : \frac{\text{state}}{\text{citizens}}$$

Moreover, the vertical relationships themselves are not causal in any specific sense, and furthermore, if the individual terms are considered apart from the total analogical set, they each possess a *variety* of connotations.

Thus the specific meaning of any of the terms within the total structure is dependent on the total set of relationships. This is surely what Lévi-Strauss in his analyses of the "savage mind" means by his obscure directive to look for meaning in relationships and not in the things themselves.[12]

This is to say that the significance of the individual terms does *not* emerge when they are viewed as having meaning as isolates, disconnected from other isolates. Rather, as individual terms they are relational terms which embody the meaning established by the set of relationships of which any term is part. Things are relationships, and these relationships are ontological rather than logical.

The individual terms are not viewed atomistically. They are not conceived of by means of the Newtonian corpuscular paradigm or what A.N. Whitehead calls a philosophy of "external relations," but instead conform to a philosophy of "internal relations" in which each of the separate terms embodies the total set of relationships of which it is part (Whitehead, 1967: 111–118; Ollman, 1971: 27–42).

Put briefly, the metaphysical doctrine of external relations is the foundation of the analytic and reductive method by means of which explanation proceeds through analyzing any given phenomenon in terms of its supposedly irreducible atomistic constituents. The explanation is completed by illustrating the mathematical laws of cause and effect that supposedly hold between these atoms, which in sum constitute the whole phenomenon. This doctrine is central to the Cartesian tradition and the view of nature with which Galileo, Descartes, and Newton propelled modern science on its successful course. Modified in theoretical physics since the early twentieth century, it still seems to

[12] In one of the few instances where Lévi-Strauss has attempted to set forth his method in a set of rules, he writes as follows: "The method we adopt, in this case as in others, consists in the following operations: (1) define the phenomenon under study as a relation between two or more terms, real or supposed; (2) construct a table of possible permutations between these terms; (3) take this table as the general object of analysis which at this level only, can yield necessary connections, the empirical phenomenon considered at the beginning being only one possible combination among others, the complete system of which must be reconstructed beforehand" (1963:16).

In our discussion of the Cauca Valley the "complete system. . . . reconstructed beforehand" is given by the use value paradigm derived from the empirical evidence and expressed both in terms of that evidence and the Aristotelian formulation.

provide the basis of most of modern *social* science and popular Western ideologies concerning society. Two important properties concern us here. As Whitehead says, "The character of each of these ultimate things is thus conceived as its own private qualification. Such an existent is understandable in complete disconnection from any other such existent: the ultimate truth is that it requires nothing but itself in order to exist" (1967:113).

In other words, the meaning or identity of a thing is given in itself alone, rather than the "living" context of which it is part. Second, by virtue of such de-contextualization, relationships between things (and changes of things or their relationships), are conceived of "externally" to the things themselves, and suggest recourse to a certain type of Deism, which is how Newton, himself regarded the problem.

In light of this the Cauca Valley beliefs, which stem from a contrary metaphysic, are paradoxically similar insofar as they also make appeals to divine or "external" agencies. Despite this apparent similarity, the concept of nature and ontology in the Cauca Valley situation is one in which the identity or character of things is seen to lie in their being embodiments of relationships and process; hence the doctrine of "internal relations" and a natural science akin to the ancient Greek view of nature, based on the principle that the world of nature is saturated or permeated by mind.

To employ another usage, the peasant epistemology is such that individual terms are conceptualized like Hegel's "moments," constitutive of the totality which constitutes them, with each "moment" containing part of the whole within itself—"internally." The *identity* of the thing springs from its relation to the whole, and is not given in the properties of the thing seen as an isolated or isolable atom. Marxism itself rests on an acute appreciation of such a perspective (cf. Ollman), and Marx expressed this throughout his writing as the foregoing quotations from his works indicate.[13]

Finally, it bears repeating that although the analogical forms can be inverted and that relationships can be transformed, the fact of the matter is that in the examples drawn from the Cauca Valley, where one mode of production is displacing another, the ethics and reason of use value are maintained. The metaphysics that underlie the analogical

[13] As an aside it is worthwhile to point out that in the formal representation of analogies of the above type,

$$\frac{A}{B} \quad : \quad \frac{C}{D}$$

A can be said to be equal or similar to C, but *only* insofar as A and C are part of the same set. In another context, A may well not be similar to C, and in this sense the law of contradiction as used by logicians is bypassed with the dialectical principle that A *is* and *is not* C.

mode are not disowned despite the fact that the peasants now own little else but their abstract labor power. The analogies are not neutral, despite the neutralizing influence of the fact-value distinction intrinsic to modern science and economic theory in which it is held that ". . . Economics is entirely neutral between ends; that in so far as the achievement of any end is dependent on scarce means, it is germane to the preoccupations of the economist. Economics is not concerned with ends as such" (Robbins, 1935:24).

Nothing could be further from the economic theory and behavior of the peasants and field hands in the southern Cauca Valley for whom economics is totally "concerned with ends as such." Reason, whether it be economic or whatever, is for them far more than the narrow concern with the maximal coordination of scarce means to alternate ends. Rather, reason is that which embodies the conditions of objective existence.[14] Their understanding of capitalist reason and the praxis it embodies, is one which leads them to conclude that it is contrary to the laws of nature, evil, and ultimately destructive of the conditions of objective existence.

To subject their reason to the instrumentality of means and ends, and to the empty formality of analogies considered apart from their content and purpose, is to merely hasten the demise of the conditions embodied in that reason. A peasant society or community can be involved in commodity production—based on exchange value—but this need not be its total culture. A community can in many ways be affected and even controlled by the wider capitalist world, but this in itself does not necessarily make such a community a replica of the larger society and global economy. Attempts to interpret pre-capitalist social formations by means of what Polanyi called "our obsolete market mentality," are misguided exercises in an ingenuous ethnocentrism that in fact is not even applicable to the market society itself, but merely a replication of its appearance.

SELECTED BIBLIOGRAPHY

Asocaña, (Asociación Nacional de Cultivadores de Caña de Azúcar) (1965) *Development of the Colombian Sugar Industry, 1967–1968*. Cali, Colombia.

Brown, Norman O. (1959) *Life Against Death*. Middletown, Conn.: Wesleyan University Press.

Burtt, Edwin Arthur (1954) *The Metaphysical Foundations of Modern Science*. New York: Anchor Books.

C.I.M. (1969) "Los Iguazos, Proletarios y Parias en el Azúcar," *Estudios Marxistas*, No. 1, pp. 43–86. Editorial Colombian Nueva Ltda., Colombia.

[14] This formulation is the subject of intensive analysis by the "Frankfurt School" of Marxist scholars, especially Max Horkheimer in his work *The Eclipse of Reason*.

Gilhodes, Pierre (1970) "Agrarian Struggles in Colombia," in R. Stavenhagen (ed.) *Agrarian Problems and Peasant Movements in Latin America*. New York: Anchor Books.

Guzman, German and O. Fals-Borda and E. Umaña Luna (1962–64) *La Violencia en Colombia*, 2 vols. Bogotá, Colombia: Ediciones Tercer Mundo.

Hesse, Mary B. (1963) *Models and Analogies in Science*. London: Sheed and Ward.

Horkheimer, Max (1974) *The Eclipse of Reason*. New York: Seabury Press.

Knight, Rolf (1972) *Sugar Plantations and Labor Patterns in the Cauca Valley, Colombia*. Department of Anthropology, University of Toronto Anthropological Series, No. 12.

Lévi-Strauss, Claude (1963) *Totemism*, Boston: Beacon Press.

Mancini, S. (1959) "Tenencia y uso de la Tierra por la Industria Azúcarera del Valle del Cauca," *Acta Agronómica* (Facultad de Agronomía, Palmira, Colombia), IV, 1.

Marx, Karl (1967) *Capital*, 3 vols. New York: International Publishers.

——— (1973) *The Grundrisse*, M. Nicolaus (trans.), Middlesex, England: Penguin Books.

Nash, June (1972) "The Devil in Bolivia's Nationalised Tin Mines," *Science and Society*, XXVI, 2.

Needham, Joseph (1956) *Science and Civilisation in China*, vol. 2. Cambridge, England.

Ollman, Bertell (1971) *Alienation: Marx's Conception of Man in Capitalist Society*, Cambridge: Cambridge University Press.

Polanyi, Karl (1947) "Our Obsolete Market Mentality," *Commentary*, Vol. 3, February 1947:109–117.

Robbins, Lionel (1935) *An Essay on the Nature and Significance of Economic Science*, 2nd Edition. London: Macmillan.

Roll, Eric (1973) *A History of Economic Thought*, 4th Edition. London: Faber and Faber.

Sahlins, Marshall (1972) *Stone Age Economics*. Chicago & New York: Aldine Atherton.

Schmidt, Alfred (1971) *The Concept of Nature in Marx*. London: New Left Books.

Smith, Adam (1967) "The History of Astronomy," J. Ralph Lindgren (ed.), in *The Early Writings of Adam Smith*. New York: A. M. Kelley.

Tambiah, S.J. (1973) "Form and Meaning of Magical Acts: A Point of View," in Robin Horton and Ruth Finnegan (eds.), *Modes of Thought*. London: Faber and Faber.

Tawney, R.H. (1954) *Religion and the Rise of Capitalism*. New York: Mentor.

Weber, Max (1927) *General Economic History*, Frank H. Knight trans., Greenberg, New York.

——— (1958) *The Protestant Ethic and the Spirit of Capitalism*, Talcott Parsons (trans.), New York: Charles Scribner's Sons.

Whitehead, Alfred North (1967) *Adventures of Ideas*. New York: Free Press.

[6]

Marshall D. Sahlins

On the Sociology of Primitive Exchange

In a discussion that has anthropological pretensions, 'provisional generalization' is no doubt a redundant phrase.[1] Yet the present venture needs a doubly cautious introduction. Its generalizations have developed out of a dialogue with ethnographic materials – many of these are appended Tylorian fashion as 'illustrative materials'[2] – but no rigorous tests have been applied. Perhaps the conclusions may be offered as a plea to ethnography rather than a contribution to theory, if these are not again the same thing. At any rate, there follow some suggestions about the interplay in primitive communities between forms, material conditions, and social relations of exchange.

I

MATERIAL FLOW AND SOCIAL RELATIONS

What are in the received wisdom 'noneconomic' or 'exogenous' conditions are in the primitive reality the very organization of economy.[3] A material transaction is usually a momentary episode in a continuous social relation. The social relation exerts governance: the flow of goods is constrained by, is part of, a status etiquette. 'One cannot treat Nuer economic relations by themselves, for they always form part of direct social relations of a general kind', Evans-Pritchard writes: '. . . there is always between them a general social relationship of one kind or another, and their economic relations, if such they may be called, must conform to this general pattern of behavior' (1940, pp. 90-91). The dictum is broadly applicable (cf. White 1959, pp. 242-245).

Yet the connection between material flow and social relations is reciprocal. A specific social relation may constrain a given movement of goods, but a specific transaction – 'by the same token' – suggests a particular social relation. If friends make gifts, gifts make friends. A great proportion of primitive exchange, much more than our own traffic, has as its decisive function this latter, instrumental one: the material flow underwrites or initiates social relations. Thus do primitive peoples transcend Hobbesian chaos. For the indicative condition of primitive society is the absence of a public and sovereign power: persons and (especially) groups confront each other not merely as distinct interests but with the possible inclination and certain right to physically prosecute these interests. Force is decentralized, legitimately held in severalty, the social compact has yet to be drawn, the state nonexistent. So peacemaking is not a sporadic intersocietal event, it is a continuous process within society itself. Groups must 'come to terms' – the phrase notably connotes a material exchange satisfactory on both sides:

> 'In these primitive and archaic societies there is no middle path. There is either complete trust or mistrust. One lays down one's arms, renounces magic and gives everything away, from casual hospitality to one's daughter or one's property. It is in such conditions that men, despite themselves, learnt to renounce what was theirs and made contracts to give and repay. But then they had no choice in the matter. When two groups of men meet they may move away or in case of mistrust or defiance they may resort to arms; or else they can come to terms' (Mauss, 1954, p. 79).

Even on its strictly practical side, exchange in primitive communities has not the same role as the economic flow in modern industrial communities. The place of transaction in the total economy is different: under primitive conditions it is more detached from production, less firmly hinged to production in an organic way. Typically, it is less involved than modern exchange in the acquisition of means of production, more involved with the redistribution of finished goods through the community. The bias is that of an economy in which food holds a commanding position, and in which day-to-day output does not depend on a massive technological complex nor a complex division of labor. It is the bias also of a domestic mode of production: of household producing units, division of labor by sex and age dominant, production that looks to familial requirements, and direct access by domestic groups to strategic resources. It is the bias of a social order in which rights to control returns go along with rights to use resources of production, and in which there is very limited traffic in titles or income privileges in resources. It is the bias, finally, of societies ordered in the main by kinship. Such characteristics of primitive economies as these, so broadly stated, are of course subject to qualification in specific instances. They are offered only as a guide to the detailed analysis of distribution that follows. It is also advisable to repeat that 'primitive' shall refer to cultures lacking a political state, and it applies only insofar as economy and social relations have not been modified by the historic penetration of states.

On a very general view, the array of economic transactions in the ethnographic record may be resolved into two types. First, those 'vice-versa' movements between two parties known familiarly as 'reciprocity' ($A \rightleftarrows B$). The second, centralized movements: collection from members of a group, often under one hand, and redivision within this group

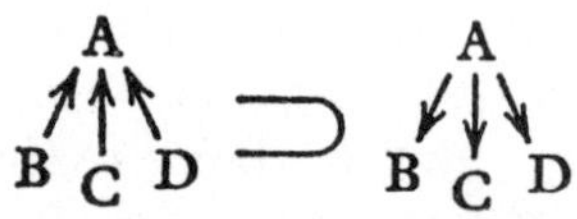

This is 'pooling' or 'redistribution'. On an even more general view, the two types merge. For pooling is an organization of reciprocities, a system of reciprocities – a fact of central bearing upon the genesis of large-scale redistribution under chiefly aegis. But this most general understanding merely suggests concentration in the first place on reciprocity; it remains the course of analytic wisdom to separate the two.

Their social organizations are very different. True, pooling and reciprocity may occur in the same social contexts – the same close kinsmen pool their resources in household commensality, for instance, also individuals share things with one another – but the precise social relations of pooling and reciprocity are not the same. The material transaction that is pooling is socially a *within* relation, the collective action of a group. Reciprocity is a *between* relation, the action and reaction of two parties. Thus pooling is the complement of social unity and, in Polanyi's term, 'centricity'; whereas, reciprocity is social duality and 'symmetry'. Pooling stipulates a social center where goods meet and thence flow outwards, and a social boundary too, within which persons (or subgroups) are cooperatively related. But reciprocity stipulates two sides, two distinct social-economic interests. Reciprocity can establish solidary relations, in so far as the material flow suggests assistance or mutual benefit, yet the social fact of sides is inescapable.

Considering the established contributions of Malinowski and Firth, Gluckman, Richards, and Polanyi, it does not seem too sanguine to say that we know fairly well the material and social concomitants of pooling. Also, what is known fits the argument that pooling is the material side of 'collectivity' and 'centricity'. Cooperative food production, rank and chieftainship, collective political and ceremonial action, these are some of the ordinary contexts of pooling in primitive communities. To review very briefly:

The everyday, workaday variety of redistribution is familial pooling of food. The principle suggested by it is that products of collective effort in provisioning are pooled, especially should the cooperation entail division of labor. Stated so, the rule applies not only to householding but to higher-level cooperation as well, to groups larger than households that develop about some task of procurement – say, buffalo-impounding in the Northern Plains or netting fish in a Polynesian lagoon. With qualifications – such as the special shares locally awarded special contributions to the group endeavor – the principle remains at the higher, as at the lower, household level: 'Goods collectively procured are distributed through the collectivity.'

Rights of call on the produce of the underlying population, as well as obligations of generosity, are everywhere associated with chieftainship. The organized exercise of these rights and obligations is redistribution:

> 'I think that throughout the world we would find that the relations between economics and politics are of the same type. The chief, everywhere, acts as a tribal banker, collecting food, storing it, and protecting it, and then using it for the benefit of the whole community. His functions are the prototype of the public finance system and the organization of State treasuries of to-day. Deprive the chief of his privileges and financial

> benefits and who suffers most but the whole tribe?' (Malinowski, 1937, pp. 232-233).

This use 'for the benefit of the whole community' takes various forms: subsidizing religious ceremony, social pageantry, or war; underwriting craft production, trade, the construction of technical apparatus and of public and religious edifices; redistributing diverse local products; hospitality and succor of the community (in severalty or in general) during shortage. Speaking more broadly, redistribution by powers-that-be serves two purposes, either of which may be dominant in a given instance. The practical, logistic function – redistribution – sustains the community, or community effort, in a material sense. At the same time, or alternatively, it has an instrumental function: as a ritual of communion and of subordination to central authority, redistribution sustains the corporate structure itself, that is in a social sense. The practical benefits may be critical, but, whatever the practical benefits, chiefly pooling generates the spirit of unity and centricity, codifies the structure, stipulates the centralized organization of social order and social action –

> '. . . every person who takes part in the *aŋa* [feast organized by a Tikopia chief] is impelled to participate in forms of co-operation which for the time being go far beyond his personal interests and those of his family and reach the bounds of the whole community. Such a feast gathers together chiefs and their clansfolk who at other times are rivals ready to criticize and slander each other, but who assemble here with an outward show of amity. . . . In addition, such purposive activity subserves certain wider social ends, which are common in the sense that every person or nearly every person knowingly or unknowingly promotes them. For instance, attendance at the *aŋa* and participation in the economic contributions does in fact help to support the Tikopia system of authority' (Firth, 1950, pp. 230-231).

So we have at least the outline of a functional theory of redistribution. The central issues are now likely to be developmental ones, the specification by comparison or phylogenetic study of selective circumstances. The economic anthropology of

Marshall D. Sahlins

reciprocity, however, is not at the same stage. One reason, perhaps, is a popular tendency to view reciprocity as balance, as unconditional one-for-one exchange. Considered as a material transfer, reciprocity is often not that at all. Indeed, it is precisely through scrutiny of departures from balanced exchange that one glimpses the interplay between reciprocity, social relations, and material circumstances.

Reciprocity is a whole class of exchanges, a continuum of forms. This is specially true in the narrow context of material transactions – as opposed to a broadly conceived social principle or moral norm of give-and-take. At one end of the spectrum stands the assistance freely given, the small currency of everyday kinship, friendship, and neighborly relations, the 'pure gift' Malinowski called it, regarding which an open stipulation of return would be unthinkable and unsociable. At the other pole, self-interested seizure, appropriation by chicanery or force requited only by an equal and opposite effort on the principle of *lex talionis*, 'negative reciprocity' as Gouldner phrases it. The extremes are notably positive and negative in a moral sense. The intervals between them are not merely so many gradations of material balance in exchange, they are intervals of sociability. The distance between poles of reciprocity is, among other things, social distance:

> 'Unto a stranger thou mayest lend upon usury; but unto thy brother thou shalt not lend usury' (Deuteronomy xxiii, 21).

> 'Native [Siuai] moralists assert that neighbors should be friendly and mutually trustful, whereas people from far-off are dangerous and unworthy of morally just consideration. For example, natives lay great stress on honesty involving neighbors while holding that trade with strangers may be guided by *caveat emptor*' (Oliver, 1955, p. 82).

> 'Gain at the cost of other communities, particularly communities at a distance, and more especially such as are felt to be aliens, is not obnoxious to the standards of homebred use and wont' (Veblen, 1915, p. 46).

> 'A trader always cheats people. For this reason intra-regional

trade is rather frowned upon while inter-tribal trade gives to the [Kapauku] businessman prestige as well as profit' (Pospisil, 1958, p. 127).

II

A SCHEME OF RECIPROCITIES

A purely formal typology of reciprocities is possible, one based exclusively on immediacy of returns, equivalence of returns, and like material and mechanical dimensions of exchange. The classification thus in hand, one might proceed to correlate sub-types of reciprocity with diverse 'variables' such as kinship distance of parties to the transaction. The virtue of this manner of exposition is that it is 'scientific', or so it would seem. Among the defects is that it is bogus, really just a metaphor of exposition, not a true history of experiment. It ought to be recognized from the beginning that the distinction of one type of reciprocity from another is more than formal. A feature such as the expectation of returns says something about the spirit of exchange, about its disinterestedness or its interestedness, the impersonality, the compassion. Any seeming formal classification conveys these meanings: it is as much a moral as a mechanical scheme. (That the recognition of the moral quality prejudges the relation of exchange to social 'variables', in the sense that the latter are then logically connected to variations in exchange, is not contested. This is a sign that the classification is good.)

The actual kinds of reciprocity are many in any primitive society, let alone in the primitive world taken as a whole. 'Vice-versa movements' may include sharing and counter-sharing of unprocessed food, informal hospitality, ceremonious affinal exchanges, loaning and repaying, compensation of specialized or ceremonial services, the transfer that seals a peace agreement, impersonal haggle, and so on and on. We have several ethnographic attempts to cope typologically with the empirical diversity, notably Douglas Oliver's scheme of Siuai transactions (1955, pp. 229-231; cf. Price, 1962, pp. 37 f; Spencer, 1959, pp. 194 f; Marshall, 1961; and others). In *Crime and Custom*, Malinowski wrote rather broadly and unconditionally about reciprocity; in the *Argonauts*, however, he developed a classification of Trobriand exchanges out of manifold variations in balance and equivalence (Malinowski, 1922, pp. 176-194). It was from this vantage-point, looking to the directness of returns, that the *continuum* which is reciprocity was revealed:

> 'I have on purpose spoken of forms of exchange, of gifts and counter-gifts, rather than of barter or trade, because, although there exist forms of barter pure and simple, there are so many transitions and gradations between that and simple gift, that it is impossible to draw any fixed line between trade on the one hand, and the exchange of gifts on the other. . . . In order to deal with these facts correctly it is necessary to give a complete survey of all forms of payment or present. In this survey there will be at one end the extreme cases of pure gift, that is an offering for which nothing is given in return [but see Firth, 1957, pp. 221, 222]. Then, through many customary forms of gift or payment, partially or conditionally returned, which shade into each other, there come forms of exchange, where more or less strict equivalence is observed, arriving finally at real barter' (Malinowski, 1922, p. 176).

Malinowski's perspective may be taken beyond the Trobriands and applied broadly to reciprocal exchange in primitive societies. It seems possible to lay out in abstract fashion a continuum of reciprocities, based on the 'vice-versa' nature of exchanges, along which empirical instances encountered in the particular ethnographic case can be placed. The stipulation of material returns, less elegantly, the 'sidedness' of exchange, would be the critical thing. For this there are obvious objective criteria, such as the toleration of material unbalance and the leeway of delay: the initial movement of goods from hand to hand is more or less requited materially and there are variations too in the time allowed for reciprocation (again see Firth, 1957, pp. 220-221). Put another way, the spirit of exchange swings from disinterested concern for the other chap through mutuality to self-interest. So expressed, the assessment of 'sidedness' can be supplemented by ethnographic observation in addition to those of immediacy and material equivalence: the initial transfer may be voluntary, involuntary, prescribed, contracted; the return freely bestowed, exacted, or dunned; the exchange haggled or not, the subject of accounting or not; and so forth.

The spectrum of reciprocities proposed for general use is defined by its extremes and mid-point:

1. *Generalized reciprocity, the solidary extreme* ($A \rightleftarrows B$)
'Generalized reciprocity' refers to transactions that are putatively altruistic, transactions on the line of assistance given and, if possible and necessary, assistance returned. The ideal type is Malinowski's 'pure gift'. Other indicative ethnographic formulae are 'sharing', 'hospitality', 'free gift', 'help', and 'generosity'. Less sociable, but tending toward the same pole are 'kinship dues', 'chiefly dues', and '*noblesse oblige*'. Price (1962) refers to the genre as 'weak reciprocity' by reason of the vagueness of the obligation to reciprocate.

At the extreme, say voluntary food-sharing among near kinsmen – or for its logical value, one might think of the suckling of children in this context – the expectation of a direct material return is unseemly. At best it is implicit. The material side of the transaction is repressed by the social: reckoning of debts outstanding cannot be overt and is typically left out of account. This is not to say that handing over things in such form, even to 'loved ones', generates no counter-obligation. But the counter is not stipulated by time, quantity, or quality: the expectation of reciprocity is indefinite. It usually works out that the time and worth of reciprocation are not alone conditional on what was given by the donor, but also upon what he will need and when, and likewise what the recipient can afford and when. Receiving goods lays on a diffuse obligation to reciprocate when necessary to the donor and/or possible for the recipient. The requital thus may be very soon, but then again it may be never. There are people who even in the fullness of time are incapable of helping themselves or others. A good pragmatic indication of generalized reciprocity is a sustained one-way flow. Failure to reciprocate does not cause the giver of stuff to stop giving: the goods move one way, in favor of the have-not, for a very long period.

2. *Balanced reciprocity, the midpoint* ($A \rightleftarrows B$)
'Balanced reciprocity' refers to direct exchange. In precise

balance, the reciprocation is the customary equivalent of the thing received and is without delay. Perfectly balanced reciprocity, the simultaneous exchange of the same types of goods to the same amounts, is not only conceivable but ethnographically attested in certain marital transactions (e.g. Reay, 1959, pp. 95 f), friendship compacts (Seligman, 1910, p. 70), and peace agreements (Hogbin, 1939, p. 79; Loeb, 1926, p. 204; Williamson, 1912, p. 183). 'Balanced reciprocity' may be more loosely applied to transactions which stipulate returns of commensurate worth or utility within a finite and narrow period. Much 'gift-exchange', many 'payments', much that goes under the ethnographic head of 'trade' and plenty that is called 'buying-selling' and involves 'primitive money' belong in the genre of balanced reciprocity.

Balanced reciprocity is less 'personal' than generalized reciprocity. From our own vantage-point it is 'more economic'. The parties confront each other as distinct economic and social interests. The material side of the transaction is at least as critical as the social: there is more or less precise reckoning, as the things given must be covered within some short term. So the pragmatic test of balanced reciprocity becomes an inability to tolerate one-way flows; the relations between people are disrupted by a failure to reciprocate within limited time and equivalence leeways. It is notable of the main run of generalized reciprocities that the material flow is sustained by prevailing social relations; whereas, for the main run of balanced exchange, social relations hinge on the material flow.

3. *Negative reciprocity, the unsociable extreme* $(A \rightleftarrows B)$

'Negative reciprocity' is the attempt to get something for nothing with impunity, the several forms of appropriation, transactions opened and conducted toward net utilitarian advantage. Indicative ethnographic terms include 'haggling' or 'barter', 'gambling', 'chicanery', 'theft', and other varieties of seizure.

Negative reciprocity is the most impersonal sort of exchange. In guises such as 'barter' it is from our own point of view the 'most economic'. The participants confront each other as opposed interests, each looking to maximize utility at the other's expense. Approaching the transaction with an eye singular to the main chance, the aim of the opening party or of both parties is the unearned increment. One of the most sociable forms, leaning toward balance, is haggling conducted in the spirit of 'what the traffic will bear'. From this, negative reciprocity ranges through various degrees of cunning, guile, stealth, and violence to the finesse of a well-conducted horse-raid. The 'reciprocity' is, of course, conditional again, a matter of defense of self-interest. So the flow may be one-way once more, reciprocation contingent upon mustering countervailing pressure or guile.

It is a long way from a suckling child to a Plains Indians' horse-raid. Too long, it could be argued, the classification too widely set. Yet 'vice-versa movements' in the ethnographic record do grade into each other along the whole span. It is well to recall, nevertheless, that empirical exchanges often fall somewhere along the line, not directly on the extreme and middle points here outlined. The question is, can one specify social or economic circumstances that impel reciprocity toward one or another of the stipulated positions, toward generalized, balanced, or negative reciprocity? I think so.

III

RECIPROCITY AND KINSHIP DISTANCE

The span of social distance between those who exchange conditions the mode of exchange. Kinship distance, as has already been suggested, is especially relevant to the form of reciprocity. Reciprocity is inclined toward the generalized pole by close kinship, toward the negative extreme in proportion to kinship distance.

The reasoning is nearly syllogistic. The several reciprocities from freely bestowed gift to chicanery amount to a spectrum of sociability, from sacrifice in favor of another to self-interested gain at the expense of another. Take as the minor premise Tylor's dictum that kindred goes with kindness, 'two words whose common derivation expresses in the happiest way one of the main principles of social life'. It follows that close kin tend to share, to enter into generalized exchanges, and distant and non-kin to deal in equivalents or in guile. Equivalence becomes compulsory in proportion to kinship distance lest relations break off entirely, for with distance there can be little tolerance of gain and loss even as there is little inclination to extend oneself. To nonkin – 'other people', perhaps not even 'people' – no quarter must needs be given: the manifest inclination may well be 'devil take the hindmost'.

All this seems perfectly applicable to our own society, but it is more significant in primitive society. Because kinship is more significant in primitive society. It is, for one thing, the organizing principle or idiom of most groups and most social relations. Even the category 'nonkin' is ordinarily defined by it, that is, as the negative aspect of it, the logical extreme of the class – nonbeing as a state of being. There is something real to this view; it is not logical sophistry. Among ourselves 'nonkin' denotes specialized status relations of positive quality: doctor-patient, policeman-citizen, employer-employee, classmates, neighbors, professional colleagues. But for them 'nonkin' principally connotes the negation of community (or tribalism); often it is the synonym for 'enemy' or 'stranger'. Likewise the economic relation tends to be a simple negation of kinship reciprocities: other institutional norms need not come into play.

Kinship distance, however, has different aspects. It may be organized in several ways, and what is 'close' in one of these ways need not be so in another. Exchange may be contingent on genealogical distance (as locally imputed), that is, on interpersonal kinship status. Or it may hinge on segmentary distance, on descent group status. (One suspects that where these two do not correspond the closer relation governs the reciprocity appropriate in dealings between individual parties, but this ought to be worked out empirically.) For the purpose of creating a general model, attention should also be given to the power of community in stipulating distance. It is not only that kinship organizes communities, but communities kinship, so that a spatial, coresidential term affects the measure of kinship distance and thus the mode of exchange.

'Brothers living together, or a paternal uncle and his nephews living in the same house were, as far as my observation goes, on much closer terms with each other than relatives of similar degrees living apart. This was evident whenever there was a question of borrowing things, of getting help, of accepting an obligation, or of assuming responsibilities for each other (Malinowski, 1915, p. 532; the reference is to the Mailu).

'Mankind [to Siuai] consists of relatives and strangers. Relatives are usually interlinked by both blood and marital ties; most of them live nearby, and persons who live nearby are all relatives. . . . Transactions among them should be carried out in a spirit devoid of commerciality – preferably consisting of sharing [i.e., "pooling" in terms of the present discussion], nonreciprocable giving, and bequeathing, among closest relatives, or of lending among more distantly related ones. . . . Except for a few very distantly related sib-mates, persons who live far away are not relatives and can only be enemies. Most of their customs are unsuitable for the Siuai, but a few of their goods and techniques are desirable. One interacts with them only to buy and sell – utilizing hard bargaining and deceit to make as much profit from such transactions as possible' (Oliver, 1955, pp. 454-455).

Here is one possible model for analyzing reciprocity: a tribal plan can be viewed as a series of more and more inclusive kinship-residential sectors, and reciprocity seen then to vary in character by sectoral position. The close kinsmen who render assistance are particularly near kinsmen in a spatial sense: it is in regard to people of the household, the camp, hamlet, or village that compassion is required, inasmuch as interaction is intense and peaceable solidarity essential. But the quality of mercy is strained in peripheral sectors, strained by kinship distance, so is less likely in exchanges with fellow tribesmen of another village than among covillagers, still less likely in the intertribal sector.

Kinship-residential groupings from this perspective comprise ever-widening comembership spheres: the household, the local lineage, perhaps the village, the subtribe, tribe, other tribes – the particular plan of course varies. The structure is a hierarchy of levels of integration, but from the inside and on the ground it is a series of concentric circles. Social relations of each circle have a specific quality – household relations, lineage relations, and so on – and except as the sectoral divisions be cut through by other

Marshall D. Sahlins

organizations of kinship solidarity – say, nonlocalized clans or personal kindreds – relations within each sphere are more solidary than relations of the next, more inclusive sector. Reciprocity accordingly inclines toward balance and chicane in proportion to sectoral distance. In each sector, certain modes of reciprocity are characteristic or dominant: generalized modes are dominant in the narrowest spheres and play out in wider spheres, balanced reciprocity is characteristic of intermediate sectors, chicane of the most peripheral spheres. In brief, a general model of the play of reciprocity may be developed by superimposing the society's sectoral plan upon the reciprocity continuum, something like this (*Figure 1*):

FIGURE 1—Reciprocity and Kinship Residential Sectors.

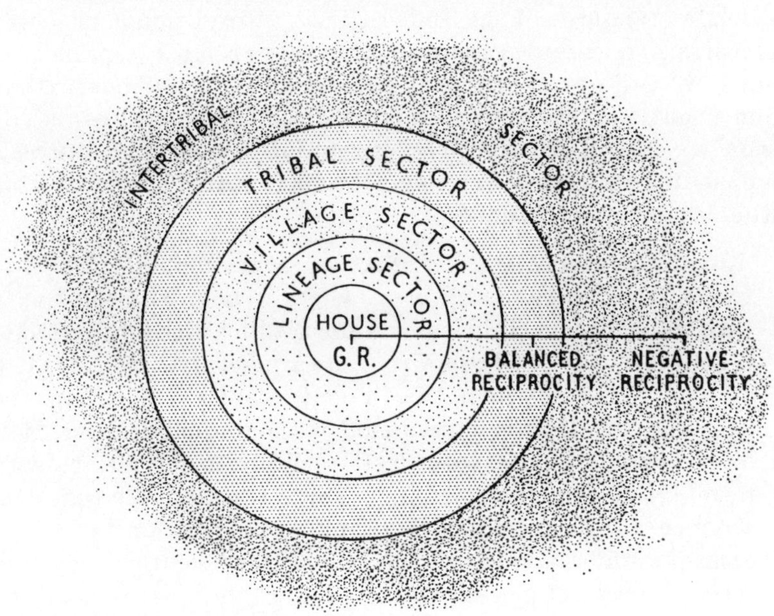

The plan does not rest alone upon the two terms of sectoral division and reciprocity variation. Something is to be said for the embedded third term, morality. 'Far more than we ordinarily suppose,' Firth has written, 'economic relations rest on moral foundations' (1951, p. 144). Certainly that must be the way the people see it – 'Although the Siuai have separate terms for "generosity", "cooperativeness", "morality" (that is, rule abiding), and "geniality", I believe that they consider all these to be closely interrelated aspects of the same attribute of goodness . . .' (Oliver, 1955, p. 78). Another contrast with ourselves is suggested, a tendency for morality, like reciprocity, to be sectorally organized in primitive societies. The norms are characteristically relative and situational rather than absolute and universal. A given act, that is to say, is not so much in itself good or bad, it depends on who the 'Alter' is. The appropriation of another man's goods or his woman, which is a sin ('theft', 'adultery') in the bosom of one's community, may be not merely condoned but positively rewarded with the admiration of one's fellows – if it is perpetrated on an outsider. The contrast with the absolute standards of the Judeo-Christian tradition is probably overdrawn: no moral system is exclusively absolute (especially in wartime) and none perhaps is entirely relative and contextual. But situational standards, defined often in sectoral terms, do seem to prevail in primitive communities and this contrasts sufficiently with our own to have drawn repeated comment from ethnologists. For instance:

> 'Navaho morality is . . . contextual rather than absolute. . . . Lying is not always and everywhere wrong. The rules vary with the situation. To deceive when trading with foreign tribes is a morally accepted practice. Acts are not in themselves bad or good. Incest [by its nature, a contextual sin] is perhaps the only conduct that is condemned without qualification. It is quite correct to use witchcraft techniques in trading with members of foreign tribes. . . . There is an almost complete absence of abstract ideals. Under the circumstances of aboriginal life Navahos did not need to orient themselves in terms of abstract morality. . . . In a large, complex society like modern America, where people come and go and business and other dealings must be carried on by people who never see each other, it is functionally necessary to have abstract standards that transcend an immediate concrete situation in which two or more persons are interacting' (Kluckhohn, 1959, p. 434).

The scheme with which we deal is tripartite: social, moral, and

Marshall D. Sahlins

economic. Reciprocity and morality are sectorally structured – the structure is that of kinship-tribal groupings.

But the scheme is entirely a hypothetical state of affairs. One can conceive circumstances that would alter the social-moral-reciprocal relations postulated by it. Propositions about the external sectors are particularly vulnerable. (For 'external sector' one can generally read 'intertribal sector', the ethnic peripherae of primitive communities; in practice it can be set where positive morality fades out or where intergroup hostility is the normal in-group expectation.) Transactions in this sphere may be consummated by force and guile, it is true, by *wabuwabu*, to use the near-onomatopoeic Dobuan term for sharp practice. Yet it seems that violent appropriation is a resort born of urgent requirements that can only, or most easily, be supplied by militant tactics. Peaceful symbiosis is at least a common alternative.

In these nonviolent confrontations the propensity to *wabuwabu* no doubt persists; it is built in to the sectoral plan. So if it can be socially tolerated – if, that is, countervailing peace-enforcing conditions are sufficiently strong – hard bargaining is the institutionalized external relation. We find then *gimwali*, the mentality of the market place, the impersonal (no-partnership) exchange of Trobriand commoners of different villages or of Trobrianders and other peoples. But still *gimwali* does suppose special conditions, some sort of social insulation that prevents the economic friction from kindling a dangerous conflagration. In the ordinary case, haggling is actually repressed, particularly, it appears, if the exchange of the border is critical to both sides, as where different strategic specialties move against each other. Despite the sectoral distance, the exchange is equitable, *utu*, balanced: the free play of *wabuwabu* and *gimwali* is checked in the interest of the symbiosis.

The check is delivered by special and delicate institutional means of border exchange. The means sometimes look so preposterous as to be considered by ethnologists some sort of 'game' the natives play, but their design manifestly immunizes an important economic interdependence against a fundamental social cleavage. (Compare the discussion of the *kula* in White, 1959, and Fortune, 1932.) Silent trade is a famous case in point – good relations are maintained by preventing any relations. Most common are 'trade-partnerships' and 'trade-friendships'. The important thing in all varieties is a social suppression of negative reciprocity. Peace is built in, haggling outlawed, and, conducted as a transfer of equivalent utilities, the exchange in turn underwrites the peace. (Trade-partnerships, often developed along lines of classificatory or affinal kinship, particularly incapsulate external economic transactions in solidary social relations. Status relations essentially internal are projected across community and tribal boundaries. The reciprocity then may lean over backward, in the direction not of *wabuwabu* but something to the generalized side. Phrased as gift-giving, the presentation admits of delay in reciprocation: a direct return may indeed be unseemly. Hospitality, on another occasion returned in kind, accompanies the formal exchange of trade goods. For a host to give stuff over and above the worth of things brought by his partner is not unusual: it both befits the relation so to treat one's partner while he is traveling and stores up credits. On a wider view, this measure of unbalance sustains the trade partnership, compelling as it does another meeting.)

Intertribal symbiosis, in short, alters the terms of the hypothetical model. The peripheral sector is breached by more sociable relations than are normal in this zone. The context of exchange is now a narrower co-membership sphere, the exchange is peaceful and equitable. Reciprocity falls near the balance point.

Now the assertions of this essay, as I have said, developed out of a dialogue with ethnographic materials. It seems worth while to append some of these data to appropriate sections of the argument. Accordingly, Appendix A*(below, pp. 186-200) sets out materials relevant to the present section, 'Reciprocity and Kinship Distance'. This is not by way of proof, of course – there are indeed certain exceptions, or seeming exceptions, in the materials – but by way of exposition or illustration. Moreover, since the ideas only gradually came over me and the monographs and articles had been in many instances consulted for other purposes, it is certain that data pertinent to reciprocity in the works cited have escaped me. (I hope this is sufficiently apologetic and that the ethnographic notes of Appendix A*are of interest to someone besides myself.)

Whatever the value of these notes as exposition of the asserted

* not reproduced here

relation between reciprocity and kinship distance, they must also suggest to the reader certain limitations of the present perspective. Simply to demonstrate that the character of reciprocity is contingent upon social distance – even if it could be demonstrated in an incontestable way – is not to traffic in ultimate explanation, nor yet to specify when exchanges will in fact take place. A systematic relation between reciprocity and sociability in itself does not say when, or even to what extent, the relation will come into play. The supposition here is that the forces of constraint lie outside the relation itself. The terms of final analysis are the larger cultural structure and its adaptive response to its milieu. From this wider view one may be able to stipulate the significant sectoral lines and kinship categories of the given case, and to stipulate too the incidence of reciprocity in different sectors. Supposing it true that close kinsmen would share food, for example, it need not follow that the transactions occur. The total (cultural-adaptive) context may render intensive sharing dysfunctional and predicate in subtle ways the demise of a society that allows itself the luxury. Permit me to quote *in extenso* a passage from Fredrik Barth's brilliant ecological study of South Persian nomads. It shows so well the larger considerations that must be brought to the bar of explanation; in detail it exemplifies a situation that discounts intensive sharing:

> 'The stability of a pastoral population depends on the maintenance of a balance between pastures, animal population, and human population. The pastures available by their techniques of herding set a maximal limit to the total animal population that an area will support; while the patterns of nomadic production and consumption define a minimal limit to the size of the herd that will support a human household. In this double set of balances is summarized the special difficulty in establishing a population balance in a pastoral economy: the human population must be sensitive to imbalances between flocks and pastures. Among agricultural, or hunting and collecting people, a crude Malthusian type of population control is sufficient. With a growing population, starvation and death-rate rise, until a balance is reached around which the population stabilizes. Where pastoral nomadism is the predominant or

exclusive pattern, the nomad population, if subjected to such a form of population control, would *not* establish a population balance, but would find its whole basis for subsistence removed. Quite simply, this is because the productive capital on which their subsistence is based is not simply land, it is animals – in other words *food*. A pastoral economy can only be maintained so long as there are no pressures on its practitioners to invade this large store of food. A pastoral population can therefore only reach a stable level if other effective population controls intervene *before* those of starvation and death-rate. A first requirement in such an adaptation is the presence of the patterns of private ownership of herds, and individual economic responsibility for each household. By these patterns, the population becomes fragmented with respect to economic activities, and economic factors can strike differentially, eliminating some members of the population [i.e., through sedentarization] without affecting other members of the same population. This would be impossible if the corporate organization with respect to political life, and pasture rights, were also made relevant to economic responsibility and survival' (Barth, 1961, p. 124).

Now, about the incidence of reciprocity in the specific case, here is something else to consider – the people may be stingy. Nothing has been said about sanctions of exchange relations nor, more importantly, about forces that countervail. There are contradictions in primitive economies: inclinations of self-interest are unleashed that are incompatible with the high levels of sociability customarily demanded. Malinowski long ago noticed this and Firth (1926) in an early paper on Maori proverbs skillfully brought to light the clash, the subtle interplay, between the moral dictates of sharing and hedonist personal interest. The widespread mode of family production for use, it might be remarked, acts to brake outputs at comparatively low levels even as it orients economic concern inward, within the household. The mode of production thus does not readily lend itself to general economic solidarity. Suppose sharing is morally called for, say by the destitution of a near kinsman, all the things that make sharing good and proper may not evoke in an affluent man the inclination to do it. And even as there may be little to gain by assisting others,

Marshall D. Sahlins

there are no iron-clad guarantees of such social compacts as kinship. The received social-moral obligations prescribe an economic course, and the publicity of primitive life, increasing the risk of evoking jealousy, hostility, and future economic penalty, tends to keep people on course. But, as is well known, to observe that a society has a system of morality and constraints is not to say that everyone acquiesces in it. There may be *biša-baša* times, 'particularly in the late winter, when the household would hide its food, even from relatives' (Price, 1962, p. 47).

That *biša-baša* is the pervasive condition of some peoples is not embarrassing to the present thesis. The Siriono, everyone knows, parley hostility and crypto-stinginess into a way of life. Interestingly enough, the Siriono articulate ordinary norms of primitive economic intercourse. By the norm, for instance, the hunter should not eat the animal he has killed. But the *de facto* sector of sharing is not merely very narrow, 'sharing rarely occurs without a certain amount of mutual mistrust and misunderstanding; a person always feels that it is he who is being taken advantage of', so that 'The bigger the catch the more sullen the hunter' (Holmberg, 1950, pp. 60, 62; cf. pp. 36, 38-39). The Siriono are not thereby different in kind from the run of primitive communities. They simply realize to an extreme the potentiality elsewhere less often consummated, the possibility that structural compulsions of generosity are unequal to a test of hardship. But then, the Siriono are a band of displaced and deculturated persons. The whole cultural shell, from rules of sharing through institutions of chieftainship and Crow kinship terminology, is a mockery of their present miserable state.

IV

RECIPROCITY AND KINSHIP RANK

It is by now apparent – it is made apparent by the illustrative materials of Appendix A* – that in any actual exchange several circumstances may simultaneously bear upon the material flow. Kinship distance, while perhaps significant, is not necessarily decisive. Something may be said for rank, relative wealth and need, the type of goods whether food or durables, and still other

* not reproduced here

'factors'. As a tactic of presentation and interpretation, it is useful to isolate and separately consider these factors. Accordingly, we move on to the relation between reciprocity and kinship rank. But with this proviso: propositions about the covariation of kinship distance or of kinship rank and reciprocity can be argued separately, even validated separately to the extent to which it is possible to select instances in which only the factor at issue is in play – holding 'other things constant' – but the propositions do not present themselves separately in fact. The obvious course of further research is to work out the power of the several 'variables' during combined plays. At best only the beginnings of this course are suggested here.

Rank difference as much as kinship distance supposes an economic relation. The vertical, rank axis of exchange – or the implication of rank – may affect the form of the transaction, just as the horizontal kinship-distance axis affects it. Rank is to some extent privilege, *droit du seigneur*, and it has its responsibilities, *noblesse oblige*. The dues and duties fall to both sides, both high and low have their claims, and feudal terms indeed do not convey the economic equity of kinship ranking. In its true historic setting *noblesse oblige* hardly cancelled out the *droits du seigneur*. In primitive society social inequality is more the organization of economic equality. Often, in fact, high rank is only secured or sustained by o'ercrowing generosity: the material advantage is on the subordinates' side. Perhaps it is too much to see the relation of parent and child as the elemental form of kinship ranking and its economic ethic. It is true, nevertheless, that paternalism is a common metaphor of primitive chieftainship. Chieftainship is ordinarily a relation of higher descent. So it is singularly appropriate that the chief is their 'father', they his 'children', and economic dealings between them cannot help but be affected.

The economic claims of rank and subordination are interdependent. The exercise of chiefly demand opens the way to solicitation from below, and vice versa – not uncommonly a moderate exposure to the 'larger world' is enough to evoke native reference to customary chiefly dues as local banking procedure (cf. Ivens, 1927, p. 32). The word then for the economic relation between kinship ranks is 'reciprocity'. The reciprocity, moreover, is fairly classed as 'generalized'. While not as sociable as the run

Marshall D. Sahlins

of assistance among close kinsmen, it does lean toward that side of the reciprocity continuum. Goods are in truth *yielded* to powers-that-be, perhaps on call and demand, and likewise stuff may have to be *humbly solicited* from them. Still the rationale is often assistance and need, and the supposition of returns correspondingly indefinite. Reciprocation may be left until a need precipitates it, it bears no necessary equivalence to the initial gift, and the material flow can be unbalanced in favor of one side or the other for a long time.

Reciprocity is harnessed to various principles of kinship rank. Generation-ranking, with the elders the privileged parties, may be of significance among hunters and gatherers not merely in the life of the family but in the life of the camp as a whole, and generalized reciprocity between juniors and seniors a correspondingly broad rule of social exchange (cf. Radcliffe-Brown, 1948, pp. 42-43). The Trobrianders have a name for the economic ethic appropriate between parties of different rank within common descent groups – *pokala*. It is the rule that 'Junior members of a sub-clan are expected to render gifts and services to their seniors, who in return are expected to confer assistance and material benefits on the juniors' (Powell, 1960, p. 126). Even where rank is tied to genealogical seniority and consummated in office-power – chieftainship properly so called – the ethic is the same. Take Polynesian chiefs, office-holders in large, segmented polities: supported on the one hand by various chiefly dues, they are freighted, as many have observed, with perhaps even greater obligations to the underlying population. Probably always the 'economic basis' of primitive politics is chiefly generosity – at one stroke an act of positive morality and a laying of indebtedness upon the commonalty. Or, to take a larger view, the entire political order is sustained by a pivotal flow of goods, up and down the social hierarchy, with each gift not merely connoting a status relation but, as a generalized gift not directly requited, compelling a loyalty.

In communities with established rank orders, generalized reciprocity is enforced by the received structure, and once in operation the exchange has redundant effects on the rank system. There is a large range of societies, however, in which rank and leadership are in the main achieved; here reciprocity is more or less engaged in the *formation* of rank itself, as a 'starting mechanism'. The connection between reciprocity and rank is brought to bear in the first case in the form, 'to be noble is to be generous', in the second case, 'to be generous is to be noble'. The prevailing rank structure influences economic relations in the former instance; the reciprocity influences hierarchical relations in the latter. (An analogous feedback occurs in the context of kinship distance. Hospitality is frequently employed to suggest sociability – this is discussed later. John Tanner, one of those 'feral Whites' who grew to manhood among the Indians, relates an anecdote even more to the point: recalling that his Ojibway family was once saved from starvation by a Muskogean family, he noted that if any of his own people ever afterwards met any of the latter 'he would call him "brother", and treat him as such' (Tanner, 1956, p. 24).)

The term 'starting mechanism' is Gouldner's. He explains in this way how reciprocity may be considered a starting mechanism:

> '. . . it helps to initiate social interaction and is functional in the early phases of certain groups before they have developed a differentiated and customary set of status duties. . . . Granted that the question of origins can readily bog down in a metaphysical morass, the fact is that many concrete social systems [– perhaps "relations and groups" is more apt –] do have determinate beginnings. Marriages are not made in heaven. . . . Similarly, corporations, political parties, and all manner of groups have their beginnings. . . . People are continually brought together in new juxtapositions and combinations, bringing with them the possibilities of new social systems. How are these possibilities realized? . . . Although this perspective may at first seem somewhat alien to the functionalist, once it is put to him, he may suspect that certain kinds of mechanisms, conducive to the crystallization of social systems out of ephemeral contacts, will in some measure be institutionalized or otherwise patterned in any society. At this point he would be considering "starting mechanisms". In this way, I suggest, the norm of reciprocity provides one among many starting mechanisms' (Gouldner, 1960, pp. 176-177).

Marshall D. Sahlins

Economic imbalance is the key to deployment of generosity, of generalized reciprocity, as a starting mechanism of rank and leadership. A gift that is not yet requited in the first place 'creates a something between people': it engenders continuity in the relation, solidarity – at least until the obligation to reciprocate is discharged. Secondly, falling under 'the shadow of indebtedness', the recipient is constrained in his relations to the giver of things. The one who has benefited is held in a peaceful, collaborative, circumspect, and responsive position in respect to his benefactor. The 'norm of reciprocity', Gouldner remarks, 'makes two interrelated minimal demands: (1) people should help those who have helped them, and (2) people should not injure those who have helped them' (1960, p. 171). (Or, as Hobbes put it: 'As justice dependeth on antecedant covenant; soe does GRATITUDE depend on antecedant grace; that is to say, antecedant free gift; and is the fourth law of nature; which may be conceived in this form, *that a man which receiveth benefit from another of mere grace, endeavour that he which giveth it, have no reasonable cause to repent him of his good will.*') These demands are as compelling in the highlands of New Guinea as in the prairies of Peoria – 'Gifts [among Gahuka-Gama] have to be repaid. They constitute a debt, and until discharged the relationship of the individuals involved is in a state of imbalance. The debtor has to act circumspectly towards those who have this advantage over him or otherwise risk ridicule' (Read, 1959, p. 429). The esteem that accrues to the generous man all to one side, generosity is usefully enlisted as a starting mechanism of leadership *because it creates followership*. 'Wealth in this finds him friends,' Denig writes of the aspiring Assiniboin, 'as it does on other occasions everywhere' (Denig, 1928-29, p. 525).

Apart from highly organized chiefdoms and simple hunters and gatherers, there are many intermediate tribal peoples among whom pivotal local leaders come to prominence without yet becoming holders of office and title, of ascribed privilege and of sway over corporate political groups. They are men who 'build a name' as it is said, 'big-men' they may be reckoned, or 'men of importance', or 'bulls' who rise above the common herd, who gather followers, who achieve authority. The Melanesian 'big-man' is a case in point. So too the Plains Indian 'chief'. The process of gathering a personal following and that of ascent to the summits of renown is marked by calculated generosity – if not true compassion. Generalized reciprocity is more or less enlisted as a starting mechanism.

In diverse ways, then, generalized reciprocity is engaged with the rank order of the community. Yet we have already characterized the economics of chieftainship in other transactional terms, as redistribution (or large-scale pooling). At this juncture the evolutionist question is posed: 'When does one give way then to the other, reciprocity to redistribution?' This question, however, may mislead. Chiefly redistribution is not different in principle from kinship-rank reciprocity. It is, rather, based upon the reciprocity principle, a highly organized form of that principle. Chiefly redistribution is a centralized, formal organization of kinship-rank reciprocities, an extensive social integration of the dues and obligations of leadership. The real ethnographic world does not present us with the abrupt 'appearance' of redistribution. It presents approximations and kinds of centricity. The apparent course of wisdom is to hinge our characterizations – of rank-reciprocities vs. a system of redistribution – on formal differences in the centralization process, and in this way to resolve the evolutionist issue.

A big-man system of reciprocities may be quite centralized and a chiefly system quite decentralized. A thin line separates them, but it is perhaps significant. Between centricity in a Melanesian big-man economy such as Siuai (Oliver, 1955) and centricity in a North-west Coast chiefdom such as the Nootka (Drucker, 1951), there is little to choose. A leader in each case integrates the economic activity of a (more or less) localized following: he acts as a shunting station for goods flowing reciprocally between his own and other like groups of society. The economic relation to followers is also the same: the leader is the central recipient and bestower of favors. The thin line of difference is this: the Nootka leader is an office-holder in a lineage (house group), his following is this corporate group, and his central economic position is ascribed by right of chiefly due and chiefly obligation. So centricity is built into the structure. In Siuai, it is a personal achievement. The following is an achievement – a result of generosity bestowed – the leadership an achievement, and the whole structure will as such dissolve with the demise of the pivotal big-man. Now I think that most of us concerned with 'redistributive economies' have come to include Northwest Coast peoples under this head; whereas assigning Siuai that status would at least provoke disagreement. This suggests that the political organization of reciprocities is implicitly recognized as a decisive step. Where kinship-rank reciprocity is laid down by office and political grouping, and becomes *sui generis* by virtue of customary duty, it takes on a distinctive character. The distinctive character may be usefully named – chiefly redistribution.

A further difference in economies of chiefly redistribution is worth remarking. It is another difference in centricity. The flow of goods both into and out of the hands of powers-that-be is for the most part unintegrated in certain ethnographic instances. Subordinates in severalty and on various occasions render stuff to the chief, and often in severalty receive benefits from him. While there is always some massive accumulation and large-scale handout – say during rites of chieftainship – the prevailing flow between chief and people is fragmented into independent and small transactions: a gift to the chief from here, some help given out there. So aside from the special occasion, the chief is continuously turning over petty stocks. This is the ordinary situation in the smaller Pacific island chiefdoms – e.g. Moala (Sahlins, 1962), apparently Tikopia – and it may be generally true of pastoralist chiefdoms. On the other hand, chiefs may glory in massive accumulations and more or less massive dispensations, and at times too in large stores on hand congealed by pressure on the commonalty. Here the independent act of homage or *noblesse oblige* is of less significance. And if, in addition, the social scale of chiefly redistribution is extensive – the polity large, dispersed, and segmented – one confronts a measure of centricity approximating the classical magazine economies of antiquity.

Appendix B*(pp. 200-215, below) presents illustrative ethnographic materials on the relation between rank and reciprocity. (See the citation from Malo under B.4.2 and from Bartram under B.5.2 on magazine economies of various scale.)

* not reproduced here

On the Sociology of Primitive Exchange

V

RECIPROCITY AND WEALTH

According to their [the Yukaghir] way of thinking, 'a man who possesses provisions must share them with those who do not possess them' (Jochelson, 1926, p. 43).

'This habit of share and share alike is easily understandable in a community where everyone is likely to find himself in difficulties from time to time, for it is scarcity and not sufficiency that makes people generous, since everybody is thereby ensured against hunger. He who is in need to-day receives help from him who may be in like need tomorrow' (Evans-Pritchard, 1940, p. 85).

One of the senses of previous remarks on rank and reciprocity is that rank distinctions, or attempts to promote them, tend to extend generalized exchange beyond the customary range of sharing. The same upshot may come of wealth differences between parties, often anyhow associated with rank differences.

If one is poor and one's comrade is rich, well, there are certain restraints on acquisitiveness in our dealings – at least if we are to remain comrades, or even acquaintances, for very long. There are particularly restraints on the wealthier, if not a certain *richesse oblige*.

That is to say, given some social bond between those who exchange, differences in fortune between them compels a more altruistic (generalized) transaction than is otherwise appropriate. A difference in affluence – or in capacity to replenish wealth – would lower the sociability content of balanced dealing. As far as the exchange balances, the side that cannot afford it has sacrificed in favor of the side that did not need it. The greater the wealth gap, therefore, the greater the demonstrable assistance from rich to poor that is necessary just to maintain a given degree of sociability. Reasoning further on the same line, the inclination toward generalized exchange deepens where the economic gap amounts to oversupply and undersupply of customary requirements and, especially, of urgent stuff. The thing to look for is food-sharing between haves and have-nots. It is one thing to demand returns on woodpecker scalps, yet one spares a dime – brother! – for even a hungry stranger.

The 'brother' is important. That scarcity and not sufficiency makes people generous is understandable, functional, 'where everyone is likely to find himself in difficulties from time to time'. It is most understandable, however, and most likely, where kinship community and kinship morality prevail. That whole economies are organized by the combined play of scarcity and differential accumulation is no secret to economic science. But then the societies involved do not wrest a livelihood as limited and uncertain as the Nuer's (and many another primitive group's), nor do they meet hardship as kinship communities. It is such circumstances precisely that make invidious accumulation of fortune intolerable and dysfunctional. And if the affluent do not play the game, they ordinarily can be forced to disgorge, in one way or another:

> 'A Bushman will go to any lengths to avoid making other Bushmen jealous of him, and for this reason the few possessions the Bushmen have are constantly circling among members of their groups. No one cares to keep a particularly good knife too long, even though he may want it desperately, because he will become the object of envy; as he sits by himself polishing a fine edge on the blade he will hear the soft voices of the other men in his band saying: "Look at him there, admiring his knife while we have nothing." Soon somebody will ask him for his knife, for everybody would like to have it, and he will give it away. Their culture insists that they share with each other, and it has never happened that a Bushman failed to share objects, food, or water with other members of his band, for without very rigid co-operation Bushmen could not survive the famines and droughts that the Kalahari offers them' (Thomas, 1959, p. 22).

Should the condition of poverty be extreme, as for food collectors such as these Bushmen, it is best that the inclination to share out one's abundance be made lawful. Here it is a technical condition that some households day in and day out will fail to meet their requirements. The vulnerability to food shortage can be met by instituting continuous sharing within the local community. I think this the best way to interpret tabus that prohibit hunters from eating game they bring down, or the less drastic and more common injunction that certain large animals be shared through the camp – ' "the hunter kills, other people have", say the Yukaghir' (Jochelson, 1926, p. 124). Another way to make food-sharing the rule, if not a rule, is to freight it heavily with moral value. If this is the case, incidentally, sharing will break out not merely in bad times but especially in good. The level of generalized reciprocity 'peaks' on the occasion of a windfall: now everyone can cash in on the virtues of generosity:

> 'They gathered almost three hundred pounds [of tsi nuts]. . . . When the people had picked all they could find, when every possible bag was full, they said they were ready to go to Nama, but when we brought the jeep and began to load it they were already busy with their endless preoccupation, that of giving and receiving, and had already begun to give each other presents of tsi. Bushmen feel a great need to give and receive food, perhaps to cement relationships with each other, perhaps to prove and strengthen their dependence upon each other; because the opportunity to do this does not occur unless huge quantities of food are at hand, Bushmen always exchange presents of foods that come in huge quantities, these being the meat of game antelope, tsi nuts, and the nuts of the mangetti trees, which at certain seasons are scattered abundantly all through the mangetti forests. As we waited by the jeep Dikai gave a huge sack of tsi to her mother. Her mother gave another sack to Gao Feet's first wife, and Gao Feet gave a sack to Dikai. Later, during the days that followed, the tsi was distributed again, this time in smaller quantities, small piles or small bagfuls, after that in handfuls, and, last, in very small quantities of cooked tsi which people would share as they were eating . . .' (Thomas, 1959, pp. 214-215).

The bearing of wealth differences upon reciprocity, of course, is not independent of the play of rank and kinship distance. Real situations are complicated. For instance, wealth distinctions probably constrain assistance in some inverse proportion to the kinship distance of the sides to exchange. It is poverty in the in-group particularly that engenders compassion. (Conversely, helping people in distress creates very intense solidarity – on the principle of 'a friend in need . . .'.) On the other hand, material distinctions between distant relatives or aliens may not commensurately, or even at all, incline the affluent party to be charitable. If the interests had been opposed to begin with, well now the desperate traffic will bear more.

The observation is frequently made that any accumulation of wealth – among such and such people – is followed hard upon by its disbursement. The *objective* of gathering wealth, indeed, is often that of giving it away. So, for example, Barnett writes of Northwest Coast Indians that 'Accumulation in any quantity by borrowing or otherwise is, in fact, unthinkable unless it be for the purpose of immediate redistribution' (1938, p. 353). The general proposition may be allowed that the material drift in primitive societies tends on the whole away from accumulation towards insufficiency. Thus: 'In general it may be said that no one in a Nuer village starves unless all are starving' (Evans-Pritchard, 1951, p. 132). But in view of foregoing remarks there must be qualification. The incline toward have-nots is steeper for more urgently than for less urgently required goods, and it is steeper within local communities than between them.

Supposing some tendency to share in favor of need, even if qualified by community, it is possible to draw further inferences about economic behavior in general scarcity. During lean food seasons the incidence of generalized exchange should rise above average, particularly in the narrower social sectors. Survival depends now on a double-barreled quickening of social solidarity and economic cooperation (see Appendix C,* e.g. C.1.3). This social and economic consolidation conceivably could progress to the maximum: normal reciprocal relations between households are suspended in favor of pooling of resources for the duration of emergency. The rank structure is perhaps mobilized and engaged, either in governance of pooling or in the sense that chiefly food reserves are now put into circulation.

Yet the reaction to depression 'all depends': it depends on the social structure put to test and on the duration and intensity of the shortage. For the forces that countervail are strengthened in these *biša-baša* times, the tendency to look to household interests especially, and also the tendency for compassion to be more-than-

* not reproduced here

proportionately expended on close kin in need than on distant kin in the same straits. Probably every primitive organization has its breaking-point, or at least its turning-point. Every one might see the time when cooperation is overwhelmed by the scale of disaster and chicanery becomes the order of the day. The range of assistance contracts progressively to the family level; perhaps even these bonds dissolve and, washed away, reveal an inhuman, yet most human, self-interest. Moreover, by the same measure that the circle of charity is compressed that of 'negative reciprocity' is potentially expanded. People who helped each other in normal times and through the first stages of disaster display now indifference to each others' plight, if they do not exacerbate a mutual downfall by guile, haggle, and theft. Put another way, the whole sectoral scheme of reciprocities is altered, compressed: sharing is confined to the innermost sphere of solidarity and all else is devil take the hindmost.

Implicit in these remarks is a plan of analysis of the normal sectoral system of reciprocities in the given case. The prevailing reciprocity scheme is some vector of the quality of kin-community relations and the ordinary stresses developing out of imbalances in production. But it is the emergency condition that concerns us now. Here and there in the illustrative materials to this section we see the two predicted reactions to depressed food supplies, both more sharing and less. Presumably the governing conditions are the community structure on one side and the seriousness of shortage on the other.

A final remark under the head of reciprocity and wealth. A community will, if suitably organized, 'tighten' not only under economic threat but in the face of other present danger, of external political-military pressure, for example. In this connection, two notes on the economics of native war parties are included in the illustrative materials appended to the present section (Appendix C:* C.1.10 and C.2.5). They illustrate an extraordinary intensity of sharing (generalized reciprocity) between haves and have-nots during preparations for attack. (Likewise, the experience of recent wars would show that transactions move a long way from yesterday's dice game in the barracks to today's sharing of rations or cigarettes on the front line.) The sudden outbreak of compassion is consistent with what has been said of

* not reproduced here

sociability, sharing, and wealth differences. Generalized reciprocity is not merely the sole exchange congruent with the now serious interdependence, it strengthens interdependence and so the chances of each and all to survive the noneconomic danger.

Ethnographic data relevant to the propositions of this section may be found in Appendix C*(pp. 215-225).

VI

RECIPROCITY AND FOOD

The character of the goods exchanged seems to have an independent effect on the character of exchange. Staple foodstuffs cannot always be handled just like anything else. Socially they are not quite like anything else. Food is life-giving, urgent, ordinarily symbolic of hearth and home, if not of mother. By comparison with other stuff, food is more readily, or more necessarily, shared; barkcloth and beads more readily lend themselves to balanced gift-giving. Direct and equivalent returns for food are unseemly in most social settings: they impugn the motives both of the giver and of the recipient. From this several characteristic qualities of food transfers appear to follow.

Food dealings are a delicate barometer, a ritual statement as it were, of social relations, and food is thus employed instrumentally as a starting, a sustaining, or a destroying mechanism of sociability:

> 'Food is something over which relatives have rights, and conversely relatives are people who provide or take toll on one's food' (Richards, 1939, p. 200).
>
> 'The sharing of food [among the Kuma] symbolizes an identity of interests. . . . Food is never shared with an enemy. . . . Food is not shared with strangers, for they are potential enemies. A man may eat with his cognatic and affinal relatives and also, people say, with the members of his own clan. Normally, however, only members of the same subclan have an unequivocal right to share each other's food. . . . If two men or the members of two sub-subclans have a serious and lasting quarrel, neither they nor their descendants may use one another's fires. . . . When

* not reproduced here

affinal relatives come together at marriage, the formal presentation of the bride and the pork and the valuables emphasizes the separate identity of the two clans, but the people actually participating in the ceremony share vegetable food informally, unobtrusively, as they might share it with intimate companions within the subclan. This is a way of expressing their common interest in linking the two groups. Symbolically, they belong now to a single group and so are "brothers", as affinal relatives should be' (Reay, 1959, pp. 90-92).

Food offered in a generalized way, notably as hospitality, is good relations. As Jochelson says, putting it for the Yukaghir with near-Confucian pith: 'hospitality often turns enemies into friends, and strengthens the amicable relations between groups foreign to one another' (1926, p. 125). But then, a complementary negative principle is implied, that food not offered on the suitable occasion or not taken is bad relations. Thus the Dobuan syndrome of suspicion of everyone save the nearest kinfolk finds its clearest expression in the social range of food-sharing and commensality – 'Food or tobacco is not accepted except within a small circle' (Fortune, 1932, p. 170; on rules proscribing commensality, cf. pp. 74-75; Malinowski, 1915, p. 545). Finally there is the principle that one does not exchange things for food, not directly that is, among friends and relatives. Traffic in food is traffic between foreign interests. (Look how a novelist quite simply suggests that one of his characters is a real bastard: 'He brought his blankets to the bare house, took silent supper with the Boss family, insisted on paying them – he could not understand why they pretended reluctance when he offered to pay them; food cost money; they were not in the restaurant business, but food cost money, you could not deny that' – MacKinlay Kantor.)

In these principles of instrumental food exchange there seems little variation between peoples. Of course, the extent to which they are employed, and which of them are employed, vary with the case. Dobuans proscribe intervillage visiting and hospitality, no doubt for good and sufficient reasons. Elsewhere, circumstances ranging from economic interdependence through political strategy enjoin both visiting and the hospitable entertainment of visitors. A detailed look at the circumstances would be beyond

Marshall D. Sahlins

the present purview: the point is that where some coming to sociable terms with visitors is desirable, hospitality is an ordinary way of doing it. And the Dobuan syndrome is by no means typical. Ordinarily, 'Savages pride themselves in being hospitable to strangers' (Harmon, 1957, p. 43).

Consequently the sphere of generalized exchange in food is sometimes wider than the sphere of generalized exchange in other things. This tendency to transcend the sectoral plan is most dramatized in the hospitality afforded trade partners, or any kinsmen from afar, who make visits the occasion for exchanging presents (see examples in Appendix A)*. Here are people whose dealings in durables are consciously balanced out – or even potentially run on *caveat emptor* – by some miracle charitably supplying one another with food and shelter. But then hospitality counters the *wabuwabu* lurking in the background and provides an atmosphere in which direct exchange of presents and trade goods can be equitably consummated.

There is logic in an undue tendency to move food by generalized reciprocity. Like exchange between rich and poor, or between high and low, where food is concerned a greater inclination to sacrifice seems required just to sustain the given degree of sociability. Sharing needs to be extended to more distant relatives, generalized reciprocity broadened beyond ordinary sectoral limits. (It might be recalled from the Appendices* to previous sections that generosity is distinctively associated with food dealing.)

About the only sociable thing to do with food is to give it away, and the commensurably sociable return, after an interval of suitable decency, is the return of hospitality or assistance. The implication is not only a rather loose or imperfect balance in food dealing, but specifically a restraint on exchanges of food for other goods. One notes with interest normative injunctions against the sale of food among peoples possessed of primitive currencies, among certain Melanesian and California tribes for instance. Here balanced exchange is run of the mill. Money tokens serve as more or less general equivalents and are exchanged against a variety of stuff. But not *food*stuff. Within a broad social sector where money talks for other things, staples are insulated against pecuniary transactions and food shared perhaps but rarely sold.

* not reproduced here

Food has too much social value – ultimately because it has too much use value – to have exchange value.

> 'Food was not sold. It might be given away, but being "wild stuff" should not be sold, according to Pomo etiquette. Manufactured articles only were bought and sold, such as baskets, bows and arrows' (Gifford, 1926, p. 329; cf. Kroeber, 1925, p. 40, on the Yurok – same sort of thing).

> '[To the Tolowa-Tututni] food was only edible, not saleable' (Drucker, 1937, p. 241; cf. DuBois, 1936, pp. 50-51).

> 'The staple articles of food, taro, bananas, coconuts, are never sold [by Lesu], and are given to kindred, friends, and strangers passing through the village as an act of courtesy' (Powdermaker, 1933, p. 195).

In a similar way, staple foodstuffs were excluded from balanced trading among Alaskan Eskimo – 'The feeling was present that to trade for food was reprehensible' – and even luxury foods that were exchanged between trade partners were transferred as presents and apart from the main trading (Spencer, 1959, pp. 204-205).

It would seem that common foodstuffs are likely to have an insulated 'circuit of exchange', separate from durables, particularly 'wealth'. (See Firth, 1950; Bohannan, 1955; Bohannan & Dalton, 1962, on 'spheres of exchange'.) Morally and socially this should be so. For a wide range of social relations, balanced and direct food-for-goods transactions (conversions) would rend the solidary bonds. Distinctive categorizations of food vs. other goods, i.e. 'wealth', express the sociological disparity and protect food from dysfunctional comparisons of its worth – as among the Salish:

> 'Food was not classed as "wealth" [i.e. blankets, shell ornaments, canoes, etc.]. Nor was it treated as wealth . . . "holy food", a Semiahmoo informant called it. It should be given freely, he felt, and could not be refused. Food was evidently not freely exchanged with wealth. A person in need of food might ask to buy some from another household in his com-

munity, offering wealth for it, but food was not generally offered for sale' (Suttles, 1960, p. 301; Vayda, 1961).

But an important qualification must in haste be entered. These food and nonfood spheres are sociologically based and bounded. The immorality of food-wealth conversions has a sectoral dimension: at a certain socially peripheral point the circuits merge and thus dissolve. (At this point, food-for-goods exchange is a 'conveyance' in Bohannan and Dalton's usage.) Food does not move against money or other stuff within the community or tribe, yet it may be so exchanged outside these social contexts, and not merely under duress but as use and wont. The Salish *did* customarily take food, 'holy food', to affinal relatives in other Salish villages and received wealth in return (Suttles, 1960). Likewise, Pomo *did* 'buy' – at any rate gave beads for – acorns, fish, and like necessities from other communities (Kroeber, 1925, p. 260; Loeb, 1926, pp. 192-193). The separation of food and wealth cycles is contextual. Within communities these are insulated circuits, insulated by community relations; they are kept apart where a demand of return on necessities would contradict prevailing kinship relations. Beyond this, in the intercommunity or intertribal sector, the insulation of the food circuit may be worn through by frictions of social distance.

(Foodstuffs, incidentally, are not ordinarily divorced from the circuit of labor assistance. On the contrary, a meal is in the host of primitive societies the customary return for labor solicited for gardening, housebuilding, and other domestic tasks. 'Wages' in the usual sense is not at issue. The feeding amounts to an extraordinary extension to other relatives and to friends of the household economy. Rather than a tentative move toward capitalism, it is perhaps better understood by a principle something to the opposite: that those who participate in a productive effort have some claim on its outcome.)

VII

ON BALANCED RECIPROCITY

We have seen generalized reciprocity in play in instrumental ways, notably as a starting mechanism of rank distinction and also, in the form of hospitality, to mediate relations between persons of different communities. Balanced reciprocity likewise finds instrumental employments, but especially as formal social compact. Balanced reciprocity is the classic vehicle of peace and alliance contracts, substance-as-symbol of the transformation from separate to harmonious interests. Group prestations are the dramatic and perhaps the typical form, but there are instances too of interpersonal compact sealed by exchange.

Here it is useful to recall Mauss's dictum: 'In these primitive and archaic societies there is no middle path. . . . When two groups of men meet they may move away or in case of mistrust or defiance they may resort to arms; or else they can come to terms.' And the terms ought to balance, insofar as the groups are 'different men'. The relations are too tenuous to long sustain a failure to reciprocate – ' "Indians notice such things" ' (Goldschmidt, 1951, p. 338). They notice a lot of things. Goldschmidt's Nomlaki Indians in fact articulate a whole set of glosses and paraphrases of Maussian principle, among them:

> 'When enemies meet they call to one another. If the settlement is friendly they approach closer and spread out their goods. One man would throw something in the middle, one man from the other side would throw in something for it and take the traded material back. They trade till one side has traded everything. The ones that have some left make fun of those who have run out, bragging about themselves. . . . This trade takes place on the border line' (Goldschmidt, 1951, p. 338).

Balanced reciprocity is willingness to give for that which is received. Therein seems to be its efficacy as social compact. The striking of equivalence, or at least some approach to balance, is a demonstrable foregoing of self-interest on each side, some renunciation of hostile intent or of indifference in favor of mutuality. Against the preexisting context of separateness, the material balance signifies a new state of affairs. This is not to deny that the transaction is ever consequential in a utilitarian sense, as it may well be – and the social effect perhaps compounded by an equitable exchange of different necessities. But whatever the utilitarian value, and there need be none, there is always 'moral' purpose, as Radcliffe-Brown remarked of certain Andaman transactions:

'to provide a friendly feeling . . . and unless it did this it failed of its purpose'.

Among the many kinds of contract closed as it were by balanced exchange, the following seem most common:

1. *Formal friendship or kinship*

These are interpersonal compacts of solidarity, pledges of brotherhood in some cases, friendship in others. The alliance may be sealed by exchange of identical goods, the material counterpart of some exchange of identities, but at any rate the transaction is likely to balance and the exchange is of distant for close relationship (e.g. Pospisil, 1958, pp. 86-87; Seligman, 1910, pp. 69-70). An association once so formed may well become more sociable over time, and future transactions both parallel and compound this trend by becoming more generalized.

2. *Affirmation of corporate alliances*

One may place in this category the various feasts and entertainments reciprocally tendered between friendly local groups and communities, such as certain of the interclan vegetable-heap presentations in the New Guinea Highlands or inter-village social feasts in Samoa or New Zealand.

3. *Peace-making*

These are the exchanges of settlement, of cessation of dispute, feud, and warfare. Both interpersonal and collective hostilities may be thus quieted by exchange. 'When an equivalence is struck' parties to an Abelam argument are satisfied: ' "talk is thrown away" ' (Kaberry, 1941-42, p. 341). That is the general principle.

One may wish to include wergeld payments, compensations for adultery, and other forms of compounding injury in this category, as well as the exchanges that terminate warfare. They all work on the general principle, the principle of fair trade. (Spencer provides an interesting Eskimo example: when a man received compensation from the abductor of his wife the two men 'inevitably' become friendly, he writes, 'because they had conceptually effected a trade' (1959, p. 81). (See also Denig, 1928-29, p. 404; Powdermaker, 1933, p. 197; Williamson, 1912, p. 183; Deacon,

1934, p. 226; Kroeber, 1925, p. 252; Loeb, 1926, pp. 204-205; Hogbin, 1939, pp. 79, 91-92; etc.).

4. *Marital alliance*

Marriage prestations are of course the classic form of reciprocity as social compact. I have little to add to the received anthropological discussion, except a slight qualification about the character of reciprocity in these transactions, and even this may be superfluous.

It does seem to miss the point, however, to view marital exchange either as 'total' or as perfectly balanced prestation. The transactions of marriage, and perhaps contingent future affinal exchange as well, are ordinarily not exactly equal. For one thing, asymmetry of exchange is commonplace: women move against hoes or cattle, *toga* against *oloa*, fish against pigs. In the absence of some secular convertability, or of a mutual standard of value, the transfer seems to an extent one of incomparables; neither equivalent nor total, the transaction may be of incommensurables. In any event, and even where the same sorts of things are exchanged, one side or the other may be conceived to benefit unduly, at least for the time being. This lack of precise balance is socially of the essence.

First, unequal benefit sustains the alliance as perfect balance could not. Truly, the people concerned – and/or the ethnographer – might muse that in the fullness of time accounts between affines even out. Or losses and gains may be cancelled by cyclical or statistical patterns of alliance. Or some balance in goods, at least, may obtain in the total political economy, where the flow of payments upwards (against a flow of women downwards) through a series of ranked lineages is reversed by redistribution from the top (cf. Leach, 1951). Yet it is socially critical that over a long term, and perhaps forever, the exchange between two groups united by a marriage has not been balanced. In so far as the things transferred are of different quality, it may be difficult ever to calculate that the sides are 'even-steven'. This is a social good. The exchange that is symmetrical or unequivocally equal carries some disadvantage from the point of view of alliance: it cancels debts and thus opens the possibility of contracting out. If neither side is 'owing' then the bond between them is comparatively fragile. But if accounts are not squared, then the relationship is maintained by virtue of 'the shadow of indebtedness', and there will have to be further occasions of association, perhaps as occasions of further payment.

Secondly, and directly related, an asymmetrical exchange of different things lends itself to alliance that is complementary. The marital bond between groups is not always, maybe not even usually, some sort of fifty-fifty partnership between homologous parties. One group surrenders a woman, another gets her; in a patrilineal context the wife-receivers have secured continuity, something at the expense of the wife-givers, at least on this occasion. There has been a differential transfer: the groups are socially related in a complementary and asymmetrical way. Likewise, in a ranked lineage system the giving of women may be a specification of the set of subordinate-superordinate relations. Now in these cases, the several rights and duties of alliance are symbolized by the differential character of transfers, are attached to complementary symbols. Asymmetrical prestations secure the complementary alliance once again as perfectly balanced, symmetrical, or all-out total prestations would not.

The casual received view of reciprocity supposes some fairly direct one-for-one exchange, balanced reciprocity, or a near approximation of balance. It may not be inappropriate, then, to footnote this discussion with a respectful demur: that in the main run of primitive societies, taking into account directly utilitarian as well as instrumental transactions, balanced reciprocity is not the prevalent form of exchange. A question might even be raised about the stability of balanced reciprocity. Balanced exchange may tend toward self-liquidation. On one hand, a series of honorably balanced dealings between comparatively distant parties builds trust and confidence, in effect reduces social distance, and so increases the chances for more generalized future dealings – as the initial blood-brotherhood transaction creates a 'credit rating', as it were. On the other hand, a renege acts to sever relations – as failure to make returns breaks a trade-partnership – if it does not actually invite chicanery in return. May we conclude that balanced reciprocity is inherently unstable? Or perhaps that it requires special conditions for continuity?

The societal profile of reciprocity, at any rate, most often inclines toward generalized modes. In the simpler hunting groups the generalized assistance of close kinship seems usually dominant; in neolithic chiefdoms this is supplemented by kinship-rank obligations. There are nonetheless societies of certain type in which balanced exchange, if not exactly dominant, acquires unusual prominence. Interest attaches to these societies, not alone for the emphasis on balanced reciprocity, but for what goes with it.

The well known 'labor exchange' in Southeast Asian hinterland communities brings these immediately to mind. Here is a set of peoples who, placed against the main run of primitive societies, offer departures in economy, and social structure as well, that cannot fail to kindle a comparative interest. The well-described Iban (Freeman, 1955, 1960), Land Dayak (Geddes, 1954, 1957; cf. Provinse, 1937) and Lamet (Izikowitz, 1951) belong in the class – some Philippine peoples may as well, but I am uncertain how far the analysis about to be suggested will work for the Philippines.

Now these societies are distinctive not only for uncommon internal characteristics of economy but for unusual external relations – unusual, that is, in a strictly primitive milieu. They are hinterlands engaged by petty market trade – and perhaps also by political dominance (e.g. Lamet) – to more sophisticated cultural centers. From the perspective of the advanced centers, they are backwaters serving as secondary sources of rice and other goods (cf. VanLeur, 1955, especially pp. 101 f, for some hints about the economic significance of hinterland provisioning in Southeast Asia). From the hinterlands view, the critical aspect of the intercultural relation is that the subsistence staple, rice, is exported for cash, iron tools, and prestige goods, many of the last quite expensive. It is suggested – with all the deference that must be supplied by one who has no research experience in the area – it is suggested that the peculiar social-economic character of Southeast Asian hinterland tribes is congruent with this unusual employment of household subsistence surpluses. The implication of an external trade in rice is not merely an internal ban on sharing it, or a corresponding requirement of quid-pro-quo in intra-community dealings, but departure from ordinary characteristics of primitive distribution in virtually all respects.

The engagement with the market makes a key minimal demand: that internal community relations permit household accumulation of rice, else the amounts required for external exchange will never be forthcoming. This stipulation must prevail in the face of limited and uncertain modes of rice production. The fortunate households cannot be responsible for the unfortunate; if internal leveling is unleashed then the external trade relations are simply not sustained.

The set of consequences for the economy and polity of the hinterland tribal communities appear to include: (i) Different households, by virtue of variations in number of effective producers, amass different amounts of the subsistence-export staple. The productive differences range between surfeit above and deficit below family consumption requirements. These differences, however, are not liquidated by sharing in favor of need. Instead (ii) the intensity of sharing within the village or tribe is low, and (iii) the principal reciprocal relation between households is a closely calculated balanced exchange of labor service. As Geddes remarks of the Land Dayak: '. . . co-operation beyond the household, except on business lines where every service must have an equal return, is at a low level' (1954, p. 34). Balanced labor-exchange, of course, maintains the productive advantage (accumulation capacity) of the family with more adult workers. The only goods that customarily move in generalized reciprocity are game and perhaps large domestic animals sacrificed in family ceremonies. Such items are widely distributed through the community (cf. Izikowitz, 1951), much as hunters would share them, but the sharing of meat is not as decisive in structuring interfamilial relations as the lack of sharing decreed by export of staples. (iv) Even household commensality may be rather rigidly supervised, subjected to accounting of each person's rice dole in the interest of developing an exchange reserve, hence less sociable than ordinary primitive commensality (compare, for example, Izikowitz, 1951, pp. 301-302 with Firth, 1936, pp. 112-116). (v) Restricted sharing of staples, demanded by articulation with the siphoning market, finds its social complement in an atomization and fragmentation of community structure. Lineages, or like systems of extensive and corporate solidary relations, are incompatible with the external drain on household staples and the corresponding posture of self-interest required *vis-à-vis* other households. Large local descent groups are absent or inconsequential. Instead, the solidary relations are of the small family itself, with various and changing interpersonal kin ties the only such nexus of connection between households. Economically, these extended kin ties are weak ones:

> 'A household is not only a distinct unit, but one which minds its own business. Perforce, it has to do so, because it has with other households no formal relations, sanctioned by custom, on which it can rely for certain support. Indeed, the absence of such structured relationships is a condition of the society as at present organized. In the main economic affairs, cooperation with others is based upon contract and not primarily upon kinship. . . . As a result of this situation, ties which persons have with others in the community tend to be widespread, but limited to sentiment and sociability, often sadly so' (Geddes, 1954, p. 42).

(vi) Prestige apparently hinges upon obtaining exotic items – Chinese pottery, brass gongs, etc. – from the outside in exchange for rice or work. Prestige does not, obviously cannot, rest on generous assistance to one's fellows in the manner of a tribal big-man. The exotic goods figure internally as ceremonial display items and in marriage prestations – thus insofar as status is linked to them it is principally as possession and ability to make payments, again not through giving them away. ('Wealth does not help a man to become chief because it gives him power to distribute largesse. Riches rarely incline a Dayak to charity, although they may to usury', Geddes, 1954, p. 50.) No one then obligates others very much. No one creates followers. As a result there are no strong leaders, a fact which probably contributes to the atomization of the community and may have repercussions on the intensity of land use (cf. Izikowitz, 1951).

In these Southeast Asian communities, the prevalence of balanced reciprocity does seem connected with special circumstances. But then the circumstances suggest that it is not legitimate to involve these peoples in the present context of tribal economics. By the same token, their use in debating issues of primitive economics, as Geddes uses the Land Dayak to argue

Marshall D. Sahlins

against 'primitive communism', seems not quite cricket. Perhaps they are best classed with peasants – so long as one does not thereupon suggest, as is unfortunately often done under the label 'economic anthropology', that 'peasant' and 'primitive' belong together in some undifferentiated type of economy distinguished negatively as whatever-it-is that is outside the province of orthodox economic analysis.

There are, however, incontestable examples of societal emphasis on balanced reciprocity in primitive settings. Primitive monies serving as media of exchange at more or less fixed rates argue this. The monies amount to the suggested special mechanisms for maintaining balance. It is worthwhile to inquire into their incidence and their economic and social concomitants.

Yet this is not to be hazarded without some formal definition of 'primitive money', a problem approaching the status of a classic dilemma in comparative economics. On one side, any thing that has a 'money use' – as we know money uses: payments, exchange, standard, etc. – may be taken for 'money'. If so, probably every society enjoys the dubious benefits, inasmuch as some category of goods is usually earmarked for certain payments. The alternative is less relativistic and therefore seems more useful for comparative generalizations: to agree on some minimal use and quality of the stuff. The strategy, as Firth suggests, is not to question ' "What is primitive money?" but "What is it useful to include in the category of primitive money?" ' (1959, p. 39). His specific suggestion, which as I understand it centrally involves the medium-of-exchange function, does indeed appear useful. ('My own view is that to entitle an object to be classified as money, it should be of a generally acceptable type, serving to facilitate the conversion of one object or service into terms of another and used as a standard of value thereby,' Firth, 1959, pp. 38-39).

Let 'money' refer to those objects in primitive societies that have token value rather than utility and that serve as means of exchange. The exchange use is limited to certain categories of things – land and labor are ordinarily excluded – and is brought to bear only between parties of certain social relation. In the main it serves as an indirect bridge between goods ('C-M-C') rather than commercial purposes ('M-C-M'). These limitations would justify the phrase 'primitive money'. If all this is agreeable, it further appears that pristine developments of primitive money are not broadly spread through the ethnographic scene, but are restricted to certain areas: especially western and central Melanesia, aboriginal California, and certain parts of the South American tropical forest. (Monies may also have developed in pristine contexts in Africa, but I am not expert enough to disentangle their distribution from archaic civilizations and ancient 'international' trade.)

This is also to say that primitive money is associated with an historically specific type of primitive economy, an economy with a marked incidence of balanced exchange in peripheral social sectors. It is not a phenomenon of simple hunting cultures – if I may be permitted, cultures of a band level. Neither is primitive money characteristic of the more advanced chiefdoms, where wealth tokens though certainly encountered tend to bear little exchange load. The regions noted – Melanesia, California, South American tropical forest – are (or were) occupied by societies of an intermediate sort, such as have been called 'tribal' (Sahlins, 1961; Service, 1962) or 'homogeneous' and 'segmented tribes' (Oberg, 1955). They are distinguished from band systems not merely for more settled conditions of life – often associated with neolithic vs. paleolithic production – but principally for a larger and more complex tribal organization of constituent local groupings. The several local settlements of tribal societies are bound together both by a nexus of kin relations and by cross-cutting social institutions, such as a set of clans. Yet the relatively small settlements are autonomous and self-governing, a feature which in turn distinguishes tribal from chiefdom plans. The local segments of the latter are integrated into larger polities, as divisions and subdivisions, by virtue of principles of rank and a structure of chieftainships and subchieftainships. The tribal plan is purely segmental, the chiefdom pyramidal.

This evolutionary classification of social-cultural types is admittedly loose. I hope not to raise an issue over it, for it has been offered merely to direct attention to contrasting structural features of primitive-money areas. They are precisely the kinds of features that, given previous argumentation, suggest an unusual incidence of balanced reciprocity. A greater play of balanced exchange in tribal over band societies is argued in part by a greater proportion of craft goods and services in the societal economic output. Foodstuffs, while still the decisive share of a tribal economic product, decline relatively. Transactions in durables, more likely to be balanced than food transactions, increase. But more important, the proportion of peripheral-sector exchange, the incidence of exchange among more distantly related people, is likely to be considerably greater in tribal than in band societies. This is understandable by reference to the more definite segmental plan of tribes, which is also to say more definite sectoral breaks in the social structure.

The several residential segments of tribes are comparatively stable and formally constituted. And a corporate political solidarity is as characteristic of the tribal segment as it is lacking in flexible camp-and-band arrangements of hunters. Tribal segmental structure is also more extensive, including perhaps internal lineage groupings in the political segments, the set (and sometimes segmentary subsets) of political segments, and the tribal-foreigner division. Now the accretion over band organization is particularly in peripheral structure, in the development of the intratribal and intertribal sectors. Here is where exchange encounters increase, whether these be instrumental, peace-making exchanges or frankly materialistic dealings. The accretion in exchange then is in the social areas of balanced reciprocity.

A chiefdom, in further contrast, liquidates and pushes out peripheral sectors by transforming external into internal relations, by including adjacent local groups within enclaving political unions. At the same time, the incidence of balanced reciprocity is depressed, in virtue of both the 'internalization' of exchange relations and their centralization. Balanced exchanges should thus decline in favor of more generalized with the attainment of a chiefdom level. The implication for primitive money is perhaps illustrated by its absence in the Trobriands, despite the fact that this island of chiefdoms is set in a sea of money-using tribes, or by the progressive attentuation in exchange-uses of shell beads moving northward from tribal California to protochiefdom British Columbia.

The hypothesis about primitive money – offered with due

caution and deference – is this: it occurs in conjunction with unusual incidence of balanced reciprocity in peripheral social sectors. Presumably it facilitates the heavy balanced traffic. The conditions that encourage primitive money are most likely to occur in the range of primitive societies called tribal and are unlikely to be served by band or chiefdom development. But a qualification must in haste be entered. Not all tribes provide circumstances for monetary development and certainly not all enjoy primitive money, as that term is here understood. For the potentiality of peripheral exchange is maximized only by some tribes. Others remain relatively inner-directed.

First, peripheral sectors become scenes of intensive exchange in conjunction with regional and intertribal symbiosis. An areal ecological regime of specialized tribes, respective families and communities of which are in trade relation, is probably a necessary condition for primitive money. Such regimes are characteristic of California and Melanesia – about South America I am not prepared to say – but in other tribal settings symbiosis is not characteristic and the intertribal (or interregional) exchange sector comparatively underdeveloped. Perhaps just as important are circumstances that put premiums on delayed exchange and so on tokens that store value in the interim. The outputs of interdependent communities, for example, may be unavoidably unbalanced in time – as between coastal and inland peoples, where an exchangeable catch of fish cannot always be met by complementary inland products. Here a currency acceptable on all sides very much facilitates interdependence – so that shell beads, say, taken for fish at one time can be converted for acorns at another (cf. Vayda, 1954; Loeb, 1926). Big-man leadership systems, it would seem from Melanesia, may likewise render delayed balanced exchange functional. The tribal big-man operates on a fund of power consisting of food, pigs, or the like, stuffs with the common quality that they are not easy to keep around in large amounts over long periods. But, at the same time, the extractive devices for accumulating these political funds are underdeveloped, and collection of goods for a climactic giveaway would have to be gradual and thus technically difficult. The dilemma is resolvable by monetary manipulations: by converting wealth into tokens and by calculated deployment of money in

Marshall D. Sahlins

loans and exchange, so that a time will come when a massive call on goods can be made and the whole pile of stuff, given away, converted into status. That's the way the money goes.

VIII

AN AFTERTHOUGHT

It is difficult to conclude with a dramatic flourish. The essay has not a dramatic structure – its main drift seems downhill. And a summary would be needlessly repetitive.

But there is a curiosity worth remarking. Here has been given a discourse on economics in which 'economizing' appears mainly as an exogenous factor! The organizing principles of economy have been sought elsewhere. To the extent they have been found outside man's presumed hedonist propensity, a strategy for the study of primitive economics is suggested that is something the reverse of economic orthodoxy. It may be worth while to see how far this heresy will get us. [186]

NOTES

1. I am indebted to Eric Wolf for many suggestions concerning this paper, and to the Social Science Research Council (Washington, D.C.), which in it may finally see some return on a most generous Faculty Research Fellowship.

2. These materials appear as Appendices to the present volume, pp. 186-225.

3. For the present purpose 'economy' is viewed as the process of provisioning society (or the 'socio-cultural system'). No social relation, institution, or set of institutions is of itself 'economic'. Any institution, say a family or a lineage order, if it has material consequence for provisioning society can be placed in an economic context and considered part of the economic process. The same institution may be equally or more involved in the political process, thus profitably considered as well in a political context. This way of looking at economics or politics – or for that matter, religion, education, and any number of other cultural processes – is dictated by the nature of primitive culture. Here we find no socially distinct 'economy' or 'government', merely social groups and relations with multiple functions, which we distinguish as economic, political, and so forth.

That economy thus presents itself as an aspect of things is probably generally acceptable. That the emphasis be the provisioning of *society* may not prove so acceptable. For the concern is not how individuals go about their business: 'economy' has not been defined as the application of scarce available means against alternative ends (material ends or otherwise). From means to end 'economy' is conceived as *a component of culture* rather than *a kind of human action*, the material life process of society rather than a rational, need-

Marshall D. Sahlins

satisfying process of individual behavior. Our purpose is not to analyze entrepreneurs but to compare cultures. We reject the historically specific Business Outlook. In terms of controversial positions recently developed in the *American Anthropologist*, the stand adopted is much more with Dalton (1961; cf. Sahlins, 1962) than with Burling (1962) or LeClair (1962). Also, solidarity is here affirmed with housewives the world over and Professor Malinowski. Professor Firth upbraids Malinowski's imprecision on a point of economic anthropology with the observation that 'This is not the terminology of economics, it is almost the language of the housewife' (Firth, 1957, p. 220). The terminology of the present effort similarly departs from economic orthodoxy. This may be justly considered a necessity born of ignorance, but something is to be said as well for the appropriateness, in a study of kinship economies, of the housewife's perspective.

Economy has been defined as the process of (materially) provisioning society and the definition opposed to the human act of satisfying wants. The great play of instrumental exchange in primitive societies underscores the usefulness of the former definition. Sometimes the peace-making aspect is so fundamental that precisely the same sorts and amounts of stuff change hands: the renunciation of opposed interest is in this way symbolized. On a strictly formal view the transaction is a waste of time and effort. One might say that people are maximizing value, social value, but such is to misplace the determinant of the transaction, to fail to specify the circumstances which produce different material outcomes in different historical instances, to hold fast to the economizing premise of the market by a false assignment of pecuniary-like qualities to social qualities, to take the high road to tautology. The interest of such transactions is precisely that they do not materially provision people and are not predicated on the satisfaction of human material needs. They do, however, decidedly provision society: they maintain social relations, the structure of society, even if they do not to the least advantage the stock of consumables. Without any further assumptions, they are 'economic' in the suggested meaning of the term.

The reader familiar with recent discussions of primitive distribution will recognize my indebtedness to Polanyi (1944, 1957, 1959) on this score, and likewise the departures from Polanyi's terminology and threefold scheme of principles of integration. It is also a pleasure to affirm with Firth that 'Every student of primitive economics, in fact, gratefully builds upon the foundations which Malinowski has laid' (Firth, 1959, p. 174).

ACKNOWLEDGEMENTS

Thanks are due to the individuals and publishers concerned for permission to quote passages from the following works:

Allen & Unwin and Oslo University Press in respect of *The Nomads of South Persia* by Fredrik Barth; The American Sociological Association and Professor A. W. Gouldner in respect of 'The Norm of Reciprocity: A Preliminary Statement', *American Sociological Review*, Volume 25, by A. W. Gouldner; The Australian National University and Melbourne University Press in respect of *The Kuma* by Marie Reay; The Free Press of Glencoe in respect of *The Gift* by Marcel Mauss; The Government Printer, Wellington in respect of *Economics of the New Zealand Maori* by Raymond Firth; Harvard University Press in respect of *A Solomon Island Society by* Douglas Oliver; Her Majesty's Stationery Office in respect of *The Land Dyaks of Sarawak*, Colonial Research Studies No. 14, by W. R. Geddes; International African Institute and Mrs Lorna Marshall in respect of 'Sharing, Talking, and Giving: Relief of Social Tensions among !Kung Bushmen', *Africa*, Volume 31, by Lorna Marshall; Oxford University Press in respect of *Land, Labour and Diet in Northern Rhodesia* by Audrey I. Richards (published under the auspices of the International African Institute); Routledge & Kegan Paul in respect of *Transformation Scene: The Changing Culture of a New Guinea Village* by Ian H. Hogbin, *Argonauts of the Western Pacific* by Bronislaw Malinowski, and with Hillary House, *Primitive Polynesian Economy* by Raymond Firth; Martin Secker & Warburg and Alfred A. Knopf in respect of *The Harmless People* by Elizabeth M. Thomas (copyright 1958, 1959 by Elizabeth Marshall Thomas); Yale University Press in respect of *The Travels of William Bartram* by William Bartram (edited by Francis Harper) and 'The Philosophy of the Navaho Indians' by Clyde Kluckhohn in *Ideological Difference and World Order* edited by F. S. C. Northrop.

REFERENCES

BARNETT, H. G. 1938. The Nature of the Potlatch. *American Anthropologist* **40**: 349-358.

BARTH, FREDRIK. 1961. *Nomads of South Persia*. London: Allen & Unwin (for Oslo University Press).

BARTRAM, WILLIAM. 1958. *The Travels of William Bartram*. Francis Harper (ed.). New Haven: Yale University Press.

BEAGLEHOLE, ERNEST & BEAGLEHOLE, PEARL. 1938. *Ethnology of Pukapuka*. Bernice P. Bishop Museum Bulletin 150.

BIRKET-SMITH, KAJ. 1959. *The Eskimos*. Second edition; London: Methuen.

BLACKWOOD, BEATRICE. 1935. *Both Sides of Buka Passage*. Oxford: Clarendon Press.

BLEAK, D. F. 1928. *The Naron*. Cambridge: Cambridge University Press.

BOAS, FRANZ. 1884-85. The Central Eskimo. *Smithson. Instn Bureau of American Ethnology Anthropological Reports* **6**: 399-669.

BOGORAS, W. 1904-09. The Chukchee. *AMNH Memoirs*, **11**, Parts I, II, III. F. Boas (ed.). New York.

BOHANNAN, PAUL. 1954. *Tiv Farm and Settlement*. Colonial Research Studies No. 15. London: H.M. Stationery Office.

—— 1955. Some Principles of Exchange and Investment Among the Tiv. *American Anthropologist* **57**: 60-70.

BOHANNAN, PAUL & DALTON, GEORGE (eds.). 1962. *Markets in Africa*. Evanston, Ill.: Northwestern University Press.

Marshall D. Sahlins

BROWN, PAULA & BROOKFIELD, H. C. 1959-60. Chimbu Land and Society. *Oceania* **30**: 1-75.

BULMER, RALPH. 1960. Political Aspects of the Moka Ceremonial Exchange System Among the Kyaka People of the Western Highlands of New Guinea. *Oceania* **31**: 1-13.

BURLING, ROBBINS. 1962. Maximization Theories and the Study of Economic Anthropology. *American Anthropologist* **64**: 802-821.

BURRIDGE, KENELM. 1960. *Mambu: A Melanesian Millennium.* London: Methuen.

CARNEIRO, ROBERT L. 1957. *Subsistence and Social Structure: An Ecological Study of the Kuikuru Indians.* Ph.D. Dissertation, University of Michigan.

CODERE, HELEN. n.d. *Fighting with Property.* Monograph of the American Ethnological Society XVIII. New York: J. J. Augustin.

COUES, ELLIOT (ed.). 1897. *The Manuscript Journals of Alexander Henry and of David Thompson, 1799-1814.* New York: Francis P. Harper. 2 Vols.

DALTON, GEORGE. 1961. Economic Theory and Primitive Society. *American Anthropologist* **63**: 1-25.

DAVIES, JOHN. 1961. *The History of the Tahitian Mission 1799-1830.* C. W. Newbury (ed.). Cambridge: Cambridge University Press for the Hakluyt Society.

DEACON, A. BERNARD. 1934. *Malekula: A Vanishing People in the New Hebrides.* C. Wedgewood, (ed.). London: Routledge.

DENIG, EDWIN T. 1928-29. Indian Tribes of the Upper Missouri. *Smithson. Instn BAE-AR* **46**: 395-628.

DRUCKER, PHILIP. 1937. The Tolowa and their Southwest Oregon Kin. *Univ. Calif. Public. in Amer. Archaeol. and Ethnol.* **36** (4): 221-300. Berkeley: University of California Press.

—— 1939. Rank, Wealth, and Kinship in Northwest Coast Society. *American Anthropologist* **41**: 55-65.

—— 1951. *The Northern and Central Nootkan Tribes.* Smithson. Instn BAE. Bull. 144. Washington: U.S. Govt. Printing Office.

DUBOIS, CORA. 1936. The Wealth Concept as an Integrative Factor in Tolowa-Tututni Culture. *Essays in Anthropology Presented to A. L. Kroeber.* Berkeley: University of California Press, pp. 49-65.

DUFF MISSIONARIES. 1799. *A Missionary Voyage to the Southern Pacific Ocean Performed in the Years 1796, 1797, 1798 in the Ship Duff . . . etc.* London: T. Chapman.

On the Sociology of Primitive Exchange

ELKIN, A. P. 1952-53. Delayed Exchange in Wabag Sub-District, Central Highlands of New Guinea, with Notes on the Social Organization. *Oceania* **23**: 161-201.

— 1954. *The Australian Aborigines: How to Understand Them.* 3rd ed. Sydney: Angus and Robertson.

EVANS-PRITCHARD, E. E. 1940. *The Nuer.* Oxford: Clarendon Press.

— 1951. *Kinship and Marriage Among the Nuer.* Oxford: Clarendon Press.

— 1956. *Nuer Religion.* Oxford: Clarendon Press.

EWERS, JOHN C. 1955. *The Horse in Blackfoot Indian Culture.* Smithson. Instn BAE Bull. 159. Washington: U.S. Govt. Printing Office.

FIRTH, RAYMOND. 1926. Proverbs in Native Life, with special reference to those of the Maori. *Folklore* **37**: 134-153, 245-270.

— 1936. *We, The Tikopia.* London: Allen & Unwin.

— 1950. *Primitive Polynesian Economy.* New York: Humanities.

— 1951. *Elements of Social Organization.* London: Watts; New York: Philosophical Library.

— (ed.) 1957. *Man and Culture: An Evaluation of the Work of Bronislaw Malinowski.* London: Routledge & Kegan Paul.

— 1959. *Economics of the New Zealand Maori.* Wellington: R. E. Owen, Government Printer.

— 1959a. *Social Change in Tikopia.* New York: Macmillan.

FORNANDER, ABRAHAM. 1880. *An Account of the Polynesian Race.* . . . London: Trubner. Vol. 2.

FORTUNE, R. F. 1932. *Sorcerers of Dobu.* New York: E. P. Dutton.

FREEMAN, J. D. 1955. *Iban Agriculture.* Colonial Research Studies No. 18, London: Her Majesty's Stationery Office.

GEDDES, W. R. 1954. *The Land Dayaks of Sarawak.* Colonial Research Studies No. 14, London: Her Majesty's Stationery Office.

— 1957. *Nine Dayak Nights.* Melbourne: Oxford University Press.

GIFFORD, EDWARD WINSLOW. 1926. Clear Lake Pomo Society. *Univ. Calif. Public. in Amer. Archaeol. and Ethnol.* **18** (2): 287-390.

— 1929. *Tongan Society.* Bernice P. Bishop Museum Bulletin 61.

GOLDSCHMIDT, WALTER. 1951. Nomlaki Ethnography. *Univ. Calif. Public. in Amer. Archaeol. and Ethnol.* **42** (4): 303-443. Berkeley: University of California Press.

GOULDNER, ALVIN W. 1960. The Norm of Reciprocity: A Preliminary Statement. *American Sociological Review* **25**: 161-178.

Marshall D. Sahlins

GRINNELL, GEORGE BIRD. 1923. *The Cheyenne Indians*. New Haven: Yale Univ. Press.

HANDY, E. S. C. 1923. *The Native Culture in the Marquesas*. Bernice P. Bishop Museum Bulletin 9.

—— 1930. *History and Culture in the Society Islands*. Bernice P. Bishop Museum Bulletin 79.

—— 1932. *Houses, Boats, and Fishing in the Society Islands*. Bernice P. Bishop Museum Bulletin 90.

HARMON, DANIEL WILLIAMS. 1957. *Sixteen Years in the Indian Country: The Journal of Daniel Williams Harmon 1800-1816*. Ed. by W. Kaye Lamb. Toronto: The Macmillan Co. of Canada.

HEARNE, SAMUEL. 1958. *A Journey from Prince of Wales' Fort in Hudson's Bay to the Northern Ocean, 1769, 1770, 1771, 1772*, ed. by Richard Glover. Toronto: The Macmillan Co. of Canada.

HENRY, JULES. 1951. The Economics of Pilagá Food Distribution. *American Anthropologist* **53**: 187-219.

HENRY, TEURIRA. 1928. *Ancient Tahiti*. Bernice P. Bishop Museum Bulletin 48.

HOGBIN, H. IAN. 1933-34. Culture Change in the Solomon Islands: Report of Field Work in Guadalcanal and Malaita. *Oceania* **4**: 233-267.

—— 1934. *Law and Order in Polynesia*. New York: Harcourt, Brace.

—— 1934-35. Native Culture of Wogeo: Report of Field Work in New Guinea. *Oceania* **5**: 308-337.

—— 1934-35a. Trading Expeditions in Northern New Guinea. *Oceania* **5**: 375-407.

—— 1937-38. Social Advancement in Guadalcanal, Solomon Islands. *Oceania* **8**: 289-305.

—— 1938-39. Tillage and Collection: A New Guinea Economy. *Oceania* **9**: 127-151.

—— 1939. *Experiments in Civilization*. London: Routledge.

—— 1943-44. Native Councils and Native Courts in the Solomon Islands. *Oceania* **14**: 258-283.

—— 1951. *Transformation Scene: The Changing Culture of a New Guinea Village*. London: Routledge & Kegan Paul.

HOLMBERG, ALLAN R. 1950. *Nomads of the Long Bow*. Smithson. Instn Institute of Social Anthropology, Public. No. 10. Washington: U.S. Govt. Printing Office.

HOWELL, P. P. 1954. *A Manual of Nuer Law*. London: Oxford University Press.

HUNTER, JOHN D. 1823. *Memoirs of a Captivity Among the Indians of North America* (new edn.). London: Longmans.

IVENS, W. G. 1927. *Melanesians of the Southeast Solomon Islands.* London: Kegan, Paul, Trench, Trubner.

IZIKOWITZ, KARL GUSTAVE. 1951. *Lamet: Hill Peasants in French Indochina.* Etnologiska Studier 17, Goteborg: Ethnografiska Museet.

JOCHELSON, WALDEMAR. 1926. The Yukaghir and the Yukaghirzed Tungus, *AMNH Memoirs* **13** (1): 1-469.

KABERRY, PHYLLIS M. 1940-41. The Abelam Tribe, Sepik District, New Guinea: A Preliminary Report. *Oceania* **11**: 233-258, 345-367.

—— 1941-42. Law and Political Organization in the Abelam Tribe, New Guinea. *Oceania* **12**: 79-95, 205-225, 331-363.

KLUCKHOHN, CLYDE. 1959. The Philosophy of the Navaho Indians. In *Readings in Anthropology*, Vol. II, M. H. Fried (ed.). New York: Crowell.

KROEBER, A. L. 1925. *Handbook of the Indians of California.* Smithson. Instn BAE Bull. 78. Washington: U.S. Govt. Printing Office.

LANDTMAN, GUNNAR. 1927. *The Kiwai Papuans of British New Guinea.* London: Macmillan.

LEACH, E. R. 1951. The Structural Implications of Matrilateral Cross Cousin Marriage. *J. Royal Anthropological Institute* **81**: 23-55.

—— 1954. *Political Systems of Highland Burma.* London: Bell.

LEACOCK, ELEANOR. 1954. *The Montagnais' Hunting Territory and the Fur Trade.* Memoir of the American Anthropological Association 78.

LECLAIR, EDWARD E., JR. 1962. Economic Theory and Economic Anthropology. *American Anthropologist* **64**: 1179-1203.

LINTON, RALPH. 1939. Marquesan Culture. In Kardiner, A., *The Individual and his Society.* New York: Columbia University Press, pp. 137-196.

LOEB, EDWIN M. 1926. Pomo Folkways. *Univ. Calif. Public. in Amer. Archaeol. and Ethnol.* **19** (2): 149-409.

MACGREGOR, GORDON. 1937. *Ethnology of the Tokelau Islands.* Bernice P. Bishop Museum Bulletin 146.

MALINOWSKI, BRONISLAW. 1915. The Natives of Mailu. *Transactions of the Royal Society of South Australia* **39**: 494-706.

—— 1921. The Primitive Economics of the Trobriand Islanders. *Economic Journal* **31**: 1-16.

—— 1922. *Argonauts of the Western Pacific.* London: Routledge & Kegan Paul (3rd imp. 1950).

MALINOWSKI, BRONISLAW. 1935. *Coral Gardens and Their Magic.* Vol. 1. New York: American Book Co.

— 1939. Anthropology as the Basis of Social Science. In Cattel, Cohen, and Travers (eds.), *Human Affairs*. London: Macmillan.

MALO, DAVID. 1951. *Hawaiian Antiquities.* (2nd edn.) Bernice P. Bishop Museum, Spec. Publication No. 2.

MAN, EDWARD HORACE. n.d. *On the Aboriginal Inhabitants of the Andaman Islands.* Reprinted from *JRAI*, 1885. London: RAI.

MANDELBAUM, DAVID G. 1940. The Plains Cree. *Amer. Mus. Nat. Hist.-Anthrop. Papers* **37** (2): 155-316.

MARINER, WILLIAM. 1827. *An Account of the Tongan Islands in the South Pacific Ocean.* (3rd edn., 2 vols.) John Martin (ed.). Edinburgh: Constable.

MARSHALL, LORNA. 1961. Sharing, Talking, and Giving: Relief of Social Tensions Among !Kung Bushmen. *Africa* **31**: 231-249.

MAUSS, MARCEL. 1954. *The Gift.* Glencoe, Ill.: The Free Press.

MCKERN, W. C. 1922. Functional Families of the Patwin. *Univ. Calif. Public. in Amer. Archaeol. and Ethnol.* **13** (7): 236-258. Berkeley: University of California Press.

MEAD, MARGARET. 1930. Melanesian Middlemen. *National History* **30**: 115-130.

— 1934. Kinship in the Admiralty Islands. *American Museum of Natural History – Anthropological Papers* **34**: 181-358.

— 1937. The Manus of the Admiralty Islands. In M. Mead (ed.), *Cooperation and Competition among Primitive Peoples.* New York and London: McGraw-Hill.

— 1937a. The Arapesh of New Guinea, In M. Mead (ed.), *Cooperation and Competition Among Primitive Peoples.* New York and London: McGraw-Hill.

— 1938. The Mountain Arapesh I. An Importing Culture. *Amer. Mus. Nat. Hist.-Anthrop. Papers* **36**: 139-349.

— 1947. The Mountain Arapesh III. Socio-Economic Life. *Amer. Mus. Nat. Hist.-Anthrop. Papers* **40**: 159-232.

MEGGITT, MERVYN. 1956-57. The Valleys of the Upper Wage and Lai Rivers, Western Highlands, New Guinea. *Oceania* **27**:90-135.

— 1957. Enga Political Organization: A Preliminary Description. *Mankind* **5**: 133-137.

— 1957-58. The Enga of the New Guinea Highlands: Some Preliminary Observations. *Oceania* **28**: 253-330.

— 1962. *Desert People: A Study of the Walbiri Aborigines of Central Australia.* Sydney: Angus & Robertson.

NILLES, JOHN. 1950-51. The Kuman of the Chimbu Region, Central Highlands, New Guinea. *Oceania* **21**: 25-26.

OBERG, KALERVO. 1955. Types of Social Structure in Lowland South America. *American Anthropologist* **57**: 472-487.

OLIVER, DOUGLAS. 1955. *A Solomon Islands Society*. Cambridge, Mass.: Harvard University Press.

POWDERMAKER, HORTENSE. 1933. *Life in Lesu*. New York: W. W. Norton.

POLANYI, KARL. 1944. *The Great Transformation*. New York: Rinehart.

—— 1959. Anthropology and Economic Theory. In M. Fried (ed.), *Readings in Anthropology*, II. New York: Crowell.

POLANYI, KARL, ARENSBERG, CONRAD & PEARSON, HARRY W. (eds.). 1957. *Trade and Market in the Early Empires*. Glencoe, Ill.: The Free Press.

POSPISIL, LEOPOLD. 1958. *Kapauku Papuans and Their Law*. Yale Univ. Public. in Anthrop. No. 54, New Haven: Yale University Press.

—— 1959-60. The Kapauku Papuans and Their Kinship Organization. *Oceania* **30**: 188-205.

POWELL, H. A. 1960. Competitive Leadership in Trobriand Political Organization. *Journal of the Royal Anthropological Institute* **90**: 118-145.

PRICE, JOHN ANDREW. 1962. *Washo Economy*. Nevada State Museum Anthropological Papers No. 6, Carson City: State Printing Office.

PROVINSE, JOHN H. 1937. Cooperative Ricefield Cultivation Among the Siang Dyaks of Central Borneo. *American Anthropologist* **39**: 77-102.

PUTNAM, PATRIK. 1953. The Pygmies of the Ituri Forest. In Carleton S. Coon (ed.), *A Reader in General Anthropology*. New York: Henry Holt.

RADCLIFFE-BROWN, A. R. 1930-31. The Social Organisation of Australian Tribes. *Oceania* **1**: 34-63, 206-256, 322-341, 426-456.

—— 1948 [1922]. *The Andaman Islanders*. Glencoe, Ill.: Free Press.

READ, K. E. 1946-47. Social Organisation in the Markham Valley, New Guinea. *Oceania* **17**: 93-118.

—— 1949-50. The Political System of the Ngarawapum. *Oceania* **20**: 185-223.

—— 1959. Leadership and Consensus in a New Guinea Society. *American Anthropologist* **61**: 425-436.

Marshall D. Sahlins

REAY, MARIE. 1959. *The Kuma.* Melbourne University Press.

RICHARDS, AUDREY I. 1939. *Land, Labour and Diet in Northern Rhodesia.* London, New York, Toronto: Oxford University Press, for the International African Institute.

RINK, HENRY. 1875. *Tales and Traditions of the Eskimo.* Edinburgh and London: Blackwood.

RODRIGUEZ, MAXIMO. 1919. Daily Narrative kept by the Interpreter Maximo Rodriguez at the Island of Amat, otherwise Otahiti, in year 1774. In Corney, B.G., *The Quest and Occupation of Tahiti by Emissaries of Spain . . . 1772-1776*, Vol. III. London: Hakluyt Society.

SAHLINS, MARSHALL D. 1958. *Social Stratification in Polynesia.* Monograph of the American Ethnological Society, Seattle: University of Washington Press.

—— 1960. Political Power and the Economy in Primitive Society. *Essays in the Science of Culture in Honor of Leslie White.* Dole and Carneiro (eds.), New York: Crowell.

—— 1961. The Segmentary Lineage: An Organization of Predatory Expansion. *American Anthropologist* **63**: 322-345.

—— 1962. Review, of *Sociological Aspects of Economic Growth* (B. F. Hoselitz), *American Anthropologist* **64**: 1063-1073.

—— 1962a. *Moala: Culture and Nature on a Fijian Island.* Ann Arbor: University of Michigan Press.

—— 1963. Poor Man, Rich Man, Big-Man, Chief: Political Types in Melanesia and Polynesia. *Comparative Studies in Society and History.* (In press.)

SAHLINS, MARSHALL, D. & SERVICE, ELMAN R. (eds.). 1960. *Evolution and Culture.* Ann Arbor: University of Michigan Press.

SCHAPERA, I. 1930. *The Khoisan Peoples of South Africa.* London: Routledge.

SCHEBESTA, PAUL. 1933. *Among Congo Pygmies.* London: Hutchinson.

—— n.d. *Among the Forest Dwarfs of Malaya.* London: Hutchinson.

SELIGMAN, C. G. 1910. *The Melanesians of British New Guinea.* Cambridge: Cambridge University Press.

SERVICE, E. R. 1962. *Primitive Social Organization.* New York: Random House.

SHARP, LAURISTON. 1934-35. Ritual Life and Economics of the Yir-Yiront of Cape York Peninsula. *Oceania* **5**: 19-42.

—— 1952. Steel Axes for Stone Age Australians. In E. H. Spicer (ed.), *Human Problems in Technological Change.* New York: Russell Sage.

SHIROKOGOROFF, S. M. 1929. *Social Organization of the Northern Tungus*. Shanghai: The Commercial Press.

SPENCER, SIR BALDWIN & GILLEN, F. J. 1927. *The Arunta*. 2 vols. London: Macmillan.

SPENCER, ROBERT F. 1959. *The North Alaskan Eskimo: A Study in Ecology and Society*. Smithson. Instn BAE Bull. 171. Washington: U.S. Govt. Printing Office.

STEWARD, JULIAN. 1938. *Basin-Plateau Aboriginal Sociopolitical Groups*. Smithson. Instn BAE Bull. 120. Washington: U.S. Govt. Printing Office.

SUTTLES, WAYNE. 1960. Affinal Ties, Subsistence, and Prestige among the Coast Salish. *American Anthropologist* **62**: 296-305.

SWANTON, JOHN R. 1928. Social Organization and Social Usages of the Indians of the Creek Confederacy. *Smithson. Instn BAE-AR* **42**: 23-472. Washington: U.S. Govt. Printing Office.

TANNER, JOHN. 1956. *A Narrative of the Captivity and Adventures of John Tanner*. Prepared for Press by Edwin James. Minneapolis: Ross & Haines.

THOMAS, ELIZABETH MARSHALL. 1959. *The Harmless People*. New York: Knopf; London: Secker & Warburg.

THURNWALD, RICHARD C. 1934-35. Pigs and Currency in Buin. *Oceania* **5**: 119-141.

TURNBULL, COLIN M. 1962. *The Forest People*. London: Chatto & Windus; Garden City: Doubleday Anchor and American Museum of Natural History.

VANLEUR, J. C. 1955. *Indonesian Trade and Society*. The Hague and Bandung: W. van Hoeve.

VANOVERBERGH, MORICE. 1925. Negritoes of Northern Luzon. *Anthropos* **20**: 148-199, 399-443.

VAYDA, A. P. 1954*ms*. Notes on Trade Among the Pomo Indians of California, mimeo., Columbia University Interdisciplinary Project: Economic Aspects of Institutional Growth.

—— 1961. A Re-examination of Northwest Coast Economic Systems. *Transactions of the New York Academy of Sciences* (Series II) **23**: 618-624.

VEBLEN, THORSTEIN. 1915. *Imperial Germany and the Industrial Revolution*. New York: Macmillan.

WAGNER, GUNTAR. 1956. *The Bantu of North Kavirondo*: Volume II: Economic Life. London: Oxford University Press for the International African Institute, 2 vols.

WALLACE, ERNEST & HOEBEL, E. A. 1952. *The Comanches, Lords of the South Plains*. Norman: University of Oklahoma Press.

Marshall D. Sahlins

WARNER, W. LLOYD. 1937. *A Black Civilization*. New York & London: Harper and Bros.

WEYER, EDWARD MOFFAT. 1932. *The Eskimos*. New Haven: Yale University Press.

WHITE, LESLIE A. 1959. *The Evolution of Culture*. New York, Toronto, London: McGraw-Hill.

WILLIAMSON, ROBERT W. 1912. *The Mafulu: Mountain People of British New Guinea*. London: Macmillan.

[7]

THE GIFT, THE INDIAN GIFT AND THE 'INDIAN GIFT'*

JONATHAN PARRY
London School of Economics & Political Science

This article criticises much of the conventional exegesis of Mauss's celebrated *Essai sur le don*, and proposes a rather different reading of the text which stresses its evolutionary aspects. The Hindu 'law of the gift' is shown to have a key role in the structure of Mauss's argument, though in fact it is quite inconsistent with his central thesis. In this particular instance he was right where anthropologists have generally thought him wrong, and wrong where anthropologists have generally thought him right. In the Maori case, however, his interpretation has much more to recommend it than has generally been recognised. Hindu and Maori ideologies of exchange represent fundamentally opposed types; and it is suggested that we might begin to account for this kind of contrast in terms of broad differences in politico-economy, and—more especially—in terms of the contrast between a World Religion and the kind of religion characteristic of small-scale tribal society. Following Mauss, an ideology of the 'pure' gift is shown to be inseparable from the ideology of the purely interested individual pursuit of utility, and to emerge in parallel to it.

Sir Raymond Firth recalls that on his way to Tikopia he had to rely for transport and hospitality on the Melanesian Mission, and was for some weeks the guest of the Bishop on the Mission yacht.

> As we travelled together among the islands we discussed many problems of human relationship in the island communities. Malinowski had only recently published his book *Crime and Custom in Savage Society* in which he stressed the importance of reciprocity as a force of binding obligation in Melanesian social organization. . . . The Bishop borrowed the book from me, read it, and strongly disagreed. He argued vehemently that Melanesians, like other people he said, performed many acts for others freely and without thought of return . . . and he denied the implication of self-interested action. . . . We argued amicably about this and other themes. . . . At last the time came for him to land me on the beach of Tikopia and leave me to my fate. He had shown me many kindnesses, which I could not repay . . . he was retiring from the Mission after many years and we both knew that it was unlikely that we should ever meet again. . . . As he said goodbye, leaving me alone in this remote community he shook me firmly by the hand, said gruffly 'No reciprocity!', turned his back and walked off down the beach to the boat (Firth 1973: 400–1).

This vignette of the knight and the bishop, sailing over a distant tropical sea engaged in earnest debate over the thesis of an expatriate Polish Professor, provides me with an apt introduction to my central theme—for I wish to speak of *ideologies* of reciprocity and non-reciprocity, of the 'Indian gift' and the Indian gift.

*The Malinowski Memorial Lecture, 1985

Man (N.S.) **21**, 453–73

In *Argonauts of the Western Pacific* (1922: 176–91), Malinowski ranges transactions along a continuum from 'pure gifts' to 'real barter'. The concept of reciprocity is central; but it has not hardened into the dogma it subsequently became in *Crime and custom in savage society* (1926), where the notion of 'pure gift' is retracted. Taking a sufficiently long-term view, we shall find that even with regard to transactions between a Trobriand man and his wife and children 'the mutual services balance' (1926: 41) for 'keen self-interest and a watchful reckoning . . . runs right through' (p. 27). Rather than being slave to custom, the 'savage' is as canny as the 'civilised businessman' and has quite as sharp an eye for the main chance. He cares more, it is true, for prestige than material pay-offs; and though he is certainly not Economic Man, he is nonetheless Maximising Man. Obligations are kept because 'the chain of reciprocal gifts and counter-gifts . . . (benefit) both sides equally' (p. 40); and because the costs of reneguing on them are too great in terms of 'self-interest, ambition and vanity' (p. 67). Supernatural sanctions are either absent altogether (p. 51), or are relatively easily evaded by means of counter-magic (p. 80).

The various elements in this model—the tendency to see exchanges as essentially *dyadic* transactions between *self-interested individuals*, and as premissed on some kind of *balance*; the tendency to play down *supernatural* sanctions, and the total contempt for questions of *origin*—all these constituted an important legacy of Malinowski's teaching, and directly or indirectly exercised a major influence over much of the subsequent literature. In Firth's writings, for example, we not only find all Malinowski's mistrust of the sanctioning power of 'recondite beliefs' (Firth 1929: 415), but also a similar emphasis on the individual choice-making actor (e.g. Firth 1967).

The same influence can also be seen in Leach's criticism of Lévi-Strauss's (1969) thesis that ranked regimes of generalised exchange are inherently unstable since they inhibit a closure of the matrimonial cycle. Although the wife-givers may not receive *women* in exchange, says Leach, the rule of reciprocity is nonetheless maintained since they are compensated by all kinds of counter-prestations of a different nature; and it is for this reason that the Kachin system is not in fact subject to the kind of instability envisaged by Lévi-Strauss (Leach 1961: 90). So while Lévi-Strauss's model of generalised exchange is based on a system of *indirect* reciprocity and—relative to systems of restricted exchange—presupposes an expansion of trust and credit, Leach's alternative invites us to view the situation in terms of an endless sequence of *dyadic* exchanges which are in the long term balanced. Instead of a speculative venture, exchange is a *quid pro quo* based on a certainty of returns.

Similar assumptions are built into Blau's (1967) discussion of exchange and power, and Weiner's (1976, 1980) criticisms of Sahlins. Both operate with a similar premiss of balance so that when—in Blau's case—the exchange itself is *not* balanced, the deficit is compensated for by an increment in power to the creditor which restores the equilibrium. Both assume that exchange takes place between calculating individuals, so that Weiner can claim that with what she calls the 'gift myth', the anthropologist is merely 'perpetuating and creating an image of "the primitive" as a person, or "primitive society" as a way of life, that has survived on some fundamental principle *other than self-interest*' (1976: 221).

It would be tedious, but not difficult, to multiply examples. The general message would be the same. The gift is always an 'Indian gift'—that is, one 'for which an equivalent return is expected'[1]—and the notion of a 'pure gift' is mere ideological obfuscation which masks the supposedly *non*-ideological verity that nobody does anything for nothing. So it is that anthropology often seems to be endlessly rediscovering the moral of Mandeville's *Fable of the bees*. Publick Benefit derives from Private Vice. Society is created by, and its cohesion results from, an endless sequence of exchanges in which all pursues their own advantage (however conceived).

All this may be obvious. But what is perhaps less so is that this habit of thought has distorted our reading of Mauss's essay on *The gift*. Though Malinowski and Mauss are commonly twinned as the joint progenitors of the anthropological understanding of exchange, it is as well to remember that the Durkheimians were one of Malinowski's main polemical targets in *Crime and custom*. Yet paradoxically Malinowskian premisses are only too often read into the Maussian text, which is unconsciously processed through a theoretical filter borrowed from his distinguished contemporary.

Mauss's gift

Mauss's essay has acquired for anthropology many of the qualities of a sacred text. It is treated with reverential awe, the greater part of its teaching is ignored, and it is claimed as the *fons et origo* of quite divergent theoretical positions. It has been cited as a forerunner of Barth's transactionalism (Kapferer 1976: 3); as demonstrating an underlying continuity between gift and commodity exchange (Firth 1973: 370) and as demonstrating the opposite (Gregory 1983: 18 sq.). It has been found to contain an implicit evolutionary model 'remarkably parallel to Marx's argument in *Grundrisse*' (Hart 1983: 46), while Lévi-Strauss—modestly avoiding claims to the mantle of Joshua—likens Mauss to Moses leading his people into the Promised Land of Structuralism, though never quite making it himself (Lévi-Strauss 1973: 37). Our undergraduate students, routinely expected to master this text in their first year, might reasonably be forgiven for wondering just how they ought to understand it.

So elliptical is his writing that Mauss himself does not always seem to be on their side. Nor is the translation, which is both carelessly inaccurate and an unconscious mirror of the prejudices of its own period[2]. Mauss says at the outset that he is concerned 'with words and their meanings', and that he has chosen to concentrate only on areas 'where we have access to the minds of the societies through documentation and philological research' (1966: 2–3; 1973: 149). The translation, however, has little patience with these preoccupations. The textual notes are often elided or even suppressed. But what is more relevant here is that I believe that Cunnison's text both reflects, and has helped to perpetuate, a 'Malinowskian' reading of Mauss's original. Let me give you just one example, taken from the very first page. Mauss writes of prestations as having a 'voluntary character, so to speak, apparently free and without cost, *and yet* constrained and interested . . . They are endowed nearly always with the form of a present, of a gift generously offered *even when* in the gesture which accompanies the transaction there is only a fiction, formalism and social deception, and *when* there is, at bottom, obligation and economic interest'. In Cunnison's version what is voluntary 'and yet constrained and interested' becomes—in the manner of Malinowski—a disinterested *theory* contradicted by an interested *practice*; 'economic interest' becomes 'economic *self*-interest'; and 'even when' the gesture of generosity is only a fiction is turned into an assertion that it *is* only a fiction[3].

In fact, of course, Mauss repeatedly stresses a *combination* of interest and disinterest, of freedom and constraint, in the gift. Nor could 'interest' possibly be a matter of *self-* (in the sense of *individual*) interest. It is not individuals but groups or *moral persons* who carry on exchanges. The *individuals* of modern society are endowed with interests as against the world. The *persons* who enter into the exchanges which centrally concern Mauss do so as incumbents of status positions and do not act on their own behalf (cf. Ekeh 1974: 32).

Nor do persons stand in opposition to the things exchanged. The gift contains some part of the spiritual essence of the donor, and this constrains the recipient to make a return—an argument which has been the source of some embarrassment to Mauss's admirers, who have tended to dismiss it as peripheral. The Maori notion of *hau* is generally taken as the exemplary, or even as the *only*, instance of this 'spirit of the gift'. Sahlins (1972), for example, suggests that in effect Mauss has two *different* answers to the question: 'why are gifts reciprocated?' The first—which is wrong—is the Maori *hau* 'raised to the status of a general explanation'. The second—which is right—is the Hobbesian State of Warre—the gift being the primitive analogue of the social contract. Similarly Lévi-Strauss sees the discussion of the *hau* as a regrettable instance of the anthropologist allowing himself to be mystified by the native, whose culturally specific rationalisations cannot possibly explain a general structural principle. Happily, however, the argument only appears at the beginning of the work, and is merely a point of departure superseded by the end (Lévi-Strauss 1973: xlvi). Firth (1929) comes to an opposite conclusion. Mauss's argument is not a Maori rationalisation but a French one—in support of which we could point, I think, to its similarity to Lévy-Bruhl's notion of 'participations' (cf. MacCormack 1982). I suspect, however—though I cannot prove—that the real source of the idea is neither Maori nor French, but Indian—for as we shall see the basic notion is clearly articulated in the Hindu texts on which Mauss had worked intensively long before Lévy-Bruhl first published his ideas.

As against Firth and Sahlins I will argue at a later stage that Mauss's interpretation of the Maori data has more to recommend it than they allow. As against Sahlins and Lévi-Strauss I should like at this stage to suggest that Mauss does not in fact advance a culturally specific ideology as a general explanation; nor is his point peripheral and limited to the opening sections of the essay. More or less the same argument recurs in relation to the pledge which must be exchanged between the parties to a contract in the law of the ancient Germanic tribes. The indebted party is constrained to make a return since he has handed over as pledge an object which is imbued with his own personality, and which therefore puts him quite literally in the hands of his creditor. By redeeming it he redeems himself (1966: 60–1; 1973: 253–5).

The general principle—of which this and the Maori *hau* are only two amongst a whole battery of *illustrations*—is the absence of any absolute disjunction between persons and things[4]. It is because the thing contains the person that the donor retains a lien on what he has given away and we cannot therefore speak of an alienation of property; and it is because of this participation of the person in the object that the gift creates an enduring bond between persons. Sahlins thus misrepresents Mauss when he suggests that the argument about 'the spirit of the gift' is independent of the argument about the gift as social contract. The gift only succeeds in suppressing the Warre of all against all *because* it creates spiritual bonds between persons by means of things which embody persons. The two aspects are inseparable; and if they were not it would be hard to understand much of Mauss's antipathy to the modern market.

What is also striking about Sahlins's commentary on the essay is that he never actually mentions its central purpose: to construct a kind of prehistory of our *modern* kind of legal and economic contract. Evolutionary speculations are at the heart of the enterprise, which displays that genetic concern for the origins of legal forms which was the dominant characteristic of Durkheimian studies of law (Vogt 1983: 31). It is this concern with the origins of the modern contract which explains why of the three obligations Mauss isolates, it is the obligation to make a return which attracts the greatest attention. Cases in which the gift is not reciprocated are virtually excluded from Mauss's purview by the way in which he has defined his problem in terms of the archaeology of contractual obligation.

The broad outline of the evolution which Mauss traces is from 'total prestations' consisting of an exchange between groups in which material goods are only one item amongst a whole range of non-economic transfers, to gift exchange between persons as representative of groups, to modern market exchange between individuals. The last of these has evolved from the first by a gradual process of attenuation or contraction. Exchanges between *groups* which had an aesthetic, religious, moral, legal and economic aspect have been *stripped down* to leave purely *economic* exchanges between *individuals*[5]. (The objects of exchange themselves undergo a parallel evolution. Ceremonial valuables of the kind represented by *kula* armshells become detached from the group and the person, and develop into the kind of depersonalised money found in modern economies [Mauss 1966: 93–4; 1973: 178–9]).

Seen in this light Sahlins's analogy with Hobbes looks problematic. Hobbes, who starts with the individual, was concerned with the creation of a wider unity out of an 'originally' atomised state of humanity; but Mauss, who starts with the group, has reversed the sequence—from an original holism, humanity and human institutions have *become* atomised. What is more the two essays in *Stone Age economics* which immediately precede Sahlins's homage to Mauss ironically reveal a striking divergence—in a Hobbesian direction—from Mauss's argument. *The gift* repeatedly stresses that there is no such thing as a 'natural economy' where production is *for use* and such exchange as occurs is of *utilities*. But Sahlins's Domestic Mode of Production is surely only a variant of the natural economy model[6], and it locates the *origins* of exchange largely in the utilitarian needs of the proportion of households which inevitably face subsistence failure[7].

To risk a different analogy, there is—I would argue—a more than superficial convergence between the evolutionary schemes of Marx and Mauss (Cf. Hart 1983); for much in Mauss's essay recalls the progressive rupture Marx discovered between man and the material world, man and his products, and man and man—this resulting in a fragmented world in which the relations of the parts to the whole can no longer be discerned, and leaving the person as a mere rump, an 'abstraction' (cf. Ollman 1976: 133f).

If the Maussian thesis is that the modern contract is the enduring remnant of archaic gift exchange, what then are modern *gifts*? Two readings of the text seem possible. The conventional one would stress a basic continuity between gifts in modern and pre-modern society. But what I understand to be the dominant proposition—which seems to have been completely overlooked—is that in our kind of society gifts come to *represent* something entirely different. *Gift-exchange* —in which persons and things, interest and disinterest are merged—has been fractured, leaving gifts *opposed* to exchange, persons *opposed* to things and interest to disinterest. The ideology of a disinterested gift emerges in parallel with an ideology of a purely interested exchange. So, for example, at the beginning of his chapter on archaic societies, Mauss writes explicitly of a clear distinction between obligatory prestations and (pure) gifts in our own cultural heritage[8], and asks rhetorically whether such distinctions 'are . . . not of relatively recent appearance in the codes of the great civilizations?' [1966: 46; 1973: 229). It is *we*, he says elsewhere (1966: 46; 1973: 229), who have opposed 'the ideas of the gift and disinterestedness' to 'that of interest and the individual pursuit of utility'; and it is because the latter have now become the guiding principles of economic life that Mauss wistfully looks back on a primitive past where interest and disinterest are combined.

The whole ideology of the gift, and conversely the whole idea of 'economic self-interest', are *our* invention; and the text explicitly acknowledges the difficulty of using these terms for societies such as the Trobriands where *prestations*—the word itself must have been chosen for its connotations of constraint—are a kind of hybrid between gifts, loans and pledges. The Malinowski of *Argonauts* was certainly in error to suggest that what is given by a father to his children is a 'pure gift'. But as the context makes entirely clear, Mauss's real purpose here is not to suggest that there is no such thing as a pure gift in *any* society, but rather to show that for many the issue simply cannot arise since they do not make the kinds of distinction that we make. So while Mauss is generally represented as telling us how *in fact* the gift is *never* free, what I think he is really telling us is how *we* have acquired a *theory* that it should be.

The interested exchange and the disinterested gift thus emerge as two sides of the same coin. Given a profound dislike of the first, mistrust of the second is only logical. The unreciprocated gift debases the recipient, and the charity of the 'rich almoner' is condemned (1966: 63; 1973: 258)—presumably because it denies obligation and replaces the reciprocal interdependence on which society is founded with an asymmetrical dependence. The remedy for our modern ills is a system of social security founded on the old morality of gift-*exchange*, to which we too are heirs.

The beginnings of the ideological revolution which destroyed this ancient wisdom are located in the late Roman Empire with the legal separation of persons from things. But the main thrust of the discussion on Rome is that this distinction—which is central to our concepts of property and market exchange—evolved out of earlier concepts strictly comparable to those of the gift economies described for the 'primitive' world. The record, however, does not allow Mauss to establish this as anything more than a 'likely hypothesis'; and it is here that India comes to his aid as showing that Indo-European law once had gift-exchange institutions like those of the Pacific and America. In a manner which is thoroughly nineteenth century in spirit, and which like much in the essay is strongly reminiscent of Maine[9], India stands in—as Trautmann (n.d) notes—for Europe's missing past. Though Maine and Mauss did not agree on whether its innovations stood for moral progress, for both it was Rome which carried the torch of history (as again it did in Mauss's essay on the person) and India which revealed the fossil record of Indo-European law. It is not perhaps so hard to see why Mauss's theories have been subjected to selective professional amnesia.

The Indian gift

The central thesis of the essay about the evolutionary origins of the modern contract thus hinges on showing that gift-exchange in the Hindu texts conforms to the model constructed for pre-literate societies. Mauss focuses here on *danadharma*, the 'law of (*religious*) gifts', and in asking how well his model in fact applies I will follow him in this (without, of course, wishing to imply that this law covers all—or even a majority—of transactions). Like Mauss, then, my main concern is with those gifts which rate as *dana*; and I shall refer only in passing to other categories of 'gift', and in order to contrast them with *dana*. Lest the restriction appear to confine me to the esoteric, let me remind you of the enormous politico-economic significance of religious gift-giving in the societies which are heirs to this law: one has only to think of the huge landed estates donated to the big South Indian temples; of the fact that at the beginning of the nineteenth century an estimated 17 to 20 per cent. of the population of Benares (then one of the largest cities in India) were Brahmans living off religious charity (Bayly 1983: 126); or of estimates of 25 to 40 per cent. of net disposable cash income being given to monks in the typical Upper Burmese village (Spiro 1970: 459).

Mauss's sources provided him with many obvious illustrations of the way in which the gift embodies the person. The donor of cattle sleeps in the byre, eats barley and cow-dung, and at the moment of transfer proclaims: 'what you are, I am; today I am become your essence, and giving you I give myself' (1966: 57; 1973: 248). More specifically the gift is held to embody the sins of the donor[10], whom it rids of evil by transferring the dangerous and demeaning burden of death and impurity to the recipient (Heesterman 1964). Nor is it without peril to the donor, for it binds him dangerously close to one who may prove unworthy. 'A Brahmana who neither performs austerities nor studies the Veda, yet delights in accepting gifts, sinks *with the* (*donor* into hell) . . .' (Manu 4: 190). The merit of the gift is thus contingent on that of a worthy recipient. And who should this be but the one who is most unwilling to receive it?

The contemporary significance of this theory has recently been documented by several ethnographers. I have described, for example, how the Brahman priests of Benares see themselves as endlessly accumulating the sin they accept with the gifts of the pilgrims and mourners who visit the city, and how they liken themselves to a sewer through which the moral filth of their patrons is passed. Theoretically they should be able to 'digest' the sin by dint of various ritual procedures of expiation, and by donating the gifts they receive to another Brahman with increment. But quite apart from the fact that this is plainly an economic impossibility, they sadly admit ignorance of the correct ritual procedures. The sewer becomes a cess-pit, with the result that the priest contracts leprosy and rots; he dies a terrible and premature death and then faces the torments of hell. The donor too is an endangered being, for if the priest misuses his gift for some evil purpose he shares in the sin. He must therefore give to a 'worthy vessel'; but the one who is prepared to accept his gifts is almost by definition unworthy to receive them (Parry 1980; n.d.).

Some of my Indianist colleagues will be as used to my recital of these data as I to their response. Such ideas, they claim, are of purely local distribution and do not reflect widespread popular attitudes in rural areas away from the major centres of Sanskritic culture, or exist much outside the Hindi-speaking region (cf. Fuller 1984: 67 sq.). In fact, however, there is evidence of very similar notions from Travancore, Tamilnadu and Gujerat[11]; and thanks to Raheja's (1985; n.d.) excellent ethnography there can now be little doubt that they are pervasive in some *rural* areas of the north.

Raheja describes two broad categories of prestation as ideologically central in the village where she lived. The first of these is characterised by reciprocity and an ideology of mutuality. By contrast with this is the category of gifts generically known as *dana*—these constituting the most important feature of most rituals and festivals, being given almost daily, and utilising enormous material resources. Such gifts 'send away' inauspiciousness from the donor to the recipient, who may be a Brahman, Barber, Sweeper or a wife-taking affine, to whom the gift will bring misfortune unless the correct ritual precautions are taken. Given that these data derive from a region on which many anthropologists had previously written, I strongly suspect that such ideas about *dana* have a far wider distribution than has so far been recognised; and that it is not because they are absent that they have not been more widely reported in the village ethnography, but rather because the fieldwork was conducted with other preoccupations in mind, and by a generation of ethnographers blinded by a deep-rooted prejudice that the spirit of the gift was merely Maussian metaphysical mystification.

In the Hindu context this notion that the gift contains the person is associated with the idea that the gift is a kind of sacrifice. It is in fact a surrogate for sacrifice appropriate to our degenerate age (Manu 1: 86; Biardeau 1976: 27). In terms of their symbolism and structure there are many obvious parallels between the two procedures[12]. But what is most relevant here is that the identification between the sacrifier and the victim—which in the classical theory is explicitly a substitute for his own person—is carried over into the theory of *dana* as an identification between the donor and his gift. As the victim is a surrogate for the sacrifier, so the gift is a surrogate for the donor. It stands moreover for what he must expiate. Now it is when the objective of the sacrifice is to eliminate *bad* sacredness that Hubert and Mauss (1964: 55) predict that the identification with the victim will be closest *before* the immolation, and that their subsequent separation will be as final as possible. Consistent with this, the identification of the donor with his gift is often highly elaborated before the transfer (as for example when he is weighed against a valuable substance which he then donates), and his separation from it afterwards is absolute.

There is no question, then, of the gift being a loan or pledge. It is alienated in an absolute way, and the very definition of the gift is that it involves the complete extinction of the donor's *proprietary* rights in favour of the recipient (Aiyar 1941: 77; Law 1926: 1). The gift threatens to cement the two together in a dangerous interdependence; but every attempt is made to sever their bond by insisting on the complete alienation of the thing. Under no circumstances, and on pain of terrible supernatural penalties, is the gift resumed. Its evil 'spirit' must *not* come back. While Mauss originally introduced this notion of 'spirit' to explain the inalienability of the object and the necessity of making a return, what it in fact explains in this context is why the gift *must* be alienated, should *never* return, and should endlessly be handed on.

The obligation to make a return is *not* therefore encoded in the *danadharma*. Mauss (1966: 123; 1973: 243) himself was uneasy here and conceded in a footnote that 'on the obligation to make return gifts—our main subject—there are few facts except perhaps Manu VIII, 213. The clearest rule consists in a rule forbidding the return of gifts'. In truth even the verse cited demands the most wilfully cock-eyed reading to make it say anything about reciprocity. 'The clearest rule' is in reality unqualified. A pure asymmetry must obtain. The donor should seek out the reluctant recipient and give freely, for the genuine gift is never solicited. No return of any earthly kind is countenanced and even an increment to the prestige of the donor weakens the gift, which should therefore be made in secret. It is as if—to paraphrase Trautmann (1981: 281–2)—the ancient Pandits had arrived at the modern theory of reciprocity, didn't like what they found, and smartly turned heel.

The pattern of affinal relations amongst the high castes in contemporary north India clearly reflects this ideology. *Kanya dana*, the 'gift of a virgin' along with her dowry, is merely the beginning of an endless series of gifts which flow unilaterally from wife-givers to wife-receivers. Not even a glass of water may be accepted in a village to which one of the daughters of the lineage has been given in marriage; and such prohibitions may even extend to those who rate as wife-takers to one's own wife-takers (Ibbetson quoted in Lewis 1958: 188–9; Parry 1979: 304–5). The chain is conceptually never closed—as is illustrated by Vatuk's (1969) analysis of the Hindi kinship terminology. Lévi-Strauss (1969: 398–9), of course, argues that this theory of marriage by gift is merely generalised exchange in an illusory guise. In the hypergamous variant of the system, however, female infanticide was in the past widespread, and the highest ranking lineages received brides but gave to none[13]. The very existence of hypergamy, of course, immediately suggests a reciprocal exchange in which the wife-givers in fact gain an increment in status. In the case of many north Indian castes, however, there is no hypergamy in the sense of a systematic ranking of descent lines, and any inferiority on the part of the bride's family is created by the marriage itself (e.g. Vatuk 1975). Clearly in such circumstances the endless stream of gifts cannot be a *quid pro quo* for an elevation in rank and there is no question of a *dyadic* exchange.

A range of quite different examples of this same denial that the gift sets up an obligation to make a return could be given. But what they would all show is that the theory is—as Trautmann (1981: 279) puts it—a 'soteriology, not a sociology of reciprocity . . .'[14]. The gift does indeed return to the donor, but it does so as the fruits of *karma*. It is this 'unseen fruit' (*adrstaphala*) which withers on the branch if any return is accrued in the here and now (cf. Aiyar 1941). The return is deferred (in all likelihood to another existence); its mechanism has become entirely impersonal, and the recipient is merely a 'vessel' (*patra*) or conduit for the flow of merit and is himself in no way constrained by the gift or bound to the donor. Even a spiritual accounting is sometimes looked upon with suspicion, and so the best gifts are given merely from a detached sense of duty and without thinking of them as gifts at all (Kane 1974: 8: 42; Mahabharata 13: 49: 3). Whether we emphasise the impersonality of the return, or the ideology which denies that a 'true' gift is made 'with desire' for *any* kind of reward, it seems clear that we are dealing with a transactional theory quite unlike Mauss's Melanesian, Polynesian and American examples. The Hindu 'Law of the gift' does not create society by instituting that constant give-*and-take* which Malinowski described for the Trobriands. The Trobriand gift may be an 'Indian gift', but the Hindu gift is not.

In passing we might note that much the same theme recurs in Theravada Buddhism, where indeed we find the gift without a recipient at all. Offerings are regularly made to the Buddha, but he has attained *nirvana*, and no longer exists. It is the gods who govern the pragmatic affairs of the world, and with them significantly the ideology is one of reciprocity—offerings for boons. The reciprocated gift belongs to the profane world; the unreciprocated gift to a quest for salvation from it (Ames 1966). Gifts made to those who carry the soteriological message of the Buddha—as they at any rate insist—are never reciprocated. Out of compassion the monk merely provides a 'field of merit' for the laity; but he is not the donor of the merit acquired through the offerings he receives (Strenski 1983).

Nor is an obligation to receive the gift entirely clear. According to the well-known textual formula it is in any case only the Brahmans who have such a duty—and this is paradoxically evaded by the best of them. The Hindu ascetic—unlike the Buddhist monk—is certainly under no such obligation. Nor is a willingness to receive gifts entirely consistent with the honour of the martial Kshatriya, who must never be a supplicant. Hence for him—as Hara (1974) shows—the most appropriate form of marriage which the texts can envisage is marriage by capture and the open exercise of violence (cf. Trautman 1981: 283). The king's duty is to *make* gifts and he should fund his generosity—as the sacrifice (Heesterman 1959)—through force and valour. Hence the king is in many symbolic ways often identified with the bandit (Shulman 1980; cf. Dirks 1982).

Danadharma thus poses a number of difficulties for our general theories of exchange. It consciously repudiates Gouldner's (1960) universal 'moral norm of reciprocity'. Nor is it clear that the unreciprocated gift produces the differentiation in power predicted by Blau (1967)—for in north India wife-giving affines are commonly required to put up with the most peremptory and disdainful treatment at the hands of those to whom they act as perpetual donors. With the hypergamous variant of this system it seems that Hindu ideology has even succeeded in periodically excluding segments of north Indian society from what Lévi-Strauss (1969: 143) calls 'the *universal form* of marriage'—one based on reciprocity. Nor does Sahlins's (1972: 185 sq.) typology of exchange, in which the 'solidary extreme' of generalised reciprocity is seen as coinciding with the closest social relations, seem wholly applicable. Here the most unbalanced exchanges are represented by the gifts made to the wandering ascetic or to the priest of a faraway pilgrimage centre; while transactions between, for example, a father and son are often talked about in the idiom of a *quid pro quo* in which the son finally settles his debts through the performance of his father's mortuary rites (Parry 1985).

As for Mauss, I think that with regard to the kinds of gifts covered by *danadharma*, that part of his thesis which anthropologists have generally found most problematic (the spirit of the gift) is—with the qualifications I have registered—in fact the most acceptable; while that part of his thesis which anthropologists have accepted most readily (the obligations to receive and make a return) is actually the most problematic. Now it is, of course, true that *danadharma* does not embrace the whole range of transactions which we would rate as gifts. As was indicated earlier in connexion with Raheja's material, there are many other kinds of prestation—most of which are explicitly reciprocal (cf. Parry n.d.). Here, however, there is little indication that the gift contains the donor—except in the loose sense that it may be interpreted as an objective manifestation of his subjective dispositions (or perhaps as material testimony to the skills with which his caste is innately endowed). Where we have the 'spirit', reciprocity is denied; where there is reciprocity there is not much evidence of 'spirit'. The two aspects of the model do not hang together.

The 'Indian gift'

I have shown, then, that the Hindu law of the gift does not display convincing evidence of continuity with the exchange systems Mauss described for Melanesia and Polynesia. But how well do these cases themselves conform to his model? Better, I think, than is sometimes claimed.

It was Mauss who originally noted the problem with Malinowski's classification of the presents made within the Trobriand domestic group as 'pure gifts'. The Trobrianders themselves describe them as *mapula*, a term which Malinowski translated as 'payment' or 'equivalent', and they clearly state that the presents which a man makes to his wife and her children are a return for her sexual and domestic services. I am aware that Weiner (1980) has denied that this is the exchange, and has questioned Malinowski's gloss for *mapula*. What she shows nevertheless is that such transfers are visualised as part of a long-term cycle of reciprocal and ultimately balanced exchanges. Gifts of descent-group property to outsiders will eventually be reclaimed, and thereby return—as Mauss said of the Maori gift—to their ancestral hearth.

In view of Johansen's (1954: 118) expert conclusion that 'a certain uncertainty' precludes 'actual certainty' on the matter of the Maori *hau*, and of Gathercole's warning (1978) that all we really have to go on is 'the detritus of an (anachronistic) discourse between various Victorian gentlemen', one might think that Ranapiri's famous parting shot should be taken seriously—'enough on that subject'. I therefore comment on the Maori case with all due trepidation.

The crucial evidence is contained in Ranapiri's explanation of a sacrificial offering of birds to the forest. This is elucidated by analogy with a gift exchange in which A gives a valuable to B who passes it on to C. When C makes a return to B, he must give it to A because it is the *hau* of the first gift, and he will become sick or die if he retains it (Mauss 1966: 8–9; 1973: 158–9; Sahlins 1972: 152). To Mauss it seemed that the gift itself is animated with the spirit of its original homeland and donor, to whom it strives to return.

This interpretation was severely criticised by Firth, who confirmed the Maori preoccupation with reciprocity, but argued that the real sanctions behind it are the threat of witchcraft and the economic and social costs of defaulting on the exchange. The *hau* is not a 'purposive entity'; nor can the *hau* of things be identified with that of persons (1929: 413). These criticisms have been generally accepted (e.g. Johansen 1954: 117; Forge 1972: 529; Parkin 1976: 171)[15]. In contesting them I pay tribute to Firth's own ethnography, and acknowledge the central importance of the sanctions he outlined.

In the Polynesian context Mauss makes it clear that the kinds of things which embody persons belong to the category of valuables known as *taonga*, which constitute the *sacra* of the family. The supreme example of *taonga* are the 'treasure items', or 'heirloom valuables', of the kinship group—with whose land and history they are identified, and into whose genealogies they enter. Johansen (1954: 104) reports that one is related to them as a kinsman, and that they are greeted and honoured like chiefs. Such valuables were exchanged as gifts between groups, and were used to conclude a peace treaty, for the *mana* inherent within them has the capacity to create a strong bond between people. These heirlooms are closely associated with rights to land (Firth 1929: 348), and the land is conceived to be the source of a Maori's spiritual well-being and identity (Hanson & Hanson 1983: 65). It therefore seems clear that in gifting such valuables a Maori was in an important sense gifting an aspect of his personhood. This identification between persons and things is again illustrated by the belief that the possessions of a man of rank—or indeed anything he called by his name or referred to as a part of his body—were permeated by his sacred power, and therefore dangerous to others (Firth 1929: 336). Given all this I cannot see how there can be any clear-cut distinction between the *hau* of persons and things. Perhaps their blending together reflects not so much the metaphysical pre-occupations of the Collège de France, as their separation reflects the pragmatic rationalism of the LSE. At least in the case of heirloom valuables the idea of the thing itself striving to return to its homeland seems perfectly consistent with Maori representations of these objects.

But there is also, I think, a more important kind of connexion between reciprocity and the *hau*. At the highest level of abstraction, Sahlins glosses the *hau* as a 'general principle of productiveness', which in specific contexts might be rendered as 'yield', 'return on' or even 'profit'. Thus the *hau* of a good is its 'yield', and when Ranapiri says that B must return the second valuable to A because it is the *hau* of the first valuable, what he is really enunciating is the precept that 'one man's gift should not be another man's capital'. 'We have', says Sahlins (1972: 162), 'to deal with a society in which freedom to gain at another's expense is not envisioned by the relations and forms of exchange'. The *hau* thus represents a kind of pre-emptive ideological strike against market principles. It is here that I find Sahlins's argument weakest. Ranapiri said nothing whatever about an equivalence in exchange. On the contrary, a 'profit' is clearly implied by the very instance he was trying to explain. The hunters return *some* of the birds to the forest, but keep the rest.

As Sahlins sees it, the great advantage of his analysis over previous ones is that it enables him to explain why Ranapiri invoked a three-party exchange—the third actor being logically necessary to illustrate the principle of a yield or profit on the original gift. Sahlins analyses accounts of three different exchanges in which the *hau* figures, and claims that all reveal a similar triadic structure. But what a close reading of these examples actually reveals is that it is only by sleight of hand that two of them can be represented in this way. The only one which in fact displays this structure is that contained in Ranapiri's text, and this is easily accounted for in other terms[16]. What was being explained after all was a sacrifice *which required the mediation of priests*. It was, in other words, a three-party transaction between hunters, priests and forest; and the economic analogy therefore had to be triadic.

What *is*, in my view, valuable in Sahlins's analysis is his stress on the *hau* as a general principle of productiveness; and this insight can—I think—be taken further. What Ranapiri is actually trying to tell us, I would argue, is that the *source* of well-being and productiveness *is* reciprocal exchange—and it is this principle that fecundity and increase stem from reciprocity which he emphasises by introducing the *hau* into his discussion at the stage of the return. That exchange *itself* is fertile and promotes increase must have appeared as a self-evident truth to the Maori, since the gift normally attracts an increment, and as it circulates it grows (Firth 1929: 416; Hanson & Hanson 1983: 110). By returning A's gift, B 'nourishes the *hau*' and thereby ensures—contra Sahlins—a future 'profit' or 'yield'. By failing to do so, by 'averting the *hau*', B would destroy the source of his own productiveness and vitality, and would therefore succumb to witchcraft or otherwise sicken and die. Again experience proves the theory, for one who defaults on his exchanges will cease to be an acceptable partner, and will be excluded from this apparently magical source of growth and productivity. The gift of a Maori valuable, I conclude, does embody the person; and what Firth dismisses as 'recondite beliefs' about the *hau* do sanction a return. By contrast with the 'spirit' of the Hindu gift which brings destitution and death to one who fails to pass it on along a chain which is conceptually never closed, the 'spirit' of the Maori gift entails like consequences for one who fails to return it to the original donor.

The ideology of the 'pure gift'

It is in any case obvious that both Trobriand and Maori exchange reveal a preoccupation with reciprocity as a norm of social conduct which contrasts with its denial in the Hindu law. In what kinds of social system, then, do we find values of this latter kind, and why? Since the notion of reciprocity has been used so uncritically that it is often unclear whether what is being described is a matter of empirical fact, indigenous theory or anthropological assumption about the nature of human behaviour (MacCormack 1976), an answer to these questions can only be tentative.

In *some* context reciprocity is surely a normative expectation in every society; and I think it probable that the vast majority also make some place for the notion of a free gift. A return, argued Simmel (1950: 392), is always ethically constrained; but the very first gift which initiates a relationship has (or better, is often seen as having[17]) a voluntary and spontaneous character which no subsequent gift can possess, and for this reason it can never be entirely reciprocated. Schwimmer (1973) describes a Melanesian society in which every social relationship is ideologically premissed on exchange. Yet how could exchange ever begin in the first place? Only, the Orokaiva myths tell us, by an original free gift of the primal ancestors[18]. Empirically, then, it is not a question of either an ideology of reciprocity or of its repudiation, but rather of a significant difference in the extent to which these possibilities are elaborated.

The premium placed on reciprocity in Melanesian societies is so striking that Lévi-Strauss (1973: 33), commenting on the convergence between Mauss and Malinowski, was led to wonder whether it was not the Melanesians themselves who were the true authors of the theory. It was the societies of Melanesia and Polynesia which first attracted explanation in these terms, and the principle does not have the same prominence in the Africanist literature (MacCormack 1976). For 'traditional' African societies, however, I can find little evidence of any elaborated ideology of the 'pure gift'. It is surely rather the ancient literate civilisations of Europe and Asia which have stressed this notion.

Mauss—as I have shown—provides some preliminary hints as to why this might be. Those who make free and unconstrained contracts in the market also make free and unconstrained gifts outside it. But these gifts are defined as what market relations are not—altruistic, moral and loaded with emotion. As the economy becomes progressively disembedded from society, as economic relations become increasingly differentiated from other types of social relationship, the transactions appropriate to each become ever more polarised in terms of their symbolism and ideology. We might therefore argue that an ideology of the 'pure gift' is most likely to arise in highly differentiated societies with an advanced division of labour—such an ideology being a logical end-product of the kind of sequence Lévi-Strauss (1969) traces from restricted to generalised to complex systems of reciprocity, where each step implies a greater indirectness of returns and an expansion of the social universe. Again, in an economy with a sizeable market sector gift-exchange does not have the material significance it has for the many tribal societies in which it provides the only access to crucial scarce resources. Gifts can therefore be given with the sole objective of cementing social relations and without any insistence on an equivalent return (cf. Schwimmer 1973: 49). Moreover if—as Mauss argues—gifts are the primitive analogue of the social contract, then they clearly carry a social load which in centralised politics is assumed by the state. In other words, gifts can assume a much more voluntaristic character as their political functions are progressively taken over by state institutions.

I am suggesting, then, that an elaborated ideology of the 'pure' gift is most likely to develop in state societies with an advanced division of labour and a significant commercial sector. But what is also in my view essential to its articulation is a specific type of belief system, as is suggested by the fact that in all of the major world religions great stress is laid on the merit of gifts and alms, ideally given in secrecy and without expectation of any worldly return.

There are, as Obeyesekere (1968; 1980) has argued, certain fundamental differences between these historical world religions and the religions characteristic of small-scale tribal society. Though the idea of salvation—defined as 'a state or condition from which suffering has been eliminated'—is found in both contexts, the majority of tribal religions are not salvation religions; and in those which are, 'compensation for suffering is meted out in the other world irrespective of the actor's behaviour in this world. Ethical considerations do not influence the topography of the other world. . . . The kingdom of heaven is for saint and sinner alike' (1968: 12, 14). In such societies social behaviour tends to be sanctioned largely by secular rather than religious morality; 'there is no systematic attempt to incorporate the secular moral code into a religious one' and hence no thoroughgoing 'ethicization' (1980: 154). Where religious norms are violated, supernatural sanctions tend to be immediate rather than saved up for the after-life[19]. In the world religions, by contrast, social behaviour *is* systematically ethicised. This 'implies the religious evaluation of moral action, actions that are morally good or bad are . . . also religiously good or bad' (1980: 147). The consequence is an elaboration of the concepts of sin (in the sense of 'a violation of the religious ethics of morality' [1968: 14]) and religious merit. These determine the individual's ultimate destiny on the principle of contingency of supernatural reward, and entail the bifurcation of the other world—hell for sinners and heaven for saints. In the South Asian context, Obeyesekere's contrast is clearly illustrated by the comparisons which Fürer-Haimendorf (1967; 1974) and Bailey (1981) have drawn between tribal religions and the Indian world religions.

An ethicised salvation religion, in which rewards are contingent on conduct, is clearly likely to have the effect of orienting the *ideal goals* of social action towards a future existence. Those whose horizons are limited by the rewards of this world will not gather the 'unseen fruits' of the next; and the ethic of intention requires that the expectation of a return in the here and now should be denied. Moreover, the notion of salvation itself devalues this profane world of suffering. The unreciprocated gift becomes a liberation from bondage to it, a denial of the profane self, an atonement for sin, and hence a means to salvation.

The more radical the opposition between this world and a world free from suffering to come, the more inevitable is the development of a *contemptus mundi* which culminates in the institution of renunciation, but of which the charitable gift—as a kind of lay exercise in asceticism—is also often an expression. In abandoning its millenarian expectations in favour of an eschatology of heaven and hell, the early Christian Church widened the chasm between this world and the Kingdom of God, and thereby enormously boosted both the spirit of asceticism and a preoccupation with charitable 'good works' (Troeltsch 1931: 113).

It is of course the case that the common fate of such 'free' gifts is to become a purchase price of salvation, resulting in the kind of actuarial calculation represented by the Merit Books of the pious Buddhist (e.g. Spiro 1970), or the arithmetical relationship between alms-offerings and the elimination of sin established by Cyprian (Westermark 1906: 555). But this same ideology may react against such reckoning in the name of an ideal of purely disinterested action.

I do not, of course, deny the important differences between the World Religions. I have spoken of an other-worldly orientation, but in the case of certain Protestant sects (and of some brands of Islam) it might have been more accurate to speak of an emphasis on creating an image of that other world in this one. The effect is nonetheless to direct action towards a transcendental ideal, and to devalue the world which actually exists along with the returns which can be expected within it. Though the stress which Hinduism and Buddhism place on the notion that the spiritual worth of the gift is contingent on that of its recipient has many parallels in medieval Christianity (Lawrence 1984), again there is certainly a difference in emphasis. To a far greater extent than in the Indian religions, Christianity—with its notion that all men are fashioned equally in the image of God—has developed a *universalistic* conception of purely disinterested giving.

But it was also, of course, the Christian world which developed the theory of pure utility, and that—as Mauss indicated—is perhaps no accident. Since the things of this world are seen as antithetical to the person's true self, his soul, an ethicised salvation religion is I think likely to encourage that separation of persons from things which is an ideological precondition of market exchange, and which significantly was first effected in the West by the laws of a *Christian* Emperor. It is surely significant that the pagan practice which the early missionary monks who Christianised the Germanic peoples were most concerned to extirpate was the burying of treasure with the dead (Little 1978: 5). 'The Christian soul', as Kiernan (1978: 374) notes, 'was purified in heaven from all taint of ownership', and not even the Toriest theologian has thought to ask 'whether each new arrival will be assigned his own personal harp'.

More importantly a *universalistic* ethic of disinterested giving can surely only encourage the creation of a separate sphere which is immune from the requirements of such a demanding precept. The ideology of the pure gift may thus itself promote and entrench the ideological elaboration of a domain in which self-interest rules supreme. It is not I think coincidental that the ideology of the 'pure gift' is accorded such prominence among groups—such as the Jews and Jains—which have a particularly close historical association with market trade, for the two spheres define each other—sometimes less, but with us today as sharply as ever. With renewed ideological stress on the autonomy of the market go renewed pleas for philanthropy to assume the responsibilities it denies. It was possibly through such speculations that Mauss arrived at his now perhaps not so quaint-sounding moral conclusion—that the combination of interest and disinterest in exchange is preferable to their separation.

Even before the publication of *Crime and custom*, Mauss had shown that *both* positions in that long-running argument sparked off by Malinowski's book, adjourned on the beach at Tikopia and endlessly resumed in the anthropological literature, are entirely given by this ideological separation and belong to a discourse peculiar to a certain kind of society.

NOTES

This article represents a slightly revised version of the original lecture, during the preparation of which Maurice Bloch, Chris Fuller, Liz Nissan and Jock Stirrat gave me some sound advice, many useful suggestions and much moral support. I am also particularly indebted to Tom Trautmann for his expert comments on the text of the lecture, permission to cite his unpublished article, the stimulus of his work and the generosity of his encouragement. Responsibility for the deficiencies of the end-product remains, of course, entirely my own.

[1] This definition is given both by the SOED and, in 1764, by Hutchinson in *The history of the colony of Massachusets-Bay* (cited in Hyde 1979: 3). One or two native informants have told me that in their understanding the expression refers to a gift which is reclaimed after it has been made; but here I follow the dictionary usage.

[2] The deficiencies of the translation have been commented on by Leach 1955; Schwimmer 1973: 10; van Baal 1975: 10; Trautmann 1981: 279 and n.d., and Fuller (in a letter to *Man* which substantiated the charge of inaccuracy in some detail, but which was not published).

[3] Mauss (1973: 147) wrote of

> 'le caractère volontaire, pour ainsi dire, apparemment libre et gratuit, et cependant constraint et intéressé de ces prestations. Elles ont revêtu presque toujours la forme du présent, du cadeau offert généreusement même quand, dans ce geste qui accompagne la transaction, il n'y a que fiction, formalisme et mensonge social, et quand il y a, au fond, obligation et intérêt économique'.

Cunnison by comparison, speaks of

> 'prestations which are in theory voluntary, disinterested and spontaneous, but are in fact obligatory and interested. The form usually taken is that of the gift generously offered; but the accompanying behaviour is formal pretence and social deception, while the transaction itself is based on obligation and economic self-interest' (Mauss 1961).

The first sentence quoted above was one of Fuller's examples of the problems with the translation.

[4] Testimony to the importance which Mauss attached to this inseparability of persons and things in primitive and archaic societies is again found in his much later essay on the person (Mauss 1979). But in view of the enormous significance for our modern concepts of property and exchange which *The gift* attributes to their eventual separation, it is perhaps surprising that in the subsequent essay he did not reverse the perspective to explore the consequences of this historical break for the concept of the person.

[5] In the context of sacrifice Mauss (1973: 167) observes that one of the first groups of beings with

whom men had to contract were the gods and the spirits of the dead. This might perhaps be taken to suggest that just as Durkheim and Mauss (1973) had discovered the origins of the theoretical classifications of modern science in religion, so the gift essay tentatively located the origins of modern secular forms of contract and exchange in sacrifice.

[6] It is, he says, 'cousin to Marx's "simple circulation of commodities", thus to the celebrated formula C→M→C' . . . primitive peoples remain constant in their pursuit of use values, related always to exchange with an interest in consumption, so to production with an interest in provisioning' (Sahlins 1972: 83).

[7] 'Almost every family living solely by its own means sooner or later discovers it has not the means to live'. Unless, therefore, 'the domestic economy is forced beyond itself the entire society does not survive' (Sahlins 1972: 101, 86).

[8] It is true that the adjective 'pure' is Cunnison's interpolation, but it seems justified in that it draws attention to the strong distinction Mauss emphasises between 'l'obligation et la prestation non gratuite, d'une part, et le don, de l'autre'.

[9] More specifically, I have in mind here their common interest in the evolution of the contract; and the ideas that ancient law knew 'next to nothing of individuals' (Maine 1960: 152), that the conflation of persons and things is characteristic of societies based on status, and that their legal separation constituted a major historical watershed (1960: 164).

[10] Mauss (1973: 249–50; 1966: 125–6) acknowledged this hastily in a footnote, only to dismiss it as an 'absurd theological interpretation'. Since what—as we shall see—the notion actually explains is why the gift should *not* be accepted in the first place, and cannot in the second place be reciprocated, Mauss clearly had difficulty in coming to terms with it.

[11] Fuller (1984: 67 sq., 196) refers to an array of sources which clearly document the extremely wide distribution of such notions, though paradoxically his own discussion is premissed on their lack of Pan-Indian significance. On the prevalence of these ideas in the South Indian literary tradition, see Shulman 1985.

[12] At the most obvious level, both require a consecration; both transform the religious state of the donor/sacrifier, and both constitute a means of communication with the divine via an intermediary. Given these parallels it is indeed curious that, as Fuller (1984: 196) notes, Mauss 'failed to tie explicitly his analysis of gifts to his earlier work on sacrifice'. In a paragraph which strikingly presages *The gift*, Hubert and Mauss (1964: 100) described sacrifice in terms of 'disinterestedness . . . mingled with self-interest. That is why it has frequently been conceived as a form of contract'. Sacrifice, they continue, presupposes an intermediary which (like the gift) simultaneously unites and separates two opposed parties who 'draw close to each other without giving themselves entirely'. They wind up, what is more, by endorsing Tylor's (1904) account of an evolution from the sacrifice made in the expectation of a return, to an ideology in which it becomes an act of self-abnegation—on my reading precisely the development which Mauss traced for the gift (or to be more precise, for one aspect of the archaic prestation).

[13] It is true that such systems are prone to the kind of instability which Lévi-Strauss predicted; but it is also the case that they have a tendency to re-establish themselves—along with the pattern of matrimonial non-reciprocity they institute (Parry 1979: 247 sq.).

[14] In the area of political values the same ideological denial of reciprocity has been documented in Mayer's (1981) fine discussion of the concept of *seva*; and it is such ideas which underlie the *Bhudan* (or 'land gift') movement of Vinoba Bhave—whose objective was quite as much to provide the landed with a route to salvation through disinterested giving as it was to provide land for the landless (Oommen 1972: 35f; Gonda 1965: 228).

[15] Two recent dissenting voices are MacCormack (1982) and Weiner (1985). Unfortunately the latter had not been published at the time of writing, for it contains much to support the view that Ranapiri was talking about *taonga*-valuables; that these valuables do indeed embody the person and that Mauss was essentially correct in suggesting that the gift is not inert. In certain other respects, however, Weiner's interesting interpretation differs from my own.

[16] The other two examples were those of the cape which Best had ordered from a weaver (Sahlins 1972: 161); and the 'payment' made to his teacher by the 'sorcerer's apprentice' (1972: 103–5). In the first case the weaver *refused* to deal with the trooper who tried to buy the cape, and thereby preserved the proper *dyadic* transaction; while the second case can only be made triadic by treating the victim as a party to the exchange (rather than as the 'thing' exchanged).

[17] The qualification is necessary, for it is surely also the case that relationships are sometimes thought to be initiated out of self-interest.

[18] It might, I recognise, be possible to argue that we should interpret these myths not so much as a statement about the impossibility of initiating exchange without priming the pump with a free gift, but more as a statement that the *only* beings capable of making such a gift were the original ancestors. Either way, my central point would stand: even in this case we find some ideological space (however minimal) for the notion of a free and unconstrained gift.

[19] We are dealing, of course, with an ideal type, and Obeyesekere (1980: 153) makes it clear that empirically there is no religion entirely devoid of ethical implications.

REFERENCES

Aiyar, K. V. Rangaswami 1941. Introduction to *Krtyakalpataru of Bhatta Laksmidhara*, vol. **5**, *Danakanda*. Baroda: Gaekwad's Oriental Series **91**.

Ames, M. 1966. Ritual prestations and the structure of the Sinhalese pantheon. In *Anthropological studies in Theravada Buddhism* (ed.) M. Nash (SE Asia Stud. **13**). New Haven: Yale Univ. Press.

Bailey, F. 1981. Spiritual merit and morality. In *Culture and morality: essays in honour of Christoph von Fürer-Haimendorf* (ed.) A. C. Mayer. Delhi: Oxford Univ. Press.

Bayly, C. 1983. *Rulers, townsmen and bazaars: north Indian society in the age of expansion, 1770–1870*. Cambridge: Univ. Press.

Biardeau, M. 1976. Le sacrifice dans l'hindouisme. In M. Biardeau & C. Malamoud: *Le sacrifice dans l'Inde ancienne*. Paris: Presses Universitaires de France (Bibl. Ecol. hautes Etud., Sci. relig. **79**).

Blau, P. M. 1967. *Exchange and power in social life*. New York: John Wiley.

Dirks, N. 1982. The pasts of a *Palaiyakarar*: the ethnohistory of a South Indian little king. *J. Asian. Stud.* **61**, 655–83.

Durkheim, E. & M. Mauss 1963. *Primitive classification* (trans.) R. Needham. London: Cohen & West.

Ekeh, P. 1974. *Social exchange theory: the two traditions*. London: Heinemann.

Firth, R. 1929. *Primitive economics of the New Zealand Maori*. London: Routledge.

——— 1967. Themes in economic anthropology: a general comment. In *Themes in economic anthropology* (ed.) R. Firth. London: Tavistock.

——— 1973. *Symbols: public and private*. London: George Allen & Unwin.

Forge, A. 1972. The golden fleece. *Man* (N.S.) **7**, 527–40.

Fuller, C. J. 1984. *Servants of the goddess: the priests of a South Indian temple*. Cambridge: Univ. Press.

Fürer-Haimendorf, C. 1967. *Morals and merit: a study of values and social controls in South Asian societies*. London: Weidenfeld and Nicholson.

——— 1974. The sense of sin in cross-cultural perspective. *Man* (N.S.) **9**, 539–56.

Gathercole, P. 1978. *Hau, Mauri* and *Utu*: a re-examination. *Mankind* **11**, 334–40.

Gonda, J. 1965. *Change and continuity in Indian religion*. The Hague: Mouton.

Gouldner, A. W. 1960. The norm of reciprocity. *Am. sociol. Rev.* **25**, 161–78.

Gregory, C. A. 1983. *Gifts and commodities*. London: Academic Press.

Hanson, F. & L. Hanson 1983. *Counterpoint in Maori culture*. London: Routledge & Kegan Paul.

Hara, M. 1974. A note on the raksasa form of marriage. *J. Am. orient. Soc.* **94**, 296–306.

Hart, K. 1983. On commoditization. In *From craft to industry* (ed.) Esther Goody. Cambridge: Univ. Press.

Heesterman, J. C. 1959. Reflections on the significance of the Daksina. *Indo-Iran J.* **3**, 241–58.

——— 1964. Brahmin, ritual and renouncer. *Wien. Z. Kunde Süd-Ostasiens* **8**, 1–31.

Hubert, H. & M. Mauss 1964. *Sacrifice: its nature and function* (trans.) W. D. Halls. London: Cohen & West.

Hyde, L. 1979. *The gift: imagination and the erotic life of property*. New York: Random House.

Johansen, J. P. 1954. *The Maori and his religion in its non-ritualistic aspects*. Copenhagen: Ejnar Munksgaard.

Kane, P. V. 1974. *History of Dharmasastra*, vol. **2**. Poona: Bhandarkar Oriental Research Institute.

Kapferer, B. 1976. Introduction: transactional models reconsidered. In *Transaction and meaning* (ed.) B. Kapferer. Philadelphia: Institute for the Study of Human Issues.

Kiernan, V. G. 1978. Private property in history. In *Family and inheritance: rural society in western Europe 1200–1800* (eds) J. Goody, J. Thirsk & E. P. Thompson. Cambridge: Univ. Press.

Law, B. C. 1926. *The law of gift in British India*. Calcutta: Eastern Law House.

Lawrence, C. H. 1984. *Medieval monasticism: forms of religious life in Western Europe in the Middle Ages*. London: Longman.

Leach, E. R. 1955. Review of M. Mauss *The gift* (trans. I. Cunnison). *Man* **55**, 30.

——— 1961. *Rethinking anthropology*. London: Athlone.

Lévi-Strauss, C. 1969. *The elementary structures of kinship* (trans.) J. Bell, J. von Sturmer and R. Needham. London: Eyre & Spottiswoode.

——— 1973. Introduction à l'oeuvre de Marcel Mauss. In M. Mauss: *Sociologie et anthropologie*. Paris: Presses Universitaires de France.

Lewis, O. 1958. *Village life in northern India: studies in a Delhi village*. New York: Random House.

Little, L. 1978. *Religious poverty and the profit economy in Medieval Europe*. London: Paul Elek.

MacCormack, G. 1976. Reciprocity. *Man* (N.S.) **11**, 89–103.

——— 1982. Mauss and the 'spirit' of the gift. *Oceania* **52**, 286–93.

Mahabharata 1905. A prose English translation by Manmatha Nath Dutt. *Anushasana Parva*, vol. **13**. Calcutta.

Maine, H. S. 1960. *Ancient law*. London: J. M. Dent.

Malinowski, B. 1922. *Argonauts of the western Pacific: an account of native enterprise and adventure in the archipelagoes of Melanesian New Guinea*. London: Routledge & Kegan Paul.

——— 1926. *Crime and custom in savage society*. London: Kegan Paul, Trench, Trubner.

Manu, The laws of, 1886; translated from Sanskrit into English by Georg Buhler (Sacred Books of the East **25**). Oxford: Clarendon Press.

Mauss, M. 1966. *The gift: forms and functions of exchange in archaic societies* (trans.) I. Cunnison. London: Cohen & West.

——— 1973. *Essai sur le don: forme et raison de l'échange dans les sociétés archaïques*. In M. Mauss, *Sociologie et anthropologie*. Paris: Presses Universitaires de France.

——— 1979. A category of the human mind, the notion of person, the notion of 'self'. In M. Mauss: *Sociology and psychology* (trans.) B. Brewster. London: Routledge & Kegan Paul.

Mayer, A. C. 1981. Public service and individual merit in a town of central India. In *Culture and morality: essays in honour of Christoph von Fürer-Haimendorf* (ed.) A. Mayer. Delhi: Oxford Univ. Press.

Obeyesekere, G. 1968. Theodicy, sin and salvation in a sociology of Buddhism. In *Dialectic in practical religion* (ed.) E. R. Leach. Cambridge: Univ. Press.

——— 1980. The rebirth eschatology and its transformations: a contribution to the sociology of early Buddhism. In *Karma and rebirth in classical Indian traditions* (ed.) W. D. O'Flaherty. Berkeley: Univ. of California Press.

Ollman, B. 1976. *Alienation: Marx's conception of man in capitalist society*. Cambridge: Univ. Press.

Oommen, T. K. 1972. *Charisma, stability and change: an analysis of the Bhoodan- Gramdan movement in India*. New Delhi: Thomson Press.

Parkin, D. 1976. Exchanging words. In *Transaction and meaning* (ed.) B. Kapferer. Philadelphia: ISHI.

Parry, J. P. 1979. *Caste and kinship in Kangra*. London: Routledge & Kegan Paul.

——— 1980. Ghosts, greed and sin: the occupational identity of the Benares funeral priests. *Man* (N.S.) **15**, 88–111.

——— 1985. Death and digestion: the symbolism of food and eating in north Indian mortuary rites. *Man* (N.S.) **20**, 612–30.

——— n.d. The moral perils of exchange in a Hindu pilgrimage city. In *The symbolism of money and the morality of exchange* (eds) M. Bloch & J. Parry.

Raheja, G. 1985. Kinship, caste, and auspiciousness in Pahansu. Thesis, University of Chicago, Illinois.

——— n.d. Auspiciousness in north Indian social life. In *Beyond purity and pollution: studies in Indic categories and everyday experience* (ed.) M. Moffat.

Sahlins, M. 1972. *Stone age economics*. Chicago: Aldine.

Schwimmer, E. 1973. *Exchange in the social structure of the Orokaiva: traditional and emergent ideologies in the Northern District of Papua*. London: C. Hurst.

Shulman, D. 1980. On South Indian bandits and kings. *Ind. econ. social Hist. Rev.* **17**, 283–306.

——— 1985. Kingship and prestation in South Indian myth and epic. *Asian Afr. Stud.* **19**, 93–117.

Simmel, G. 1950. *The sociology of Georg Simmel* (ed.) K. H. Wolff. Glencoe, Ill.: Free Press.

Spiro, M. 1970. *Buddhism and society: a great tradition and its Burmese vicissitudes*. Berkeley: Univ. of California Press.

Strenski, I. 1983. On generalized exchange and the domestication of the *sangha*. *Man* (N.S.) **18**, 463–77.

Trautmann, T. 1981. *Dravidian kinship*. Cambridge: Univ. Press.

——— n.d. *The gift* in India. Paper delivered before the eleventh Annual Conference on South Asia, University of Wisconsin, November 1982.

Troeltsch, E. 1931. *The social teachings of the Christian churches*, vol. **1**. London: George Allen & Unwin.

Tylor, E. B. 1904. *Primitive culture*, vol. **2**. London: John Murray.

van Baal, J. 1975. *Reciprocity and the position of women: anthropological papers*. Assen: Van Gorcum.

Vatuk, S. 1969. A structural analysis of the Hindi kinship terminology. *Contrib. Ind. Sociol* (N.S.) **3**, 94–115.

——— 1975. Gifts and affines in north India. *Contrib. Ind. Sociol.* (N.S.) **9**, 155–96.

Vogt, W. P. 1983. Obligation and right: the Durkheimians and the sociology of law. In *The sociological domain: the Durkheimians and the founding of French sociology* (ed.) P. Besnard. Cambridge: Univ. Press.

Weiner, A. 1976. *Women of value, men of renown: new perspectives in Trobriand exchange*. Austin: Univ. of Texas Press.

——— 1980. Reproduction: a replacement for reciprocity. *Am. Ethnol.* **7**, 71–85.

——— 1985. Inalienable wealth. *Am. Ethnol.* **12**, 210–27.

Westermark, E. 1906. *The origin and development of moral ideas*, vol. **1**. London: MacMillan.

[8]

Physiocracy: a natural economics

Like a brilliant meteor the Physiocrats burst upon the scene of pre-Revolutionary France and for two decades had the attention of fashionable and influential society. By the late 1770s, however, real events fatally undermined their theoretical constructions. A century later Marx revived interest in their work, but in general the Physiocrats have been dismissed as forerunners of a discipline which has since shown them to have been in error.[1]

The term 'physiocracy' means rule of nature, and no label could have been more apt for this school of economists and social theorists. The key figure François Quesnay (1694-1774), doctor to the king, was taken under the protection of Madame de Pompadour. His *Tableau économique* is the central Physiocratic work, hailed now as a precursor of modern numerical techniques, capital theory and general equilibrium theory. A less central yet consequential figure was Turgot (1727-1781), whose *Réflexions sur la formation et la distribution des richesses* clearly states the fundamentals of Physiocracy. Although Turgot also discusses such topics as capital, profit and interest, only from a modern perspective might one claim that his Physiocratic concepts are alien 'to the argument into which they are inserted' (Schumpeter 1954:243).

Like Ricardo, the Physiocrats developed a model of the economy; but this is not quite how they would have seen it. The Physiocrats would have denied a distinction between their model and the facts, for according to their epistemology human formulations were derived from reality through the application of reason. Gaps between the two were transitory in that through discussion and thought the human constructions themselves would come to match the realities of nature. To call Physiocracy a model, therefore, distorts their own understanding of their efforts.

The Physiocrats portrayed the economy as a total, circulating system of wealth. But unlike the mercantilists they identified the source of this wealth as lying in agriculture or production, not within circulation. According to Physiocratic thought, agriculture was almost the only activity which yielded a material output that exceeded its input. They posited a three-order or three-class society, consisting of cultivators or peasants, landowners and artisans. At the start of the year, the cultivators have in hand the stock necessary to support their labors; at year's end output is sufficient to cover all costs of production and to provide an excess. This extra amount was termed the *produit net*. The 'net product' or excess comprises the rent and flows to the landowners who consume it and use part to purchase items from the artisans. The cultivators or husbandmen use their return as foodstuffs and for exchange with the artisans, who in turn use their receipts for direct consumption and as raw materials for the goods they fashion. The only increment coming into the system of circulation is from agriculture, and this yearly injection flows to the social class who possesses the factor which produced it.

Physiocracy, of course, was only one of several local, economic models in Enlightenment France, and it had real influence for only a brief time. Turgot, for example, was named Contrôleur Général in 1774 and instituted several Physiocratic-inspired reforms; but within twenty months he was dismissed by the King, and nearly all his innovations were opposed by one or another segment of the society. Physiocracy is therefore sometimes dismissed on account of its historical failure to become an accepted paradigm. It is also generally thought to have been mistaken in identifying agriculture as the sole productive source within the economy. But, leaving issues of evaluation aside, there remains the cultural question: why did the Physiocrats accord such primacy to agriculture? This was the keystone of their model which, when destroyed, brought down the entire edifice. Even if the Physiocrats were correct to pay special attention to agriculture in pre-Revolutionary France, this does not account for their particular construction of it. What *cultural* sense did it make for the Physiocrats to place agriculture at the very center of their model?

The Physiocrats as seen by others

We do not lack interpretations of Physiocracy, but most are attempts to assess its validity. I shall review three of these as representative of a broader triangulation of positions.[2]

Joseph Schumpeter, in his historical account of economic theories (1954), is generally concerned to relate the intellectual milieu to the discipline as it was developing. In the case of Quesnay, however, he insists that no facet of his economics was buttressed by a theological or extra-empirical belief. 'This proves ipso facto the purely analytic or "scientific" nature of his economic work' (Schumpeter 1954:233). This is odd not only because Schumpeter here departs from his own method of analysis but also in that he consequently does not (and cannot) explain the crucial shift in Quesnay's argument which Schumpeter himself succinctly outlined: 'He took it for granted that the fact of physical productivity implied value productivity, and he shifted in midstream from the one to the other' (1954:238). Schumpeter would consider the Physiocrats solely in terms of their 'scientific' merit, which means that he assumes the existence of prediscoursive facts. By granting his knowledge of these facts priority over the constructions of others, Schumpeter suspends judgment about the verisimilitude and relativity of his own formulations while blocking access to other perspectives on Physiocracy.

Marx (1963[1905-10]) was much more sympathetic. He saw that the Physiocrats were expressing a form of materialism, and had shifted the focus of attention from circulation to production. Marx's central criticism, of course, was that the Physiocrats had failed to see that only labor creates value. Value became confounded with physical substance. Marx held that although the Physiocrats were the first economists to analyze modern capitalism, they did so through the lens of feudalism. For the Physiocrats, everything appeared through the perspective of land, which is to say landed property, and this was a vestige of feudalism. Capitalism had not – so to speak – fully broken its feudalistic bonds. Feudalism was made bourgeois, while capitalism was cloaked in a feudalist wrap. Thus, surplus value was explained 'in a feudal way, as derived from nature and not from society, from man's relation to the soil, not from his social relations' (Marx 1963[1905-10]:52).

When Marx opposed real relations in society to the Physiocratic emphasis on relations with nature, he was not presenting a vision of 'society with ideas' but of society as the context in which material labor was extracted by one human from another. Marx did not oppose the materialism of the Physiocrats, he shifted its locus. For Marx, the Physiocratic emphasis on land obscured labor's real powers, and this, of course, served to justify the aristocrats' source of wealth. Thus, Marx interpreted or remodeled the ideas of the Physiocrats principally in the light of what he saw to be their class interest. Physiocracy was a clear instance of a mystification or ideology.

The Physiocratic model may have been motivated in this fashion, but the same class interest could have produced other models, and Physiocracy itself is not entirely reducible to class interest. It was an attempt to understand and to constitute emerging social relationships by placing them within an accepted cultural vision. To say that a model has a particular 'explanatory' function does not account for the pattern it has. This is a matter of historical influences and human inventiveness. The form and semantics of the Physiocratic model were part of a cultural tradition.

One anthropologist has already attempted to place the Physiocrats in an historical and cultural perspective. Louis Dumont (1977) argues that Quesnay was the first to visualize the economy as a distinct entity, as a separate domain made up of interrelated parts, and he traces this view to Quesnay's interest in the human circulatory system and to his version of natural law theory. More broadly, Dumont argues that a connection can be found between Physiocracy and the work of John Locke. But Dumont disrupts the historical link by considering Quesnay prior to Locke, while his discussion of the philosopher is limited almost entirely to his *Two Treatises* (Locke 1823[1690]). Dumont neglects the impact which Locke's epistemological work, *An Essay Concerning Human Understanding* (1975[1690]), had upon the Physiocrats.

Leading constructs in the Physiocratic model

The Physiocratic model is built around three metaphors which offer a mechanistic view of economic behavior. Unlike Ricardo's early model, however, the Physiocratic one does not contain a linear, step-by-step, sequence. Rather the metaphors overlap. They are all based upon the human body, two having been suggested by Quesnay's medical experience. Quesnay drew the concept of *circulation* from Harvey's researches and the imagery of the flow of blood. Similarly, he probably took the notion of *reproduction* from the birth process. In the model these are projected as the circulation and reproduction of wealth.[3] The third scheme was drawn from Locke's concept of *mind*, in which external sensation is distinguished from, and understood to be prior to, internal operations. This was represented in the model as the division of human effort into productive and nonproductive activities. The Physiocrats conjoined the three metaphors in the domain of agriculture, which they considered to be the productive sphere of the economy.

The notion that only agriculture is productive was central to Physiocracy. Mirabeau, for example, asserted that 'The land is the mother of all goods' and added that 'wealth' comes only from the land (Meek 1973:120-1). With Quesnay he also wrote of 'the spontaneous gifts of nature' (Meek 1963:60). Quesnay himself stated the assumption firmly in the 'Dialogue on the work of artisans': 'The origin, the principle, of all expenditure and all wealth is the fertility of the land, whose products can be increased only through these products themselves' (1963a[1766]: 209). Only agricultural products represent a 'true *generation* or *creation* of wealth' (Quesnay 1963a[1766]:223). Similarly, for Turgot nature was a storehouse which offers a 'superfluity' to humans as a 'pure gift' (Turgot 1898[1770]:9,12,13,14,51).

The Physiocratic construction actually has two facets. Agriculture, or nature, is the source of wealth; and it is the source of a surplus, a conclusion which is not necessarily entailed by the first view. The idea that a surplus accrues in agriculture places the Physiocrats within the ambiance of modern economic theory, but it also raised a question of agency. What was the origin or source of the productive excess? The Physiocrats cited the Deity as the agent behind nature, but perhaps this is not so different from evoking human labor as a causal force. Both are modes of solving the riddle which arises when it is claimed that production is a material movement from a lesser to a greater quantity.

The Physiocratic view of agriculture defined, by implication, a second and complementary category of activities, those which are nonproductive. These were called 'barren' or 'sterile.' This was not to say that such activities are not useful or even without honor (Turgot 1898[1770]:7). On the contrary, they are necessary for the social order; but they are not productive in the special Physiocratic sense. Sterile and productive activities are distinguished by reference to the object on which labor is performed. Only work that is done on material things which reproduce is productive, while work performed on objects which do not reproduce, alone or under human guidance, is barren. In a positive sense, sterile work may re-form or shape existing materials, but such activity only represents the combining of other, already present, wealth forms. Manufacturing, for example, is never productive, because it is not creative of material.

The opposition between productive and sterile work is not, however, entirely dependent on the reproductive nature of materials. For example, at the outset of his *Tableau* Quesnay offered the following classification:

> Productive expenditure is employed in agriculture, grasslands, pasture, forests, mines, fishing, etc., in order to perpetuate wealth in the form of corn, drink, wood, livestock, raw materials for manufactured goods, etc. (1972[1758-9]:i)

According to Quesnay, fishing is productive while cattle raising is not. This seems puzzling, for cattle obviously reproduce. Quesnay's classification, however, depends on the assumption that cattle are machines and providers of fertilizer, not sources of foodstuffs. The question that concerned him was whether man-made machines could be substituted profitably for cattle (1963a [1766]:218). More broadly, and in modern terms, we might say that Quesnay was trying to sort primary from secondary and final goods. But he formulated his division by applying simultaneously the two metaphors of reproduction and mind. To be productive, an activity had to be performed on material that was both reproductive and secured from 'outside' the social order. Fishing and logging, for example, both fall within the area of overlap and were considered to be productive; but cattle raising – for the Physiocrats – had only one of the critical attributes. Cattle were seen as being domestic, machine-like beasts. This reasoning, incidentally, should also disqualify mining from being a productive activity. But Quesnay was inconsistent about mining, and it was precisely this activity which gave rise to disagreement among several of the Physiocrats (Weulersse 1910,1:277-80).

A third and closely related construct in the model is that of labor. Labor is a form of consumption, a destruction of produced wealth. Humans use up wealth whether they are idle, making handicrafts, or farming. The three expenditures are distinguished not by the activity itself but by the material on which it is performed. The landowner simply consumes wealth. The artisan, because he conveys wealth from one repository to another, preserves it. The farmer is productive because he both conveys wealth and harnesses nature's special powers.

In the Physiocratic model, then, labor is the immediate cause but not the source of wealth (Turgot 1898[1770]:5,7,17). The function of labor is to transport wealth, from one larder to another. This is a passive labor, a machine for changing inputs to outputs. Like the early Ricardo, but unlike Marx, the Physiocrats did not construct the human as a material or ideational creator.

This same passivity of the human contribution recurs in the Physiocratic construct of productivity. The Physiocrats clearly recognized that work might be performed more or less efficiently; and in a remarkable passage anticipating Adam Smith, Turgot extolled the division of labor (1898[1770]:4-5). But advances in productivity posed no conceptual problem for the Physiocrats; they encouraged it in practice without linking it to an active conception of work. Labor efficiency, like good household management, cut costs rather than raised output. The source or fount of wealth, they maintained, was nature, regardless of how well humans used it.

The focus of Physiocracy was upon how wealth was augmented and then circulated through the social order. Landowning was a form of pure consumption or use. Artisanship was a mode of trade or the exchange of equivalent for equivalent. Only agriculture yielded a net product. But even the husbandman was more like a midwife than a producer in that he only attended to the given, reproductive powers of the land. The farmer was productive because he engaged in an unequal exchange, an appropriation from nature.

A natural economics

The Physiocrats denied a creative role to the human, but for them nature was an irreducible force in society. The Physiocrats were constructing not an economics of nature, whose form might be ecology or evolution, but a natural economics. Their concept of nature provided a cosmological warrant or justification for the formulations in the model.

Nature confronted humans first as internal necessity. Humankind, the Physiocrats argued, has three needs: to subsist, to preserve itself and to continue the species (Turgot 1898[1770]:7; Mirabeau and Quesnay 1973[1763]:106). These needs constitute the a priori or material requirements of the organism, and they lie at the foundation of the social order. In *Rural Philosophy*, for example, Mirabeau and Quesnay (1973[1763]:104-5) provide an essentialist view of the relation between material and social organization.

> We must consider the common weal in terms of its essence, and humanity as a whole in terms of its root, *subsistence*. All the moral and physical parts of which society is constituted derive from this and are subordinate to it. It is upon subsistence, upon the means of subsistence, that all the branches of the political order depend. Religion, in a sense, is purely and simply spiritual, but natural law inspires us and also tells us about duties relative to our needs; the civil laws, which originally are nothing more than rules for the allocation of subsistence; virtues and vices, which are only obedience to or revolt against natural or civil law; agriculture, trade, industry – all are subordinate to the means of subsistence. This is the fundamental force.

The Physiocrats, like Ricardo, were providing a foundational view of the economy, but their model was not derivational. They simply asserted that a connection had to exist between natural needs and the remainder of the economy and the social order. In some respects, this is an empiricist counterpart to the more rationalist model of Ricardo.

The Physiocratic model also incorporated a naturalistic view of history. History led inevitably to eighteenth-century French society; the social order could not have been different. By assuming that society was naturally determined, the Physiocrats also chartered their own argument as a direct reading of natural processes rather than as an historically influenced construction.

The principal role of nature in Physiocratic theory, however, was to account for economic value. The agricultural net product was a real substance provided by nature. Everything else was a reworking of it. Nature yielded the materials, while humans shaped them for consumption.

> The crops which the land produces to satisfy the different wants of man cannot serve the purpose, for the most part, in the state in which nature gives them; they must undergo various changes and be prepared by art. Wheat must be converted into flour. (Turgot 1898[1770]:5)

Today we would draw the line between nature (wheat) and culture (flour) at an earlier stage than did Turgot, or we might visualize the entire agricultural process as a cultural shaping of nature. Agricultural inputs usually are transformed outputs of a prior state; they are not themselves raw materials. Wheat, for example, has long been shaped by human intentions; the centuries of human use, seeding and harvesting of the crop have helped to form its current features (Harlan 1975,1976). And this human shaping of nature was as true of the land utilized by eighteenth-century French farmers as it was of their crops.

This same opposition between natural substances and their human shaping appears in the Physiocrats' purely economic calculations. In agriculture, the Physiocrats thought they could perceive a natural, quantitative difference between inputs and outputs, the latter being larger than the former. But the means and ends of agriculture are heterogeneous, and any comparison of the two must be based upon a measure different from the substances themselves, such as money, labor or calories. These are cultural scales of value. Thus, the supposed power of nature to grant a gift to humans actually hinges upon the human way of constructing this superfluity. This conclusion, however, hardly fits the Physiocratic epistemology. For them the material increase was an existent fact.

A similar observation applies to the wage level. For nature to provide a surplus, it must be assumed that the wants of the farmers are less than what nature yields in return for the expenditure of their labor. If the cultivator consumes too much, there is no net product. The Physiocrats had to postulate that wants – the expenses of labor – are determined by nature and not by society (Turgot 1898[1770]:5,7,9,12). The sentient human with his needs and wants was constructed as a natural being.

In Physiocracy, nature provided the foundation for society. Implicit in their construction, as in Ricardo's Essay, was the moral argument that the political sphere had to bend to the economic, the naturally given; its 'first care must be to procure subsistence' (Mirabeau and Quesnay 1973[1763]:107). To us, the construction appears vacuous and abstract, because it reveals little about the formation of social and economic value; yet, for the Physiocrats, it was significant and real, precisely because it had a basis in natural processes. Why, then, did they believe that the invocation of nature constituted a satisfactory explanation? What cultural sense did it make that society and the economy were seen as derived from the facts of nature?

Quesnay's cosmos: the world of Locke

The intellectual milieu of the Physiocrats had been deeply influenced by the Cartesians and by Locke. But they themselves were not totally in sympathy with the Cartesian tradition (Neill 1948,1949), while Locke had a special impact upon them (Albaum 1955; Sewell 1980). Locke's epistemological views provided not only a charter for their model but one of its primal metaphors.

Quesnay's essay on 'Natural right' (1963b[1765]) offers some useful clues to the link between his economic model and world view. Quesnay began his essay with the proposition that man has a natural claim upon those things which he has 'procured' through his labor (1963b[1765]:43,46,47). Nearly a century earlier Locke had offered a similar though rather more elaborated notion in the *Two Treatises*, arguing that everyone has a property in his own person, therefore in his own labor, and therefore in that with which he has mixed his labor (1823[1690]:354).

The remaining portion of Quesnay's 'Natural right' helps to elucidate some of the metaphysical foundations of his economic argument. Quesnay held that there is such a thing as a natural order, independent of human intention and with its own laws. The natural order has two dimensions. Quesnay posited, first, the existence of physical law, meaning 'the regular course of all physical events in the natural order which is self-evidently the most advantageous to the human race' (1963b[1765]:53). But physical laws are not social laws, and Quesnay also proposed the existence of moral law by which he meant 'the rule of all human action in the moral order conforming to the physical order which is self-evidently the most advantageous to the human race' (1963b[1765]:53). Together these two orders, the physical and the moral, comprise natural law which itself is given by the 'Author of Nature' or the Supreme Being.

Quesnay's constructions reveal, to begin with, an empiricist position. The notion of 'self-evidence,' for example, is used to justify his argument; and he expresses an unshakeable belief in the inherent orderliness of nature. Quesnay also assumes that a relation exists between the physical and social realms; invariable and 'real' building blocks, according to his empiricist belief, underpin the social order. Natural law is the work of the Deity, the 'mythical' source of the rules which exist outside and prior to any social formation. But despite the allusions to the ultimate 'Co-author' or 'Supreme Being' scattered throughout Physiocratic writing, the emphasis remains on the empirically visible, natural order.

A concept of the normative was also embedded in Quesnay's vision. The rules of human behavior, which exist apart from society, are possessed of more good than evil. Humans should follow them, for 'self-evidently' this is advantageous. Nature, in fact, conveys its own punishments and rewards.

> If a government deviated from the natural laws which assure the success of agriculture, would we dare lay the blame on agriculture itself for the fact that we lacked bread? (Quesnay 1963b[1765]:48)

Morality, derived from the Deity, exists in nature, and society must adapt accordingly. The general argument echoes Locke, from the emphasis on nature to the linking of natural law and ethics, although the details are Quesnay's.

In the economic model itself, the Physiocratic emphasis upon agriculture made sense from this natural law perspective. Within a natural law construction of the world, farming – the human interaction with nature – had to assume a dominant position, for this was the 'first' place in which physical laws had a social influence. Farming was the empirical link between given, natural essences and social action, which to be useful had to conform to the physical.

Between Locke's epistemology and the economics of the Physiocrats, however, there was a different and more subtle connection. Quesnay provides a clue to it when in one paragraph he jumps from economic processes to verbal categories.

> The idea of *production*, or of *regeneration*, which here forms the basis of the differentiation between the general classes of citizens, is confined within physical limits which are so rigorously reduced to reality that they no longer conform to the vague expressions used in ordinary language. But it is not for the natural order to conform to a language which expresses only confused and ambiguous ideas; it is for the expressions to conform to the exact understanding of the natural order, in distinctions which are rigorously regulated by reality. (1963a [1766]:204)

This juxtaposition of riches and reason goes to the foundation of the Physiocratic model. A central duality in Locke concerning human understanding became a schema in Physiocracy. When Locke sought the sources of ideas – the materials of all knowledge – he found them in experience, and such experience came either from sensation or mental operations.

> *External Objects furnish the mind with the* Ideas *of sensible qualities*, which are all those different perceptions they produce in us: And the *Mind furnishes the Understanding with* Ideas *of its own Operations*. (1975[1690]:106)

Locke here distinguishes sensation from operation. The first is a mode of apprehending real-world objects; the second is a manipulation of those given sensations. The Physiocratic distinction between the capture of material wealth by farmers and the shaping of that wealth by artisans is a metaphor of Locke's bifurcation. The first is an appropriation of objects while the second is an operation upon the objects already appropriated: farming is to artisanship as sensation is to operation.

This same Physiocratic distinction between agriculture and artisanship bears an equally striking similarity to Locke's division between simple and complex ideas. Simple ideas are 'the Materials of all our knowledge' (1975[1690]:119), in the reception of which the mind is passive. Complex ideas are those which the mind has actively 'gained by combining, joining and separating simple ideas' (1975[1690]:163). Quesnay similarly contrasts 'a *real* production of wealth' in agriculture to 'a simple production of forms' by artisans (1963a[1766]:205).

> We have to distinguish an adding together of items of wealth which are combined with one another, from a *production* of wealth. That is, we have to distinguish an increase brought about by combining raw materials . . . which were in existence prior to this kind of increase, from a *generation* or creation of wealth, which constitutes a renewal and *real* increase of renascent wealth. (Quesnay 1963a[1766]:207)

The opposition between agriculture and artisanship is a metaphor of the distinction between simple and complex ideas.

A parallel can also be drawn between the Physiocratic model and the noninteractionist theory of mind proposed by Locke according to which mind operates upon the given sense qualities of things. The Physiocrats erected a noninteractionist economics in that nature was seen to offer items of wealth prior to human desire and understanding.

In Physiocracy, then, human 'productive' activity was neither seamless nor homogeneous. It was bifurcated into farming and artisanship, and this duality was not one of equality but asymmetry. This way of modeling human endeavors made sense to the Physiocrats and their audience because it was formed in the pattern of a known image, although the connection was perhaps never consciously formulated. The Physiocrats offered an organic analogy according to which economic practices were a metaphor of mind. In this 'intellectual' economics, agriculture was to artisanship as sensation was to mental operation as the simple was to the complex idea. The first term in each pair was primary.

But my argument that the Physiocrats were influenced by Locke's epistemological as well as his political work raises a problem about the Physiocratic construction of labor in relation to the consistency between Locke's two works. Just as there exists an intellectual tension between the *Two Treatises* and the *Essay*, is there a comparable hiatus in the Physiocratic model? In economic terms, the problem takes the form of reconciling the notion that labor creates property but land creates value.

Locke had proposed in the *Two Treatises* that 'it is labour indeed that put the difference of value on everything' (1823[1690]: 361). Quesnay likewise argued that labor performed on a natural object annexes that object and conveys a right of possession. Can this belief, held by the Physiocrats and derived from the *Two Treatises*, be reconciled with the other claim (influenced by the *Essay*) that only land is productive? Whether or not Locke actually 'formulated the labor theory of value' (Samuelson 1973:840), the Physiocratic claim that property is created by labor appears to contradict their central thesis, that land is the source of wealth.

Locke's idea of labor, however, was a very special one; it was an *additive*, not a *generative* principle. Labor only brought about a human imprinting on an object. Similarly, for the Physiocrats labor conveyed but did not create value. Certainly, it could appropriate that which 'nature produces spontaneously' (Quesnay 1963b[1765]:46), but in so doing it only transported value from one object to another. Labor could create property without generating fresh value. In the Physiocratic construction, labor was passive just as, for Locke, mind was the passive receptor of experience.

The economic model of the Physiocrats, therefore, was not only consistent with Locke but a projection of his imagery. Their construction was part of a meaningful conception of mind and cosmos. A world view was brought into conjunction with the facts of Enlightenment France to generate an economic model.

Artisanship

There remains the question of how commodities themselves were seen by the Physiocrats. The Physiocrats were primarily interested in agriculture, but how did the work of the artisans and their products fit into the model?

Physiocracy might be termed a proto-phonological or early structuralist economics, for it constituted goods by opposing content to form, regardless of function (Lévi-Strauss 1963:21). Objects as substances represented the unique reproductive and regenerative power of nature, while as forms they signaled a kind of human rationality. Agriculture provided the material substance, artisanship yielded the shape. Or,

content : form ::
substance : shape ::
nature : reason ::
agriculture : artisanship.

Where a modern structuralist, however, regards form as more important, the Physiocrats believed that content was primary.

Goods as fresh or new substances in the economy were a sign of nature's inherent fertility and the power of the 'co-author.' But this was a quiet co-author, a ghost writer, a silent agent; and as He was easily forgotten, the economics and understanding of the commodities could take a materialist turn. Explanation by natural laws also implies that objects convey little social information. Definitively separated from people, the commodities communicated little about social groups, social *persona* or social history. Effectively, Physiocracy denied any inherent social significance in the goods as material things. Objects represented their natural foundation.

The form of the objects also had a meaning even if, unlike the substance, it was not a source of economic value. This form was conferred by the artisans. But what did their work signify? On the analogy with Locke's image of mind, farming is passive activity, while artisanship is active. In what sense could the work of the artisans have been active and yet nonproductive?

The Physiocrats paid little attention to artisanship, but their views on the subject were shared by some of their contemporaries. Their inattention to the work of the artisans, and the resulting gap in their model, could be compensated for by others who held the same general outlook. The exemplar of such contemporaries was undoubtedly Diderot, and the general tone of thought was well represented by the massive work he edited, the *Encyclopédie*. 'Whoever believes at all in the concept of the "spirit" of an age will be inclined to look upon the *Encyclopédie* as the very incarnation of the eighteenth-century spirit. . . . The philosophy is mainly empiricist' (Schumpeter 1954:137-8). Diderot, who was intellectually close to the Physiocrats, was also influenced by Locke (Wilson 1972); and the Physiocrats contributed a number of selections to his *Encyclopédie*.

Diderot accorded a central place in his thought and in the *Encyclopédie* to the category 'art.' This referred to a broad range of activities, covering all human skills and industries. Art meant orderliness and rule-governed behavior but not the inspiration of genius (Sewell 1980:22-3). It was also closely allied to science. Both represented the use of human reason. 'It is the industry of man applied to the productions of nature either for his needs, or for his luxury, or for his amusement, or for his curiosity, etc., that has given birth to the Sciences and to the Arts' (Diderot 1751:714). Art was not, however, equivalent to science. For Diderot, if a good was made, then the rules by which it was fabricated were art; if the object was but studied, the techniques pertained to science. We might understand this as a distinction between applied and abstract science (Wilson 1972:110).

Diderot paid special attention to the mechanical arts, not all art, for a statement about these could best convey his views about human capacities (Sewell 1980:66). He meant by the mechanical arts, however, precisely what Quesnay meant by artisanship.[4] Art or artisanship was reasoned activity, performed to achieve specific objectives. The emphasis was less upon the end product than on the fact that behavior was organized to accomplish a material goal. The mechanical arts represented an orderly process.

> The purpose of all *art* in general, or of all systems of instruments and of rules leading to a similar end, is to imprint certain determined forms on a base given by nature. (Diderot 1751:714)

The satisfaction offered by an object did not lie solely in its physical consumption or accumulation but also in the contemplation of its production. The form of commodities represented reasoned activity, for it was this which raised them to the point of utility.

Diderot also specified the human faculties which he thought were involved in artisanship:

> In the mechanical arts . . . the power of man is reduced to bringing together [*rapprocher*] or to separating [*éloigner*] natural substances. Men can do all or nothing, according to whether this drawing together [*rapprocher*] or that separating [*éloigner*] is or is not possible. (Diderot 1751:714)

The similarity to Quesnay and Locke is evident. For Diderot, applied reason in the mechanical arts combined and separated but did not create; and this is exactly how Quesnay viewed the work of the artisans, and Locke defined complex ideas. Diderot's construction of artisanship fitted the Physiocratic model.

Clearly, Diderot's assertion that artisans provided form was liberating and exhilarating; but form itself has no meaning. Was artisanship indicative of a human capacity to construct a world of significance? According to the modern structuralist perspective, form is imposed on a large range of possibilities; however, in Diderot's view the human freedom to construct was bounded, for the material order was given. Diderot expressed an humility about the potential of the mechanical arts precisely because the possibilities nature offered were limited. 'Man is no more than the minister (*la ministre*) or interpreter of nature' (Diderot 1751:714). The goal was to produce by discovering the natural order which humans could then arrange and compose (Sewell 1980:71). The creative source of order lay outside society, in nature. Diderot's view, like that of the Physiocrats, presupposed a natural law perspective.

The forms produced by artisans were the product of human reason operating upon orderly nature, and the capacity to reason was itself part of nature. But if form was pre-existent, humans nevertheless had to discover it. Even if they did not create shape, it was not directly presented to them. Ample room existed for improvement – which was one theme of Enlightenment thought.

Artisanship was consequently an active but not a productive endeavor, as it was constrained to operate upon the given. Physiocracy was not without a view of what we label 'rationality,' but this rationality was encompassed within a broader construction. The complete Physiocratic model employed a four-part analogy, only one side of which featured combinatorial logic. Objects conveyed information about reason and riches, artisanship and agriculture. This construction does sound modern, but it is also distant from us. For example, the duality within the Physiocratic model was to be doubly opposed by Marx. The creative power behind substances and forms was to be shifted from the Deity and nature to humans. Only by standing the Physiocrats on their heads can goods come to symbolize socially formed labor, not an abstract reason nor a dehumanized natural riches.

The Physiocrats in a comparative context

By examining the Physiocrats after Ricardo I have intentionally disrupted an historical sequence, for it seems to me that the Physiocrats take us a step closer to exotic models. Certainly, the Physiocrats and Ricardo are similar in their emphasis upon material circulation, upon the passivity of labor, and upon the determining role of agriculture and nature. Like the early Ricardo, the Physiocrats were concerned less with growth and accumulation than with the proper management of the economy. But there are also significant differences. Terms such as 'regulation' are not found in the Physiocratic discourse. No single feature characterizes all economic practices; artisanship is formed in one image, agriculture in another. More generally, the Physiocratic model is woven together not by derivation but by conjoining three separate metaphors: circulation, reproduction, and sensation versus operation. Their point of overlap provides the foundation for the economy and society.

In the next chapters I shall examine several exotic models in which emphasis is also placed upon nature as opposed to the live human laborer. But there are some large differences between Physiocracy and the nonWestern models. In Physiocracy the economy is modeled after the human body, and the environment is an intentionless physical world whose continuing inner structure is unaffected by social agency. The ultimate force, the Deity, is a quiet agent. With the Physiocrats we encounter a mechanistic perspective in which material objects have essential features apart from humans. The natural order expresses nothing other than its own laws, which are independent of humankind. By contrast, in the exotic models nature is constituted rather through social metaphors. Material objects and economic practices come to represent social relationships in a way quite different from the Western pattern.

For the Physiocrats, economic morality consists in conforming to natural laws; as with Ricardo, it is a moral duty and a necessary act for the social world to bend to the natural order. In the exotic cases, however, economic morality consists in conforming to the social order. The Physiocrats, after all, constructed their model within a post-Newtonian world. They did not fully extend causal explanations to society, but causal laws were regarded as facts of nature to which humans had to adapt. In this respect their model resembles that of later economists. By contrast, the exotic models are mostly situated within a nonNewtonian world, and in them the environment is frequently constituted through noncausal or intentional modes of agency.

Notes

1 I am indebted to William Sewell and Stephen Holmes for advice and comments on this chapter.

2 Two general sources on Physiocracy are the recent Fox-Genovese (1976) and the standard Weulersse (1910,1931). For one view concerning metaphysics and Physiocracy, see Robinson (1964), and Robinson and Eatwell (1973:9-10). For an empiricist-inductionist and materialist-deductionist explanation of Physiocratic theory, see Meek (1963,1968). Eagly (1969) provides an analysis of Physiocracy in terms of capital theory, while Eltis gives 'a modern reconstruction' (1975:169) of Quesnay's *Tableau*.

3 Lüthy argues:

> The title of his [Quesnay's] best-known medical work, *L'Essai physique sur l'économie animale*, is there to remind us of the exceedingly broad character of the term 'economy,' which embraces all the functions of a living organism. (1970:165)

To this he adds:

> Scholars have often tried to establish analogies between Quesnay's economic doctrine and his views on medicine, and especially between his *Tableau* and the system of the circulation of the blood. But the relation between them is deeper than a mere analogy. Physiocracy . . . was the last powerful manifestation of the 'organic' and 'total' medieval view of society. (1970:166) [159]

4 Sewell cites a pamphlet (*What is the Third Estate?*) by the Abbé Sieyés which was highly influential in the political discussion of 1789. This was a new conception of the social order much of which fits the Physiocratic model.

> For Sieyès, the essential activity of the nation was the transformation of natural substances into useful goods . . . [He] established production as the central activity of the nation. . . . The source of order was not spirit but nature, and the categories of citizens proceeded outward from the productions of nature to personal services. (Sewell 1980:80-1) [160]

Bibliography

ALBAUM, M. 1955. 'The moral defenses of the Physiocrats' laissez-faire.' *Journal of the History of Ideas*, 16:179–97.

DIDEROT, D. 1751. 'Art.' *Encyclopédie, ou Dictionnaire Raisonné des Sciences, des Arts et des Métiers*, ed. Diderot and D'Alembert, 1:713-17. Paris: Briasson, David, Le Breton, Durand.

DUMONT, L. 1977. *From Mandeville to Marx: the Genesis and Triumph of Economic Ideology*. Chicago: University of Chicago Press.

EAGLY, R. V. 1969. 'A Physiocratic model of dynamic equilibrium.' *Journal of Political Economy*, 77:66-84.

FOX-GENOVESE, E. 1976. *The Origins of Physiocracy*. Ithaca, New York: Cornell University Press.

HARLAN, J. R. 1975. *Crops and Man*. Madison, Wisconsin: American Society of Agronomy.

HARLAN, J. R. 1976. 'The plants and animals that nourish man.' *Scientific American*, 235:88-105.

LÉVI-STRAUSS, C. 1963. *Structural Anthropology*, trans. C. Jacobson and B. Schoepf. New York: Basic Books.

LOCKE, J. 1823 [1690]. *The Works of John Locke*, 5. London: J. Johnson.

LOCKE, J. 1975 [1690]. *An Essay Concerning Human Understanding*, ed. P. H. Nidditch. Oxford: Clarendon Press.

MARX, K. 1963 [1905-10]. *Theories of Surplus-Value*, Part I. Moscow: Progress Publishers.

MARX, K. 1967 [1867]. *Capital*, I, trans. S. Moore and E. Aveling. New York: International Publishers.

MARX, K. 1968 [1905-10]. *Theories of Surplus-Value*, Part II. Moscow: Progress Publishers.

MEEK, R. L. 1963. *The Economics of Physiocracy: Essays and Translations*. Cambridge, Mass.: Harvard University Press.

MEEK, R. L. 1968. 'Ideas, events and environment: the case of the French Physiocrats.' *Ideology and Economic Theory*, ed. R. V. Eagly: 44-64. Detroit: Wayne State University Press.

MEEK, R. L. 1973. *Precursors of Adam Smith*. London: Dent.

MIRABEAU, MARQUIS de and QUESNAY, F. 1973 [1763]. *Precursors of Adam Smith*, ed. R. L. Meek: 104-13. London: Dent.

NEILL, T. P. 1948. 'Quesnay and Physiocracy.' *Journal of the History of Ideas*, 9:153-73.

NEILL, T. P. 1949. 'The Physiocrats' concept of economics.' *Quarterly Journal of Economics*, 63:532-53.

QUESNAY, F. 1963a [1766]. 'Dialogue on the work of artisans.' *The Economics of Physiocracy*, ed. R. L. Meek: 203–30. Cambridge, Mass.: Harvard University Press.

QUESNAY, F. 1963b [1765]. 'Natural right.' *The Economics of Physiocracy*, ed. R. L. Meek: 43-56. Cambridge, Mass.: Harvard University Press.

QUESNAY, F. 1972 [1758-9]. *Tableau Économique*, trans. and ed. M. Kucynski and R. L. Meek. London: Macmillan.

RICARDO, D. 1951-2. *The Works and Correspondence of David Ricardo*, ed. P. Sraffa, vols I,III,IV,VI. Cambridge: Cambridge University Press.

ROBINSON, J. 1964. *Economic Philosophy*. New York: Doubleday.

ROBINSON, J. and EATWELL, J. 1973. *An Introduction to Modern Economics*. London: McGraw-Hill.

SAMUELSON, P. 1973. *Economics*, 9th edn. New York: McGraw-Hill.

SCHUMPETER, J. 1954. *History of Economic Analysis*. New York: Oxford University Press.

SEWELL, W. H. 1980. *Work and Revolution in France: the Language of Labor from the Old Regime to 1848*. Cambridge: Cambridge University Press.

TURGOT, A. R. J. 1898 [1770]. *Reflections on the Formation and the Distribution of Riches*. New York: Macmillan & Co.

WEULERSSE, G. 1910. *Le Mouvement Physiocratique de 1756 à 1770*, 2 vols. Paris: Félix Alcan.

WILSON, A. M. 1972. *Diderot*. New York: Oxford University Press.

[9]
THE HOUSE

Both the house and the corporation are found in the countryside, but from the most distant and marginal zones to the edges of fertile plains near towns the house predominates. The arresting feature of the house is that its activities are modeled on the layout of the dwelling itself.

Rural houses take many forms. Some are constructed of sticks and thatch, others of adobe, wattle and daub (*bajareque*), tapia, or brick and cement. Shapes also vary; simple ones with a room or two may have a veranda on one or all sides, while more elaborate houses, with four sides and an internal patio, recall the Roman villa. Nearly every material activity can be witnessed inside and around a dwelling: sorting seeds and sharpening knives; drying a harvest of tobacco or coffee; eating, conversing, and tending children. A small garden usually surrounds the house, and frequently one of the major agricultural plots is located nearby. Houses may contain single individuals, married pairs, nuclear families, or larger agglomerations of kin and nonkin. Whatever its size or physical shape, the house itself provides a plan for the economic group.

The principal features of the house model can be quickly summarized. A rural economic group is known as the "house" (*la casa*). It has a "base" (*una base*) or "foundation" (*un fundamento*), which is its wealth. It also has "doors" (*puertas*), as is signaled by the expressions "from the doors inward" (*de puertas para adentro*) and "from the doors outward" (*de puertas para afuera*). The people use shorthands to talk about material transactions of the group: goods are produced by the house and kept "inside" (*de adentro*), pass "from inside to outside" (*de adentro por afuera*), and come "from outside to inside" (*de afuera por adentro*). Any shift of the house's base through the doors, from inside to outside or outside to inside, is termed a "movement" (*un movimiento*), just as people themselves are said to move through the doors.

A house has two projects. Its first is to "maintain" (*mantener*), "sustain" (*sostener*), "support" (*soportar*), or "keep" (*guardar*) itself.

These frequently used words are themselves employed in two contexts, each evoking or implying the other. The physical aspects of a house must be "maintained," and the members of the house must be "kept" or "sustained" with food. "We work to support ourselves," said a man in Nariño.

> We need foods. They come first, but support includes clothes; otherwise you are like an animal. These are the house expenditures.

Normally, when people speak of "maintaining a house" the physical image is taken to mean supporting the members with food, but this social application implies the need for keeping up the dwelling. The model works from the physical to the social to the physical, conjoining the two.

An elaboration of the house model is used when the group hires outside laborers. A house usually feeds its "outside" workers and is said to "support" them. But a special terminology is employed for one of the meals served late in the day: the repast is said to "buttress" (*apuntalar*) the hired workers, to "prop them up," just as a buttress on the outside of a building gives it extra strength. In the people's precise usage, the food is an "auxiliary support," limited in time and scope, given at that moment in the day when the strength to work is ebbing; and it is an "outside" support, being provided from without the worker's domestic group. The elaboration of the house figure playfully models the limits and purposes of the household obligation and practice.

The second project of a house is to "augment" or "increase" (*aumentar*) its base. The rural folk try to expand both the wealth of a house and its physical foundation. To accomplish these two goals people try "to keep" or "hold" (*guardar*) household products (*la base*) "inside the doors"; they practice "householding" and "housekeeping." The figure of a physical house is consistently and creatively used to model the parts and the project of the economic group.

A conversation: models and metaphors

In the house model a figure from the built world – with foundation, supports, and doors – is used to talk about and organize material practices. Between physical house and material processes there is no a priori connection, but through the model, physical houses are turned into economic centers, while economic units are realized as houses. The model is built around a metaphor.

The domestic metaphor in Colombia is, as we have suggested, a key one, for it has a central place in structuring material activities and helps shape other domains of discussion. For example, the expression about the doors of the house is used to express political control of information. The government voice that speaks "from the doors outward" provides information for public "consumption"; this is filtered news, though not necessarily false. The political voice that speaks "from the doors inward," however, offers "inside" information for private "consumption," as does an "in-house publication." In this "government-as-house" metaphor, the doors mark the edges of the controlling group and signal its ability to control the flow of information. The political expression is a projection of the "economy-as-house" metaphor. Thus, one figure (the physical house) is used in a metaphor (the domestic economy) that itself is applied within a new domain (the polity); information flow is modeled after wealth "movements," which are modeled after human movements through the doors of a house. By such projections models invade each other, and conversations become ever thicker over time. Within a culture, however, some figures seem to hold a persistently central place, and the "polity-as-house" example suggests something of the persuasive power that the "economy-as-house" metaphor still has in Colombia.

In the domestic metaphor itself the figure of a house is not fully exploited. The metaphor does not utilize the roof or walls, although the existence of both is implied by the expression about the "doors." A metaphor seldom, if ever, consists of a point-for-point mapping from domain to domain. It seizes upon certain characteristics of a figure, leaving others aside for later elaboration or oblivion. In discourse also, the house metaphor is not a totality. Only by the fiction of inscription or within an extended conversation does it appear as a whole. Normally, the metaphor is used in bits or is called forth by parts, the naming of a house feature serving in everyday conversation as a shorthand for the whole and for an economic function. The word "base" implies the physical house, the house economy, and the wealth of the group.

The rural folk, of course, do not speak of a domestic

metaphor, and what an outsider might term "figure" (the house as physical structure) and "application" (the house as economic organization) are mixed together. This is part of the model's persuasiveness. For example, according to the metaphor, land and crops are part of the foundation and fall within the doors of the house. But the people also say that one leaves the house to work on the land, that one has work outside the house, and that one brings the crops to the house for storage: "You bring from outside what you gather up from the land." In the one usage, the crops and land are inside the house; in the other the land is outdoors and the crops are brought from outside to inside. Clearly, the various parts of an economic "house" are not always held within the physical house, and certainly they are never kept underneath it as a foundation; conversely, an existent structure may contain people or things that are not part of its economic organization. But in conversation the two are intermixed and cause no confusion.

There is more to the several uses of the word "base." The people say that the base as wealth does not include the physical house itself. For example, a day laborer may possess a house on its foundation without having a base, and it is possible to have a base of wealth without having a dwelling. In such instances, the economic or "figurative" application of the term contradicts its "literal" or original use. According to some views on metaphor (Beardsley 1981; Henle 1981; Ricoeur 1977), when figurative use contradicts literal application a metaphor is in play, and this seems to be true of the case at hand. "Base" does and does not mean the physical underpinnings of a house, and it does and does not mean the undergirdings of an economy. Its use for the latter depends upon its use for the former yet denies it.

HOUSE CONNECTIONS

A house has two arenas of contact with the larger world, the land and other humans. New wealth moving into the house normally consists of agricultural produce or pastoral products. We initially thought that because land and cattle are part of the base, new crops and progeny must be "inside the doors," too; it seemed inconsistent to claim that they came from outside to inside. The rural folk explained, however, that crops and cattle (via pasture) depend for their growth on the earth's strength, which is never owned. The "giving," therefore, comes from "outside," and wealth "moves into the house" from agriculture or pastoralism. This wealth is then used up or expended, which diminishes the base.

The house's connection to the material world is marked by a gender difference. A woman is said to perform "domestic work," a man "material work." The construction fits the household way of getting things from the land and using them up inside. The male works principally in the fields, the female primarily in and around the house.

A household also engages in material exchanges with other humans outside the doors. Any movement of labor or goods into the house is termed an "entry" or "entrance" (*una entrada*) as well as a "gain," while a movement out is a "departure" (*una salida*). When a man trades labor with another, he says he is "gaining a peon" (*ganar un peón*), and when he works for someone else he speaks of "leaving to work" (*salir a trabajar*).

In transactions that involve a movement of the base, the people have different expectations for the earth and the market. With market transactions, they try to recover their initial position, not to make a gain. Market trade involves movements in which a material good leaves the house and is traded for money and then the money is used to purchase a different item, which reenters the doors. The aim of the movements, from inside to outside and outside to inside, is to "replace" (*reponer*) the base. Money is a means of transfer, and the house is engaged in what we term the base→money→base′ circuit.

The word "replace" is used similarly with animals. Sometimes an animal, such as a calf, is obtained to be raised for sale. When the animal is sold a young one may immediately be purchased. This is "replacing" the animal, meaning having what one started with a year before. Replacing the base, however, means being able to purchase a young animal plus the equivalent volume of food given to the old and its caretakers during the previous year. Anything that remains above replacement of the base is "an increase" (*un aumento*).

Replacing the base through trade is an uncertain process, for price changes are beyond the control of the rural folk. As one person voiced it, "You expend today and wait until tomorrow to see if you can replace it, and if it doesn't come, what then?" She continued, "Often you use up what is inside for outside without knowing what will happen – that is occurring now. To go forward, you have to have more inside for the future. But money cannot be replaced inside like the base."

In addition to moving the base through the doors to change it, processing of the base takes place inside the house. For this the terms "return," "maintain," "keep," and "hold" are used. After the harvest of a crop, one portion is set aside for "returning to" (*volver a*) seeding in the next year. This is not a replacement of the base, for the entire harvest is already part of it; rather, the earmarked volume (and its planting) allows the base to be "maintained." Similarly, within the house, the base may be shifted from one form to another to hold it better. For example, the foundation is "kept" by feeding maize to chickens or a hog. If the maize were sold to purchase animal feed, then the people would speak of "replacing" the base through market trade. Of course, maize physically leaves the house when it is fed to chickens and hogs or taken to the fields for seeding, but according to the model the crop does not "move through the doors." To distinguish this second way of shifting the base from the first, we label it base→base′. The two circuits are alike in that they begin and end with base, but the base→base′ circuit, as opposed to the base→money→base′ one, keeps processes within the house and does not require the use of money.[1]

When the doors are closed or allow entries only, the house is engaged in the base→base′ circuit and is self-supporting. In many respects, this is the project of the house. We were often told, "I am working to sustain the place" or "I am maintaining the food plate." A frequently used phrase was "I am working to live, to eat," and some said, "The land gives for living, for maintaining, nothing more." The people do not speak of goals or finishing points but of what they are doing or what "it is necessary to do" (*hay que hacer*). When a house has "increased" and accumulated sufficient wealth to maintain itself, its owner or someone else may finally say, "It is done" (*está hecho*), but this does not mean the work is finished, for continuing management and effort are always needed.

Goods that flow into a house from the land are used first for maintenance. We translate the frequently used verb, *gastar* as "expending," "using," or "using up." An "expenditure" [*un gasto*], said one person, "is all that you consume." One uses up one's work in the fields, uses up health and energy in work, and uses up food to restore the body's strength. (Ultimately, all are expenditures of force.) Money too is "used up," although a money use, unlike a material use, is a "cost" (*un costo*). The people also distinguish the general use of the word "expenditure" from its house application by employing the lexical modifier "of the house" (*de la casa*) for the material expenditures that a house makes to support its members and activities. When the goods or useful things (*utilidades*) that come to the house are directed to self-maintenance, they are "expenditures of the house" or "uses from the doors inward." As one woman said, "One uses it up for the house, but in order to avoid buying."

The rural folk are normally thrifty with goods, but sometimes the base is used without being replaced. One morning in northern Boyacá a woman who was shelling maize for animals in the house patio explained that two weeks previously she and her husband had purchased a dozen small chickens to "replace" grown ones that had been sold. Along with the chicks she had purchased some pigeons, for she liked to watch them, and they were being fed with maize, too. The pigeons, like the chickens, were an "expenditure of the house," but unlike the chicks they were a "luxury," as they ate but were not for consumption or sale. They did not "return" the base.

A part of the base is also lost through waste. Spoiled food, disposed of beyond the walls of the house, is said to be "lost to use" or "thrown away" (*echado a perder*). Once or twice in its lifetime, however, a house may lavishly use its resources by entertaining others or celebrating the passage rites of a member; this is known as "throwing the house out the window" (*echar la casa por la ventana*). Rather than moving part of its base through the doors in an orderly trade, the house throws its entirety "inside out" for public display.

The flow of goods in the base→base′ circuit may quickly turn negative, for a house uses up base to undertake agriculture; and if the earth does not return the expenditures, more goes out the doors than comes in. The balance is always precarious. But with declining productivity of the soil, ever more fertilizer must be used, and the money for this is gained by selling something from inside. Say the people, one can no longer "keep the base inside the doors."

Labor patterns fit these constructions in various ways. The rural folk say that the base is expended to "support work" (*mantener el trabajo*), and the work is intended to yield more base. Members of the household, who are supported by its expenditures and work for it, "help" the group, for they "help the earth" to produce. Help is performed "inside the doors." For example, "children help but do not collect from one. They are inside help." But help is not performed exclusively by house members, for hired laborers are also used. If outside laborers are paid with cash already held inside the house, both their cash cost and their labor are "inside the doors." If the money is borrowed, however, their cost is "outside the doors" while their labor is "inside help." Outside workers also may be fed during the day, which is a "house expenditure" from "inside the doors," unless the food has had to be bought with borrowed money, which makes it "from the outside."

Thus, the two movements of the base, toward the earth (base→base′) and toward the market (base→money→base′), are alike as ways of maintaining the house but also different, for market trade requires that parts of the base leave house control before returning.

Linked to this difference in use of the base is a distinction made between crops "for eating" (*para comer* or *para consumir*) and crops "for sale" (*para vender*). The distinction applies to the uses of a harvest; but it also sorts different crop types. Some crops, such as herbs, fruits, and yucca, rarely leave the house for the market; these are raised for eating inside the doors. Crops such as maize and potatoes are raised principally for eating, but portions may be for sale. Still other crops, such as sugarcane, are raised almost entirely for sale; however, when sugarcane is locally refined into the brown sugar cake known as *panela*, a portion of the harvest may return to its owner in processed form. Finally, tobacco, onions, and coffee are grown only for sale; they are raised inside the house but move through the doors for money. The rural folk note that they do not control the price of a harvest for sale: "In tobacco the campesino serves to cultivate it [*beneficiarlo*] but he does not put the price on it." With respect to raising a new and more costly variety of tobacco, one person said:

> Where does this money come from? Where does one get the money to raise it? Blond tobacco doesn't even give back the base that has left the house. With tobacco you cannot replace what you have used up.

The opposition between "for eating" and "for sale," thus, is an elaboration upon the distinction between "returning to" and "replacing" the base. It has to do with diverging movements and uses of crops relative to the house, with varying control over them, and with varying power to determine the size of their returns.

Other expressions also serve to place the house within the market world. In most rural towns there is a weekly market, and the people talk about going to market "every week" (*cada ocho días*) or "every two weeks" (*cada quince días*). The marketplace itself is situated in the town plaza, which is usually near the church and government offices. The rural folk speak of the market by its location, "the plaza," and generally any market activity, including purchasing at everyday stores, is known by the shorthand "going to the plaza." The market is a place rather than a conceptual entity, with the circumscribed town locale forming an opposition to the bounded house in the "countryside" (*el campo*).

The people say of an active market that it has much "movement," therby modeling it as a place where the "inside" wealth of many houses is traded. But they also distinguish between the aims of a house in the countryside and those of a "business" (*un negocio*) in the market. In English, "business" comes from "busy-ness," and in Spanish "*negocio*" comes from *negar ocio* or "negating inaction." This is marketplace activity, the "busy-ness" consisting in buying and selling and buying again. For the people, a *negociante* is a trader or "intermediary" (*intermediario*), who makes purchases and sales to gain money. We term this set of transactions the "money→base→money′" circuit. It is quite different from the house one. As one person explained, "The land gives for sustaining oneself, but the market does not give useful things." A harvest is sold to purchase a needed item, not for profit.

This difference between market and house activity is linked to an opposition between "making savings" (*hacer economías*) and "making money" (*hacer plata*). Use of the base→base′ circuit is closely tied to "making savings." As the people say, if nothing goes out the doors, one is "making savings" or "being thrifty." They add that "making savings" means replenishing or "returning" something within the house itself. A principal example is self-sufficient agriculture, for if a house's foodstuffs come directly from its base, and the holdings are "returned" through agriculture, then the provisioning process is contained "within the doors" and money is saved. In contrast, "making money," the intent of a business, is accomplished through trade. The opposition is between two projects and two circuits of exchange. One of them starts and ends with money in order to have an enlarged sum; this is "making money," or money→base→money′. The other begins with material holdings and their uses in order to maintain and augment them within the house; this is "making savings," or base→base′.

But the two circuits are intermixed, because trade to replace the base involves the use of cash, the base→money→base′ circuit. For the people, money always comes "from the doors outward," while what is traded for it comes "from the doors inward." Trade, interlinking the house and business, is necessary to secure salt and clothes; but a house has no assurance of being able to replace its holdings once it is engaged in the market. Today, a house is even less able than before to provide itself with the materials needed for agriculture; yet purchasing inputs to transform them and sell the product (money→base→base′→

money′) is precisely what the rural household is unable to do. The land available for farming is either marginal or fully "off-the-margin," and when it occasionally does become profitable (often through the initial colonizing activities of the rural folk) the house is usually squeezed off it by market actors (LeGrand 1986). The house cannot persist as a pure market participant but is increasingly forced to attempt to do so, with the result that it must lower its consumption or raise its work input. As one person observed, "There is no margin here."

Conversations: circuits, the house, and the corporation

The people's distinctions between "from the doors inward" and "from the doors outward," the house and business, crops "for eating" and crops "for sale," the house and the plaza, and "making savings" and "making money" find corresponding voices in the texts of economists. For example, in the first volume of *Capital* (1967[1867]), Marx makes analytical use of the difference between two exchange cycles that he labels the "commodity→money→commodity" circuit and the "money→commodity→money′" circuit. The first involves the circulation of commodities in which a sale is made in order to buy, money serving only as a medium of exchange. His examples are drawn primarily from the world of the peasant, who is said to enter the market with a commodity, such as a harvest, which he exchanges for money that is then converted to a different commodity, such as clothing. For Marx, the peasant producer engages in market exchange to fulfill limited material goals. Transactions come to an end with their accomplishment. In contrast, the second circuit is typical of the capitalist producer. The profit maker exchanges money for a commodity that is held or transformed and then sold for more money. The capitalist starts with money in order to expand it; purchase is made with the end of sale. The commodity bought can be a good that is then sold, as in mercantile capitalism, or a raw material (including labor) that is transformed into something else, as in industrial capitalism. The money→commodity→money′ circuit never reaches a conclusion, for each end point is a new beginning. The money circuit is the dialectical completion of the commodity circuit. One has to do with exchange that uses goods, the other with uses of goods in relation to exchange.

Marx's discussion is in fact an elaboration of earlier writings by David Ricardo, Adam Smith, and the Physiocrats. In the *Wealth of Nations* (1976[1776]), for example, Smith distinguished between "value in use" and "value in exchange," and this was taken over by Ricardo (1951[1817]). John Stuart Mill, who in some respects carried on the Ricardian tradition, also discussed the distinction (1929[1848]:437), but after his summary volume it fell by the wayside with the marginalist revolution and the rise of neoclassical economics. The analytical division between use, value, and exchange has remained a central theme only in Marxist economics.

But this capsule summary of the textual history of use and exchange foreshortens the conversation. Two thousand years before Smith, Aristotle had drawn an opposition between the oeconomic and the chrematistic, and it is this distinction that profoundly influenced the subsequent textual conversation from Roman writers through Aquinas and the Scholastics right up to the early modern theorists. The opposition is also relevant to rural Colombia today. In the *Politics* (1946), Aristotle developed the distinction by pointing out that a shoe has two "uses," one "proper" to it, the other not; a shoe can be worn by its owner or it can be exchanged for something else. The first use leads to the "acquisition" of shoes solely for the satisfaction of limited needs, the second to "acquisition" itself as a boundless goal. Aristotle saw "exchange for use" as a function or feature of householding while "exchange for gain" was the goal of retail trade. But the context of his discussion is important. Aristotle was examining the relation between the domestic economy and the market, and his discussion of use and exchange is situated within a consideration of the household as a unit in "political society." He was not writing about capitalism, the market, or the economy itself. Marx (1967[1867]:152), while using Aristotle's distinction, situated his discussion differently. He located both exchange for use and exchange for gain within capitalism and omitted the institutional connection that Aristotle drew between the house economy and exchange for use. Marx, concerned with the world of capitalism, left off a discussion of householding as an economic process, replacing the household group with "the peasant" as actor or participant in the capitalist and business-dominated market.

This is a long and complicated conversation with many mediating voices, both written and verbal. Marx, certainly versed in Aristotle and other early writings, shifted the conversation for his purposes. These changes aside, we surmise that he and his conversational predecessors were influenced by distinctions made by European folk and that it would have made little sense for them to deploy these distinctions unless they had first been voiced in social life. As seen from Colombia, for example, Marx appropriated part of the domestic model in order to construct a critical view of capitalism: his critique – from notions about the force of labor to the importance of exchanging for use versus exchanging for gain – was influenced by the world of the peasant house. Yet this was not simply a one-way movement from practice to text, for the living culture of European folk had been inscribed in a different form two thousand years earlier by Aristotle, and his inscriptions had their persuasive effect on succeeding practices and conversations as they did on Marx. There has been a continual oscillation of models from practice to inscription to practice. Our suggestion is that the house is a folk institution of long standing and for this reason has been a source of ideas for inscription ever since Aristotle. Furthermore, as a European institution, the house model early on became a component of Latin American life, where it has since developed and changed. Colombian rural life and the inscriptions of European theorists are part of the same conversation.

But if the similarities with Marx's views help illuminate the campesinos' conversation, the differences are illustrative, too. For Marx the word "commodity," even when used in the context of the commodity→money→commodity circuit, implies something made for sale and gain. This is the more evident when the Spanish term for "commodity" is used, for *la mercancia* is derived from *mercado*, "market." In Marx the commodity→money→commodity circuit starts and ends with commercial or market items. By contrast, the Colombian rural folk speak of getting needed "provisions" (*las provisiones*) and of trading the base or foundation, not of securing market "commodities." The rural model of exchange takes the perspective of – as Aristotle suggested – the house and not the market. From the Colombian folk perspective, Marx's discussion subsumes the house project within the market model. Also, the rural people model two circuits involving the house. One takes place solely within it: this is the notion of returning to seeding (base→base′). The second, in which base materials move from house to market and back, is replacing the base (base→money→base′).

This difference between the folk and economists' models returns us to the general, institutional distinction between means of grouping: the house and the corporation. Our view is that European history has witnessed a broad movement from a house to a corporate economy. This movement has not been without reversals, and many economic formations, such as slavery, feudalism, and mercantile society, have served as the larger matrix for the domestic economy. But the house has persisted throughout, counterposed in later history to the corporation (Bloch 1966; Braudel 1986; Duby 1968, 1974; Postan 1972). The initial written division between householding and gain, adumbrated by Aristotle, was continued by a variety of Roman authors, such as Cato (1933), and, as Tribe (1978) has shown, found its way into the early texts on "the economy." At times, the "domestic economy" meant the household itself, and at other periods the house model was applied to the state, the entire nation being seen as a self-sufficient household. From the fourteenth century onwards, the corporate mode of organization developed and expanded, but the transition from the one to the other was not a simple function of time's arrow. Historians, for example, have been discovering that self-sufficient economies existed on the "frontiers" of North American economy and society during the nineteenth century (Clark 1979; Faragher 1986; Hahn and Prude 1985; Merrill 1977; Pruitt 1984); these house economies developed or were reproduced "after" the historical rise of the corporation and yet before its "arrival" in an area. Everything depends upon the market and the way in which the two means of grouping are linked to exchange.

A corporation – like a house – must always provide for

its necessary expenses, funding them perhaps from a past accumulation. But a corporation is not self-reproducing in a material sense, for it exchanges part of its product to secure its necessary means; and it operates on the assumption that sales, by more than covering purchases, will generate a profit. The corporation is surrounded on its input and output sides by buying and selling, or market exchange. In addition, corporate profit is a social phenomenon in that it is partly distributed to those who own the corporation as property; it cannot be fully kept "inside the doors." The balance sheet of a corporation makes public its ties with others, as assets and liabilities. These are the current yet enduring exchanges it maintains on the input and output sides. In an older but felicitous terminology, assets and liabilities were known in English as active debts and passive debts, while in contemporary Spanish they are *los activos* and *los pasivos* – apt expressions because they recall both Mauss's (1954 [1925]) well-known argument that debts of exchange link humans and groups and Leach's (1954) claim that social structure is a system of lasting debts. The balance sheet of a corporation – its "double-entry bookkeeping" – displays these debts by focusing on their momentary conjunction within the corporation itself. The market participant is enmeshed in persisting exchanges, developed in the past and projected into the future, in which buying is a means for selling. A breakdown of trust with loss of confidence in the future undermines this network of ties, yielding business cycles of the Keynesian and Kondratieff variety. More generally, if debts "make" the market world, their liquidation unmakes ties and produces autarky. The house, unlike the corporation, has no assets and liabilities, no enduring relationships. It does not need debts to "make it work." Quite the reverse; if the house did exchange or buy in order to sell, it would undermine its project of survival. The house is not susceptible to economic cycles, for it represents a distancing from the economic intentions of others, although it is vulnerable to ecological changes. A house can enter the market to sell some of its product if this represents the amount above what is needed for reproduction, for then changing market prices have no effect on the perpetuation of the unit, determining only the volume realized in trade. In the market context, the house takes its place in opposition and relation to the corporation.

But the interconnection of these two models is always complex. The house has occurred separately and before the corporation; and it has been prompted by the market economy, on the edges and beyond the border of profit. In European history there has been a dialectical tension (in both inscriptions and practice) between the "body" model and the "house" model. Clearly, in market societies the house model has been shrinking in scope, particularly in recent years. Yet we still use much of its lexicon: "housekeeping," "householding," "maintaining a house," "housewife," and even "kept woman"! The recipes of domestic economy, including ways to be thrifty and the art of home baking, that used to be so avidly taught in land-grant universities, are the remnants of this once vibrant way of life. In the United States, "fast foods" sold by corporations and bought in the market have replaced the slow foods that used to be prepared in pots on the stove, but the house economy is still alive in many parts of Latin America today.

REFERENCES

Aristotle. 1926. *The Nicomachean Ethics*, trans. H. Rackham. London: Heinemann.
1946. *The Politics*, trans. Ernest Barker. London: Oxford University Press.
Beardsley, Monroe C. 1981. "The Metaphorical Twist," *Philosophical Perspectives on Metaphor*, ed. Mark Johnson, pp. 105–22. Minneapolis: University of Minnesota Press.
Bloch, Mark. 1966. *French Rural History*. Berkeley: University of California Press.

Braudel, Fernand. 1986. *The Wheels of Commerce*, trans. Siân Reynolds. New York: Harper and Row.

Cato. 1933. *On Farming*, trans. Ernest Brehaut. New York: Columbia University Press.

Clark, Christopher. 1979. "Household Economy, Market Exchange, and the Rise of Capitalism in the Connecticut Valley, 1800–1860," *Journal of Social History*, vol. 13, pp. 169–89.

Duby, Georges. 1968. *Rural Economy and Country Life in the Medieval West*, trans. Cynthia Postan. Columbia: University of South Carolina Press.

1974. *The Early Growth of the European Economy*, trans. Howard B. Clarke. Ithaca, N.Y.: Cornell University Press.

Faragher, John Mack. 1986. *Sugar Creek: Life on the Illinois Prairie*. New Haven: Yale University Press.

Hahn, Steven, and Jonathan Prude. (eds.) 1985. *The Countryside in the Age of Capitalist Transformation*. Chapel Hill, N.C.: University of North Carolina Press.

Henle, Paul. 1981. "Metaphor," *Philosophical Perspectives on Metaphor*, ed. Mark Johnson, pp. 83–104. Minneapolis: University of Minnesota Press.

Leach, Edmund. 1954. *Political Systems of Highland Burma*. London: G. Bell.

LeGrand, Catherine. 1986. *Frontier Expansion and Peasant Protest in Colombia, 1850–1936*. Albuquerque, N. Mex.: University of New Mexico Press.

Marx, Karl. 1963. (1905–10). *Theories of Surplus Value*, vol. I. Moscow: Progress Publishers.

1967 (1867). *Capital*, vol. I, trans. S. Moore and E. Aveling. New York: International Publishers.

Mauss, Marcel. 1954 (1925). *The Gift*, trans. Ian Cunnison. London: Cohen and West.

Merrill, Michael. 1977. "Cash is Good to Eat: Self-Sufficiency and Exchange in the Rural Economy of the United States," *Radical History Review*, vol. 4, pp. 42–71.

Mill, John Stuart. 1929 (1848). *Principles of Political Economy*, ed. W. J. Ashley. London: Longmans, Green.

Postan, M.M. 1972. *The Medieval Economy and Society*. Harmondsworth: Penguin Books.

Pruitt, Bettye Hobbs. 1984. "Self-Sufficiency and the Agricultural Economy of Eighteenth-Century Massachusetts," *The William and Mary Quarterly*, vol. 41, pp. 333–64.

Ricardo, David. 1951 (1815). *The Works and Correspondence of David Ricardo*, vol. IV, ed. P. Sraffa. Cambridge: Cambridge University Press.

1951 (1817). *On the Principles of Political Economy and Taxation*, ed. P. Sraffa. Cambridge: Cambridge University Press.

Ricoeur, Paul. 1977. *The Rule of Metaphor*, trans. R. Czerny. Toronto: University of Toronto Press.

Smith, T. Lynn. 1967. *Colombia: Social Structure and the Process of Development*. Gainesville, Fla.: University of Florida Press.

Tribe, Keith. 1978. *Land, Labour and Economic Discourse*. London: Routledge and Kegan Paul.

CURRENT ANTHROPOLOGY Volume 33, Number 1, February 1992

Beyond "The Original Affluent Society"

A Culturalist Reformulation[1]

by Nurit Bird-David

This paper examines Marshall Sahlins's "Original Affluent Society" in relation to recent developments in modern hunter-gatherer studies and reveals a theoretical confusion of ecological and cultural perspectives within it which has hitherto been overlooked. Drawing comparatively on three case studies—the Nayaka of South India, the Batek of Malaysia, and the Mbuti of Zaire—it then reformulates Sahlins's argument using the culturalist method of economic analysis. At the same time it demonstrates the explanatory and analytical dimensions of this new method.

NURIT BIRD-DAVID is Lecturer in Social Anthropology at Tel Aviv University, Tel Aviv, Israel. Born in 1951, she was educated at Hebrew University of Jerusalem (B.A., 1974) and at Cambridge University (Ph.D., 1983). She has been Research Fellow of New-Hall and Smutz Visiting Fellow at Cambridge. Her research interests are hunter-gatherer studies and economic anthropology. She has published "The Giving Environment: Another Perspective on the Economic System of Gatherer-Hunters" (CURRENT ANTHROPOLOGY 31:189–96); "Hunter-Gatherers and Other People," in *Hunters and Gatherers*, vol. 1, edited by T. Ingold, D. Riches, and J. Woodburn (Oxford: Berg, 1988); "The Kurumbas of the Nilgiris: An Ethnographic Myth?" (*Modern Asian Studies* 21:173–89); and "Wage-Gatherings: Socio-economic Change and the Case of the Naiken of South India," in *Rural South Asia: Linkages, Change, and Development*, edited by P. Robb (Salem, N.H.: Merrimack Publishers Circle, 1983). The present article was submitted in final form 5 VII 91.

The idea of "the original affluent society" was first presented during the 1966 "Man the Hunter" conference, which laid the foundations for the anthropological study of modern hunter-gatherers. The participants—social anthropologists, archaeologists, human biologists, ecologists, and demographers—were struck by the brief contribution of Marshall Sahlins, a non-specialist invited discussant, in response to their papers (Sahlins 1968*a*). Sahlins later produced a much longer essay on the idea for *Les temps modernes* (1968*b*), and this became the basis for the first chapter of his *Stone Age Economics* (1972). The book was a highly controversial text on tribal societies, and the essay itself—which proposed, essentially, that the hunting-and-gathering way of life provided unparalleled affluence for its followers—became notorious both inside and outside anthropology. It was hotly debated by scholars from a broad spectrum of disciplines that shared an interest in the evolution of human society. It has since become the representative text on hunter-gatherers in introductory courses (see, e.g., Cole 1988) and appears on the reading lists of most anthropology departments. Despite their initial enthusiasm, however, up to the 1980s specialists gave Sahlins's essay little serious or direct attention. It was rarely challenged or further explored through empirical research. It is fair to say, in fact, that in their research—as opposed to their teaching—many anthropologists made an effort to ignore it.

The explanation for the fate of "The Original Affluent Society" during this period is complex. The general interest in it no doubt reflected our symbolic and ideological needs and our (Western) construction of the prehistoric past. Furthermore, the essay was timely in dispelling certain inadequate conceptions of "primitive" economic life and disclosing anthropologists' ethnocentric biases. Beyond this, it marked the inception of modern hunter-gatherer research and constituted certification of its legitimacy. Above all, most specialists, and many other scholars as well, recognized, if only intuitively, that Sahlins "had a point." We sensed that he had touched on something essential to the hunting-and-gathering way of life, although—and this is the problem—we did not know quite what it was.

The ambivalence of specialists had to do with gaps between data and conclusions. Intended to provoke as well as to document, the essay soared beyond conventional scientific discourse, appealing directly to Western fantasies about work, happiness, and freedom. It offered, as a result, a peculiar synthesis of theory and data, insight and banality, breadth of view and gimmicky wit, all so craftily blended together as to make it extraordinarily resistant to analysis. Had specialists attempted to engage with Sahlins's essay in the years immediately following its publication, they would have encountered three problems in particular.

First, despite the paucity of reliable data, Sahlins drew quantitative and pseudo-quantitative conclusions concerning hunter-gatherers' work ("a mean of three to five hours per adult worker per day in food production" [1972:34]) and leisure ("a greater amount of sleep in the day time per capita than in any other condition of society" [p. 14]). In addition to the anecdotal observations—perceptive in their own terms—of explorers and missionaries he relied upon three professional studies. Two of these had been undertaken in the course of a 1948 American-Australian expedition in Arnhem Land by McCarthy and McArthur (1960)—the first a nutritionist, the second an anthropologist. The third, a remarkable

1. My thanks go to Barbara Bodenhorn, Ernest Gellner, Keith Hart, Caroline Humphrey, Tim Ingold, Marilyn Strathern, and James Woodburn for comments on the early version of the paper and to Alan Barnard, Harvey Feit, Stephen Gudeman, and Richard Lee for their support of the earlier paper in which I began to explore these ideas.

and pioneering work on the Dobe !Kung by Lee (1968, 1969), was influenced as much by Lee's evolutionary objective as by his actual fieldwork experience, which only in subsequent years came to include a more rounded study of the !Kung way of life. These case studies provided samples too small to be statistically meaningful: they concerned 13 and 9 individuals in the two Arnhem Land camps and an average of about 30 individuals in the Dobe !Kung camp, studied for one, two, and three weeks respectively.[2] Nor were Sahlins's conclusions capable of further testing. It is difficult enough to study "work time" among time-illiterate peoples who scatter across rough terrain as they go hunting and gathering, singly or in small groups, not only for need but for leisure, let alone to construct a comparable parameter for other peoples that pursue activities of an entirely different kind.

Second, Sahlins integrated into the argument concepts which specialists would have found difficult to use in economic analysis at that time. How could they address in analysis and pursue in the context of fieldwork suggestions that hunter-gatherers follow the "Zen way" to affluence or that "a pristine affluence colors their economic arrangements, a trust in the abundance of nature's resources rather than despair at the inadequacy of human means" (1972:29)?

Finally, and most important, although Sahlins acknowledged the difficulties involved in studying contemporary peoples as descendants or representatives of prehistoric hunter-gatherers, in discussing evolutionary processes of the macro- time scale, he projected ethnographic observations of the micro- time scale—which left much to be desired. Extraordinary as it now seems, a close examination of the published sources, McCarthy and McArthur (1960) and McArthur (1960), shows that even the nine adults who constituted the Fish Creek group were in fact encountered in a missionary station and invited to participate in an "experiment" (McArthur 1960:91). Not only that, but they "became so tired of the diet, the greater part of which was animal food, that on 12 October, the fifth day of the survey, two of the men walked into Oenpelli to get flour and rice." Luckily, they acquiesced to the researchers' wishes and "willingly handed over these foods until the conclusion of the experiment"—and so "the quantitative survey was continued" (McCarthy and McArthur 1960:147). As for Lee's early quantitative study, while it was more sophisticated and less contrived, it nevertheless focussed on a selected group that represented 58% of the 425 !Kung counted in the Dobe area in 1964—the others were involved in other activities or did not stay for the four-week survey (Lee 1969:52–54)—and Lee later found that even these selected people had previously been working for wages and had occasionally grown their food (1979:409; 1976:18).

In short, "The Original Affluent Society," in spite of its importance, remained too complex for straightforward examination by students of modern hunter-gatherers for many years after its publication. It thus became a kind of a sacred text. It was left untouched and unapproached, and there evolved an oral tradition, passed down from teacher to student, which gave it an acceptable meaning (see Barnard and Woodburn 1988: 11–12). We continued to include it in our reading lists, as much for its historical importance as for that "something" which we felt it had and also because we had nothing better to offer. Occasionally a (bright) student would exclaim, "The king is naked!," but we considered it a king even if indecently dressed.

Recently, however, ecologically oriented specialists have taken up the essay and, drawing on advances made during the intervening years in both fieldwork and theory, read it as a hypothesis to be tested by means of empirical research (e.g., Hayden 1981, Hawkes and O'Connell 1981, Hawkes et al. 1985, Gould 1982, Hill et al. 1985, Headland 1987, Smith 1987). A major session was devoted to their work at the recent Sixth International Conference on Hunting and Gathering Societies in Fairbanks, Alaska. Making use of quantitative data collected within research projects informed by optimal foraging theory (Winterhalder and Smith 1981), these specialists have focussed mainly on hunter-gatherers' work time. They have reported that Sahlins's argument does not apply universally, because some peoples—for example, the Ache, the Alyawara, the Agta, and even the !Kung (see esp. Hawkes and O'Connell 1981; Headland 1987; Hill et al. 1985; Hayden 1981; Lee 1979: 278)—work on average at least six hours a day. They have argued that the studies Sahlins used were not universally representative (a charge which can be made against virtually any anthropological work) and, moreover, that they take account neither of the societies concerned at large nor of the full seasonal cycle, let alone of irregular ecological changes. They have also addressed the construction of the parameter "work time" and argued that it is misleading because it does not include time devoted to constructing and maintaining tools, the preparation of food, child care, and the informal exchange of information. While most of these scholars have challenged "The Original Affluent Society" on these grounds, some have concentrated on Sahlins's idea of "limited wants," reframing it within evolutionary-ecological theory (e.g., Hawkes et al. 1985, Smith 1987, Winterhalder 1990) and asking whether "limited needs" had any ecological rationale in terms of optimal foraging theory ("time minimizing," "opportunity maximizing," and "energy maximizing").

Twenty-five years after the idea was introduced, it is indeed time to revisit "The Original Affluent Society." Yet it is not enough to pick up components of the argument such as "work time" and "limited needs" and pursue them piecemeal. To understand what Sahlins was trying to get at, we must first penetrate the essay analytically and strip the argument of its rhetorical and polemical excesses. This is the first objective of this paper. The second objective is to offer an up-to-date culturally

2. Lee's output-input study was carried out over a period of four weeks, but he excluded one week during which his own contribution to subsistence effort was too great to be overlooked.

oriented analysis of hunter-gatherers' work and material welfare. In recent years a culturalist method of economic analysis (following Gudeman 1986) has developed, and its application to the study of hunter-gatherer economy has already begun (see Bird-David 1990). Drawing on culturally oriented data, new and old, concerning three groups—the Nayaka of South India, the Mbuti of Central Africa, and the Batek of Malaysia—I will argue that Sahlins's argument, duly updated and reconceptualized, does indeed hold.

I will, however, confine myself to the modern dimension of "The Original Affluent Society," leaving the evolutionary dimension to be pursued separately at a different analytical level of abstraction and with due care for the massive problems involved. The recent debate on the status of modern hunter-gatherers (e.g., Solway and Lee 1990, Wilmsen and Denbow 1991), which I have addressed elsewhere (Bird-David 1988, n.d.), lies outside the concern of the present paper, since it does not deal with how the modern peoples in question have come to be the way they are—through evolution or as a result of colonialism.

An Analysis of "The Original Affluent Society"

Along with all other observers of modern hunter-gatherers, Sahlins was struck by what he described as their "peculiar" economic behaviour. In his terms, they have only a few possessions, which can be manufactured easily from materials which lie in abundance around them, and display a notable tendency to be careless about them and to lack interest in developing their technological equipment. Lack of foresight is apparent in "their propensity to eat right through all the food in the camp, even during objectively difficult times," and in their "failure to put by food surpluses and develop food storage" (pp. 30–31). Many of these features have since been combined by Woodburn in a single construct, "the immediate-return system" (1980, 1982, 1988).

In "The Original Affluent Society" Sahlins intended to offer a culture-specific explanation of this "peculiar" economic behaviour. Referring to the formalist/substantivist controversy of the 1960s, he set himself against the use of "ready-made models of orthodox Economics, especially the 'microeconomics' taken as universally valid and applicable *grosso modo* to primitive societies" (1972:xi). He expressed, instead, a commitment to "a culturalist study that as a matter of principle does honour to different societies for what they are" (p. xi) and to a view of the economy as "a category of culture rather than behaviour" (p. xii). Any lingering uncertainty about his theoretical position is dispelled by *Culture and Practical Reason* (1976), where he argued for an economic analysis that takes into consideration peoples' cultural constructions of the material world and challenged the assumption that there is an economic sphere which is regulated by practical reason. Interestingly, he specifically criticized analyses which present a "naturalization of the hunter-gatherer economy" and concern themselves with the "naturalistic ordering of culture" instead of "the cultural order of nature" (1976:100).

What he did in "The Original Affluent Society" was, however, precisely the reverse of his intention: he discussed hunter-gatherers' work in terms of practical reason and ecological constraints and analysed their economy with none other than a microeconomic model focussing on individuals' optimal, rational behaviour. He argued, in fact, that the imminence of diminishing returns shaped the hunter-gatherer economy, first imposing mobility and then enforcing prodigality (pp. 31–33). "Hunters and gatherers," he concluded, ignoring their culture altogether, "have *by force of circumstances* an objectively low standard of living" (p. 37, emphasis added).

How did this happen? It was not for lack of trying. Sahlins offered two promising cultural propositions. The first was that affluence is a culture-specific relation between material wants and means and that hunter-gatherers achieve it by reducing their material wants through cultural processes: "Want not, lack not." This would have been a good starting point from which to explore the ideas of hunter-gatherers in relation to their economic conduct and thereby to provide a culturalist framework for understanding their economic arrangements. But Sahlins did not pursue it, in part because of lack of relevant data and conceptual apparatus and in part, unfortunately, because he sacrificed the issue to wit and glossed this proposition as the "Zen way." In so doing, he diverted attention from the hunter-gatherers' own ideas, since, needless to say, "honour[ing] different societies for what they are" means projecting upon them neither Western nor Zen ideas.

Sahlins's second cultural proposition was, essentially, that hunter-gatherers have confidence in their environment and that their economic conduct makes sense in relation to that confidence. In "Notes on the Original Affluent Society" he put this boldly, arguing that "a certain confidence, at least in many cases, attends their economic attitudes and decisions. The way they dispose of food on hand, for example—as if they had it made" (1968*a*:86). Notably, most of the speakers in the discussion that followed (1968*a*:89–92) addressed their comments to this proposition, designated by one of them as the "thesis of confidence in the yield of the morrow" (Helm 1968:89). Although they discussed it in a preliminary way, in impressionistic terms, and did not find it equally applicable to all cases, the consensus was that this proposition did apply to peoples whose economies were later to be characterized as "immediate-return systems" and in restricted ways to other groups as well.

When Sahlins made the same point again in "The Original Affluent Society," however, he added a qualifier which brought to an end the interest he and others had shown in this proposition. He wrote: "My point is that the otherwise curious heathen devices become understandable by the people's confidence, a confidence which is the *reasonable* human attribute of a generally successful economy" (p. 29, emphasis added). He later indicated that by "successful economy" he meant gaining a livelihood while retaining a low ratio of work time to leisure time. While the initial proposition could clearly have led to a culture-sensitive analysis—because confidence in the natural environment reflects cultural representations as much as objective, ecological conditions—this addition reduced it to a practical reason and prepared the way for the ecological proposition.

Sahlins did not, I think, go back on the explanatory importance of hunter-gatherers' confidence in their environment. He simply laid his bet on another proposition which he had come to believe would make his case more strongly. Reputed to be central and crucial to "The Original Affluent Society," this proposition was that hunter-gatherers work an average of three to five hours per adult per day. In retrospect, and taking into account the recent work discussed briefly above, it is clear that he bet on the weaker horse. However, even in the essay itself one can see how the illusion evolved and, moreover, that this proposition is not a necessary condition for Sahlins's argument.

Pre-1968 theory had explained hunter-gatherers' economic dispositions in terms of their unrelenting quest for food. Sahlins's attack on this theory was what made his essay historically important, but he addressed it only to pave the way for his own. It would have been sufficient for that purpose to point out—in a general way, and, without going into the problematic statistics—that what were then new and exceptionally rich empirical findings conclusively showed that hunter-gatherers did not work relentlessly. (This would also have confirmed the impressions of attentive travellers and missionaries.) However, Sahlins chose a more polemical and dramatic approach, and as a result, while he debunked the old theory sensationally, he lost control of his own.

He overprocessed the ecologically oriented quantitative data from the aforementioned studies and in the course of that adopted the analytical construct of "work time"—a modern Western construct par excellence that is meaningful within the ecological paradigm but not in a culturalist study. Moreover, with the zeal of the newly converted, he further quantified the quantitative measures of work time that, with considerable caution, Lee and McArthur and McCarthy had provided and so arrived at estimates of "four or five hours" (in the case of the Arnhem Land Aborigines [p. 17]) and "an average of 2 hours and 9 minutes per day" (in the case of the Dobe !Kung [p. 21]). The simplistic reduction of the data to these two figures was unfortunate, because when he then turned to his other sources he found in them suggestive comparable estimates: "two or three hours," "three or four hours," and "an average of less than two hours a day" (p. 26, citing Grey 1841, vol. 2:263; Eyre 1845:254–55; Woodburn 1968:54). He himself was aware that the estimates were "very rough," but —lo and behold!—they were similar to each other and to the estimates just mentioned. (Sahlins further highlighted the similarity by printing the estimates in boldface.) These were similar enough, in any case, for scholars who had just discovered what has been called the "magic number" in hunter-gatherer studies—the 25-strong hunter-gatherer band—and suggested a second magic number, "a mean of three to five hours" of work per adult worker per day.

This seeming fact was sufficient for Sahlins's case: if they worked so little, they indeed enjoyed unparalleled affluence. Furthermore, it made the cultural propositions simple corollaries of this fact: if hunter-gatherers could gain an adequate livelihood by working so little, it was obvious that they could easily get what they wanted and did not want more than they could easily get, and, furthermore, it was obvious ("reasonable") that they had confidence in their environment. Thus, Sahlins centered his concluding theory on the ecological proposition, which should not have been offered (since there was neither sufficient evidence nor any theoretical need for it), and abandoned the cultural propositions.

It is as a result of this that he provided a theory of *abundance with cost* (owing to ecological dictates) when he had set out to offer the opposite, a theory of *affluence without abundance* (owing to cultural influences). His theory was, in Winterhalder's terms, "the neoclassical formulation preceded by a minus sign" (1990:498)—a neat formula in the best formalist fashion that lacked culture-sensitive depth. Worst of all, the whole argument came to appear doubtful in the light of subsequent work because the ecological proposition upon which it rested had been called into question. I would argue, however, that in drawing attention to the explanatory power of hunter-gatherers' trust in their environment, Sahlins did point the way towards a culturally oriented theory of hunter-gatherers' economic behaviour. He was on the threshold of what can now be pursued by using the culturalist method of economic analysis.

The Cosmic Economy of Sharing

No one can seriously suppose either that all modern hunter-gatherers will be the same or that any point needs to be made of this. It seems, however, that not only do hunter-gatherers with immediate-return systems share the economic features which perplexed Sahlins (whilst other modern hunter-gatherers differ from them in various ways) but at least some of them view their natural environments in a similar way: they have, in Gudeman's (1986) terms, very similar primary metaphors. These metaphors are drawn from their social institutions and constitute the cores of the metaphorical models that Gudeman has called local economic models. I shall move on to discuss these metaphorical models and then show that this ethnographic material provides substance for Sahlins's cultural propositions, a basis on which to refine them, and, in addition (and as Sahlins suspected) a means of making sense of these hunter-gatherers' economic behaviour.

I began to explore the primary metaphors of hunter-gatherers with immediate-return systems in an earlier paper (Bird-David 1990), where I examined one metaphorical model—the giving environment—in relation to patterns of exchange and ownership in the context of a contrast between the South Indian Nayaka and their shifting-cultivator neighbours the Bette and Mullu Kurumbas. Here I discuss a closely related metaphorical model—the cosmic economy of sharing—in relation to subsistence activities in the context of a comparison between the Nayaka and two other groups with immediate-return systems, the Mbuti of Zaire and the Batek of Malaysia. Each group has animistic notions which attribute life and consciousness to natural phenomena, including the forest itself and parts of it such as hilltops, tall trees, and river sources. I shall examine the way in which they construct their relationship with these agents—at once natural and human-like—by looking eclectically at their ritual and myth and their everyday discourse and conduct and by paying special attention to the metaphors which they use. Four features in particular are prominent:

First, the natural (human-like) agencies socialize with the hunter-gatherers. The Mbuti *molimo* festival, for example, is, in fact, precisely about this: the Forest visits the Mbuti camp, plays music, and sings with the people (Turnbull 1961). The Batek similarly say that the supernatural spirits, called *hala'*, "come to earth merely for the pleasure of sharing a good singing session with the Batek." During the fruit season, Batek frequently sing for—and with—the natural spirits (Endicott 1979:219). The Nayaka confine the merriment of a communal get-together with the natural agencies to a festival normally held once a year. However, throughout this festival, which lasts 24 hours, they converse, dance, sing, eat, and even share cigarettes with natural-cum-ancestral spirits, which they invoke by shamanistic performances.

Second, the natural agencies give food and gifts to everyone, regardless of specific kinship ties or prior reciprocal obligations. The Mbuti, for example, explicitly say that "the forest gives them . . . food and shelter, warmth and clothing" (Turnbull 1976 [1965]:253; 1978:165). They view game, honey, and other natural foods as "gifts" (Turnbull 1976 [1965]:161, 180, 277; 1961:61, 237). The Batek, according to their origin stories, hold that the *hala'* created most of the plants and animals especially for the Batek (Endicott 1979:54–55, 72) and now demand nothing in return, not even (with a few exceptions) sacrifices or offerings (p. 219). According to some versions, some *hala'* even turned themselves into the plants and animals that the Batek eat (p. 67). The *hala'*, the Batek say, keep large quantities of fruit blossoms in their abodes, "like goods on a shop shelf" (p. 44), and release the fruit in season, "freely bestowing their bounties" (p. 219).

Third, the people regard themselves as "children of" the forest, the term connoting generic ties rather than simply bonds of emotion and care. For example, not only do Mbuti often refer to the forest as "father" and "mother" (Turnbull 1965:252; cf. Mosko 1987) and say that it "gives them . . . affection" (1965:253) but also they describe it as the source of all spiritual matter and power, including the vital essence of people's lives (*pepo*) (Turnbull 1976 [1965]:247, 252). They describe the forest as a "womb" (Turnbull 1978:167, 215; 1983:30, 32, 44) which plays a part in the conception and development of a Mbuti foetus (Turnbull 1978:165, 167–70; 1976 [1965]:178; cf. Mosko 1987:899). In a similar vein, although from the opposite perspective, the Nayaka not only refer to natural agencies (especially hilltops and large rock formations) by the terms *dod appa* (big father) and *dod awa* (big mother) and to themselves correspondingly by the terms *maga(n)* and *maga(l)* (male and female children) but also say that dead Nayaka become one with the forest spirits. They do not exclude their own immediate forefathers, and furthermore, they perform secondary mortuary rituals to help their deceased relatives join the forest spirits. The Batek also address the end point of the life-cycle, though they depict a two-stage transformation. They say that the spirits of their dead relatives first go to the land of the dead, where superhuman friends and relatives transform them into superhumans and teach them the skills and songs of the *hala'*; thereupon they become *hala'* and move to the *hala'* place (Endicott 1979:111–15, 219).

Finally, these groups not only depict their ties with the natural agencies as ties of sharing between relatives but also explain experiences which could be seen to be at odds with this cultural representation in its own terms, as temporary, accidental, and remediable exceptions. The Mbuti, for example, say that mishaps occur when the forest is asleep. Then they have to awaken it by singing and "draw the forest's attention to the immediate needs of its children" (Turnbull 1961:87; 1976 [1965]:257). The Batek even go in for a preventive measure and believe that as long as they sing, the *hala'*, who like the songs, will send food in abundance (Endicott 1979:54, 56, 219). The Nayaka explain mishaps in another way, though they too effectively relocate the volition outside the natural agencies. They maintain that the natural agencies are generically benign but, interestingly, "people from far away," through sorcery, have affected them. Nevertheless, as for the Mbuti, it is simple enough for Nayaka to restore the order of goodness. Through divination they make it known that the natural agencies are not at fault, and the natural agencies turn back into their normal, benign selves.[3]

While we will never know for certain how Nayaka, Mbuti, or Batek relate to their environments, it is clear enough that the metaphor of sharing provides an important clue to it. Drawn from the institution of sharing so common in these hunter-gatherers' social life, it is a primary metaphor which can help us to loosen slightly the bonds of our own Western ways of viewing the world. Whereas we commonly construct nature in mechanistic terms, for them nature seems to be a set of agencies, simultaneously natural and human-like. Furthermore, they do not inscribe into the nature of things a division between the natural agencies and themselves

3. In the case of extreme and lingering problems, it is believed that a local Nayaka has interfered with the natural agencies and has made them harmful. There is a more elaborate way of addressing this problem.

as we do with our "nature:culture" dichotomy. They view their world as an integrated entity. While many other non-Western peoples view the world in this fashion, it seems that hunter-gatherers with immediate-return systems distinctively view their ties with the natural agencies in terms of visiting and sharing relationships. We can say that their world—according to the metaphorical template carried by the image of sharing—is a cosmic system of sharing which embraces both human-to-human and nature-to-human sharing. The two kinds of sharing are constituents of a cosmic economy of sharing.

Hunting and Gathering as Aspects of the Cosmic Economy of Sharing

The culture-specific dimensions of hunting and gathering can be brought into relief by examining them through the metaphorical model of the cosmic economy of sharing. Within it, they are constructed as acts of nature-to-human sharing which stimulate further acts of sharing in the world.[4] During the past 20 years, we have learnt a great deal about hunter-gatherers' human-to-human sharing. We have learnt that sharing is a social event which demonstrates relatedness, affection, and concern. In economic terms, the value of sharing often lies in its occurrence—in that it secures recurrence—rather than in the value of the resources involved in the particular transaction. Verbally, agents praise generosity in general and generous individuals in particular, but at the same time, in what has come to be called demand sharing (see Bird-David 1990, Peterson 1988), they moan excessively about their poverty and needs. Practically, would-be-recipients request what they *see* in the possession of others and do not request them to produce what they do not appear to have. With these aspects of sharing in mind, we can see that these hunter-gatherers do indeed engage with their natural environments as with sharing partners in at least four ways.

First, as in the case of human-to-human sharing, they care about going on forays just as they do about the value of their products. For example, on some days they collect items of no immediate use and of no great value, and, having collected something, return to the camp, even in the middle of the day. A concern with the activity itself—as much as, and sometimes more than, with its yield—is even more conspicuous when people engage temporarily in other subsistence activities. They continue to go on expeditions in the forest every now and then, even though they often collect little or nothing at all and could do without it. When they forage in the forest, they feel that they are in touch with the natural agencies. The Batek, for example, "feel they are being brought closer to the *hala'*" (Endicott 1979:67). The Mbuti experience a communion with the forest in that "the moment of killing . . . [is] . . . a moment of intense compassion and reverence" (Turnbull 1976 [1965]:161). In some of their stories, the Nayaka even tell of encounters with their supernatural relatives during the course of gathering. According to one story, for example, a woman dug up roots and came upon an elongated stone (the Nayaka point out that it resembles the human body in its shape and refer to it as *kalu* [deity]). She brought the stone to the hamlet (where it still is) and placed it with the other items, including other stones as well as personal mementoes of deceased relatives, that are ceremonially entertained and fed once a year.

Second, like sharing, hunting and gathering are social events and contexts for socializing. The Batek, for example, do not "view work as a burden. . . . Most men and women approach their economic activities enthusiastically" (K. L. Endicott 1980:650). "Women often go fishing with their children as a way of filling an hour or two after other work has been completed" (p. 634). They often say when they go that "they are tired of sitting around camp" and when they return that "they were just playing around at fishing" (Endicott 1979:21). Nayaka families often walk in the forest, each on its own, at a slow, indulgent pace. While picking up usable items, they observe what has happened since last they were there, what has blossomed and what has wilted, and talk about it in a leisurely way. Mbuti approach their hunting in a similar way, as is vividly evident in the following example (which is especially interesting in that it is provided by an ecologically oriented ethnographer [see Hart and Hart 1986], who is here describing a hunt for commercial ends): "The overall pace of the hunt is so leisurely that old people and mothers with infants may join. Between casts of the nets, the hunters regroup . . . to share tobacco or snacks of fruit and nuts gathered along the way . . . to flirt and visit, to play with babies" (Hart 1978:337).

Third, as in human-to-human sharing, seeing constitutes a crucial moment in hunting and gathering activities.[5] These hunter-gatherers tend to appropriate what they see rather than to search for something they want. They often set off from their huts with no particular sense of what they want to acquire in mind and collect what they happen to see on their way. Moreover, although it is impossible to see far ahead in the forest, they often do not even plan their route, instead going in the direction which seems best at the time. Again, they rarely request the natural agencies to produce more resources. They use, for example, very few if any magical means to try to improve their luck in hunting, fishing, and other endeavours (Endicott 1979:22). Seeing also establishes right of first access to resources in the forest, and this is particularly noticeable with respect to certain valued resources—for instance, certain kinds of

4. It should also be useful to look at hunting and gathering from the perspective of the sociology of work, which since the 1950s has gone well beyond the examination of work as labour.

5. Among the !Kung and some northern hunters individuals "see" game in divinatory dreams and then set out to get it, or they "see" where it will be best to go foraging (e.g., Lee 1979, Tanner 1979).

honey—which can be collected repeatedly in the same place. The individual who first sees the tree on which it is annually found owns the tree, which means that he has the right to initiate the collection expedition.

Finally, echoing demand sharing in the human realm, these hunter-gatherers both praise the goodness and generosity of the natural agencies and (regardless of what they actually have) frequently complain of hunger and other insatiable needs. During their 24-hour shamanistic sessions, the Nayaka, for example, repeatedly do both. Similarly, the Mbuti complain of food shortage, although they also frequently sing to the goodness of the forest as they walk in it and as they hunt and gather alone and in groups (Turnbull 1976 [1965]:167, 256; 1961:57, 79; 1978:164). As in human-to-human sharing, complaints and praise are but complementary idioms in an economic discourse premised on giving (see Bird-David 1990).

From this ethnographic glimpse of hunter-gatherers with immediate-return systems it appears that the metaphor of sharing is a clue both to their views of their environment and to their action within it. Recent theory—from diverse perspectives—indeed shows that cognition (concepts, especially metaphorical ones, and percepts) is interrelated with action (Lakoff and Johnson 1980; Gibson 1979, 1982; Ingold 1989), and this is, of course, in harmony with our own most commonplace experience. For example, our use of the metaphor "a dog is a friend" indicates that through close interaction with the dog we have come to perceive and approach it as a friend. Even when we represent the dog as an animal, in the course of what Marx called the life activity we engage with the dog as our friend and express this in various ways in our conduct and discourse.

The primary metaphor of "sharing" is thus a concept with which *we* can make sense of the hunter-gatherers' economic arrangements (Gudeman 1986) and, moreover, a metaphorical concept by which *they* make sense of their environment, one that guides their action within it. Through their close interaction with the environment they have come to perceive it, and act with it, as with a friend, a relative, a parent who shares resources with them. Though in certain contexts they talk about aspects of their environment in "knowledge of" terms, for the most part in the course of their life activity they normally engage with it as if they were in a sharing relationship.

The metaphor "the natural environment is a sharing partner" thus constitutes an analytical tool (to be used with caution, in awareness of the inevitable uncertainty of our own authorship, continually checked and refined as we use it) to examine the issues which Sahlins raises in "The Original Affluent Society." For example, how do hunter-gatherers with immediate-return systems construct their needs vis-à-vis their environment in culture-specific terms? Do they trust their environment, and in what culture-specific sense? How does this metaphor make sense of their seemingly "peculiar" economic behaviour?

Rewriting Sahlins's Cultural Propositions

Do hunter-gatherers have "confidence in the yield of the morrow"? Being keen observers of nature's vicissitudes and ecological variations, hunter-gatherers with immediate-return systems are as cognisant of uncertainties in the "yield of the morrow" as we are, and probably more so. They have experienced periods of hardship in the past and know only too well that such periods may recur. Nevertheless, as in a sharing relationship, although they do not know—and know that they cannot know—what the natural environment will provide, they are confident that under normal conditions it will give them food. Moreover, irrespective of what they obtain in any particular hunting and gathering event—in any momentary episode of the life-long engagement of sharing—the very fact that they have obtained something in their eyes reaffirms their relationship with the natural agencies and therefore secures the recurrence of sharing. In a sense, then, they do have "confidence in the yield of the morrow"—a confidence born of the view that the environment is morally bound to share food and other material resources with them and that under normal conditions it will.

There is a certain truth in Sahlins's suggestion that hunter-gatherers have "limited needs," although it is empirically—not merely theoretically—inaccurate to say that they restrict their material desires in the way that Zen believers do. True, they are not interested in possessions and do not go to a great deal of bother to obtain and accumulate them. However, it is equally apparent that they delight in abundance when circumstances afford it and that they consume ostentatiously what they have. Furthermore, to quote Barnard and Woodburn (1988:12), their "demand for food and other goods from anthropologists, as well as from members of their own societies, is very great, indeed at times almost insatiable." Although these observations seem contradictory, they make sense given that these peoples construct their material requirements from their natural environment—and also, in many ways, from their social environment—in the way in which they construct their demands in a sharing relationship. They culturally construct their needs as the want of a share. Therefore, they require of their environment what they see when they see it and do not request it to produce more. But at the same time they enjoy and exhaust what they have obtained, however much it is, and persist in their demands for shares, irrespective of what they already have. They thus restrict their material wants, but in the way in which one does within a sharing relationship.

Not only food but also technological means are constructed as objects which are shared between the environment and people. This means that they are also regarded as items which can be appropriated from the environment, used without effecting modifications, and then returned to it, directly or via other people. As Woodburn has pointed out, these people often pick up tools just before, and for, the imminent collection of a

32 | CURRENT ANTHROPOLOGY *Volume 33, Number 1, February 1992*

resource and then leave them behind. They do not concern themselves with developing their technological equipment, although, if the environment provides sophisticated equipment, such as a gun or a Land Rover, they will readily use it, while showing the same remarkable (but not "peculiar") disposition to be careless about it. Their expertise has come to be the sophisticated use of the material means which the environment provides.

With one critical proviso, there is also value in Sahlins's suggestion that hunter-gatherers' economic dispositions are predicated on abundance. The proviso is that "abundance" is an assumption of their economic model—homologous with and opposite to the assumption of scarcity in Western economic models. In non-extreme situations, irrespective of what we have, the assumption of scarcity has a bearing upon our decisions, choices, and actions. In the case of these hunter-gatherers, the assumption of abundance has the same function. It is consistent with their view of the natural environment as a sharing partner, which implies that as human agents appropriate their shares they secure further sharing. The assumption of scarcity is consistent with Westerners' mechanistic view of the natural environment, which implies that in the course of time, as human agents use up resources, the total stock is depleted.

In conclusion, then, Sahlins suggested that hunter-gatherers follow the "Zen way" to affluence, which presupposes that "human material wants are few and finite, and technical means unchanging, but on the whole adequate" (1972:2). This way contrasts, he argued, with the modern Western one (the "Galbraithian way"), whose assumptions are appropriate to market economies—"that man's wants are great, not to say infinite, whereas his means are limited, although improveable." Hunter-gatherers with immediate-return systems in fact follow a third way—the "sharing way"—to affluence. Their way is based on assumptions appropriate to their sharing economy—that material wants are linked with material means which are available for sharing. (They want a share of however much is available.)

Further, Sahlins observed that in the Western market economy "all economic activity starts from a position of shortage. . . . one's resources are insufficient to the possible uses and satisfactions" (1968*a*:86). In this respect, the hunter-gatherers' case is the reverse. All economic activity starts from a position of affluence (affluence as a premise). One expects to obtain sufficient resources—at times of abundance even in excess of possible uses and satisfactions.

Finally, Sahlins wrote that "otherwise curious heathen devices become understandable by the people's confidence" (1972:29) and that hunter-gatherers behave "as if they had it made" (1968*a*:86). He was right on both points—if read to say that just as Westerners' behaviour is understandable in relation to their assumption of shortage, so hunter-gatherers' behaviour is understandable in relation to their assumption of affluence. Moreover, just as we analyze, even predict, Westerners' behaviour by presuming that they behave as if they did not have enough, so we can analyze, even predict, hunter-gatherers' behaviour by presuming that they behave as if they had it made.

Towards New Ecological Propositions

In terms of the cosmic economy of sharing, then, the "peculiar" economic behaviour of hunter-gatherers with immediate-return systems makes sense. Moreover, reconceptualized in this way, Sahlins's cultural propositions hold. But the reader is likely to ask: under what ecological conditions can people maintain, and live by, such an economic model? Furthermore, do they in fact have abundant resources, or do they merely think that they do? These are our questions, framed within our models; the people in question would not ask them. Nevertheless, most of our colleagues in the world of learning and in policy-making circles—let alone most students of hunter-gathering peoples—think in Western terms. We therefore have to address these questions, especially since Sahlins's implicit assumption that hunter-gatherers' confidence in the environment is explained by abundance (albeit under conditions of enforced mobility and prodigality) does not hold.

Unfortunately, much as we might want to explore the ecological dimension of these hunter-gatherers' cultural-economic system in their own terms, we cannot do so. In the case of the farmers of the eastern Andes, Gudeman and Rivera (1990) have shown that Westerners, and even certain Western economists, can engage in direct conversation with the local people, but this is possible only because of the close affinity between the local model, the folk Western model, and the model of certain Western economists (they argue for a historical link dating to the Iberian conquest of the Americas). In the case of the hunter-gatherers, in contrast, there is a fundamental disjuncture between the Western and the local model: the terms of each exclude the other. While the Western model presupposes a detached observer concerned with an inanimate nature, the local one presupposes an actor personally involved with an animate natural environment (see Ingold 1989).

However, as I have shown above, the local model relates experientially to action and, moreover, to the same physical reality—the natural environment—with which we are concerned. Therefore, although we cannot translate their experience into our terms, we can come to understand it (see Lakoff 1987:chap. 17) by finding a new way of looking at the natural environment. We need to create a new metaphor of our own and use it as an imaginative cognitive model. Ideally, this metaphor will evoke the way in which these hunter-gatherers relate to their environments in terms equivalent to their own. From such a metaphor we should be able to deduce new, testable propositions and gain novel perspectives on their economy.

I think that there is a metaphor which fills the bill, and it involves the Western institution of the bank. Not only is it the major institution of exchange in the Western economy, and therefore equivalent to sharing, but we draw on it metaphorically, just as the hunter-gatherers draw on sharing, when we are dealing with resources which, for us, are ambiguously placed between the animate and the inanimate (we have, for example, blood banks and semen banks).

Furthermore, the bank is a system which is both concerned with the circulation and use of resources and founded on trust. Individuals save resources for future need, but instead of keeping their valued resources privately they deposit them in the bank, in trust, so that when the time comes they will be able to repossess either them or their exact equivalent instantaneously. For the most part, however, these resources are meanwhile accessible to the public for gainful use, on the basis of the statistical fact that at any given time only a fraction of the savers will claim their deposits. Now, the hunter-gatherers not only have trust in their natural environment and regard its resources as their due shares but, indeed, also make intermittent claims on those shares. They engage in occasional opportunistic pursuit of other subsistence activities (for example, labouring for their neighbours) and frequently shift between these and hunting and gathering (see Bird-David n.d.). Moreover, the bank is a system which can only work if people do not withdraw proceeds from it in order to hoard or circulate them within restricted, private circles. This is precisely the case among the hunter-gatherers and is, after all, what the social institution of sharing is all about. It seems, therefore, that the metaphor "nature is a bank" captures the essence of these hunter-gatherers' engagement with the natural environment while embodying the material basis as well as the cultural aspect of their economy.

Among the many possible propositions which can be deduced from this metaphorical model, there is one which is relevant to the question of the ecological foundations of the local economic model. This is that the hunter-gatherers can maintain their trust in the natural environment—and a successful economy—even when the natural environment cannot, in fact, provide sufficient resources for everyone simultaneously. This hypothesis may seem paradoxical, but it is no more so than the case of the Western bank (see Samuelson 1951:323). The crucial ecological condition may be, as it is in the banking system, a minimum threshold of resources which corresponds to the fraction of the group that is likely to make claims on its shares instantaneously. To explore this possibility, we will need to move away from the goose-chase study of "near pure" hunter-gatherers and look instead at the temporal and idiosyncratic structures of hunting and gathering in the heterogeneous groups that we encounter. We will need to find out what portion of the group pursues foraging at any given period of time, how frequently individuals within the community shift between subsistence activities, and how often they hunt and gather. We may then be able to work out the minimum ecological threshold for a successful economy premised on trust in the natural environment. There is a related proposition of which we must be aware: this kind of economy can collapse as a result of a breakdown of confidence even when there is no crucial decline in the level of natural resources. The history of banking systems provides examples of this, and we may find also hunter-gatherer cases.

The second question, and the more intriguing one, concerns the extent to which these hunter-gatherers' cultural-economic system generates wealth. Does the fact that they view their environment as rich make it richer? Ecologically oriented scholars have already explored the proposition that sharing—human-to-human sharing—constitutes a kind of collective insurance against unpredictable natural fluctuations and argued that it safeguards individuals from poverty (e.g., Wiessner 1982, Cashdan 1985, Smith 1988, Gould 1982). They have not, however, gone far enough. They ignore both a fundamental part of the ecological equation and the way in which the actors themselves view their environment. Since these scholars view natural resources as an independent variable, they take into account neither the stochastic link between past human use and present level of natural resources nor the fact that, like money in a bank, natural resources left in nature can grow.

The metaphorical model "nature is a bank" implies a more complex development of their proposition, namely, that sharing constitutes an insurance scheme which also involves investment in a banking system. Not only does it safeguard individuals from unpredictable troubles but also it increases their resources. The simpler way in which this may happen can be best explained by an example drawn from a non-monetary banking system. For instance, with the blood bank each individual protects himself by giving blood when he can and receives blood when he needs it. However, the total volume of blood in the bank meanwhile increases as well, because what may not have been a resource before now becomes one. For example, blood which may have been the wrong type for one's friends and relatives becomes a usable resource once it is deposited in the bank. We need to explore whether these hunter-gatherers' economy works in a similar way. For instance, does the general sharing of large game generate wealth because a large amount which would have been wasted on one's own friends and close relatives stretches farther when it is divided among all members of the group?

The second and more complex way in which a banking system generates wealth can be illustrated by our monetary banking system, in which money in fact generates more money. The folk explanation is simple enough: we say that money grows, and, noticeably, we ourselves use the metaphor "money in the bank is like a plant in nature." The technical explanation is complicated and lies in the paradoxical nature of circulation and ownership in this system (put simply, it has to do with the fact that for each pound sterling in the bank, there are about four individuals who simultaneously own it and use it). We need to explore the ways in which this may happen within these hunter-gatherers' economic system. The sharing of large game, for example, may also generate wealth in an additional way: recipients of meat are likely to postpone hunting, since they have had a share and since they are confident that meat is secured in the bank of nature until they need it, meanwhile allowing more time for natural increase. I suspect that if we examine the temporal and idiosyncratic patterns of foraging, as well as patterns of ownership and circulation, with these aspects of the banking system in mind, we will find that in many other ways these hunter-gatherers' economic system, premised on trust in the natural environment, does generate wealth. Sahlins summarized his case by the catch phrase "Want not, lack not." It may well be, however, that the hunter-gatherers' case is "Think rich, be rich."

Conclusions

The fundamental flaw in "The Original Affluent Society" was Sahlins's conflation of cultural and ecological perspectives. As shown here, however, this problem can be resolved, and the relevant empirical studies then show that Sahlins did indeed "have a point"; his essay is a king that could—and should—be scientifically reclothed. The evocative title of his essay was inspired by John Kenneth Galbraith's *The Affluent Society* (1969 [1958]). It is ironic that Galbraith in fact emphasized the impact of ideas on the economy, arguing—in a mirror image of what I have argued for the hunter-gatherers in question—that the assumption of scarcity continues to influence economic conduct in the increasingly wealthy West and thereby acts to preserve poverty. The irony is doubled, for in the second edition of his book Galbraith criticized those who misread his argument and overrated his point on the shortening of work hours. His main argument was that the way to the really affluent society lies in an ideological disengagement between production and economic security and between production and income. These ideas are precisely the ideas which are embodied in the cosmic economy of sharing. In respect to their cultural ideas, therefore, hunter-gatherers with immediate-return systems constitute the original affluent society in a more comprehensive sense than Sahlins envisaged.

References Cited

ALTMAN, J. C. 1984. Hunter-gatherer subsistence production in Arnhem Land: The original affluence hypothesis re-examined. *Mankind* 14:179–90. [JA]

———. 1987. *Hunter-gatherers today: An Aboriginal economy in North Australia.* Canberra: Australian Institute of Aboriginal Studies. [JA]

ARCAND, BERNARD. 1981. The Negritos and the Penan will never be Cuiva. *Folk* 23:37–43. [ESB]

BARNARD, A., AND J. WOODBURN. 1988. "Introduction," in *Hunters and gatherers*, vol. 2, *Property, power, and ideology.* Edited by T. Ingold, D. Riches, and J. Woodburn, pp. 4–31. Oxford: Berg.

BICCHIERI, M. G. 1990. From Eurocentric to geocentric: The perspective from small-scale societies. *Anthropos* 85:1–9. [MGB]

BIRD-DAVID, N. 1988. "Hunter-gatherers and other people: A reexamination," in *Hunters and gatherers*, vol. 1, *History, evolution, and social change.* Edited by T. Ingold, D. Riches, and J. Woodburn. Oxford: Berg.

———. 1990. The giving environment: Another perspective on the economic system of gatherer-hunters. CURRENT ANTHROPOLOGY 31:183–96.

———. n.d. Beyond "Man the Hunter": Hunter-gatherers between nature and nation. *Man.* In press.

BODENHORN, B. "The animals come to me, they know I share": Niupiaq kinship, changing economic relations, and enduring world views on Alaskan north slopes. Ph.D. diss., Cambridge University, Cambridge, England.

BURCH, ERNEST S., JR. 1980. "Traditional Eskimo societies in northwest Alaska," in *Alaska native culture and history.* Edited by Yoshinobu Kotani and William B. Workman, pp. 253–304. Senri Ethnological Studies 4. [ESB]

———. "Modes of exchange in northwest Alaska," in *Hunters and gatherers*, vol. 2, *Property, power, and ideology.* Edited by T. Ingold, D. Riches, and J. Woodburn, pp. 95–109. Oxford: Berg. [ESB]

CASHDAN, E. 1985. Coping with risk: Reciprocity among the Basarwa of northern Botswana. *Man* 20:454–74.

COLE, J. B. Editor. 1988. *Anthropology for the nineties: Introductory readings.* New York: Free Press.

Cross-cultural and comparative research: Theory and method. 1991. Behavior Science Research 25. [CRE]

DAMAS, D. Editor. 1969*a*. *Contributions to anthropology: Band societies.* National Museums of Canada, Anthropological Series 84, Bulletin 228. [MGB]

———. 1969*b*. *Contributions to anthropology: Ecological essays.* National Museums of Canada, Anthropological Series 86, Bulletin 230. [MGB]

———. 1972. Central Eskimo systems of food sharing. *Ethnology* 11:220–40. [GWW]

EMBER, C. R. 1983. The relative decline in women's contributions to agriculture with intensification. *American Anthropologist* 85:285–304. [CRE]

ENDICOTT, K. 1979. *Batek Negrito religion: The world view and rituals of a hunting and gathering people of peninsular Malaysia.* Oxford: Clarendon Press.

ENDICOTT, K. L. 1980. Batek Negrito sex roles: Behaviour and ideology. Paper presented at the Second International Conference on Hunting and Gathering Societies, Quebec, Canada.

ERASMUS, C. J. 1980. Comment on: Does labor time decrease with industrialization? by W. Minge-Klevana. CURRENT ANTHROPOLOGY 21:289–91. [JA]

EYRE, E. J. 1845. *Journals of expeditions of discovery into Central Australia, and overland from Adelaide to King George's Sound, in the years 1840–41.* 2 vols. London: Boone.

FIENUP-RIORDAN, ANN. 1983. *The Nelson Island Eskimo: Social structure and ritual distribution.* Anchorage: Alaska Pacific University Press. [GWW]

GALBRAITH, J. K. 1969 (1958). *The affluent society.* Harmondsworth: Penguin.

GIBSON, J. J. 1979. *The ecological approach to visual perception.* Boston: Houghton Mifflin.

———. 1982. *Reasons for realism: Selected essays of James J. Gibson.* Edited by E. Reed and R. J. Jones. Hillsdale: Lawrence Erlbaum.

GOULD, R. 1982. "To have and have not: The ecology of sharing among hunter-gatherers," in *Resource managers: North American and Australian hunter-gatherers.* Edited by N. Williams and E. Hunn. Boulder: Westview.

GREGORY, C. A., AND J. C. ALTMAN. 1989. *Observing the economy.* London: Routledge [JA]

GREY, SIR GEORGE. 1841. *Journals of two expeditions of discovery in north west and western Australia during the years*

1837, 38 and 39. 2 vols. London: Boone.
GRINKER, ROY RICHARD. 1990. Images of denigration: Structuring inequality between foragers and farmers in the Ituri Forest, Zaire. *American Ethnologist* 17:111–30. [RRG]
GROSS, D. R. 1984. Time allocation: A tool for the study of cultural behavior. *Annual Review of Anthropology* 13:519–58. [CRE]
GUDEMAN, S. 1986. *Economics as culture: Models and metaphors of livelihood.* London: Routledge and Kegan Paul.
GUDEMAN, S., AND A. RIVERA. 1990. *Conversations in Colombia.* Cambridge: Cambridge University Press.
HART, J. A. 1978. From subsistence to market: A case study of the Mbuti net hunters. *Human Ecology* 6:325–53.
HART, T. B., AND J. A. HART. 1986. The ecological basis of hunter-gatherer subsistence in African rain forests: The Mbuti of western Zaire. *Human Ecology* 14:29–55.
HAYDEN, B. 1981. "Subsistence and ecological adaptations of modern hunter/gatherers," in *Omnivorous primates: Gathering and hunting in human evolution.* Edited by Robert S. Harding and Geza Teleki, pp. 344–421. New York: Columbia University Press.
HAWKES, K., AND JAMES F. O'CONNELL. 1981. Affluent hunters? Some comments in light of the Alyawara case. *American Anthropologist* 84:622–26.
HAWKES, K., JAMES F. O'CONNELL, KIM HILL, AND ERIC L. CHARNOV. 1985. How much is enough? Hunters and limited needs. *Ethology and Sociobiology* 6:3–15.
HEADLAND, T. N. 1987. The wild yam question: How well could independent hunter-gatherers live in a tropical rain forest ecosystem? *Human Ecology* 15:463–91.
HELM, J. 1968. Comment on "Does hunting bring happiness?" in *Man the hunter.* Edited by R. B. Lee and I. DeVore, p. 89. Chicago: Aldine.
HILL, K., H., KAPLAN, K. HAWKES, AND A. M. HURTADO. 1985. Men's time allocation to subsistence work among the Ache of eastern Paraguay. *Human Ecology* 13:29–47.
ICHIKAWA, M. 1987. The food restrictions of the Mbuti Pygmies, eastern Zaire. *African Study Monographs,* suppl. 6, pp. 97–121. [ML]
INGOLD, T. 1989. Culture and the perception of the environment. Paper presented at the Sixth EIDOS Workshop on Cultural Understanding of the Environment, London, June.
JOHNSON, A. 1975. Time allocation in a Machiguenga community. *Ethnology* 14:301–10. [JA]
JONES, R. 1980. "Hunters in the Australian coastal savanna," in *Ecology in savanna environments.* Edited by D. Harris. London: Academic Press. [JA]
KEMP, WILLIAM B. 1971. The flow of energy in a hunting society. *Scientific American* 225(3):105–15. [GWW]
KUHN, T. 1962. *The structure of scientific revolutions.* Chicago: University of Chicago Press. [SG]
LAKOFF, G. 1987. *Women, fire, and dangerous things: What categories reveal about the mind.* Chicago: University of Chicago Press.
LAKOFF, G., AND M. JOHNSON. 1980. *Metaphors we live by.* Chicago: University of Chicago Press.
LAUGHLIN, WILLIAM S. 1968. "Hunting: An integrating biobehavior system and its evolutionary importance," in *Man the hunter.* Edited by R. B. Lee and I. DeVore, pp. 304–20. Chicago: Aldine. [ESB]
LEE, R. B. 1968. "What hunters do for a living, or, How to make out on scarce resources," in *Man the hunter.* Edited by R. B. Lee and I. DeVore. Chicago: Aldine.
———. 1969. "!Kung Bushman subsistence: An input-output analysis," in *Environment and cultural behavior.* Edited by A. P. Vayda, pp. 47–79. New York: Natural History Press.
———. 1976. "Introduction," in *Kalahari hunter-gatherers: Studies of the !Kung San and their neighbours.* Edited by R. B. Lee and I. DeVore, pp. 3–27. Cambridge: Harvard University Press.
———. 1979. *The !Kung San: Men, women, and work in a foraging society.* New York: Cambridge University Press.
LEE, R. B., AND I. DEVORE. Editors. 1968. "Discussions, pt. 2: Does hunting bring happiness?" in *Man the hunter.* Edited by R. B. Lee and I. DeVore, pp. 89–92. Chicago: Aldine. [GWW]
LONNER, THOMAS D. 1980. *Subsistence as an economic system in Alaska: Theoretical and policy implications.* Alaska Department of Fish and Game Division of Subsistence Technical Paper 67.
LUHMANN, N. 1988. "Familiarity, confidence, trust: Problems and alternatives," in *Trust: Making and breaking cooperative relations.* Edited by D. Gambetta. Oxford: Blackwell. [TI]
MCARTHUR, M. 1960. "Food consumption and dietary levels of groups of Aborigines living on naturally occurring foods," in *Records of the American-Australian Scientific Expedition to Arnhem Land,* vol. 2, *Anthropology and nutrition.* Edited by C. P. Mountford. Melbourne: Melbourne University Press.
MCCARTHY, F. D., AND M. MCARTHUR. 1960. "The food quest and the time factor in aboriginal economic life," in *Records of the American-Australian Scientific Expedition to Arnhem Land,* vol. 2, *Anthropology and nutrition.* Edited by C. P. Mountford. Melbourne: Melbourne University Press.
MEEHAN, B. 1982. *Shell bed to shell midden.* Canberra: Australian Institute of Aboriginal Studies. [JA]
MINGE-KLEVANA, W. 1980. Does labor time decrease with industrialization? A survey of time-allocation studies. CURRENT ANTHROPOLOGY 21:279–87. [JA, CRE]
MOSKO, M. 1987. The symbols of "Forest": A structural analysis of Mbuti culture and social organization. *American Anthropologist* 89:896–913.
NUTTALL, MARK. 1991. Sharing and the ideology of subsistence in a Greenlandic sealing community. *Polar Record* 27(162): 217–22. [GWW]
PETERSON, N. 1988. Reciprocity and the demand for generosity. Paper presented at the Fourth International Conference on Hunting and Gathering Societies, London, England.
SAHLINS, M. 1968*a*. "Notes on the original affluent society," in *Man the hunter.* Edited by R. B. Lee and I. DeVore, pp. 85–89. Chicago: Aldine.
———. 1968*b*. La première société d'abondance. *Les temps modernes,* no. 268, pp. 641–80.
———. 1972. "The original affluent society," in *Stone Age economics,* pp. 1–39. London: Tavistock. [46]
———. 1976. *Culture and practical reason.* Chicago: University of Chicago Press.
SAMUELSON, P. A. 1951. *Economics: An introductory analysis.* New York: McGraw-Hill.
SAWADA, M. 1990. Two patterns of chorus among the Efe, forest hunter-gatherers in Northeastern Zaire: Why do they love to sing? *African Study Monographs* 10:159–95. [MI]
SCHEBESTA, P. 1936. *Revisiting my Pygmy host.* Translated by G. Griffin. London: Hutchinson. [MI]
SERVICE, ELMAN R. 1966. *The hunters.* Englewood Cliffs: Prentice-Hall. [ESB]
SMITH, E. A. 1987. On fitness maximization, limited needs, and hunter-gatherer time allocation. *Ethnology and Sociobiology* 8:73–85.
———. 1988. "Risk and uncertainty in the 'original affluent society': Evolutionary ecology of resource-sharing and land tenure," in *Hunters and gatherers,* vol. 1, *History, evolution, and social change.* Edited by T. Ingold, D. Riches, and J. Woodburn. Oxford: Berg.
SOLWAY, J., AND R. B. LEE. 1990. Foragers, genuine or spurious? Situating the Kalahari San in history. CURRENT ANTHROPOLOGY 31:109–146.
TANNER, A. 1979. *Bringing home animals: Religious ideology and mode of production of the Mistassini Cree hunters.* London: Hurst.
TERASHIMA, HIDEAKI. 1985. Variation and composition principles of the residence group (band) of the Mbuti Pygmies: Beyond a typical/atypical dichotomy. *African Study Monographs,* suppl. 4, pp. 103–20. [RRG]
TESTART, ALAIN. 1982. The significance of food storage among hunter-gatherers: Residence patterns, population densities, and social inequalities. CURRENT ANTHROPOLOGY 23:523–37. [ESB]
TURNBULL, C. M. 1961. *The forest people: A study of the Pygmies of the Congo.* New York: Simon and Schuster.

———. 1976 (1965). *Wayward servants: The two worlds of the African Pygmies.* Westport: Greenwood Press.

———. 1978. "The politics of non-aggression (Zaire)," in *Learning non-aggression: The experience of non-literate societies.* Edited by A. Montagu, pp. 161–222. Oxford: Oxford University Press.

———. 1983. *The Mbuti Pygmies: Change and adaptation.* Holt, Rinehart and Winston.

USHER, PETER J. 1976. Evaluating country food in the northern native economy. *Arctic* 29(2):105–20. [ESB]

WENZEL, G. W. 1981. *Inuit ecology and adaptation: The organization of subsistence.* Canadian Ethnology Service Mercury Paper 77. [GWW]

———. 1991. *Animal rights, human rights: Ecology, economy, and ideology in the Canadian Arctic.* London: Belhaven. [GWW]

WIESSNER, P. 1982. "Risk, reciprocity, and social influence on !Kung San economics," in *Politics and history in band societies.* Edited by E. Leacock and R. Lee. Cambridge: Cambridge University Press.

WILMSEN, E., AND J. DENBOW. 1991. Paradigmatic history of San-speaking peoples and current attempts at revision. CURRENT ANTHROPOLOGY 31:489–524.

WINTERHALDER, B. 1990. "An ecological explanation for limited effort foraging," the *Sixth International Conference on Hunter-Gatherers, Fairbanks, Alaska, May 1990 (Precirculated Papers and Abstracts),* vol. 1, pp. 489–503.

WINTERHALDER, B., AND E. A. SMITH. Editor. 1981. *Hunter-gatherer foraging strategies:* Chicago: University of Chicago Press.

WOODBURN, J. 1968. "An introduction to Hadza ecology," in *Man the hunter.* Edited by R. B. Lee and I. DeVore. Chicago: Aldine.

———. 1980. "Hunters and gatherers today and reconstruction of the past," in *Soviet and Western anthropology.* Edited by E. Gellner. London: Duckworth.

———. 1982. Egalitarian societies. *Man* 17:431–45.

———. 1988. "African hunter-gatherer social organization: Is it best understood as a product of encapsulation?" in *Hunters and gatherers,* vol. 1, *History, evolution, and social change.* Edited by T. Ingold, D. Riches and J. Woodburn, pp. 31–64. Oxford: Berg.

Part II
Processes: Production

[11]

Capital, Investment and the Social Structure of a Pastoral Nomad Group in South Persia

BY FREDRIK BARTH

In this essay, I shall present a summary analysis of some aspects of the pastoral nomad economy of the Basseri tribe of Fars, South Persia. I shall discuss the nature of pastoral capital and its implications for the social structure of the nomads, granted certain cultural premises current among the Basseri. In this discussion I shall draw on material collected in the field during the winter and spring of 1958.

The Basseri are a tribe of 15,000–20,000 pastoral nomads, divided residentially into camps of ten to fifty tents, who migrate between winter pastures in the steppes and deserts of southern Fars and summer pastures in the high mountains 300 miles further north. A general picture of this tribe has been presented elsewhere (Barth, 1961), and certain aspects of the prevailing system of land use and migration have been analysed (Barth, 1960). In general, the following description may be taken as representative of conditions among the pastoral nomads of the whole South Persian area, a population of about half-a-million nomads.

A pastoral nomadic subsistence is based on assets of two main kinds: domesticated animals, and grazing rights. The recognition by the sedentary authorities of traditional grazing rights vested in distinct tribes is basic to the pastoral adaptation in Fars. Such tribes mostly have centralized political organizations based on chiefs, as do the Basseri, and are further united into large confederacies, which were formerly integrated into the semi-feudal traditional organization of Persia, and which are still recognized by the authorities. The association of every tribe with a corporate estate in the form of shared grazing rights has important implications for the political forms developed in the area. But in this essay I shall concentrate on the internal organization of the tribe, particularly the structure of local camp units. Within camps, all members share equal access to

Capital, Saving and Credit in Peasant Societies

pastures; so for my present purposes I shall concentrate my analysis on the other main form of asset, the *herds*, and try to show the connection between features of this form of capital, and the internal structure of camps and of the tribe.

CAPITAL FORM

Animals are individually owned private property, and a Basseri household makes its livelihood from the production of the animals owned by its members. A certain minimum of additional property is necessary in a nomadic adaptation, mainly a tent, bedding, saddle-bags, ropes, and leather sacks for milk and water, all produced by household members, and clothes, shoes, cooking and eating utensils, obtained from the towns. The total value of such equipment is slight compared to that represented by the animals. Of them the most important producers are sheep, subsidiarily goats, while donkeys are necessary for transport. Every household also has a watchdog.

In South Persia in 1958, the market value of a live adult female sheep was around 80 Tomans (£4). Its product per annum was estimated at:

clarified butter ..	*c.* 25 T.
wool	20 T.
lamb: skin	15 T.
total	60 T. or £3.

In addition, there were the lambs' meat, buttermilk and curds, to which the nomads could not give a money value of any meaning since these products are not regularly marketed. The corresponding values for goats are somewhat lower, and there is no market for their hides. On the other hand, twinning is much more frequent among them. The main reason why some goats are kept in every herd, however, is to provide goathair for the production of tent cloth.

The productive capital on which the pastoral adaptation is based is thus a large herd of sheep and goats. Of these a 10 per cent population of rams and he-goats is sufficient to ensure the fertility of the ewes and she-goats.

Certain features of this form of capital appear to have fundamental implications for the economic and social organization of the nomads:

(a) *Essentially all productive capital is in consumable form.* The livestock may at any time be slaughtered and eaten; and thus the main productive asset of a household may be consumed without the necessity of conversion through a market.

(b) *A significant fraction of the income is in the form of capital gains.*

Lambs reach maturity in two years, and a female sheep is estimated by the Basseri to have a productive period of about seven years. To maintain the full capital value of the herd, about 15 per cent of the lambs must thus be set aside each year to ensure replacement of stock; the remaining female lambs and a proportionate fraction of male lambs may be regarded as capital gains and give a possible capital increase rate of nearly 40 per cent per annum. As in the case of point (a), no market mechanism is necessary to effect a conversion from consumable product to productive capital.

(c) *There is a continual risk of total or partial loss of capital.* Since all nomadic property is movable, total loss through robbery or warfare is a continual and real danger in the weakly administered areas frequented by the nomads. Furthermore various other disasters may strike the herd: accidents and predatory animals threaten the sheep, particularly when they stray from the main flock, so constant vigilance is required to keep the animals together and protect them; and at times epidemic disease, drought or famine may strike the herds, reducing the total animal population by as much as 50 per cent.

(d) *The rate of income decreases with increased capital.* This is mainly a consequence of the herding and management techniques known to the Basseri. Unassisted by dogs, a shepherd cannot control a flock larger than about 400 head; the man who owns more animals is forced to divide his flock and entrust other persons with shepherding duties. In fact, since shepherding is a strenuous and exacting occupation, owners of herds larger than about 200 animals already tend to hire a shepherd. A recognized consequence of this is somewhat less careful herding and more frequent losses, as well as a continual pilfering of the produce. The larger the total number of animals, the less effective is the owner's supervision of his shepherds, and the greater is the decrease in the rate of income. Standard shepherding contracts, especially the long-term ones in which there is no supervision, reflect these expectations in their stipulations:
(i) *dandune* contract: the shepherd pays 10–15 Tomans per animal per year and takes all produce. At the expiration of the contract period, he returns a flock of the same number and age composition as he originally received;
(ii) *nimei* contract: the shepherd pays 30 Tomans per animal per year for a period of 3–5 years. He takes all produce, and at the expiration of the contract returns half the herd as it stands, and keeps the other half (cf. Lambton 1953, pp. 351 ff., Barth, 1961).

In addition to these characteristics of the pastoral form of capital, certain other aspects of the economic situation of the Basseri should

Capital, Saving and Credit in Peasant Societies

be described before discussing social implications, namely consumption patterns, borrowing, and investment.

A striking feature of the consumption patterns is the importance of agricultural produce to a nomad household. Wheat is the main staple; rice, dates, sugar and tea are also consumed in large quantities. Together with the considerable needs for cloth and clothing, various equipment, and luxuries, this implies a strong productive specialization and a dependence on market exchanges. A few family budgets in the nomad camp best known to me suggest an average rate of consumption in agricultural and industrial products to a value of more than 3,000 Tomans, or nearly £200, per annum per household of about six persons.

These products are paid for by the marketing of pastoral products, which only among the very poor is augmented by seasonal labour. Marketing and purchases usually take place through the medium of 'village friends'—small peddlers who live in predominantly agricultural villages where they sell industrial goods to the peasants, while supplying nomads with both agricultural and industrial produce. A nomad householder establishes a relation with such a village friend in every area where he spends a long period; during his time there he is provisioned by the peddler, and before his departure he usually settles the accumulated debt by delivery of butter, wool and hides. Though money is rarely used in these transactions, all values are estimated in terms of fluctuating current market prices.

Where the nomad does not have accumulated stores to cover his purchases, he is usually granted a half-year's or one year's credit. While such debts are usually paid for by villagers at a rate of 5 per cent per month, nomads are rarely charged more than 20–30 per cent per annum, and this is often waived when payment is made. Some nomads' debts run up to 4,000 to 5,000 Tomans.

Though this would appear to represent borrowing for current consumption, such credit serves in fact to conserve the productive asset represented by the herd: payment could be made by delivery of livestock, but by obtaining credit with security in the flock, this loss of productive animals is prevented. With a rate of income on mature sheep of nearly 100 per cent per annum (value: 80 T., product: 60 T. plus various foodstuffs), such borrowing is clearly advantageous for the nomad even when full interest is charged; and nomads often succeed in recouping in the course of a year or two in spite of heavy indebtedness.

There are thus outside sources of credit available to members of a nomadic group; likewise, outside investments are open to them. There is, in Fars, an open market in land, and standard land tenancy contracts secure a considerable income for the absentee landowner (one sixth to two-thirds of the crop, according to the quality of the

Social Structure of a Pastoral Nomad Group in South Persia

land). However, there are difficulties in converting capital in herds into capital in land which partially prevent such investments. Animals may be freely sold, but the market for livestock is severely restricted. The strains of sheep owned by the nomads, though larger and more productive than those of the villagers, are less robust, and experience shows that only some 30 per cent survive if kept in one locality through the whole year. Old sheep are of course sold for slaughter to the villages, but they fetch only a small price; animals for breeding and use can only be sold to other nomads. But since fellow nomads have very few sources of income other than their own herds, those who wish to increase their flocks by purchase have relatively limited means and represent only a very small market. The marketing of livestock is thus inevitably a rather slow process.

On the other hand, income from the sale of wool, butter and hides beyond what is required to pay for the household's consumption may freely be accumulated in the form of money, and can be invested in land. The advantages offered by this investment are security, in that the land cannot be lost through epidemics or the negligence of herdsmen, and the fact that income from land is in the form of the very agricultural products which a nomad household requires.

SOCIAL IMPLICATIONS

The above sketch of some relatively simple features of the economic situation of the Basseri pastoral nomads highlights factors of relevance to the economic choices faced by nomadic householders. I shall now try to show the social implications which they have for (a) the family development cycle, (b) processes which maintain social homogeneity within the nomad camp, and (c) attitudes and practices with respect to saving and investment.

(a) *Family development cycle.* A pastoral household requires flocks to subsist as an independent productive unit; among the Basseri at the time of my visit the nomads estimated that a herd of sixty adult sheep/goats was about the minimum required by an elementary family, while the average size of flock was at that time nearly 100 head. But a pastoral adaptation also implies certain labour requirements, and the tasks that are necessary are among the Basseri traditionally divided in such a way as to require the co-operation of at least three persons: a male head of the household, who loads the pack animals and directs the migration, erects the tent, fetches water and wood, and keeps most equipment in repair; a woman who does the cooking and housework, assists in packing and camping, and milks the flock; and a man who herds the animals, driving them to camp to be milked at about 12 a.m. and 5 p.m.

Capital, Saving and Credit in Peasant Societies

These capital and labour requirements define conditions which a family must satisfy if it is to live as an independent household. It is immediately apparent that an elementary family can only expect to satisfy these conditions with regard to labour force for a limited period of its natural development cycle, i.e. from the time the first son reaches the age of about eight to ten years, till the last son marries; and that it can obtain the necessary capital, if not on credit, then only through inheritance, i.e. normally at the dissolution of the parental household(s). Yet the value placed in Basseri culture on the elementary family as an independent household has called forth certain standardized adjustments, the forms and wider consequences of which may be analysed as social implications of pastoral capital forms and uses, granted the ideal of elementary family households.

The labour requirements of such small households are safeguarded among the Basseri by the formation of co-operative herding units of two to five tents. Since a single shepherd, as noted above, can control a herd of up to 400 head, several households can usually combine their flocks and still remain below this critical number, thus together requiring only one shepherd. Families which are short on personnel establish herding co-operation with families with several adolescent sons, thereby securing the additional labour assistance they need. The increased work involved in shepherding a flock say of 300 instead of 100 is negligible, and so the payments for this service are small: a household which supplies no herdsman for the flock of its co-operative herding unit generally gives the boys from the other tents who perform this duty one or two lambs a year and occasional small presents.

The capital requirements of a newly established family, on the other hand, are obtained by a different pattern, essentially a pattern of anticipatory inheritance. Only sons, subsidiarily collateral agnates or adopted sons, receive a share of their father's flock. This share they are given at the time of their marriage, thereby losing further claims on the estate. Each son receives at the time of his marriage the share which he would have received if his father had died at that moment, with no subsequent adjustments. An example will illustrate this: A man had 200 sheep when the eldest of his three sons married. He first paid the brideprice of 20 sheep, leaving 180; of this estate the groom received his rightful third, or 60 head, leaving 120 for the father and remaining two sons. If the father's flock subsequently increases to 200 again before the next son marries, that son will, assuming the same brideprice, receive 90 sheep at his marriage; and there is no attempt to correct the disparity between the 60 and the 90 sheep received respectively by the first and second son—because, the Basseri argue, his 60 sheep may meanwhile have grown to 600, or have been lost. The marriage of the last son is usually delayed until the parents are old, or one parent dies, so the son can become head of the new household in which the old parent(s) are permitted to live. If the son or only son reaches maturity while the father is still in his prime, the two often divide the flock 'as brothers' and separate.

In a culture where elementary families should live apart in separate tents, the capital forms and management patterns described above thus have clear social implications: certain technical patterns of herding co-operation and inheritance rules are developed, and these again have wider implications. Since the establishment of a household unit depends on the allocation to it of independent productive capital, the separation of men from their fathers and brothers is already completed when they marry—no vested economic or managerial interest ties them to their parental household. They are free to join whichever co-operative herding unit they wish, for personal or economic reasons—the practices prevent the formation of minimal or potential patrilineal nuclei on the basis of shared economic interests.

(b) *Social homogeneity*. The Basseri constitute a population of striking social homogeneity—apart from the unique position occupied by the quite small chiefly dynasty, which is based on a number of unique features such as private title to lands, political functions, and taxation rights. Nearly all Basseri commoners are independent small herd owners, and this homogeneity of the population has extensive implications for the political organization of the tribe. There is no effective hierarchy of authority in camps or sections, and groups of every size experience great difficulties when trying to reach corporate decisions, unless these are dictated by the tribal chief (cf. Barth, 1960a). This basic social homogeneity may be analysed as the result of a number of processes, to a large extent implicit in the economic features I have outlined. I shall try to show (i) that these features are such as to inhibit the concentration of wealth, and thus the emergence of status differences based on wealth, and furthermore (ii) that they tend to encourage the elimination from the group of persons who deviate significantly in wealth from the average.

(i) A number of different factors tend to inhibit the accumulation of capital in the form of large herds. The continual risk of capital losses has been noted: epidemics, famines, and losses of young animals in case of late frost may all strike as sudden disasters and reduce the herd in a fashion which is unpredictable, and which thus the herd owner cannot anticipate in his stock management. All herds will thus experience intermittent setbacks, sometimes gross reductions.

While this control on herd growth strikes large and small flocks alike, other controls, implicit in Basseri consumption patterns, have increased effects with growing herds. The household with larger herds not only increases its consumption of luxuries and of foodstuffs—that is lambs, as well as tea, sugar, rice, etc. With greater capital in herds, an increasing amount of the wealthy household's labour is also diverted from pastoral production and management to other pursuits: the men require greater leisure, and their efforts are taken up by training and tending horses, hunting, and political activity; the women weave and tie rugs (which are never marketed); and the increased weight of household belongings and larger tents requires more beasts of burden, including camels, which again means a need for a separate camel herder. All these activities and persons depend on the herd without significantly contributing to its care and production; their presence will serve as a brake on the rate of herd increase.

Greater wealth also generally leads to an earlier fragmentation of the household. The pattern of anticipatory inheritance noted above means that the marriage of sons effects a dispersal of the household's capital; furthermore, such a marriage is only possible if the son can be equipped with a share of animals sufficient to support his wife and himself—i.e. about fifty animals or more. The expected marriage age of men is in their twenties; among poor people it may be postponed till the man is as much as thirty-five to permit the necessary accumulation of capital. Wealthy people, on the other hand, have no reason for such delay; and pressure from the boy and the community at large assure a marriage age of eighteen to twenty for the sons of the large herd owners. In other words, within about twenty years of his own marriage, the dispersal of the successful herder's flock commences, giving only a brief period of accumulation for the wealthy, and nearly twice that time for the poorer and less successful. For the wealthy this means also an early loss of the cheap and dependable labour represented by adult, unmarried sons.

Finally, it is common for wealthy herd owners to contract plural marriages; they may after some years take a second, younger wife, and sometimes even a third and fourth. This means a significant increase in the size of household which must be supported by the flock, and the increased consumption will represent a drain on that flock. Furthermore, since plural marriage extends the herd owner's fertile period, it affects the distribution of wealth by inheritance. The elder sons will wish to be married at a time when their father's younger wife is still bearing children—this means that they will receive unduly large shares of their father's estate, since the shares of as-yet unborn half-brothers will not be deducted. In short, the effects of all these different and partly interconnected factors—accidental capital losses, differential consumption rates and the diversion of labour from pastoral production, accelerated division of household and capital, polygyny and increased family size without corresponding reduction of the inheritance shares of elder sons—these all act together to

Social Structure of a Pastoral Nomad Group in South Persia

inhibit the concentration of wealth in the form of large herds.

(ii) These factors are not, however, completely effective checks on the accumulation of wealth. Even less are they an effective guarantee against impoverishment, though reduced consumption, postponement of the fragmentation caused by the marriage of sons, etc., will facilitate cases of rehabilitation, just as their obverse hampers accumulation. The homogeneity of the tribe with respect to wealth will not result from these processes alone. But there are other features of the economic situation which also tend to produce homogeneity, though by a different process: there is a distinct tendency and clearly observable frequency of elimination from the tribe of households with unusually great and unusually small capital. This is possible because the Basseri, like other Persian nomads, are but a segment of a larger population where assimilation by sedentarization into peasant villages and urban centres is possible and frequent, and for different reasons sedentarization is the normal result of great capital accumulation, or capital losses.

Firstly in the case of accumulation: factors which tend to reduce the rate of income with increased size of herd have been noted. This means that while the risk of capital losses remains or increases, the increment to a large herd owner's income which results from the addition of further animals to his flocks decreases significantly. Consider, then, the possibilities of alternative investment. In nomadic activities they are nil; but the possibility of investment in agricultural land is always present. I should emphasize that sedentarization is never regarded as an ideal among the nomads; they value their way of life more highly than life in a village. But the economic advantages of land purchase are palpable: the risk of capital loss is eliminated, the profits to an absentee landowner are large, and they are in the form of products useful in a nomadic household. There is thus no feeling that land purchase implies sedentarization—a small plot of land can be let out on tenancy contracts and is merely a source of economic security and useful products. The difficulty in such investment is to convert the capital in animals to money capital by which land may be purchased. As noted, this is a relatively slow process, unless the owner is willing to take a considerable loss; none the less, with some patience it may be done, and banking facilities are available in the towns for accumulating savings, though no credit is available to nomads for investment in land.

Once a piece of land has been bought, the wealthy herd owner's money income increases rapidly, since production in marketable goods such as wool, butter and hides continues while expenses for the purchase of agricultural produce are reduced or eliminated. If a herd owner continues to be successful, he will thus accumulate wealth more rapidly, with little promise of profit through further investment in herds, but increasingly in a form which may be directly invested in land. Furthermore, title to land is held in a sedentary legal system where sons upon their marriage have no rights to anticipatory inheritance—which makes it an attractive form of capital from the owner's point of view and prevents a premature dispersal of the wealth.

This gradual process of land accumulation was observed in the field in its various stages. Only towards the very end do informants see sedentarization as its natural end result: they have a house built on their property and become increasingly concerned with the need for management of house and land, they develop a taste for many comforts that can only be satisfied by sedentary residence, etc. Sudden stock losses at this stage seem to be a common precipitating factor which drives them into the village; and even when they are well established as petty landowners they generally erect their old tent in their compound, and reside in it in the summer months.

Cases of sedentarization through capital accumulation and land purchase are by the nature of things relatively rare, and my material for the above description consists mainly of a handful of life histories. Sedentarization through impoverishment, on the other hand, is a constant threat for many and has a high empirical frequency, of the order of one person in every three in the groups of my censuses. Here the process is very simple: accident, sickness or poor management of a small herd leads to losses, and thus to an annual production below what is required for the purchase of food and clothing. But the herd itself is a large food store, and hunger easily drives the nomad to invade this his only productive capital, reducing the pastoral output further, in a vicious circle. The only alternative is to seek additional sources of income. Since shepherding contracts are relatively few (because they are, as we have seen, unprofitable for the herd owner), such sources are mainly found in sedentary society: as seasonal labourer, shepherd for the village flocks, doing local transport with donkeys, etc. To be successful, these activities must give the nomad income both to support his household *and* to increase his flock (thereby constituting a market for rich herd owners who wish to buy land). But frequently such work for a village community disturbs the nomad's migratory cycle, and thus leads only to reduced pastoral production and further animal losses, which makes him all the more dependent on sedentary sources of income. The Basseri feel that once a household's flock falls significantly below the minimal level of sixty adult head, this downward spiral is pretty inevitable and quite rapid; and there is a steady flow of impoverished settlers from every South Persian tribe to the villages and towns of their area.

These features of capital form and management thus tend, in the wider economic situation of the Basseri, to maintain a general economic homogeneity among the nomads, both by inhibiting the concentration of pastoral wealth, and by a constant elimination through sedentarization of the top and the bottom of the economic spectrum. As a consequence, social differentiation based on, or accompanied by, economic differences becomes impossible; and the nomad population becomes characterized by a striking social homogeneity, consisting of independent, economically self-sufficient small herd owners.

(c) *Saving and investment.* A final implication of these features may be seen in attitudes and practices relating to saving, thrift, and capital accumulation. I have noted the fact that pastoral capital is in a directly consumable form and consists of animals with a short life span. This creates a situation where a certain minimum of thrift is necessary in capital management—the capital can only be maintained through a systematic policy of reserving lambs for the replacement of stock. Whereas in agriculture the distinction between produce and land is clearly apparent, among pastoralists nearly every instance of consumption threatens the productive capital itself, and must be considered and evaluated by the nomad. What is more, many of the factors involved are unknown. Disease may strike so that even a conservative policy of slaughter of lambs and yearlings still results in a reduction of stock. Milking practice is also a field of continual economic choice: not only the question of how many sheep should be left with lambs, but also how much sheep with lambs should be milked, and how much should be left to those lambs. In a good year, near-starvation of lambs gives a greater yield in butter to the nomad and does not appear to have great ill effects; on the other hand, if such lambs are subject to special strain or mild disease, they are lost in much higher frequency than are well-fed, robust lambs. In short, the management of pastoral capital requires a constant awareness of savings and investment policy; it breeds an attitude of continual and thrifty concern for the herd in its practitioners.

The Basseri are very aware of the economics involved in these choices, and discuss such policy at length within the household, though rarely in public, except in the form of gossip about third persons. The basic guiding principle which they adopt comes out in an almost obsessive desire to postpone every incident of consumption—to let each lamb gain weight one more day, or week, or season, to have one more lamb from an old sheep, to make a worn-out pair of shoes last till the next market town, or till arrival in the summer area, or till next spring equinox (the Persian New Year, when it is customary to put on new clothes).

Yet—or perhaps precisely as a correlate of these interests—hospitality is a highly valued virtue. The hospitable man is admired and people speak highly of him whether he is present or absent. Men seek his company and flock to his tent, though without importunity. By their own standards, then, most Basseri are miserly; and a few glaring examples are held up for public ridicule. Thus one of the largest herd owners in the group is popularly known as D.D.T. Khan because, they say, he is such a miser he eats his own lice.

But this failure in good manners (by Basseri canons) caricatured by some and prevalent in most need not be explained only in terms of the special habits of thrift developed as a result of pastoral life. There are also clear social reasons why a pattern of conspicuous consumption and hospitality is not only economically unwise, but also socially and politically unprofitable—in contrast to most of the local societies in the Middle East. These are found in the very features of social structure described in the previous section: the great economic and social homogeneity within Basseri camps. Where wealth differences are small, a policy of social aggrandizement through public consumption of wealth is bound to bring very limited returns. Nearly all the tents of a camp remain independent and self-supporting units; a hospitable man may gain influence in his camp through hospitality, but never to the extent of being able to dominate his camp fellows, or to expect economic support or advantage from them at a later date. On the contrary, the homogeneity itself is valued, and lampoons are sung about anyone who puts on airs and assumes an authoritative manner. For the Basseri commoner, there is little to gain by spendthriftness, and thus few inducements, but many controls, on the practice of hospitality.

CONCLUSION

The material presented in this brief paper can hardly be drawn together further, since the paper itself is already a summary of select features of the economic and social organization of a pastoral tribe which show a clear relation to certain features of sheep and goat herds as a form of capital. As noted in the introduction, other economic features (e.g. relating to pasture rights and the organization of migrations) have not been discussed, though they appear to have methodologically analogous implications for centralized authority and other features of the political organization of the tribe. In the present essay I have merely attempted to show how certain elementary characteristics of capital in the form of herds are related to a limited range of features of family organization, social homogeneity within camps, and common saving and consumption patterns—granted certain cultural values and conceptions held by the Basseri people. The characteristics of pastoral capital which I have discussed are, I believe, of a type familiar in conventional economic analysis, though here admittedly in a very elementary and rough form. What is interesting, and perhaps surprising, to a social anthropologist is the fact that it should be possible at all to show their social implications by a discussion involving relatively few 'cultural' facts—that the processes by which they are made relevant to social action and features of a local social system seem to implicate few of the other basic premises of Basseri culture. Admittedly, some of these premises are contained in the specific economic definitions and characterizations used; and it would seem a hopeless, and perhaps fundamentally impossible, task to state them all in a manner so that their implications would have the form of a deductive system. But it does seem possible to show how specific social forms are related as a product to simple constellations of determining factors, and thus how partial features of Basseri social structure are directly related to specific characteristics of pastoral capital and other economic facts.

BIBLIOGRAPHY

Barth, F., 1960: 'The Land use pattern of migratory tribes of South Persia', *Norsk Geografisk Tidsskrift*, vol. 17.

—1961: *Nomads of South Persia*, Oslo.

Lambton, A. K. S., 1953: *Landlord and Peasant in Persia*, London.

[12]
Farms and Produce (*Yiagh*)

ONE OF THE PIVOTAL WORDS in the Tiv language is *yiagh;* in it their ideas of well-being and economy and work and society meet. *Yiagh* means subsistence in its broadest sense: food in the field, in the granary, in the pot, and in the belly; the farms that produce the food; the work that is required to plant, tend, and harvest it; and the whole range of activities that center around physical nourishment and comfort.

Crops and Crop Rotation

TIV COUNTRY lies between the yam-growing areas of the Guinea Coast and the grain-growing areas of the sudan. They are in the "middle belt" which is fortunate enough to have both roots and grains as staples. The staple crops are yams (*discorea* spp), millet (*pennisetum* spp), and guinea corn (*sorghum* spp). Tiv attitudes toward these and lesser crops are given in detail in *Akiga's Story* (1939:65–82).

Some parts of Tivland practice a three-year cropping cycle, other parts a two-year cycle. In the southern areas for which data is available (MbaDuku and Shangev MbaShaya), the third year is devoted to the important cash crop, beniseed. However, in the northwest (Iharev/ Ityoshin), beniseed is interplanted with guinea corn, and a two-year cycle results. In both areas plots of peanuts, sweet potatoes, and cassava are planted on fallow land especially cleared for the purpose; these crops are not part of the crop rotation. The quantity of such subordinate crops in proportion to the "staples" rises decidedly with increase in density of population.

To explain fallow periods and rotations merely in terms of years is to misrepresent the Tiv viewpoint. Southerners consistently say that land should lie fallow for at least six years and bewail the fact that such long periods of fallow are no longer possible. In the northwest, where there is no land shortage, Tiv do not think of fallow in terms of years at all, but actual practice seems to have varied from two years to sixteen years. Generally Tiv do not compute fallow periods in years; rather, they say that land should lie fallow until it is rejuvenated, a state which can be judged by grasses, trees, and earthworms. Tiv have told us that different types of soil take varying periods of years to rejuvenate, but none was able to give proportionate times. Since one can always determine the condition of any given piece of soil by examining it, there is no need to calculate time.

When discussing crop rotations, Tiv seldom talk in terms of years; instead they refer to the phases a particular farm goes through in a complete rotation cycle. Examination of the words for these phases provides a key to Tiv farming and land usage. They are summarized in Table 5.

All land which has obviously once been farmed is called "fallow" (*tsa*). It continues to be called that between the time that the final crops of one rotation are removed from it and the time it is again prepared for yams.

When the grass is pulled preparatory to making a new yam farm, the land is "cleared ground" (*ihyande*). As soon as the mounds for the new yams are well started, the land is called "mounds" (*avom*). After seed yams have been planted, it becomes a "yam field" (*sule*). Only a yam field can be called a "field"; all cultivated land can, however, be referred to as "farm" (*tiev*). As soon as the yams are harvested the farm becomes a "second-year field" (*akuur*). When the last crop (usually guinea corn) of the second-year farm has been harvested, the land

TABLE 5

WORK CALENDAR FOR KUNAV/MBADUKU

Aug.	Sept.	Oct.	Nov.	Dec.	Jan.	Feb.	Mar.	Apr.	May	June	July
IHYANDE ——	——	——	——	→ ← AVOM ——	——	→ ← SULE ——	——	——	——	——	——
SULE ——	——	——	——	——	——→	←AKUUR ——	——	——	——	——	——
AKUUR ——	——	——	——	→ ← TSA	——	——	——	——	——	——	——
MEN'S WORK CALENDAR: SOUTHERN TIV											
CLEARING FIELDS		——	——	——	——	——	——	——	——→	←——	—Millet harvest Sweet potato mounds
	HOEING MOUNDS		——	——	——	——	——	——	——→		
				Guinea corn harvest		Corn→ Plant yams	——	—— Plant millet and beniseed	——→	Plant guinea corn	Pluck beniseed
WOMEN'S WORK: SOUTHERN TIV											
CLEARING FIELDS		——	——	——	——→		PLANT YAMS	——	——→	Weed yams	Millet and beniseed harvest
Second weeding		Weeding sweet potatoes									
YAMS DUG AS NEEDED		——	——	——	→ YAM HARVEST		Weed and level *akuur*	Peanuts ——	——	——→	Clear and plant sweet potatoes
			Rice harvest	Guinea corn and sweet potato harvest	Dry cassava and vegetables		Weeding in *pagh*				

becomes fallow again. Any crops of a third year of rotation are said to be planted on fallow (Figs. 8, 9, and 10).

Progression from one of these phases to another is marked by activities in the agricultural cycle. Pulling grass turns land from "fallow" into "cleared ground"; harvesting yams changes land from a "field" into an "old field." Tiv thus see their farming and their farmland in terms of these key activities.

Cleared Ground (*Ihyande*)

A FEW DAYS before the time to pull grass for new fields—about the last half of August in southern Tivland, November in the north—the compound head calls together all the other adult males in the compound to discuss selecting sites for new farms (*nema sule*). (We have never seen such a meeting, and we believe that Tiv over-formalize it in the telling.) Following conversations over several months, it is generally known and agreed where new farms are to be made: in the land-hungry areas of southern Tivland, on that piece of land which has been longest fallow; in the swampy northwest, on the piece of land which is not submerged in the normal year and which is close enough to the compound to allow easy access, but far enough not to be menaced by goats.

Tiv say that the compound head has final and complete control of the size and location of the farms of each man in the compound. Actually, practice varies markedly in different compounds: in some the head makes no attempt to correlate agricultural activities, each subordinate group within the compound farming where it sees fit. However, agreement is usually reached quite informally among all the adult males of the compound. Tiv insist that, should there be a dispute, the compound head has the final word, but a domineering and unreasonable compound head would soon find himself "sitting alone"—the worst fate that can overtake a Tiv.

When asked what sort of requests a compound head will refuse, Tiv answer in terms of labor. A man who wants to make a larger yam farm than he can control without stinting his obligations to the group will be refused permission by the compound head. If he wants to plant many more yams than his wives and children need, so that he can sell them to get more money and goods than others in the compound, he is likely to be refused, first on the ground that he will shirk communal work,

Farms and Produce (Yiagh)

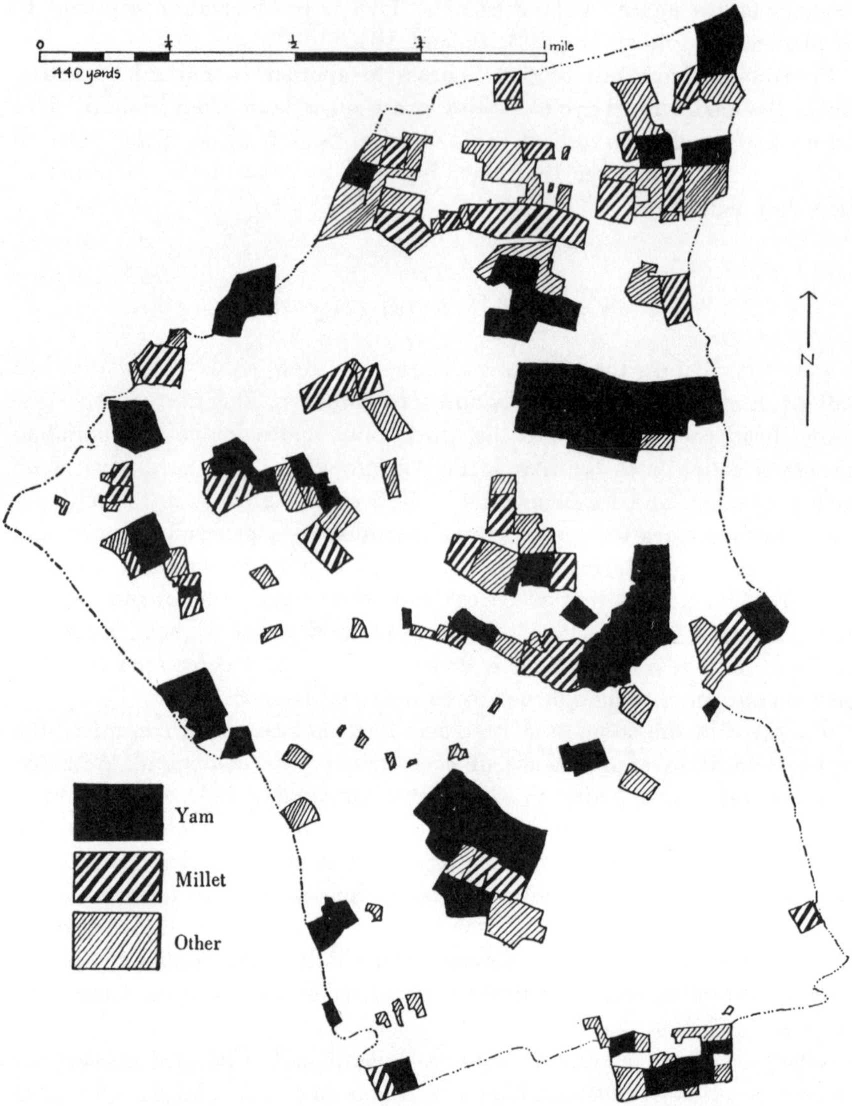

Fig. 10.—Land under cultivation, by crops—MbaGor.

43

second on the ground that if any person in the compound besides the compound head has a great deal of money the compound "spoils" (*vihi*). However, no reasonable compound head will refuse to let a man make an extra patch of ground nuts, beniseed, or cassava for sale, because the amount to be realized on them is small, and the work minimal.

On the day that grass-pulling begins, the compound is left in the care of a sick person or a child or two—in case of small compounds, often only the goats—while all of the others go out to pull grass. Women bring food to cook there; young women and girls bring pot after pot of water from the streams for cooking, for drinking, and for washing before eating. "Nurses"—children between seven and eleven—bring their infant charges out to be with their mothers who are cooking or pulling grass. All children above the age of eleven are working. But there is a definitely festive air; grass-pulling is a noisy time, with plenty of laughter and singing as well as plenty of work.

The people of the compound do not divide up into small labor groups to pull grass as they do for most other work in the fields. Younger men cut down the saplings with matchets and lop the lower branches off the large trees; the compound head, especially if he is an elder, may take little part in the work he oversees. But everybody—men and women, boys and girls—pulls grass. They form a long line, each person two or three yards from those nearest him; they bend from the waist, grabbing the tufts of grass in the left hand and pulling and cutting into the roots with hoes and matchets. The line keeps pretty well abreast as it goes from the top to the bottom of the field. The gay, picnic atmosphere lasts only for a day or two. After this, the women divide their time between the new clearings and their yam fields, and the work goes more slowly.

After a considerable portion of the land has been cleared, the compound head, with the advice and assistance of his brothers and sons, stakes out the new farms. Laying out a farm is done differently in the south than in the north.

In the southern lineages, the compound head first of all makes a large yam heap on which he will then erect an *akombo*, or magical emblem.[1] This mound, with the *akombo* set either on it or just in front of it, is the center point of the "top" (*ityough*) side of the field of the senior woman of the compound, usually the mother or wife of the compound

1. For discussion of *akombo*, see Akiga 1939:176–234; Abraham 1940:84–101; Downes 1933:63–67; L. and P. Bohannan 1953:85–90.

Farms and Produce (Yiagh)

head. He then takes 58 (more or less) paces in a straight line to the bottom (*ityo*) of the field and marks the spot.

Most Tiv say that yam mounds should be one pace (32 in.–33 in.) apart and that there should be 58 mounds in a row (*iba*); hence, the compound head should take 58 steps. There is some variation in the number of mounds said to compose a row; although the most common number is 58, the range is from 50 to 80. There is even greater variation in the numbers of heaps actually found in rows.

Dechi

The line that the compound head paces off becomes the *dechi,* or center row of the field of the senior woman. Since it is important as a reference point, Tiv say it should be straight. In one case the compound head, after pacing off about 60 paces, pushed a pointed stick into the ground, returned to his mound, and sent three of his sons to different points along the line: one to the stake at the bottom of the field, the other two at interim points. He got them into a straight line by shouting instructions to each boy in turn to move a bit to left or right. The boys were not lined up directly behind one another; rather each was just visible to the left of the one in front of him. When the row was straight, each boy drove a stake into the ground as a guide for the men who were to hoe mounds of the *dechi.*

Southerners inspect and check the straightness of this line conscientiously. They hail every passer-by to inspect the line of the markers and if one demands a change of a few inches in one of the stakes, the change is made in the full knowledge that the next passer-by will probably move it back. The compound head sights down the stakes again and makes his own alteration, then finally announces that he is satisfied. He then paces off, at approximate right angles, the full width of the field, going in each direction from the *dechi* mound. If the senior woman of the compound is to have 80 rows of yams, he sets a stake 40 paces from each side of the original mound (actually 39 paces, for Tiv count the rows, not the paces). The *dechi* itself is counted twice: they always count the rows of yams in a field from the center to one edge, including the *dechi,* then multiply by two. There are thus 79 rows of yams in a field said to contain 80. If you point this out to them, they tell you that what you say is quite true, but the mounds in the *dechi* are bigger than the mounds in the other rows.

TIV ECONOMY

Only after the field of the senior women has been staked can the limits of the other fields be staked, usually with somewhat less care.

Southerners count yam rows to determine the size of a man's field or the status of one of his wives. One hears such comments as, "I see that WanGajo has 20 more rows of yams this year than last—is she pregnant?" Or, "Dzungwe has hoed 10 fewer rows for his senior wife this year—yes, her daughter was married and went to her husband." These are indicative of the fact that the size of a woman's fields is usually in direct proportion to her needs. A woman with many children or one who has many attached junior wives, daughters-in-law, or grandchildren may have 100 or more rows of yams. A new wife, who has borne only one child or none, will have only 20 or 30 rows. The favorite wife of an important man may have a larger farm than her co-wives, but all the persons in the compound, including her co-wives, say that this is because she supplies the major portion of the food which her husband shares with friends and guests.

The fields in the northwest have no *dechi*. They are laid out from one side to the other and "squared" on the "path row" (*iba-ndoro*, sometimes called *gwendor* in Iharev dialect). Iharev/Ityoshin people count all the rows in a farm; all the farms are larger, and the size of a woman's farm tends to be associated with the number of seed yams she can get together rather than with her status or the number of her dependents.

Mounds (*Avom*)

The day after the field of the senior wife has been laid out, the young men—including her sons, if she has any of working age—begin hoeing mounds, while the other men and the women continue to pull grass. The center row of mounds is usually completed before any other mounds are begun. Mounds of the *dechi*, like all yam mounds, are a pace apart, but *dechi* mounds are taller than others: they are usually about 30 inches in height, while the ordinary mound is about 18 or 20 inches.

The "small *dechi*"[2] are made next: rows of ordinary-sized yam heaps, one on each side of the *dechi*. The small *dechi* need not be finished before the other rows are made.

The mounds in a row of yams are set off from those in the next row, as shown in Figure 11. A well-laid-out field forms rows in both directions,

2. Translated "*dechi's* children" (*wan dechi*) by East in Akiga 1939, passim. As Akiga says, only Kparev make yam fields in this way.

Farms and Produce (Yiagh)

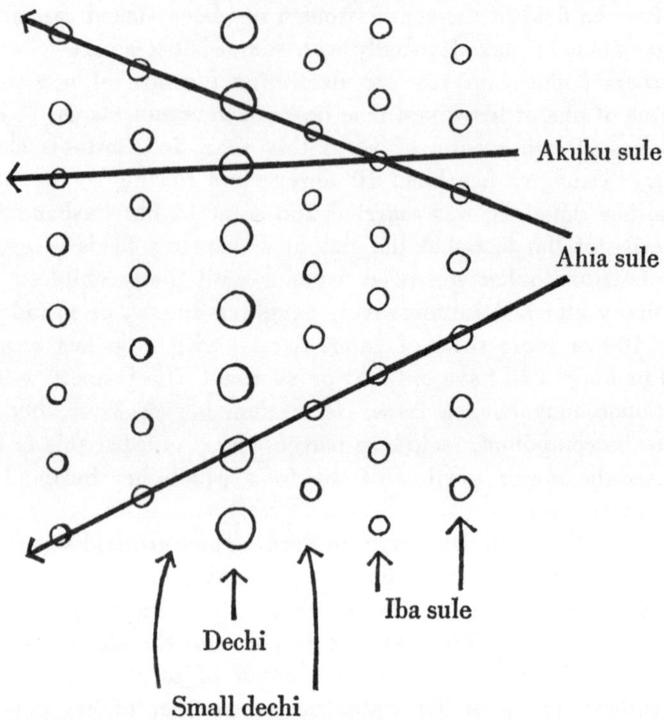

Fig. 11—Mounding of yam field.

as well as diagonally. Tiv describe this by reference to the top, bottom, and sides of the field. The rows which run from top to bottom are called *iba sule* in Kunav dialect; the rows from side to side are called *akuku sule;* while diagonal rows are called *ahia* (interstices) *sule.*[3]

Though the top of a field is usually higher in altitude than the bottom, it need not be so. Nor are "top and bottom" necessarily correlated with

3. Iharev dialect is somewhat different. An *iba sule* is a row running in any direction; the row from top to bottom is called *lyembe sule. Akuku sule* means diagonal row instead of cross row, while cross rows are called *gwambe sule.*

direction. In Ityoshin there is a cleared space some five feet wide around all yam fields to keep wild animals out. We have never seen this cleared space (*kpi sule*) in the south.

The work of making mounds is done by men with a heavy hoe. The actual operation of constructing the mound seems a simple one, but it is not. The legs are placed well apart, then the hoe is dug into the soil between the feet in such a way that a clod of about eight inches wide by two or three inches thick is scooped on to the hoe. This clod is then flipped, moist side out, into position on the mound which is being built up.

When the mound has been finished, dried grass and leaves—left on the field after clearing—are gathered into small bundles and set on top of the mound, weighted down with a hoeful of soil. This may be done by the man who digs the mound, or it may be done by younger boys. The purpose of this bit of grass is to prevent erosion of the mound and to afford protection from the sun for the sprouting yam.

Soon after the mounds have been made, often on the same day, a piece of cassava stalk, freshly cut, is placed rather low on the side of the mound. The cassava, planted thus several weeks or months before the yams, is given a chance to grow up high enough to provide a trellis for the yam vine to climb. Tiv point out that more than one stalk of cassava per mound stunts the yams planted there.

Clearing the grass is usually finished by the end of November (the end of December in Iharev/Ityoshin). Digging the mounds takes longer. Kparev say it is best to finish them a month or so after the dry season sets in; after that the ground is hard and mounds made from dry soil will crumble. This ideal is seldom realized. A light rain during the dry season (there are usually three or four) is followed by a few days of feverish activity in the new fields, before the soil again gets too hard to work. Although the best and biggest yams are those which are planted in February, many people do not finish digging their mounds until the new rainy season is well under way—sometimes the middle of May. This latter practice is the norm in Iharev/Ityoshin.

When a man has finished his yam fields he cuts a branch of a plant known as "man's ikula" (*ikula i nomsu;* in Iharev, *kwakula*) if he is living with his agnatic lineage, or "woman's ikula" (*ikula i kase—sarcocephalus esculentis*) if he is living with his mother's agnatic lineage. This branch is placed across the most important patch which borders or traverses the field; the symbol of an *akombo* may be put beside it. The branch is covered with a hoeful or two of soil to keep it in place.

Farms and Produce (Yiagh)

Tiv say that this notifies persons going down the path that a farm has been finished, so that they will examine it and remark on it. The man who puts up such a symbol will himself first scrutinize his fields closely. He will look down each row to see that it is straight; he asks advice of passers-by. We have seen a man change the position of two mounds slightly because he was convinced they were a bit out of position on the diagonal, thereby spoiling the symmetry of his field. A well-laid-out field in which all the rows—vertical, horizontal, and diagonal—are straight is a source of aesthetic satisfaction. We have been told, "Nothing so gladdens the heart as a field in which all the rows are straight." We have seen Kparev Tiv spend an hour or so admiring their own fields, if they were well done, and almost as long admiring those of a kinsman. If one walks in a strange area with Tiv at any time during the growing season, one is given a continuous commentary which can be summarized, "That field is a good one; this one is not."

The Field (*Sule*)

THE ACTIVITY which turns the mounds into a field (*sule*) is the planting of the seed yams. Seed yams are sometimes stored in the compound but more often in special trenches or in last year's mounds. They are carried to the new field by women, who sort them by types and lay them out, one seed yam or section on top of each mound. Both men and women do the actual planting—men with the heavy hoe, women with a digging stick. The grass crown is removed and the hoe is sunk into the top of the mound just behind the seed yam (only the inept first remove it; more skillful men jeer at those who do so, or those who injure a seed yam with the hoe). The hoe is then held in the left hand and pulled forward to leave a gap; the seed yam is slipped into the gap with the right hand and the hoe removed easily, allowing the soil to fall back gently. The most skillful men can perform this operation without losing any of the soil from the top of the mound.

When a woman plants seed yams, she takes her digging stick in both hands, and with a sharp downward stroke forces it into the top of the mound. Then by twisting and working it about, she creates a hole into which the yam will fit, inserts it, and closes the top by hand. In all cases the grass cap is replaced and again weighted with soil.

In May, after the rains are well under way and all the yams should have sprouted, those which prove infertile are removed from the mounds and replaced.

Planting completes men's work with yams. The major part of women's agricultural work is with yams. Yams should be weeded two or three times—most Tiv agree that three times is best, but many compounds manage only two weedings. Women perform this work with the small hoe (see Chap. 8)*.

Many side crops are grown in yam fields. We have counted as many as eight crops in a single mounded field: yams, cassava, peanuts, okra, sorrel (both red and white), *ahuma* beans, *adenge* beans, and pepper. Cotton, corn, gourds and cucurbits of several kinds, and a great many "soup plants" may be grown as well. Most of these side crops (cassava is the obvious exception) are planted low on the sides of the mounds by women during and after the first weeding. They are harvested as they ripen or are needed.

Harvest

The first yams are usually ready to be dug and eaten in early July in Kparev; in Ityoshin, not until early September. First yams are said to be associated with various rites in different parts of the country (East 1939:90–92). These rites are casual; they affect only adult males and are commonly omitted.

After the "first yams" are dug (and often before), women harvest those they need for food. The general harvest takes place in late December when the dry season is well advanced, after the guinea-corn harvest is completed. It is carried out by the basic labor group of women: a senior woman with attached co-wives and daughters-in-law. Most of the digging is done by young women with digging sticks. The stick is held in both hands and driven into the top of the dry mound; then with a forward motion one whole side of the mound is peeled off, leaving the yam exposed. The dry soil can be loosened the rest of the way round the yam and the whole thing lifted out undamaged. For a few weeks after the yams have been removed, the field looks like a series of half-domes. The younger women bring the yams to one of several collection points in the field, where the senior woman separates them carefully by types. Eating yams are separated from seed yams, then dry yams (*iyough*) from water yams (*agbo*), and there is a further separation into red and white yams. There are well over fifty types of yams, with names known only to

* not reproduced here

women; except for a half dozen of the simplest and most common, few women agree on identifications.

In Kparev, after separating and grading, the yams are cached about the field in trenches, covered with a matting of dried grass. They are not simply dumped into the trenches, but are carefully and symmetrically laid in, graded by type and size.

In Kparev, seed yams are carried either to the compound or to the cache in the new fields, whichever is nearest. Women divide their time between old farms and new farms at this time of the year. The men, who are probably still working at hoeing mounds in the new fields, build field shelters (singular, *tumbe*) for their wives, and a woman and her young children often spend many nights in her fields watching over the harvest, with only an occasional trip back to the compound. These shelters are about ten feet in diameter, comprised of six or eight uprights with a thatched conical roof. They have built-up, pounded floors; the sides may be open or mats may be tied along one side. A fire is kept going in these shelters and cooking is done here. There is usually a single shelter for all the women in the basic labor group.

Even in Ityoshin, where all other crops are safely stored in the fields, it is risky to leave seed yams unattended in a cache. People say that they are short almost every year and that yams are likely to be stolen no matter how strong a magical emblem protects them. They add, however, that when yams are laid out on mounds before planting, they will not be stolen—though they may be eaten by cattle or monkeys.

The yams for eating are gradually, over a period of weeks, transported by women to the compound, a headload at a time. The ordinary headload of yams varies between fifty and seventy pounds in weight; it is sometimes over a mile from farm to compound but usually half a mile.

Second-Year Fields (*Akuur*)

As soon as the yams and cassava have been removed, the land on which they grew becomes a second-year field (*akuur*). In March or April, usually after the harmattan has stopped but before the rains, what remains of the old mounds is leveled by the men. Then, after the first big rain which is considered to be the start of the rainy season proper (there may be two or even three heavy rains before this time, perhaps separated by dry periods of a fortnight or more), bulrush millet (*amine*) is planted by broadcasting the seed; the soil is then turned and worked quickly to bury the seed. This is men's work, though women often assist.

When the millet has been planted, a man again puts *ikula* leaves on the path to indicate that he has finished a farm. It is not so important an occasion as finishing a yam field. Tiv appreciate a neat millet field, but not with the same zeal with which they appreciate a well-made yam field.

Millet is a tricky crop, Tiv say, because minor changes in the weather affect it. Millet must be planted after a soaking rain, and should then have about five days of cloudy weather, but no rain. Without these conditions for germination, the yield is poor and the grains—if they form—are brown and bitter. Tiv are always in doubt as to just when millet should be planted, and they emphasize the element of luck involved. What was conceded by all to be the best millet crop in MbaGor—the only really good one in 1950—was planted almost two weeks before any of the others. Almost everybody else in MbaGor told the compound head who had planted so early that he would get no yield at all. Iyon planted millet even later than MbaGor, and the yield was even poorer.

The crop most commonly interplanted with bulrush millet is guinea corn (*wua*), which is planted a month or six weeks after the millet, being broadcast into the field, usually with no subsequent turning of the soil. Kparev people broadcast guinea-corn seed from their hands, walking through the field. Iharev people take a mouthful of mixed guinea-corn seed and beniseed and walk along the rows blowing it out in a fine spray. Most people say that millet should be weeded immediately prior to the planting of the guinea corn, but it often is not done. Tiv in the north do not plant guinea corn until the millet has been harvested.

Other crops found interplanted with millet include cassava (usually to be found growing in the field before the millet itself is planted) and beniseed. Planting beniseed and guinea corn together is somewhat more common in the south and is standard practice in the north, where beniseed is planted late in July (if planted earlier in this swampy, fertile soil, it goes to stem and does not bear well).

At millet harvest, men break down the stalks with an arrangement of rope and pole (*aga*), cut them with matchets, and then lay the stalks in rows running from top to bottom of the field, about eight to ten feet apart. Women then go down the rows, cut off the heads, tie them into bundles, and carry them back to the compound.

Millet is harvested about two months or slightly longer after planting—usually in June. It is valued by all Tiv because it makes the best beer; it is especially valued by southern Tiv because it is a hunger-breaker, ready between the time that the guinea corn is exhausted and the new yams are dug. It shares this role of hunger-breaker with corn, which is grown as a side crop in the main fields, in the kitchen gardens, or in stream beds.

In those parts of southern Tivland which we know, millet stalks are used for fuel. In the areas of Ityoshin where we worked, however, and in all those we walked through, there is plenty of firewood; there millet stalks are laid in rows in the fields, and the soil is piled over them, making ridges in which the next crop, guinea corn, is planted. Iharev people recognize that this makes the soil more fertile but say the effects are not noticeable the year it is done.

Beniseed is harvested by plucking each spike, then tying several together and hanging the bundle over rails to dry. It is, when thoroughly dry, pounded in a mortar and winnowed.

Guinea corn is harvested in the same way as millet; it is trod down with the *aga*, and the heads cut off with a knife. People in the south say that guinea-corn harvest begins the morning after the first harmattan arrives; this was true on December 1, 1949. Northerners do not make this correlation, and in late 1951 the guinea-corn harvest followed the arrival of the harmattan by more than three weeks.

Fallow (*Tsa*)

As soon as the guinea corn has been cut, the land is referred to as "fallow." In the south, wet season beniseed (that is, planted in April and harvested in June) is grown on "fallow" in the third year of a rotation. Peanuts, sweet potatoes, Bambara groundnuts, and cassava may be grown on "fallow" without necessitating a lengthened fallow period, Kparev people say. Iharev, however, say that Kparev grow these crops in quantity only because of land shortage, and that they themselves like these foods only for occasional snacks.

In the south, when fallow land is cleared for planting fallow crops, grass and small trees are allowed to dry and are burned. The ashes are mixed with the soil when mounds or ridges are made. Some Tiv say this increases the yield; others say that burning the grass and brush is the easiest way to get rid of it, adding that if you wanted it for fertilizer you would bury it rather than burn it.

TIV ECONOMY

Clearing for fallow crops is usually done by women, though men assist by making the mounds. Sweet potatoes (*atsaka*) are planted from runners in round, flat-topped mounds about eight or ten inches high. Southerners plant sweet potatoes late in June; northerners plant the few they want at any time during the agricultural year. Weeding and harvesting sweet potatoes is woman's work.

Peanuts are planted by women on three or four inch high ridges made by men; Bambara groundnuts are planted by women on small rounded mounds about ten inches high. Both are harvested by women. Cassava, when grown alone, is planted by either sex in ridges a foot or so high made by men.

These fallow crops are of great importance in the diet of southern Tiv; they are not highly regarded, however, and much less care is given to them than to yams, millet, guinea corn, or the "swamp crops."

One of the ways to tell that a piece of fallow is ready for recultivation is by the type of grass it produces. Tiv say that after a piece of land has been cropped, the grass which it grows is predominantly sword grass (*ihila*). The next year, *agom* grass begins to replace it. For the next few years *agom* clumps get larger and heavier until they are about a foot in diameter at the base and there is no sword grass left; then it is ready to be farmed again. Another grass which is said to be indicative of good soil is *aper*.

In central parts of Tivland, according to informants in Jengba/Ipav, trees and earthworms are used as the indicators of rich soil. Large undergrowth trees and large-size grass clumps with plenty of earthworm mounds mark fallow which is ready for recultivation.

Reclaimed Swamp (*Pagh*)

In Iyon there are fifteen or twenty acres of irrigated land in stream beds, which do much to ameliorate conditions of severe land shortage. This land (see Figs. 9 and 12) is in production for ten months or more of the year, affording as much as three crops of quick-maturing corn and one of rice. During the rains, proper care of this reclaimed land insures fresh supplies of silt, and the quick decay of luxuriant vegetation, constantly being cut back and left to rot, has made a deep, thick soil.

Tiv call the irrigated land along a stream bed *pagh*. *Pagh* also means to prepare land in such a way that water is retained or redirected. The

Farms and Produce (Yiagh)

heavy work of keeping such land clear, and the almost constant work on ditches and the building of ridges and beds, falls on the men. Most of it is done with the heavy hoe and the matchet. Corn—the most important crop grown in such reclaimed swamp—is planted in slightly raised ridges by stamping a hole in the soft moist soil with the heel of one foot, dropping in two grains of corn, then brushing soil back into the hole with the toes. Rice is planted by broadcasting it among the stalks of the second or third crop of corn.

There are no large areas of such irrigated land in MbaGor, although we believe all compounds have small corn and rice fields along the streams. The first crop of corn is planted as early as February, maturing in April.[4] Corn ears are sold in local markets during the season, to be eaten on the spot. Rice, in 1949, was primarily a woman's cash crop which eventually found its way to the Ibo and Cross River peoples in the Eastern Provinces. By 1952, men had taken over the rice, and acreage was vastly increased.

Reclaimed swamp land of this sort is highly prized by southern Tiv; they say that a good piece of such land need never be left fallow for more than a few months at a time. It is also highly important because the corn it produces ripens when food is short, and because the rice which can be grown on it is a ready source of cash. We found no reclaimed swamp land in the northwest of Tivland.

Kitchen Gardens (*Ikongo*)

THE GARDENS which surround southern compounds—and are in turn often surrounded by a ring of trees—provide Tiv not only with most of their green vegetables, tobacco, indigo, cotton, and fruit, but with small amounts of staples, particularly millet and corn. The *ikongo* also symbolizes privacy and discreteness. The kitchen gardens, forming a ring round the compound, are a buffer between the people of the compound and their neighbors. Encroaching on someone else's land to make a new

4. During the time the map of MbaGor was made, there was no activity in the stream farms, and most were fallow. We did not map them, since pacing these muddy paddies is almost impossible. Those in Iyon (see Fig. 12) are all indicated, but are in such tiny blocks that we did not have time to get exact distribution.

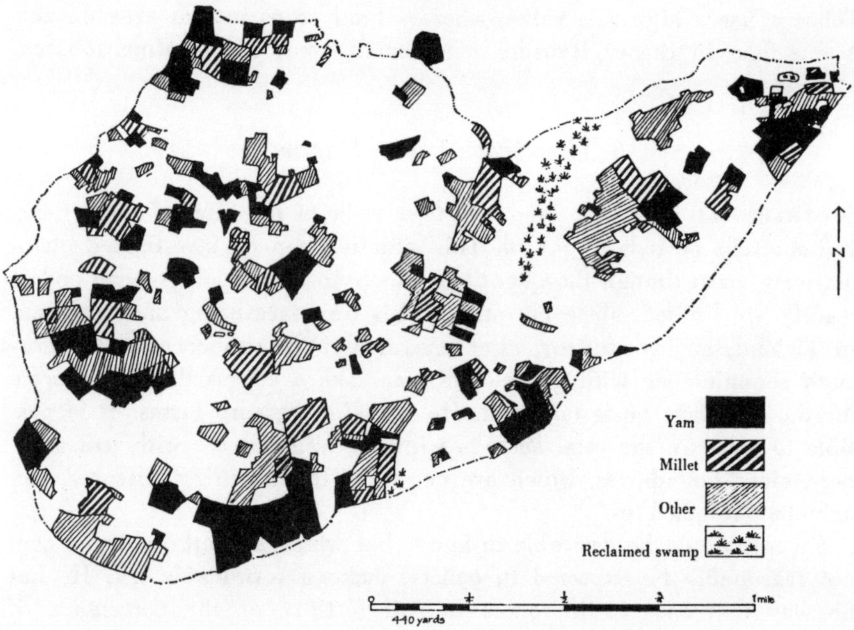

Fig. 12.—Land under cultivation by crops—Iyon.

farm is common; but encroaching on kitchen gardens is a serious breach of etiquette.

Every man is entitled to a plot just behind his wives' huts for his kitchen gardens. He may give each wife a patch or he may keep it all for himself, telling the wives what work to perform.

Kitchen gardens and the trees that surround them are important in some rituals; they are the scene of assignations; they symbolize the unity and discreteness of the compound; they are kitchen middens and latrines.

Ikongo, in Iharev dialect, means only the area surrounding the compound. It is seldom used for kitchen gardens because the goats (more numerous than in the south) eat any crops planted close to the compound. Crops which Kparev people plant in their kitchen gardens are planted by Iharev in their fields—except tobacco, which would be stolen.

Farms and Produce (Yiagh)

Tobacco has a high sale value, whereas food crops in that area do not. A few men in Iharev/Ityoshin fence small areas for planting tobacco.

The Size of Tiv Farms

SOUTHERN TIV say that land shortage reduces the size of their fields and shortens periods of fallow. This situation can be investigated quantitatively, even though the quantities which an anthropologist can collect readily are limited, since he must do his own measuring and counting. In Tivland, an investigator, after several months' residence and a thorough acquaintance with genealogies, can take a census that is accurate for the few days he is taking it. He can also measure farms. It is possible to measure the total acreage within a minimal *tar* with less accuracy, since boundaries, which are necessary to measuring acreages, can only be "roughed in."

Facts it would be desirable to know, but which an anthropologist cannot reasonably be expected to collect, make a formidable list. He has no way to measure differences in soil fertility or the percentage of cultivable land. It is impossible for him—in Tivland, at least—to obtain accurate data on crop yields. Tiv do not have a general harvest in which all of any single crop is put in one place. Millet and guinea corn, which are cut all at once, are seldom stored in such a way that the investigator can do more than estimate weight roughly. Yams are dug as needed until the middle or late dry season. Tiv do not measure the yield of their farms. Therefore, any attempt to do so meets misunderstanding, mistrust, active opposition, or resentment. The agricultural department of the colonial government could supply yield statistics from its own experimental farms, but conditions on the farms for which these figures are available do not correspond with those of an ordinary Tiv farm, and the statistics are useless for our purposes. The 1951 agricultural census was much too general. In short, obtaining accurate yield statistics would require one assistant per woman whose farm was included in the survey. He would have to follow her about from morning to night to weigh and record what she picked or harvested to eat or cook. Needless to say, Tiv women would not put up with this sort of thing, even if the assistants could be found.

In order to investigate Tiv statements about land shortage, it has been necessary to adopt different methods. We can ask, "What percentage of

TIV ECONOMY

a total area of a minimal *tar* is under cultivation each year, and what is the relationship between this percentage and the density of population?"

Table 6 shows quantitatively that as the density of population rises, the percentage of land in cultivation also rises. If the same proportion of land per person were used in Iyon as in MbaAliko, 62 per cent of Iyon would be under cultivation constantly. Since it is impossible, if fertility is to be maintained by fallowing, for 62 per cent of the land to be under cultivation at a given time, the land shortage is obviously severe. The actual figure is about half that: 35 per cent. Hence, some adjustment must be made. Several things can be done: (1) The cultivation period can be shortened; (2) the size of the fields can be decreased; (3) a change in crops can be introduced; (4) the length of the fallow period can be reduced; and (5) new farming methods can be introduced.

TABLE 6

CULTIVATED ACREAGE AND POPULATION DENSITY

Location	Acres in Cultivation	Total Acreage	Percentage of Land in Cultivation	Density of Population per Square Mile
Southern Tivland				
MbaGor	327.75	1,145	28	267
Iyon	426.05	1,217	35	552
Northern Tivland				
MbaAliko	125.27	c. 1,700	7	65

In both MbaGor and Iyon the cultivation period has been reduced. In this part of the country, where beniseed is normally planted as the third-year crop in the rotation, many farmers plant beniseed on second-year fields in place of millet, rather than on fallow in the third year. When these two crops are harvested in late June or early July, the entire acreage is put into guinea corn. This practice definitely reduces the amount of food available, especially millet, a hunger-breaker. Moreover, not all land that is planted to yams in the first year of a rotation cycle is used during the second year. Some is allowed to revert to fallow after a single year, thus further reducing food supplies. All these practices lead to greater reduction of grain than of yams in land-hungry areas.

The size of fields has also been reduced, especially in Iyon. The yam acreage per person is given in Table 7.

Farms and Produce (Yiagh)

TABLE 7

YAM ACREAGE

Location	Acres in Yams	Population	Acres of Yams per Person
Southern Tivland			
MbaGor	152.35	477	.30
Iyon	163.50	1,047	.16
Northern Tivland			
MbaAliko	57.56	167	.33

Though Iyon have reduced the size of yam fields to about half that of the other areas, MbaGor have not. MbaGor people say that they would increase the size of their yam fields if they had sufficient land to do so. If Iyon yam fields were the same size per person as those of MbaGor, and all other factors were equal, Iyon would require almost three times the total amount of land available at present.

Much the same picture emerges from an examination of the total cultivated acres per person (see Table 8).

TABLE 8

CULTIVATED ACREAGE PER PERSON

Location	Total Cultivated Acreage	Population	Acres per Person
Southern Tivland			
MbaGor	327.75	477	.68
Iyon	426.05	1,047	.42
Northern Tivland			
MbaAliko	125.27	167	.75

MbaGor have cut the size of their fields very little. Iyon, who have only about half the amount of yam acreage per person as MbaGor, have two-thirds the amount of total cultivated acreage per person. This leads to the next point: the possibility of a change of crops.

If, by change of crops, new and different crops are meant, there has been no change. Iyon grow the same crops as do the rest of the Tiv. However, a change of proportion in the crops has taken place. The data in Table 9, as well as Table 10 and Figures 12 and 13, give some indication of the extent of the change.

The most obvious difference is the decreased acreage in millet and guinea corn in the land-hungry areas, and the concomitant increase in fallow crops, such as beniseed and cassava. These figures support our

TIV ECONOMY

TABLE 9
Acreage in Various Crops
(percentages)

Location	Yams	Millet and Guinea Corn	Beniseed (3d year)	Cassava	Fallow Crops
Southern Tivland					
MbaGor	46.5	30.3	10.0	3.1	10.1
Iyon	38.4	29.9	17.5	4.4	9.8
Northern Tivland					
MbaAliko	46.0	51.0	—	—	3.0

TABLE 10
Beniseed Acreage per Adult Male

MbaGor	.24
Iyon	.27

observations that in the north guinea corn lasts until the new yams are ready to eat, leaving almost all the millet for brewing, whereas southerners are lucky if the guinea corn lasts until the millet is harvested and, further, if the millet lasts until the new yams are ready to eat.

Northerners usually have no hungry season. This fact is largely attributable to a much greater grain supply. Although the yam supply is somewhat larger, yams are staple for fewer months of the year.

The increase in fallow crops in the southern areas is in all probability the obverse of this comparative shortage of grain. Peanuts, Bambara groundnuts, and sweet potatoes are all grown extensively in the south. Although some northern women plant one or all of these crops, they seldom plant more than can comfortably be grown as side-crops on their yam mounds. They are used in the north as flavoring or snacks; in the south they form an important part of the diet. Northerners say they do not like them, that they are not proper food. Southerners, however, say that they do like them and that they are good solid food.

The increase in cassava proportionate to the shortage of land does not show up as clearly in these figures as it might if there were a more detailed breakdown. Cassava can be and is interplanted with all the other crops. In collecting the data on which these figures were based, it was necessary, therefore, to eliminate cassava when it was intermixed with other crops, lest the number of categories become utterly unwieldy; only those patches in which cassava was planted alone appear

Farms and Produce (Yiagh)

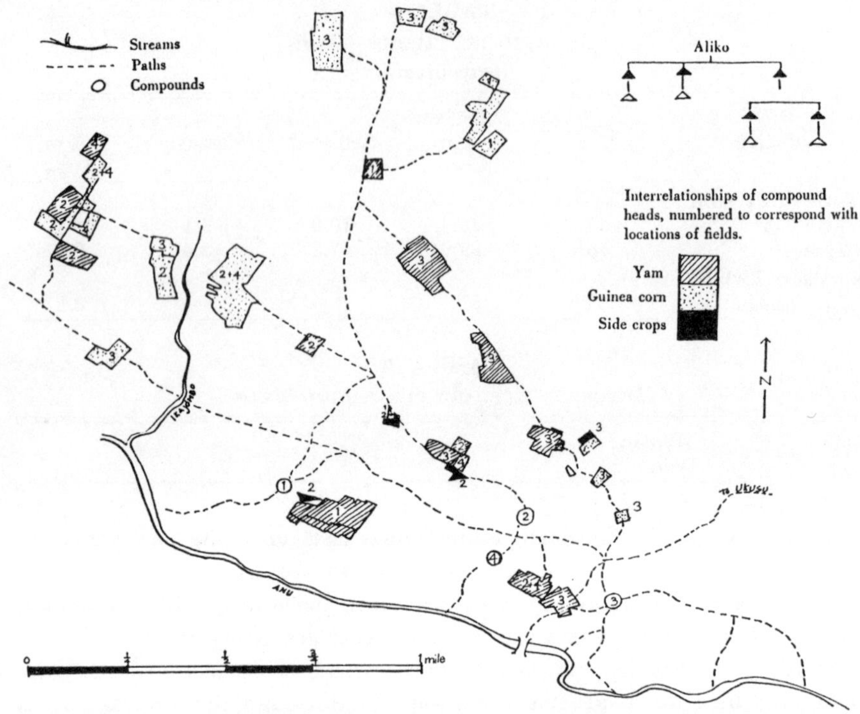

Fig. 13.—Land and compounds of MbaAliko.

in the figures. What is more apparent is that there is some cassava grown in Ityoshin, but only that grown on yam mounds, and by no means in all yam fields. In MbaGor there is much more cassava grown in yam fields than in Ityoshin, both in amount per field and in the number of fields, for in MbaGor almost all yam fields had cassava. Sometimes cassava was interplanted with kitchen garden crops; it was almost always done in Iyon. MbaGor seldom or never interplanted cassava with guinea corn; it was standard practice in Iyon. In almost no place in MbaGor was cassava interplanted with beniseed; it was common in Iyon. One man in Iyon knowingly took a chance of reducing the yield of his yam field by planting two cassava roots instead of one in each mound.

TIV ECONOMY

Tiv do not like cassava. Southerners say that a small portion of it can be added to yam porridge (*luam*) without hurting it; northerners say that the yam porridge containing cassava and sweet potatoes made by the people of central and southern Tivland gives them headaches and stomach-aches. No Tiv like cassava alone; all say that if you eat too much of it, stomach-ache and indigestion result. This is due in part to the fact that Tiv do not leach cassava to make flour of it as do Ibo, Hausa, and other Nigerian peoples. They usually eat it roasted. They know the techniques used by these other peoples, but do not employ them.

Another important, but not so obvious, divergence which comes to light in Table 9 is the beniseed acreage. It would seem unusual—at least it would demand explanation—that in an area as hard pressed for land as Iyon, almost one-fifth of the land is devoted to a "cash crop." This can be explained, however, by reference to another set of figures (see Table 10). Throughout Tivland there is a direct relationship between beniseed and tax. Beniseed is called "tax" (*kpandegh*) and not "food" (*yiagh*). This is the one crop for which the acreage per male is nearly the same in the two lineage areas. Men in both areas say they plant only enough beniseed for tax.

In the 1950 season the price of beniseed was 20*s*. per hundredweight, and the agricultural census figures made that year indicated that the average yield in Tiv Division was 200 pounds per acre. This figure was said to be below average because of unseasonal rains. We were in MbaGor and Iyon at the time and recorded no statements that a bad crop was harvested. If these figures are correct, each male received about 10*s*. for his beniseed, while the tax was 8*s*. 6*d*. per adult male that year. We left the field before beniseed sales began on a large scale, and before taxes were due, so we did not learn whether the amount of beniseed actually did cover the tax. We did learn, however, that when the tax was announced—it had been 6*s*. 6*d*. the year before—increases were made in the amount of land allotted to beniseed.

Beniseed acreage in the north is not strictly comparable because it is interplanted with guinea corn and ripens at a different time of the year. During the 1951 season, when everyone said the beniseed crop was poor because of heavy rains in October, the dozen or so men we asked about sales reported that they got about 15*s*. for their beniseed—enough to pay their 10*s*. head tax in addition to a cloth for the wife who carried it to town to sell it.

Farms and Produce (Yiagh)

Any reduction which may have occurred in the length of the fallow period is not so easy to quantify. Tiv in MbaGor said that they had extensively reduced their fallow periods—too much to allow for proper revitalization of the soil. Iyon people said that they had nearly done away with fallow. One Iyon man whom we knew well planted millet and guinea corn in 1950 on a farm which had been cleared of yams the year before. Instead of planting beniseed there the following year, or letting the land revert to fallow, he intended to put a new crop of yams on it in 1951. They wouldn't be very big yams, he said, but by eating them mixed with cassava and sweet potatoes, he could leave some of his other fallow idle or in fallow crops for an additional year. He said this would make one year out of three more difficult. During that year he would have to sell cassava to the Hausa and Ibo in Obudu in order to buy yams from the Uge, but he would be better fed in the long run, because his land would have longer in fallow or fallow crops.

The last alternative for bringing into accordance agricultural practice and the amount of land available for cultivation—that of new and improved agricultural methods—needs careful consideration. Tivland is (except for a few places which have been cleared) tsetse-infested, and as a result animals in sufficient number to provide manure for fields cannot be kept. Most Tiv use no form of fertilization on their farms. Some of them do use human and animal excreta in their kitchen gardens when planting fruit trees, but they regard the idea with repugnance. The government agricultural service tried to introduce green manure crops and compost heaps. In Shangev and southern Kunav these methods were not successful. Tiv so far have not been made to see that if they plant part of their land with a crop which will be dug under to provide green manure, they will get much better yields from the land (though the northern practice with millet stalks indicates that the idea is not foreign to them). To Tiv, such a practice represents hard work with no visible gain, and—more important to them—it would (they say) reduce even further the amount of land available. Composting has been even less successful: Tiv are indifferent to green-manure crops. They are downright anti-compost: "Have *you* ever tried to carry such stuff on your head?"

When discussing the introduction of new agricultural methods, Tiv always come back to fallow. They insist that if there were enough land available, it could lie fallow until it grew the right grasses. It would then be as good as it ever was for growing food. They say they do not need green-manure crops or compost heaps but the abolition of the boundary between themselves and the Udam and Uge, their neighbors to the south, thus making it possible for them to take sufficient land to prolong the fallow periods.

Both points of view are correct: either longer fallow periods, with accompanying expansion, or fertilizers and improved farming methods will increase agricultural production in southern Tivland. Proponents of each view are not prepared to accept that the other has any virtue while the alternative exists. Here is a real clash of cultural values.

We have seen that there is a wide variation in the size of farms in various minimal *utar* and that the amount of land under cultivation per person and the proportions of crops are, generally speaking, directly correlated with the density of population and resulting land shortage. The variation in size of farms within the minimal *tar* is also greater in those areas in which land shortage is most severe (Table 11).

TABLE 11
Total Cultivated Acreage per Person

Location	Compound with Maximum	Compound with Median	Compound with Minimum	Ratio of Maximum to Minimum
MbaAliko (including a sample from Ukusu)	.77	.74	.58	1.33:1
MbaGor	1.79	.65	.40	4.48:1
Iyon	.92	.41	.14	6.57:1

In the northern sample, the compound with the most acreage per person has only 33 per cent more than that with the least. In the southern area of greatest land shortage, the compound with the greatest acreage per person has 650 per cent as much land as that with the least. Though a ratio of 6.5:1 between poorest and richest is truly very small, it is noteworthy that land shortage is one of the primary correlates of a growing economic differentiation.

Both median and minimum acreages per person decrease as the density of population increases. Yet the maximum acreage of cultivated land per person is higher in both areas of land shortage than in the area in which there is no land shortage. The cases discussed in Chapter 5 will help to explain this fact.

Bibliography

ABRAHAM, R. C.
1940 *The Tiv People* (2d ed.). London: Crown Agents for the Colonies.

AKIGA (B. AKIGA SAI)
1939 *Akiga's Story*. Trans. Rupert East. London: Oxford University Press for International African Institute.

BOHANNAN LAURA AND PAUL
1953 *The Tiv of Central Nigeria*. London: International African Institute.

DOWNES, R. M.
1933 *The Tiv Tribe*. Kaduna: The Government Printer.

EAST, RUPERT (trans.)
1939 *Akiga's Story*. London: Oxford University Press for International African Institute. (Items of the text are footnoted "Akiga 1939"; those from the notes, "East 1939.")

[13]
Land Rights: Social Relations in Terrestrial Space

IDEAS ABOUT SPACE reflected in English and related languages are so specialized—so refined to fit specific institutional situations—that it is difficult to understand other cultural perceptions of social ecology (Hall 1963; 1966). The concepts of "ownership" and "property" are highly specialized and are dependent on specific technological, social, and legal institutions which are by no means universal. Nevertheless, a large number of writers dealing with "land tenure" have assumed the English and American specifics and then tried to understand the general and the exotic in terms of them. Needless to say, it has not worked well.

The literature on land tenure is one of the largest—and one of the poorest—in all of social and legal science. Its poor quality is comparable only to that of the late nineteenth-century writings on "primitive religion," with the difference that "land tenure" had no Tylors, Robertson-Smiths, or Durkheims. Lévi-Strauss (1963) recently claimed that "totemism" could be understood in terms of nineteenth-century Western needs and philosophies, but scarcely in folk terms or in terms of twentieth-century social and cultural theory. In analogy, we claim here that "property" and "land tenure" and "ownership" studies in the ethnographic literature can be explained in terms of Western legal philosophy and economic history from the waning of the Middle Ages until about World War II. Only if we first consider Western history a specific example of a generalized phenomenon can we bring into focus the problems and data of essentially different systems of arrangement of society in terrestrial space, and exotic economic, political, and mythopoeic arrangements for linking men and space together.

Land Tenure

WHAT IS IT, then, that Westerners mean by "land tenure"? What do we mean by "land," and what by "tenure"?

Every people must have some view of the physical milieu—the "folk geography" of the world and their part of it. Westerners divide the earth's surface by use of an imaginary grid, itself subject to manipulations and redefinitions. We then plot the grid on paper or on a sphere, and correlate the physical features of the land and sea with this grid. We have developed instruments for locating ourselves on the earth's surface in relation to the positions of the stars. There are precise rules for symbolizing the information from the instruments. We have perfected a system of measurement which allows us to repeat precisely operations carried out in the past; thus we have been able to locate and measure pieces of the earth's surface and to record our computations on gridded maps. These measured pieces become, for some purposes at least, identifiable "things."

Land, whatever else it may be, is for Westerners a measurable entity divisible into thing-like "parcels" by means of mathematical and technical processes of surveying and cartography. This complex notion of "land," with its accompanying technology, is an essential of present-day Western land tenure, as well as of the Western market-oriented economy.

The ideas of "tenure" in our own system are even more tangled. First of all, "tenure" assumes a conception of "land" of the sort we have already described. Only if it is divisible and the divisions stable and measurable can "land" be "held." Only if land is cut up into definable units can it enter the market or, as the jurist sees the same phenomenon, be subject to contract. Contract and a land market constitute specific types of relationships between men and land.

However, holding a piece of "real property" is more than a mere relationship between a man and a thing-like piece of land. As the best jurisprudential opinion has long told us, it is a relationship among persons. "Tenure" has to do with rights *in* land *against* or *with* other persons. Thus, in addition to the man-land unit, usually called a "property system" by Westerners, we have a man-man unit, which is part of the social system in general and of the legal system in particular.

When Westerners discuss land in terms of the social or legal system, they do so in terms of "rights." "Rights" are attributes of persons against other persons. But in European languages, with the particular notions of land they reflect, "rights in land" can become attributes *of the land.* This "land right" links a person and a piece of land.

The equation of rights of people with rights in land, making one the obverse of the other, does not occur in most African societies. Therefore, when we turn from the Western to the Tiv situation, we must ask how we can classify Tiv attitudes toward "land" and Tiv versions of "tenure."

This matter can best be examined by generalizing the factors we have found so they can guide our work in exotic cultures. The three factors are: a concept of geography, a mode of correlating man with his physical environment, and a social system with a spatial dimension. These factors can be restated as axioms: (1) A people has a representation of the country in which it lives; that representation can be analyzed in analogy to the Western map. (2) Members of any society have a set of concepts for speaking about and dealing with the relationships between themselves and the earth they exploit. (3) The spatial aspect of any social organization has some overt expression in word and deed. The study of land in society is the way in which any people associates map, property, and spatial relationships.

Land Maps

IT IS, WE BELIEVE, a fact that no African societies used indigenously an astrally based map such as our own, although a few peoples elsewhere, notably the Polynesians, did do so. Astral maps are, of course, seafarers' maps. A few African peoples did divide up the earth's surface into pieces by using terrestrial landmarks. The Kikuyu (Sluiter 1960) and the Haya (P. Reining: personal communication) are notable examples. In both cases, some form of land transfer similar to "sale" did exist under limited conditions; in at least the Kikuyu case, however, land "tenure" was regarded as part of the kinship system.

Other African societies have "tenure" relationship to land of a sort

TIV ECONOMY

very different from "ownership" or "contract." Two of probably many types can be distinguished here. The first is represented by rain shrines among the Tonga (Colson 1954) or saints' graves among the Cyrenaican Bedouin Arabs (Evans-Pritchard 1949). Rather than pieces of land with boundaries, there are points on the land, marked by shrines, that form the center of activity of a social group; the "map" is a juxtaposition of geographical points intruded into the social system by a religious idiom.

In the second type of "non-property" system, of which the Tiv are an example, the social organization is conceived in terms of pure space, and is only incidentally linked with the physical environment for comparatively short periods of time by activities such as farming. Tiv see geography in the same terms in which they see social organization. As we have noted (Chap. 3), the idiom of descent and genealogy provides not only the basis for lineage grouping, but also for territorial grouping.

This "genealogical map" of Tivland moves about the surface of the earth in sensitive response to the demands of individual farmers as those demands change from year to year. Association of the genealogical map with specific pieces of ground is of brief duration only; a man or woman has what we have called "farm tenure," i.e., precise rights to a farm during the time it is in cultivation. But once the farm returns to fallow, the specific rights lapse. However, a man always has rights in the "genealogical map" of his agnatic lineage, wherever that lineage may happen to be on the terrain. These rights, which are part of his birthright, can never lapse. A mathematician has suggested that whereas the Western map, based on surveys, resembles geometry, the Tiv notion resembles topology—"geometry on a rubber sheet." The Western map must be rigid and precise if the principle of contract is to work; the Tiv map must constantly change if the principle of kinship grouping is to work.

Instead of seeing maps in terms of man-thing units such as property, Tiv axiomize the spatial aspect of their social groups. This "social map" leaves them free to question the ways in which social groups or individuals are attached to exploitational rights in the earth. This is the exact opposite of Westerners, who axiomize their maps in terms of their property norms and values and see the social system which results as fundamentally a series of contracts and hence open to change and to question. In short, Westerners can question the social group more easily than a concept of property, while Tiv can question their property-like concepts more easily than their social groups.

Land Rights: Social Relations in Terrestrial Space

Land Rights

WITHIN THE MINIMAL *tar* every piece of cultivated ground, from the largest yam field to the most insignificant patch of cassava, can be referred to by somebody as "mine." Such a statement does not imply "ownership" of the land, but rather the "farm tenure" which gives that person some rights in the crops then growing on that farm. Such rights can be defined closely.

If the investigator is standing beside a farm in a minimal *tar*, A, and asks a man of a different minimal *tar*, B, "Whose farm is this?" he will be told, "It is the farm of minimal *tar* A," giving the patronymic. One is not likely to be successful in getting a more precise reply. If, however, one is standing beside the same farm in minimal *tar* A and asks a man of the segment associated with minimal *tar* A, "Whose farm is this?" the first reply will probably be, "It is ours." If the investigator asks which compound head the farm belongs to, the name will be given; the name of the woman who works the land and who will harvest and sell the crops or the name of her husband may be volunteered.

Again, if the ethnographer asks a woman whom he finds weeding a farm, "Whose farm is this?" she will say, "It is mine." In order to get further information one must ask, "Whose wife are you?" If, however, one asks this woman's husband, "Whose farm is this?" he will say, "It is mine." In order to get any further information one must ask, "For which wife did you hoe it?" or, "Who is your compound head?" If one further asks the compound head whose farm it is, he will reply, "It is mine." To get more precise information one must ask, "For which woman did you hoe it?" or "Which of your youngsters hoed his wife a farm here?"

In these answers are found the cluster of rights in a particular farm. A woman has rights in the farm: she owns and controls most of the produce which is grown on it; she has corresponding obligations to feed her husband and her children from the produce of her farm. Her husband also has his rights in the farm: he made it for his wife with the help of some of his kinsmen; millet or beniseed grown on it during its cultivation cycle belongs to him; he will eat from it and pay his tax from it. The compound head has other rights in the farm: he allotted it to the husband for him to make his wife a farm there; he has a right to a small portion of the crop for purposes of hospitality and ritual if he needs it; he has the final word in determining the size of the farm.

That farm is the symbol of the compound head's good faith in fulfilling the needs of his subordinates.

The map of Figure 2 shows the farms of most of the people of a large compound in MbaGor. It is meant to bring out the different portions claimed by different women, the juxtaposition of farms of the various women making up a basic labor group of attached wives or daughters-in-law, the larger portions claimed by the husbands of the women, and the whole claimed by the compound head.

Besides these rights in specific pieces of cultivated land, Tiv also claim rights to *sufficient* land. (1) Every wife or widow of a compound member has a right to a farm from which to feed herself and her dependents. (2) Every adult male who lives in the compound has a right to a farm sufficient to feed himself and his dependents. (3) Every compound head has a right to sufficient land to feed himself and all the members of his compound, including the rights of sufficient fallow land to allow for revitalization of exhausted soil.

Sanctions

BOTH SETS OF RIGHTS—to specific farms and to sufficient land—have easily recognized sanctions. Rights to specific farms are protected by ritual sanctions. Tiv erect magical emblems called *akombo* to protect farms against interlopers, thieves, and witches. This emblem consists of a bundle of sticks or a braided palm frond, a stone or a potsherd, placed on the ground or hung on a pole at the "top" of a field. The *akombo* are said to inflict disease or misfortune on anyone who meddles with the farm. The right to erect this magical emblem on a specific field is part of the basic cluster of rights in the field: a woman can erect an *akombo* on her own field; and her husband or the compound head can erect an *akombo* on this field. A woman may ask her husband to erect one on her farm, though more often he simply does it. A man can ask his compound head to erect an *akombo* on his farm; the compound head would not do so without being asked. No one else dares do so (unless he is paid by one of these three) lest the *akombo* attack the person who put it up.

In southern areas an *akombo* is usually found on any piece of cultivated ground, although some men do not erect them until late in the season. Except for *akombo* hung on economically valuable trees, they are rarely found on uncultivated ground. Fallow is not in need of *akombo* protection, although in some boundary disputes the emblems are brought into play.

Although an *akombo* would seize (*kor*) any person within the compound who took food he was not entitled to, it serves primarily as a protection against outsiders. Within the compound, moral sanctions of family (including co-wives) and co-residence are usually sufficient protection of one's rights to specific land.

Rights to sufficient land also have obvious sanctions and reciprocal obligations. A woman has a right to a farm sufficient to feed herself and her children. If she doesn't get it, she leaves. Her husband must either make her a farm or lose his wife and bridewealth. If a man is too ill to make his wife's farm, his brothers or age-mates hoe for her. Every adult male in the compound, then, must have a right to land on which to make farms for his wives.

An agnatic member of the lineage associated with the minimal *tar* has rights to sufficient land within that minimal *tar* because of his agnation. A man who is not an agnatic lineage member is given such rights for the period of his residence. If a compound head does not provide fields—and provide them willingly, with no fussing, nagging, or fighting—an aggrieved agnate follows one of two courses: he either moves out and builds a compound for himself, after which he can claim a part of "his father's fallow" and have the claim settled by the elders of the minimal segment; or he moves his family to his mother's people, where he is given fields. A non-agnate simply leaves. The sanction is the same as in the case of a wife: physical separation. The fear of "sitting alone" is acute among the Tiv. A man who wrangles with his sons and brothers soon finds himself "sitting alone," without labor, unable to work his fields. A bad temper or a surly, stingy nature "spoils the compound."

The right of every compound head to sufficient land to feed his dependents is of a basically different kind: a "right against the world." Generally speaking, the only sanction among Tiv to enforce a right against the world is self-help, traditionally in the form of fighting or "fighting by night" (the Tiv euphemism for witchcraft). Self-help calls into play all sorts of subsidiary rights and duties, the sanctions of which are found in lineage, kinship, religious, economic, and other values.

If a compound head does not have sufficient land to feed the members of his own compound, he exercises his right against the world and takes more land. His right to do so is limited only by the possibility of his being driven from it. The procedure for taking more land, however, is circumscribed. Except for migration—a very different matter—it is always accomplished by extension of "present holdings."

The following example of such an extension shows its main points. The boundaries of fallow are almost never marked. Markers, especially within the minimal *tar*, are universally deplored. It was, however, known throughout the minimal lineage that Andza had rights to land next to Ikpaor, Doga, and Iyorver (see Table 13). Andza, Doga, and Iyorver had a common father's father's father, but their agnatic link with Ikpaor was still another generation removed. When the time came for Andza to farm fallow he had used several years previously, he therefore extended his former holdings toward Ikpaor, not toward his closer agnates, Doga and Iyorver. In areas of land shortage Tiv say, "Would you cause hunger in the compound of your mother's son (*wanngo*, 'a close relative') if you can get land from your father's son (*wanter*, 'a more distant relative')?"

TABLE 13

LINEAGE RELATIONS IN A LAND DISPUTE

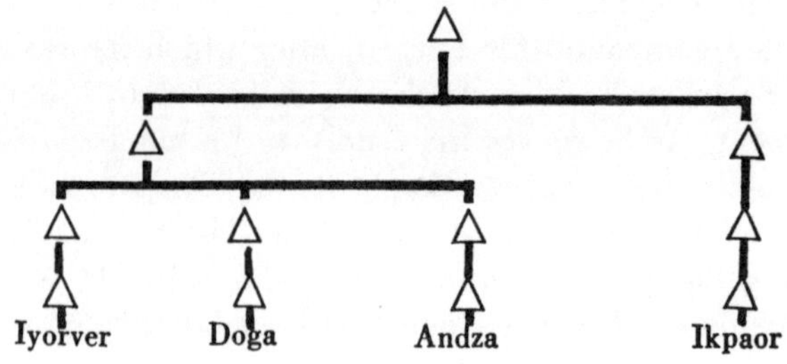

This pattern was vividly apparent when a group of Hausa established a village at a market site within the area of MbaDuku. The presence of resident Hausa is the mark of a big market. Most MbaDuku favored a Hausa settlement. After considerable negotiation, a site was selected in the *tar* of MbaKov (a lineage of MbaDuku/MbaIkaa; see Table 1). MbaKov people agreed to have the Hausa on this site, but they foresaw a problem sooner than did the others. At this site a market place and the Hausa village were laid out. About twenty acres were taken out of cultivation. No food crops were destroyed; all were harvested. But the fallow and fields covered by this area were claimed by six different compounds.

We asked one of these compound heads if the new settlement did not run him short of farm land. "Oh, no," he replied. "All MbaDuku has given land to the Hausa."

We didn't understand. "You *saw* us," he continued. "All MbaDuku met and decided that this was the place for the market and the village to be built."

"But it's *your* food land!" we insisted.

His reply stated the Tiv view precisely: "All MbaKov [the minimal segment] are the sons of one mother. When you need more land you go to your brother and you say, 'My brother, give me land on which to make a farm for my wife so that she may eat.' The brother says, 'Of course' (*Ka sha mi*), and if he in turn is short of land he goes to the brother at his back [i.e., the person who bounds his land but who is more distantly related than the first man, to whom he gave land] and says, 'My brother, will you give me land so that I may hoe a farm for my wife, so that she and her children may eat?' He says, 'Of course,' so the man hoes the farm. That man then goes to his brother in MbaAji [the companion minimal segment] and says, 'My brother [using the same term, *wanngo*], will you give me land . . . ?' " and so on.

Discussing this later we received a fuller explanation. Our informant drew a diagram on the ground. First, he said that MbaKov land looks like this (a circle), and it is surrounded by other *utar* (which he named; see the larger concentric circle of Fig. 14[A]). Then he explained again the process of extending holdings at the expense of the genealogically most distant kinsmen whose land adjoins your own. As he went on he changed the diagram until it had the appearance of that shown in Figure 14(B). "You see," he ended, "all MbaDuku—all Kunav [for the concentric circle surrounding MbaKov could represent either]—are giving land to the Hausa!"

While the Hausa community was being laid out, the men who were being dispossessed from part of their farms shouted and argued foot by foot. They were opposed by the government chief and a few of the more vocal elders; the Hausa very wisely stayed out of the dispute. On the surface one might have assumed that the chief had a right to move his people off a given piece of land or that he had some sort of superior right in it. No Tiv, including this chief, saw it that way. By shouting over this specific piece of land the farmers were impressing on all comers their

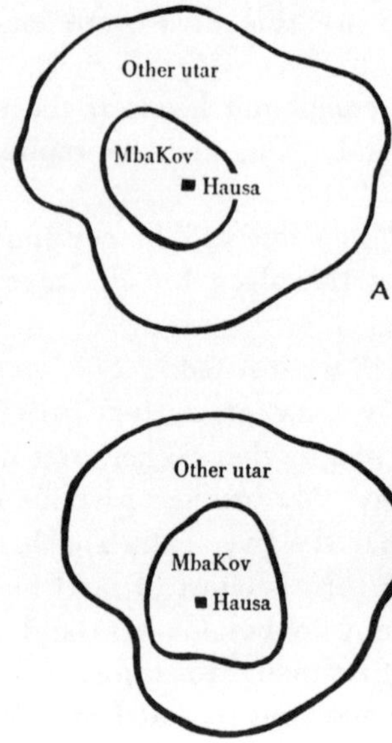

Fig. 14.—Sketch of land adjustment for a Hausa market.

rights to sufficient land. When the time came for them to take more land, they wanted their case to be remembered. The shouting and argumentation were, in a way, a mnemonic formality.

Rights of women always depend on residence and marriage. A woman has rights in her farms in the *tar* of her husband as long as she is resident there. She has a right to sufficient land in her husband's minimal *tar* as long as she is married to him (or her levir), whether the right is exercised or not. Women have no land rights in their natal *utar*, and few live there once they have married. If one does, she works on "the farms of her mother." Her brothers may hoe her a very small farm for a year or two, but she is still said to be "tending" the farm of her mother. No one has an obligation to her; such an obligation to an unmarried woman is incumbent only on sons and brothers.

Rights of men depend on agnation or matrilateral kinship and residence. A man has rights to sufficient land, as well as to specific cultivated land, in the *tar* of his agnatic minimal segment. Although these rights can be exercised only while he is resident in this *tar*, they never lapse. Rights of agnates can be revoked only by ritual exclusion from the agnatic lineage. This was formerly possible if a man changed lineages when the children of complementary exchange marriages were equalized (Akiga 1939:118–20), or if he were sold into slavery for his crimes. Today both these possibilities are prohibited by law. If a man is accepted as a resident by a non-agnatic kinsman or friend, he is given land. His rights lapse when he leaves that *tar*.

The right of an agnate to a specific piece of land within the minimal *tar* is often in question, but in the several score of land disputes we saw from 1949 to 1953, the right of an agnate to sufficient land was never questioned. No informants could discuss, even hypothetically, a situation in which an agnate was refused land in his minimal *tar*. None got beyond the platitude, "You can never refuse your father's son." To do so would be an act canceling agnation.

Thus land rights are a part of the birthright of every man; they are an aspect of his social and political status. To be without land is to be without kin. But a man has specific land only when he is in residence. On his return after an absence, he settles among his full brothers, beside his half-brothers. This agnatic birthright carries with it rights to land intermixed with, but distinct from, that of a man's full brothers. Their land is intermixed with, but distinct from, that of their half-brothers. The land of the entire group is intermixed with, but distinct from, that of other men of the compound. Land rights are a spatial aspect of agnatic filiation.

Land rights are simple among Tiv; they are, in fact, so simple that the anthropologist must state some of the things which they are *not* in order to avoid being misunderstood.

"Communal Tenure"

TIV LAND TENURE is *not* communal tenure. It is a matter of regret that this concept, which Malinowski (1935 1:319) called "the undying fallacy of anthropological work," has refused to die. In a fully developed, contractually oriented society like our own, communal ownership can and does exist. That is to say, the commune, whatever its nature, is regarded as a jural person—a corporation aggregate capable of legally owning property. The difficulty arises when this legal fiction is applied to African land systems. "Communal tenure" is an illusion that results from viewing the systematic exploitation by kinship groups of their environment through the distorting lens of Western market-oriented and contract-dominated institutions of property and ownership. Sir Henry Maine pointed out long since that in a community based on kinship, land is an aspect of the group, but *not* the basis for grouping.

Rights are attributes of persons. "Titles" are attributes of land. Tiv rights of persons in specific farms and to sufficient land are all individual rights. Tiv do not recognize any concept of "title." No matter how many other persons have another right to a piece of land in which X has a right, X's individual right still remains. A woman, her husband, and their compound head each has an individual right in a given farm. No one else has those particular rights. To change the frame of reference from the people to the farm by saying that the farm is the "community" property of some members of the compound is to distort the Tiv view so greatly as to make comparative study banal.

Tiv always use a *person's* frame of reference. They never use the *land* frame of reference with its insistence on some concept of "ownership." There are several references in this report to "our field" and "our fallow." This meaning of "our" is analogous to the commonly heard "our wife." "Our wife" means a woman who is the wife of a man with whom the speaker is identified, usually by lineage membership. It certainly does not indicate polyandry. Equally, "our farm" means one to which one or several individuals with whom I am associated can claim rights. It does not indicate "communal ownership" or even collective rights.

Inheritance, Rental, and Sale

LAND RIGHTS can be acquired in two ways: by status and by gift. "Inheritance" cannot give one greater rights than one already has. To make this point completely clear, we shall discuss inheritance briefly. Tiv do not have a word in their language which corresponds to the English word "inherit." Both Tiv dictionaries define *dyako* as "heritage"; nevertheless, it has this meaning only by extension. While a man is alive his *dyako* is his property: wives, spears, reception hut, clothing, crops, and livestock. When he dies, his heir is said to "eat" (*ya*) the *dyako*. One may also "eat the *dyako* of so-and-so" before the death of the owner. This sentence refers to major gifts from one's elders, and was said of gifts we made

Land Rights: Social Relations in Terrestrial Space

from our belongings before leaving the field. Basically, *dyako* means "personal property." It includes seed yams, but not land or farms.

To succeed a man to a status or position is to "sit on his head." This phrase is also used when a man's son, younger brother, or recognized agent deputizes for him. A new compound head either "sits on the head" of his deceased predecessor, or, most commonly, is said to "eat the compound" of his predecessor.

Land is relevant in the context of splitting a compound or splitting the field (see Chap. 2)* but not in the succession to the status of compound head or inheritance of *dyako*. The Tiv state two "rules" which sound enough like "inheritance laws" that they should be examined carefully: (1) At the time the fields are "split" a man has a right to that portion of his father's land which was farmed by his mother, and (2) if full brothers split their land, they say it is split on the basis of what has been farmed by their respective wives.

We were discussing inheritance with a son of a polygynist who had three sets of sons. The young man assured us that each set of sons would take the land of their mother; he pointed out the actual yam fields of these women as the indication of where each group of sons would farm. We asked, "What will happen if your group gets larger than that of your half-brother? What if you become twenty, but they become only ten?" His immediate reply was "He will give me land; we would not split the field." But we asked what would happen if the half-brothers too were short of land; would he still get land from them? "That would spoil the compound," he said seriously. "I would get it from my father's son" (i.e., from a still more distant agnate).

What Tiv are in fact saying is that they take their position in the lineage and the rights that go with it from their fathers, and that their separate mothers account for the internal structure of the group. Although they see the lineage in spatial terms, they do not see any correlation between genealogy and specific farms. They see the genealogy as evidence of rights to sufficient land.

These concepts do not pretend to allow for equal sharing of farms among all of a man's sons and brothers; rather they allow for every man's right to land, in view of his genealogical position. Indeed given the migration patterns of the Tiv (Chap. 7)*, it would be impossible for a man actually to use the ground that his mother farmed. He does, however, "inherit" his position in the system through her and through his father.

* not reproduced here

TIV ECONOMY

A Tiv may be given temporary rights to reside and farm in areas where he has no agnatic rights to the land. He pays no one for this land; his kinsmen say that they "gave him a farm." However, his rights lapse when he leaves. In a few exceptional cases a farm is "given" for the length of a rotation cycle to non-residents. In the land-hungry areas of southern Tivland, a compound head who finds himself with many absent dependents—hence a nominal right to more land than he can use without making his fields too big to work (thereby leading to envy and witchcraft)—grants the right to make a farm to a man living in a neighboring minimal *tar*, and filiated to the lineage of the neighboring *tar*.

In MbaGor, Tsavkor found himself "sitting alone" because people were convinced that he had perpetrated a particularly heinous piece of witchcraft. He knew that if his farms lay fallow for more than the minimal time for bare recovery, he would lose them through occupation by his neighboring agnates. His problem, then, was to keep enough land in legitimate use to be able to retain it against the day when his people returned to him or to his successor. He solved his problem by giving land to four different individuals who were living in the companion minimal lineage, MbaWandia. Two of these men were his matrilateral kinsmen. The third recipient was a daughter's son of MbaWandia, whose position there was weak and who was not a strong enough personality to gain as much land from his host as he thought he needed. The fourth was an agnatic member of MbaWandia: a quiet, meek man who was the younger full brother of one of Tsavkor's most cherished adversaries.

These men hoed farms for their wives on Tsavkor's land. The trilogy of rights to these farms shows some important differences from the ordinary. Tsavkor had no right to any of the produce, and certainly he received no rent in money. He had no obligation to see that a non-resident farmer of his fields had *sufficient* land. The non-resident farmer had no obligation to take part in any land action brought by or against Tsavkor, although his interest might lead him to do so. The rights of the non-resident farmer are temporary, almost never exceeding a single crop rotation.

To call such persons "tenants" seems a marginal usage of the term. No question of residence is involved, no question of rent—even in kind or as token—enters into the matter. It is solely a device on the part of the "giver" to maintain his rights in a specific farm against the rights of his agnates to sufficient land.

Tiv are unequivocal (once you have made them understand the question) in saying that they cannot and do not rent or sell land. There is no word in Tiv which even remotely approximates the English word "rental," nor is there a word that can be used in respect to land that might be translated as "pledge" or "mortgage." Tiv of Kunav and Shangev are not unfamiliar with the idea of rental, however. They knew the Hausa colony in Obudu paid a small annual ground rent which went into the Native Treasury of the Obudu District. Tiv consider this procedure immoral. To them it smacks of taking money for hospitality, thereby nullifying the hospitality. One Tiv summed it up by saying, "Isn't a guest a guest?"

The Hausa settlers in MbaDuku certainly paid no land rent; they said so themselves, the Tiv all said so, and we believe that we obtained enough information on the money that changed hands among them to be sure that nothing even resembling a rental for the village site was ever considered. They did pay for labor performed and for building materials, but they did not pay for the land on which they lived or had their garden plots.

Whenever we asked too insistently about rentals, Tiv always asked, "Are *you* paying anything for permission to live here?" and we had to admit that we were not.

Though no cases were found in 1950 of land being farmed for money or produce rent, we were told that about three years before our study one Iyon man had offered the Uge £6 for the right to farm a complete crop cycle in their country. The particular people whom he approached agreed to the arrangement, but the elders of the Uge refused to give their permission, so nothing had ever come of it.

When we returned to MbaDuku in 1952, we discovered one case in which a man of MbaGor had accepted 3*s*. from a man of MbaWandia for permission to clear some swamp land and plant rice. The MbaGor man said it was for one year only, and his swamp land would be cleared for him.

We also found an account in old administrative files about an occasion on which Gav (companion lineage to Kunav) encroached on Ogoja Division tribes: they were fined heavily but were allowed to retain the farms they had planted. As soon as the people and administration of Ogoja Division discovered that the Tiv thought this an excellent bargain, they no longer allowed Tiv to retain the farms.

All Tiv deny that they sell land. When pressed they are likely to ask, "What would we sell?" To Tiv, such an answer is sufficient. Land is, for them, a unique category. Nothing is exchangeable for it. Tiv could not exchange land for wealth to use as bridewealth as do the Jaba Kwoi (Cole 1949) because land and such wealth (or women themselves) have, in the Tiv view, nothing in common to make them exchangeable. On the other hand, they do not exchange land for other land (Cole 1949 cites such cases among the Kagoro; Jones 1949 mentions it as an Ibo practice) because land is associated with a segment in a lineage system, and hence with agnation.

There is one other, and even more important, reason why Tiv cannot sell land. We have seen that rights to land follow residence rights and are of two kinds: permanent rights to land and temporary rights to farms. No one can *buy* rights to land in a *tar* in which he is living; he has a right to sufficient land already. No one can *buy* land in a *tar* in which he is not living, because he is not living there. No one can buy a farm because it is a part of his living arrangements.

If land runs short in one's own *tar*, one takes land from an adjoining *tar*. All Tiv see the *tar* as expanding with the synchronous processes of passage of time and increase of population (proved to Tiv satisfaction by reference to lineage genealogies). This has led to the doctrine, *not* of transfer of land, but of movement of people and social groups, as the next chapter will show.

Summary

THE TASK of this chapter has been to examine the ways in which "land" and territoriality are institutionalized by the Tiv in the absence of market allocation. In carrying out that task we saw that the relationship between people and things, which in English is translatable into a set of "ownership" ideas, backed by "property" law and deep regard for the property of others, is seen as a social relationship by Tiv. Such a task is one of the most difficult that anthropology presents: understanding phenomena as they are manifested in the absence of simplifying ideas. Yet only by so doing can we see the significance of the simplifying idea as well as the need for it.

Bibliography

AKIGA (B. AKIGA SAI)
1939 *Akiga's Story*. Trans. Rupert East. London: Oxford University Press for International African Institute.

COLE, C. W.
1949 *Report on Land Tenure, Zaria Province*. Kaduna: Government Printer.

COLSON, ELIZABETH
1954 "Ancestral Spirits and Social Structure among the Plateau Tonga," *International Archives of Ethnography*, XLVII, 21–68.

EVANS-PRITCHARD, E. E.
1949 *The Sanusi of Cyrenaica*. Oxford: Clarendon Press.

HALL, E. T.
1963 "A System for the Notation of Proxemic Behavior," *American Anthropologist*, LXV, 1003–26.
1966 *The Hidden Dimension*. New York: Doubleday.

JONES, G. I.
1949 "Ibo Land Tenure," *Africa*, Vol. XIX.

LÉVI-STRAUSS, C.
1963 *Totemism*. Boston: Beacon Press.

MALINOWSKI, B.
1935 *Coral Gardens and Their Magic*. 2 vols. London: George Allen and Unwin, Ltd.

SLUITER, G.
1960 "Kikuyu Concepts of Land and Land Kin." Master's thesis, University of Chicago.

[14]

Human Ecology, Vol. 1, No. 1, 1972

The Wet and the Dry: Traditional Irrigation in Bali and Morocco

Clifford Geertz[1]

Received April 14, 1971; revised September 10, 1971

The comparative perspective is of central importance to effective analysis in human ecology. The present paper compares "traditional" irrigation systems in two quite disparate settings: east central Morocco and southeastern Bali. Bali, which has a tropical climate and a plentiful water supply, displays a highly collective approach to the organization of irrigation facilities. Morocco, which is essentially an arid country, displays, on the contrary, a much more individual, property-based approach to water regulation. The internal organization of these two regimes is described and their connection with more general cultural and ecological factors is traced, in an attempt to demonstrate that patterns of adaptation are susceptible to the same pattern of analysis as other aspects of social and cultural life. The contrast between the strongly group-oriented Balinese approach to water control and distribution and the highly individualistic Moroccan one is said to extend in an overall way to the two societies as a whole.

INTRODUCTION

The pioneer studies made by the anthropologist Julian Steward in what he later came to call cultural ecology were expressly comparative, either as between different sorts of hunting-gathering bands or different sorts of irrigation civilizations (Steward, 1955). More recent studies have tended to lose this dimension, however, and concentrate on monographic analysis of single societies in the conventional anthropological manner. Yet, as Steward realized, any

Supported by the Rockefeller Foundation and the Center for International Studies, Massachusetts Institute of Technology, Cambridge (Indonesian study) and by the National Institute of Mental Health (Moroccan study).

[1] Institute for Advanced Study, Princeton, New Jersey.

attempt to discover broader generalities in the relationships between natural processes and cultural ones demands an at least implicitly (and, preferably, explicitly) comparative perspective. Any long-established adaptive regime considered only in itself tends to take on the look of not only inevitability but also optimality. The doctrine that whatever is is right is no more attractive in anthropology than it is in ethics. But it comes only too easily to hand when one looks too fixedly at a single case.

A comparative approach in human ecology restores the sense that things could quite easily be otherwise than they are, which is not the same as saying that they could be anything at all. It prevents the cultural aspects from decaying into a mere reflection of the ecological and the whole enterprise into another exercise in reductive materialism. When generally similar adaptive regimes are viewed in generally unlike cultural contexts, the recognition that those regimes are multiply determined is very difficult for even the most monomanic of theorists to escape. The original intent of Steward's program was to integrate physical and biotic variables into cultural analysis, not to segment them off as extrahuman determinants of culture within which unconditioned laws would then be sought. By dramatizing the fact that cultural presuppositions stemming from sources whose connections with adaptive constraints are (to the extent they exist at all) very distant can have a profound effect on adaptive responses, comparative analysis tends to keep that intent in the center of attention. Single case studies may, of course, do that as well, and a number have. But the proposition that landscape, weather, rice, or pigs make the man can be rendered much more readily plausible when there are no contrast cases to challenge inferences from the exhaustively detailed immediate instance.

In this spirit, partly polemical, partly constructive, partly, I must admit, merely wistful, I will discuss here "traditional" irrigation in two settings—east central Morocco and southeastern Bali—about as different from one another as two settings can be. And I will attempt to show how the equally radically different ways in which water is handled in the two settings leads to some general insights into the again strikingly different cultures situated in them.[2]

SOME GENERAL CONTRASTS BETWEEN MOROCCO AND INDONESIA

Whatever Morocco and Indonesia have in common—Islam, poverty, nationalism, authoritarian rule, overpopulation, clean air, spectacular scenery, and a colonial past—the one thing they do not have in common is climate.

[2] The fieldwork on which this article is based was carried out in Indonesia during 1957-1958 and in Morocco during 1965-1966 and 1968-1969. Also, it should be noted that all vernacular terms, Balinese or Moroccan Arabic, are given in the singular form only, plurals being indicated by English endings.

At base, the contrast is almost Lévi-Straussian in its simplicity: wet and dry.[3] The annual rainfall in central Java, the classical heartland of Indonesia, averages around 2000 mm (i.e., about twice that of Chicago), while in parts of Sumatra and Borneo it gets up over 3500 mm. In the Fez-Meknes-Marrakesh triangle, the classical heartland of Morocco, it averages about 500 mm (i.e., about half that of Chicago), while in the South, Pre-Sahara, it drops as low as 50 mm a year.

Further, not only are the annual mean totals near the opposite ends of the world scale, but also the rhythmicity with which rain falls is also out near the extremes. In Indonesia, year-to-year variation is very small, as is variation in the shape of the rainfall regime from one year to the next. In Morocco, not only is year-to-year variation in rainfall enormous, but also is the within-year shape of it. To be a weatherman in monsoon Indonesia, all you *do* need to know is which way the wind is blowing; in Morocco, to be one you need to be able to penetrate the mind of God.

In the Balinese area studied, the annual rainfall over a 10-year period varied between about 2200 mm and about 2500 mm, with a coefficient of variation of 5.8%. In the Moroccan area, over a similar period, the variation was from 350 mm to about 900 mm, for a coefficient of variation of 29.4%. Where the monthly Balinese totals over the same period–how much it rained in July, January, or whenever–were also extremely consistent, almost invariant, they were astonishingly unpredictable in Morocco. In January 1959 there were 15 mm of rain; in January of the following year, there were 190 mm. There was more rain in July (i.e., mid-summer of 1959) than in February (i.e., mid-winter) of 1961, though those two yearly totals happened to work out nearly identically.

One gets the same picture with all the other climatic measures–temperature (a constant 80 F in Bali year round, a 55 F mid-summer/mid-winter swing in Morocco, and similarly for diurnal variations), wind, sunshine, and so on. The same contrast could be extended throughout all the established metereological parameters: constancy, regularity, homogeneity in the one place; inconstancy irregularity, and heterogeneity in the other.

Without going into the reasons for these systematic differences, nor into other environmental contrasts (soils, relief), it is clear that they are going to provide rather different sorts of habitats for agrarian man to live in. Bali is, of course, largely paddy country; central Morocco, largely wheat and olive (and, on the pastoral side, sheep) country. The thousands of small, squared off, carefully irrigated mud diked rice terraces sunk like ancient ruins into the sculptured

[3] For a general review of the Indonesian climate and natural setting, see Dobby (1954); for one of the Moroccan, see Martin *et al.* (1964).

landscape of the former, the thousands of narrow, little, medieval-like dirt-farming strips scratched on the baked surfaces of the latter can almost stand as paradigm images (and, in tourist posters, often do) of the two countries.

One can carry these contrasts forward in many directions–population density, cultivation methods, settlement patterns, trade.[4] But so far as our focus here is concerned (irrigation), the main difference is that there is a great deal of water in Bali, most of the time, and there is a great deal less–indeed, from the farmers' point of view, an absolute water shortage–irregularly distributed, both temporally and spatially, in Morocco.

Speaking generally, in south Bali irrigation is widespread to the point of being universal; in central Morocco it is confined to well-demarcated, commonly very constricted localities, micro-environments in the micro-est sense of the word. Where Bali, from this point of view, is a kind of giant outdoor aquarium, or, rather, a multitude of little aquariums pressed tightly up against one another, Morocco is–again from *this* point of view–a collection of scattered (or anyway discontinuous) oases, garden spots in a dessicate landscape.[5]

Balinese irrigation is a huge, homogeneous, very precisely calibrated, multi-leveled, extraordinarily effective system. Moroccan irrigation (and, again, to re-emphasize, the overwhelming bulk of Moroccan agriculture is not irrigated at all) is a small-scale, quite heterogeneous, broadly at best, calibrated, single-level, but, at best, moderately effective system. These general differences in long-established irrigation regimes are determinately related to similar differences in technological, sociological, and cultural patterns in such a way that two quite contrasting ecosystems with quite different properties are created. Environment is, therefore, and long has been, more than a passive, residual, limiting sort of factor in shaping Moroccan and Balinese life.[6] It is and has been an active, central, and creative one.

THE BALINESE *SUBAK*

The defining feature of the Balinese irrigation system, something which

4 For an attempt to pursue some of these matters for Indonesia generally, and Java particularly, see Geertz (1963).

5 It needs continually to be remembered in what follows that irrigation plays a role in only a small proportion, though the most productive, of Moroccan agriculture. In particular, nowhere does irrigated agriculture form the exclusive or even nearly exclusive basis of the subsistence regime, but is always set in a broader context of rainfull farming and/or pastoralism. The implication of this fact in a general assessment of the Moroccan adaptation is profound, but it cannot be pursued here.

6 Balinese irrigation, apparently organized along lines extremely similar to the present, is mentioned in inscriptions dating as early as 896 (Goris, 1954). For a description of Moroccan-introduced irrigation patterns substantially identical to those described below in medieval Valencia, see Glick (1970).

makes it, if not wholly unique, certainly unusual, is that it is organized into a separate, independent, completely autonomous social form, called the *subak*, and unusually translated well enough, if awkwardly, as "the irrigation society."[7] A *subak* is, first and foremost, a differentiated, corporate, self-contained social organization, devoted specifically and exclusively to irrigated farming, mainly (though not exclusively) of paddy–a kind of "wet village," as opposed to the "dry" one in which people reside. Indeed, this idiom is commonly employed by the Balinese to refer to it.

In spatial terms, a *subak* consists of all the rice terraces irrigated from a single major water canal (*telabah gde*). This canal runs down the steep volcano-to-beach slope of Bali from a single mud and stone river dam. (Southern Bali is laced with very deep cut gorges plunging down this slope every thousand yards or so, and it is across them that these dams, one every three or four miles, are thrown.) The dam (*empelan*), which is usually five or ten miles, sometimes even more, upslope from the *subak* it serves, is the property of the *subak* as a corporate body. So also is the canal, which, often aided by underground tunnels, overhead aquaducts, and reservoirs, runs off from it to the fields proper.

The fields proper, the terraces, are contiguous and form a clearly bounded domain. (Like "dry" villages, *subaks* are individually named.) All people owning land, which they do in simple freehold fashion, in that domain are members of the *subak*. This membership is completely independent of any other social characteristic–residence (all *subaks* have people from various villages, and any one individual with much land at all will belong to several *subaks*), caste, kinship position, and so on.

Thus, the *subak* is at once a technological unit, marked out by the collectively owned dam and canal; a physical unit, an expanse of terraced land with a defined border around it; and a social unit, a corporation consisting of people owning land in that expanse, serviced by the dam and canal. It is also, as we shall see, a religious unit.

As the main canal approaches the fields, it usually is split by very ingenious bamboo water dividers into two smaller canals, and subsequently those smaller canals are again divided into halves or thirds by a second rank of dividers, a process which may, in large *subaks*, be repeated a third or even fourth time.[8]

7 For other descriptions of the *subak*, see Grader, 1960: 268-288; Liefrinck, 1886-1887: 1033-1059, 1213-1237, 1557-1568, 17-30, 182-189, 364-385, 515-552; Geertz, 1959: 991-1012; and Geertz, 1967: 210-243. *Subak* terminology varies over the island; that given here is the Klungkung one.

8 In general, *subak* increase in size as one moves from the top of the drainage area downard toward the sea. The very highest are extremely small; those near the strand, large and sprawling. A full description of the interaction of landscape, *subak* structure, and political organization will be presented in a monograph on the traditional Balinese state now in preparation.

The final result of this before-the-terrace distribution is the creation of between six and twelve separate inlets to the terraces as a whole. Each such inlet defines a distinct subsection of the *subak* as a whole called a *tempek*, which, if the *subak* is a water-village, would be the water-quarter or hamlet, and indeed is sometimes thus referred to. This pre-terrace organization can get very intricate, but the essential point is that this dividing and redividing and thus water allocation by *tempek* is fixed and unchanging (or, at most, very, very gradually and marginally changing), embodied in hallowed custom, which here in fact is actually written down in palm-leaf *subak* constitutions (*awig-awig subak*). The technical grid, the crystalized canal and water gate structure, gives thus the form of the whole system, its skeleton. Alterations are occasionally made, but they are not done either easily or often.

After the water reaches the terraces proper it is further divided into halves, thirds, or fourths, occasionally sixths, to create yet smaller subunits (*ketjoran*), water neighborhoods, so to speak, which may consist of anywhere from six to seventy or eighty terraces and which is again named. And finally, within these subunits, smaller dividers, capable, given the mere rivulets they are by this stage faced with, of divisions as fine as a tenth, segment the water out into terminal canals defining the elementary unit of the *subak*, called a *tenah*.

Within any one *subak* (*not* between them, of course) such final *tenah* units represent, in theory, and given the technical precision involved, pretty much in fact as well, exactly the same share of the water supply, whatever that may be either in general or from moment to moment, the overall grid being very carefully arranged to produce such a result.[9]

This, then, is the physical structure of the *subak*. But it is, as I say, also the social structure, because the organization of the *subak*, and thus of wet rice agriculture generally, parallels this technical pattern with virtually perfect and explicit exactitude. The structure of the *subak* as a corporate body, as a social system, and as a cultivation regime is given by—or, if that is too deterministic a way to put it, is congruent with—the structure of the *subak* as a physical mechanism for moving water between rivers and fields.

The best way to see this is to look briefly at cultivation as such. The actual ploughing, planting, weeding, and harvesting of terraces is organized and carried out by the individual terrace owners, independently of the *subak* structure, *except*, and this is, as we shall see, a critical point, *with respect to timing. When*

[9] A *tenah* is, in fact, at once a water measure, a land measure, a seed measure, and a rice measure. A *tenah* of land is the amount a *tenah* of water irrigates; a *tenah* of seed, the quantity needed to plant that much land; and a *tenah* of rice, the yield thereby produced. For more of this, see Geertz (1967).

to plant is not a matter of individual choice: everyone in the *subak* must plant at the same time.[10]

As for irrigation proper, a technically complex matter here, it is wholly a collective *subak* matter. The upkeep of the various works, from the large main dam down to the smallest canal, is carried out by work groups of *subak* members, the details of whose formation, mode of operation, and compensation we can ignore here. The structure of the work group is socially extremely complex, and it is tiered like the grid itself into larger and smaller units devoted to tasks at different levels of the *subak*. The main point is that these are not mere ad hoc groups, but official arms of the *subak*. The opening and closing of water gates is similarly a *subak* matter. Thus, except for work entirely confined to the individual terrace, and even indirectly there, cultivation is regulated, paced, if you will, by the *subak* as a set of larger and smaller groups of its members organized into work groups under appropriate officials.

At the peak of this political-social-technical hierarchy there is the *subak* chief (*klian subak*), elected by the members, and the *subak* council, consisting of all the members, each with a single vote irrespective of size of holding. The council sets general policy within limits of the written constitution and elects the various officials. It can, and does all the time, fine people for infraction. (For severe contumacy it can even take away a man's land, though matters but rarely come to such a pass.) It collects taxes for support of the *subak* and disburses moneys out of them for improvements. It appoints priests to conduct the appropriate rituals in the *subak* shrines. With a miniature bureaucracy, a parliament of the whole, specially focused task groups, police and tax powers, and a ritual encasement, the *subak* is not only a technically developed unit but also clearly a very organic social unit, a corporation, with a form and direction of its own.

Yet, at the same time, it must also be stressed that the *subak* is in no sense a collective farm. On his own land (which he can sell, rent, tenant, or whatever, as he wishes), within the regulations set by the *subak*, the individual peasant is his own master working in his own way, consuming (or selling) his own produce. The *subak* never engages in the actual process of cultivation as such, nor, as I say, of marketing; it regulates irrigation, and that's all that it does. And in order to do so (with results that for Southeast Asia are the most productive in the entire region), it exercises important constraints on the decisions of the individual cultivator. But the actual process of cultivation within those constraints has always been a matter specifically (and this too is written, like some agrarian bill of rights, into the palm-leaf constitutions) beyond both its competence and its interest. The *subak* is a technically specialized, cooperatively owned public utility, not a collective farm.

[10] Traditionally, this was true only for rice, but with increased population pressure and crop diversification it is increasingly true for nonrice "dry" crops as well. For details, see Geertz (1967).

Since, as south Bali has, in simple quantitative terms, if not all the water it could conceivably use, then about all it can in fact effectively use, it is less the absolute amount of water overall that is at issue than the timing of its application to the fields. For this reason, the very elaborate ritual system, to which I have several times alluded, is as critical in the *subak's* operation as the technical, social-structural, and political aspects of it I have just reviewed.

The focus of this ritual system is a rice-goddess cult, whose precise content we need not go into here, and it is conducted at every level of the *subak* from the individual terrace, through the various subsections of the *subak*, to the *subak* as a whole.[11] At the higher levels there are specific temples, with assigned priests, special ceremonies at special times, and specific altars, gods, offerings, and prayers. These various ceremonies are symbolically linked to cultivation in a way which locks the pace of that cultivation into a firm, explicit rhythm.

Even more interestingly, however, the ritual system not only does this internally within the *subak*, but also reaches beyond the individual *subak* to ensure inter*subak* coordination within a given drainage region—a region, say, ten to fifteen miles wide and thirty-five or so long, fanning out as you descend from mountain to sea. To see how this occurs, it is necessary to give a very generalized and overstandardized description of the cult.

The cult consists of nine major named stages. These stages follow in a fixed order at a pace generally determined, *once the first stage is initiated,* by the intrinsic ecological rhythms of rice growing. This cult is uniform over the entire region and it refracts to all levels of the system from the terrace to the supra*subak,* i.e., concurrent rituals are conducted at all levels. The nine stages are: (1) water opening; (2) terrace opening; (3) planting; (4) purifying the water; (5) "feeding" the gods with holy water and other offerings; (6) budding of the rice plants (about 100 days after planting); (7) "yellowing" (that is, approaching fruition) of the rice; (8) harvesting; (9) placing the harvested rice in the granary.[12]

Now, the "water opening" day, stage one, for the various *subak* in the drainage (i.e., the day on which, amid ceremonies at the dam temple, water is diverted at the river dam into the *subak's* main canal) is staggered in such a way that the higher the *subak* along the mountain-to-sea gradient, the earlier the opening day. *Subaks* at the top of the system begin the ceremonial cycle, and with it the cultivation sequence, in December; *subaks* at the bottom, near the

[11] For general description of Balinese religious life see Swellengrebel (1960). For a description of the rice cult as such, see Wirz (1927).

[12] The Balinese names for these ceremonies are: (1) *Amapeg Toja;* (2) *Njamu Ngempelin Toja;* (3) *Mubuhin;* (4) *Toja Sutji;* (5) *Ngerestiti* (or, more colloquially, *Ngrahinin*); (6) *Membiju Kukung.* Stages, (7), (8), and (9) are all included under the general term *Ngusaba,* plus appropriate qualifiers, and are really, thus, seen as three phases of a single stage.

coast, begin it in April; those in between topographically are in between temporally as well.

The result is that, at any one point in time, the drainage area as a whole shows a step-by-step progression in the cultivation sequence as one moves downslope. When a higher *subak* is flooding its terraces preparatory to ploughing, a lower is clearing its. When a lower is flooding a higher is planting. When a lower is celebrating the yellowing of the rice and thus the promise about a month hence of harvest, the higher is already carrying the sheaves to the barns.

The temporal progression built into the ceremonial cycle (which is set off and continued by a kind of superpriest at a regional river cult temple at the volcanic lake at the very top) is thus laid out on the ground as well, and in addition to pacing the cultivation sequence in each *subak* separately, it also intermeshes those separate sequences in such a way as to provide for an overall sequence for the region as a whole.

The main ecological effect of this system is to stabilize the demands upon water over the crop year, rather than allowing it, as it would in the absence of such a system, to fluctuate widely. Simplifying somewhat, terraced wet rice growing requires maximum water input at or just after the initiation of the cycle, and then a steadily decreasing input as the cycle proceeds, until, at the end, harvesting is carried out in a fully drained, dry field. If the cycles of all the *subaks* in a single drainage, or, worse, along a single river, were coincident, the result would be that water resources would be enormously overtaxed during the earlier phases of the cycle and about as enormously underutilized during the later ones, especially as, again simplifying somewhat, the amount of water naturally available does not vary greatly over the year. Indeed, as water is the central limiting factor in the *subak* ecosystem, if *subak* cycles were not staggered, wet rice cultivation in Bali could never have attained, and could not maintain, a fraction of its actual extent, which is, as I have said, extremely great.

THE MOROCCAN IRRIGATION SYSTEM

In turning to the central Moroccan pattern, I am going to do something which, at the level of principle, I would prefer not to do: namely, describe it in opposition to something else, the Balinese pattern, rather than independently prior to comparison. As a developed, articulated, and in its own way and own place, not ineffective system, it deserves a more positive characterization, one in terms of what it is rather than in terms of what it is not. But for purposes of exposition it is nonetheless useful to describe it in a kind of negative design way. This is less than ideal, but even the negative design approach can bring out the main features of the system, and in briefer compass, so long as it is remembered that the Moroccan irrigation system is not just a very inferior version of the Balinese. Indeed, it is not a version of the Balinese at all, which could never work in Morocco, but a particular adaptive form, a distinctive ecosystem of its own.

Having said that, the quickest way into the Moroccan system is to say that there is nothing like the *subak* here, no corporate group organization of irrigation at all. Indeed, the underlying principle in Morocco is individual personal ownership of water. This works out in a variety of ways, but underneath them all is the concept that water, like land, houses, clothing, women, children, friends, sheep, sanctity, and anthropologists, is *property*, something that someone owns.

As it is also, unlike land, women, anthropologists, and so forth, not a fixed entity but a fluid resource, this raises some important problems of coordination and even, in an agonistic sort of way, cooperation. But these problems are not met by any version of the public utility method, but by a precise and elaborate system of customary property law, a system of common-law type legal concepts defining individual rights in something which one can possess only as an agency, not as an object, but no less firmly for that.

In any case, rather than deep-cut ravines pouring water down the sides of volcanic slopes every thousand yards, what you have, at least in the area I studied, are irregularly scattered springs, some voluminous, some trivial, and a great many in between, irrigating sharply circumscribed areas—oases, in the broad sense of the term. There are other sources, but the spring sort of irrigation system is, in the region I am concerned with, overwhelmingly the main one, and I shall confine my attention therefore to it.[13]

The particular area involved—a small city plus its hinterlands about thirty kilometers south of Fez—is marked by three fairly distinct subregions. Behind the city, the Middle Atlas mountains rise immediately, and in them the major mode of adaptation is sheep and goat pastoralism. There is some extremely small-scale cultivation, mainly of maize, and even here and there in a favorable locality a spot of irrigation. But, in general, springs are few, scattered, and thin. Northward, toward Fez, the country is rolling prairie, prologue to the great Sais plain which forms the country's bread basket, and on the prairie there is a mixture of large capital intensive farms, formerly French, now mostly nationalized or bought up by members of the Moroccan elite, and hundreds of small strip farms, most of them (as are the large farms) in wheat. Though a few of the capital intensive farms have installed mechanical pumps for irrigation, this area also lacks more than a few scattered springs and depends almost entirely on rainfall for water. Between these two areas, in the piedmont, however, there is a thin band, ten to fifteen miles wide, where a very large number of springs, many of them sizeable, and what is even more important, reliable, exist. It is in this subregion where almost all the intensive irrigation in the area as a whole takes

[13] Elsewhere in Morocco both river-flooding and well irrigation are important, as are such technological inventions as the Persian water-wheel, dams, and the famous covered canals (*gana*). For a general review, see Martin *et al.* (1964).

place, where there are intensive truck farming (vegetables, olives, grain), large villages, small garden-surrounded towns, and relatively dense population (though, of course, nothing like the Balinese).

Given the microenvironmental variation of this piedmont region particularly, each specific system differs somewhat from the next, because the problems it is faced with differ. But the family resemblance among them is for all that overwhelming. Thus, rather than using the ideal-type approach I employed for the *subak*, where there is also some variation, but less fitful in expression, I will describe, and that sketchily, a particularly well-developed specific example from this area, adding merely the remark that other systems in the area I could as well have described would have displayed little kinks of their own, but come, in general, to the same sort of thing.

The area involved consists of four or five, depending on how you count, clustered settlements, scattered several hundred yards apart down over five miles or so of the foothills to the mountains, just before they flatten out into the prairie.[14] The core of these settlements consists in four Arab-speaking lineages considered each to have descended from one of the sons of a famous seventeenth-century saint who is buried, so they say, in a shrine in the largest of the settlements. There is some tendency for the lineages to be correlated with the settlements, but this is far from absolute. There is also some tendency for them to be both separately and collectively endogamous, but that is not absolute either. In addition, there are other people living in the settlements who are not members of these saintly lineages.

It is unnecessary to go further into social structure here, except to say that though the area—the four or five settlements—is a rather well-defined one in kinship and religious terms (that is, essentially in terms of self-image), it is not as a whole a political unit of any reality, nor, for that matter, are the separate settlements; there is very little corporate quality to any of the social groupings—lineage, settlement, settlement cluster. Conceptually the area is an entity, socially it is rather profoundly not, a paradox, or apparent paradox, which tends to be characteristic of Morocco generally.

So far as irrigation is concerned, the important point is that, although the people of this area draw upon common water resources, they do so in a way about as far from the public corporation Balinese *subak* as it is possible to get and still not fall into a Hobbsean war.

Beginning, as I did with Bali, at the specifically technical level, the first point is that rather than a single irrigation source, the river dam, there are here a multiplicity, the various local springs. One of these, called "Sultan Spring" (*'ayn seltan*), is the most important, because it produces the most water and is the

[14] For a full sociological description of this settlement, see Rabinow (1970).

most reliable, but there are a number of others, large, small, and medium-sized as well. From these springs run canals, here hardly more than crude ditches as compared with the elaborate Balinese ones, whose form and direction can be changed, if not at will, at least relatively easily within a fairly wide range. It is not the structure of the grid that organizes the water distribution here, but rather the water distribution that organizes the grid.

There are, to be less aphoristic, two methods by which fields are irrigated from the springs. In some cases, here mostly the smaller ones irrigating local clumps of fields, there is an order of succession in terms of which individual fields are watered. That is to say, field A is watered until it has sufficient water, then B, C,...,N, and then back to A. How fast the cycle goes around depends upon the amount of water, the number and size of the fields, and, not least, the rhetorical skills of the owners. In other cases, especially in connection with the larger springs, such as the Sultan Spring, water is rotated by the clock among various fields: section A gets three hours; B, three hours; then C, six; D, two; and so on, in a similarly cyclical fashion. Although the second pattern is more complicated, and now that there are clocks rather than prayer times to measure by, perhaps more precise, and probably more flexible, the underlying principle is the same: individual men have defined individual property rights in water.[15]

A man owns his place in the cycle, whether measured in hours or in queue terms, as he owns anything else, and though there are natural constraints on what he can do with these rights–for one thing Bali and Morocco do have in common is that water runs downhill in both places–there are none which stem from any overall community determination of the public utility sort. There is no "water village" here. There are rules; a very great many of them. But they are phrased in terms of individual rights, not collective necessities, as contractual, not civic, obligations.

In the first place, water rights and land rights are here not fused. One can sell either without the other, can own water rights from which one has no appropriate land, and can rent it to somebody who does. One also can–and it goes on constantly–borrow and lend water from one field to another, sometimes several miles away. (For example, a man who owns three hours downstream can as well apply it upstream if he wants and topography permits, and vice versa.) When a man dies, one of his heirs may get his land and another his water. And so on.

Second, there is no superordinate political structure of any significance connected with irrigation. There are a few, quite unimportant officials (*jarri*) to

[15] The timed system in called *l-ma dyal s-sa'a* ("water by the hour") or *b-l magana* ("by the clock"; there is a large clock in the mosque which is the standard, though most men have watches of their own as well); the queue system is called *mubih.* For the same contrast between these two systems in old Spain, see Glick (1970).

keep time and track (though everyone does this for himself as well), but there is no meeting, irrigation head, constitution, fines, taxation, organized collective labor, authorities with sanctioning power, etc. When canals (*sāqiya*) need to be cleaned, open, shut, or whatever, those concerned merely do it themselves; in the absence of elaborate works, most jobs are minor and involve but a few people. On the rare occasion on which a larger task appears, some sort of ad hoc group is formed, or the owners pay laborers to do it. And where there are differences of opinion, which is just about all the time, people merely argue, occasionally even come to blows.

What *does* control this system is an elaborate property law. The simplest way to clarify this fact without getting into the formal details, which are numerous and intricate, of the matter is to give two quite typical examples from, on the one hand, the farmer's viewpoint, and on the other, from the viewpoint, so to speak, of the water.

As a prelude, it is necessary to know that all land plots, even uncultivated ones, and all water units have individual, proper, so to speak, "personal" names (*Ḥariga, Ḥasun,* etc.). In the water case, these units are shares in the output of a particular spring, say, Sultan Spring, determined, as I say, either in temporal or queue fashion; in the land case they are specific fields. For simplicity, I shall represent these named land or water units by letters A, B,...,Z.

Take, then, Muhammad. Muhammad has four irrigated plots, scattered in various parts of this miniregion.[16] He owns four-what can we call them? waters? One of these, A, is three nighttime hours in Sultan Spring which comes around to him once every six nights. Another, B, is four daytime hours in the same spring which comes around to him every ten days. A third, C, is one daytime hour in another spring which comes to him every twelve days. Finally, for D, he has queue type rights in another small spring whose cycle depends upon how much water there is.

Now, Muhammad waters his four irrigated fields W, X, Y, and Z thusly: W–the four day-hours of B, once every four times they come around (i.e., every forty days) and one night-hour of the four of A every time it comes around; X–one night-hour of A's four each time it comes, the four day-hours of B once every four times they come around, and the queue right more or less as needed and/or available; Y–one night-hour of A's four every time around, the four day-hours of B every four times around, plus the one hour of C every other time it comes around (i.e., every twenty-four days); Z–the same as Y.

This is not only a quite ordinary example, but also a rather simpler than usual one. Further, I have ignored all the borrowing and lending of water, temporary renting in or out of rights, and so on, which goes on constantly.

[16] Muhammad also has nine unirrigated plots. We will ignore them here, though he doesn't, and a full ecological analysis wouldn't either.

Indeed, how Muhammad deploys his resources differs according to time of year, what is planted where, and the like, so this is a rather reduced and too static version of Muhammad's actuality.

If you look at the situation the other way around, from the point of view of a water unit–call it N, a nighttime one which has a six-night cycle–the same complexity emerges. There are seven holders, owners, whatever you want to call them, owning, respectively, 3, ¾, ¾, 1, 1, 1, ½ hr of the total 8 hr. And this, too, is a simpler than average case.

The point of all this, again, is not the details as such; it is what they say, especially against the background of the *subak,* about what kind of system this is, what the social form of it is. It is a system in which individual private ownership of water is the organizing principle, a principle developed to levels of legal complexity which stand in marked contrast to the technical simplicity of the actual system which underlies it.

This whole area covers only a few hundred hectares, lying in three main discontinuous patches in this little cup of hills, but the number of major units of water rights involved in the main spring, the Sultan Spring, alone is twenty-three (ten "days"; thirteen "nights") and these, as we have seen, are then fractionated hour by hour, or even by half-, third-, or quarter-hours.[17] Add in the half dozen or so other springs, one of which at least is also quite large and complexly subdivided, and something of the social intricacy of this system can, I trust, at least be sensed.

COMPARISON OF THE BALINESE AND MOROCCAN IRRIGATION SYSTEMS

On just about every dimension, the southeast Bali and east central Moroccan patterns contrast. Where the Balinese is technologically complex, the Moroccan is almost technologically embarrassing. Where the Balinese is enclosed in a tightly corporate, superordinate group which explicity and firmly enforces regulations, the Moroccan is entangled in an elaborate code of laws which provides as much a framework for disputation, a vocabulary of argument, as anything else. Where the Balinese system is exactly adapted and structurally very firmly fixed, the Moroccan is very generally and loosely adapted and structurally very flexible. Coordination, in the Moroccan system, is not only low in absolute terms, but also, insofar as it exists, it is confined to small well-demarcated systems, or even parts of systems, not extended to large regions, as the Balinese.

[17] There are even 80- and 50- min units on occasion. This hyperfractionation is most likely a recent development, brought on by population pressure and made possible by modern clocks.

Even the religious dimensions, which I have not gone into in the Moroccan case, so contrast. There is nothing like the Balinese rice cult in Morocco. There are mass prayers at times of drought, certain symbolic connections between water sources, sacred places, gardens, and Paradise, too elusive and complicated to describe in short compass, and a highly developed, religiously supported (i.e., by Islam) sense for the objective reality of codified personal law.

So, what our two cases have in common is that physical, social, and cultural factors are integrated into quite distinctive ecosystems, ecosystems with human beings in them. What they differ in is how that system is organized and functions. But, even more interesting, however, is the fact that *this general order of difference within a single cultural dimension--adaptation to the setting--extends in an overall way to the two societies as a whole.*

The Balinese have a passion–that is the only word for it–for organizing everything into specifically focused, highly corporate, structurally articulate, mutually independent, autonomous groups and then seeking to adjust relations among them in terms of a highly developed ritual system. This way of "doing things" runs through the entire society, from kinship and village organization to temple worship and state structure. Similarly, the Moroccan passion for organizing everything in terms of the head-on encounter of individuals within a general, universalistic moral-legal code, which is used as a basis for forming contracts, arguing issues, deciding conflicts, maximizing options, and adjusting opportunistically to passing reality, runs through every aspect of local life there. Had I discussed family life, or the market, or the civil administration, a picture more than a little reminiscent of the one I have given for irrigation would emerge, and not solely because I was giving it.

Balinese social integration comes down to a matter of adjusting the relations among a sizeable number of differently based but similarly organized, highly corporate, cross-cutting membership groups–*subaks,* lineages, hamlets, castes, temple groups; Moroccan integration comes down to mediating relations among a field of competing individuals, each with a somewhat different basis of power and each scrambling to make his way within the general rules of the game by his own wit and resources. The pluralistic collectivism, as I have called it elsewhere, of Bali, is matched, as a pervasive theme, by, to have another phrase, the agonistic individualism of Morocco.

This is not geographical determinism. It is an argument that the kind of sociocultural analysis that applies to kinship, village politics, child raising, or ritual drama applies equally, and not just in these two societies, to human transactions with the environment. In the formation of Balinese and Moroccan civilization, environment is but one variable among many–or, better, one set of variables among many. And it is one whose actual force must be empirically determined, not a priori declaimed.

But it is one variable, or set of them, and the familiar split between nature and culture which renders the former a stage upon which the latter performs cannot any longer be maintained. As a chameleon tunes himself to his setting, growing into it as though he were part of it, just another dun rock or green leaf, a society tunes itself to its landscape, mountain-side, river fan, or foothill oasis, until it seems to an outside observer that it could not possibly be anywhere else than where it is, and that, located where it is, it could not be otherwise than what it is. This is an illusion, of course, though certain kinds of Marxists and certain kinds of Romantics are habitually taken in by it. What this illusion arises from is the fact that an established society is the end point of such a long history of adaptation to its environment that it has, as it were, made of that environment a dimension of itself. If a people live in a place long enough the quality of it enters into the substance of their life.

To connect the restless irregularity of much of Moroccan life, the tense expectancy and aggressive opportunism of it, to the uncertain, capricious climate is not, therefore, to yield to a vulgar materialism, for it is in part that climate which projects the aura of irregularity and tension, at least to anyone with a sensuous imagination, in the first place. Similarly, the dogged, deliberate, unwavering—as they themselves say, "straight-line"—quality of Balinese peasant life, moving along one foot after the other in its fixed furrows, is not a mere product of the hanging monotony of the wet heat, but more a kind of comment on it, as it, the heat, in turn is upon that life. The environments of societies such as the Moroccan or Indonesian are no more external to them than the storms in *Lear* are external to the play or the moors in *Wuthering Heights* are external to what passes between Cathy and Heathcliffe.

Though perhaps more apparent in so-called "traditional" civilizations, this sort of infolding of setting and society is hardly confined to them. It used to be thought that, although environment might shape human life at primitive levels, where men were, it was said, more dependent upon nature, culture-evolutionary advance, especially technical advance, consisted of a progressive freeing of man from such conditioning. But the ecological crisis has divested us all of that illusion; indeed, it may be that advanced technology ties us in even more closely with the habitat we both make and inhabit, that having more impact upon it we in turn cause it to have more impact upon us. It is not just the Balinese, looking out at the perfected geometry of their rice terraces, or the Moroccans, looking out on the ad hoc irregularity of their irrigation ditches, but us, looking out on the nervous, smoky confusion of our streets, who see the image of themselves.

REFERENCES

Dobby, E. H. G. (1954). *Southeast Asia* (4th edition). University of London Press, London.
Geertz, C. (1959). Form and variation in Balinese village structure. *American Anthropologist* **61**: 991-1012.

Geertz, C. (1963). *Agricultural Involution.* University of Chicago Press, Berkeley.

Geertz, C. (1967). Tihingan: a Balinese village. In Koentjaraningrat, R. M. (ed.), *Villages in Indonesia,* Cornell University Press, Ithaca.

Glick, T. F. (1970). *Irrigation and Society in Medieval Valencia.* Harvard University Press, Cambridge.

Goris, R. (1954). *Prasasti Bali,* Vol. 1. Kirtya Liefrinck-van der Tuuk, Bandung, Bali.

Grader, C. J. (1960). The irrigation system in the region of Jembrana. In Swellengrebel, J. L. (ed.), *Bali: Life, Thought and Ritual,* The Hague and Bandung.

Liefrinck, F. A. (1886-1887). De Rijstcultuur op Bali. *Indische Gids.*

Martin, J., Sover, H., Le Coz, J., Mauver, G., and Woin, D. (1964). *Geographie du Maroc.* Hatier, Paris and Casablanca.

Rabinow, P. (1970). The social history of a Moroccan village. Unpublished doctoral dissertation in anthropology. University of Chicago.

Steward, J. (1955). *Theory of Culture Change.* University of Illinois Press, Urbana.

Swellengrebel, J. L. (1960). Introduction. In Swellengrebel, J. L. (ed.), *Bali: Life, Thought and Ritual,* The Hague and Bandung.

Wirz, P. (1927). Der reisbau und die reisbaukulte auf Bali und Lombok. In *Tijdschrift voor Indische Taal-, Land- en Volkenkunde,* G. Kolff and Co., Batavia.

[15]

THE SINHALESE OF THE DRY ZONE OF NORTHERN CEYLON

E. R. LEACH
Cambridge University

The concept of social structure, as it is used by British social anthropologists, is closely linked with the notion of social continuity. It is an established convention among anthropologists that a "people" can survive the most startling changes of external circumstance. The Iroquois who build skyscrapers in New York are "the same" Iroquois that introduced Morgan to the mysteries of matrilineal kinship organization. Clearly, if we use such a terminology, the notion of sameness requires cautious analysis.

Over a period of time the actual composition of any "society" changes; the old die, children grow old, and new children are born. Customs change too, in primitive as well as in sophisticated cultures; in a single generation the head-hunters of Sarawak have become prosperous rubber planters touring their rivers in outboard motorboats. In the face of such change, what is it that persists? The total situation is plainly very complex, for the perpetuation of language alone entails the maintenance of an elaborate mesh of "tradition" which is, to a high degree, impervious to immediate changes in the local situation. In developing their special theory of social structure the British social anthropologists have laid stress on only one particular aspect of this total problem.

If we consider a community of people at any given point in time, we can readily see that most interpersonal relations are governed by conventional rules which, in themselves, apply to statuses rather than to individuals. There are rules about how the young should respect the old, how men should treat women, how parents should deal with their children, and so on. Such rules, as a whole, can be said to form a "system." In principle, the system will not be altered by any mere progression of time, for at every point in time there will always be old and young, men and women, parents and children.

Going further, the British social anthropologists have claimed that, in societies where unilineal descent is given marked cultural emphasis, the continuing system of jural relationships to which I have referred turns out to be very largely a matter of kinship organization. The continuity of the society as a whole rests on the continuity of the system of lineages, each of which is a "corporation," the life span of which is independent of the individual lives of its individual members.

This mode of analysis has proved so fruitful, particularly with regard to African materials, that it has been easy to overlook its limitations. The argument is one which has developed specifically with regard to societies possessing clear-cut unilineal descent groups (Fortes, 1953), and this poses two questions. First, what kind of ongoing corporation takes the place of the lineage in societies which lack unilineal descent groups? Second, if we are to distinguish societies with unilineal descent groups as a special type, where do we draw the line? For, considered as an organizing principle, unilineal descent is never simply present or absent; it can be present in varying degrees.

The justification for including a paper on Ceylon in a symposium on Southeast Asia is precisely that Sinhalese society may be considered a marginal case. Generally speaking, the tribal peoples of Borneo and the Philippines have kinship systems which are fully cognatic. Nothing could be more "bilateral" than the pattern described by Barton (1949) for the Kalinga or by Freeman (1958) for the Iban. Sinhalese society, however, though broadly speaking cognatic in type, also contains marked elements of unilinearity, and one authority (Ryan, 1953, p. 26) has even alleged that the Sinhalese have a lineage system. A discussion of the nature of structural continuity in the Sinhalese case may therefore serve to discriminate some of the critical issues.

The notion of a corporation, as derived from Maine, is that an estate comprises a "bundle of rights" over persons and things. At any one time the corporation embraces a number of individuals who share in the assets of the estate according to their particular relative status. Recruitment to such a property-owning corporation may be acquired in a variety of ways, e.g., by purchase, by initiation, or by inheritance. It is the general characteristic of unilineal descent groups that a child automatically inherits corporation membership from one or the other of its recognized parents, but not from both.

Clearly the principle of unilineal descent is a convenient one, but this should not blind us to the fact that several other kinds of "inheritance" are theoretically possible. A system in which all children inherited equal rights from both parents would plainly lead to total confusion, but a system in which children could choose to take particular rights from either the father or the mother (though not from both at once) would not, in principle, lead to a structure any more complex than one of straight unilineal descent. Alternatively, the status might depend not so much upon parentage as on place of residence. Ethnographic examples of both these alternatives have been recorded. The Sinhalese case contains something of both.

Sinhalese culture is by no means uniform. Common usage distinguishes the low-country Sinhalese of southwestern Ceylon from the Kandyans of the central and north central areas. Within the Kandyan category it is useful to distinguish further the population of the mountainous, and relatively densely populated, Central Province from that of the flat Dry Zone lying to the north and east.

The reasons for cultural differences here are partly historical, partly ecological. European colonialism made its impact upon the coastal regions and upon the southwest several centuries before the Kandyan kingdom was subjugated. Within the Kandyan area, on the other hand, the climatic contrast between the Dry Zone and the rest is very great, and in consequence quite different residential patterns have developed in different sections.

Formally considered, the whole Kandyan area possesses a unified system of customary law, much of which now has judicial sanction. The principles of this law, especially as regards matters of marriage and inheritance, have been described in a number of textbooks, notably that of Hayley (1923). Patterns of residence in relation to kinship have received less attention, but Tambiah (1958) has recently published an excellent account of the situation prevailing in hill villages close to Kandy itself. Still more recently Yalman (1960) has reported on other Kandyan hill communities.

Kandyan hill communities are mostly of substantial size, with populations exceeding 1,000 individuals. They usually include members of a number of different castes, and there is wide economic differentiation between rich and poor. The wealthier sections of the society set considerable value on the maintenance of the family estate as an intact entity. The *gedera*, i.e., the family house and its associated lands, is looked upon as a patrimony to be handed down mainly to the male heirs, who should ideally continue to reside in, or close to, the parental home. With this patrilineal ideology, however, is associated a bilateral principle of inheritance. Daughters as well as sons inherit from both parents, and in equal degree. The patrimonial landed estate can therefore be conserved on behalf of the sons only if the daughters can take their share of the inheritance in some other form, usually that of money or other movable assets given as a dowry at the time of the daughter's marriage.

Although the same ideology concerning property rights prevails throughout the community, it is in general only the wealthier families that are able to provide their daughters with cash dowries. Hence it is only among the wealthy that the *gedera* emerges as a named group with many of the attributes of a corporate patrilineage. Among poorer families, property in land, such as it is, is dispersed among both sons and daughters, and the appearance of unilinearity disappears.

The situation in the northern Dry Zone is rather different. The general region of Anuradhapura has a very long history of human occupation. It was the site of the classical kingdom of Ceylon, the virtues of which are extolled in the Mahavamsa. What is relevant in a highly complex history is only that a sophisticated civilization flourished there from the third century B.C. until the thirteenth century after Christ. It was a "hydraulic civilization" in the sense in which Wittfogel (1957) uses the term; the whole countryside was very intensively developed by a great variety of irrigation works of various types and sizes.

In later centuries the more elaborate of these works fell into decay, but village life continued to be possible on a limited scale. If we ignore the consequences of the intensive reconstruction work over the past thirty years, the general ecological pattern of the North Central Province today may be summarized as follows. Each village constitutes a separate economic entity. Its population subsists by the cultivation of irrigated rice in a small permanent field which is watered from a rain-fed reservoir (tank) which is particular to that village alone. The villagers are alone responsible for the maintenance of the tank and, subject to certain supervisory governmental controls, have sole rights in its water.

The village field necessarily lies below the level of the tank where it is easily irrigated with a controlled water supply. The houses of the village are clustered together immediately below the earthwork of the tank, where water seepage makes it possible to grow fruit trees and moisture-demanding vegetables. Although the total annual precipitation is considerable—50 to 75 inches—it is concentrated in brief periods, and the rate of evaporation in dry weather is very high. Some cultivation in unirrigated areas is possible, but only erratically so. Generally speaking, permanent human habitation is impossible without irrigation.

It follows that there is a peculiarly intimate relationship between any particular tank and the village and field that are associated with it. The size of any tank depends upon its position. Once the main earthwork has been constructed the capacity of the tank is fixed within quite narrow limits. This sets consequential limits on the size of the field which can be irrigated, and more indirectly on the size of the village population which can derive its subsistence from that field.

Since the field is fixed in size and position, it is not surprising to find that land is owned according to rules which we might describe as "freehold private tenure," i.e., which allow land to be bought and sold, leased, and mortgaged. Such a description, however, masks the really crucial element in the situation. The scarce valuable is not land but water. Although the villagers appear at first sight to be concerned with the ownership of land, closer investigation shows that land is measured in terms of the water to which it is entitled. This fact has considerable social implications.

While plots of land can be divided, the unity of the tank is permanent and inescapable. The villagers who derive their sustenance from a single tank may have their petty rivalries, but in larger matters, such as the maintenance of the tank earthwork and the proper operation of the tank sluices, they must cooperate closely lest disaster befall them all. We consequently find that, although the ownership of land (i.e., water) is meticulously fragmented into small individual parcels, the work of the agricultural cycle is closely coordinated and operated according to a strict collective timetable. We find too that the villagers who derive their sustenance from a single tank are almost invariably members of a single small sub-caste (*variga*), that they tend strongly to be endogamous, and that they are consequently all close kin.

Although both men and women own and inherit property, it is the husband who is normally its manager. Since it is humiliating for a man to be exclusively dependent upon his wife's property, every man endeavors to marry virilocally (*diga*). If he must marry uxorilocally (*binna*), he looks for a girl from his own village, where he is likely to have assets of his own. While the ideal preference for *diga* as opposed to *binna* marriage is quite explicit, the actual numerical proportion of *binna* marriages may be 40 per cent or more.

Binna marriages belong to several clearly defined types. There is the *binna* husband who is himself landless and makes himself the servile dependent of his father-in-law; there is the *binna* heiress who has no brothers and whose parents have insisted that she stay at home to maintain the family estate; and there is the *binna* marriage where the spouses are cross-cousins. In this last instance there is again an economic motive. Since a man normally inherits land both from his father and from his mother, he may be co-heir with his mother's brother's daughter of land located in his mother's village of birth, so that by marrying her he consolidates the estate. Sinhalese even say that a man has a "right" to marry his mother's brother's daughter for this purpose. In practice, although cross-cousin marriages occur quite frequently, they are in no special sense preferred or prescribed.

Properly speaking there is no dowry system. What is sometimes called a dowry (*dävädda*) is simply an advance of inheritance in the form of land. There is in this region no technique of preserving the patrimonial estate for males by giving movable assets to the daughters. Nevertheless, since it is the more prosperous families who marry *diga*, there is observable among them a statistical tendency in the direction of patrilineal rather than cognatic inheritance. What happens is roughly as follows. Both the male head of a household and his wife may separately own property in land. Both parcels will be separately inherited by the sons and daughters. Those who remain resident in the village will all receive equal shares, but those who marry far away will, in practice, get smaller shares or even nothing at all.

It is mainly a question of the practicability of fragmentation. A poor man with several children can not in practice divide his assets equally, and the family usually disperses, leaving a single son to inherit the patrimony and buy out his co-heirs as the occasion demands. A wealthy household with only one son and one daughter, on the other hand, is likely to arrange an exchange marriage with some equally wealthy household in a nearby village or even in the same village. The property may be fragmented for the time being, but the possibility, indeed the probability, exists that it will be brought together again by further marriages between the same two families at a later date. Such procedures do not have the effect of conserving property within a patrilineage, but they do tend, in the long run, to conserve property within particular co-resident compound groups. The heads of such groups are normally male and are usually descended from previous owners by male rather than female links.

If the total population of a cluster of closely adjacent villages is analyzed over a period of time, it will be found that, in each village, the occupants of a small number of particular compounds (*watte*) persistently retain most of the economic and political influence. None of the various positions of influence and title which villagers can hold, either by governmental appointment or in their own private affairs, are hereditary, but the constancy with which such positions remain within a narrow circle of kin plainly demonstrates that, among the wealthy, the strategy of marriage can be used to circumvent the apparently disruptive influence of bilateral inheritance.

In one village studied, for example, the leadership over a period of about half a century was transmitted successively (the dates are approximations) as follows:

In 1905 to A, a resident in Compound 1;
In 1925 to B, a resident in Compound 2, son-in-law to A;
In 1938 to C, a resident in Compound 1, son of a cross-cousin of A's wife;
In 1948 to D, a resident in Compound 2, sister's son to C and cross-cousin's son to B;
In 1952 to E, a resident in Compound 1, cross-cousin to D and son to C.

There were nine compounds in the village, but the other seven were entirely excluded from positions of influence during the period in question. This was not because Compounds 1 and 2 had any special hereditary right but was directly due to the fact the A and B arranged a series of highly astute marriages both for themselves and for their descendants. In 1886 the occupants of Compounds 1 and 2 had both been nearly bankrupt; by 1954 their successors owned all the best land in the village.

It is against this background of property maneuver that we can best understand the peculiar attitude of the Dry-Zone Sinhalese toward marriage. By European standards the villagers are scandalously promiscuous. A girl ordinarily starts having love affairs as soon as she reaches puberty, and most women have been pregnant at least once by the time they reach sixteen. According to customary law the resulting children are always legitimate, provided always that the girl is not foolish enough to have a liaison with a man of the wrong sub-caste.

This kind of "marriage" can be entered into in the most casual manner. Any woman who cooks for a man is considered to be his wife for the time being, and the relationship can be broken off as easily as it is started. When a child is born, the villagers go to great pains to see that the birth is registered and that the father's name appears on the birth certificate, for this may potentially affect the child's ultimate status as an heir. The ordinary obligations of parents toward children, however, are treated in a highly casual way. It is quite common to find that a man and woman who are living together and rearing a family have each had several other children by several different spouses. One consequence of this is that half-brother and step-brother relationships are extremely common.

In addition to these casual "common-law" marriages, we find that the villagers sometimes turn a wedding into a ceremony of the utmost elaboration. Ceremonial weddings are the occasion for expensive feasting and the demonstrative gathering of rival groups of kinsmen. From a legal point of view the formal wedding is no more binding than an informal liaison, though in practice the collapse of a formally established marriage is likely to lead to bitter recriminations. The formal marriages, as one might expect, are mainly those of influential people, or of those who are seeking to gain influence. In terms of village politics they represent treaties of alliance between potentially hostile groups of kinsmen. The two types of marriage are identical from the point of view of the children, who are legitimate in either case. They differ in the fact that, whereas informal marriage is a private affair between husband and wife, a formal marriage is arranged by the parents. Formal unions are part of the long-term strategy whereby property and influence are conserved within particular compound groups.

Since all the inhabitants of a Sinhalese Dry-Zone village are likely to be related to one another in several different ways, it would be misleading to suppose that kinship behaviors conform to rigid stereotypes. Nevertheless, some general tendencies deserve to be noted. Relations between a man and his children are never close. As soon as a young man marries he begins to be treated as a separate householder, and his relations with his parents become increasingly formal and remote. Separation of the sexes is extreme. Although men and women sometimes work together in the field, there are few other occasions when they can, with propriety, be seen close together.

Relations between co-resident siblings, who are likely to be heirs to the same property, are formal rather than friendly. In contrast, the relationship between brothers-in-law, which is assimilated to that of cross-cousins, is characteristically one of cooperative equality. Where brothers-in-law reside in the same compound their friendship often assumes the form of a joking relationship. This stereotyped pattern is, however, complicated by the high incidence of half-sibling and step-sibling relationships alluded to above. Since the total area of irrigated land available to the villagers is unalterable, the inheritance of land inevitably becomes a source of bitter jealousy. The restrained formality with which a younger brother is expected to treat an elder brother is in accord with this. Co-resident "brothers," however, may well be of partly or completely different parentage, so that their potential rights of inheritance are quite different. In such cases much of the potential strain inherent in the sibling relationship disappears, and half-brothers who are not co-heirs to the same property are often close allies.

Neat summary of these facts is difficult, but underlying the whole complex one can discern two contradictory, yet complementary, structural principles. On the one hand there is the principle of bilateral inheritance by all sons and all daughters in roughly equal proportions. While property can be transmitted in other ways, e.g., by will or by sale, inheritance remains the main process by which rights in land are transferred from one generation to another. Considered simply in kinship terms, bilateral inheritance must lead to the fragmentation of holdings and to rivalry between co-heirs. It thus stands in contradiction to the ideology which requires the co-heirs of an estate to remain co-resident in the same ancestral compound, and which presupposes that a band of brothers will always act together as a united family.

On the other hand, the principle that women, despite their inferior political status, have rights to land means that the transmission of property to children serves to unite disparate holdings as well as to fragment them, for the separate properties of a man and his wife are unified in their children. Heirship separates property; marriage brings it together. It is a reflection of this that full brothers, though formally united, seldom cooperate, whereas brothers-in-law, though formally opposed, are characteristically close allies.

Space is lacking for more than the barest outline of the system of land tenure which provides the economic basis for Sinhalese Dry-Zone society, but its essence can be briefly summarized. The village field is not only fixed in size; it is also fixed in layout. It consists of a set number of permanent shares (*pangu*), which are so laid out on the ground that each share receives a precisely equal proportion of the total available tank water. One share may be divided among several owners, or one owner may possess several shares, but the layout of the field, which is plain for all to see, remains the same from generation to generation.

Let me sum up. The study of social structure in societies organized according to unilineal descent has not only thrown the emphasis on kinship but has given the impression that kinship structures can be considered in isolation, without reference to the economic background. It has also suggested that social structure is a matter of clearly defined rules, e.g., of descent, of inheritance, and of preferential marriage. In the society considered in this essay social structure is likewise a matter of kinship, but kinship arrangements are not clearly constrained by rules. In all issues of inheritance, succession, marriage, and residence the individual is faced with choice. It is not implied that choice is random, but by and large choices are governed by economic ends.

In such a society the continuing entity is the pattern of the man-made economic context—the village tank, the compounds, the layout of the village field. Within narrow limits these are unalterable facts to which each generation of inhabitants must adjust their domestic lives. Although, as in other primitive and peasant societies, the language of kinship plays a dominating role in the expression of social relationships, social behavior is not constrained by the prior existence of kinship corporations. It is not so much that the Sinhalese order their economic lives in accord with kinship relations as that their kinship relations are an expression of the way in which they order their economic lives.

The relevance of this analysis in the present context of a survey of Southeast Asian societies is that it should make us cautious of embarking upon typological generalizations. Freeman's analysis of Iban society might, on first inspection, suggest a polarization of types—the social structure of bilateral societies in contrast to the social structure of societies with unilineal descent groups. But we need to be careful. My analysis of Sinhalese social structure has followed lines closely analogous to those of Freeman for the Iban, even though less quantitative evidence has been provided. But Sinhalese society, though lacking a fully developed lineage system, is by no means fully cognatic in a sense applicable to the Iban and the Kalinga. More important than typology is the implication, in both

Freeman's work and my own, that social structures are sometimes best regarded as the statistical outcome of multiple individual choices rather than a direct reflection of jural rules. For this approach both of us are indebted to a highly germinal essay by Fortes (1949).

KINSHIP TERMINOLOGY

It will be apparent from the foregoing analysis that in my personal view the kinship terminology is not of any great significance for the understanding of Sinhalese social structure. By request, however, and for comparison with the data in other papers, I append a list of the kinship terms used colloquially by the Sinhalese of the northern Dry Zone, followed by a summary of the facts. Unless otherwise noted, all terms are subject to rather wide collateral extension as discussed hereinafter.

1 *kiriättā:* grandfather, either paternal or maternal.
2 *kiriamma:* grandmother, either paternal or maternal.
3 *appa:* father.
4 *loku appa:* father's elder brother; mother's elder sister's husband.
5 *bāppa:* father's younger brother; mother's younger sister's husband.
6 *amma:* mother.
7 *loku amma:* mother's elder sister; father's elder brother's wife.
8 *kudamma:* mother's younger sister; father's younger brother's wife.
9 *māmā:* mother's brother; father's sister's husband; spouse's father. Not subject to collateral extension.
10 *nändā:* father's sister; mother's brother's wife; spouse's mother. Not subject to collateral extension.
11 *ayiyā:* elder brother; elder male parallel cousin; elder female cross-cousin's husband.
12 *malli:* younger brother; younger male parallel cousin; younger female cross-cousin's husband.
13 *akkā:* elder sister; elder female parallel cousin; elder male cross-cousin's wife.
14 *namgi:* younger sister; younger female parallel cousin; younger male cross-cousin's wife.
15 *massinā:* male cross-cousin; brother-in-law. Not subject to collateral extension.
16 *nänā:* female cross-cousin; sister-in-law. Not subject to collateral extension.
17 *putā:* son; sister's son (w.s.); brother's son (m.s.).
18 *duvā:* daughter; sister's daughter (w.s.); brother's daughter (m.s.).
19 *bänā:* sister's son (m.s.); brother's son (w.s.); daughter's husband. Not subject to collateral extension.
20 *leli:* sister's daughter (m.s.); brother's daughter (w.s.); son's wife. Not subject to collateral extension.
21 *munuburā:* grandson. Not subject to collateral extension.
22 *minibiri:* granddaughter. Not subject to collateral extension.

An accurate and adequate brief summary of Sinhalese kinship terminology is given by Tambiah (1958). The other principal accounts are those of Ariyapala (1956), Hocart (1928), and Pieris (1956). Superficial differences between the various descriptions are due to several factors. First, certain literary terms (e.g., *piyā*, father) are seldom used in colloquial speech. Second, some terms which occur in Low-Country Sinhalese are not used by the Kandyans, and *vice versa*. Third, the language is particularly prolific in terms of endearment. Thus where colloquial English has such terms as "dad," "daddy," "pa," "papa," and "pop" as alternatives for the formal "father," Sinhalese has *appa*, *appocci*, and *tatta* as alternatives for *piyā*. Analogous alternatives exist for most other terms, e.g., *bālappa*, *bāpocci*, and *kudāppa* for *bāppa* (father's younger brother). Such variations differ somewhat by caste as well as by region, but usage is not necessarily standardized even among households of the same caste group within the same village.

When complications of this sort are ignored, the structural pattern of Sinhalese kinship terminology is identical to that of the Tamil, which was first fully analyzed by Morgan (1870) and classed by him as Turanian. This circumstance may be partly responsible for the widespread belief that the Sinhalese have or have had a patrilineal descent system (cf. Pieris, 1956, p. 219). At the present time Sinhalese society is "patrilineal" only to about the same extent as is English society, i.e., with surnames normally derived from the father rather than from the mother, and there is no evidence that patrilinearity was any more emphatic in the past.

It must be remembered that Sinhalese kinship terminology is associated with a system of sub-caste endogamy; all recognized kinsmen are members of the same sub-caste. The functional purpose of the terminological categories is not to divide up the total society into discrete unilineal descent groups but rather to distinguish, among the general body of kinsmen, those who are classed as affines from the rest. Marriage establishes an affinal (*massinā*) relationship between a man and his brother-in-law, and this relationship is perpetuated in the next generation so that the sons of brothers-in-law are likewise *massinā* to one another. The structural facts have been correctly analyzed by Dumont (1957), who points out that in societies of this type the sociological facts are better expressed by saying that "my cross-cousin is the child of my father's brother-in-law" than by the more conventional statement that "my cross-cousin is the child of my mother's brother or of my father's sister."

Tambiah (1958, p. 22) has summarized the Sinhalese terminological system so succinctly that it seems advisable to quote him directly:

"All kin within Ego's own and adjacent generations fall into one or other of two major categories. On the one hand own patrilineal kin constitute a theoretically exogamous grouping consisting of fathers (*appa*) and father's sisters (*nändā*); elder brothers (*ayiyā*) and elder sisters (*akkā*); younger brothers (*malli*) and younger sisters (*namgi*); sons (*putā*) and daughters (*duva*). Ranged against these are the categories of affinal relatives: mothers (*amma*) and mother's brothers (*māmā*); male cross cousins (*massinā*) and female cross cousins (*nänā*); sons of siblings of opposite sex (*bänā*) and daughters of siblings of opposite sex (*leli*). The terminology is used as if the entire society consisted only of two intermarrying exogamous patrilineal groups. Thus the wives of all *appa* are *amma*; the husbands of all *nända* are *māmā;* and so on. One consequence of this is that Ego's mother's sister's child is classed as a sibling even if there is no real patrilineal link at all. It will be observed that any term category is specific as to the sex and the generation of the individual referred to. Within each sex-generation category individuals are further distinguished by various prefixes, e.g., father's elder brother, *loku appa* (big father); father's younger brother, *kudā appā* (little father)."

Practical usage does not correspond strictly to this formal design. For example, I found that *bāppa* (a variant form of *kudā appā*) was often given a very wide extension, being applied to any male of Ego's sub-caste of the senior generation whose precise kinship status was unknown. Similarly the terms *ayiyā* (elder brother) and *malli* (younger brother) may be used indiscriminately, even of individuals who should, according to formal principles, be classed as *massinā* (cross-cousin). The term *hūrā* is often used in addressing a cross-cousin who is considerably older than Ego. It is, I think, less formal and respectful than *ayiyā*. Its reciprocal is to address the younger *massinā* by his personal name.

In general the "matrilateral" or "affinal" terms (*māmā, nändā, massinā, nänā, bänā,* and *leli*) have a much more restricted usage than their "patrilateral" counterparts (*appa, amma, ayiyā, malli, akkā, namgi, putā* and *duva*). The former group of terms are applied only to relatives who are effectively in an affinal relationship with Ego. Since affinal relationship entails various kinds of obligation, the use of affinal kinship terminology implies an assertion of kinship rights. In certain kinds of polite society, indeed, the use of the terms *massinā, nänā,* and *leli* seems to be altogether taboo except in reference to third parties. In this connection it should be remembered that, although marriage with a true cross-cousin is not particularly common, all of a man's legitimate mates are his *nänā*, so that the use of this term has definite sexual connotations. The distinction between "patrilineal" kinsmen and "affines" disappears in the second ascending and descending generations.

Rights of domicile in the Dry Zone are a jealously guarded privilege which, in theory, can only be derived by inheritance from an ancestor. There is thus a set of terms denoting ancestors of different generations without regard to sex. My informants professed to distinguish seven such terms for as many degrees of ancestry: *āttā*, grandparent; *nāttā*, great grand-parent; *panāttā*, ancestor of the fourth ascending generation; *kittā*, ancestor of the fifth ascending generation; *kirikittā*, ancestor of the sixth ascending generation; *kirikimuttā*, ancestor of the seventh ascending generation; and *dōvikittā*, ancestor of the eighth ascending generation. While I do not think these terms were invented simply to amuse the anthropologist, I got no evidence that they are ever actually used.

BIBLIOGRAPHY

BARTON, R. F.
1949. *The Kalingas*. Chicago.

DUMONT, L.
1957. Hierarchy and Marriage Alliance in South Indian Kinship. *Occasional Papers of the Royal Anthropological Institute*, XII, 1–45.

FORTES, M.
1949. Time and Social Structure: An Ashanti Case Study. *Social Structure*, ed. M. Fortes, pp. 54–84. Oxford.
1953. The Structure of Unilineal Descent Groups. *American Anthropologist*, LV, 17–41.

FREEMAN, J. D.
1955. Iban Agriculture. *Colonial Research Studies*, XVIII, 1–148. London.
1958. The Family System of the Iban of Borneo. *Cambridge Papers in Social Anthropology*, I, 15–52.

HAYLEY, F. A.
1923. *A Treatise on the Laws and Customs of the Sinhalese*. Colombo.

HOCART, A. M.
1928. The Indo-European Kinship System. *Ceylon Journal of Science*, Section G, I, 179–186.

MORGAN, L. H.
1870. Systems of Consanguinity and Affinity of the Human Family. *Smithsonian Contributions to Knowledge*, XVII, 1–590.

PIERIS, R.
1956. *Sinhalese Social Organisation: The Kandyan Period*. Colombo.

RYAN, B.
1953. *Caste in Modern Ceylon*. New Brunswick.

TAMBIAH, S. J.
1958. The Structure of Kinship and Its Relationship to Land Possession and Residence in Pata Dumbara, Central Ceylon. *Journal of the Royal Anthropological Institute*, LXXXVIII, 21–44.

WITTFOGEL, K. A.
1957. *Oriental Despotism*. New Haven.

YALMAN, N.
1960. The Flexibility of Caste Principles in a Kandyan Community. *Cambridge Papers in Social Anthropology*, II, 78–112.

[16]

Rice and sugar: local models of change

When I first went to Panama in the latter part of the 1960s, I chose to live in a small community that appeared to be undergoing a radical change in agricultural practices. Within less than a decade the people in the village of Los Boquerones shifted from 'subsistence' farming of rice and maize to raising sugar-cane for cash sale, to working for a government sugar mill that had taken control of their land. At the time of my principal fieldwork I was able to study the first two of these economic patterns. By intention I did not focus on topics such as who adopts new agricultural practices first, the motivational characteristics of 'entrepreneurs' or the role of information in promoting change; rather, I attempted to characterize each economy as a distinct form and to explore the nature of the transitions between them. The theoretical tools I eventually employed were a blend of anthropological concepts and what has become known as neoRicardianism, for it seemed to me then – and I would still support the position – that a neoRicardian economics overlaps in important ways with an anthropological perspective (Gudeman 1976a, 1978a, 1978b).

But now I wish to reconsider some of this published material, as well as some unreported ethnography, in order to display more clearly the people's own economic constructions; at each historical period in Panama the villagers had a set of coherently arranged economic categories. Obviously, these local models were constructed in relation to a more powerful economy whose tendrils were encountered but not controlled; and the economic concepts as well as their patterning shifted in response to changing external forces. But the local concepts and schemas constituted the everyday economic activities of the villagers. The Panama material provides an initial example of three separate yet linked schemas of livelihood. Of particular interest is the first set of categories, for these comprised an *oikos* model, a pattern which has not yet been fully explored from a people's perspective. But more generally my purpose is to illustrate the existence, importance and coherence of local constructions. Themes and images from this initial example will find their counterparts in later analyses.

I shall first consider the models separately and then look at the relations between them. For each I first describe the situation from an external perspective and then provide the local view, precisely because the external context itself was locally modeled.

A household economy

The first economic pattern had endured for several hundred years. To provide it with a term, it might be called a household, domestic or *oikos* model (Gudeman and Whitten 1982). The household, based on a division of labor between the sexes, was the central institution of the economy and constituted the primary unit of production and consumption. Goods were produced primarily for use within the household, and they were evaluated in terms of their productive and consumptive qualities; the exchange sector was not highly developed. Overall, the economic pattern was cyclical and goods were seen as flowing through domestic units. Any use of them was defined as an expense, for consumption represented a drain upon the basic reproductive cycle. Close attention, therefore, was given to household economy or the domestic management of goods.

The productive system was based upon agriculture, although some animals were kept. A variety of crops were raised, the most important being rice and maize. Rice, consumed at every meal, was said by the people to be a 'necessity.' All crops were grown by swidden or shifting agriculture. The usual practice was to cut down the forest, burn it, farm a plot for two years in succession and then allow it to regenerate for eight to ten years. The machete and digging stick were the primary tools, while the seed stock was taken from the prior year's harvest; the agricultural system required little 'capital accumulation.' A key technological practice was the use of fire. Burning the forest released nutrients to the soil, and it obviated the need to possess heavy equipment for clearing the land.

Rice and sugar: local models of change 3

Each household used one to one-and-a-half hectares of land. But the work site of a household changed every few years, and in any single year a group usually farmed several pieces of land simultaneously, for by selecting plots with varying characteristics it would have some insurance against the uncertainties of the environment. Even if a household harbored sufficient labor, it often secured outside help during the year. The motivation for obtaining such aid varied from the desire for conviviality to the need for rapidly harvesting a ripened crop. The work itself was repaid by labor, in kind or by cash.

Although the economy of the countryside was founded upon self-sufficient household units, the overall pattern – or model – was not independent of the broader society. The 'domestic economy' itself was generated by an encompassing 'political economy.' It was set into a larger pattern property and a capitalist system. The central or mediating link between this more powerful economy and the countryside was the land.

Throughout the rural areas land was owned predominantly by absentee landlords (Figueroa Navarro 1978). Most used their land to raise cattle. In the area of Los Boquerones the land was owned by the descendants of an army general who had helped lead a revolution against Colombia in the nineteenth century. The owners used it for grazing cattle but also permitted peasants to live on and to farm it. The peasants were allowed to cut down and burn the forest; to keep out the cattle, they would construct wooden fences around their plots. After two years of use, the fences would be demolished so that the cattle might forage in the cleared area while the shrub and brush grew once again. Thus, in return for the right of usufruct, the landowners received the benefit of pasture clearance. In addition, the peasants paid a small rent of either $1.00 or a day of labor per year, regardless of field size or land quality.

The landowners, however, also placed a constraint upon this use right – a limitation designed to protect their own interests. They prohibited permanent investments in either houses or land. The peasants were never allowed to seed a crop that was a perennial or to construct permanent homes; all had to be of the stick and thatch variety. By creating a situation of temporal scarcity in relation to the land, the landowners protected themselves against possible claims by right of improvement. The result was that the peasants had to practice shifting agriculture, if they wanted to have access to the land. Furthermore, they had no reason to improve the land for future use, for they could not benefit from such an investment. The technological practice of swidden agriculture represented not so much an ecological as a socio-economic adaptation to the conditions in which the peasants found themselves.

Within this context of outside control and ownership, how did the people construct their relationship to the land? In the first place, it was said that the forest was freely available for use; everyone had equal rights of access to it. Rights, in fact, were secured by erecting crosses about the area one wished to work. While the land was being used, one had exclusive rights to it, but these lapsed when the agricultural cycle was completed. As one person said: 'In the old times one was owner only of what he planted or worked.' In effect, the land was continuously being cycled from the public to the private to the public domain. The public domain, of course, was not a true commons; the land was not a publicly held benefice. No one owned it and everyone had equal access to it precisely because it was outside local social control.

The people's construct of the land itself was closely linked to this pattern of external control and internal use. Above all, the land was said to have a 'force.' It had powers which could be drawn upon in production. Land – the people would say – needed to be 'rested'; and good land had 'strength,' it would 'give' a good crop. Particular areas 'lent' themselves for certain uses. Overall, the land was modeled as if it were a natural pool or reservoir which could be drawn upon to support the agricultural cycle. The land was an external power the people used but did not control. In these respects, the peasants' model was strikingly similar to that of the Physiocrats and the early Ricardo, both of whom also modeled the land as a natural power that sustained the economic cycle. The Physiocrats, however, justified their focus on the land as fertilizing agent in the economic process by natural law theory and Locke's epistemology of mind. In Ricardo's corn model, land assumed a special importance partly because he relied upon a derivational form of analysis. Clearly, the Panamanian peasants' focus upon land as a natural force arose within a different epistemological context. All three models, however, were about class-structured agricultural societies in which land was a central resource. In all three, furthermore, land was controlled by those who did not directly cultivate it. In particular, for the Panamanian peasants, outside power and control was felt and made known first through the land. The so-called force and fecundity of nature was, in some respects, their way of modeling the external economic powers.

This image of the land as a natural reservoir was elaborated by a remarkable metaphor that the peasants used in their everyday agricultural practices. According to this metaphor, which had an analogical form, crops were to the land as human hair was to the head. The metaphor appeared in the verbal expressions used for practical activities.

According to the people, in the first stage of the agricultural cycle, the *monte* or bush had to be knocked down (*tumbar*) or cut down (*socolar*) so that it could be burned and then seeded (*sembrar*). At this point, precisely when the land was seeded and usufruct rights took effect, the terminology shifted and became humanized. The next step in the agricultural process was to weed. But this was known as 'cleaning,' not weeding, for it was said that the land became 'dirty'. (The term 'cleaning' was also used in the context of demarcating the domestic space of the household from its natural surroundings; each day the patio of the house had to be swept clear of debris.) One cleaned the land so that the rice and other crops would grow and 'throw off children.' The weeding itself was done with different degrees of skill. The poorest was to botch or bungle (*guachapear*) the job by cutting too high with the machete. To cut the weeds at their bases, however, was known as 'trimming the hair slightly' (*sobrepeine*). Best of all was to cut the weeds at their roots by digging the machete several inches into the ground; this was described as *casqueado* – which means cutting the roots by breaking the casing of the head!

The next major task after the weeding was to harvest, but this was known as cutting (*cortar*) the crop. Then, if the same land was to be used in the same year for a second crop (i.e. double cropping), the dead stalks that remained had to be cleared by machete before planting. This activity was known as 'shearing off hair' (*pelar*).

The dead stuff remaining in a field after a crop had been

gathered was termed 'stubble' (*rastrojo*). In the second year of a field's use this stubble was cleared for burning by 'beating' it (*aporrear*). After this second burning, the same sequence of barbering terms was used until the land again became stubble. Finally, a plot remained as stubble for several years until the forest had grown back and the land was again termed *monte*.

Thus, subsistence crops grow as does human hair. The metaphor fitted the cycle by which land moved from equal access to temporary usufruct and back to nature. Agriculture is an activity in which nature is temporarily tamed or humanized by removing the forest cover. Although both human hair and crops are cultivated under the guidance of persons, their force for growing comes not from themselves (the hair, the seed) nor from their cultivator (the barber, the laborer) but from that in which they grow (the head, the earth). Agriculture is a crafting of nature; it entails the use of an external source which must be 'rested' when it becomes 'tired.' Humans contribute their barber-like skills, but the crops are not labor-generated; this is a natural process which depends upon a force that is outside local control.

The peasants had an unwritten land map which made use of this same imagery. The home-made map used in the village consisted of designation by natural features. In the people's terms these were names of 'workplaces' (*trabajaderos*). The entire land surface of the community, including house locales, was divided conceptually into irregular patches, almost all of which bore the names of unchanging natural features. All areas were included, there were no empty spaces, and each was of equivalent importance, whether house site or work site. As one person told me, 'All the places have names, names are equal in this respect.'

The various, designated, real sites had no physical boundaries; the topography was also represented as continuous, and one patch shaded into another. The name of each land piece was taken – or was said to have been taken – from a natural feature found in the area. One region, for example, was termed 'Dark

Notes to Table 1.1

* 'This word, of Galicia – Portuguese origin, is frequent in Panamanian vocabulary and is not uncommon in toponymy' (Robe 1960: 22).

** This was the name of a house and farm site, taken from the person who 'first' worked the area. The individual and family are no longer in the region, and the name is used here in a de-personalized manner.

Rice and sugar: local models of change 7

TABLE 1.1: Land names

Natural referents	*Supernatural referents*	*Social referents*
La Alta Laja* – Large Flat Stone	El Duende – Goblin	Antonina – diminutive of personal name
Los Cagajones – Dungheap		Ciriaca – personal name
Cerca de Piedra – Stone Fence		Juarez – family name
Cerro de Carmen – Carmen's Hill		
Cerro de Guavita – Guavita Hill		
Cienegon – Marsh, Bog		
Coiba – name of island in Pacific Ocean, south of Province		
La Coloma – Heaped up, Overflowing (The Cemetery)		
La Cucha – Lagoon		
Charco El Tronco – Log Pond		
Guayabal – Grove of Guava Trees		
Mataprieta – Dark Shrub		
Mirador – Vantage Point		
Palo Verde – Green Tree		
Picorales – Place of Sharp, Pungent Taste or Things		
Pinto – Spotted		
La Playa Prieta – Dark Beach		
Pozohondo – Deep Pool		
Pozolindo – Pretty Pool		
La Sementera – Sown Land		
Sitio Campo** – Campo (name) Site		

Shrub,' after a large shrub found in the general domain. 'Vantage Point' referred to a locality surrounding a hill which afforded a vision of the entire community. The names are listed in Table 1.1.

The land map was used primarily in providing directions to the changing work sites of the people. The community extends for 2800 hectares, and with approximately twenty-six topographic names, including that of the village itself, each region designated on average more than one hundred hectares. But residential areas, as well as some of the less usable land, were not finely differentiated. A named work locale might cover only sixty hectares and this was an area within which sight and sound could be used to pinpoint a work site. Orientation was provided by combining the label for an area with a cardinal direction; one man might say to another, 'I am working to the north of Deep Spring.' Work sites were easily designated in terms of their distance to and direction from or within a geographic feature or space.

According to the people, the names were there when the first inhabitants of the village arrived. No one knew when the labels originated nor who conferred them upon areas. Given to society, the names were – for the people – outside their volition. In a double respect, the names were a natural terminology. The names themselves referred to natural features; they also possessed no social history and were deemed always to have existed.

As I soon found out through trial and error, however, the map was not fully referential. It was not a direct representation or coding of nature. Many of the labels, for example, had no topographic referent or correlate in the landscape. At certain points only did the labels coincide with the visible features of the land surface, as if the map were a canvas tacked down here and there by a stake or two. Upon enquiry I found that the peasants adopted a rather nominalistic view. For them, the map was something to be used; pragmatically, it was simply a way of marking differences. As one individual put it: 'People put on the names to distinguish them, to call your attention, so you know where to go to work. Like a dog needs a name: if you say "dog," any dog may come.'

None the less, the map labels did fall within the general category 'nature,' which raises the question: why did the peasants draw names from this as opposed to other possible categories? I suggest that selecting labels from the category of nature was fitting in the context of the peasant's local model. The natural map, on the one hand, stood for the fact that the land was free from individual or village appropriation. The land was a part of nature and available to everyone. It was unbounded by a social grid. Being impermeable to human history, to human intervention, to human control, the land remained constant while people moved and used it on a short-term basis. At the same time, the natural map was one way of modeling external control. The natural strength of the land to which the peasants gained occasional access was the force of the landowners. The land map was one of the peasants' ways of constructing and of mediating their relation to the larger society.

The land, however, was important primarily because it provided the foundation or reservoir for the annual seed cycle. Above all, the people were interested in the quantity and quality of the real items which they could produce and reproduce. The peasants were not addicted to quantitative measurements; but they always measured their crops, particularly the input and output or the flows of the seed cycle. By historical knowledge or 'custom' – as they said – they knew that a certain input of seed would yield roughly a certain volume of output. When I enquired about production, the first quantity a person would discuss was the volume of seed he had planted or would plant, not his land size or labor requirements. Furthermore, the peasants made use of a complex system for measuring the volumes of rice and maize. This system was partly of Spanish origin, partly of their own devising; in contrast, nothing so elaborate was used for measuring the land or labor.

Land, in fact, was frequently measured or calculated in terms of the seed. An often-repeated rule of thumb was 'one *lata* (a large tin holding about twenty-five pounds) of rice seeds one hectare.' Actually, some of the 'land measurements' I have were based upon this rule which translates volume of seed to spatial dimension; land size was expressed in terms of a seed quantity. As one person said, 'Before the sugar-cane came, that is how people figured.' Seed measurement dominated land calibration; the land was subordinated to the crops.

Despite the risk of causing some confusion, I am tempted to

label the peasants' model a 'commodity economy.' Their interests were focused upon the commodity, the real items, which they could produce. Rice was a topic of everyday conversation and was discussed in terms of its uses and supply. Different strains were evaluated according to their ease of preparation and eating qualities. Some strains, for example, were said to be softer, others had less tendency to break or chip, while still others were known to preserve well after cooking. Each year seed strains were chosen to secure these qualities. But the reliability of the strains and their suitability for different soils were yet more important. Regardless of consumption qualities, it was crucial to raise enough product to support the household for a year. Agricultural practices were directed to assuring sufficiency, not accumulation or growth through reinvestment. Overall, the seed harvest as a consumable entity was the purpose or finality of the system. To support this cyclical pattern of seed yielding seed, the peasants drew upon the natural power of the land.

Labor, like land, was measured in terms of the seed. The primary labor calculation was by task, rather than time, and this was a way of measuring work performance by the commodity. The focus was upon the material to be transformed – a volume of bush to be cut down, a number of weeds to be cleaned, a quantity of harvest to be gathered. I collected a whole series of labor 'tasks' (*tareas*): for each stage of each crop there was a different task size. For rice weeding there was one task size, and for rice seeding another. Both these tasks differed when done on the maize. The tasks themselves were measured spatially, the human body providing the measuring stick. One undertook a certain number of 'handfuls' or 'arm lengths' of work, where the body length measured the work to be done on the crop, not the land itself. 'The task signifies the quantity of work,' one person said, 'it does not signify land.'

In general, then, labor was not modeled as a homogeneous entity, measured by time. Labor like land was calibrated in terms of crop size. Certain work had to be completed for the harvest to be obtained; given this purpose, the time that a person expended was not of immediate importance nor was it always calculated.

These constructions of the seed, land and labor were closely related to the people's notions about private property and value. No one was said to own the land or forest, even while it was being used: 'the *monte* has no value and one is not the owner.' But everything which was elaborated upon or raised from nature was the property of the laboring individual 'because of the work you have put in – the work from the beginning.' The land (or head) was outside local appropriation, but the crops (or hair) were individually possessed. Possession resulted from the work expended upon an object. In this sense, labor created property.

The peasants never held, however, that property was created because labor itself generated something beyond its brute powers or that humans had a special capacity to coax from the means more than they, the humans, consumed in the process of doing so. This was not a generative but a passive construction of labor. Work added value but only by transporting or moving it from one item to another. When the people bought and sold crops in a field among themselves, they said they were transferring the work or the expenses represented in the objects. And the expenses were calculated in terms of real items. Expense meant the consumption or use of goods. For example, when a man said that in the past maize had more expenses than rice, he was referring not to the cost of producing it but to the fact that maize used to be consumed by horses, pigs and other animals; previously it had more uses. Humans, animals, anything that used up an item was an expense. A good that was consumed not in leisure but in the process of working sustained a useful activity, but it did not and could not help generate extra value. An item was worth the expenses it contained, and these designated a quantity of goods, whether they had been expended directly in the item or indirectly through human labor. Thus, private property was generated not by work itself but by ownership of the expenses which had been impacted into an object. In this respect, too, the villagers' model resembled that of the Physiocrats: the core of both was the cyclical reproduction of agricultural goods which sustained or 'passed through' labor and yielded property rights.

As a totality, the peasants' local economy was based upon household units. This was an *oikos* economy, for the domestic group was the social unit where goods were produced and through which they were cycled. The people, in fact, did not use the term 'economy'; they spoke instead of 'economizing' within the household. Specifically, they would speak of 'expenses of the house' or 'house expenses' (*gastos de la casa*). The expenses were the material needs of the group; by economizing or keeping these uses of the goods under control, the household could maintain itself from year to year. Household plans were predicated upon a cyclical pattern of goods. A surfeit of goods in one year was not seen as accumulation for reinvestment but as pure savings or, more precisely, deferred use. The term 'capital,' for example, was not used by the people; it was not considered to be a productive factor.

Households, as units through which goods flowed, also were not profit centers. As the people said, profit 'is not a thing of the countryside.' Theirs was an expense-conscious, not a profit-directed, economy. For them, profit arose only in trade, not production. Yet, the people did not have a purely exchange conception of profit. Here it is necessary to distinguish between rural exchange and rural-urban trade. Among themselves, the peasants traded both labor and goods. These transactions were modeled as the exchange of equivalents. When you sell, they would say, you recover your expenses – where expenses again were the volume of goods used to produce something. By contrast, outsiders did make profits in rural-urban exchanges. How this happened was a 'mystery' for the peasants, but it was the commodity buyers and traders who could turn a profit. In fact, this metaphoric construction of profit fitted the local model very well; because the peasants had a cyclical, use model, they had no way of constructing profit except as a mysterious entity secured by outsiders or nonparticipants in their economy.

This same rural/urban distinction was seen in the peasants' categorization of the commodities which they consumed. Roughly, goods produced in the countryside were classified as 'necessities' or items needed to meet household expenses. Commodities purchased by cash – obtained through sales of their own goods on the market – were categorized mostly as 'luxuries' and as 'vices,' for their consumption detracted from meeting the necessities of the household. Market commodities signaled a diversion of local goods from the use-expense cycle to sale; they were luxuries precisely because they were not needed to maintain the basic, subsistence cycle and represented a dangerous drain upon it.[1] There was, furthermore, a vague ideological or theological metaphor forged between market commodities and evil. It was sometimes said that one could obtain the power to purchase luxuries only by falling under the Devil's influence. To limit one's 'tastes' (*gustos*) to the 'expenses' (*gastos*) of the household, therefore, was not only prudent but also a moral act.

Overall, then, this was a model of reproduction but not increase or accumulation. To sustain the cycle, the people had to draw on the special power of the land. They constructed this as a force in nature outside their control. The land, when properly tended, would 'give' its strength to the crops which in turn were produced for use or consumption. The act of working was crucial in maintaining this cycle, but labour itself was modeled as a form of crafting – like barbering – and as an expense or use of the goods that were produced. This was a true 'domestic' or 'necessity' economy whose dialectical relation to the larger 'political' or 'luxury' economy was mediated through the land and 'mysterious' exchanges.

A cash crop economy

Beginning in the 1940s the rural area began to experience a more direct penetration by the outside economy. In particular, sugarcane began to be raised as a cash crop. The household remained the central unit in the economy, but in addition to managing a flow of material goods it had to manage a flow of money. Households acted to increase their money income as well as control their real expenses of consumables. Several changes also combined to make the land a scarce and potentially more durable resource.

This period witnessed, first, a shift in control of the land. Throughout the decade the landowners allowed their herd to decline in size, and eventually in the early 1950s they took the first steps toward selling the land to another cattle grazier, who himself threatened to remove the people. The peasants began to react to the possibility of losing usufruct. Ultimately, they found that power through arms was the only way to alter the situation, although their objective was only to restore the status quo. After confrontations and negotiation, in 1963 the government purchased the land, through its land reform agency, with the intention of apportioning the terrain to its users. In the 1960s the future of the area remained uncertain and the people could not predict what entitlements they would hold, but a shift of some land rights from the outside to the local economy had been set in motion.

At the same time the population density of the area increased, due to a slackening in infant mortality and a predominance of in-migration over out-migration. In addition, as the cattle were removed, the forage grasses began to dominate; and the bush, which previously had grown back rather rapidly, now regenerated itself more slowly. Consequently, whether measured absolutely or per household, the amount of usable forest land was decreasing.

In the late 1950s – when the road network was improved – two sugar-cane mills introduced the growing of sugar as a cash crop. Sugar-cane had always been raised, but only in small amounts for immediate consumption and local processing. The peasants rather quickly took up seeding the cash crop, because it could be done in the leisure time generated by their subsistence crops and because any cash received for the sugar-cane was an extra gained at low risk. They used the cash to buy market goods.

Sugar-cane is a perennial which, as grown in Panama, produces a profitable harvest for some five years. But the crop carries on yielding something even in after years and wears out the soil. The effect of seeding sugar-cane was to reduce even further the amount of land available for subsistence crops, both because at a particular time the cane occupied some of the land and because over time it diminished the land's capacity to regenerate the forest.

Overall, then, a change in social organization allowed the villagers to have greater control over the land, but the shift was accompanied by ecological transitions which made the land more scarce. The result of this dialectic between expanded control and diminishing availability was a local land-enclosure movement. During the late 1940s the people began to construct wire fences around plots in the fields. Barbed wire, because of its ease in use, earlier had begun to replace wooden fences, but now the fences changed in their purpose. They were erected not to keep cattle from damaging crops but to stake visible and permanent claims. Each man began to have 'his' own piece or pieces of land in subsistence crops, forest and sugar-cane. By the mid-1960s nearly all the land was fenced, and the economy was caught between subsistence farming and cash cropping.

The impact of the sugar-cane mills, however, was not limited to heightening the ecological dilemma. They had a direct impact on the pattern of the local economy itself.

The principal constraint on the expansion of the mills was land. With ample grinding capacity and financial resources, they wished to increase their raw cane supply; their objective was to secure a larger volume of low-cost, sugar-rich cane. But the mills did not want to commit their own funds to the purchase of more land, while the peasants controlled the only other available land close to the grinding facilities.

Through a system of cash advances, which financed each segment of the cane cycle, the mills were able to gain access to the land of the peasants. Costless money was advanced to the local suppliers on the basis of its being used as the mills prescribed. A century and a half later than the classic British practice, this was a putting-out system in which the supplier had to control not a cottage and loom but a plot of land. The remainder of the means were controlled by the mills' capital advances, although these were conveyed to the suppliers under the label of 'no interest loans.'

The amount the mills loaned was based on the amount of land that a grower made available. Size of loan did not depend upon past yield or the 'entrepreneurial' abilities of the recipient. The mills matched loaned means to land means. 'Inspectors' came out and walked or sighted the land to determine its size and potential. Thus, a different kind of land control came into effect with the sugar-cane. The financial funds of the mills allowed them to gain access to and control some of the peasants' land. Access to such financial funds was precisely what the peasants lacked.

Within this context of monetary power, how did the peasants model the land and the cash crop itself?

In the first place, for the peasants, having permanent control over a plot of land was the ticket of admission to the cash crop. Accordingly, their definition of what constituted private property expanded. Prior to the sugar-cane, an individual possessed the objects which he placed in a field, such as fencing, and the improvements which he added to a field, such as preparing it for seeding. No one possessed the land itself. The local enclosure movement began as a response to ecological pressures and diminished external control, but eventually it became something more than a way of securing permanent usufruct. Fencing an area became a claim to the land itself. Previously, no one had owned the *monte* and it was said to have no value; in land purchases and sales a person was paid only for the improvements he had added to the land. In the 1960s, however, land transactions began to include an extra sum to cover an entitlement which the people called 'respect' or 'consideration.'

What the peasants intended to convey by these terms was not clear; in fact, they disagreed over the meaning of the words, an indication that their local model was in transition. The problem they faced was an interesting one. It was agreed that everyone had a right to 'his' crops, work and fences; but how were the people to justify their appropriation of the land itself? Upon what experience and knowledge could the villagers draw to legitimate their actions? Not surprisingly, their new model was inchoate, and land rights were justified in various ways. For some, fencing the land was a sufficient claim. In effect, this claim was based not upon the fencing itself but on the control of funds which were used to purchase the fencing. For others, having worked in an area gave the right to claim that area; the claim was based on historical use and association. For still others, the imprecise land sightings of a privately paid surveyor – an individual who had claimed to represent the government – constituted a proper claim. Finally, some of the people asserted that only a state-issued title represented a claim – and such titles were not held by anyone in the village.

Regardless of the legitimation invoked, this period did witness an expansion in the power to appropriate. In the earlier use-expense economy only improved things, such as crops, fences or field betterments, were possessed. In the cash crop or commodity context, however, personal property could include nonfabricated objects which formerly had been seen as lying in nature and available for general use. The lines between the public and private, and between the natural and social, shifted.

In spite of these transitions, the subsistence economy was still in existence, and in terms of this economy the metaphor of the land as containing a force was still voiced. But this construct of the land also served well for the cash crop; here, too, land had a pivotal role in that landholding was a prerequisite to the earning of cash.

The mental map of the land did undergo a change, however. The terrain was mapped as being divided into parcels, each marked by boundaries. Personal names were used to designate the fenced pieces; and a plot, regardless of size, was known by the first name of the person who had fenced and claimed it. The map enshrined land claims.

This map was also used to provide spatial directions, but now everyone needed more social information, for the new terms of the map emanated from society. In the first system a person had to possess topographical information only, but in the second he had to have information about the people of the village, about plots, and about the interrelation of the two. A classification of people had to be coordinated with a classification of the land. When information was incomplete, the second map might be supplemented by use of the first, which was still in existence: 'I shall meet you on Juan's land.' 'Where?' 'Near Green Tree.' To send the message clearly, people would shift from one map to the other, but in doing so they were also shifting from one economy to another.

The second map altered, where the first was static. In the second system, rights to plots were sold, and plots themselves were split and joined in fresh ways. As these property rights shifted, boundaries and labels on the land map had to be changed. Unlike the natural map with permanent names, this was an historical map, a map encompassing change, a social map linked to a living community.

The way of measuring the crop also changed. With the subsistence crops measurements were made in terms of the seed, from seed input to seed output or from seed input to land input. This pattern was inverted for the cash crop, which was seen in terms of the land; each hectare, it was said, would yield so much sugar-cane. In a series of interviews I once had with a neighbor, he gave me seed to seed measures for rice, maize, beans and a host of other subsistence crops; but each time we shifted the discussion to sugar-cane, he changed the input parameter from seed to land.

This method for calibrating the crop fitted the new economic pattern. With sugar-cane the objective was to obtain cash, rather than the crop itself. The largest sums received came from the cash advances, and these varied according to the amount of land devoted to the crop. In consequence, the crop was modeled through the land which determined the principal cash flows.

The sugar-cane itself, like rice and maize, was a frequent topic of conversation, but it was evaluated according to different criteria. The people would discuss the different strains of cane in terms of their sugar content, weight, thickness of stalk, ease of harvesting (which was a major cost), and how many years they yielded a profitable harvest. The crop was modeled and selected in terms of its exchange qualities – that is, its cash value – rather than its consumption features.

The peasants' construct of labor also changed with the advent of the sugar-cane. In the first place, a completely different work terminology was used in the sugar-cane. Similar acts of physical labor were performed on the subsistence and cash crops, but they had different labels. No barbering terms were employed in the sugar-cane; work was called 'seeding,' 'weeding' and 'harvesting.' The physical movement when clearing the weeds with a machete was almost identical in the domestic and cash crops, but in the cane this was called 'weeding' while in rice it was 'trimming the hair.'

Furthermore, much of the work in the sugar-cane was performed by hired laborers. The workers were paid by the day and in cash. In the sugar-cane, labor was a quantity of effort measured by time.

The people, however, did not have a generative notion of labor, and this had to do with the way they saw their relationship with the mills. Peasant suppliers did not use the constructs of capital, profit or return on investment for the sugar-cane. Actually, a sugar-cane supplier never received a true profit. At the end of the harvest he received a sum that represented the balance between his revenues for the harvest, whose costs had been paid in prior years, and his current cash costs, which would pay off in the future. A supplier received a funds flow as opposed to a profit result. Even a trained observer could not calculate profit, loss or return on investment for a sugar-cane plot from the information locally available.

Still, to achieve this funds flow result, a supplier had to hire laborers from other rural areas to work in his fields. The people were very aware that the less they paid the hired workers, the more that remained for them. In effect, sugar-cane suppliers held a mini-power of distribution based on land control. They used this power to their advantage but did not see it as a source of profit. The extra amount that a supplier could keep from his workers was a 'trick' which increased his cash returns. In this respect, labor was not seen as value- or profit-generative. There was no notion that profit derived or was an extraction from labor. Extra cash was gained through careful management or economizing of money flows, just as the flow of goods in the domestic economy could be carefully managed.

The people did say, however, that the mills had capital and that they made a profit: 'The mills get rich from our sweat.' Profit, then, was a construct for the people but outside their control. Again, it arose in the asymmetric exchange between the rural and urban sectors; it was not a thing of the countryside.

Overall, sugar-cane was seen in terms similar to rice and maize, in that it afforded increased household consumption. It was never modeled in terms of profit, investment, reinvestment, productivity, growth or any other 'development' concepts. The difference was that consumption in this economy was mediated by the receipt of cash, which was used to purchase market goods.

A wage goods economy

Following the 1968 elections in Panama, a revolution occurred and a new government assumed power. Led by a general who had been born in the rural area, this government took a fresh interest in the countryside. As part of its development plan in Veraguas Province, it prevailed upon the peasants who lived within one 10,000-hectare area, a region including the village of Los Boquerones, to take part in a government program and to raise only sugar-cane. By 1973 the government was operating a modern cane-mill in the area.

Originally, the mill was to be a part of a large cooperative which would include all the villagers and suppliers. In fact, it has been administered by government appointees. The mill's power has been immense and the changes it has instituted have been far-reaching. At the outset it acquired the terrain of Los Boquerones from the land reform agency. The existing, private mills were told to search elsewhere for suppliers of raw cane. Government surveyors recorded approximately how many hectares each person had encircled; then all the old fences were torn down. The entire area was converted to growing sugar-cane. New roads were cut through the region, a few hills were leveled, and the raising of subsistence crops was prohibited. The sugar-cane is grown in large parcels which have passageways and irrigation canals between them. Modern technology is employed, including the use of heavy equipment, aerial spraying and seed selection based on experimentation.

As previous users of the land, the men all have the right (which they exercise) to work for the mill. Because it is impossible to raise subsistence crops, they are completely dependent upon earning wages and purchasing market commodities. They also have lost control over the organization of the work process. Each day the men report to the mill and are then transported to one or another field area. Only occasionally does a man work in his own community, and village land is frequently worked by others.

In addition, each landholder receives a set 'rent' ($70 per hectare) for the area he has under cultivation. Some of this return will be used to pay for actual title to the land.

This new context has brought into being a different local model of the economy. In the first place, the household is no longer the unit of production, and it has lost the function of controlling the reproductive flow of goods. The people no longer speak of 'expenses of the house.' It serves now as a base for participants in the larger productive system and as the locale for consummatory activities. In the future it may also function as the unit through which inheritance and rights to property are transmitted.

Labor is constructed entirely as a quantity, measured by time. As opposed to the land or usable goods, it is the basis of economic survival. Labor itself has become a kind of commodity, for only through the performance of labor and the receipt of a wage can needed market goods be obtained. Thus, in place of the consumable qualities of rice or the exchangeable qualities of sugar-cane, the people now talk about how long they work, how hard they work, how much they earn, the rate of inflation and the purchasing power of their wages; they have all the typical 'wage grumbles.' In the past they would and did fight over control and possession of the land; now if it were possible, they would strike over the wage. The focus of their struggles has shifted significantly.

In addition to modeling themselves as wage earners and market consumers, the people also state that they are landowners who receive a rent. The rationale for this construction, however, is not immediately apparent. In the first place, they no longer have specific or demarcated plots of land which could be said to receive a rent; and the set return they do receive is unrelated to the particular fertility of a plot. Clearly, the villagers are not receiving a rent in the technical, Ricardian sense. In fact, actual landownership has disappeared, the land having been swallowed up by the mill. The people have neither right of use nor control over their land, any more than a shareholder of a corporation may appropriate a piece of equipment from his company. In effect, a 'landowner' has title to a fractional share of the assets of the enterprise; and what the local owner receives is not a rent but a set share of the sugar mill profits, rather like a return on a long-term corporate debenture. Unlike most lenders of capital, however, the villagers have obtained their assets on 'margin.' With the returns generated they may hope to pay off their accounts due. 'Landownership' is really a way of speaking about a share of financial assets, held but not controlled.

Why, then, do the people see themselves as landowners receiving a rent? In this respect it may be useful to consider the new land map. The area itself is divided into large rectangular blocks of cane. An old private plot may now fall within several of the new cane parcels, while one of the new parcels may contain what were once separate plots. In addition, most of the physical landmarks have been obliterated, and the new ones, such as roads, fire-breaks and the land parcels themselves, physically resemble one another. The older mapping systems are remembered, but with the new mill and techniques, the old natural and personal names are of little use. In fact, for the villagers there is little need to give directions outside the settlement area, which itself has been concentrated along a central roadway. Each land parcel, however, does bear a plaque with a number, and in the infrequent conversations concerning land – among villagers or between villagers and outsiders – the number is used to designate a work site. People now refer to geographic space by number rather than nature or society. This third map is a technical and depersonalized representation of the terrain, conveying nothing about local possession of the land.

Traditionally, land has been the focus of the relation between the rural and urban sectors in Panama. How the people map the land is a way of modeling this link. For the villagers, the land is no longer an animate force, a human head or a personal possession. The numbers were given by the mill, and the map is a reflection of the impersonal and administrative conditions under which they now work. At the same time, the map does serve to remind the villagers that they have a right to work at the mill and to participate in the distribution of the mills' profits, because they 'contributed' the land. The mental map perhaps is akin to the bond certificate hidden in the safety deposit box but occasionally removed and gazed upon fondly. Although the map may no longer signal access to the means, it does suggest some rights of access to the ends. Thus the concept of rent, which the people employ, emphasizes that it is only through the land that they have some permanent rights in relation to the external enterprise. Land and rent are the idioms by which and through which the people are able to voice a legitimate and enduring claim on the jobs and returns of the sugar mill. As in the earlier situations, a rural-urban asymmetry in power and control is evident, only now the people speak explicitly of 'the power of the mill.'

A succession of models

Let us now consider the three models as an historical series, for each was partly built from the preceding. Although no common thread runs through them, it is possible to find continuities and transformations between the three.

The first two models were closely related in their purpose or end (see Table 1.2). The primary purpose of raising both the subsistence and cash crops was home consumption, either via the foodstuffs raised or through cash purchases of goods. The two systems, however, did not have an equivalent standing in that work in the sugar-cane was originally done in the leisure time generated by the subsistence crops which had first call upon a man's time.

This ranking of the two systems was related to the difference between the kind of goods and consumption yielded by them; at

TABLE 1.2: Three local models

	Land	*Seed*	*Labor*	*Configuration*
Household	Externally owned 'Freely available' A 'force' Land: crops :: Head: hair Land map – natural names, unbounded, outside society	The measure for input – output Qualitative features A 'necessity'	Heterogeneous Performs 'tasks' Measured by body sizes and crop needs Consumes and transfers value	Reproductive schema: Land-based, seed cycle Home consumption which is an expense Household-focused Profits in external trading
Cash crop	Individually appropriated Ticket of admission Determines loan and crop size Has 'value' Land map – personal property, bounded, personal names, historical and social A force	Measured by land input Exchange features	Hired (irregular) Paid cash Homogeneous quantity usually measured by time	Linear schema: Land-based, Crop-grown, Cash return, Market consumption Profits earned by external mills
Gov't mill	Individually owned as claim on enterprise Provides a rent Technical map – technical boundaries, numbered plots	No personal crop	Wage laborers 'Wage grumbles' Externally and administratively organized	Linear schema: Wage-based, Cash return, Market consumption Power of gov't mill

first, one provided necessities while the other satisfied vices. The cash crop was an 'extra.' It enabled the people to indulge in commodity vices without endangering the flow of subsistence goods. But as ecological degradation (caused by the cash crop) increased, the cash received for the sugar-cane was used more and more for the purchase of necessities, such as rice. The sugar-cane was seen as supplementing, not complementing, the subsistence cycle. Not surprisingly, the villagers eventually formed a dialectical or contradictory set of ideas about the mills: they claimed at the same time that the mills had 'saved' them by providing cash for necessities and 'ruined' them by causing the situation in the first place.

In addition, some of the constructions in the first two models were metaphorically related. In both, the land was said to give 'force' to the crop. This similarity between the models had implications for practical actions. When I asked the peasants why they used fertilizer for sugar-cane but not the subsistence crops, they pointed out that fertilizer took the place of the ash which fell to the soil when trees were burned in the swidden. Both gave 'strength' to the land. The earlier model provided a schema for organizing new experience.

A similar transfer occurred with the notion of profit. In the first model, profit was seen as arising in rural-urban relationships and as accruing to outsiders. In the second model it also fell outside the people's control, but what in the earlier situation had been 'traders' profits' became the 'mills' profits' in the later.

There were also important changes between the first two models. The crop was the measure for quantities of land and labor in the first model, but land – which determined the cash flow – was the measure in the second. Labor consequently was transformed from a task measurement for crops to a quantity of effort measured by time. To use a shorthand terminology, there was a shift from a crop-focused to a land-focused model or from a system of use to a system of exchange. A cyclical and reproductive schema of seed to crop to seed was transformed into a linear schema of land to commodity to cash to market goods.

Elements of the third model, in turn, were patterned after the first two. Home consumption was still the primary purpose of productive activities; turning a profit was never a goal. Furthermore, time work, cash use, and the purchase of market goods all had occupied an important place in the second model. In the third model also a crucial part of the relationship between the rural and urban sectors was constituted through the land, which was precisely the role it had played in the first two models. In addition, the construct of 'rent' used originally in the first model was employed in the third. But in the first it referred to the claims which outsiders had upon the peasants through the land, whereas in the third it designated the claims the villagers had through the land upon the government sugar cooperative. The earlier concept was used and in a sense inverted for the later experience.

The third model, however, was quite different in its principal focus. In its linear pattern wage labor was central, for this provided the cash return upon which all consumption depended. In consequence, the ideological seam between the local and the larger economy was eradicated. Commodities were no longer separated into necessities and vices or into use-expense and market goods. They pertained to the same category in that they all had to be purchased. The domestic economy disappeared.

The changes among the three models were externally induced, through such influences as road improvement, better sugar-cane technology and an expanded sugar quota to the United States. Specifically, the changes were mediated through external control over one or another productive means. In each model, however, the peasants constructed this external control ecologically, via the land, and through the notion of profit. They modeled themselves as being penumbral to a larger economy which had a controlling influence upon their lives.

Thus, at each stage the peasants' current model became a way of constructing or seeing their new experience, even though they did not initiate that experience. At each point also the people creatively transformed their models such that there were continuities and discontinuities, metaphors and gaps, between them.

Local models of development

In this chapter I have been examining a situation of change or what is sometimes known as 'development.' My interest has been in the local models of this change. But do these give us a different perspective on development? I have sometimes been taxed by development economists with the question: 'You anthropologists always tell us why things go wrong, but what can you offer us in a positive way? Have you no theories?' Perhaps the material of this chapter suggests why I find the question itself to be inappropriate.

I would argue that one part of the development process should include the explicit examination of local constructions. A people's model is their life and history, their historical consciousness, their social construction. To a far greater degree than we sometimes realize, it is a part of what we call 'development.' But such local models are not to be examined through the perspective of our models. These are not, as it is sometimes said, 'externalities,' 'constraints,' 'causes for failure' or 'political and social blockages to technological change.' The use of such terms implies a valuation based upon a Western model. Local models are simply the conditions of and for 'development.' They can hardly be evaluated, unless the observer claims to have privileged knowledge.

One might envision, then, a different way of thinking about development. I would shift the discussion from a focus on material exploitation and the measurement of value to the deeper and more perplexing issue concerning the relation between models and power. If development is fundamentally about models and their changes, the central question must be: who is the modeler? To what degree, for example, has an initial local model been self-constituted and to what degree has it been constrained by the models and actions of others? Are subsequent models of change representative of those for whom they are intended? What place should formal, academic models have in both understanding and directing a situation of development? Indeed, who should have the right to construct a development model? Here perhaps we might envision a shift toward the conception of a 'community of modelers' (Aris and Penn 1980). Models are never the product of a single individual but are part of an historical and cultural tradition. Development situations, however, are particularly complex, because they must involve mixing together several different cultural discourses. The challenge is not to try to uncover and then use general laws of development, nor is it simply to figure out what agricultural or monetary techniques can be employed in a particular situation of change; rather it is to define who belongs to and how to organize a community of modelers. What is a fair balance of representation as between local persons, government appointees and outside technicians? What conditions need to be specified so that equitable participation may occur? These are difficult questions, for they concern the distribution of power; and they make an even more difficult task of development than it already is. But perhaps this perspective indicates an alternative and potentially more successful formulation of the development process.

Regardless, development contexts are particularly interesting because they represent a confrontation and mixture of local and global power as well as folk and Western knowledge. They graphically illustrate the differences between local constructions and modern models, a distinction to which I now turn.

Notes

1 As I have argued elsewhere (Gudeman 1978a,1978b) there is a fascinating parallel between the peasants' division of goods into necessities and luxuries and the Sraffian division into basics and luxuries. Previously, I used a Sraffian-like model to analyze the productive system in rural Panama.

Bibliography

ARIS, R. and PENN, M. 1980. 'The mere notion of a model.' *Mathematical Modelling*, 1:1-12.

FIGUEROA NAVARRO, A. 1978. *Dominio y Sociedad en el Panama Colombiano (1821-1903)*. Panama: Impresora Panamá.

GUDEMAN, S. 1976a. *Relationships, Residence and the Individual*. London: Routledge & Kegan Paul.

GUDEMAN, S. 1978a. 'Anthropological economics: the question of distribution.' *Annual Review of Anthropology*, 7:347-79. Palo Alto, Calif.: Annual Reviews.

GUDEMAN, S. 1978b. *The Demise of a Rural Economy: From Subsistence to Capitalism in a Latin American Village*. London: Routledge & Kegan Paul.

GUDEMAN, S. and WHITTEN, N. E. 1982. 'Introduction.' *American Ethnologist*, 9:223-9.

LOCKE, J. 1823 [1690]. *The Works of John Locke*, 5. London: J. Johnson.

LOCKE, J. 1975 [1690]. *An Essay Concerning Human Understanding*, ed. P. H. Nidditch. Oxford: Clarendon Press.

RICARDO, D. 1951–2. *The Works and Correspondence of David Ricardo*, ed. P. Sraffa, vols I,III,IV,VI. Cambridge: Cambridge University Press.

ROBE, S. 1960. *The Spanish of Rural Panama*. Berkeley: University of California Press.

Part III
Processes: Exchange

[17]

THE ESSENTIALS OF THE KULA

I

HAVING thus described the scene, and the actors, let us now proceed to the performance. The Kula is a form of exchange, of extensive, inter-tribal character; it is carried on by communities inhabiting a wide ring of islands, which form a closed circuit. This circuit can be seen on Map V, where it is represented by the lines joining a number of islands to the North and East of the East end of New Guinea. Along this route, articles of two kinds, and these two kinds only, are constantly travelling in opposite directions. In the direction of the hands of a clock, moves constantly one of these kinds—long necklaces of red shell, called *soulava* (Plates XVIII and XIX)*. In the opposite direction moves the other kind—bracelets of white shell called *mwali* (Plates XVI and XVII)*. Each of these articles, as it travels in its own direction on the closed circuit, meets on its way articles of the other class, and is constantly being exchanged for them. Every movement of the Kula articles, every detail of the transactions is fixed and regulated by a set of traditional rules and conventions, and some acts of the Kula are accompanied by an elaborate magical ritual and public ceremonies.

On every island and in every village, a more or less limited number of men take part in the Kula—that is to say, receive the goods, hold them for a short time, and then pass them on. Therefore every man who is in the Kula, periodically though not regularly, receives one or several *mwali* (arm-shells), or a *soulava* (necklace of red shell discs), and then has to hand it on to one of his partners, from whom he receives the opposite commodity in exchange. Thus no man ever keeps any of the articles for any length of time in his possession. One transaction does not finish the Kula relationship, the rule being

* not reproduced here

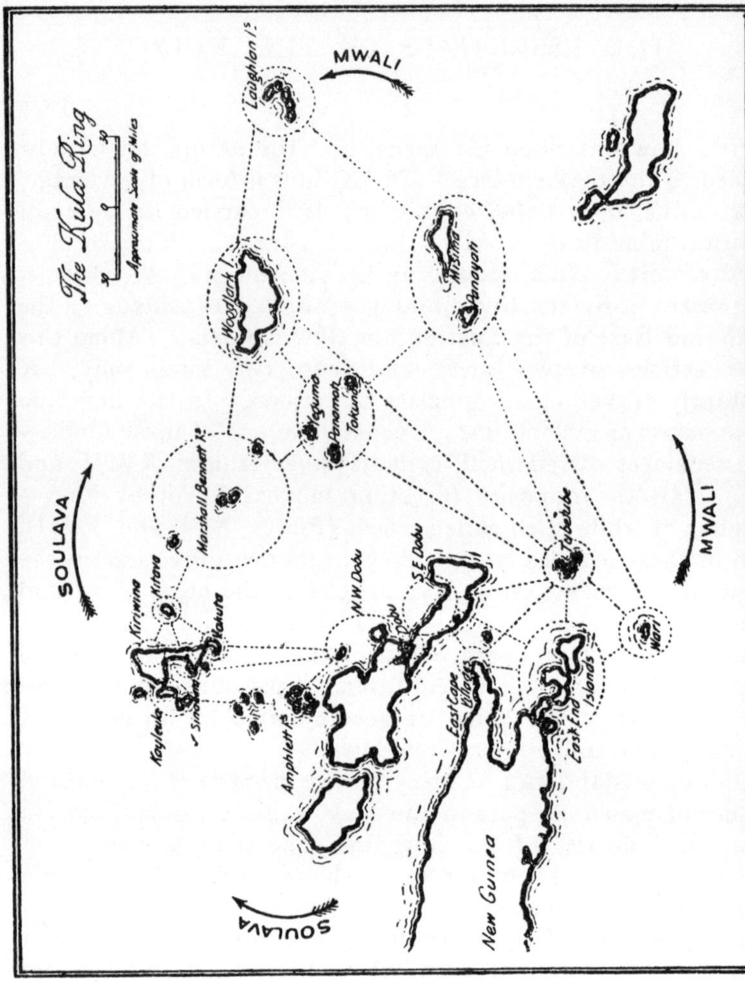

Map V—The Kula Ring.

" once in the Kula, always in the Kula," and a partnership between two men is a permanent and lifelong affair. Again, any given *mwali* or *soulava* may always be found travelling and changing hands, and there is no question of its ever settling down, so that the principle " once in the Kula, always in the Kula " applies also to the valuables themselves.

The ceremonial exchange of the two articles is the main, the fundamental aspect of the Kula. But associated with it, and done under its cover, we find a great number of secondary activities and features. Thus, side by side with the ritual exchange of arm-shells and necklaces, the natives carry on ordinary trade, bartering from one island to another a great number of utilities, often unprocurable in the district to which they are imported, and indispensable there. Further, there are other activities, preliminary to the Kula, or associated with it, such as the building of sea-going canoes for the expeditions, certain big forms of mortuary ceremonies, and preparatory taboos.

The Kula is thus an extremely big and complex institution, both in its geographical extent, and in the manifoldness of its component pursuits. It welds together a considerable number of tribes, and it embraces a vast complex of activities, interconnected, and playing into one another, so as to form one organic whole.

Yet it must be remembered that what appears to us an extensive, complicated, and yet well ordered institution is the outcome of ever so many doings and pursuits, carried on by savages, who have no laws or aims or charters definitely laid down. They have no knowledge of the *total outline* of any of their social structure. They know their own motives, know the purpose of individual actions and the rules which apply to them, but how, out of these, the whole collective institution shapes, this is beyond their mental range. Not even the most intelligent native has any clear idea of the Kula as a big, organised social construction, still less of its sociological function and implications. If you were to ask him what the Kula is, he would answer by giving a few details, most likely by giving his personal experiences and subjective views on the Kula, but nothing approaching the definition just given here. Not even a partial coherent account could be obtained. For the integral picture does not exist in his mind ; he is in it, and cannot see the whole from the outside.

The integration of all the details observed, the achievement of a sociological synthesis of all the various, relevant symptoms, is the task of the Ethnographer. First of all, he has to find out that certain activities, which at first sight might appear incoherent and not correlated, have a meaning. He then has to find out what is constant and relevant in these activities, and what accidental and inessential, that is, to find out the laws and rules of all the transactions. Again, the Ethnographer has to *construct* the picture of the big institution, very much as the physicist constructs his theory from the experimental data, which always have been within reach of everybody, but which needed a consistent interpretation. I have touched on this point of method in the Introduction (Divisions V and VI),* but I have repeated it here, as it is necessary to grasp it clearly in order not to lose the right perspective of conditions as they really exist among the natives.

II

In giving the above abstract and concise definition, I had to reverse the order of research, as this is done in ethnographic field-work, where the most generalised inferences are obtained as the result of long inquiries and laborious inductions. The general definition of the Kula will serve as a sort of plan or diagram in our further concrete and detailed descriptions. And this is the more necessary as the Kula is concerned with the exchange of wealth and utilities, and therefore it is an economic institution, and there is no other aspect of primitive life where our knowledge is more scanty and our understanding more superficial than in Economics. Hence misconception is rampant, and it is necessary to clear the ground when approaching any economic subject.

Thus in the Introduction we called the Kula a " form of trade," and we ranged it alongside other systems of barter. This is quite correct, if we give the word " *trade* " a sufficiently wide interpretation, and mean by it any exchange of goods. But the word " trade " is used in current Ethnography and economic literature with so many different implications that a whole lot of misleading, preconceived ideas have to be brushed aside in order to grasp the facts correctly. Thus the *a priori* current notion of primitive trade would be that of an exchange of indispensable or useful articles, done without much ceremony

* not reproduced here

or regulation, under stress of dearth or need, in spasmodic, irregular intervals—and this done either by direct barter, everyone looking out sharply not to be done out of his due, or, if the savages were too timid and distrustful to face one another, by some customary arrangement, securing by means of heavy penalties compliance in the obligations incurred or imposed * Waiving for the present the question how far this conception is valid or not in general—in my opinion it is quite misleading —we have to realise clearly that the Kula contradicts in almost every point the above definition of "savage trade." It shows us primitive exchange in an entirely different light.

The Kula is not a surreptitious and precarious form of exchange. It is, quite on the contrary, rooted in myth, backed by traditional law, and surrounded with magical rites. All its main transactions are public and ceremonial, and carried out according to definite rules. It is not done on the spur of the moment, but happens periodically, at dates settled in advance, and it is carried on along definite trade routes, which must lead to fixed trysting places. Sociologically, though transacted between tribes differing in language, culture, and probably even in race, it is based on a fixed and permanent status, on a partnership which binds into couples some thousands of individuals. This partnership is a lifelong relationship, it implies various mutual duties and privileges, and constitutes a type of inter-tribal relationship on an enormous scale. As to the economic mechanism of the transactions, this is based on a specific form of credit, which implies a high degree of mutual

* By "current view," I mean such as is to be found in text-books and in passing remarks, scattered through economic and ethnological literature. As a matter of fact, Economics is a subject very seldom touched upon either in theoretical works on Ethnology, or in accounts of field-work. I have enlarged on this deficiency in the article on "Primitive Economics," published in the *Economic Journal*, March, 1921.

The best analysis of the problem of savage economy is to be found, in spite of its many shortcomings, in K. Bücher's "Industrial Evolution," English Translation, 1901. On primitive trade, however, his views are inadequate. In accordance with his general view that savages have no national economy, he maintains that any spread of goods among natives is achieved by non-economic means, such as robbery, tributes and gifts. The information contained in the present volume is incompatible with Bücher's views, nor could he have maintained them had he been acquainted with Barton's description of the Hiri (contained in Seligman's "Melanesians.")

A summary of the research done on Primitive Economics, showing incidentally, how little real, sound work has been accomplished, will be found in Pater W. Kopper's "Die Ethnologische Wirtschaftsforschung" in *Anthropos*, X—XI, 1915-16, pp. 611-651, and 971-1079. The article is very useful, where the author summarises the views of others.

trust and commercial honour—and this refers also to the subsidiary, minor trade, which accompanies the Kula proper. Finally, the Kula is not done under stress of any need, since its main aim is to exchange articles which are of no practical use.

From the concise definition of Kula given at the beginning of this chapter, we see that in its final essence, divested of all trappings and accessories, it is a very simple affair, which at first sight might even appear tame and unromantic. After all, it only consists of an exchange, interminably repeated, of two articles intended for ornamentation, but not even used for that to any extent. Yet this simple action—this passing from hand to hand of two meaningless and quite useless objects—has somehow succeeded in becoming the foundation of a big inter-tribal institution, in being associated with ever so many other activities, Myth, magic and tradition have built up around it definite ritual and ceremonial forms, have given it a halo of romance and value in the minds of the natives, have indeed created a passion in their hearts for this simple exchange.

The definition of the Kula must now be amplified, and we must describe one after the other its fundamental characteristics and main rules, so that it may be clearly grasped by what mechanism the mere exchange of two articles results in an institution so vast, complex, and deeply rooted.

III

First of all, a few words must be said about the two principal objects of exchange, the arm-shells (*mwali*) and the necklaces (*soulava*). The arm-shells are obtained by breaking off the top and the narrow end of a big, cone-shaped shell (*Conus millepunctatus*), and then polishing up the remaining ring. These bracelets are highly coveted by all the Papuo-Melanesians of New Guinea, and they spread even into the pure Papuan district of the Gulf.* The manner of wearing the arm-shells is illustrated by Plate XVII,* where the men have put them on on purpose to be photographed.

The use of the small discs of red spondylus shell, out of which the *soulava* are made, is also of a very wide diffusion.

* Professor C. G. Seligman, op. cit., p. 93, states that arm-shells, *toea*, as they are called by the Motu, are traded from the Port Moresby district westward to the Gulf of Papua. Among the Motu and Koita, near Port Moresby, they are highly valued, and nowadays attain very high prices, up to £30, much more than is paid for the same article among the Massim.

* not reproduced here

There is a manufacturing centre of them in one of the villages in Port Moresby, and also in several places in Eastern New Guinea, notably in Rossell Island, and in the Trobriands. I have said " *use* " on purpose here, because these small beads, each of them a flat, round disc with a hole in the centre, coloured anything from muddy brown to carmine red, are employed in various ways for ornamentation. They are most generally used as part of earrings, made of rings of turtle shell, which are attached to the ear lobe, and from which hang a cluster of the shell discs. These earrings are very much worn, and, especially among the Massim, you see them on the ears of every second man or woman, while others are satisfied with turtle shell alone, unornamented with the shell discs. Another everyday ornament, frequently met with and worn, especially by young girls and boys, consists of a short necklace, just encircling the neck, made of the red spondylus discs, with one or more cowrie shell pendants. These shell discs can be, and often are, used in the make-up of the various classes of the more elaborate ornaments, worn on festive occasions only. Here, however, we are more especially concerned with the very long necklaces, measuring from two to five metres, made of spondylus discs, of which there are two main varieties, one, much the finer, with a big shell pendant, the other made of bigger discs, and with a few cowrie shells or black banana seeds in the centre (see Plate XVIII).*

The arm-shells on the one hand, and the long spondylus shell strings on the other, the two main Kula articles, are primarily ornaments. As such, they are used with the most elaborate dancing dress only, and on very festive occasions such as big ceremonial dances, great feasts, and big gatherings, where several villages are represented, as can be seen in Plate VI. Never could they be used as everyday ornaments, nor on occasions of minor importance, such as a small dance in the village, a harvest gathering, a love-making expedition, when facial painting, floral decoration and smaller though not quite everyday ornaments are worn (see Plates XII and XIII).* But even though usable and sometimes used, this is not the main function of these articles. Thus, a chief may have several shell strings in his possession, and a few arm-shells. Supposing that a big dance is held in his or in a neighbouring village, he will not put on his ornaments himself if he goes to

* not reproduced here

assist at it, unless he intends to dance and decorate himself, but any of his relatives, his children or his friends and even vassals, can have the use of them for the asking. If you go to a feast or a dance where there are a number of men wearing such ornaments, and ask anyone of them at random to whom it belongs, the chances are that more than half of them will answer that they themselves are not the owners, but that they had the articles lent to them. These objects are not owned in order to be used ; the privilege of decorating oneself with them is not the real aim of possession.

Indeed—and this is more significant—by far the greater number of the arm-shells, easily ninety per cent., are of too small a size to be worn even by young boys and girls. A few are so big and valuable that they would not be worn at all, except once in a decade by a very important man on a very festive day. Though all the shell-strings can be worn, some of them are again considered too valuable, and are cumbersome for frequent use, and would be worn on very exceptional occasions only.

This negative description leaves us with the questions : why, then, are these objects valued, what purpose do they serve ? The full answer to this question will emerge out of the whole story contained in the following chapters, but an approximate idea must be given at once. As it is always better to approach the unknown through the known, let us consider for a moment whether among ourselves we have not some type of objects which play a similar rôle and which are used and possessed in the same manner. When, after a six years' absence in the South Seas and Australia, I returned to Europe and did my first bit of sight-seeing in Edinburgh Castle, I was shown the Crown jewels. The keeper told many stories of how they were worn by this or that king or queen on such and such occasion, of how some of them had been taken over to London, to the great and just indignation of the whole Scottish nation, how they were restored, and how now everyone can be pleased, since they are safe under lock and key, and no one can touch them. As I was looking at them and thinking how ugly, useless, ungainly, even tawdry they were, I had the feeling that something similar had been told to me of late, and that I had seen many other objects of this sort, which made a similar impression on me.

And then arose before me the vision of a native village on coral soil, and a small, rickety platform temporarily erected under a pandanus thatch, surrounded by a number of brown, naked men, and one of them showing me long, thin red strings, and big, white, worn-out objects, clumsy to sight and greasy to touch. With reverence he also would name them, and tell their history, and by whom and when they were worn, and how they changed hands, and how their temporary possession was a great sign of the importance and glory of the village. The analogy between the European and the Trobriand *vaygu'a* (valuables) must be delimited with more precision. The Crown Jewels, in fact, any heirlooms too valuable and too cumbersome to be worn, represent the same type as *vaygu'a* in that they are merely possessed for the sake of possession itself, and the ownership of them with the ensuing renown is the main source of their value. Also both heirlooms and *vaygu'a* are cherished because of the historical sentiment which surrounds them. However ugly, useless, and—according to current standards—valueless an object may be, if it has figured in historical scenes and passed through the hands of historic persons, and is therefore an unfailing vehicle of important sentimental associations, it cannot but be precious to us. This historic sentimentalism, which indeed has a large share in our general interest in studies of past events, exists also in the South Seas. Every really good Kula article has its individual name, round each there is a sort of history and romance in the traditions of the natives. Crown jewels or heirlooms are insignia of rank and symbols of wealth respectively, and in olden days with us, and in New Guinea up till a few years ago, both rank and wealth went together. The main point of difference is that the Kula goods are only in possession for a time, whereas the European treasure must be permanently owned in order to have full value.

Taking a broader, ethnological view of the question, we may class the Kula valuables among the many " ceremonial " objects of wealth ; enormous, carved and decorated weapons, stone implements, articles of domestic and industrial nature, too well decorated and too clumsy for use. Such things are usually called " ceremonial," but this word seems to cover a great number of meanings and much that has no meaning at all. In fact, very often, especially on museum labels, an article is called " ceremonial " simply because nothing is known about its uses and general nature. Speaking only about museum exhibits from New Guinea, I can say that many so-called ceremonial objects are nothing but simply overgrown objects of use, which preciousness of material and amount of labour expended have transformed into reservoirs of condensed economic value. Again, others are used on festive occasions, but play no part whatever in rites and ceremonies, and serve for decoration only, and these might be called *objects of parade* (comp. Chap VI, Div. I).* Finally, a number of these articles function actually as instruments of a magical or religious rite, and belong to the intrinsic apparatus of a ceremony. Such and such only could be correctly called *ceremonial.* During the *So'i* feasts among the Southern Massim, women carrying polished axe blades in fine carved handles, accompany with a rythmic step to the beat of drums, the entry of the pigs and mango saplings into the village (see Plates V and VI). As this is part of the ceremony and the axes are an indispensable accessory, their use in this case can be legitimately called " ceremonial." Again, in certain magical ceremonies in the Trobriands, the *towosi* (garden magician) has to carry a mounted axe blade on his shoulders, and with it he delivers a ritual blow at a *kamkokolà* structure (see Plate LIX; compare Chapter II, Division IV).*

The *vaygu'a*—the Kula valuables—in one of their aspects are overgrown objects of use. They are also, however, *ceremonial* objects in the narrow and correct sense of the word. This will become clear after perusal of the following pages, and to this point we shall return in the last chapter.

It must be kept in mind that here we are trying to obtain a clear and vivid idea of what the Kula valuables are to the natives, and not to give a detailed and circumstantial description of them, nor to define them with precision. The comparison with the European heirlooms or Crown jewels was given in order to show that this type of ownership is not entirely a fantastic South Sea custom, untranslatable into our ideas. For—and this is a point I want to stress—the comparison I have made is not based on purely external, superficial similarity. The psychological and sociological forces at work are the same, it is really the same mental attitude which

* not reproduced here

makes us value our heirlooms, and makes the natives in New Guinea value their *vaygu'a*.

IV

The exchange of these two classes of *vaygu'a*, of the arm-shells and the necklaces, constitutes the main act of the Kula. This exchange is not done freely, right and left, as opportunity offers, and where the whim leads. It is subject indeed to strict limitations and regulations. One of these refers to the sociology of the exchange, and entails that Kula transactions can be done only between partners. A man who is in the Kula—for not everyone within its district is entitled to carry it on—has only a limited number of people with whom he deals This partnership is entered upon in a definite manner, under fulfilment of certain formalities, and it constitutes a life-long relationship. The number of partners a man has varies with his rank and importance. A commoner in the Trobriands would have a few partners only, whereas a chief would number hundreds of them. There is no special social mechanism to limit the partnership of some people and extend that of the others, but a man would naturally know to what number of partners he was entitled by his rank and position. And there would be always the example of his immediate ancestors to guide him. In other tribes, where the distinction of rank is not so pronounced, an old man of standing, or a headman of a hamlet or village would also have hundreds of Kula associates, whereas a man of minor importance would have but few.

Two Kula partners have to *kula* with one another, and exchange other gifts incidentally ; they behave as friends, and have a number of mutual duties and obligations, which vary with the distance between their villages and with their reciprocal status. An average man has a few partners near by, as a rule his relations-in-law or his friends, and with these partners, he is generally on very friendly terms. The Kula partnership is one of the special bonds which unite two men into one of the standing relations of mutual exchange of gifts and services so characteristic of these natives. Again, the average man will have one or two chiefs in his or in the neighbouring districts with whom he *kulas*. In such a case, he would be bound to assist and serve them in various ways, and to offer them the pick of his *vaygu'a* when he gets a fresh supply. On the other hand he would expect them to be specially liberal to him.

The overseas partner is, on the other hand, a host, patron and ally in a land of danger and insecurity. Nowadays, though the feeling of danger still persists, and natives never feel safe and comfortable in a strange district, this danger is rather felt as a magical one, and it is more the fear of foreign sorcery that besets them. In olden days, more tangible dangers were apprehended, and the partner was the main guarantee of safety. He also provides with food, gives presents, and his house, though never used to sleep in, is the place in which to foregather while in the village. Thus the Kula partnership provides every man within its ring with a few friends near at hand, and with some friendly allies in the far-away, dangerous, foreign districts. These are the only people with whom he can *kula*, but, of course, amongst all his partners, he is free to choose to which one he will offer which object.

Let us now try to cast a broad glance at the cumulative effects of the rules of partnership. We see that all around the ring of Kula there is a network of relationships, and that naturally the whole forms one interwoven fabric. Men living at hundreds of miles' sailing distance from one another are bound together by direct or intermediate partnership, exchange with each other, know of each other, and on certain occasions meet in a large intertribal gathering (Plate XX).* Objects given by one, in time reach some very distant indirect partner or other, and not only Kula objects, but various articles of domestic use and minor gifts. It is easy to see that in the long run, not only objects of material culture, but also customs, songs, art motives and general cultural influences travel along the Kula route. It is a vast, inter-tribal net of relationships, a big institution, consisting of thousands of men, all bound together by one common passion for Kula exchange, and secondarily, by many minor ties and interests.

Returning again to the personal aspect of the Kula, let us take a concrete example, that of *an average man* who lives, let us assume, in the village of Sinaketa, an important Kula centre in the Southern Trobriands. He has a few partners, near and far, but they again fall into categories, those who give him arm-shells, and those who give him necklaces. For it is

* not reproduced here

naturally an invariable rule of the Kula that arm-shells and necklaces are never received from the same man, since they must travel in different directions. If one partner gives the arm-shells, and I return to him a necklace, all future operations have to be of the same type. More than that, the nature of the operation between me, the man of Sinaketa, and my partner, is determined by our relative positions with regard to the points of the compass. Thus I, in Sinaketa, would receive from the North and East only arm-shells ; from the South and West, necklaces are given to me. If I have a near partner next door to me, if his abode is North or East of mine, he will always be giving me arm-shells and receiving necklaces from me. If, at a later time he were to shift his residence within the village, the old relationship would obtain, but if he became a member of another village community on the other side of me the relationship would be reversed. The partners in villages to the North of Sinaketa, in the district of Luba, Kulumata, or Kiriwina all supply me with arm-shells. These I hand over to my partners in the South, and receive from them necklaces. The South in this case means the southern districts of Boyowa, as well as the Amphletts and Dobu.

Thus every man has to obey definite rules as to the geographical direction of his transactions. At any point in the Kula ring, if we imagine him turned towards the centre of the circle, he receives the arm-shells with his left hand, and the necklaces with his right, and then hands them both on. In other words, he constantly passes the arm-shells from left to right, and the necklaces from right to left.

Applying this rule of personal conduct to the whole Kula ring, we can see at once what the aggregate result is. The sum total of exchanges will not result in an aimless shifting of the two classes of article, in a fortuitous come and go of the arm-shells and necklaces. Two continuous streams will constantly flow on, the one of necklaces following the hands of a clock, and the other, composed of the arm-shells, in the opposite direction. We see thus that it is quite correct to speak of the *circular* exchange of the Kula, of a ring or circuit of moving articles (comp. Map V). On this ring, all the villages are placed in a definitely fixed position with regard to one another, so that one is always on either the arm-shell or on the necklace side of the other.

Now we pass to another rule of the Kula, of the greatest importance. As just explained " the armshells and shell-strings always travel in their own respective directions on the ring, and they are never, under any circumstances, traded back in the wrong direction. Also, they never stop. It seems almost incredible at first, but it is the fact, nevertheless, that no one ever keeps any of the Kula valuables for any length of time. Indeed, in the whole of the Trobriands there are perhaps only one or two specially fine armshells and shell-necklaces permanently owned as heirlooms, and these are set apart as a special class, and are once and for all out of the Kula. Ownership,' therefore, in Kula, is quite a special economic relation. A man who is in the Kula never keeps any article for longer than, say, a year or two. Even this exposes him to the reproach of being niggardly, and certain districts have the bad reputation of being ' slow ' and ' hard ' in the Kula. On the other hand, each man has an enormous number of articles passing through his hands during his life time, of which he enjoys a temporary possession, and which he keeps in trust for a time. This possession hardly ever makes him use the articles, and he remains under the obligation soon again to hand them on to one of his partners. But the temporary ownership allows him to draw a great deal of renown, to exhibit his article, to tell how he obtained it, and to plan to whom he is going to give it. And all this forms one of the favourite subjects of tribal conversation and gossip, in which the feats and the glory in Kula of chiefs or commoners are constantly discussed and re-discussed."* Thus every article moves in one direction only, never comes back, never permanently stops, and takes as a rule some two to ten years to make the round.

This feature of the Kula is perhaps its most remarkable one, since it creates a new type of ownership, and places the two Kula articles in a class of their own. Here we can return to the comparison drawn between the *vaygu'a* (Kiriwinian valuables) and the European heirlooms. This comparison broke down on one point : in the European objects of this class, permanent ownership, lasting association with the hereditary dignity or rank or with a family, is one of its main features.

* This and the following quotations are from the Author's preliminary article on the Kula in *Man*, July, 1920. Article number 51, p. 100.

In this the Kula articles differ from heirlooms, but resemble another type of valued object, that is, trophies, gauges of superiority, sporting cups, objects which are kept for a time only by the winning party, whether a group or an individual. Though held only in trust, only for a period, though never used in any utilitarian way, yet the holders get from them a special type of pleasure by the mere fact of owning them, of being entitled to them. Here again, it is not only a superficial, external resemblance, but very much the same mental attitude, favoured by similar social arrangements. The resemblance goes so far that in the Kula there exists also the element of pride in merit, an element which forms the main ingredient in the pleasure felt by a man or group holding a trophy. Success in Kula is ascribed to special, personal power, due mainly to magic, and men are very proud of it. Again, the whole community glories in a specially fine Kula trophy, obtained by one of its members.

All the rules so far enumerated—looking at them from the individual point of view—limit the social range and the direction of the transactions as well as the duration of ownership of the articles. Looking at them from the point of view of their integral effect, they shape the general outline of the Kula, give it the character of the double-closed circuit. Now a few words must be said about the nature of each individual transaction, in so far as its *commercial technicalities* are concerned. Here very definite rules also obtain.

V

The main principle underlying the regulations of actual exchange is that the Kula consists in the bestowing of a ceremonial gift, which has to be repaid by an equivalent counter-gift after a lapse of time, be it a few hours or even minutes, though sometimes as much as a year or more may elapse between payments.* But it can never be exchanged from hand to hand, with the equivalence between the two objects discussed, bargained about and computed. The decorum of the Kula transaction is strictly kept, and highly

* In order not to be guilty of inconsistency in using loosely the word "ceremonial" I shall define it briefly. I shall call an action ceremonial, if it is (1) public; (2) carried on under observance of definite formalities; (3) if it has sociological, religious, or magical import, and carries with it obligations.

valued. The natives sharply distinguish it from barter, which they practise extensively, of which they have a clear idea, and for which they have a settled term—in Kiriwinian : *gimwali*. Often, when criticising an incorrect, too hasty, or indecorous procedure of Kula, they will say : " He conducts his Kula as if it were *gimwali*."

The second very important principle is that the equivalence of the counter-gift is left to the giver, and it cannot be enforced by any kind of coercion. A partner who has received a Kula gift is expected to give back fair and full value, that is, to give as good an arm-shell as the necklace he receives, or vice versa. Again, a very fine article must be replaced by one of equivalent value, and not by several minor ones, though intermediate gifts may be given to mark time before the real repayment takes place.

If the article given as counter-gift is not equivalent, the recipient will be disappointed and angry, but he has no direct means of redress, no means of coercing his partner, or of putting an end to the whole transaction. What then are the forces at work which keep the partners to the terms of the bargain ? Here we come up against a very important feature of the native's mental attitude towards wealth and value. The great misconception of attributing to the savage a pure economic nature, might lead us to reason incorrectly thus : " The passion of acquiring, the loathing to lose or give away, is the fundamental and most primitive element in man's attitude to wealth. In primitive man, this primitive characteristic will appear in its simplest and purest form. *Grab and never let go* will be the guiding principle of his life."* The fundamental error in this reasoning is that it assumes that " primitive man," as represented by the present-day savage, lives, at least in economic matters, untrammelled by conventions and social restrictions. Quite the reverse is the case Although, like every human being, the Kula native loves to possess and therefore desires to acquire and dreads to lose, the social code of rules, with regard to give and take by far overrides his natural acquisitive tendency.

* This is not a fanciful construction of what an erroneous opinion might be, for I could give actual examples proving that such opinions have been set forth, but as I am not giving here a criticism of existing theories of Primitive Economics, I do not want to overload this chapter with quotations.

This social code, such as we find it among the natives of the Kula is, however, far from weakening the natural desirability of possession ; on the contrary, it lays down that to possess is to be great, and that wealth is the indispensable appanage of social rank and attribute of personal virtue. But the important point is that with them to possess is to give —and here the natives differ from us notably. A man who owns a thing is naturally expected to share it, to distribute it, to be its trustee and dispenser. And the higher the rank the greater the obligation. A chief will naturally be expected to give food to any stranger, visitor, even loiterer from another end of the village. He will be expected to share any of the betel-nut or tobacco he has about him. So that a man of rank will have to hide away any surplus of these articles which he wants to preserve for his further use. In the Eastern end of New Guinea a type of large basket, with three layers, manufactured in the Trobriands, was specially popular among people of consequence, because one could hide away one's small treasures in the lower compartments. Thus the main symptom of being powerful is to be wealthy, and of wealth is to be generous. Meanness, indeed, is the most despised vice, and the only thing about which the natives have strong moral views, while generosity is the essence of goodness.

This moral injunction and ensuing habit of generosity, superficially observed and misinterpreted, is responsible for another wide-spread misconception, that of the *primitive communism of savages*. This, quite as much as the diametrically opposed figment of the acquisitive and ruthlessly tenacious native, is definitely erroneous, and this will be seen with sufficient clearness in the following chapters.

Thus the fundamental principle of the natives' moral code in this matter makes a man do his fair share in Kula transaction and the more important he is, the more will he desire to shine by his generosity. *Noblesse oblige* is in reality the social norm regulating their conduct This does not mean that people are always satisfied, and that there are no squabbles about the transactions, no resentments and even feuds. It is obvious that, however much a man may want to give a good equivalent for the object received, he may not be able to do so. And then, as there is always a keen competition to be the most generous giver, a man who has received less than he gave will not keep his grievance to himself, but will brag about his own generosity and compare it to his partner's meanness ; the other resents it, and the quarrel is ready to break out. But it is very important to realise that there is no actual haggling, no tendency to do a man out of his share. The giver is quite as keen as the receiver that the gift should be generous, though for different reasons. Then, of course, there is the important consideration that a man who is fair and generous in the Kula will attract a larger stream to himself than a mean one.

The two main principles, namely, first that the Kula is a gift repaid after an interval of time by a counter-gift, and not a bartering ; and second, that the equivalent rests with the giver, and cannot be enforced, nor can there be any haggling or going back on the exchange—these underlie all the transactions. A concrete outline of how they are carried on, will give a sufficient preliminary idea.

" Let us suppose that I, a Sinaketa man, am in possession of a pair of big armshells. An overseas expedition from Dobu in the d'Entrecasteaux Archipelago, arrives at my village. Blowing a conch shell, I take my armshell pair and I offer it to my overseas partner, with some such words as ' This is a *vaga* (opening gift)—in due time, thou returnest to me a big *soulava* (necklace) for it ! ' Next year, when I visit my partner's village, he either is in possession of an equivalent necklace, and this he gives to me as *yotile* (return gift), or he has not a necklace good enough to repay my last gift. In this case he will give me a small necklace—avowedly not equivalent to my gift—and he will give it to me as *basi* (intermediary gift). This means that the main gift has to be repaid on a future occasion, and the *basi* is given in token of good faith—but it, in turn, must be repaid by me in the meantime by a gift of small arm-shells. The final gift, which will be given to me to clinch the whole transaction, would then be called *kudu* (clinching gift) in contrast to *basi* " (loc. cit., p. 99).

Although haggling and bargaining are completely ruled out of the Kula, there are customary and regulated ways of bidding for a piece of *vaygu'a* known to be in the possession of one's partner. This is done by the offer of what we shall call solicitary gifts, of which there are several types. " If I, an inhabitant of Sinaketa, happen to be in possession of a pair of arm-shells more than usually good, the fame of it spreads, for it must be remembered that each one of the first-class armshells and necklaces has a personal name and a history of its own, and as they circulate around the big ring of the Kula, they are all well known, and their appearance in a given district always creates a sensation. Now, all my partners—whether from overseas or from within the district—compete for the favour of receiving this particular article of mine, and those who are specially keen try to obtain it by giving me ***pokala*** (offerings) and ***kaributu*** (solicitary gifts). The former (***pokala***) consist as a rule of pigs, especially fine bananas, and yams or taro ; the latter (***kaributu***) are of greater value : the valuable, large axe-blades (called ***beku***), or lime spoons of whale bone are given " (*loc. cit*, p. 100). The further complication in the repayment of these solicitary gifts and a few more technicalities and technical expressions connected herewith will be given later on in Chapter IV.*

VI

I have enumerated the main rules of the Kula in a manner sufficient for a preliminary definition, and now a few words must be said about the associated activities and secondary aspects of the Kula. If we realise that at times the exchange has to take place between districts divided by dangerous seas, over which a great number of people have to travel by sail, and do so keeping to appointed dates, it becomes clear at once that considerable preparations are necessary to carry out the expedition. Many preliminary activities are intimately associated with the Kula. Such are, particularly, the building of canoes, preparation of the outfit, the provisioning of the expedition, the fixing of dates and social organisation of the enterprise. All these are subsidiary to the Kula, and as they are carried on in pursuit of it, and form one connected series, a description of the Kula must embrace an account of these preliminary activities. The detailed account of canoe building, of the ceremonial attached to it, of the incidental magical rites, of the launching and trial run, of the associated customs which aim at preparing the outfit—all this will be described in detail in the next few chapters.

Another important pursuit inextricably bound up with the Kula, is that of the *secondary trade*. Voyaging to far-off countries, endowed with natural resources unknown in their

* not reproduced here

own homes, the Kula sailors return each time richly laden with these, the spoils of their enterprise. Again, in order to be able to offer presents to his partner, every outward bound canoe carries a cargo of such things as are known to be most desirable in the overseas district. Some of this is given away in presents to the partners, but a good deal is carried in order to pay for the objects desired at home. In certain cases, the visiting natives exploit on their own account during the journey some of the natural resources overseas. For example, the Sinaketans dive for the spondylus in Sanaroa Lagoon, and the Dobuans fish in the Trobriands on a beach on the southern end of the island. The secondary trade is complicated still more by the fact that such big Kula centres as, for instance, Sinaketa, are not efficient in any of the industries of special value to the Dobuans. Thus, Sinaketans have to procure the necessary store of goods from the inland villages of Kuboma, and this they do on minor trading expeditions preliminary to the Kula. Like the canoe-building, the secondary trading will be described in detail later on, and has only to be mentioned here.

Here, however, these subsidiary and associated activities must be put in proper relation with regard to one another and to the main transaction. Both the canoe-building and the ordinary trade have been spoken of as secondary or subsidiary to the Kula proper. This requires a comment. I do not, by thus subordinating the two things in importance to the Kula, mean to express a philosophical reflection or a personal opinion as to the relative value of these pursuits from the point of view of some social teleology. Indeed, it is clear that if we look at the acts from the outside, as comparative sociologists, and gauge their real utility, trade and canoe-building will appear to us as the really important achievements, whereas we shall regard the Kula only as an indirect stimulus, impelling the natives to sail and to trade. Here, however, I am not dealing in sociological, but in pure ethnographical description, and any sociological analysis I have given is only what has been absolutely indispensable to clear away misconceptions and to define terms.*

* It is hardly necessary perhaps to make it quite clear that all questions of origins, of development or history of the institutions have been rigorously ruled out of this work. The mixing up of speculative or hypothetical views with an account of facts is, in my opinion an unpardonable sin against ethnographic method.

By ranging the Kula as the primary and chief activity, and the rest as secondary ones, I mean that this precedence is implied in the institutions themselves. By studying the behaviour of the natives and all the customs in question, we see that the Kula is in all respects the main aim: the dates are fixed, the preliminaries settled, the expeditions arranged, the social organisation determined, not with regard to trade, but with regard to Kula. On an expedition, the big ceremonial feast, held at the start, refers to the Kula; the final ceremony of reckoning and counting the spoil refers to Kula, not to the objects of trade obtained. Finally, the magic, which is one of the main factors of all the procedure, refers only to the Kula, and this applies even to a part of the magic carried out over the canoe. Some rites in the whole cycle are done for the sake of the canoe itself, and others for the sake of Kula. The construction of the canoes is always carried on directly in connection with a Kula expedition. All this, of course, will become really clear and convincing only after the detailed account is given. But it was necessary at this point to set the right perspective in the relation between the main Kula and the trade.

Of course not only many of the surrounding tribes who know nothing of the Kula do build canoes and sail far and daringly on trading expeditions, but even within the Kula ring, in the Trobriands for instance, there are several villages who do not kula, yet have canoes and carry on energetic overseas trade. But where the Kula is practised, it governs all the other allied activities, and canoe building and trade are made subsidiary to it. And this is expressed both by the nature of the institutions and the working of all the arrangements on the one hand, and by the behaviour and explicit statements of the natives on the other.

The Kula—it becomes, I hope, more and more clear—is a big, complicated institution, insignificant though its nucleus might appear. To the natives, it represents one of the most vital interests in life, and as such it has a ceremonial character and is surrounded by magic. We can well imagine that articles of wealth might pass from hand to hand without ceremony or ritual, but in the Kula they never do. Even when at times only small parties in one or two canoes sail overseas and bring back *vaygu'a*, certain taboos are observed, and a customary course is taken in departing, in sailing, and in arriving; even the smallest expedition in one canoe is a tribal event of some importance, known and spoken of over the whole district. But the characteristic expedition is one in which a considerable number of canoes take part, organised in a certain manner, and forming one body. Feasts, distributions of food, and other public ceremonies are held, there is one leader and master of the expedition, and various rules are adhered to, in addition to the ordinary Kula taboos and observances.

The ceremonial nature of the Kula is strictly bound up with another of its aspects—magic. "The belief in the efficiency of magic dominates the Kula, as it does ever so many other tribal activities of the natives. Magical rites must be performed over the sea-going canoe when it is built, in order to make it swift, steady and safe; also magic is done over a canoe to make it lucky in the Kula. Another system of magical rites is done in order to avert the dangers of sailing. The third system of magic connected with overseas expeditions is the *mwasila* or the Kula magic proper. This system consists in numerous rites and spells, all of which act directly on the mind (*nanola*) of one's partner, and make him soft, unsteady in mind, and eager to give Kula gifts" (loc. cit., p. 100).

It is clear than an institution so closely associated with magical and ceremonial elements, as is the Kula, not only rests on a firm, traditional foundation, but also has its large store of legends. "There is a rich mythology of the Kula, in which stories are told about far-off times when mythical ancestors sailed on distant and daring expeditions. Owing to their magical knowledge they were able to escape dangers, to conquer their enemies, to surmount obstacles, and by their feats they established many a precedent which is now closely followed by tribal custom. But their importance for their descendants lies mainly in the fact that they handed on their magic, and this made the Kula possible for the following generations" (loc. cit., p. 100).

The Kula is also associated in certain districts, to which the Trobriands do not belong, with the mortuary feasts, called *so'i*. The association is interesting and important, and in Chapter XX* an account of it will be given.

The big Kula expeditions are carried on by a great number of natives, a whole district together. But the geographical

* not reproduced here

limits, from which the members of an expedition are recruited, are well defined. Glancing at Map V, " we see a number of circles, each of which represents a certain sociological unit which we shall call a Kula community. A Kula community consists of a village or a number of villages, who go out together on big overseas expeditions, and who act as a body in the Kula transactions, perform their magic in common, have common leaders, and have the same outer and inner social sphere, within which they exchange their valuables. The Kula consists, therefore, first of the small, internal transactions within a Kula community or contiguous communities, and secondly, of the big over-seas expeditions in which the exchange of articles takes place between two communities divided by sea. In the first, there is a chronic, permanent trickling of articles from one village to another, and even within the village. In the second, a whole lot of valuables, amounting to over a thousand articles at a time, are exchanged in one enormous transaction, or, more correctly, in ever so many transactions taking place simultaneously" (loc. cit., p. 101). " The Kula trade consists of a series of such periodical overseas expeditions, which link together the various island groups, and annually bring over big quantities of *vaygu'a* and of subsidiary trade from one district to another. The trade is used and used up, but the *vaygu'a*—the armshells and necklets—go round and round the ring" (loc. cit., p. 105).

In this chapter, a short, summary definition of the Kula has been given. I enumerated one after the other its most salient features, the most remarkable rules as they are laid down in native custom, belief and behaviour. This was necessary in order to give a general idea of the institution before describing its working in detail. But no abridged definition can give to the reader the full understanding of a human social institution. It is necessary for this, to explain its working concretely, to bring the reader into contact with the people, show how they proceed at each successive stage, and to describe all the actual manifestations of the general rules laid down in abstract.

As has been said above, the Kula exchange is carried on by enterprises of two sorts; first there are the big overseas expeditions, in which a more or less considerable amount of valuables are carried at one time. Then there is the inland trade in which the articles are passed from hand to hand, often changing several owners before they move a few miles.

The big overseas expeditions are by far the more spectacular part of the Kula. They also contain much more public ceremonial, magical ritual, and customary usage. They require also, of course, more of preparation and preliminary activity. I shall therefore have a good deal more to say about the overseas Kula expeditions than about the internal exchange.

As the Kula customs and beliefs have been mainly studied in Boyowa, that is, the Trobriand Islands, and from the Boyowan point of view, I shall describe, in the first place, the typical course of an overseas expedition, as it is prepared, organised, and carried out from the Trobriands. Beginning with the construction of the canoes, proceeding to the ceremonial launching and the visits of formal presentation of canoes, we shall choose then the community of Sinaketa, and follow the natives on one of their overseas trips, describing it in all details. This will serve us as a type of a Kula expedition to distant lands. It will then be indicated in what particulars such expeditions may differ in other branches of the Kula, and for this purpose I shall describe an expedition from Dobu, and one between Kiriwina and Kitava. An account of inland Kula in the Trobriands, of some associated forms of trading and of Kula in the remaining branches will complete the account.

In the next chapter I pass, therefore, to the preliminary stages of the Kula, in the Trobriands, beginning with a description of the canoes.

[18]

HEADS OR TAILS? TWO SIDES OF THE COIN*

KEITH HART

University of Cambridge

Money has two sides, symbolised as heads and tails. It is the product of social organisation both from the top down ('states') and from the bottom up ('markets'). It is thus both a *token* of authority and a *commodity* with a price. Most economic theories of money focus on one extreme to the exclusion of the other. The current ideological debate between Keynesians and monetarists leads to unnecessarily wide swings in public policy. It is time for anthropologists too to abandon our predilection for polarised argument when making a comparative study of institutions such as money. The article has three main sections. The first locates the problem of money in contemporary economic history, showing how the rise of Eurodollar banking, barter and plastic credit cards is undermining state control of money in the industrial societies. The second traces two influential strands in the history of western monetary theory, linking them to the contrast in nineteenth-century economic thought between English utilitarianism and the German romantic reaction. These strands are brought together in the work of Keynes, whose ideas dominate our century. The third section applies these findings to a reanalysis of Malinowski's Trobriand ethnography, suggesting that the commodity/token opposition has relevance for the organisation of exchange there. The ethnography of stateless societies adds an essential dimension to our search for effective understanding of the forces shaping the modern world.

The first modern ethnography, *Argonauts of the western Pacific*, told of a complicated exchange economy which functioned without money and markets as we know them. Malinowski used his findings to berate the insularity of contemporary models of 'economic man', in effect the ideology which represents an image of western civilisation as universal. We, his successors in British social anthropology, have retained a penchant for juxtaposing exotic facts and western folk theories. But Malinowski's example is deficient in several ways. First, we should be more explicitly aware of the concrete conditions which stimulate our interest in some abstract problems rather than others. This means asking what it is in the world as we experience it that informs our researches, whether directly or indirectly. Second, it is no good taking potshots at vulgar reductions of economic ideas, when the intellectual history of western economic thought is itself extremely plural, even contradictory. A constructive reading of that intellectual history might have served Malinowski's ethnographic analysis better than the straw man he chose to attack. Finally, when historical awareness and a more sophisticated intellectual apparatus are combined with our discipline's standby of ethnographic fieldwork, the resulting anthropological

*The Malinowski Memorial Lecture, 1986

Man (N.S.) **21**, 637–56

analysis offers a more secure foundation for critical understanding of the world in which we live.

As a synthetic vehicle for this task I have chosen the topic of *money*, specifically how we are to assess its changing role in exchange economies as diverse as the Trobriand Islanders' and our own.[1] Malinowski insisted that the idea of money as 'currency' should be limited to that universal means of exchange and standard of value which is typically found in the form of 'coin of the realm'.[2] Mauss took him to task for this, claiming that Melanesian valuables should also be thought of as a sort of money.[3] In our own day, cash is rapidly being displaced by plastic credit cards; and computerised barter networks have arisen as alternatives to markets based on money. If we want to make sense of such phenomena, it will not do to cling to a restrictive definition of money which explains more the preindustrial roots of modern civilisation than its continuing evolution and potentialities.

The monetary theories of economists ought to offer a more effective framework for this analysis than popular beliefs and vernacular expressions. But a cursory inspection of the metaphysics of monetary theory reveals a state of affairs more akin to theology than science.[4] Here we find two broad camps, each fixing on one side of money to the exclusion of the other and claiming a monopoly of truth on the subject. The current labels for these camps are 'Keynesians' and 'monetarists'; but they have existed under other names at least since the Enlightenment and took definite form in the nineteenth century.

Their relative positions are summarised in my lecture title. Look at a coin from your pocket. On one side is 'heads'—the symbol of the political authority which minted the coin; on the other side is 'tails'—the precise specification of the amount the coin is worth as payment in exchange. One side reminds us that states underwrite currencies and that money is originally a relation between persons in society, a token perhaps. The other reveals the coin as a thing, capable of entering into definite relations with other things, as a quantitative ratio independent of the persons engaged in any particular transaction. In this latter respect money is like a commodity and its logic is that of anonymous markets. Heads and tails stand for social organisation from the *top* down and from the *bottom* up, epitomised in modern theory by the state and the market respectively. Most theories of money give priority to one side over the other. It is as if, not content with exploring the ambiguous unity of heads and tails, politics and markets, economists felt compelled like gamblers to toss the coin—heads or tails?—and, having opted for the one that lands up, then denied the existence of the other side, except in the minds of devil-worshippers. This Manichaean medieval impulse is deeply embedded in modern economic thought, and our century has seen the two sides inflated into an ideological struggle between state socialism and the free market that could be the death of us all. Malinowski was part of this ruinous polarisation; and, if we are to do better in future, anthropologists have to be capable of comparing their exotica with a more profound picture of ideas and realities in the modern industrial world which sustains us.

Conventional economic reasoning fails to enlighten us because it is so unremittingly one-dimensional. The coin has two sides for a good reason —both are indispensable. Money is at the same time an aspect of relations between persons and a thing detached from persons. If we forget this, we encourage social disasters and perpetuate the wild oscillation between extremes which has dogged monetary policy over the last century. For too long now economic anthropologists have been, at best, brokers between two separate disciplines. Today's effort is an act of *bricolage* rather than brokerage, formed from a vision of the anthropologist as a handyman who can help repair the damage done by professionals.

The modern evolution of money

This is a time of unprecedented dynamism in the form and institutional organisation of money. Here I will offer some brief notes indicative of the transformation we are living through.[5] Most of us have access to five forms of money—coins, banknotes, cheques, savings accounts and plastic. The relationship between the five is inherently unstable. The traditional money form, known as 'specie'—i.e. coins containing precious metals equivalent to their nominal value—now survives only in a specialist hoarders' market for gold coins. For two and a half millennia the only alternative to specie were notes of credit, which took the precise form of bills of exchange in Europe about 600 years ago. Coins were first mass-produced in Britain around 1800. Then, in the second half of the nineteenth century, national paper money emerged as a widespread substitute for both specie and promissory notes issued by private banks. Base metal coinage was introduced after the second world war, so that both paper and metal versions of the national currency now became equally worthless, being distinguished largely by function rather than cost of production. In the meantime, private individuals have continued to issue cheques against their bank accounts; and this source of personal liquidity has recently been augmented by the phenomenon of plastic credit cards. It is tempting to predict that before long this decentralised form of money will also be nationalised, perhaps through an adaptation of existing arrangements for national insurance and taxation.

In the course of these developments, the state monopoly of money has been subjected to pressure from both above and below, from the international sphere of banking and commerce, as well as from internal devolution of control over liquidity within the national economy. I wish to take these two aspects of modern monetary institutions in order.

Galbraith (1975) reminds us of the insubstantial basis of banking. Banks take money from one party and give it to another; they then try to persuade both that they still have it. The real reserves of wealth supporting a bank's promise to pay are normally minuscule and, in the case of national banks, mostly illusory. Seen from this point of view, money is founded on credit—it is a token, symbol of something intangible. The principles of finance are not those of commodity exchange; and it could be argued that during the modern period banking has assumed an increasingly dominant role in the management of economic affairs at all levels from the international to the domestic.

During the nineteenth century credit was based on the convertibility of money to gold, thereby, it was hoped, subordinating the scope for financial manipulation to the need for a stable means of international exchange.[6] The gold standard broke down between the two world wars; and it was replaced by the agreement known as Bretton Woods just over forty years ago. This was a system of state-guaranteed money with fixed parity exchange rates anchored on the reserve currencies, principally the dollar and sterling. In other words, international trade was based on confidence in the world's strongest economy, that of the United States. Bretton Woods was undermined by high US balance of payments deficits at the time of the Vietnam war; and international monetary crises were already predictable annual events by the end of the 1960's.[7]

The OPEC oil price increase and the attendant convulsions of world commodity markets in 1973/74 put paid to the fixed parity system; and the 1970's saw a shift towards acceptance of a relatively free market in currencies. This was a time of unprecedented global inflation rates, fuelled by progressive devaluation of the dollar, the oil trade's unit of account. Fear of runaway inflation prompted a decisive shift in western monetary policy away from Keynesian techniques of state management to what was thought to be the safer ground of a free market in money. The next turning point was 1979, when OPEC sought to recoup the erosion of its dollar earnings with a second major price rise. This triggered off a run on the dollar which was met by a rapid escalation of US interest rates to over 20 per cent. The United States remains a magnet for free-floating capital and this deflects the worst domestic effects of a regime based on budget deficits and high interest rates. The recent collapse of oil prices introduced another shock to a world economy already suffering from damaged confidence and lower growth rates than during the boom years of Bretton Woods.

The last two decades have also seen the flowering of the Eurodollar banking system. In consequence an incalculable proportion of all the currency in circulation is now beyond the control of the states who issue the money—in offshore banking transactions. After the second world war the Russians and the Chinese, legitimately fearing seizure of their New York dollar deposits by a hostile US government, transferred the money to London and Paris. The financial crisis of the early 1970's led to a more widespread use of this procedure, with London emerging as the main centre for 'Eurodollar banking'—i.e. dollars held by a non-resident of the US, usually in the form of a deposit with a bank outside the US.[8]

Offshore banking has on average a one per cent. edge in the interest rates it can afford to offer, this being the cost of keeping the minimum deposit required as security by law when banks are subject to national regulation. The oil price rise depressed demand for loans in the industrial countries and generated an OPEC financial surplus much of which found its way into the offshore system. In consequence the Third World became the target of a massive sales drive for loans by private banks.[9] A decade later the prospects for Third World development are generally bleak and offshore investors must be wondering what their paper assets are really worth. What then is the basis of the Eurodollar banks' credit? Not commodities nor state power, to be sure. Their credit is based on the value of outstanding loans. Default on any major loan would call into question the creditworthiness of all the offshore banks, which are of course often subsidiaries of the domestic banks—Barclays, Chase Manhattan, Crédit Lyonnais etc. The banks invented what they hope is a form of insurance against default. Each loan is farmed out to a consortium of up to 200–300 banks. If that loan were declared in default, the banks would lay claim to any foreign assets of the country involved, including all its exports. More important, their customers might be stampeded into a collective run on the bank which would make the bank failures of the Depression years seem trivial in comparison. It is not surprising then that the principal capitalist states periodically reschedule Third World private debts, rather than invoke this spectre of default.

In this inherently unstable situation, money itself has become a commodity traded in a purely speculative way. The total volume of money sales is now vastly in excess of the amount needed to finance international trade. Credit is grounded neither in real values nor in state-made money. On the Chicago Mercantile Exchange money is traded alongside pork-belly futures;[10] and the continuing world depression piles up idle money capital to fuel an endless round of speculative surges. While most people, ostrich-like, hope that the problem will go away, vast fortunes are made by those who keep their eyes open and the international monetary crisis deepens.

Nor is money standing still on the home front. The virtue of traditional money forms—coinage and later banknotes—was that they could be transported easily and spent anonymously in a wide variety of commodity transactions. Since their value was objective, there was no need to introduce questions concerning an individual's creditworthiness. Moreover, complex networks of exchange could be articulated without requiring the simultaneous two-way transfer of commodities associated with barter systems. A further feature of conventional money is closely linked to the activities of those preindustrial states who did most to promote 'coin of the realm'. Governments have long depended on cash transactions for their own sources of liquidity. Taxation and markets are symbiotic. Internal revenues today are still levied almost exclusively on the exchange of goods and services for money. But the technical and institutional underpinnings of state-made money in its classic form have been eroded by postwar developments in telecommunications and computers—the so-called 'information revolution'.[11]

It is now easier to evade state control at all levels of the economy; and money has become less anonymous, more personalised. One sign of the first tendency is the revival of barter in the industrial economies.[12] Multinational corporations swap bulk quantities of unsold commodities through brokers: thus, for example, an oil company offloads 100,000 gallons of surplus paint in direct exchange for an off-season lease of an airline's hotel in the Bahamas. Meanwhile tax lawyers argue with the Internal Revenue Service about the income represented by this non-market transaction. Barter has, of course, long been the mainstay of trade between nations of the eastern and western blocs, ever since the Bolsheviks pulled Russia out of the international system of commodity-based currencies. Today Third World countries who lack the dollars to participate in normal trade reach barter agreements among themselves. The largest of these to date is a deal involving Nigerian oil and Brazilian manufactures over a number of years.

More routinely, impoverished neighbours in West Africa swap meat for grain. A recent report of The Group of Thirty estimated that barter now accounts for 8–10 per cent. of international trade, a half of all arms sales. They conclude that barter does not *yet* pose a threat to the monetary system.

At a lower level, barter networks for individual businesses are springing up throughout North America.[13] Some of these appear to originate in Oklahoma City, where there is a large Mormon community. (Mormons were forced into the federal political economy more or less at gunpoint a century ago and now they are leading the backlash against state control of business.) In California old age pensioners exchange services for points registered on a Social Services Department computer: gentleman willing to mow lawns meets lady anxious to knit jumpers—and no money changes hands. In British Columbia an alternative trading system known as LETS (Local Exchange Trading System—with echoes of *laissez-faire*?) has taken root in several communities (Gabel *et al.* 1985). Members need a home computer and a telephone to trade with each other in 'green dollars', an imaginary currency equivalent to federal dollars. Credit and debt are always exactly balanced in the system and anyone can inspect the banking record of another member. Such local initiatives are not entirely new; less sophisticated substitutes for scarce dollars in the Great Depression, according to a report of *The Times* of 20 June, 1933, included wooden cash and notes stamped on real buckskin in denominations of 'one buck' and 'half a buck'.[14] Barter, of course, is less vulnerable to inflation than trading mediated by state-backed currencies. It is possible to discern in phenomena such as these the seeds of a tax revolt, with large chunks of the North American economy withdrawing from the cash/tax nexus and public finances being subjected to a cumulative squeeze comparable to the fiscal crisis of the later Roman empire.[15]

The second tendency—personalisation of money as information technology catches up with the proliferation of transactions—is typified by the spread of plastic money in our lives.[16] Now a seller can phone a computer and decide on the spot whether to extend credit to someone he has never seen before. Below I will suggest that personal identity is intrinsic to the functional equivalent of money in primitive economies such as that of the Trobriand Islands. Now money is once more bound up with tokens of personal identity; but credit is extended to something rather less than the whole person, to a formal abstraction of individual human beings, to a cipher in a universe of numbers. To all the other manifestations of our alienation we must now add the fear of being defined by machines processing digitalised identities. At the same time most of us now experience greater freedom in opening up personal lines of credit; and the control exercised by governments over the money supply is made to a corresponding degree weaker. I have explored this aspect of what I call 'commoditization' in another place (Hart 1982). The continuing evolution of money is as double-sided a phenomenon as coinage. The information revolution clearly exposes us to the threat of ever more centralised access to our personal credit rating, while at the same time offering a partial escape from state-made money on a scale unequalled in western economic history since bills of exchange superseded coin of the realm for medieval merchants.

Let us next see what light is thrown on these matters by the discourse of modern economists.

Modern theories of money

The great historian of economic ideas, Joseph Schumpeter, once said, 'There is no denying that views on money are as difficult to describe as shifting clouds' (1954: 289).[17] My hubristic aim here is to reduce this elusive skyscape to a few simplified sketches. The problem of money was intrinsic to the birth of English economics. Locke and his contemporaries were faced with a crisis of confidence in the coin of the realm (the so-called 're-coinage crisis'), following the triumph of Parliament over absolutism.[18] By the eighteenth century mercantilist theory leaned towards a position later dubbed 'metallism'. This stated that the value of currency should be tied to precious metals such as gold and silver, thereby subordinating its circulation to the functioning of markets. This 'commodity theory' of money held sway in Britain right into this century. Anti-metallists, such as Barbon, held that 'money is a value made by law'. The special term 'chartalism' was later coined for this school which stressed the several forms that money could take, including paper promises made by private individuals or by the government. The 'quantity theory' of money associated with Bodin and Hume took the metallist position to the point of asserting that public intervention in the money supply, with the aim of stimulating economic expansion, was bound to fail in its intention. Hume argued that the volume of commodity exchange was logically independent of money supply, so that, in a closed economy, twice the amount of money in circulation would merely double prices. This has led him to be claimed as an ancestor by Milton Friedman and to be satirised by Karl Polanyi (1944), who tartly asks how much of society would be left intact by such a quantitative adjustment.[19]

The classical theory systematised by Ricardo (1817) and Mill (1848) drew from these preclassical antecedents the notion that money was the servant of the 'Law of Value', a mere technical prerequisite of commodity exchange which should be removed as far as possible from the threat of political manipulation by being tied to precious metals. The liberal synthesis of the nineteenth century found institutional expression in the promotion of free markets based on the gold standard under British financial and industrial hegemony. Adherence to the gold standard made it impossible for governments to protect their populations from excessive fluctuations in markets; and this point was made sporadically by an undercurrent of populist opposition throughout the Victorian era, exemplified by Major Douglas whose theory of underconsumption receives a doubled-edged endorsement from Keynes in the *General Theory*.[20]

In matters of monetary theory Marx adhered broadly to classical orthodoxy. The opening passages of *Capital* (1887) make it clear that money is a commodity whose use is to facilitate exchange and capital is money put to accumulative ends within the exchange circuit. Marx's main innovation was to draw from Hegel's theory of alienation the notion of money and commerce as an estranged burden on the freedom of modern man. This allowed him to develop a phenomenological analysis of money's fetishised role in our understanding of social agency.[21]

He also, of course, placed great emphasis on extraction of surplus value as the key source of money capital. But in essentials he subscribed to the prevailing classical view that money was subordinate to the laws of commodity exchange and as such best thought of as a specialised commodity itself. This was monetary orthodoxy in the heyday of British industrial expansion.

The most systematic challenge to this orthodoxy came from Germany. One man deserves to be recognised as the author of a fully-fledged romantic theory of money—Adam Muller, who wrote *A new theory of money* in 1816.[22] Muller negated everything that British political economy stood for—free trade, division of labour etc.—in favour of national self-sufficiency, the virtues of working the land and so on. Money for him derives its value from the trust generated within a community and is more specifically an expression of the national will. Schumpeter vehemently rejects Muller's claim to the rank of an economist, speaking of '. . . a number of wholly inoperative metaphysical conceptions' (1954: 421). This is an inevitable reaction once the intellectual historian is committed to teleological reconstruction of a process culminating in twentieth-century anglophone economic science. Such an approach reduces German economic ideas to the status of an aberrant sideshow for their refusal to extrude the social and cultural context of economic life into the analytical dumping-ground known normally as *ceteris paribus* assumptions.[23]

The first years of this century saw the culmination of German monetary theory in Knapp's *State theory of money* (1924) and Simmel's *Philosophy of money* (1978); Weber devotes a long passage of *Economy and society* (1978: 166–93) to a discussion of money which draws heavily on Knapp. G. F. Knapp gave us terms such as 'metallism' and 'chartalism', so that it is his work that has done most to crystallise the opposition between commodity and token in the history of monetary theory. Being an anti-metallist, Knapp set out to put flesh on Barbon's dictum that 'money is a value made by law'. He believed that money was a standard of credit issued by the state and that the state's freedom of manoeuvre in monetary policy should not be restricted by an international system anchored in the timeless exchangeability of gold.

The common intellectual inheritance of Knapp, Weber and later Polanyi was Kant's dialectic of form and content (in essence the relationship between mental construct and material substance). For Kant our world is made up of two constituents—a form supplied by the structure of the mind and a content supplied by the senses. In continental social thought this analytical distinction was later made to inform a contrast between on the one hand the self-conscious rationality of state-made law and markets and on the other the anonymous everyday influence of customs whose force was presumed to derive from ancient mechanisms of collective survival. Weber (1978: 85–6) argued that formal and substantive rationality were in conflict, i.e. that the growing dominance of calculation in public life impaired our ability to make adequate social provision for material welfare. This distinction was taken up by Polanyi (1957*b*) and made the basis for the mind-bogglingly reductionist formal-substantive debate which dogged economic anthropology in the 1960's and 70's.

At this point the issue becomes more complicated than a simple opposition between English utilitarianism and German idealism. For one thing, Victorian

Britain had its romantics too—but this is no place to explore the monetary theories of Morris and Ruskin. More significantly, British liberals were as likely to draw on the moral sentiments of Adam Smith as on Benthamite principles. For example, John Stuart Mill simultaneously plays down the importance of money in relation to free commodity exchange and decries the emphasis on money-making for its own sake in England and America. Thus in one place he says 'There cannot in short be intrinsically a more insignificant thing in the economy of society than money' (1848: 488); and elsewhere he inveighs vigorously against the subordination of public morality to the mindless accumulation of money.[25] Money was not just an instrument of trade, repository of universal natural impulse, a gold-based bulwark against absolutism. It was also the object of money-making and as such shaped by all the abuses that anti-social capitalists could inflict on their contemporaries. Bagehot's lesser known work on Lombard Street (1910) represents a counter-current which emphasised the moral dimensions of bourgeois accumulation. Here trust, debt, banking, 'the Englishman's word'—in a word, credit—defined money as an aspect of relations between persons, not as a thing, mere cash. We are reminded of Durkheim's refutation of utilitarian abstraction in *The division of labour in society* (1933), when he speaks of the non-contractual element of the contract —the nexus of humane institutions and values that makes market behaviour possible. It is as well to remember that not all Victorians were unreconstructed Benthamites and social Darwinists.

Simmel reflects this position as a German liberal.[26] For him money encapsulates all the main strands of social life. There is no essential contradiction between capitalism and society, as both Marx and Weber held. Above all Simmel emphasised the morality of exchange, echoing Muller and prefiguring Mauss. The rationalism of statists such as Knapp and liberal economists such as Ricardo equally abstract commodity exchange from its moral source—the human wisdom of an anonymous economy based on trust.

What started as a simple opposition between commodity and token theories of money—between anglophone economism and the German romantic reaction—clearly needs to be modified to take account of two cross-cutting nineteenth century ideologies. These are first the perceived contradiction between markets and states which supposed that anyone who was in favour of one must be against the other; and second Kant's analytic of form and substance, which explicitly shaped much European discourse and was implicit in the moral discourse of some British liberals. I have summarised what is a rather dense section of my argument in fig. 1.[27] The liberal pro-market side equates social progress with capitalism, but splits into formal economics and a substantive emphasis on trust. The statist side sees capitalism and society as contradictory, but splits into a formal theory looking to rational law and government policy for antidotes and a substantive construct of the state as nation, *Volk* or *narod*, in a word—populism.

There are thus three types of theory opposed to the classical orthodoxy which regards money solely as a commodity, subject to the laws of competitive markets. These are all *token* theories which insist that money is a symbol for something intangible, an aspect of human agency, not just a thing like a lump of

	MARKET	STATE
FORMAL	C Economics	T Policy Law
SUBSTANTIVE	T Credit Trust	T National Institutions

C = Commodity Theory
T = Token Theory

FIGURE 1. *Theories of money c. 1900.*

coal. Money as trust locates value in the morality of civil society; its fulcrum is the management of credit and debt in human relations—as illuminated, for example, by Mauss's great work *The gift* (1967), so revealingly interpreted by the last Malinowski lecturer, Jonathan Parry.[28] Money as the expression of state policy emphasises the role of law and government intervention—a tradition stretching from Barbon to Knapp and beyond. The populist theory of money stresses the accumulated institutions of a nation as a necessary framework for markets and finance. American institutionalist economics—with its roots in the politics of William Jennings Bryan and Henry George and the writings of Veblen, Commons and Ayres[29]—is a major vehicle for this tendency; as are the Russian Narodniks whose theories so infuriated Lenin.[30]

This discussion prepares the way for an assessment of the pivotal figure in twentieth century social thought. In seeking to overthrow English monetary theory between the wars, Keynes was bound to recapitulate elements of the predominantly German critique. The details of Keynes's recommendations are unimportant here.[31] He proposed that the state manipulate demand and investment through control of the interest rate and the size of the public debt. This represented explicit recognition that unemployment could not be brought down by adherence to the practices of the gold standard years. For all his credentials as a social democrat, Keynes belongs squarely with Knapp in the elitist box of formal statism. Not for him the folk wisdom of mass social action or even that of a humanised bourgeoisie. He wrote for the chosen few who effect policy and thought himself with some reason to be one of them. In characterising the motives of the capitalist class as 'animal spirits' he both echoed the Scottish enlightenment's emphasis on the role of the passions in human nature and the recent attention given to the non-rational foundations of supposedly rational behaviour, a recurring theme of late nineteenth-century German sociology and of Max Weber's work in particular.[32]

Keynes's greatest legacies are Bretton Woods, the postwar monetary order which was smashed in the 1970's,[33] and the welfare states which were built from the proceeds of those boom years. Richard Nixon's announcement, just before his downfall, that 'we are all Keynesians now', is as good a marker as any of the end of the great economist's influence. The confidence of western nations in state fiscal policy was shattered by an inflation which undermined the price mechanism and much else in their market economies. By the mid-1980's conservative regimes dogmatically opposed to 'Keynesianism' run the United States, Britain, Germany and Japan. Their creed is 'monetarism', a revival of the old liberalism and of the commodity theory of money. Its most vigorous exponents are Milton Friedman and other members of the Chicago school.[34] They make an explicit link to the quantity theory of two centuries ago. Money is just a thing with a function and a price; any government interference will have unintended consequences whose effects are on balance likely to be negative; so that it is best to concentrate on ensuring that markets are efficient. As always, political practice is more confusing than professed ideology. One has only to think of Reagan's massive Keynesian reflation of demand through expansion of the US public debt in the light of his alleged adherence to 'supply-side economics'.

There is thus a long history underlying contemporary fashions in monetary theory. Anthropologists are not immune to absorbing these polarised currents of modern ideas; but prior exposure to their history might help to make our borrowings from economic thought less vulgar than before—less confused and more self-conscious. While being more respectful of a plural intellectual tradition, we should also be open to the notion of economics as a form of secular theology. Relations between persons and things are typically fetishised as two contradictory camps, thought of as states and markets, abstract actors in a Manichean universe of good and evil which only has room for one side of the coin at any time. It is surely the case that the coin has two sides and that what matters is their relationship, the mutual constitution of politics and markets in a moving social whole.

I now turn to an ethnographic setting where money and markets as we know them are apparently absent—Malinowski's Trobriand Islands.

Ethnographic analysis

Throughout *Argonauts of the western Pacific* (1922), Malinowski emphasises the contrast between *kula* and *gimwali* in Trobriand economy.[35] The first is a ceremonious exchange of gifts (personal ornaments) and it carries great social prestige. The second is an undignified haggling, individual barter; its social significance is minimal and it frequently accompanies the *kula*, perhaps under the latter's umbrella. Trobrianders say that the two types of exchange are in the starkest possible contrast: the one epitomising generosity, the other selfishness. Malinowski lists seven types of transaction from pure gift to trade (1922: 177–91). The last two are 'ceremonial barter with deferred payment' (including the *kula*) and 'trade, pure and simple' (typically *gimwali*). But rather than rehash the well-known *kula* story here, I want to draw your attention to two subsidiary examples noted briefly by Malinowski in this context.

Coastal and inland villages on Kiriwina are in the habit of exchanging fish for yams or vegetables, allowing a measure of division of labour between fishing and agriculture. Sometimes this exchange takes the form of ceremonial prestations (*wasi*) involving community leaders on the pattern of *kula*. But we are told that, where no *wasi* relationship exists between villages, individual barter at the household level (*vava*) is normal. So, whereas in one case a big man hands over a job lot of fish to his counterpart, allowing him to ration them out among his followers and to organise a future return of yams in similar fashion, in the other individuals wander from house to house trying to get a reasonable deal for the quantity of commodities they have to sell.

Three features of this opposition are worth noting. 1) The degree of formalisation of the social processes involved—the presence and absence of ceremony.[36] 2) The time interval between the two moments of exchange (giving and the return)—their separation by a delay in *wasi*, their collapse into a simultaneous equivalence in *vava*.[37] 3) The level of conflict tolerated in the price-setting mechanism—the generosity of gift-giving as a means of avoiding conflict and haggling as an expression of confidence in the partners' ability to contain aggression. The fact that the two institutions fall neatly into paired sets, each the other's negation, suggests a routinised resolution of social ambivalence. Formalisation of exchange—ceremony, separation of the moments of exchange, conflict avoidance—reflects high social distance and weak political order, bringing big men and corporate organisation into play. Informal interpersonal haggling reflects low social distance and strong political order. The issue is whether individuals belonging to different groups feel free to risk the conflict inherent in barter without invoking all the danger, magic, prestige and hierarchy that go with ceremonial exchange. Thus one form is a temporary social framework erected in the relative absence of society; the other is an atomised interaction predicated on the presence of society. This has to be spelled out, following the example of both Marx and Mauss, because it is often assumed that individualism is in contradiction with social order, rather than, as this case suggests, being predicated on it.[38]

My argument, which is admittedly a speculative extrapolation from incomplete ethnography, is that the two types are different means of securing the same ends, namely circulation of commodities between independent communities. Individual barter is favoured when the general peace is such as to allow commodities to flow at their equivalent values; whereas ceremonial exchange is a temporary construct of peace based on alliance between leaders of communities at war, with political intervention in the distribution of commodities an inevitable corollary. Thus the *kula* valuables are tokens of personal responsibility, naming the networks of big men whose reputations secure peace for the trade.[39] Obviously barter can and does take place within the temporary framework of *kula*, which should be seen as a highly visible version of that social glue that Durkheim (1933) insisted lies more invisibly behind the anonymity of market contracts.

One further point. Although Malinowski speaks as if these institutional arrangements were congealed in aspic forever, my analysis lends itself to a more dynamic interpretation. Thus a breakdown of political relations between coastal and inland villages (i.e. war) might occasion a shift from *vava* to the more formal *wasi*. Equally, unpredictable fluctuations in supply (failure of the fish catch or a yam glut) might undermine the price-setting mechanism of barter and require the intervention of big men as rationing or stockpiling agents. The Trobriand economy may thus be represented as oscillating between two types of organisation of commodity exchange in response to imperfections both of the political order and of supply and demand. Normal conditions grant low-level agents considerable autonomy which is superseded by high-level regulation when the environment is especially uncertain. Big men may affect to despise haggling—it is not, after all, their stock-in-trade—but we would be ill-advised to take at face value statements that formal exchange and ordinary barter have nothing whatsoever to do with each other, a rhetorical exaggeration of their conceptual and practical complementarity.[40]

So, although there are no coins in Trobriand economy, the two sides of the coin have their counterparts in local economic institutions. There is political authority and there are markets of a sort. Their interaction is flexible according to variable conditions affecting trade. The question has been asked from time to time whether the *kula* valuables are a form of money.[41] Malinowski answers emphatically that they are not, by which he means that they are not money as defined by the commodity theory of liberal orthodoxy. Clearly they are tokens of interpersonal relations, a sophisticated device for ranking political credit in an unstable environment of trade and war between communities. In consequence one of the most complex commercial organisations in the preindustrial world is carried out without benefit of states or merchants under considerable handicaps of transport, communications and ecological instability. Perhaps Mauss (1967: 94) was right to suggest that enabling exchange in this way ought to be counted one of the functions of money. When states invented coin of the realm, credit was shifted from a personal basis to the objective value of the contents of a man's pockets. Private notes of credit, such as cheques, supplied a personal dimension to money; and today advanced information systems have expanded this dimension in the form of plastic credit cards. It may not then be ridiculous to think of *kula* valuables as money after all.

I should add some brief comments on the possible application of my dualistic perspective to the preindustrial states whose economy rested so heavily on coins made from precious metal. The path of commodity exchange appears to have been universally problematic for archaic civilisations.[42] Usury, debt bondage and gross inequalities of wealth provoked popular revolutions at regular intervals in the ancient Mediterranean[43]. The emergence of democratic political theory in the Greek city state was thus, as Fustel de Coulanges (1866) and Weber (1976) insist, largely a response to the class polarisation and economic chaos of the preclassical period (roughly 800–500 B.C.). Later, conservative theorists such as Plato and Aristotle promoted economic models based on self-sufficiency and low division of labour as an antidote to Athens's escalating dependence on maritime trade. This in turn was canonised by the medieval scholastics as a bias against markets in favour of a system of landed property where the natural harmony of God, king and the earth rested on responsible self-management.[44]

The point of this excursion is to reveal the true source of the idea that heads and tails are in irreconcilable conflict—the Aristotelian theodicy of Europe's middle ages—which Adam Smith (1776) stood on its head by preferring the rational anarchy of markets to the clumsy dirigiste efforts of a corrupt court and its clientele of oafish landowners. To summarise, commodity economy was understood to be in contradiction with sound public policy throughout the era of agrarian states. Oscillations between the two produced both revolutions and institutions designed to contain the contradiction. Economic thought was overwhelmingly interventionist and hostile to trade. Modern liberal orthodoxy is best thought of as the negation of all that. But the contradiction continues, as do its attendant oscillations. Modern monetary policy, however, is less flexible than Trobriand institutional practice because it is still governed by a quasi-theological dogmatism.

Concluding remarks

I have suggested that ethnographic analysis needs to be complemented by greater openness to intellectual history and by a journalistic awareness of the events unfolding in our time. Moreover, I am committed to the proposition that the ethnography of stateless societies adds an essential dimension to our search for effective understanding of the major forces shaping the modern world.[45]

Many of the distinctive features of our civilisation were formed during the 5,000 years of agrarian states. Far from being the enlightened offspring of industrialism that we fondly imagine ourselves to be, we are rather the confused by-product of social and technical processes whose implications are masked by the persistence of preindustrial cultural assumptions and institutions. There can be little doubt that the legacy of agrarian society is unravelling before our eyes; but we need the benefit of long-run, wide-angle vision—of an anthropological vision—if we are to have much chance of sorting out the elements of the era our generations are setting in train.

The chief characteristic of preindustrial states is their preoccupation with *states*, i.e. with fixity, permanence, the absolute. Their religions anchor all experience in the single, aprioristic truth of a universal Creator. Their monarchs provide a central point of coherence in a fragmented society. Their cities are centred on the 'pivot of the four quarters' (Wheatley 1971). So it is too with their money, which is presumptively immutable, objective, a thing uniting a quasi-divine royal authority with the timeless value of gold and silver.

Much of the monetary history of the last 150 years has been a losing battle to retain a fixed standard for money. The role of economists in this process has largely been to divide into two warring camps split by the definition of what money 'really' is. Some have sought to pin money down as a commodity and others have sought refuge in the power of nation-states. Their intellectual rigidity has precluded a dialectical synthesis of money's two sides, namely the relationship between persons and things in a social world dominated by both states and markets.[46] Instead we have witnessed the unseemly debacle of wide oscillations between polarised policies which court disaster through systematic rejection of the opposite point of view. This is what I mean by referring to one strand of economic thought as 'secular theology'.

Keynes is a crucial figure, not just for his influence on modern economic institutions, but because he set himself firmly against the pretence that economic science can protect us from confusion and error with its deductive logic and mathematical techniques.[47] In this respect he deserves to be placed alongside Max Weber as a sympathetic critic of the liberal tradition in economics. One of the inferences to be drawn from my argument is that German dialectical reason offers at the very least a conceptual framework for resolving intellectual difficulties posed by the Anglo-Saxon preoccupation with naming unambiguous entities in the real world.[48] If we remain fixated on what money 'really' is, we shall be unable to grasp the interplay of forces that makes up its history and continuing evolution.

This is the value of Trobriand ethnography. The Melanesians are not bound by a static doctrine of social principle. They have not developed states and are extremely wary of established political office in any form. Yet they are aware that commodity exchange depends on flexible substitution of free individual barter and regulated communal transfers. This is, roughly speaking, the practice of modern treasury departments—pragmatic reconciliation of opposing aims in response to changing circumstances. But at the highest theoretical level it seems that pragmatism is insufficient. We need to know on what solid foundation money rests—on commodities or states or what? I believe that the core of an answer lies in the shifting hierarchy of credit relations that make up modern markets—a less substantial foundation than most of us seem willing to live with. In this respect our plastic-toting yuppie culture is nearer to Malinowski's *kula* ring than either is to traditional 'coin of the realm' or to the nineteenth century experiment in gold-backed currency which has done so much to shape modern western attitudes to money.[49]

NOTES

With one or two very minor changes, the present text is the same as the original lecture, given on March 13th, 1986 at the London School of Economics and Political Science under the title 'The two sides of money'. Subsequent elaboration and documentation of the argument are restricted to the notes and text citations. I am grateful to Mick Brown, John Bryden, John Coates, Eduardo da Fonseca, Ernest Gellner, Tony Giddens, Chris Hann, Carrie Humphrey, Johnny Parry and Marilyn Strathern for their comments on earlier drafts.

[1] This is not the place to review the anthropology of money. Crump's *The phenomenon of money* (1981) is a remarkable synthesis which has influenced my own enterprise more diffusely than can be acknowledged in footnotes. Einzig's *Primitive money* (1949) is still an indispensable introduction to the subject. Gregory's *Gifts and commodities* (1982) addresses some of the more general issues raised here. Those readers who would prefer more explicit reference to the major figures of economic anthropology—Firth, Sahlins, Douglas, Godelier, Bohannan and Dalton—will generally be disappointed. My debt to these colleagues is, however, immense.

[2] See his article 'Primitive currency' (1923) and the comment in *Argonauts* on Seligman's usage: '*Currency* as a rule means a medium of exchange and standard of value, and none of the Massim valuables fulfil these functions' (1922: 499).

[3] Mauss (1967: 93–4) adds a long footnote to *The gift* 'on the principle adopted in discussing the idea of money'. 'In this view . . . there is money only when precious objects . . . are made into money—when they are named, impersonalized, detached from any relationships with moral, collective or individual persons other than the authority of the state which mints them . . . The above definition can cover only a secondary type of money—our own'. (p. 93) He prefers to stress the purchasing power of primitive valuables—'. . . these purchasing instruments could serve as a

means to count wealth and make it circulate' (p. 94); and concludes that the forms of money are more plural than Malinowski's restrictive definition implies.

[4] I use neither expression as a term of abuse. Economics, like evolutionary biology, stands as a bridge between medieval cosmology and the modern aspiration to place our collective affairs on a rational footing. The economics of money is a discipline all by itself; Clower (1971) is one means of entry.

[5] This is not a scholarly guide to modern monetary institutions; and references are kept to a minimum. My sources range from recent journalism to an unsystematic selection of economic history textbooks. The most recent British monograph on the extraordinary monetary developments during our times is Hamilton's *The financial revolution* (1986), which contains a glossary of what is truly a fast-breaking terminology. Moffitt's *The world's money* (1983), Samson's *The money-lenders* (1981) and Galbraith's *Money: whence it came, where it went* (1975) offer a range of popular introductions to the subject. Institutional innovation is now so rapid that up-to-date knowledge can only be gained from a daily reading of the *Financial Times* or *Wall Street Journal.*

I believe that anthropologists must offer inexpert summaries of the industrial world, if our ethnographic findings are not to be ghettoised. It is easier to be proved wrong when a topic commands the attention of hundreds of professionals from several disciplines, safer by far to stick to reporting unknown tribes with the interpolation of occasional abstract commentary on the great divide between 'them' and 'us'. My point is that 'we' are extremely diverse and are caught in the middle of profound upheavals. Anthropologists can and should make a concrete contribution to understanding these developments.

[6] Polanyi's masterpiece, *The great transformation* (1944), represents the gold standard, along with the balance of power system, the liberal state and the self-regulating market, as an institutional bulwark of the first industrial civilisation.

[7] The Bretton Woods system was effectively abandoned in 1947–48 and rediscovered, along with convertible currencies, a decade later. Its heyday was 1958–71. For most of the period immediately following the second world war national protectionist regimes dominated monetary management, in violation of the international spirit of Bretton Woods.

[8] The definition is Hamilton's (1986: 245). Eurobanking in general refers to non-residents holding deposits of any currency somewhere other than the national territory of the state issuing that currency. The Eurodollar market has grown within a decade from a few hundred million dollars to $300 billions a year today.

[9] Samson (1981) provides a vivid account of loan peddlers hawking their wares around some of the Third World's less savoury regimes in the 1970's.

[10] Whereas markets were once traditionally specialised and Chicago was hog-butcher to the world, the recent trend has been towards 'financial supermarkets' competing across the board worldwide. Financial futures now represent 90% of total volume on the Chicago Mercantile Exchange, which was a frontrunner in the money market revolution of the mid-1970's.

[11] For a recent summary, see Office of Technology Assessment, US Congress *Effects of information technology on financial services systems* (1984); also Hamilton (1986: 30–49) who cites Walter Wriston's maxim 'The information standard has replaced the gold standard as the basis of world finance'.

[12] There have been several recent conferences on barter within and between industrial nations; but serious academic analysis of emergent economic institutions of this sort has not come to my notice.

[13] These examples were gathered informally during a period (1975–83) spent teaching in North America.

[14] Deerskin was a unit of account in the early North American fur trade; hence the popular term for a dollar—'buck'.

[15] Weber's classic essay, 'The social causes of the decline of ancient civilization' (1976: 389–411). .shows how the flight from central taxation contributed to the feudalisation of the Roman empire from within.

[16] The spread of plastic money deserves more attention than it appears to get from social scientists. Crump (1981: 129) mentions the phenomenon, with special reference to taxation.

[17] Readers who wish to explore the history of economic ideas should start with Schumpeter's magisterial *History of economic analysis* (1954).

[18] For Locke's economic thought and its historical context, see Vaughn (1980).

[19] See Schumpeter (1954: 311–17) on the quantity theory; also Friedman & Schwarz (1963) and Polanyi (1944: 192–93). Polanyi's critique of liberalism in *The great transformation* is devastating. Money, he says, is a fictitious commodity, since it is not produced by labour. It should rather be conceived of as an expression of society's need for commerce. Money is both a commodity for purposes of international trade and a token of domestic policy. In this latter capacity its supply is bound to be used to protect citizens from depression, war-induced shortage and various forms of economic calamity. Such measures would in turn undermine attempts to found the international economic order on gold or some other commodity.

[20] 'Major Douglas is entitled to claim, as against some of his orthodox adversaries, that he at least has not been wholly oblivious of the outstanding problem of our economic system. Yet he has scarcely established an equal claim to rank—a private, perhaps, but not a major in the brave army of heretics—with Mandeville, Malthus, Gesell and Hobson, who, following their intuitions, have preferred to see the truth obscurely and imperfectly rather than maintain error, reached indeed with clearness and consistency and by easy logic but on hypotheses inappropriate to the facts.' (1936: 371)

[21] The fetishism of commodities (*Capital Vol. 1* 1970: 71–83) is an idea whose day has certainly arrived in anthropology. See Taussig (1980), Bloch (in press) and Appadurai (1986) for interesting commentary on Marx's phenomenology.

[22] *Versuche einer neuen Theorie des Geldes*. Schumpeter's distaste for Muller as a German romantic is extreme: 'Such interpretations of metaphysical meanings are by nature incapable of telling us anything that we do not already know about the relations subsisting in the empirical world . . . I have no intention of paralleling the ignorance that fails to appreciate the tasks and methods of analysis by equally ignorant failure to appreciate the tasks and methods of philosophic vision or interpretation of meanings . . . these are two different worlds that do not touch anywhere' (1954: 422).

[23] The most common word for economics in nineteenth-century Germany (*Sozialpolitik*; cf. also *Nazionaloekonomie*) speaks of the huge gulf between national intellectual traditions. One of the earliest uses of the term 'economics' is in the name of the institution which sponsored this lecture (founded in 1891).

[24] A good selection of arguments from the formalist-substantivist debate in its heyday is Leclair and Schneider (1968). Economic anthropology today boasts of almost as many positions as practitioners. (See Ortiz 1983). Weber repeatedly made the point that any work of comparison requires the dialectical ability to make empirical distinctions within a unifying conceptual framework, that is, to embrace both sameness and difference—a point that was lost in the heat of academic polarisation.

[25] Of Americans Mill wrote '. . . the life of the whole of one sex is devoted to dollar hunting and of the other to breeding dollar hunters' (Mill 1965: 755).

[26] Simmel's *The philosophy of money* (1978), recently revived in English translation, is a complex masterpiece which deserves to be placed among the classics to which anthropologists pay routine homage. Frankel's *Money: two philosophies* (1977) draws on Simmel, along with Marx and Keynes, to make a neo-liberal case for emphasising trust in monetary theory.

[27] The typology of theories is ideal. Great thinkers never fit easily into such boxes, but their epigones often split into opposed camps along simplified lines of the sort identified here.

[28] See *Man* (N.S.) **21**, 453–76. My lecture was designed in part to be complementary to his: whereas I emphasise the outside context of economic anthropology, Parry focuses on the inside story of our discipline's preoccupation with exchange.

[29] Veblen (1904), Commons (1934) and Ayres (1944) are the most prominent members of this school. Their followers sustain the *Journal of economic issues*.

[30] Lenin *The development of capitalism in Russia* (1899). See also Hussain and Tribe (1981) for the wider political context.

[31] Keynes's two great theoretical works, the *Treatise on money* (1930) and *The general theory of employment etc.* (1936), are reasonably accessible to non-specialists. But his *Essays in persuasion* (1931) offer a readable point of entry to his thought.

[32] Before the romantics gave the word its modern meaning, 'the passions' referred mainly to internalised sources of passivity—in the work of Hume and Smith (e.g. *The theory of moral sentiments* 1793) to those natural and cultural constraints within each of us which stand opposed to the exercise

of freedom through reason. In this respect the Scottish Enlightenment anticipated a central tenet of German idealism—the tension between the rational and the non-rational, between the conscious and the unconscious, that we tend to associate with Nietzsche, Freud and Weber.

[33] Although Keynes was undoubtedly one of the two major figures at the Bretton Woods conference in 1944, the final version of the new international order that emerged owed more to American interests than to his own preconceived scheme.

[34] See e.g. Friedman and Schwarz (1963) and Hayek (1973–79).

[35] Although the distinction is basic to his argument, Malinowski provides only a few scattered glimpses of trade in his ethnography. There is a generalised description of *gimwali* on pp. 189–190 of *Argonauts*. The examples of trade between *kula* visitors and hosts on pp. 362–364 leave it uncertain how far fixed rates of exchange or a sliding-price mechanism operate. Malinowski emphasises haggling, but it would not be remarkable if some long-distance exchanges were based on normalised ratios. *Wasi* and *vava* are mentioned only briefly on pp. 188–190. Much of my analysis, therefore, is an invention for which the essential information is largely missing. I have been able to draw for comparative insights on the recent explosion in Melanesian ethnography (especially J. Leach & E. Leach 1983), on several films about the Trobriands and on a visit to Papua New Guinea in 1972. My debt to Marshall Sahlins's *Stone-age economics* will be obvious—see especially his chapter 'Exchange value and the diplomacy of primitive trade' (1972: 277–314). Nevertheless, I reject the conceptual opposition of social totality and individual anarchy which informs much of the book. My prime purpose in telling the story this way is to cast doubt on the prevailing utilitarian orthodoxy in anglophone economic anthropology which in a sense stems from Malinowski (see Parry 1986). I do *not* wish to suggest that ceremonial exchange and barter institutions everywhere correspond to the idealtypical contrast drawn in this section.

[36] 'I shall call an action ceremonial, if it is (1) public; (2) carried on under observance of definite formalities; (3) if it has sociological, religious or magical import, and carries with it obligations' (Malinowski 1922: 95).

[37] Mauss (1967) makes the timing of the two moments of exchange *the* formal criterion for distinguishing between gifts and market purchases. Rejecting the ideological appearance of a contrast between the two based on altruism and egoism, he emphasises the social inequality inherent in gift-giving and the equality made possible by simultaneous commodity exchange.

[38] Humphrey (1985) links individualised barter to economic disintegration on the Nepal-Tibet border. The collapse of political authority and poverty combine there to inhibit the use of money in trade. See also my short essay on barter (Hart in press). The empirical permutations of social organisation and trading mechanisms are more plural than my present analysis may be taken to imply.

[39] Uberoi's (1962) reanalysis of the Trobriand ethnography stresses this point.

[40] Parry (1986) argues convincingly that Malinowski's opposition between 'pure gifts' and 'trade, pure and simple' belongs more securely to the ideologies of commercial civilisations than to tribal societies such as the Trobriands. Nevertheless, I am convinced that some such dualism is recognised in Trobriand cultural categories—'He conducts his Kula as if it were *gimwali*' (Malinowski 1922: 96)—even if the contrast is exaggerated both by the ethnographer and by his more aristocratic informants.

[41] See notes 2 and 3 above.

[42] Most of the standard works on ancient economy (e.g. Finley 1973; Heichelheim 1964) stress order more than disorder. But Weber (1976: 38–79) was well aware of the pathologies attending commodity exchange.

[43] The Hebrew institution of *jubilee* was one routinised response to these pathological features of economy in the city states and kingdoms of Mesopotamia, Iran and the Levant. This was the custom of freeing debt slaves once every fifty years and allowing people who had been evicted from their homes back to their own land. The implication of this and more radical measures of debt cancellation was that an economy based in part on commodities and money led to impoverishment of citizens on a scale insupportable by a polity claiming popular legitimacy.

[44] See Polanyi (1957a). Mandel (1968: 690–8) provides a breezy and polemical history of economic ideas in preindustrial civilisations. Polanyi epitomises the Aristotelian tradition in economic anthropology.

[45] British social anthropology's historical mission, triumphantly announced in *African political*

systems (Fortes & Evans-Pritchard 1940)—namely to expose the intermediate levels of corporate social life obscured by modern theories of the state and, I would add, by market theories—is even more necessary today than half a century ago, since postwar developments have made these public ideologies more pervasive, more deeply entrenched in popular understandings of the world.

[46] Such a rigid pattern may be more true of the British two-party system and of rivalry between the superpowers than of some other industrial and industrialising nations. It could be argued that in Germany and Japan the contradiction between states and markets has never been a prominent feature of political economy. Bismarck invented the welfare state as a necessary adjunct of industrial capitalist expansion; Hitler took the idea further; and the postwar *Wirtschaftswunder* rests on the idea that social democracy and capitalism reinforce each other. As the British contemplate their own creeping deindustrialisation, they might also dwell on the historical symbiosis of state and capital in Japan which has so far allowed that nation to avoid the excesses of *laissez faire* that are so dear to anglophone neo-conservatives.

[47] See note 20 above.

[48] 'Nominalism' is the philosophical position (associated with the medieval heretic Duns Scotus) which denies that universals have any objective reference in the real world, being rather mere abstractions. Leach (1961) took up such a position when he accused Radcliffe-Brown and his followers of 'butterfly collecting'. Despite this, the habit of conducting ethnographic comparison with reference to supposedly objective analytical categories, such as 'money' or 'unilineal descent groups', dies hard in British social anthropology.

[49] A short poem, which I composed some time ago, bears on the central philosophical theme of this lecture:

Two sides to every point.
Well fancy that—
A point that's flat.

REFERENCES

Appadurai, A. (ed.) 1986. *The social life of things*. Cambridge: Univ. Press.

Ayres, C. 1944. *The theory of economic progress*. Chapel Hill: Univ. of North Carolina Press.

Bagehot, W. 1910. *Lombard Street: a description of the money market*. London.

Bloch, M. in press. The symbolism of money in Imerina. In M. Bloch & J. Parry (eds) in press, *Money and market morality*.

Clower, R. (ed.) 1971. *Monetary theory: selected readings*. Harmondsworth: Penguin.

Commons, J. 1934. *Institutional economics*. New York.

Crump, T. 1981. *The phenomenon of money*. London: Routledge & Kegan Paul.

Durkheim, E. 1933. *The division of labour in society*. New York: Free Press.

Einzig, P. 1949. *Primitive money in its ethnological, historical and economic aspects*. London.

Finley, M. 1973. *Ancient economy*. Berkeley, Los Angeles: Univ. of California Press.

Fortes, M. & E. Evans-Pritchard (eds) 1940. *African political systems*. London: Oxford Univ. Press.

Frankel, S. H. 1977. *Money: two philosophies*. Oxford: Blackwell.

Friedman, M. & A. Schwartz 1963. *A monetary history of the United States 1867–1960*. Princeton: Univ. Press.

Fustel de Coulanges, N. 1956 (1866). *The ancient city*. New York: Doubleday.

Gabel, M., E. Pahl, R. Shegda & R. Rodale 1985. *Local regeneration: examples to build on*. (The Regeneration Project, Paper 5). Emmaeus, Pa: Rodale Press.

Galbraith, J. K. 1975. *Money: whence it came, where it went*. London: Deutsch.

Gregory, C. 1982. *Gifts and commodities*. New York: Academic Press.

Hamilton, A. 1976. *The financial revolution*. London: Viking.

Hart, K. 1982. On commoditization. In *From craft to industry* (ed.) E. Goody. Cambridge: Univ. Press.

Hart, K. in press. Barter. In *The new Palgrave: dictionary of economics*. London: Macmillan.

Hayek, F. 1973–79. *Law, legislation and liberty* (3 vols). London: Routledge & Kegan Paul.

Heichelheim, F. 1964. *An ancient economic history*. Leiden: Sijthoff.

Humphrey, C. 1985. Barter and economic disintegration. *Man* (N.S.) **20**, 48–72.

Hussain, A. & K. Tribe 1981. *Marxism and the agrarian question* (2 vols). London: Macmillan.
Keynes, J. M. 1931. *Essays in persuasion*. London: Hart-Davis.
——— 1936. *The general theory of employment, interest and money*. London: Macmillan.
——— 1971 (1930). *A treatise on money* (2 vols). London: Macmillan.
Knapp, G. 1924. *The state theory of money*. London.
Leach, E. 1961. *Rethinking anthropology*. London: Athlone Press.
Leach, J. & E. Leach (eds) 1983. *The kula: new perspectives on Massim exchange*. Cambridge: Univ. Press.
Leclair, E. & H. Schneider (eds) 1968. *Economic anthropology*. New York: Holt, Rinehart & Winston.
Lenin, V. I. 1974 (1899). *The development of capitalism in Russia*. Moscow: Progress Publishers.
Malinowski, B. 1923. Primitive currency. *Econ. J.*
——— 1961 (1922). *Argonauts of the Western Pacific*. New York: Dutton.
Mandel, E. 1968. *Marxist economic theory*. London: Merlin.
Marx, K. 1970 (1887). *Capital Volume 1*. London: Lawrence & Wishart.
Mauss, M. 1967. *The gift*. New York: Norton.
Mill, J. S. 1848. *Principles of political economy*. London.
——— 1965. *Collected works* (ed.) J. M. Robson, Toronto: Univ. Press.
Moffitt, M. 1983. *The world's money*. London: Michael Joseph.
Office of Technology Assessment 1984. *Effects of information technology on financial servicing systems*. Washington DC: US Congress.
Ortiz, S. (ed) 1983. *Economic anthropology: topics and theories*. Lanham, Md.: Univ. Press of America.
Parry, J. 1986. *The gift*, the Indian gift and the 'Indian gift'. *Man* (N.S.) **21**, 453–76.
Polanyi, K. 1944. *The great transformation*. Bosto: Beacon.
——— 1957a. Aristotle discovers the economy. In *Trade and market in the early empires* (eds) K. Polanyi *et al*. New York: Free Press.
——— 1957b. The economy as instituted process. In *Trade and market in the early empires* (eds) K. Polanyi *et al*. New York: Free Press.
———, C. Arensberg and H. Pearson (eds) 1957. *Trade and market in the early empires*. New York: Free Press.
Ricardo, D. 1970 (1817). *Principles of political economy and taxation*. Cambridge: University Press.
Sahlins, M. 1972. *Stone-age economics*. Chicago: Aldine.
Samson, A. 1981. *The money lenders*. London: Hodder & Stoughton.
Schumpeter, J. 1954. *History of economic analysis*. London: Oxford Univ. Press.
Simmel, G. 1978. *The philosophy of money*. London: Routledge & Kegan Paul.
Smith, A. 1961 (1776). *An inquiry into the nature and causes of the wealth of nations* (2 vols). London: Methuen.
——— 1976 (1793). *The theory of moral sentiments*. Oxford: Clarendon Press.
Taussig, M. 1980. *The devil and commodity fetishism*. Chapel Hill: Univ. of North Carolina Press.
Uberoi, J. S. 1962. *Politics of the kula ring*. Manchester: Univ. Press.
Vaughn, K. 1980. *John Locke: economist and social scientist*. London: Athlone Press.
Veblen, T. 1904. *The theory of business enterprise*. Clifton, N.J.: Kelley.
Weber, M. 1976. *The agrarian sociology of ancient civilisations*. London: New Left Books.
——— 1978. *Economy and society* (eds) G. Roth & C. Wittich. Berkeley, Los Angeles: Univ. of California Press.
Wheatley, P. 1971. *Pivot of the four quarters*. Edinburgh.

[19]

BARTER AND ECONOMIC DISINTEGRATION

CAROLINE HUMPHREY

University of Cambridge

The mainstream economists' view that barter should be seen as a 'natural' phenomenon of human nature and as the origin of money is rejected. Barter occurs in specific socio-economic conditions which may obtain also in economies which know money. When there is a very low supply of currency, money may cease to function as an index of value for all goods and itself become an item bartered. This is likely to occur when small discrete social groups wish to maintain autonomy. Unlike money payment, which requires a further transaction before value is realised, barter satisfies demand immediately and is of its nature discontinuous. As with car trade-ins in our economy barter occurs when people cannot afford to keep money, and it becomes a system when society is atomised to the extent that people do not exploit the variations in exchange ratios between different communities. Using the case of the Lhomi of north-east Nepal, it is shown that although the exchange of common produce, as opposed to rare valuables, is most likely to approximate to a notional 'equilibrium price', the practice of barter with no established measures of weight and volume means that there can be no underlying index of value / numeraire. Each transaction exists virtually on its own. Thus, although barter is an egalitarian mode, it contains no protection against changing exchange ratios which may harm one partner. Barter tends to take place between people who know one another, because it is only by the establishment of customary times and places for exchange that the costs of searching for partners, waiting etc. are avoided. Delayed barter, which often occurs with valuables, requires non-economic means of ensuring repayment, but the ritualised trade-partnerships which the Lhomi employ are self-limiting: restricted relations cut traders off from the wide, unpredictable world of the capitalist end sale. Business often fails and the traders suffer.

Barter is at once a cornerstone of modern economic theory and an ancient subject of debate about political justice, from Plato and Aristotle onwards. In both discourses, which are distinct though related, barter provides the imagined preconditions for the emergence of money. Why should anthropologists be interested in logical deductions from an imagined state? No example of a barter economy, pure and simple, has ever been described, let alone the emergence from it of money; all available ethnography suggests that there never has been such a thing. But there are economies today which are nevertheless *dominated* by barter, and here anthropology can both learn from and add to the ancient debate.

In Plato, non-monetary exchange provides the first means of satisfying complementary needs established by the division of labour, which is a condition of the ideal Republic (Plato 1908: II, 369–72). Aristotle develops the idea of 'proportional exchange', relative to social evaluations of the worth of persons and their products, in his consideration of what is just. Here money, which can measure everything, is introduced by convention as a 'kind of substitute for

Man (N.S.) **20**, 48–72

need or demand', its value being derived not from nature but from law (Aristotle 1895: 5, 1–17). Economists of the contemporary orthodoxy, on the other hand, which stems at least from Adam Smith and was revived in the marginalist economics of Menger and Jevons and reaches Clower in the present, propose an evolutionary development of economies which places barter, as a 'natural' human characteristic, at the most primitive stage, to be superseded by monetary exchange as soon as people become aware of the latter's greater efficiency.

Anthropologists have also tended to see barter as a transaction of the primitive economy, although in the classic examples, such as Malinowski (1922), Thurnwald (1934–5) and Sahlins (1972) the ethnographic diversity and complexity of distribution is recognised. Dominated by other activities considered to be 'more socially embedded', such as ceremonial exchange, gift-giving, sharing of food, or dues to chiefs, barter is found in a corner of the economy —and one that is despised by the people and anthropologists alike. Barter, according to Sahlins summarising a wide range of ethnography, is 'negative reciprocity, the unsociable extreme'. Characterised as 'haggling', barter is held to take place with outsiders, along with 'chicanery' and 'theft', each participant trying to outwit the other with an eye to his own benefit (1972: 195).

There is something unsatisfactory about each of these modern arguments. If we take barter to be the more or less simultaneous exchange of one good for another with the possibility of bargaining, the anthropologists have no justification in regarding it as 'negative reciprocity'. By definition, barter is a complementary exchange in which each participant bargains until he or she is satisfied. It does not necessarily imply antagonism. As far as the economists' argument is concerned, we know from the accumulated evidence of ethnography that barter was indeed very rare as a system dominating primitive economies.[1] Money of various kinds has been around for over two millennia, and in the last century, in its purest, non 'commodity-money' form, has penetrated virtually every economy on earth, and yet barter is common *today* in economies which also know money. I shall propose in this article that barter *in the present world* is, in the vast majority of cases, a post-monetary phenomenon (i.e. it coexists with money), and that it characterises economies which are, or have become, de-coupled from monetary markets. In these circumstances barter can become a dominant principle of transaction, to which money itself is subject. As was well known to Marx and even Aristotle (1895: 5, 14), but has somehow escaped the general attention of anthropologists, currency may be bartered like any other commodity.

As an idea 'barter' is part of the history of economics and anthropology, and the assumption that it was the forerunner of monetary exchange is crucial in the way it is normally conceptualised. Polanyi's suggestion, in *The great transformation*, that the evolutionary doctrine of the economists preoccupied with the emergence of markets might virtually be reversed, has been largely ignored (1957: 58).[2] His own view is considerably closer to that of the ancient philosophers, suggesting as he does the prior existence of long-distance trade as a result of regional environmental differences and only later the emergence of local markets and bargaining or barter. In this article I should also like to escape from the notion of 'truck' or 'barter' as a natural human propensity which still appears as a myth of our subject. This implies the disentangling of two concepts of barter, (a) the notion of a simple exchange of goods without money and without specifying the mode of the non-monetary transaction, and (b) the process of barter in time as a practice which involves bargaining. It is the latter that will be my focus.

The word barter as I use it implies an open-ended, potentially innovative, negotiable, transaction, in which need not only answers need but can also create a new demand: 'If you don't want these potatoes, perhaps you would like this pair of scissors?' Furthermore, barter, which in itself refers only to a social relation of transaction and not to economic values, can encompass the idea of an exchange of goods which have one value to one side and another to the other. I use 'barter' in this sense to differentiate it from 'primitive trade' in which, as Malinowski showed, socially determined rates of exchange outweigh bargaining in the great majority of types of transaction.

For barter to become dominant in an area, such that it can incorporate even pure money, we must suppose not only economic but also some particular social and cultural conditions which allow the 'construction' of barter as a system. I shall attempt to describe this on the basis of the economy of the Lhomi[3] and their neighbours of the Nepal-Tibet border in 1979–80. The Lhomi are farmers but also traders, and clearly their historical role as intermediaries between the highland pastoral economy of the Tibet hills and the agriculture of the Nepali hills, is a basis for the culture of trading which they find so attractive. I would argue, however, that it is not because the Lhomi *were* traders that they *now* engage in barter. Similar Himalayan peoples are now almost entirely monetised. Clearly there are many conditions ranging from negative consequences of using money[4] to regulated systems of distribution in centralised economies[5] which might impel people to barter as it were by default. In other cases, themselves differing from one another greatly in ideological context, barter may be positively preferred in itself. We may cite the example of East Coast American farmers of the late eighteenth to mid-nineteenth centuries, where products were exchanged between independent households and even cash was bartered just outside New York. Merrill (1977: 42–71) explains this rejection of capitalist, functionally monetised farming as an expression of radical republicanism, based on essentially individualistic household production. It is certainly not the case that such examples are simply 'survivals' of early forms of economy. From historical and comparative materials in the Himalayan region it can be seen that alternations between increasingly monetised trade in periods of accumulation, and barter, which in my view is here a phenomenon of economic disintegration in the vertical economy, have been highly unstable.

To show theoretically why this is the case we must look at the economic ideas in more detail. The prevalent theory of barter in the economic literature looks at barter, not in itself, but with the primary aim of elucidating the role and origin of money. Clower (1969), following Jevons (1910), states that barter is abandoned because of its high transaction costs. In an imagined island economy without money it is assumed that people have a natural desire to acquire goods they do not produce themselves and therefore engage in exchange. With an elegant series of curves, Clower suggests that the costs involved in simple barter (searching for exchange partners, establishing a double coincidence of wants, postponing a desired transaction, and wasting time in bargaining) would lead people first to barter at fairgrounds, then to establish trading-posts for particular goods, then to make use of the one most common item as a means of exchange at all the posts and, finally, to establish this commodity also as a standard of value, means of payment and store of wealth, in other words, as money. Here the primary function of money is assumed to be as a means of exchange.

Thomas Crump, who has made a survey of both the economic and the anthropological literature, argues convincingly, however, that Clower is wrong (1981: 85). Because the supply of money must be under some control,[6] it is unlikely that any good emerging as the primary means of exchange through frequency of use in barter—which is what Clower suggested—would ever 'turn into' money.

There is an alternative theory, again dealing with barter only as a seed-bed for the emergence of money, but one which is, I think, more useful to us in understanding barter itself. The economist Charles Goodhart argues against the Clower school on the grounds that money as *the* means of exchange emerging from primitive barter cannot be the initial key, since this already assumes the existence of a market economy and market mentality. He is concerned to make a distinction between money as a means of exchange and its narrower function as a means of payment. He sees the latter as primary. Barter could distribute goods (and thus render payment unnecessary) but, because of transaction costs, most exchanges will not be simultaneous but will involve the extension of credit. The existence of time means that even in an economy rigidly bound by custom there must be uncertainty, e.g. about weather, future technology, or the honesty of people. Delayed barter could only exist generally in face-to-face communities in which every exchange partner has knowledge about others such that he can trust payment to be made for items given. But this is unlikely ever to be the case, and lack of information about the future credit standing of prospective purchasers would in some cases force people to use a specialised means of payment, money. The proportion of transactions settled by monetary exchanges will rise with the growing complexity and dispersion of the economy because of the greater liklihood of *not* having adequate information about other people. Conversely, the use of money declines with the development of methods, such as credit cards, to increase the amount of personal information available (1975: 7–8).[7]

All this is very formalistic, but it does help us to see something of the essential nature of barter. Barter makes payment unnecessary. Payment is the transfer from one person to another of an interest which is expressed in terms of a standard of value. It is money which makes payment possible, as Crump has forcefully pointed out. The key point about money is that, whatever functions it may have, the payee is in a position to perform them by virtue of the payment, but he can only do so by making a further payment. Thus it is of the nature of money to circulate indefinitely (Crump 1981: 3–4). Barter, on the other hand, entails no further transaction. It is, in principle, a one-off affair, because the objects exchanged are mainly objects for use. Barter agreements are made by individuals or groups separately and discontinuously, and without any implicit standard of value (this is discussed further on p. 60). The implication is that, unlike the use of money, barter exchange will have the effect of dis-integration in the regional economy.

This gives some clues as to which economies are likely to be dominated by barter. Barter will occur when economies are atomised (when money ceases to function as a standard of value). 'Delayed barter', which in practice may range from something close to 'primitive trade' to the activities of professional merchants intent on keeping people in thrall (Leach 1959: 145–6 and Gorer 1938: 113–18) can only occur when there is a large amount of information about partners (or other social pressures for repayment). A further important condition is suggested by an early paper of Helms. She proposed the idea of the 'purchase society' which characterises groups on the fringes of incompletely centralised states (Helms 1969). Such groups exist in a complex relation between political autonomy from and economic dependence on the central society. Her point is that the people are 'hooked' on goods from outside and characteristically quickly become monetised. However, there are societies in a similar political situation which resist monetisation (Harriss 1982), in particular as represented by money markets in land and labour.

Other groups may be forced out of the money economy. Crump has suggested a useful model based on the notion of upper and lower limits to the supply of money (1981: 83–96). As we have noted in the case of cowries (note 6), an object cannot function as 'pure money', in Crump's terminology, if the supply is unlimited (upper limit). Only after supply of the money-stuff has been subject to limitation, either by transport to a different region or because it is manufactured in a situation of control, will it function as money. Flowing through this area, money passes to other regions in progressively smaller amounts, ending up in what Crump calls a 'sink' (the lower limit), 'represented by a population which imports these objects, but not so as to use them for any recognisable monetary purpose' (1981: 86). In the sink, money-stuff cannot be used as money because there is not enough of it around. A peripheral self-contained sub-economy must maintain a positive balance of payments in its external trade with the national economy if it is to import enough money to maintain its own monetary system. In practice, simple poverty makes this very problematic in many regions of the world, even in places adjacent to monetised market towns (1981: 212).

It is what goes on in this 'sink' that we shall be concerned with. I agree with Crump that the supply of money is crucial. Simply to say that an economy operates below the lower limit of money supply tells us little, however, of what actually happens. As we shall see (p. 62) the level of the supply of money does not explain the value which money has in a barter economy. For this we must look at barter itself, and here I turn to the Lhomi ethnography.

The Lhomi

The Lhomi are a small community of farmers and traders living in the valley of the Arun River close to the Tibetan border. They are Buddhists and speak a dialect of Tibetan. Separated by a precipitous, uninhabited jungle from their neighbours to the south, they live in a dozen or so compact villages perched on the steep mountain slopes. This is a 'vertical economy' with many similarities to the Andean case. The lands attached to villages range from yak pasturage above the tree-line (16,000 ft), through cattle and sheep pasture, swidden, and fields for potato, wheat and barley on the upper levels (10–12,000 ft), maize, millet, buckwheat, fruit-trees and vegetables at village level (6,000–10,000 ft), and terraces of rice right down near the river at approximately 3,000 ft. Although each village produces a range of crops, even slight differences in height, sunlight and rainfall magnify the variations in what they can produce as surplus.

The Lhomi farm is owned by and production is organised on the basis of the household. Patrilineal clans have rights to pastures and residual rights to fields, and land is not freely available for sale.[8] The more senior of the clans also provide the inherited positions of village headman (*goba*) and tax-collectors (*gyembu*). Only in the last 10–15 years has the authority of these leaders been superseded by that of elected panchayat officials of the Nepalese state. About 3 per cent. of households have no land, just a few more than the number of families of '*gara*', i.e. those of 'unclean mouth'. Otherwise, the overt ideology today is egalitarian, despite the fact that those clans calling themselves '*jimi*' (original settlers) still tend to have more rice land than later arrivals. These latter, known as 'Kampa' although they come from various parts of Tibet, are, however, sometimes rich in livestock, since they arrived with herds of yaks and yak-crosses which have still not yet been entirely depleted. Though most households have a few cattle, pigs and chickens, only around 20 per cent. have sheep, and very few indeed have yaks. There is virtually no wage-labour. Exchange-labour (*nga-lak*) is by far the predominant form, though poorer men and women may work for the odd day or two for pay in cash, grains, salt or garlic. Basically, Lhomi expect to live off the produce of their farms and to barter or, occasionally, sell the surplus.

There is evidence that the people of the upper Arun valley were richer in the nineteenth century than they are today. Referring to the period around 1810, Hamilton describes Hatiya on the Arun and Alangchang (Wallungchung) on the Tamar River as the two great 'marts' for the important Tibet–India trade, which passed through north-east Nepal. Goods were brought to the northern marts from the town of Chayenpur (Chainpur), where there was a fort and the residence of the administrative officer of the Gorkha government (Hamilton 1819: 156–7). Hatiya today has no market of any kind, and Wallungchung, which was still an important trade entrepot in the 1950's (von Fürer-Haimendorf 1975: 125), was largely swept away by a landslide around 1970.

It is not clear to what extent the early nineteenth century trade was monetised. Hamilton distinguishes between periodic markets (*hat*), where money was used, for which he gives a list for east Nepal, and 'marts', such as Hatiya and Wallungchung, which were not markets but entrepots, where goods were exchanged primarily by barter. Hooker remarks for Wallungchung in the 1840's that it had no market or bazaar and that it was only by threats that he could obtain rice there (Hooker 1854: 218). It is to Sagant that we owe the useful distinction between the bazaar, the market and the fair, all of which use money, and the 'mart' which operates primarily by barter. Sagant suggests that Hatiya was probably not a market (Sagant 1968–9: 111–12), but against this we have the fact of its name which was surely derived from the Nepali word for market (*hat*). In any case, money was of course present in north-east Nepal in the early nineteenth century. The headmen (‘*guobah*’) of the Upper Arun and Wallungchung collected taxes on trade-goods and transport animals in rupees (Hooker 1854: 160; von Fürer-Haimendorf 1975: 116). They were politically powerful enough to maintain monopolies on trade through these valleys and keep strangers out (Hamilton 1819: 154 and Hooker 1854: 230–1). Also, the wool trade was always monetised. Traders paid money in advance to the Tibetan shepherds, the advantage of this from their point of view being that in this way they could stabilise prices. In the early twentieth century, the volume of the wool trade was so great that it determined the value of Tibetan currency. If there was a large wool crop one year so many Indian rupees flowed into Tibet that the value of the rupee would fall as against the Tibetan *trang-ka*. Conversely, if the crop was poor, the value of the rupee rose (Bell 1928: 117). The wool trade became important in north-east Nepal in the middle of the nineteenth century.

What does seem apparent is that the monetisation of particular places could rise and fall quite rapidly in this region of the Himalayas. Das mentions, for example, that in 1901 there was only a cowshed at Gok, northeast of Darjeeling, where formerly there had been twelve shops (Das 1902: 21).

In the Lhomi area further evidence of previous prosperity is the large number of Buddhist temples (*gompa*) attached to each village. Many of them are now virtually unused, and all are poverty-stricken. Their lands have shrunk to small plots, and the buildings are bare shells. The valuable statues and paintings, which some Lhomi maintained had been stolen, were perhaps sold by the lamas, as I was told by others. In the past, land was more freely bought and sold than it is today. The *gompas*, which acquired substantial wealth from donations, engaged in trade and bought land. Temple land was worked by the villagers in return for the religious services of the lamas.

Let us look now at the modern barter economy. Before the virtual closure of the Tibetan border by the early 1970’s which followed the Chinese invasion, the Lhomi engaged in three kinds of barter. First, there was inter-village direct exchange of surplus foods, handicrafts and items gathered from the forests, e.g. maize for potatoes, wool for tobacco, wild garlic for rice, etc. This small-scale barter was carried out not only between Lhomi villages but perhaps more importantly between Lhomi and their neighbours to the south, Gurungs, Rais, Limbus, Bahuns and Chhetris, all of whom are relatively prosperous grain farmers.

Secondly, regular and large-scale barter of agricultural produce took place each year in exchange for the produce of the Tibetan livestock economy, butter, dried fats and meats, woven woollen clothes, ropes, sacks, rugs, and blankets of yak hair. The Lhomi still see pastoral products as essential for existence in their culture, providing their own kind of food, dress, utensils and objects of value, radically different from those of the ‘Gorkha’ (Nepalese) peoples to the south. In their own eyes the Lhomi themselves (*shing-sa-wa*, ‘field-earth-people’) provide only a half-life from their farming produce, and the inferior half at that. But the Tibetan nomadic pastoralists (*drog-pa*) retreated *en bloc* to the northern side when the border was closed, because that is where the good high-altitude pastures are.

Only these pastures are suitable for herding yaks, yak-crosses and Tibetan types of sheep and goats.

Thirdly, there was long-distance trade of salt, acquired by the nomads in Tibet, for grains (mainly rice) acquired by the Lhomi in the Nepalese middle hills. This salt-grain trade, supplemented by other valuable items on either side, such as medicinal herbs, musk, vegetable dyes, pashmina wool, paper, coral, turquoise, silver and gold, was not primarily for use but for onward trading. The goods exchanged were very similar to those of the early nineteeth century (Hamilton 1819: 156–7). By the mid-twentieth century, however, there were no marts or entrepots. Tibetan salt was acquired in the border region for *x* amount of rice and then transported to the middle hills where it was bartered with Gurung, Rai, etc. farmers for *y* amount of rice. This rice was then taken north and bartered again for salt at a rate which would give the Lhomi an operational surplus for the next cycle. This barter was carried out between 'known families' and often involved delay or debt (*bulon*).

There is evidence from the Dolpo region further west that in the early twentieth century the salt-grain trade was conducted with established exchange rates and an absence of competition, i.e. it had features of 'primitive trade' (Jest 1975: 164). But this was fragile. The disastrous effect on exchange ratios of the flood of Indian salt in the south from the 1920's onwards, and of the shutting down of Tibetan salt supplies by the Chinese in the 1960's–70's, have been described by Rauber (1982) for the Khyampa, a group of Himalayan traders in north-west Nepal.[9] An exactly similar process was recounted by the Lhomi when I visited in 1979. The result is that the profitable 'business' end of their barter has been drastically reduced. It has ceased to be profitable to trade Tibetan salt in the south, and the Lhomis fetch it now only for personal consumption and for their animals. The main items of 'business' trade from Tibet today are medicinal herbs and musk, which fetch high money prices in the bazaars of southern Nepal and northern India. Supplies of other valuables and foods from the North have dwindled too. The Chinese have official trading posts where Lhomi can barter or sell grain and hides for salt, consumer goods, or Chinese currency, but the rates are less good than private barter with Tibetans in the communes at Lungde or further away at Karta. The Tibetans, however, can only openly trade the personal shares of wool, butter, salt, etc. allowed them by the communes; anything else is illegal. Since very few Tibetans now come over the border into Nepalese territory, the Lhomi have to travel north on foot, carrying heavy baggage over high passes, sleeping in the open or in caves, in order to obtain the pastoral products. Formerly they waited at harvest time for the nomads, who used sheep as transport, to come to them. Now, the most valued and prestigious products in their culture are in short supply. The Lhomi, like the Humli Khyampas described by Rauber, have had to fall back on their own farms for subsistence. To them, this means not only back-breaking toil and a wretchedly reduced diet but also a sense of injustice.

In this same period the Lhomi political system has fallen apart. In the 1930's and 40's the villages had been more or less united under one paramount *goba* who managed to subordinate the others. Goba Sinon was born in the village of Pang-Dok, but later moved to the southernmost Lhomi village of Syaksila which stands on a craggy outcrop dominating the trail. He controlled the area from Hedagna to the border. Here, apparently, he was able to keep control of all traffic and take a tax on goods moving through, as did his predecessors of the early nineteenth century. He maintained his position through force of arms and was able to keep officials of the Nepali state at bay. His power was probably already diminished by the time of von Fürer-Haimendorf's visit in the 1950's (von Fürer-Haimendorf 1975: 116), and today his descendants are *gobas* of separate villages and have little but ancestral prestige left.

Regional barter in the Arun Valley has also been affected, since the Lhomi are no longer able to give Tibetan salt in exchange for rice. Many more people than previously now travel down to the middle hills for two to three months in winter, doing menial work on Gurung, Rai, etc. farms for payment in rice, other grains, hides and animal carcasses. In principle, the Lhomis' pay, which is always in kind, can be taken north again in spring for trade with Tibet during the summer, but in practice many of them have such small farms that they need it all for subsistence. The rates of pay are highly variable. If a Lhomi arrives with a large number of dependants he may receive nothing for the winter's work except food and shelter for his family. Richer Lhomi, on the other hand, can either remain in their villages or use the winter months in trading ventures in the southern bazaars.

From this we see that the large-scale effects of a barter economy, like any economy based on 'commodity' transactions, may be unequal, even though each particular exchange is by definition equal in the circumstances. In barter there are no social mechanisms strong enough to ensure a stabilisation of exchange ratios in the face of externally produced changes in supply. This is unlike the kind of 'primitive trade' network alluded to by Polanyi and analysed by Sahlins, where, despite rises in the external 'prices' of items, they were still traded for the same number and type of goods in the interior over a considerable period of time. We also see from the annual cycle of production and exchange that the modern economists' suppositions about 'transaction costs' in a barter economy are mistaken. Who produces what, where and when, is customary and well-known in the region. The search for coincidence of wants is not necessary, since the time and place of barter for common items was established long in the past. Activities are dovetailed and combined, such that transport, storage and waiting costs are minimised.

The inter-village barter of farming and forest produce has probably been least affected by the decline in long-distance trade. It continues as before, dominated by the barter of Lhomi potatoes (introduced *c.* 1840's, Hooker 1854: 240) for grains from the lower villages. In autumn a stream of people from all over the nearby middle hills trudge up to the Lhomi villages bearing baskets of grain for exchange. They trade usually with 'known people', though otherwise wherever they can.[10]

One common argument of economists for the efficiency of money is that it limits the number of price quotations necessary. All items can be quoted in money, whereas in a barter system everything has to be quoted against everything else. In practice, this is not the case. Although there are no clear 'spheres of exchange', many items are never traded for one another. The reasons for this are usually purely practical, e.g. cattle are too valuable to barter for transportable amounts of grain. Barter, in practice, follows limited and well-known 'tracks'.

The Lhomi today have relatively little everyday contact with money. Chinese money is not accepted in Nepal, nor vice versa. But more important than this is the fact that money is not needed for subsistence farming: the Lhomi do not use bought tools, fertilisers, etc., and while they would buy ploughing oxen or cows if they could, the average farm inherits its livestock. Even state land taxes, which are small, are paid to the *gyembus* if necessary in grains. In everyday life money is only absolutely necessary for buying bazaar items such as cooking oil, kerosene and lamps, iron, cotton cloth, and Western or Ayurvedic medicines. Lhomi are not yet in the transistor belt. But once in a while every Lhomi needs large sums of money to pay for a wedding, a funeral or a sacrifice. On these occasions they take out loans, a subject to which I shall return later.

The nearest bazaar is at Khandbari in the middle hills, some five days walk from the Lhomi villages. People make occasional trips there to sell Chinese manufactured goods, medicinal herbs (Humphrey 1980; Burbage 1981), eggs, garlic, pigs, bristles, or beer made from rice or millet. Most people make no surplus money from this. Some Lhomi, both men and women, take portering jobs in the middle hills to earn money, but this again has limited possibilities: there is little time to spare from the farms, and the Lhomi are in competition for this work with the Rais, Gurungs, etc. who live on the spot. Also, Lhomi dislike and resent having to take paid work of any kind. All of this means that the flow of money into the Lhomi villages is very limited.

From this brief survey we can see some of the conditions for a barter economy. (1) There is a low money supply, and absence of markets in land and labour. Culturally, the people are not 'hooked on' goods imported from the national economy. (2) The region, because of its ecological diversity, has a certain specialisation of production. (3) There is an absence of state control of the economy which would siphon off surplus into a large system of redistribution, as was the case for example in the Inca vertical economy. Lhomi political control has now disintegrated. (4) There is no widely institutionalised system of 'gift exchange', nor is there socially regulated control of trade rates, i.e. bargaining is possible for all goods. (5) Barter is carried out by individuals belonging to households which do not require money for essential subsistence. (6) Regional production and exchange is well-known and predictable, so that there are established patterns of dovetailing the times and places of barter. Partners are known to one another, especially in delayed exchange (cf. Goodhart 1975).

Exchange ratios

I now take up the question of barter exchange ratios in greater detail, as I believe them to be subject to different conditions through the range of products. It was stated above that the possibility of bargaining is a condition for barter, but does this imply that exchange rates are dominated by supply and demand?

The Lhomi material seems to show that the more widely produced an item is, the less likely it is to be subject to 'interference' with the workings of supply and demand. This appears to be only common sense. It is also a point well-known in 'economic anthropology', e.g. Bohannan's lowest 'sphere of exchange' among the Tiv (Bohannan & Bohannan 1968). However, we can only say that barter ratios for such products appear to correspond *more or less* with what a 'market equilibrium' rate might be. In fact, of course, no such rate is visible. It is somewhat complex to demonstrate this, but let us start with maize-salt barter in autumn 1979. Maize becomes cheaper in relation to salt as one travels southwards in the Arun Valley.

Kimathanka (north)	1 maize = 1 salt
Pang Dok	1 maize = 1 – salt
Syaksila (south)	1 maize = ⅓ salt[11]

This in itself tells us little because these ratios might indicate that maize becomes scarcer as one goes north, or that maize is equally common in all of the villages, but that salt, which we know is obtained in Tibet, becomes progressively more expensive the further away it is bartered. Or they might indicate both. Indian salt can be bought in Khandbari bazaar for money. In Pang Dok the two kinds of salt have more or less equal value against other things, despite the fact that Tibetan salt is preferred for its taste. The explanation for this is that Indian salt has to be paid for in money and can only be acquired some six days walk away, while the border with Tibet is only two days away. The supply of maize is equally problematic. No adequate survey of the countless tiny fields of the producers has ever been made. We can best try to explain the ratios by looking at maize in relation to another item, e.g. potato seed.

Kimathanka	1 maize = 2 potato seed
Pang Dok	1 maize = 1½ potato seed
Syaksila	1 maize = 1 potato seed
Angla (near Khandbari)	1 maize = ½ potato seed

We see that maize varies against potato seed as it goes north in much the same proportion as it does against salt (maize become three times more expensive against both salt and potatoes from Syaksila to Kimathanka). This concurrence would suggest that maize does actually become scarcer the further north one goes, and this would seem to be confirmed by Lhomi impressions of the amount of maize planted. The rates change from year to year: in Pang Dok in a year of poor maize harvest 2 units of potatoes obtain only 1 of maize, but 3 in a year when maize is plentiful. All of this suggests that there is a gross correspondence between barter rates and supply and demand.

Within each village, barter rates for these basic products are consistent with one another. I shall give here rates for 1979 in Pang Dok as stated by the villagers. This may be confusing to read but it is an accurate representation of ethnographic reality. The data are re-expressed in terms of 1 unit of rice as numeraire in the table. However, it is important to realise that Lhomi do not think in terms of a numeraire.

3 potato seed = 2 maize / millet
1 salt = 2 maize / millet

If rates were consistent we would expect to find that 1 salt would exchange for 3 potato seed, and this is confirmed from the data:

1 salt = 3–4 potato seed.

Rice was preferred to maize or millet for food, but fetched almost the same rate in barter because it was possible to exchange it in Tibet at equal rates.

1 rice = ½ salt

Consistent with this is:

1 rice = 1+ maize / millet
2 rice = 3 potato seed

Work also entered the barter economy:

1 day's labour = 2 units maize / millet
hire pair ploughing oxen per day = 4 days labour
hire pair ploughing oxen per day = 8 units maize / millet

Barter rates in Pang Dok in 1979 expressed in one unit (kathi) of rice.
* represents absence of transaction.

	Rice	Maize	Millet	Pots.	Work day	Oxen hire	Salt
Rice	*	1+	1+	1½	½	⅛	½
Maize		*	1–	1½	½	⅛	½
Millet			*	1½	½	⅛	½
Potatoes				*	*	*	⅔
Work day					*	¼	1
Oxen hire						*	*
Salt							*

There is consistency in the *internal* village barter exchange ratios for common produce (e.g. all grains, salt, chillies, garlic, vegetables, butter and local meat) which would suggest that 'market forces' are at work here. But, other items, such as clothes, Tibetan woven aprons, boots, yak tails, Tibetan dried meat, rugs, gem stones, etc., which are bartered less frequently, exchange for one another and for the agricultural products on an *ad hoc* basis and without any consistency. This can be explained conventionally by lack of information about comparable transactions, the cost of obtaining information being greater than the estimated saving of a lower price (the 'thin market'; cf. Stigler 1961) but I would account for it rather by the social practice of barter: some degree of comparison, and hence competition, is unavoidable in frequent local exchanges, but not in distant or infrequent barter. But in either case it is not lateral comparison, but the process of bargaining between two people, which determines the 'price'.

But let us look more clearly at what is really going on. There are two important points: (a) the lack of standard units of measurement, and (b) the hidden inequalities behind the 'traditional' places and times of barter.

In the Upper Arun there are three different scales of measurement operative: (1) Nepali measures of weight and volume; (2) Tibetan measures of weight and volume; (3) Lhomi measures of volume, the main one being the *kathi*, a round pot with straight sides. While Nepali and Tibetan weights and measures are more or less standardised, this is far from true in the case of the Lhomi ones. (Jest

(1975: 168) remarks for Dolpo, 'A chaque maison, sa mesure'.) The kathi in particular is often described as 'a large kathi', 'a small kathi', etc. Some goods are commonly measured in one series and others in another. Lhomi use different series at the Tibetan border, in their own villages, and in the south. This makes it difficult for them (or us) to compare exchange rates for different goods. This is an important factor behind the absence of a common standard of value in barter. Barter, though equally 'commodity exchange' is radically different from the monetary mentality. Most Lhomi could only make approximate guesses as to the conversion of one set of measures into another. The same lack of abstract measurement applies to production as well as exchange. Lhomi usually estimate field sizes by the amount of *x* or *y* grain they sow in them. But this is largely guesswork, as they rarely weigh the seed and almost never weigh the harvest.[12] No doubt, if they sold their harvest in a bazaar the Lhomi would weigh it. But they do not, they barter it. This means that it is impossible for them to assess 'profit' against costs of production.

Let us take the example of a poor farmer, Kun-top, from Pang-Dok. His main crop was potatoes, which he grew for his own consumption and for barter. He obtained in exchange rice, maize, millet and chillies, mostly from people from outside the village. He knew that 3 kathis of potatoes were equal to 2 of maize that year (1979) and that millet and maize were the same 'price'. However, he actually bartered his potatoes in a unit called a *tobo*, a kind of large basket. He thought that one tobo was equal to about 30 kathis, but some were up to 40 kathis in size. His own tobo was a small one, around 20 kathis, he thought. What he was certain of was that he aimed to barter two tobos of potatoes that year and then he would have enough grains for his consumption.

In barter, the participants only have to examine what is offered. In the monetised economy, on the other hand, it is not the amount of goods but the money price which fluctuates. Thus the Lhomi reach an impasse in the bazaar of Khandbari. No-one in the bazaar trusts the *kathi*, and the Lhomi therefore, if they are to sell anything, are required to hire a Nepali measure of volume, the *kurwa*. Prices in the bazaar are well-known and there is a certain social pressure not to raise them.[13] Lhomi grumble at this and say that this relative inflexibility is one of the main reasons why they prefer barter.

The effect of the absence of exact measurement is to make village barter rates as quoted by the Lhomi more or less notional, almost ideological. They represent merely the beginning of the bargaining process. As I have suggested in the case of maize, the state of supply of products can only really be guessed at. In barter, what people *know* is demand, and the mutual adjustment of demands is a social relation. For this reason, the most important fact about barter is that it takes place between individuals who are socially 'understood', whether they belong to the same or different 'ethnic groups'. Part of the calculation is the extent to which people can trust one another.

Let us look now at relations of domination in barter.[14] In the case of common produce perhaps any disadvantage (in transport costs, timing of the transaction, etc.) takes an 'economic' form which can be adjusted via exchange ratios. But in the case of goods for which something like a monopoly can be maintained, for example the vestiges of the wool trade in the Upper Arun, the customary 'track' of barter might seem to establish a persistently unequal relation between ethnic groups, such that one side can dictate terms of trade. It is significant that it is here that relationships of debt also flourish.

The wool trade: emergence of a monopoly

By the late nineteenth century the trade in wool from Tibet was one of the most important economic activities in the region. Certainly by the beginning of the twentieth century and probably earlier this trade was monetised (Bell 1928: 117–18). Since the Lhomi always obtained most of the wool for their own use from the exchange with the Tibetan nomads they have never owned many sheep themselves, nor did they place much value on their own inferior pastures on this side of the Himalaya. At the beginning of this century their leaders sold the rights of use in the pastures to the Gurungs. The position today is that Gurung sheep swamp the only available pastures, which are Lhomi pastures.

Sheep in the Upper Arun today are of the Nepali Baruwal variety, different from the Tibetan sheep, and Lhomi have no expertise in the washing, dyeing, spinning, and weaving operations for wool of the Baruwal type. The Gurungs, on the other hand, are the regional specialists in the manufacture of Baruwal woolen rugs (*radi*), jackets, capes, etc. Virtually all Gurung households spin and weave, even if they do not own sheep. The few Lhomi who own sheep hand over all of their wool to the Gurungs, either to women who come up to fetch it, or to shepherds passing through Lhomi villages on their way to and from the pastures. Lhomi take money, or goods measured in money, for their wool. They can expect to gain fairly large sums (some 350 Rs for the wool from ten sheep in a year). Wool prices in rupees reflect transport costs to Gurung villages, and are identical for everyone. Although they have risen in the last five years (1975–80) by about ⅓, this is only keeping step with the rise in wool prices in Kathmandu (see note 20).

But in fact it is relatively rare for Lhomi actually to sell wool in a simultaneous transaction, since they have usually taken out a loan in advance against each season's wool crop. The Gurung farmers know exactly how many sheep each owner has, and they are prepared to pay in advance at slightly lower rates than normal, a time-honoured practice in the Himalayan wool trade. Other families can obtain a loan of 300 Rs in advance payment for herding a Gurung flock for a season. But most Lhomi are forced at one time or another to take out money loans *tout simple*. Interest rates are very high: 5 RS a month or 60 RS a year for a loan of 100 RS, with a surcharge (*tekki*) of 12 RS.[15] Avoidance of repayment is frequent. Such loans are very rarely taken out by one Lhomi from another and then only with a good deal of persuasion. In such cases loans are often in grain rather than money and the rates are lower (25 RS a year on 100 RS loan, with a tekki of 5 RS or one day's labour). The giving of loans is accompanied by a blessing from the donor. Loans are usually taken out at life crises, when it is necessary to buy in pigs, chickens, liquor, etc. for feasts. But they can also be used, like other valuables, such as jewellery or livestock, to start off a trading venture. Such loans and valuables are the spring which enable a few individual Lhomi to jump clear from the maze of petty barter operations.

It is the Gurung farmers with an interest in the north who give out loans and it is apparent that the operation is not unconnected with the pasture situation. The Lhomi have begun to make claims that they are legally entitled to have their pastures back. In any case, Gurung shepherds are dependent on Lhomi for allowing them passage, for storing provisions, and giving shelter in the north. The ultimate ownership of the pastures is the lever which Lhomi can use to counterbalance the Gurung wool trade monopoly and to ensure the continued availability of loans. Lhomi avoid taking loans from people they work for in winter and they spread the number of creditors as widely as possible, i.e. they are careful not to become too dependent. Lhomi maintain a defiantly separate culture from the Gurungs. Nevertheless, it is perhaps the increasing Gurung control of the money supply to the Lhomi which is reflected in the recent election of a Gurung as a panchayat official for a Lhomi ward.[16]

I have been discussing the wool trade in the context of 'barter' and this may seem odd in view of the fact that even Lhomis sell wool for money. In fact, money itself enters the barter 'system'.

Money has a different value in different villages, in terms for example of rice or labour.[17] It also has a different value in the same village in relation to one type of product rather than another, just as other valuables do.[18] The variation in the value of money in different villages could be explained simply by the money supply. We could remember here the situation described by Bell for Tibet in the 1920s (see p. 54): in years when there was plentiful wool for export, rupees flooded in, and the value of Tibetan goods against rupees went up (i.e. they cost more rupees). On this analogy we could explain the high money price of rice in certain Lhomi villages by the greater volume of sales from these villages resulting in a larger money supply in them. But in this case, the money prices of *all* goods would be high in these villages. But this is not so.

The explanation of the facts lies in the strategic position occupied by various goods and money in the different villages in the barter system. In Pang Dok, although a relatively fertile village, people simply do not normally accept money for rice. Rice can be used both as high prestige food and as a barter good in the trade with Tibet two days walk away. Money, on the other hand, is only useful in the bazaar, five days arduous walk away. Potatoes and garlic are occasionally sold for money in Pang Dok because they are produced here specifically for trade, and are no use in the Tibetan barter. The same is true of wool. But people here want wages in grains, not money. Contrary to orthodox economic views on money, even in terms of exchange-value, it is much better in the 'sink' to be paid in grains than money. The fact that wage labour is normally paid in grains thus reflects the relatively strong bargaining position of employees. This is what one would expect in a village with so few landless households.

Unfortunately we do not have the data to discuss prices and exchange ratios in relation to productive capacities and regional demand. However, it is possible to make some general conclusions. The amount of grain or money paid in wages does not correlate with the fertility of the location (Syaksila is a poor village and yet has high grain wages and low money wages[17]), nor with an equal subsistence level for workers in all villages (the difference between Pang Dok or Chemtang and Syaksila is considerable). Essentially, money, grain, and work are bartered for one another in each location. Lhomi do not exploit the differences between villages. The extent of lack of consistency in rates is an indication of the lack of integration of society and hence of the economy.

Barter in society and culture

Money is not used to measure the common products which are bartered. A corollary of this is that small amounts of money are not added up or saved to acquire things. The 'windfall mentality' of Lhomi with regard to money is often commented upon by their neighbours. If they have money, they spend it, often on drink. If they need a large amount of money, they borrow it or sell something so as to obtain the amount they require. I cannot possibly agree, for such a case, with the economists who argue that barter gives rise to monetisation. On the contrary, money has a tendency to sink into barter.

Of course, money is not always, or necessarily, used in this 'barter' fashion. Lhomi can operate in the bazaar as cannily as anyone else, not that the bazaar is a perfect market by any means (Sagant 1968–9; Jones 1980). But inside the Lhomi economy money 'disappears' because it is not accumulated as a goal of wealth. A Lhomi counts himself rich by virtue of ownership of land, livestock, and valuables such as jewellery. A rich man or woman is honoured for sponsoring special rituals, requiring beer, grains, butter, meat, etc., at the numerous *gompa* temples. But virtually no-one can afford to do this now. The richer Lhomi, of the *jimi* (original) clans, are members of associations attached to temples for the payment of the costs of regular monthly rituals. These associations are egalitarian in the sense that a group of wealthy families takes it in turn to provide the expenses, and all members of the village participate in the feast whether they have made provision or not.[19] Money thus tends to be rapidly converted into goods. Recent severe inflation in lowland Nepal may well play a part in this.[20] The expectation that in the future one will be poorer, not richer, and that other people also will be poorer, which is the Lhomi experience of the past decades, inclines people to prefer the immediacy of barter. Poor people, indeed, who experience hunger in bad years, have little choice.

In the past there was not such a marked tendency to convert out of money. This is because two kinds of money, as metallic value and as state currency, were still linked. Until quite recently the Indian silver rupee had an intrinsic melt down value, as did various Tibetan and Chinese coins (up to 1939 the rupee was 92 per cent. silver, thereafter 50 per cent. until the end of British rule). But this was less important than their cultural role as signifiers of 'treasure'. Among ordinary Lhomi, silver coins were melted down to make bracelets or belts, but often they were used in jewellery *as coins*. All Lhomi still use old Indian rupees as indications of wealth, sewn onto women's hats. In Khandbari there is a flourishing trade in old coins, and Lhomi craftsmen know how to weld rings to them and polish them up for display purposes. Goodhart's logical deduction that the absence of monetary payment as the normal form of economic transaction would require the demonstration of credit-worthiness seems to be borne out by the Lhomi practice—paradoxically by the use of 'money-turned-into-treasure' as a signifier.

To some extent modern Nepalese currency still retains an internal role as a 'valuable'. This is at odds with the mentality of the bazaar, but less so either with barter or with ceremonial-status payments. A ritual gift of 61 RS is still an essential transfer from the bridegroom's side to the bride's at marriage (a transaction between groups of different status). But in barter the money exchanged for a valuable comes itself to have something of the valuable about it. This is because the mentality of barter is one of *equal* exchange. In a fully monetised economy it is better to hold money than goods. But in a barter economy, having money rather than goods may or may not place someone at a direct advantage, and the Lhomi always behave to one another as if money is just another, rather honourable, 'good'. This must be determined by a psychology tending towards 'immediate returns' (cf. Woodburn 1980), since Lhomi disregard what we know from Aristotle: that 'even if we happen to want nothing at the moment, money is a sort of guarantee that we shall be able to make an exchange at any future time when we happen to be in need' (1895: 5, 14).

It is perhaps because of the impossibility in barter of calling upon an abstractly expressed 'just price' (this illusion being created by the idea of money as a measure of value) that bargaining itself is decorous, marked by silences or absences, as people retreat to 'consider'. We may compare this with the confrontational mode of higgling described by Geertz for the monetised Moroccan *suq*, where the intensive determining of the realities of the particular deal coexists with some sort of extensive search for the going price which also seems to be the 'fair price' (1979: 206–7). In the *suq* the 'generally acknowledged' and the 'equitable' are the same, though admittedly it is a vexed and problematic matter to establish what this might be. But the Lhomi do not even try. They ensure that the reference to 'fair price' becomes an impossibility by their attitude to money and to measurement. Barter thus abolishes abstract justice (and the need to appear 'honest' in relation to general or external criteria), and replaces it with whatever is considered by the parties to be just in their circumstances. This is arrived at by bargaining. This same feature is true in a somewhat hidden sense of the *suq*, but in barter it becomes overt and dominant. We could see this again as a feature of atomised society.

Among the Lhomi there is a continuum from petty money transactions or direct barter, though regular and then delayed trade by barter, to the occasional 'big business'. All this can be contrasted with those transfers of value which are concerned with reproducing differences in status between clans and maintaining hierarchical institutions (see Clarke 1951). But these kinds of payment have declined to a minimum among the Lhomi today, and the question does arise whether this is a simple result of increased poverty or something in the nature of a 'social choice' engendered by ideological change. I do not at present have enough information to disentangle these two factors. Certainly, egalitarianism is what the Lhomi today admire. People even grumble about others who keep a servant. It is notable that Lhomi egalitarianism includes relations between the sexes. Women have never previously been eligible for inherited political position, but today several of the elected representatives in the panchayat system are women with their own households. Two of these were ebullient personalities, not especially rich, but 'merry widows' with several lovers. A wealthy and influential man, on the other hand, told me that he would not stand for the panchayat because office was held only for a short period. In sum, the Lhomi are in the process of reformulation of political values, to some extent induced by their gradual incorporation in the state of Nepal, but also fuelled by an anarchic individualism of their own. It seemed to me in 1979 almost as though, alien to Western practice, economic transactions were undertaken with seriousness bordering on solemnity, while politics, at any rate of the panchayat, was a realm of disrespect and hilarity. Going down the trail to attend meetings, the closer the Lhomi deputies approached the 'Gorkha' centre of Khandbari the more outrageous their behaviour became.

For the Lhomi, the pinnacle of barter is the occasional big business deal. This is normally conducted between 'known people', often distant kin, or 'ritual friends',[21] or kinsmen of ritual friends. A deal is often preceded by the giving of minor solicitory gifts and a ritual scarf. The arrangements require discussion and time. Much of this trade is illegal and so the partners have to trust one another. The watch-musk barter trade, between India and Tibet, is the most valuable of all. The same channels are used for lesser valuables, such as Tibetan carpets or religious objects. They go, perhaps via southern towns such as Dhankuta or Dharan, to Lhomi contacts in Darjeeling or Kathmandu. A trade chain of this kind does not consist of people trying to outwit one another, but of friends and accomplices. It is a gesture of friendship to be asked to participate (unlike Western society, where 'friendship' has a different meaning and is considered inimical to business).

In all this there are, and can be, no set prices. The only guide is the distant chimera of a notion of what the market in the end will bear. The ultimate buyer is part of the capitalist system, Indian traders, French perfume houses, West German carpet importers, or Western tourists. This is the part of the Lhomi barter system which is least subject to the 'traditional' channels of the regional productive economy: prices can vary wildly and yet it is the most involved with relations of friendship and trust. Sahlins made the perceptive remark, for 'primitive trade', that where rates are more or less fixed, the only way to adapt to changes in supply and demand in the long run is to revise the partnerships rather than the rates (1974: 312–13). Again it appears that the 'barter economy' differs radically from 'primitive trade' systems. Exchange rates in barter trade are decided upon separately for each transaction, i.e. there is no expectation of a 'standard rate' over time. This does not, however, have the effect of destroying trade partnerships, which often include prolonged periods of negotiation. The time allowed for repayment, in the case of a delayed transaction, can be very elastic and much depends on the energy and social weight of the individual. Some people makes disastrous losses and their partnerships lapse, not because the social relationships have ended, but because they have, for the time being, no trade to conduct. I knew of one man, Lhagpa, who arrived from Tibet with three yaks, worth several thousand rupees, which he entrusted to a distant Lhomi Khampa relative for a trade deal. The business failed. Five years later, Lhagpa, a mild man, was still waiting for the Khampa to make a successful deal and repay him. Lhagpa moved to Kathmandu and took paid work. Living like a churchmouse with the friends of kin, he spent his first month's wages on a second-hand sleeping-bag which he sent off, via a trusted friend, to the same Khampa for a deal which was to involve medicinal herbs. Some months later when I left Kathmandu the outcome of this trade was still not known.

There is no radical break between this trade kind of barter and the rest. Essentially it is still conducted within the community, and the commercial biting edge, the final sale, is done by middlemen of other ethnic groups. Economically, everything depends here on the internal gains of each transactor bearing some relation to the outside price. Lhomi have fairly good channels of information, but in fact they are not very good 'big businessmen' precisely because they themselves seldom have the opportunity or boldness to make the final sale (in this they are much more retiring than other 'Bhote' groups of Nepal). Losses are absorbed into the complex web of unfinished transactions which link exchange partners. It is highly probable that there is not enough wealth around for these ever to be resolved in the foreseeable future. The consciousness of this is one factor among many that makes Lhomi refuse to give one another loans and to prefer, whenever possible, the simultaneous transaction.

Conclusion

The conditions in which barter emerges as a dominant form of transaction are discussed on p. 52. Here I mention characteristics of barter which appear to be important.

1) The relation between actual exchange ratios in barter and presumed 'equilibrium rates' (i.e. the prices representing equilibrium between supply and demand, cf. Marshall 1890: Appendix F* on barter) depends on the volume and frequency of exchange of the items in question. Goods widely produced and bartered are likely to be exchanged at ratios most nearly approximating to notional 'equilibrium rates', while those infrequently transacted may be bartered at quite arbitrary rates. Among the Lhomi, money falls into this latter category *in the local economy* (the essentially non-monetised 'sink' in Crump's terminology). In effect, the practice of barter including money renders speculation about 'equilibrium rates' pointless. The notion of a general 'just price' in Aristotelian terms is therefore absent.

2) One reason for arbitrary rates lies in the fact that barter is immediate, and being immediate is by its very nature discontinuous. For relatively infrequent exchanges people do not concern themselves with what prices might be elsewhere. Even when barter is delayed and part of a complex of debts, the participants do not compare transactions with one another or against a standard of value (see also Leach 1954: 145–6).

4) The requirement of immediate satisfaction of demand is paramount in barter systems. This is one of the explanations of the rejection of monetisation. Very poor people literally cannot afford to keep wealth in money. In this situation, the absence of exact measurement is not a feature of low cultural development but a deliberate strategy to ensure the persistence of one-to-one transactions. The

* not reproduced here

subjection of money to the same rationality indicates the strength of the barter system. Here even money has no temporality. The 'windfall mentality' thus does not indicate irresponsibility, as the stereotypes of other ethnic groups about the Lhomi maintain, but a desire for freedom.

5) Immediate barter is an expression of autonomy and therefore is likely to be insisted upon in relations with outsiders. Direct barter also dispenses with the need for payment, i.e. it will be used when there is little information about the credit-standing of purchasers, or when there is a lack of trust. These advantages of direct barter are so great that they outweigh the transaction costs involved. Thus we find that Gurung farmers, who need seed potatoes and do not trust the Lhomi to bring them down in time for the planting season, will trudge for days up and down the craggy Arun slopes to get to the Lhomi villages for *direct* barter of their grains for potatoes.

6) Delayed barter occurs where credit is required, and there is a correlation with the more valuable goods because these also tend to be less frequently transacted (see Douglas and Isherwood, 1978). However, delayed barter, as Goodhart pointed out, can only work in a relationship of knowledge and trust. In the case of the Lhomi, despite the existence of trading friendships with other ethnic groups, this feature limits trade networks and results in a curtailing of trade in valuable goods. The general implication of Marx's work is that wealth accrues through control of production. Here, however, we see that there are ways of profiting through strategic domination of barter-trade, the control of the means of exchange. However, if barter rather than monetary sale is the means of exchange we can see that it is self-limiting: the trust required for barter to include credit effectively circumscribes economic operations.

7) The preference for barter is therefore related to underlying political conditions which make autonomy a paramount consideration. The Lhomi have entered a cycle of internal political disintegration such that the economic transfers reproducing hierarchy, whether in the context of affinal relations, chiefship, or the Lamaist church, have all but ceased. Many different social groups (villages, clans, old settlers/new settlers, lamas, households, etc.) coexist and do not wish to be subjected to one another. This situation has complex antecedents, both in the earlier economic collapse of the salt-grain trade, which drastically reduced the amount of surplus the Lhomi could produce, and in the advent of Nepali political institutions, which are displacing the Lhomi ones. In relation to outside political power, the Lhomi still wish to maintain an autonomy allowing them some degree of control over the Arun route and their monopoly of the Tibetan trade.

8) While it is true that barter is conducted in an egalitarian mode, and most customary or relatively long-standing barter arrangements adjust exchange-ratios to transaction costs, nevertheless in the long run barter, unlike certain systems of 'primitive trade' described in the literature, cannot save people from the effects of external changes in supply and demand. In an atmosphere of perfect friendliness, as between the Lhomis and their respected Tibetan nomad friends, exchange rates may still inexorably drop. Indeed, barter, by hindering the emergence of integrative economic institutions, may make the situation worse. Barter is a response to increasing poverty on the part of people who wish

nevertheless to maintain their autonomy. Thus, while preserving the same 'benign' culture of economic independence, barter may actually preside over real economic desperation and instability.

NOTES

The fieldwork on which this article is based was carried out in collaboration with the Kosi Hill Area Rural Development Programme in Nepal in 1979. I am grateful to the Nepali coordinator, Mr Kayastha, and to Dick Jenkin, Jit Man Gurung, Prem Subba, Samdup Lama, Jit Bahadur Gurung, Ambar Bahadur Rai, Prem Dutt and Dorje Bhote for the very great help they gave me. Sean Conlin, Edgar Keller, Jonathan Zeitlin, Stephen Hugh-Jones, Samdup Lama, Simon Strickland, Lionel Carter and Mrs Tsering Sangmo brought materials to my attention during the writing of this article. I am indebted especially to Quentin Outram and Istvan Hont, and also to Edmund Leach, Keith Hart, Stephen Gudeman, Wynne Godley, Parker Shipton, Charlotte Hardiman, Paul Sant Cassia and Graham Clarke for discussions relating to barter. I wish to thank my mother, Margaret Waddington, without whose support I would never have written this article.

[1] Crump in his survey of the literature could find only three 'primitive' economies dominated by barter (1981: 54).

[2] 'The logic of the case is, indeed, almost the opposite of that underlying the classical doctrine. The orthodox teaching started from the individual's propensity to barter; deduced from it the necessity of local markets, including division of labour; and inferred, finally, the necessity of trade, eventually of foreign trade, including even long-distance trade. In the light of our present knowledge we should almost reverse the sequence of the argument: the true starting point is long-distance trade, a result of the geographical location of goods, and of the "division of labour" given by location. Long-distance trade often engenders markets, an institution which involves acts of barter, and, if money is used, of buying and selling, thus eventually, but by no means necessarily, offering to some individuals an occasion to indulge in their alleged propensity for bargaining and haggling'. (Polanyi 1957: 58).

[3] I use the term 'Lhomi' for this community in the Upper Arun because it is established in the literature (von Furer-Haimendorf 1975; Bista 1967). In fact ethnicity in the region is complex and shifting. The Lhomi use both Bhote (local Tibetan) and Nepali names for people and places, and this is reflected in the paper.

[4] For example, in cases of hyper-inflation, or the quite different situation where money is avoided in order to evade the attention of tax institutions of the state, as in present-day California.

[5] As in socialist economies where scarce goods are allocated, often without the use of money, to social categories, and frequently pass from these groups to the population at large via barter transactions.

[6] Crump notes that, quite apart from the functions of money mentioned by Clower, 'true money' can only exist under certain real conditions: it must be physically capable of circulating indefinitely (i.e. it links the present to the future); it must have a distinctive idenity as money and no real importance for non-monetary purposes (e.g. it should not be consumable); and it should be in limited supply. If these conditions do not obtain the money-stuff can appear and disappear in an uncontrolled way which plays havoc with its role of storing value, etc. For example, cowries, the most widely used 'true money' of the specie (non-manufactured) type, never circulated as money on the shores of the Indian ocean where they could be simply picked up on the beach, but only in distant places where the supply was controllable (1981: 85).

[7] It might appear that Goodhart, in suggesting that barter takes place *inside* the face-to-face community, is reversing Marx's well known proposition that the origin of commodity exchange is the barter of products *between* communities (Karl Marx 1887 vol. 1: 91–2). Only in dealing with the outside world, Marx wrote, are individuals freed from the social obligations ('property rights') which render their goods inalienable inside their own communities. Commodity exchange, i.e. transaction of alienable products, therefore has to take place with outsiders. This idea has taken root in anthropology and been elaborated in many influential theories (Sahlins 1972; Servet 1981–2; Gregory 1980). Goodhart, however, really agrees. He is saying that barter as simultaneous exchange is so difficult as to be virtually an impossibility and that what would occur is delayed exchange, i.e. credit and debt. Comparatively little of the movement of goods within a community would use the price mechanism (i.e. barter), as opposed to internal distribution by direction, and these few debts

would be settled in the context of general mutual knowledge. Transactions outside the community would be forced to use money. Although we need not agree with him about the virtual impossibility of barter, it is clear that in both cases we are talking about 'commodity exchange' in Marxist terms.

[8] Lhomi own land in '*kipat*' (communal) tenure as defined in Nepali law (see Caplan 1970: McDougal 1979). Kipat tenure is in the process of being transformed into individual rights, but the legal situation was uncertain when I visited the Lhomi in 1979 and almost no land was bought or sold. The main reason the Lhomis gave for this was the unhelpful attitude of Nepali officials at the land registration office where Lhomi feel at a disadvantage, as very few of them are literate in Nepali. Land is in fact transferred mainly by *bandhaki* (Nep.): grain or money is given to the owner in return for use, and if the payment is not returned by a specified time the land is acquired by the user.

[9] Rauber says that, around 1900, one unit of rice obtained 10 of salt at the Tibetan mart of Purang, while it got ⅓ of salt in the district of Bajura some 50 miles to the south, and only ⅕ or ⅙th in Accham, another 20–30 miles south. With the infiltration of Indian salt into the hills from the 1920's onwards, exchange ratios of Tibetan salt with rice declined steadily in the southern district of Accham:

1900	1 rice = ⅕th or ⅙th salt
1925	1 rice = ¼ salt
1935	1 rice = ⅓ or ½ salt
1965	1 rice = 1 salt

By the 1960's, the effect of the Chinese invasion of Tibet began to be felt at the other end of the trade route, and the amount of salt given for rice at Purang went rapidly down:

1964	1 rice = 8 salt
1974	1 rice = 7 salt
1976	1 rice = 4–5 salt
1977	1 rice = 3–4 salt

In 1977, one unit of rice could still be bartered for only one of salt in the southern districts of Baljura and Accham (Rauber 1982: 151).

[10] Baumgartner (1980: 135) notes that Sherpa elders of each village meet annually to discuss the exchange potential of their potato crop and then set a minimum exchange ratio as against grains for that year. There is a constant danger that richer households would agree to lower rates.

[11] These are the accepted annual rates in kathis. There was no mention of changes during the season, which suggests that something like the Sherpa practice may have been in force (see above).

[12] Henry Osmaston (personal communication) notes a similar lack of precision in measurement among Ladakhis, despite knowledge of standard Tibetan rates. Harris suggests, in a paper with many themes in common with this one, that 'measurement by volume rather than by weight is an index of the degree to which monetary equivalence in exchange is avoided' (Harris 1982: 77).

[13] Bazaar prices are fixed nationwide by the Nepali government for paddy and wheat, and in Dhankuta there is also price fixing over a wide range of basic products by a group of large traders. Sellers are prevented from trading at lower but not higher prices. The reason for this is the desire of traders in general to keep purchasers from travelling down to the Terai where prices would otherwise be lower (Jones *et al.* 1982: 33–5). Although such institutionalised price fixing does not occur in Khandbari the same factors apply there.

[14] The question of 'unequal exchange' in partially monetised peripheral economies has been discussed by Platt (1982) and Harris (1982). Platt maintains that the very features which look least affected by the capitalist economy, such as payment of wages in maize, ensure the reproduction of households lacking maize production. Low agricultural prices in markets result in an unequal exchange between the peasants and the rest of the economy. The effect is to transfer value, but the peasants are not thereby pressured to leave the land. The result is the maintaining of a reserve of labour available at times of seasonal demand. This argument clearly has relevance for the Lhomi. However, in this article I am discussing the question of 'unequal exchange' between Lhomi and their immediate tribal neighbours, rather than between the Lhomi and the capitalist economy as a whole, mainly because there are so many steps between the Lhomi and anything resembling capitalism in Nepal. 'Unequal exchange' is not a phenomenon of capitalism alone. It remains true, however, that were capitalism (labour markets) to penetrate into the middle hills the Lhomi would find themselves in the position described by Platt.

[15] The *tekki* or *thegi* (surcharge, deducted from the initial loan or paid in labour, grain, etc.) is

known throughout Nepal and is standardised in given regions. Simon Strickland noted an interesting case among Gurungs of Siklis in Central Western Nepal of a 'strike' by debtors caused by the sudden raising of the tekki rate by creditors. The debtors belonged to one set of clans and the creditors to another higher group. The 'strike' consisted in refusing ritual services to the upper groups of clans (Strickland, personal communication).

[16] Elections to the panchayat are expensive. One of the main lamas of Hatiya managed to get his son elected, but only by selling almost all of his cattle in order to give the electors presents, etc.

[17]

Chemtang	1 day's work is paid 1.6 kathis grains or 10 RS
Pang Dok	1 day's work is paid 2 kathis grains or 8–10 RS
Hatiya	1 day's work is paid 2.4 kathis grains or 15 RS
Syaksila	1 day's work is paid 2.6 kathis grains or 4–5 RS

Of course, work is not usually paid at all—exchange labour prevails. Employers differ in what they offer (the figures above are averages). There is no free labour moving from village to village. We see that as one proceeds northwards from Syaksila, a day's work is paid progressively less in grains, and this is what we might expect given the increasing value of grains vis-à-vis other products from south to north. But the money pay is much less clear. For one thing, grains often cost more to buy separately for money than their money value as wages. These prices do *not* reflect transport costs—the money price of rice in Pang Dok, for example, is far higher than the cost of buying rice in the bazaar and paying porters to carry it north. When we compare the money price of grains in different villages and the payment for work in the same places there is a marked inconsistency. One day's work is paid:

Pang Dok	2 kathis grains or 8–10 RS pay, but money price of grains in 16 RS
Hatiya	2.4 kathis grains or 15 RS pay, but money price of grains is 15 RS
Syaksila	2.6 kathis grains or 4–5 RS, but money value of grains in 13 RS

The point is that it is virtually impossible to buy grains for money in the northern villages.

[18] Because money is virtually never exchanged for common produce it can maintain values which are inconsistent. For example, in Pang Dok 1 kathi of potatoes had a price of 2 RS, and as we saw, 1 kathi of rice barters for 1.5 of potatoes. We would expect the money price of rice to be 3 RS, but in fact it is 8 RS. There is the same effect with maize. With a money price for potatoes of 2 RS per kathi and a barter rate of 1 maize to 1.5 potatoes, we should expect the money price to be 3 RS per kathi. However, in fact it is 7 RS per kathi, which is consistent with the cultural preference for rice (8RS per kathi) and with the fact that, because of difficult conditions in the Tibetan communes, it is possible to barter all grains in Tibet at equal rates, e.g. against salt.

[19] These groups are known as *go* ('door') and seem to be similar to the Tibetan '*kidu*' discussed by Miller (Miller 1956) (my Tibetan assistant assumed that they were identical).

[20] I am indebted to Edgar Keller for the following information from West German government sources. Prices in Kathmandu (1972–3 = 100):

	1977	1978	1979	1980	1981
Meat and fish	166	180	187	235	290
Ghee and cooking oil	141	201	185	202	275
Herbs	194	266	262	231	227
Vegetables	161	190	205	243	262
Cloth	144	152	158	170	177
Wool	153	161	178	203	239

Between 1972/3 and 1978/9 the price of raw coarse rice in Dhankuta rose from 1.90 to 2.71 Rs/Kg, ghee from 15.54 to 20.75 Rs/Kg, mutton from 7.50 to 12.54 Rs/Kg and sugar from 3.48 to 8.28 Rs/Kg. The price of the main item produced by the Lhomi, potatoes, rose by far less: from 1.32 ro 1.85 Rs/Kg (Jones *et al.* 1982: 37). Lhomi were aware of inflation and constantly mentioned the rise in wool prices, money (as opposed to grain) wages, and livestock prices.

[21] The Lhomis have trading friends (*trogpo* male, and *trogmo* female) among the Tibetan nomads. These relationships are inherited patrilineally, but they are not exclusive. An active trader might have 5–6 such friends. A few Lhomi also have more ritualised friendships (*mit*) with people of 'Gorkha' ethnic groups. The *mit* ritual friendship is commonly established between people belonging to hierarchically distinct groups, or between endogamous groups, allowing an extension of close ties in a society which is divided and ranked. The relation involves an initiating ritual in the presence of a priest, promises of help in times of trouble, the use of respectful terms of address,

avoidance of the mit's spouse, no marriage between descendants, and funerary obligations. There is some debate in the literature as to whether *miteri* are commonly involved in trade with one another, and the evidence seems to suggest that regions of Nepal differ in this respect (Gorer 1938; Miller 1956; Okada 1957; Caplan 1970; McDougal 1979). In the case of Lhomi *mit* do trade with one another, and the kinsmen of *mit* are also involved. In my experience, Lhomi set up *mit* relationships in order to trade.

REFERENCES

Aristotle (translated by F. H. Peters) 1895. *The Nicomachaean ethics* London: Kegan Paul.

Baumgartner, R. 1980. *Trekking und Entwicklung ins Himalaya: die Rotwaling Sherpa in Ost-Nepal.* Diessenhofen: Rüegger.

Bell, Charles 1928. *The people of Tibet.* Oxford: Clarendon.

Bohannan, P. & Laura Bohannan 1968. *The Tiv economy.* Evanston: Northwestern Univ Press.

Burbage, M. B. 1981. *Report on a visit to Nepal: the medicinal plant trade in the KHARDEP area: a study of the development potential.* London: Tropical Products Institute.

Caplan, Lionel 1970. *Land and social change in east Nepal.* London: Routledge.

Clarke, Graham E. 1951. The lama people of Nepal: the temple and kinship among a Buddhist people of the Himalaya. Thesis, University of Oxford.

Clower, R. W. 1969. Introduction. In *Monetary theory* (ed.) R. W. Clower. Harmondsworth: Penguin.

Crump, Thomas 1981. *The phenomenon of money.* London: Routledge & Kegan Paul.

Das, Sarat Chandra 1902. *Journey to Lhasa and central Tibet.* London: Murray.

Douglas, M. D. & B. Isherwood 1978. *The world of goods.* London: Allen Lane.

Geertz, C. 1979. Suq: the bazaar economy in Sefrou. In *Meaning and order in Moroccan society* (eds) C. Geertz *et al.* Cambridge: Univ. Press.

Goodhart, C. A. E. 1975. *Money, information and uncertainty.* London: Macmillan.

Gorer, G. 1938. *Himalayan village.* London: Nelson.

Gregory, C. 1980. Gifts to men and gifts to god: gift exchange and capital accumulation in contemporary Papua. *Man* (N.S.) **15**.

Haimendorf, C. von Fürer 1975. *Himalayan traders.* London: Murray.

Hamilton, F. 1919. *An account of the kingdom of Nepal.* Edinburgh: Constable.

Harris, Olivia 1982. Labour and produce in an ethnic economy, northern Potosi, Bolivia. In *Ecology and exchange in the Andes* (ed.) D. Lehmann. Cambridge: Univ. Press.

Helms, Mary W. 1969. The purchase society: adaption to economic frontiers. *Anthrop. Q.* **42**, 325–42.

Hooker, J. D. 1854. *Himalayan journals*, vols **1** & **2**. London: Murray.

Humphrey, Caroline 1980. *Report on a field study in north Sankhuwasabha (Nepal)* (KHARDEP Rep. **7**). Kathmandu: KHARDEP.

Jest, Corneille 1975. *Dolpo: communautes de langue tibetaine du Nepal.* Paris: Editions CNRS.

Jevons, W. S. 1910. *Money and the mechanism of exchange.* London: Kegan Paul.

Jones, S. F. 1980. *Kosi Hill Area Rural Development Programme: agricultural marketing survey*, vols **1** & **2**. London: Tropical Products Institute.

———, J. B. Innes, M. Pant & S. Subba 1982. *Agricultural marketing survey* vol. **3**: Survey results. Kathmandu: KHARDEP.

Leach, E. R. 1954. *Political systems of highland Burma.* London: Bell.

——— 1960/1. The frontiers of 'Burma'. *Comp. Stud. Soc. Hist.* **3**, 49–68.

McDougal, Charles 1979. *The Kulunge Rai.* Kathmandu: Bibliotheca Himalayica.

Malinowski, B. 1967. *Kula*: the circulating exchange of valuables in the archipelagoes of A New Guinea. In *Tribal and peasant economies* (ed.) G. Dalton. Austin, London: Univ. of Texas Press.

Marx, Karl 1954. *Capital*, vol. 1 (1887 edn). London: Lawrence & Wishart.

Marshall, A. 1920. *Principles of economics.* London: Macmillan.

Merrill, M. 1977. Cash is good to eat: self-sufficiency and exchange in the rural economy of the United States. *Radical Hist. Rev.* **1:1**. New York: John Jay College.

Miller, Beatrice D. 1956. Ganye and Kidu: two formalized systems of mutual aid among Tibetans. *SWest. J. Anthrop.* **12**.

Okada, Ferdinand E. 1957. Ritual brotherhood: a cohesive factor in Nepalese society. *SWest. J. Anthrop.* **13**.

Plato (translated by B. Jowett) 1908, *The Republic*. Oxford: Clarendon Press.

Platt, Tristan 1982. The role of the Andean *ayllu* in the reproduction of the petty commodity regime in northern Potosi, (Bolivia). In *Ecology and exchange in the Andes* (ed.) D. Lehmann. Cambridge: Univ. Press.

Polanyi, K. 1957. *The great transformation*. Boston: Beacon Press.

Rauber, Hanna 1982. Humli-Khyampas and the Indian salt trade: changing economy of namadic tribes in far west Nepal. In *Contemporary nomadic and pastoral peoples: Asia and the north* (ed.) P. S. Salzman. Williamsburg: College of William & Mary.

Sagant, Philippe 1968–9. Les marches en pays Limbu (notes sur les trois hat bajar de Taplelung et de Terhathum). *Ethnographie* **62**, 90–111.

Sahlins, Marshall 1972. *Stone age economics*. London: Tavistock.

Servet, J.-M. 1981–2. Primitive order and archaic trade. *Econ. Soc.* **10**, 451–66, **11**, 22–59.

Stigler, George G. 1961. The economics of information. *J. polit. Econ.* **69**, 212–25.

Thurnwald, Richard 1932. *Economics in primitive communities*. London: Oxford Univ. Press.

Woodburn, James 1980. Hunter-gatherer economies. In *Soviet and western anthropology* (ed.) E. Gellner. London: Duckworth.

[20]

'Salt money' and the circulation of commodities among the Baruya of New Guinea†

PRECIOUS GOODS AND MONEY IN PRIMITIVE SOCIETIES: A FEW PRELIMINARY REMARKS

At the beginning of this century Boas[1] and Malinowski,[2] uncovering and analysing the potlatch of the Kwakiutl Indians and the *kula* of the Melanesians in the Trobriand Islands, began to destroy the traditional image of primitive man worn down by the forces of nature and trying hard to stay alive. He was seen to be busy, apart from his subsistence activities, accumulating precious objects, feather head-dresses, pearls, pigs' and dolphins' teeth, copper plaques and transforming them, by clever strategy of gifts and various kinds of presentations, into 'stores of wealth' (Malinowski), into a means of acquiring the most valued roles or status in his society. Within the complex network of kinship relations, relations of production and power in primitive societies, the gift was revealed to be the dominant form of exchange and competition between individuals or groups. It was found necessary to elaborate the theory of the gift.

Mauss, the first (1924)[3] to apply himself to the task was followed by Firth,[4] Einzig,[5] Polanyi,[6] Dalton,[7] Sahlins,[8] etc. In carrying it out an ideological difficulty immediately became apparent, which has not yet been entirely overcome. At first sight all the ethnographic material suggested that to understand it we would have to revive notions of political economics and see in primitive forms of competition and exchange 'archaic' forms of commercial competition and consider the gift as a kind of 'compound interest loan' and precious objects as types of currencies. Primitive transactions seen in the light of market-economy categories, seem to differ only in degree and not in kind from modern capitalist economies.[9] A close look however showed that primitive transactions do not easily fit into such readymade categories. It had to be admitted that the Trobriand islanders, far from confusing *kula* with normal trade distinguished it from barter, since they had another term for this (*Gimwali*).

It also had to be admitted that potlatch was unlike a loan since it is the lender who forces his rival to accept the gift, while with the loan it is the debtor who asks to borrow.[10] Above all the fact could not be ignored that precious objects, primitive 'currencies', were only rarely exchanged and hardly ever for land or labour;[11] also that their accumulation and circulation among individuals and groups did not lead to a general development of productive forces as is the case with the accumulation of capital in capitalist trading societies.[12]

Precious objects in primitive societies were not capital and rarely functioned within these societies as a form of currency, i.e., as a means of commercial exchange;[13] they were objects to show off, to give away or redistribute in order to create a social relationship (marriage, admission to a secret society, intertribal political alliances); they were objects for healing breaks in social relations (ancestral offerings, compensation for murders or other offences); for creating or symbolising a superior social position (potlatch deluxe objects accumulated and redistributed by important people, chiefs or kings). They served as a means *of social exchange*, of multiple and complex value in a distinct and separate sphere of circulation, within limits determined by the very structure of the social relations of production and power.

Nevertheless, we generally forget that all these precious objects, whether fabricated or obtained at the price of great labour or large payments, were *rare* products, which when bartered, possessed an *exchange value*.[14] In Malaïta, for example, currency armbands of white pearl came from the Kwaio who exported them to their neighbours. From the barrier reefs, one person could not collect, polish or pierce more than two armbands of pearls (at the most) per month. Dolphin teeth came from the Lau, fashioned by fishermen of remarkable skill who lived on small islands where agriculture was impracticable, and who exchanged these teeth for pigs and vegetable foods. The Yap millstones came from far distant islands and veritable sea expeditions were undertaken to extract them, hew them and bring them back.[15] Throughout the interior of Africa, Asia and New Guinea cowries circulated which came from distant shores, generally from India, and were obtained through the exchange of local, rare products.[16] Therefore when *entering or leaving* these societies, precious objects provisionally took the form of bartered commodities at fixed, or barely fluctuating prices. *Within* each society they usually ceased to circulate as commodities, and became objects to *give or distribute* in the social process of social life, kinship relations, relations of production and power, etc.

Therefore, if our analysis is correct, we must perforce conclude that *very often* the precious objects we encounter in primitive societies have a *dual nature*: they are both goods and non-goods, 'money' and gifts, according to whether they are bartered between groups or circulate within the group.

They function primarily as commodities if they have to be imported or produced for export. Subsequently they function as prestige objects, as objects of social exchange when circulated within a group through the mechanism of gifts and other forms of distribution. The same object, therefore *changes* its function; of the two functions, the second is the *dominant* one because it takes *root* and *meaning* within the requirements of *dominant structures* in primitive social organisation, kinship and power.[17]

In addition, it should be noted that a precious object does not simply function as a commodity when imported or exported between groups, but each time it is bartered between members of a group, when not given or distributed. It then circulates within this group as a commodity, even though it might circulate mostly as a non-commodity – as an object to give or an object of social exchange.

Finally, it should be made clear that when a precious object circulates as a commodity, this does not necessarily mean that it becomes 'money'. An additional condition is required for this: the possibility of exchanging it for *several* goods of various kinds. For example in Malaïta, a necklace of red pearls may be exchanged in return for pigs or tools of carved stone, or in return for food, raw or cooked, etc., and in this case it functions as money.

To sum up, more often than not, precious objects circulating between and within primitive societies were both objects of commercial exchange and objects of social exchange, goods for bartering and goods to exhibit or use as gifts, commodities which sometimes turned into money or symbols, visible signs of the history of individuals or groups receiving their innermost meaning from the social structures. They were, therefore, multifunctional objects whose functions did not merge even when superimposed or combined, objects which circulated always within strict limits, determined by the very structures of these primitive societies where labour and, more especially, land were never transformed into commodities obtainable by the exchange of other goods.

If this is correct, we can now understand why the analyses or statements made by economists or anthropologists about primitive currency are contradictory, or appear to be.[18]

There may be two basic reasons for these contradictions. When taken on the level of the facts themselves, the object described by the anthropologist has been perceived either functioning primarily as bartered merchandise[19] or functioning primarily as an object of adornment or as a gift; secondly, in the anthropologist's very way of thinking, the theoretical distinctions between commodities, money and objects of social exchange have not been clear and have made for confusion in the perception and analysis of the facts themselves.[20] Now, on the basis of these distinctions a very thorough rereading of the vast documentation which has accumulated on 'primitive money' becomes necessary and, indeed, possible.

We can also understand why most primitive peoples, right from first contacts, have shown that they understood the reasoning behind both gifts and bartering in the simple circulation of goods and why some of their precious objects have been called archaic forms of our money, even though it was rare for their money to be manipulated as capital invested for profit or accumulation.[21]

Finally, we can understand why, under certain circumstances, from Antiquity to the present day, these precious objects became ever more divested of their dominant characteristic as gift objects and came increasingly to be regarded as commercial objects,[22] retaining for a long time the 'traditional', or as is sometimes said, 'ethical'[23] aspect.

With these preliminary remarks we can now present the material collected in New Guinea on the fabrication and circulation of salt money among the Baruya.[24]

BARUYA SOCIETY

The Baruya[25] number about 1500 people spread over a dozen or so villages or hamlets in the subdistrict of Wonenara, which in June 1960, was the last region in the Eastern Highlands of New Guinea to come under Australian administration. Their language, material culture and social organisation all belong to an original ensemble of tribes now known under the name of 'Kukakuka', an offensive term used by some of their neighbours and made general since its adoption by the Australian government. Linguistically, the Kukakuka are not related to the Highland tribes or to the Melanesian languages of the coastal tribes of Papua or New Guinea.[26] Their number is estimated at about 50 000, the majority living in the northern part of a vast, extremely rough and hilly territory, stretching from the Vailala river in the West to the River Bulolo in the east and the River Watut in the North on the outskirts of Kerema on the Papuan coast. In Papua, some groups, under little administrative control, lead a 'nomadic' existence in a forestal region which is extremely difficult of access and protected from contacts because of its great distance from the patrol-posts of Menyamya, Kantiba and Kerema.

The Kukakuka are warlike tribes, mostly cannibal, whose raids sow terror amongst the neighbouring tribes and they live in a state of perpetual war.[27] Victims of the discovery of gold deposits on their eastern frontier in the Wau region, at the beginning of the century, they now make it difficult for gold-seekers to enter the country and put up a lively resistance to the Australian government's efforts to control and pacify them.[28]

The Baruya claim descent from the refugees of the Yoyué tribe living in the Menyamya region, who had to flee their original territory after a conflict which put them in opposition to other segments of their tribe, who on that occasion had become allies of their former enemies. The exodus took place, according to our calculations, about two centuries ago. The refugees settled in the Marawaka region, some three days' march to the north-west of Menyamya and gradually, through wars and matrimonial alliances, took possession of part of the territory of the local tribes, the Andjé and Usarumpia. At the beginning of the twentieth century they penetrated the neighbouring valley of Wonenara driving back the former inhabitants. Together with the Baruya, they constitute the frontier groups of Kukakuka to the west. Beyond them are the Awa, Taiora and Fore tribes, profoundly different in language and culture though similar in other ways to the tribes of the Eastern Highlands studied by Read, Watson, Langness and Salisbury.

The social organisation of the Baruya is that of an acephalous tribe composed of thirteen patrilineal clans, eight of which descend from the first refugees and seven from segments of the lineage of enemy or neighbouring tribes, with whom the Baruya once exchanged women and who chose to reside with their allies. Lineages are the basic social unity. Each village consists of from three to five lineage segments belonging to different clans. Individuals enjoy considerable freedom to choose their place of residence, even though patrilocal residence is preferred. A hierarchical division of the male population into four age-classes makes for a further break in the ensemble of clans and lineage descents, bringing together all the villages and unifying the society in ideological (the initiations' cycle) and military spheres.

Agriculture is the principal economic activity, along with pig-breeding and production of vegetable salt in considerable quantities. The villages are situated between 1600 and 2000 metres up in the high valleys of the Kratke Range, a mountainous chain which reaches 3720 metres in height. Vegetation is *rain-forest* type with large expanses of grassy savannah (*kunai*) resulting from slash-and-burn farming. Rain is abundant with seasonal variations quite marked. Hunting and gathering plays a minimum role with regard to food supplies but has great ceremonial significance. Until about 1940, the polished stone adze, the digging stick, the bamboo knife and bone chisel, constituted the main elements of the Baruya equipment. Before the arrival of the Whites, the steel axe and machete penetrated the region through intertribal commercial routes and rapidly took over from the neolithic equipment.

The staple food is sweet potatoes, cultivated in a relatively intensive way with periods of short fallow, mainly in the deforested zone. Cassava is much less important than the sweet potato as a food, but it is of prime importance in the ceremonial and social spheres. It is cultivated in the minor forest soils which are left fallow for twelve to twenty years. Drainage techniques, irrigation with bamboo pipelines and the bark of the screw-pine, lightly-banked terraces against the sloping levels to prevent surface soil erosion on the steepest inclines, are all evidence of a more complex type of farming than simple burning and superficial scratching out of the soil.

The lineage is the collective owner of the soil. Hunting and farming territories are shared by all the clans and lineages. Right of ownership is clearly fixed, but the use of the soil is extremely flexible. Ownership is founded, for each tribe as such, on rights of conquest and, for each lineage, on the work done by ancestors in clearing the forest. Work is based on a sexual division of labour and is done both collectively and individually.

SALT PRODUCTION

Technology

The diet of New Guinea natives is based chiefly on the consumption of tubers and, apart from a few communities with abundant resources of meat or fish, this entails a high sodium deficiency. Salt must be got by some means or other. On the coast, salt is obtained from sea water and is often exchanged with hinterland tribes. The state of the terrain, the distance and the constant war between tribes prevent sea-salt from reaching tribes living far inland. The latter, or at least some of them, produce their own salt either from salt mines or by extracting it from plants gathered or cultivated in the bush.[29]

The Kukakuka tribes all manufactured salt, but nowhere did it reach the amplitude and degree of specialisation as among the Baruya. They made their salt from the ashes of the *Coix gigantea* Koenig ex Rob, a plant[30] which originated in south-east Asia; as seedlings it is planted in areas naturally or artifically irrigated (by means of canals or ditches).[31] The cultivated areas vary from 2 to 30 acres divided into small plots, boundaries being marked off by different varieties of flowers or shrubs.

This salt plant is cut each year during the dry period and then springs up again. It is left to dry for a week or two; it is then mounted on a stake compiled of special kinds of wood and burnt for a day or two. The heap of ashes is protected under a thatched roof and remains there for several months. A filter is then constructed, composed of a row of gourds, blocked at the bottom by a wad of *Triumfetta nigricans*, which retains all impurities. The gourds are filled with the ashes (600 to 800 grams) and fresh water is slowly poured over them. The water, in passing, becomes saturated with the mineral elements and flows into a gutter made of leaves which discharges the water into long bamboo canes, which are subsequently transported to the place where the salt is manufactured. From time to time the water flowing from the gourd is tasted and when there is no longer any salty flavour, the gourd is emptied and refilled with new ashes.

The salt-making equipment is the property of a specialist. It includes an oven, composed of a tunnel 3.50 metres in length, 30 cm high and 30 cm wide. The walls are made from fire-proof, flat stones, cemented with the hardened deposit of the salt plant ashes. At the top of the oven a series of 12 to 15 moulds have been hollowed out, each 80 cm long and 12 cm wide in the middle. Each mould contains a bucket of impervious banana leaves and the top is kept open under pressure of a framework of light bamboo-cane. The salty water is poured into the buckets when the oven reaches a suitable temperature. This is maintained at a constant heat during the five days and nights which it takes for the evaporation and crystallisation of the salt solution.

The specialist supervises the oven temperature to ensure that the solution in the buckets does not boil (the temperature is kept between 55 and 65° C). With a special spatula, he stirs the water surface to prevent any skin formation. He removes any impurities which form or fall into the buckets. Finally and what is more important, he is the master of salt magic. At the end of five to six days evaporation is complete and the crystallised salt appears as very hard bars, 60 to 72 cm long and 10 to 13 cm wide. The bars are then carefully lifted out and the sides scraped to present a perfectly regular shape. A group of men wrap them in dried banana leaves and long narrow strips of wettened bark, carefully tied with overcast stitch, which harden as they dry out. The packing affords adequate protection against humidity and makes for easy transport without danger of breakage. The bars are stocked in the huts on a support above the hearth.

15 bars on average represent 25 to 30 kg of salt. The oblong shape of the oven means that the bars at the two side ends are shorter than those in the centre. The Baruya classify the bars into three categories according to size, giving them different names and allocating them different rates of exchange. Out of 15 bars, four or five are small, four or five medium-sized, six are large.

The social division of labour

The process of salt production, therefore, is divided into two phases separated by quite a long period. The first consists in gathering, incinerating the salt plants and building a cover to protect the ashes from bad weather. The second consists, strictly speaking, in the manufacture of the salt, namely, the filtering, the evaporation and the packaging. Both men and women participate in the work of the first phase and according to the importance of the task, the work is performed individually or collectively. On the other hand, the manufacture of salt is essentially man's work, surrounded by independent rituals and sexual prohibitions which ward off any risk of female pollution. It also brings in a specialist for the delicate operations of evaporation and crystallisation. These specialists are few in number, two to five for each village out of a population averaging 30 adult males. Their recognition as such is due to their magical powers and technical know-how. If their descendants also manifest a disposition and the ability for it, they transmit their secrets to them.

In Table 1 we have drawn up the basic data showing the duration of each operation and the kinds of work, individual or collective, male and/or female which each require. We then calculated, from the duration of the operations, the amount of social work necessary for the production of fifteen bars of salt. For this we abstracted the difference between male and female labour, which we felt justified in doing since, in the tasks of cutting, collecting, transport, stacking of the salt-plant stalks (in all of which they participated), the women showed practically the same efficiency as the men. A more delicate problem is that of the conversion into days of straightforward work, the supervision work of the specialist (discontinuous supervision over a period of five days and five nights). We have reduced this specialist work to three days of simple continuous work.

Table 1 reveals that work of any complexity is essentially male, which is also the case in the construction of houses, the digging of canals for irrigation, the installation of pipelines, the manufacture of weapons, etc. It can also be seen that collective work prevails slightly over individual work and that the number of individuals working collectively is quite few, varying from two to six. Taken as a whole the manufacture of salt requires the participation of eight to ten men and eight to ten women, in other words, twenty-one people.

What was the effect of the introduction of steel equipment to replace the traditional methods of production based on neolithic equipment? Without going into details, let it be noted that the technological changes have only diminished the time spent on cutting the canes and the wood for burning. Before 1940, the salt plants were cut with long knives of tapered bamboo cane and the wood for burning with the stone adze. It can be estimated that 50 per cent more time was needed to cut the plant, i.e., three days instead of two. The whole process must have required approximately twenty-seven days instead of twenty-one, which corresponds to 30 per cent supplementary labour.

In comparison, agricultural work, tree-felling, clearing the undergrowth, the construction of fences round gardens to protect them from domestic or wild pigs, the digging of drainage and irrigation ditches, have undergone much more significant changes. In the social sphere, the increase in productivity of individual work has diminished the social significance of collective labour by making cooperation in work less necessary. Cooperation is based on the mutual aid certain individuals owe to the salt owner through kinship ties, or which they provide as friends or neighbours on the understanding that he will do the same for them on another occasion.

Table 1

	Process of production								
	Production of raw material						Salt manufacture		
	(1)	(2)	(3)	(4)	(5)	(6)	(7)	(8)	(9)
Nature and order of operations	Cutting and laying-out the canes	Cutting and transporting the wood for burning on the pile and in the oven	Making the pile	Collecting and stacking up the dry canes	Supervising incineration	Making a shelter for the ashes	Filling the bamboos with fresh water for filtering and transporting to workshop	Supervising evaporation	Packaging the bars
Transformation of product	*Coix gigantea* Koenig				Ashes		Solution	Crystallised salt	
Forms of work	Collective – women (2)	Individual – Male		Collective – male and female (10 people)	Individual – male		Individual – male		Collective – male
Time taken for each operation	2 days	2 days	1/2 day	1/2 day	1 night	1 day	2 days	5 days and nights	1½ hours per bar
Quantity of social labour	2×2 = 4 days	2 days	1/2 day	1/2×10 = 5 days	1/2 day	1 day	2 days	3 days	22 hours = 3 days
	Total quantity of social labour to produce 15 bars of salt = 21 days						Quantity of social labour per bar = 1¼ days		

Table 2

Distribution of the quantity of social labour = 21 days	
(a) According to the sexual division of labour	
Male 13 (61%)	Female 8 (39%)
(b) According to type of work	
Individual 9 (42%)	Collective 12 (58%)
Specialised 3 (14%)	Non-specialised† 19 (86%)
If we take operations (3, 5, 7, 8, 9) of Table 1 as more complex forms of work than operations (1, 2, 4, 6) we get:	
Simple 9 (42%)	Complex 12 (58%)

† By non-specialised work we mean work which may be undertaken by any worker within the limits of the sexual division of labour.

Salt manufacture terminates with a collective meal (*tsàmouné*), generally offered by the beneficiary of this mutual aid. Sweet potatoes and cassava are served in abundance and eaten with bits of salt collected from the moulds or scraped from the bars during the process of smoothing the edges before packing them. Juicy sugar-canes complete this 'deluxe' meal, and the guests, whether they have helped or not in the salt manufacture, will linger on for a long time talking and discussing, their discourse only barely interrupted to masticate betel or to inhale enormous puffs of green tobacco from their long bamboo pipes.

SALT TRADE AND DISTRIBUTION

Salt circulation among the Baruya assumes two forms: redistribution and commercial exchange.[32]

Redistribution

Salt lands. All lands adapted to salt culture (flat and well-irrigated zones) were appropriated by different lineages during the conquest of the Marawaka and, later, Wonenara valleys. The desire to seize salt lands is one of the acknowledged reasons for certain wars with the Andjé and the Usarumpia, neighbours of the Baruya. In theory, all lineages have salt lands; in practice this does not work for a large number of their segments. The reason for this is the history of the group itself, its expansion toward the north-west at the beginning of the twentieth century and the invasion of the Wonenara valley. The first occupants of this valley divided and reclaimed lands suitable for salt production and because of the distance, ceased working on those they possessed at Marawaka. These continued to be worked by members of their lineage who had not emigrated, by allies or simply by friends.

Then, about 1940, following the Marawaka valley invasion by enemy groups from the east and south-east, a small band of refugees went to join the Wonenara valley inhabitants. A large number of them no longer wished to return to Marawaka after the enemies had been forced to cede their conquered territory. They settled in the Yanyi and Wiaveu villages, but unlike the colonists who had arrived at the beginning of the century, they came too late to find new salt lands in the vicinity, and they lived too far away from the old ones to make working on them feasible.

In the Wonenara valley therefore there is an unequal distribution of salt lands between the different segments of lineages which is advantageous to the first colonists. However, inequality in the owning of salt lands does not lead to any inequality in the redistribution of the salt itself and this can be explained in two ways: firstly, the proprietors frequently allow their in-laws, their maternal relatives or friends the right to use their lands (i.e., to cut and burn the canes). Sometimes even, they authorise permanent use of a plot by a relation or friend. Secondly, those who cut the salt (whether owner or user) are obliged to redistribute a part of their product.

Redistribution of the product. Salt is redistributed by the owner among his in-laws (brothers- and sons-in laws), his cross-cousins, mainly those on the maternal side, sometimes a few friends (particularly his co-initiates). Out of fifteen, five or six bars will be redistributed. The remainder are destined for family needs and for himself, and sometimes, if they are still living, for his father and mother. The bars are kept above the hearth and will be produced on various ceremonial occasions (approximately half a bar per year), or used as a form of exchange.

Salt exchange

Exchange for services. Out of those that remain, the salt owner must again deduct one or two bars for the salt specialist. Occasionally he will give one or two bars to a sorcerer, if he has cured a member of his family or himself. Finally and even more infrequently, if he himself is not able to go to neighbouring tribes to trade his salt and should he have need of some important article (a steel axe), he will entrust a friend to go and barter in his place giving him one salt bar for his trouble.

Exchange for goods. (1) Bartering within the group. In certain cases, bartering is practised among the Baruya. When a man has a son, or younger brother, who has to go through the initiation rites which will make him a man,

Table 3

	Objects and their use		Rate of exchange	Trading partners
Means of production	Split stones	large	1–2 LB*	Tchavalié, Kokwayé,
	Adzes	medium		Yopénié, Yoyué,
		small	1 MB*	Youndouyé
			⅓, ¼, ⅕, ⅙ of a bar according to length of stone	
	Steel axes		From 1–4 LB, on average 2 or 3	Nangravanié, Tchaégananié, Nondanié, Watchakè, Yoyué
	Machetes		1 LB	Yoyué
Weapons	Round pierced stone for stonecrushing		1 MB	Yoyué
	Bow			
	Barbed arrows (20–30)		½ LB	Youndouyé
Luxury goods	*Ceremonial attire*			
	(1) Necklace of pigs' teeth		½ LB	Youndouyé, Wantékia, Yopénié
	(2) Shells			
	(*a*) gamshell (polished mother-of-pearl)		3 LB or 1 cowrie bracelet 3–4 metres long	Tchavalié, Kokwayé Yopénié, Yoyué
	(*b*) cowries		1 SB*	Youndouyé, Nangravanié,
	narinna (young girls)			Tchaégananié, Yoyué, Nondanié
	small cowries		6–7 necklaces = 1 LB	Youndouyé, Yoyué, Tchavalié
	tambu		1 set = 1 LB	Tchavalié, Kokwayé, Yopénié, Yoyué
	(*c*) ampwakameunié		1 cowrie bracelet 3–4 metres long	Kokwayé
	(*d*) ndjammeunié		1 set = 1 LB	Kokwayé
	(3) Feathers			
	(*a*) aralla		1 set = ¼ LB	Demboulié, Wantékia,
	(*b*) niutniuvé		1 set = ½ LB	Tsimbari

Table 3 continued

	(*c*) kalavé	1 wing = ½ LB	Youndouyé, Tsimbari, Andjé, Usarumpia, Boulakia, Tchavalié, Kokwayé, Yopénie, Wantékia
	(*d*) bané	1 wing = ½ LB	Wantékia, Tsimbari, Boulakia, Watchaké
	(*e*) worié	10 feathers = ½ LB	Youndouyé, Wantékia, Tsimbari, Andjé, Usarumpia, Boulakia
	(*f*) willa	10 feathers = ½ LB	Yopénié
	(4) Pearls		
	pearl seeds	1 article = 1 LB	Kokwayé, Yoyué
	European	1 article = 1 LB	Andjé
	Magical charms		
	nuts (niaka) bark of	Bits of salt	Yoyué, Tchavalié
	cinnamon tree	Bits of salt	Tsimbari, Wantékia, Boulakia
	Pigs		
	male	2–3 LB	} Yoyué
	female	4–6 LB	
	Dogs		
	male	1 MB	} Tchavalié, Yoyué, Yopénié
	female	1 LB+1 MB	
Current consumption goods	Bark cloths	1 LB = 5 large cloaks 5 loin cloths with Wantékia, Boulakia 1 LB = 6 large cloaks with Youndouyé	Wantékia, Demboulié, Tchavalié, Kokwayé, Yopénié, Boulakia
	Salt from other groups	1 large bark cloak	Kokwayé, Tchavalié
	Small knives	⅙ LB	Watchakès, Yoyué
Services	Salt specialist	2 LB	} Baruya
	Friend 'commercial traveller'	1 LB	
	Sorcerer	1–2 LB	

* LB = large bar, MB = medium bar, SB = small bar.

he must provide him with a cross-belt of pigs' teeth, an emblem of his new status. If he himself does not own a cross-belt, he will offer pieces of salt to the pig killers in exchange for the jaw bones. Often, he also gets a piece of the meat. He makes the cross-belt himself. In fact, the Baruya prefer to get hold of small necklaces of pigs' teeth from their neighbours and mount these on the cross-belt. In other instances, extremely rare, a man may offer salt to a friend in exchange for the stone in a ceremonial mace.

In reality, exchanges inside the group are of little importance, since the circulation of goods is primarily regulated by the play of reciprocal loans between relations or between neighbours and friends.

(2) Exchanges with foreigners. Salt was the object of very active exchanges between the Baruya and neighbouring tribes, some of whom lived over a four days' march away. Except for the Youndouyé, whose language and customs are different and with whom the Baruya maintained a constant state of trade and peace, all the Baruya neighbours were alternatively their allies or their enemies.

The exchanges related to a range of products which we have classed in four categories.

(*a*) Production resources: split stones for the fabrication of adzes (small picks) and, since 1945, steel axes, machetes,

(*b*) Weapons: bows, arrows, stone bludgeons,

(*c*) Luxury goods: ceremonial adornments made from feathers, shells, pearls, magic charms, pigs,

(*d*) Current goods for consumption: bark wrappers, lime for chewing betel.

Salt is also exchanged for dogs, which may be classed in the category 'weapons', because they are principally used for chasing marsupials, who figure obligatorily in the most important ritual acts. Rates of exchange vary according to the products exchanged. A large piece of split stone is worth one or two salt bars, a male pig from two to three, a female from three to six, a steel axe from three to six, a feather headdress only one. Rates differ according to tribes, but once a rate is established with a particular tribe, it tends to remain the same (See Table 3).

The trading routes were opened by daring individuals whose names pass down to posterity. They ran the risks (being killed or eaten) involved in making first contacts with a neighbouring tribe, managed to establish friendly relations with certain members of the group and to effect a form of trade-and-protection pact with them. Normally this pact carries over from generation to generation and a man inherits the trading partners of his father. Each partner undertakes to house, feed and protect his guest and, if unable to provide it himself, will do his best to find the merchandise the other desires from within his own group. Transactions between his partner and possible purchasers are carried out inside, or at the door of, his house. This space, both geographical and social, restricted to the confines surrounding the dwelling of a segment of the lineage, and where the stranger is assured in advance of being able to meet possible purchasers with complete safety, functions therefore like a 'miniature market', each time a seller is present. This type of market (space and transaction) which is somewhat 'sporadic', is distinct from the periodical or permanent type of market habitually described by anthropologists and economists (See Table 4).

Table 4

Distance (in days on foot)	Names of trading partners	Distance (in km)
½	Youwarrounatché (N.), Youndouyé (N.W.) Andjé (S.), Usarumpia (S.W.)	10–15
1	Tchavalié (E.), Wantékia (W.), Nangravanié (N.)	15–20
2	Nondanié (N.), Watchakès (N.E.), Boulakia (S.W.), Yopénié (S.E.)	20–35
3	Kokwayé (S.), Yoyué (S.)	35–50
3+	Wéiaganatché (E.), etc.	50+

However, even when normalised and peaceful, exchanges continue to be dangerous. If the visitor has shown himself to be too hasty during the bargaining, he risks becoming the victim of acts of witchcraft directed against him by the discontented purchaser or by another witch whom the purchaser has engaged to avenge him. Often, for this reason, the visitor carefully covers his stomach and chest with special bluish-coloured clay, which diverts poisons or sickness against him.

Thus, trade signifies peace, even if it is more often an armed peace. From this aspect, therefore, the network of exchanges at any given period expresses the political relations between tribes and simultaneously reveals the complementarity of their economies. Therefore, apart from a description of mechanisms, microeconomic exchanges which link small groups of partners in pairs, it is essential to make an analysis of the overall mechanism of Baruya exchanges; this makes them appear to be a decisive link in a vast intertribal and interregional system of exchanges (See Table 5).

Before the introduction of steel tools, the Baruya did not have at their disposal stone-beds or quarries where the stone was of the required hardness or quality to fabricate their tools of production or their maces. They, therefore, had to import them and to do this they had to possess or produce an

Table 5

Friends	Friends and/or enemies	Neutral
Youndouyé* Yoyué†	(1) All immediate neighbours: Usarumpia, Andjé, Wantékia, Youwarrounatché, Goutlutché, Tchavalié	Nangravanié Nondanié Boulakia Tsimbari
	(2) Distant groups: Watchakès, Yopénié, Kokwayé	Wéiaganatché

* Legend has it that between the ancestors of this group and the Baruya there was a trade and peace contract.
† They descend from Baruya ancestors.

exportable resource. There is little need to emphasise that, seen in this light, intertribal exchange was not based on the economic decisions of any individual, but was a practical necessity both anonymous and collective. The stones came from the north-west and south-west of the Okapa region (tribes of the interior) and the south-east along the route leading to the Yoyué in the Menyamya region.

Moreover, the Baruya live at a high altitude, 2000 metres up, and it is too cold to grow the tree varieties used in making their bark cloaks (*ficus*). In addition, and for the same reason, their forests are lacking in the kinds of birds whose iridescent feathers serve as ceremonial adornments (different varieties of birds-of-paradise: *Paradisaea raggianna, Paradisaea Rudolfi, Paradisaea minor*, etc., or the cassowary, *Casuarius unappendiculatus*).[33] On the other hand, trees and birds are plentiful in the lower valleys, to the west and south-west, leading towards the marshlands of the Papuan Gulf or, in the north-east, over the slopes descending to the River Markham.

Thus, to procure for themselves the means of production indispensable to their agriculture, to protect themselves from the cold, and to ensure that, in the functioning of their social life, there are present the material resources of its symbolic expression, the Baruya had to find, in their environment, a precious resource to exploit and exchange. This resource was found in the very morphology of their habitat, in the vast flat areas of the valley beds and the alluvial banks descending in tiers to the River Wonenara. The Baruya, it seems, immediately recognised which sections they had to draw off for irrigable surfaces and decided to exploit (and conquer) them systematically. One person confided to us that the Baruya clans of the Yoyué tribe, after taking refuge with the Marawaka, were visited by representatives of brother tribes who had stayed in the Menyamya district after the war against Tépadéra. The visitors had come to look for the refugees in order to resettle them on their territory. When they saw the Marawaka salt lands, they counselled the Baruya against returning and strongly encouraged them to remain where they were and produce salt. And that is what happened. Not only did the Baruya *plant* huge areas with salt, creating a kind of primitive commercial agriculture, but they *improved on* the production techniques known to most Kukakuka groups and invented the ovens with moulds capable of producing twelve to fifteen bars at a time and which constituted permanent workshops under the control of specialists. Thus, faced with the objective necessity of trading in order to live, the Baruya responded by showing intelligent utilisation of their environment and with technological and social invention. In so far as this invention revolved around trade, one can say that they 'enhanced' the value of their material resources.

Since the salt trade is destined to satisfy the needs of a population which today numbers about 1500 people, we may roughly calculate the volume of these exchanges. Suppose each member of the society requires one bark cloak per year and if we assume the average rate of exchange to be 1 bar for 6 cloaks, the group must annually produce 250 bars of salt to protect themselves from the cold. If we take 12 bars of salt as the average oven batch then at least 21 people would have to make salt in order to distribute 250 bars and knowing the average rate of yield for a hectare of salt planted, it is possible to calculate the area which must be cultivated to afford protection from the cold.

On the other hand, there must be 1500 cloaks available for Baruya in neighbouring tribes. As, according to our calculations, a tree aged six to ten years provides the raw material for 3 cloaks, these tribes must use up 500 of their trees each year to satisfy the Baruya demands (therefore they would plant them some years in advance). We shall see later how much work this exchange of 'salt–bark cloaks' represents for the groups concerned. But, to be complete, a total analysis of a system of exchange must be historical.

About 1920, different varieties of cowries and glass beads appeared among the populations in the north and south, to such an extent that they came under the control of the Australian government who used these articles instead of money. Steel axes and machetes arrived in 1940.

From all the information we received, it would seem that from 1920 to 1960, in order to procure pearls, shells, steel tools, the Baruya, who were not yet under White control, planted, produced and exchanged more salt than ever before. During this time, they went still farther afield to trade and came in contact with groups (five or six) who up till then were unknown to them and spoke different languages. Therefore, with *no outside pressure*, the Baruya had changed their production technique by sustituting the steel axe for the stone adze; they had enlarged the scope of their luxury objects (pearls, shells) and, at the same time, they had had to intensify their salt production and increase their commercial contacts. The present period is witnessing a rapid disintegration of their system of exchange, even though the Baruya salt, consumed principally during ceremonies, is not directly in competition with European salt, which can be bought in the Lutheran Mission shop. Construction works at the Wonenara landing-strip and *patrol-post* were paid in cowries, axes, machetes. Work on the plantations brought in ready cash which immediately found its way to a shop opened by a Kainantu commercial company and, later (1967) to the Lutheran Mission shop. Exchanging salt for bark cloaks remains the last solid remnant of the system, but already the Baruya partners are demanding to be paid in shillings. Finally, the ceremonial adornments and magic charms, which formed a small part in the business of exchange, are less and less required, since the government stopped wars, and the missions have morally discredited initiation rites.

By 1967, it was already too late to discover the traces of stone-axe exchange or to resuscitate the spectre of neolithic economy. Tomorrow the Baruya salt will be a useless accessory stowed away for ever in the museum of primitive cultures.

SOME THEORETICAL ANALYSES

Taking our ethnographical analysis as a basis, we may attempt the reply to three inevitable questions. (1) Is Baruya salt a primitive form of 'money'? (2) What is the basis for the exchange value of this money? (3) If there is both money and exchange, is there also profit?

Is Baruya salt a primitive form of 'money'?

When salt production first started, there was, as we have seen, an objective necessity for the Baruya to export in order to import the necessary means of production for their agriculture; the means to protect themselves from the cold (which constitutes a serious problem at an altitude between 1500 and 2300 metres); the means to satisfy their need for symbolic expression in social relations (ceremonial adornments) and to ensure their control over supernatural forces (magic charms). By reason of its variety of basic functions (subsistence, ideology), the exchange does not constitute a marginal activity, an occasional supplement of the functioning of Baruya society, but a strategic element of its structure. To go further, we might say that this society cannot subsist without exchange. We have arrived, therefore, at the antipodes of primitive, so-called 'subsistence' economies.[34] In the historical and archaeological sense, Baruya society constitutes an important example in that it throws light on the economies of neolithic societies, many of whom had to import raw material to make their tools and equipment. Theoretically speaking, its example brings to light all the difficulties in the concept of surplus in the way that economists of classic Marxist or Keynesian schools often deal with it. It was not after being sure of their subsistence that the Baruya turned to exchange and selling off their surplus. In fact, salt for them was a product primarily destined for exchange, and therefore a commodity.

This merchandise has an exchange value primarily because it has a use value: it is consumable.[35] Certainly, what salt is consumed by the Baruya themselves is minimal; it is not because salt is physically scarce, but because it is exclusively an object of ritual consumption. Therefore, salt is a commodity whose use value is that of a highly-prized ritual object by its ideological and social significance as much as by its biological usefulness, its gastronomic flavour and the difficulties in production. Salt is therefore a 'price' commodity, a luxury, which one usually does without, but which must make its appearance every time daily life gives way to ceremonial activity. Moreover, though salt is not physically scarce among the Baruya, it is among all groups who do not manufacture it and who also reserve it for ceremonial occasions and requirements.

Salt is a price commodity, but is it 'money'?

In order for a commodity to function as 'money', it must be able to be exchanged for a *whole lot* of other goods, it must function as a *general* equivalent for the lot. Let us go back to Table 3 and look at the example showing the circulation of a cross-belt made from pigs' teeth. It cannot be exchanged for a stone axe or a pig, dead or alive. It could be exchanged for feathers, but the possibilities for its conversion to another product stop there. Its circulation therefore involves a simple swop and if it is a commodity, it is not money. Stone axes and pigs could, virtually, be converted into any other commodity, but this is not the case, perhaps because they are too scarce.[36] On the other hand, only salt may run the whole gamut of possible conversions. Therefore it functions as money.

Because bird-of-paradise feathers, stone axes and even the services of a witch may be converted into salt, they become comparable to a certain extent. Salt in the form of bars, big and small, capable of being divided into pieces, offers a convenient unit of measurement for initiating business relationships. Its extremely careful packaging means it may be easily transported and will last for years. Salt has, therefore, a general equivalence, and is an inevitable intermediary for the acquisition of all goods which are socially available or necessary. A general equivalence does not imply a universal equivalence, since common consumption goods, sweet potatoes, cassava, etc., land and labour are not commodities and stand outside the sphere of 'salt money' exchange. This general equivalence does not only apply to the Baruya, but also their neighbours, the Youndouyé, for example, who come first to exchange their bark cloaks for Baruya salt before trading the latter for stone axes with the Awa and Tairora.

Baruya salt is therefore a primitive form of money and, since it is 'primitive', this money offers us an exceptional opportunity to probe the mysteries of the theory of value.

Baruya 'salt money' and the basis for its exchange value: labour or scarcity?

If you ask a Baruya his reasons for exchanging 1 salt bar for 5 or 6 bark cloaks, instead of 1, 2 or 18, you generally get a reply in the form of two answers, neither of which excludes the other. First he will emphasise that he doesn't trade for himself alone, but also for his wife or wives, his children, his brother's children, etc. In this way he is referring to the importance of collective needs. On other occasions, on the contrary, he refers explicitly to the long and arduous work entailed in the production of salt. According to our observations, in a bargaining situation, the former type of argument is generally employed first, aimed at appealing to his partner's sense of compassion: 'My children have nothing to wear . . ., etc'., and, later, when the other remains impassive, he will bring work into the picture. A Baruya once told us: 'When we bargain, work is invoked only in the last resort. Work belongs to the past, it has almost been forgotten. We only bring it up when the other man goes too far.'

The balance of exchanges is therefore primarily regulated by the volume of social needs. In any one exchange, bargaining determines a position of equilibrium between supply and demand. If it is thought that the visitor has laid down an insufficient number of cloaks before a bar of salt, or that the cloaks are of poor quality, then the salt will not be offered to him. The latter will then add one or two more cloaks and the salt bar will be handed over. If one or the other asks too much, the transaction will be cut short. Nevertheless, bargaining or haggling is rare and generally each partner knows what he *must* give in order to receive. The two act as if there were a 'normal' rate, a 'correct price' for the goods exchanged and this rate is known by the tribe and all its members. However, it is worth noting that rates are not the same for all tribes. The Wantékia, for a bar of salt, give five large cloaks and five bark loin-cloths (all of which corresponds to 7 cloaks), that is to say a rate slightly higher than the Youndouyé give (5 or 6). In this connection innumerable problems present themselves which we can only touch on. For the Baruya, though their trade with other tribes was of vital importance, it was at the same time constantly threatened and interrupted by fluctuation in their political relations, alternately peaceful and warlike. For this reason they did not solely trade with groups who offered them the 'best prices'. Moreover, those tribes who offered the best prices frequently had little to exchange, except the Yoyué with whom the Baruya would constantly speak of their common origin, their blood ties (which rule out pettiness). Finally, another reason why some groups would trade their products for low rates with the Baruya was their infrequent contact with them, their ignorance of the rates which other groups had settled with the Baruya and their lack of knowledge concerning the terms of salt production. For example, when the Baruya made contact with the Watchakès for the purpose of obtaining stone axes, they offered them one bar of salt for one axe and this rate was accepted until, one day, a Baruya, who had not taken advice from those who had been before and who was terrified by the cannibal Watchakès, threw three bars of salt on the ground and fled with the axe proferred him. He had applied the rate which the Baruya used for the Yoyué. After this the Watchakès refused to exchange for less than three bars of salt and the guilty one was copiously reviled for his cowardice and stupidity.

This is a very important example, because it shows exactly under what circumstances a 'normal' rate is established. It is fixed when regular and important exchanges exist between neighbouring, yet foreign, groups, who do not know the circumstances of production or the efforts required by their partners to procure the merchandise. It is not perhaps by chance, that the Baruya describe those groups with whom they trade the most – the Youndouyé, Tchavalié, the Kokwayé – as being 'hard, miserly'.

However, once fixed, what do the objectivised social conditions for forming a normal rate of exchange consist of? Is it the relationship between two equivalent quantities of work output, as certain economists recalling Marx, even Ricardo, never cease to hope?

In order to explore this problem, we shall take a trading example of the present day which is both the most regular and the most important – salt traded for bark cloaks between the Baruya and a tribe with whom they are tied by a pact of 'eternal friendship', the Kénasé (whom the Baruya call Youndouyé and the Australian administration, Asana). According to our calculations, making a bark cloak requires five hours of intensive labour which can be broken down into three distinct operations (See Table 6).

Every man and woman knows how to make the bark cloaks. There is no specialisation in the work beyond the simple sexual division of labour. The most delicate work (thinning the bark without making holes in it), and the hardest (the stone-beater weighs between 800 and 1000 grams) is done by the women. A woman can beat out a loin cloth or a cloak in one day, but this represents eight hours of intensive and continuous labour.

Table 6

Nature and order of operations	The process of production (1) Cutting and removing the bark from the tree	(2) Scraping the bark inside and out with a bamboo knife	(3) Beating the bark with a stone to make it supple
Form of Labour	Individual male	Individual male	Individual female
Hours of work	½	1½	3

If we analyse, in terms of labour, the exchange of 1 average bar of Baruya salt, which equals 6 Youndouyé bark cloaks, we get:

1½ days ⟷ 4 days of work (5 hours×6)

The *normal* rate of exchange is therefore an *unequal* rate since the Baruya receive almost three times more than they give. The normal exchange is not an equivalent exchange.

Leaving aside the substitution of steel knives for bamboo, which has practically no effect on productivity, the production process of bark cloaks has remained entirely traditional. If we take two days as being the amount of time required for producing a Baruya bar of salt, before the introduction of steel tools, the exchange still remains unequal:

2 days ⟷ 4 days

The Baruya must know this, because they say that they 'gain', and their salt, agreed unanimously by their trading partners, is considered dear. From this, the last question we must ask if we are to throw light on the fundamentals of salt value is as follows:

Why is it that the Baruya and Youndouyé, knowing each other as they do and having lived always at peace with one another, consider this unequal rate as normal? (Unequal to our mind and in terms of the exchange of social labour.)

We suggest the following answer, which tallies with what we have been told: salt is dear because it is a 'luxury' product and its production requires a knowledge of technique and magic which other neighbouring tribes do not possess. What the Baruya ask for and what their partners normally agree to pay for, is the *monopoly of a double rarity*–product and know-how. By the same logic the Baruya were paying a lot for certain things like stone axes, *gamshells*, which were precious to them. The exchange was established on a level which expresses both the need and the labour involved (or the effort to procure a resource), but labour seems to play a secondary role; this could only be defined as a kind of minimum below which the rate of exchange must not descend, while the need, the rarity of the product, could be defined at the maximum limit attainable.[37]

'Primitive', therefore, does not mean 'simple'. Primitive reality not only contains the seeds of some future, therefore complex, conditions, but may also present 'developed' forms of social practice, the *analogy* for which may be found in other moments of historical evolution. This conclusion will be reinforced once we have analysed two other cases of Baruya salt exchange.

In the Menyamya district, the Baruya obtain certain nuts (*niaka*), which, used with cinnamon sticks, possess the magical power of attracting 'crowds' of possums on roads used by hunters. These nuts are also sucked, during ceremonies, by young married men who have just had their first child, in order to purify their mouths and bodies against the dangerous pollutions which result from sexual relations with their wives. These nuts are exchanged in the Menyamya district for pieces of salt. Probably they come from south of Menyamya, from Papua, where they are collected by local tribes. Here, we have an example of a thing which has 'social utility', which is a commodity, and therefore has a relatively high price corresponding to the amount of work involved in collecting nuts and transporting them in small quantities.

We shall conclude with another 'complex' example. If a man wishes to buy a young sow from the Yoyué, he will need at least four large (Tchameunié) bars of salt. Very often, he lacks the required number and will borrow a couple or so from a brother or brother-in-law. Later, when the sow has given birth, he gives in return one piglet for each bar of salt borrowed. If this is translated into salt money, he will have borrowed one bar of salt and returned the equivalent of two or three bars of salt, if the young pig is male, and four or five if female. This corresponds to an 'interest rate' of 100 to 400 per cent. However, this is a rare case and it is more important to note that no one, to our knowledge, *accumulates* salt *in order to lend it*. This example brings us to our last question: Is the Baruya salt exchange governed by profit seeking?

Exchange. Money and profit

The constituents for an answer are already there; they merely have to be put together. We have seen that in the Wonenara valley there exists, in favour of the first colonists, an unequal distribution of salt lands among the different lineage segments. This situation does not mean unequal distribution of the salt itself, since the owners allow their families, relations or friends the right to use temporarily or permanently their salt lands, and more especially since every person who cuts salt is obliged to redistribute part of his takings. A widow, an old man, an orphan will receive salt and necessary goods, bark cloaks, knives, etc. The 'interest rate' example, when salt bars are borrowed in order to buy a pig, reveals a fact which betrays the essence of the exchange process: no one accumulates salt for the purpose of lending out or making profit. There is certainly a material advantage and moral prestige to be had from lending, but no profit is sought to the detriment of the debtor. The underlying principle and aim of exchange lies in the satisfaction of social needs, consumption and not profit-seeking. Political authority and social prestige in a clan, lineage or an individual resides less in land wealth or salt than in ritual or war-like functions, the number of wives or children. Baruya society recognises a certain hierarchy of clans and individuals, but nothing resembling the 'big-man' of the Western Highlands societies, where a vast network of men and merchandise are manipulated and, of course, there is nothing which evokes the noble Trobriand lineages or the Polynesian aristocracies.[38]

Is it the same in the relations between the Baruya and their commercial partners, and does the profit which they draw from certain unequal exchanges signify exploitation of one group by another?

The answer seems negative to us for two reasons. The inequality, as we have seen, lies in the unequal exchange of work.[39] Now, with the Baruya, as with most primitive societies, *labour is not a scarce resource.* Productive activities occupy, at least for men, only a part of the time available (we estimate a third of their time is devoted to productive activities). What counts in group exchanges is the reciprocal satisfaction of their needs and not a well-kept balance of their labour expenditure. For this reason, the inequality of exchange expresses the comparative social utility of exchanged products, their *unequal importance in the scale of social needs and the diverse monopolist positions of exchange groups.* What counts is that there is *enough* to satisfy their needs and, recalling the words of one of them: 'If we receive enough, then work belongs to the past, it is forgotten.'

There is therefore *inequality without the exploitation* of man by man. Baruya salt exchange belongs to the sphere of the *simple* circulation of commodities. It constitutes *a case of simple market economy, welded to a non-market economy,* based on the individual and collective works of direct producers redistributing their products by way of kinship channels and neighbourly intercourse.

CONCLUSION

Our analysis of Baruya 'salt money' illustrates the previous theoretical comments. Salt, to the Baruya, is:

(1) A precious object, of a particular kind, because it enters, along with pigs, into the category of things 'good to eat, yet scarce and essential', i.e., meat and salt.

(2) A precious object, because it is consumed exclusively during vital moments of social life: birth, initiation, marriage, i.e., within the framework of ceremonies and rites 'celebrating' them. Salt is, therefore, invested with all the significance attached to the most solemn and decisive moments in the life of individuals and of the group.

(3) A precious product because its manufacture cannot be effected without the art of specialists who must possess both technical and magical know-how in order to bring about its crystallisation. In short, it is to the salt maker's magical powers that salt-field owners must turn if they wish to get that 'white and heavy' salt which other tribes covet and are ready to 'pay' a good price for.

(4) A precious product, because, thanks to it, the Baruya can procure all *that they lack*, and which to them is necessary for subsisting (stone axes), protection from the cold (bark cloaks), adornment and finery (feathers, pearls), compensation for murder, initiation of their daughters and warriors (magic nuts), arming themselves, etc. Salt is therefore precious, because it allows the Baruya to overcome the limits of their resources, limits imposed by their ecology and economy.

Salt is, thus, both a commodity produced for others and an object given 'among themselves'. In so far as it is the only commodity which is exchanged for all others, it plays the role of money. Conversely, all goods substituted for it *become by this exchange* commodities and leave neighbouring tribes, *in this form*, passing to the Baruya where they again lose their quality of commodities in order to become objects for display or for giving in the same way as salt itself; among the Baruya, salt is never an object for barter, it is an object for giving or distributing, an object of social exchange.

We can understand now why, in some Baruya huts, suspended above the fire-place there are bars of salt a generation old, blackened from soot and shrivelled. '*Not for anything in the world*' would their owner exchange or eat this salt because for him, it is a symbol of past friendship, of a pact sealed with his enemies, a dumb language which at every moment reminds him of a past which must never fade away. The bars are now no longer any good to eat, to barter or to give away. They are only 'good for thinking'.

5 'SALT MONEY' AND THE CIRCULATION OF COMMODITIES AMONG THE BARUYA OF NEW GUINEA

† *Cahiers Vilfredo Pareto*, No. 21, Droz, Geneva, 1970. The material for this study was put together during a mission to New Guinea (1967–9) subsidised by the *Centre national de la recherche scientifique*. The author would also like to thank the Wenner Gren Foundation for the personal help extended to him. A more descriptive version of this study was published in *L'Homme*, Vol. IX, No. 2, 1969, pp. 5–37.

1 Boas, 'The Social Organization and the Secret Societies of the Kwakiutl Indians', *Report of the U.S. National Museum for 1895*, Washington, 1897, pp. 341–59.

2 Malinowski, 'The Primitive Economics of the Trobriand Islanders', *Economic Journal*, 1921, pp. 1–15; 'Kula', *Man*, art. 51, 1920–1.

3 Mauss, 'Essai sur le don, forme archaïque de l'échange', *Année sociologique*, 1923–4.

4 Firth, 'Currency, Primitive' and 'Trade, Primitive', *Encyclopaedia Britannica*, pp. 345, 346, 881.

5 Einzig, *Primitive Money*, Eyre & Spottiswoode, 1948.

6 Polyani, 'The Semantics of Money Uses', *Primitive, Archaic and Modern Economies*, 1968.

7 Dalton, 'Primitive Money', *American Anthropologist*, vol. 67, 1965, pp. 44–65.

8 Sahlins, 'On the Sociology of Primitive Exchange', *The Relevance of Models for Social Anthropology*, ASA Monographs, New York, Praeger, 1965.

9 Herskovits, *Economic Anthropology*, New York, A. Knopf, 1952, pp. 487–8.

10 Goldmann, 'The Kwakiutl of Vancouver Island', *Cooperation and Competition among Primitive Peoples*, Margaret Mead (ed.), McGraw-Hill, 1937, pp. 180–209.

11 Moore, 'Labor Attitudes Toward Industrialization in Under-Developed Countries', *American Economic Review*, No. 45, 1955, pp. 156–65.

12 Forde, 'Primitive Economies', *Man, Culture and Society*, NY Oxford Press, p. 342. See particularly: L. Lancaster, 'Crédit, épargne et investissement dans une économie non monétaire', *Archives européennes de sociologie*, III, 1962, pp. 156–65.

13 Dalton, *Primitive Money*, op. cit., p. 59.

14 Davenport, 'Red Feather Money', *Scientific American*, vol. 206, March 1962, pp. 94–105.

15 A. Senft, 'Ethnographische Beitrage über Karolinen-Insel Yap', *Dr A. Petermann's Mitteilungen*, 1903, pp. 50–151, and W. H. Furness, *The Island of Stone Money*, Philadelphia, 1910, p. 96.
16 K. Polanyi, Arensberg, Pearson, *Trade and Market in the Early Empires*, Glencoe, 1957.
17 M. Godelier, 'Objet et méthodes de l'anthropologie économique', *L'Homme*, vol. v, No. 2, 1965, and *Rationalité et irrationalité en économie*, op. cit., pp. 262–79.
18 Einzig, *Primitive Money*, op. cit., pp. 24–5.
19 Sahlins, 'Exchange value and the Diplomacy of Primitive Trade', *American Ethnological Society*, 1965 annual meeting, pp. 95–129.
20 See the use of the concept of capital by Salisbury, *From Stone to Steel*, op. cit.; and our critique in 'Economie politique et anthropologie économique', *L'Homme*, vol. IV. no. 4, 1964, pp. 118–32; and Bessaignet, 'An Alleged Case of Primitive Money', *Southwestern Journal of Anthropology*, 1965, pp. 333–45.
21 Take the case of the Tolaï in New Britain: cf. T. S. Epstein, 'European Contact and Tolaï Economic Development, A Schema of Economic Growths', *Economic Development and Cultural Change*, April 1963, pp. 283–307; and R. Salisbury, 'Politics and Shell-Money Finance in New Britain', *Political Anthropology*, Aldine, 1966, pp. 113–28.
22 Davenport, 'When a Primitive and a Civilized Money Meet', *Proceedings of the American Ethnographical Society*, Spring Meeting Symposium, Seattle, 1961, pp. 64–8.
23 On the gift and trade in Homeric times, see M. Finley, *The World of Odysseus*, Viking Press, NY, 1954, ch. 3; E. Will, 'De l'aspect éthique des origines grecques de la monnaie', *Revue Historique*, 1954, pp. 212–31; and Benvéniste, *Le Vocabulaire des institutions indo-europénes*, Editions de Minuit, Paris, 1969, vol. 1, ch. 2: 'Donner et prendre', and ch. 11: 'Un métier sans nom: le commerce'.
24 Salt usage in different societies and at different times should be compared. See Mahieu, *Numismatique du Congo*, 1924, p. 57; and for the salt bars in Abyssinia, Salviac, 'Les Gallas', *Geographical Journal*, 1901, p. 159.
25 The Baruya were discovered by J. Sinclair in 1951. He called them Batia in his book, *Behind the Ranges* (ch. 3: 'The Saltmakers'). Cf. J. Sinclair, *Behind the Ranges*, Melbourne Univ. Press, 1966.
26 S. A. Wurm, 'Australian New Guinea Highlands Languages and the Distribution of their Typological Features', *Amer. Anthrop.*, New Guinea, August 1964, pp. 77–97.
27 J. P. Murray, *Papua or British New Guinea*, T. Fischer-Unwin, 1912, pp. 170–1.
28 Cf. Demaitre, *New Guinea Gold: Cannibals and Goldseekers in New Guinea*, London, Geoffrey Bles, 1936. The only scientific publications concerning the Kukakuka are those of B. Blackwood, 'Use of Plants among the Kukakuka of Southeast Central New Guinea', *Proceedings of the Sixth Pacific Science Congress*, IV, Berkeley, 1939, pp. 111–26 and *The Technology of a Modern Stone Age People in New Guinea*, Oxford, Pitt-Rivers Museum 1950 (60 p.). Note also H. Fischer, 'Ethnographien von de Kukukuku' *Baessler Archiv*. 7 (neue Folge), pp. 99–122; description of a collection in the Hamburg museum by a missionary, J. Maurer.
29 Cf. J. M. Meggitt, 'Salt Manufacture and Trading in the Western Highlands of New Guinea', *The Australian Museum Magazine*, XII, 10, 1958, pp. 309–13.
30 Spectroscopic examination shows that this salt has a high percentage of potassium and, in high doses, is a violent poison.
31 A. Freund, E. Henty, M. Lynch, 'Salt Making in Inland New Guinea', *Transactions*, Papua and New Guinea Scientific Society, 1965, pp. 16–19.

32 In their language the Baruya distinguish: *moumbié*, bartering in the sense of both buying and selling; and *yanya*, giving; the generous man is the one who goes halves.

33 From A. L. Rand and E. T. Gilliard, *Handbook of New Guinea Birds*, Weidenfeld and Nicholson, London, 1967 (612 p.).

34 A. Deluz & M. Godelier, 'A propos de deux textes d'anthropologie économique', *L'Homme*, vol. VII, 3, 1967, pp. 78–91.

35 When the Baruya were paid for the first time in cash, they did not understand the utility of the coins. Some threw them in the bush, others pierced them and wore them round their necks like shells. However as soon as a 'counter' was opened at Wonenara, where for these pieces, they were offered shorts, shirts, canned foods, chewing-gum, they had no doubts about the usefulness of this metallic money. Perhaps the above anecdote explains why the Baruya, in their language, designate for the White Man's money, the very same term they give to their cowries: *nounguyé*; no one has been able to tell us the reasons for this assimilation. It is useful to note that when the Baruya want to make the value and functions of salt understood, they like to compare it with the White man's 'big money', i.e., pound sterling notes or dollar bills.

36 This merits separate treatment which is beyond the scope of this article.

37 Marx clearly indicated the *restrictive* conditions under which, in a developed market economy, a commodity may be exchanged for its value: 'For prices at which commodities are exchanged to approximately correspond to their values, nothing more is necessary than (1) for the exchange of the various commodities to cease being purely accidental or only occasional; (2) so far as direct exchange of commodities is concerned, for these commodities to be produced by both sides in approximately sufficient quantities to meet mutual requirements; (3) so far as selling is concerned, for no natural or artificial monopoly to enable either of the contracting sides to sell commodities above their value or to compel them to undersell.' *Capital*, op. cit., Vol. 1, p. 175. See also M. Godelier, 'Théorie marginaliste et théorie marxiste de la valeur et des prix: quelques hypothèses', article cited.

38 M. Sahlins, 'Poor Man, Rich Man, Big-Man, Chief: Political Types in Melanesia and Polynesia', *Comparative Studies in Society and History*, 5, op. cit., pp. 285–303. See also by the same author 'On the Sociology of Primitive Exchange'; M. Banton, ed., *The Relevance of Models for Social Anthropology*, New York, Praeger, 1965.

39 In the Baruya language, work is not an abstract notion, unaffected by the concrete matter of laborious activity. The verb *waounié*, to work, to make, is always used in a practical context: make a house, salt, palisade, etc. Let us remember what Marx said, having stressed the immense progress made by A. Smith, when the latter broke away from the ideas of the physiocrats in order to define work simply and independently of its concrete forms: agricultural (to the physiocrats the only productive kind of work), manufacturing, commercial work: 'It might seem that in this way merely an abstract expression was found for the simplest and most ancient relation in which human beings act as producers, irrespective of the type of society they live in. This may appear true, but is, in fact false. 'Labour' from the simplest economic point of view is a category just as modern as the social relations which give rise to this pure and simple abstraction.' Cf. Introduction to a Criticism of Political Economy, from *The German Ideology*, Lawrence and Wishart, 1970 and *Capital*, Book III, 1, pp. 173–94.

[21]

The cultural biography of things: commoditization as process

IGOR KOPYTOFF

For the economist, commodities simply are. That is, certain things and rights to things are produced, exist, and can be seen to circulate through the economic system as they are being exchanged for other things, usually in exchange for money. This view, of course, frames the commonsensical definition of a commodity: an item with use value that also has exchange value. I shall, for the moment, accept this definition, which should suffice for raising certain preliminary issues, and I shall expand on it as the argument warrants.

From a cultural perspective, the production of commodities is also a cultural and cognitive process: commodities must be not only produced materially as things, but also culturally marked as being a certain kind of thing. Out of the total range of things available in a society, only some of them are considered appropriate for marking as commodities. Moreover, the same thing may be treated as a commodity at one time and not at another. And finally, the same thing may, at the same time, be seen as a commodity by one person and as something else by another. Such shifts and differences in whether and when a thing is a commodity reveal a moral economy that stands behind the objective economy of visible transactions.

Of persons and things

In contemporary Western thought, we take it more or less for granted that things – physical objects and rights to them – represent the natural universe of commodities. At the opposite pole we place people, who represent the natural universe of individuation and singularization. This conceptual polarity of individualized persons and commoditized things is recent and, culturally speaking, exceptional. People can be and have been commoditized again and again, in innumerable societies throughout history, by way of those widespread institutions known under the blanket term "slavery." Hence, it may be suggestive to approach the notion of commodity by first looking at it in the context of slavery.

Slavery has often been defined, in the past, as the treatment of persons as property or, in some kindred definitions, as objects. More recently, there has been a shift away from this all-or-none view toward a processual perspective, in which marginality and ambiguity of status are at the core of the slave's social identity (see Meillassoux 1975, Vaughan 1977, Kopytoff and Miers 1977, Kopytoff 1982, Patterson 1982). From this perspective slavery is seen not as a fixed and unitary status, but as a process of social transformation that involves a succession of phases and changes in status, some of which merge with other statuses (for example, that of adoptee) that we in the West consider far removed from slavery.

Slavery begins with capture or sale, when the individual is stripped of his previous social identity and becomes a non-person, indeed an object and an actual or potential commodity. But the process continues. The slave is acquired by a person or group and is reinserted into the host group, within which he is resocialized and rehumanized by being given a new social identity. The commodity-slave becomes in effect reindividualized by acquiring new statuses (by no means always lowly ones) and a unique configuration of personal relationships. In brief, the process has moved the slave away from the simple status of exchangeable commodity and toward that of a singular individual occupying a particular social and personal niche. But the slave usually remains a potential commodity: he or she continues to have a potential exchange value that may be realized by resale. In many societies, this was also true of the "free," who were subject to sale under certain defined circumstances. To the extent that in such societies all persons possessed an exchange value and were commoditizable, commoditization in them was clearly not culturally confined to the world of things.

What we see in the career of a slave is a process of initial withdrawal from a given original social setting, his or her commoditization, followed by increasing singularization (that is, decommoditization) in the new setting, with the possibility of later recommoditization. As in most processes, the successive phases merge one into another. Effectively, the slave was unambiguously a commodity only during the relatively short period between capture or first sale and the acquisition of the new social identity; and the slave becomes less of a commodity and more of a singular individual in the process of gradual incorporation into the host society. This biographical consideration of enslavement as a process suggests that the commoditization of other things may usefully be seen in a similar light, namely, as part of the cultural shaping of biographies.

66 Igor Kopytoff

The biographical approach

Biographies have been approached in various ways in anthropology (for a survey, see Langness 1965). One may present an actual biography, or one may construct a typical biographical model from randomly assembled biographical data, as one does in the standard Life Cycle chapter in a general ethnography. A more theoretically aware biographical model is rather more demanding. It is based on a reasonable number of actual life histories. It presents the range of biographical possibilities that the society in question offers and examines the manner in which these possibilities are realized in the life stories of various categories of people. And it examines idealized biographies that are considered to be desirable models in the society and the way real-life departures from the models are perceived. As Margaret Mead remarked, one way to understand a culture is to see what sort of biography it regards as embodying a successful social career. Clearly, what is seen as a well-lived life in an African society is different in outline from what would be pronounced as a well-lived life along the Ganges, or in Brittany, or among the Eskimos.

It seems to me that we can profitably ask the same range and kinds of cultural questions to arrive at biographies of things. Early in this century, in an article entitled "The genealogical method of anthropological inquiry" (1910), W. H. R. Rivers offered what has since become a standard tool in ethnographic fieldwork. The thrust of the article – the aspect for which it is now mainly remembered – is to show how kinship terminology and relationships may be superimposed on a genealogical diagram and traced through the social-structure-in-time that the diagram mirrors. But Rivers also suggested something else: that, for example, when the anthropologist is in search of inheritance rules, he may compare the ideal statement of the rules with the actual movement of a particular object, such as a plot of land, through the genealogical diagram, noting concretely how it passes from hand to hand. What Rivers proposed was a kind of biography of things in terms of ownership. But a biography may concentrate on innumerable other matters and events.

In doing the biography of a thing, one would ask questions similar to those one asks about people: What, sociologically, are the biographical possibilities inherent in its "status" and in the period and culture, and how are these possibilities realized? Where does the thing come from and who made it? What has been its career so far, and what do people consider to be an ideal career for such things? What are the recognized "ages" or periods in the thing's "life," and what are the cultural markers for them? How does the thing's use change with its age, and what happens to it when it reaches the end of its usefulness?

For example, among the Suku of Zaire, among whom I worked, the life expectancy of a hut is about ten years. The typical biography of a hut begins with its housing a couple or, in a polygynous household, a wife with her children. As the hut ages, it is successively turned into a guest house or a house for a widow, a teenagers' hangout, kitchen, and, finally, goat or chicken house – until at last the termites win and the structure collapses. The physical state of the hut at each given age corresponds to a particular use. For a hut to be out of phase in its use makes a Suku uncomfortable, and it conveys a message. Thus, to house a visitor in a hut that should be a kitchen says something about the visitor's status; and if there is no visitors' hut available in a compound, it says something about the compound-head's character – he must be lazy, inhospitable, or poor. We have similar biographical expectations of things. To us, a biography of a painting by Renoir that ends up in an incinerator is as tragic, in its way, as the biography of a person who ends up murdered. That is obvious. But there are other events in the biography of objects that convey more subtle meanings. What of a Renoir ending up in a private and inaccessible collection? Of one lying neglected in a museum basement? How should we feel about yet another Renoir leaving France for the United States? Or for Nigeria? The cultural responses to such biographical details reveal a tangled mass of aesthetic, historical, and even political judgments, and of convictions and values that shape our attitudes to objects labeled "art."

Biographies of things can make salient what might otherwise remain obscure. For example, in situations of culture contact, they can show what anthropologists have so often stressed: that what is significant about the adoption of alien objects – as of alien ideas – is not the fact that they are adopted, but the way they are culturally redefined and put to use. The biography of a car in Africa would reveal a wealth of cultural data: the way it was acquired, how and from whom the money was assembled to pay for it, the relationship of the seller to the buyer, the uses to which the car is regularly put, the identity of its most frequent passengers and of those who borrow it, the frequency of borrowing, the garages to which it is taken and the owner's relation to the mechanics, the movement of the car from hand to hand over the years, and in the end, when the car collapses, the final disposition of its remains. All of these details would reveal an entirely different biography from that of a middle-class American, or Navajo, or French peasant car.

One brings to every biography some prior conception of what is to be its focus. We accept that every person has many biographies – psychological, professional, political, familial, economic and so forth – each of which selects some aspects of the life history and discards others. Biographies of things cannot but be similarly partial. Obviously, the sheer physical biography of a car is quite different from its technical biography, known in the trade as its repair record. The car can also furnish an economic biography – its initial worth, its sale and resale price, the rate of decline in its value, its response to the recession, the patterning over several years of its maintenance costs. The car also offers several possible social biographies: one biography may concentrate on its place in the owner-family's economy, another may relate the history of its ownership to the society's class structure, and a third may focus on its role in the sociology of the family's kin relations, such as loosening family ties in America or strengthening them in Africa.

But all such biographies – economic, technical, social – may or may not be culturally informed. What would make a biography cultural is not what it deals with, but how and from what perspective. A culturally informed economic biography of an object would look at it as a culturally constructed entity, endowed with culturally specific meanings, and classified and reclassified into culturally constituted categories. It is from this point of view that I should like to propose a framework for looking at commodities – or rather, speaking processually, at commoditization. But first, what is a commodity?

The singular and the common

I assume commodities to be a universal cultural phenomenon. Their existence is a concomitant of the existence of transactions that involve the exchange of things (objects and services), exchange being a universal feature of human social life and, according to some theorists, at the very core of it (see, for example, Homans 1961; Ekeh 1974; and Kapferer 1976). Where societies differ is in the ways commoditization as a special expression of exchange is structured and related to the social system, in the factors that encourage or contain it, in the long-term tendencies for it to expand or stabilize, and in the cultural and ideological premises that suffuse its workings.

What, then, makes a thing a commodity? A commodity is a thing that has use value and that can be exchanged in a discrete transaction for a counterpart, the very fact of exchange indicating that the counterpart has, in the immediate context, an equivalent value. The counterpart is by the same token also a commodity at the time of exchange. The exchange can be direct or it can be achieved indirectly by way of money, one of whose functions is as a means of exchange. Hence, anything that can be bought for money is at that point a commodity, whatever the fate that is reserved for it after the transaction has been made (it may, thereafter, be decommoditized). Hence, in the West, as a matter of cultural shorthand, we usually take saleability to be the unmistakable indicator of commodity status, while non-saleability imparts to a thing a special aura of apartness from the mundane and the common. In fact, of course, saleability for money is not a necessary feature of commodity status, given the existence of commodity exchange in non-monetary economies.

I refer to the transaction involving commodities as discrete in order to stress that the primary and immediate purpose of the transaction is to obtain the counterpart value (and that, for the economist, is also its economic function). The purpose of the transaction is not, for example, to open the way for some other kind of transaction, as in the case of gifts given to initiate marriage negotiations or to secure patronage; each of these cases is a partial transaction that should be considered in the context of the entire transaction. While exchanges of things usually involve commodities, a notable exception is the exchanges that mark relations of reciprocity, as these have been classically defined in anthropology. Here, gifts are given in order to evoke an obligation to give back a gift, which in turn will evoke a similar obligation – a never-ending chain of gifts and obligations. The gifts themselves may be things that are normally used as commodities (food, feasts, luxury goods, services), but each transaction is not discrete and none, in principle, is terminal.

To be saleable for money or to be exchangeable for a wide array of other things is to have something in common with a large number of exchangeable things that, taken together, partake of a single universe of comparable values. To use an appropriately loaded even if archaic term, to be saleable or widely exchangeable is to be "common" – the opposite of being uncommon, incomparable, unique, singular, and therefore not exchangeable for anything else. The perfect commodity would be one that is exchangeable with anything and everything else, as the perfectly commoditized world would be one in which everything is exchangeable or for sale. By the same token, the perfectly decommoditized world would be one in which everything is singular, unique, and unexchangeable.

The two situations are ideal polar types, and no real economic system could conform to either. In no system is everything so singular as to preclude even the hint of exchange. And in no system, except in some extravagant Marxian image of an utterly commoditized capitalism, is everything a commodity and exchangeable for everything else within a unitary sphere of exchange. Such a construction of the world – in the first case as totally heterogeneous in terms of valuation and, in the second, as totally homogeneous – would be humanly and culturally impossible. But they are two extremes between which every real economy occupies its own peculiar place.

We can accept, with most philosophers, linguists, and psychologists, that the human mind has an inherent tendency to impose order upon the chaos of its environment by classifying its contents, and without this classification knowledge of the world and adjustment to it would not be possible. Culture serves the mind by imposing a collectively shared cognitive order upon the world which, objectively, is totally heterogeneous and presents an endless array of singular things. Culture achieves order by carving out, through discrimination and classification, distinct areas of homogeneity within the overall heterogeneity. Yet, if the homogenizing process is carried too far and the perceived world begins to approach too closely the other pole – in the case of goods, that of utter commoditization – culture's function of cognitive discrimination is undermined. Both individuals and cultural collectivities must navigate somewhere between the polar extremes by classifying things into categories that are simultaneously neither too many nor too embracing. In brief, what we usually refer to as "structure" lies between the heterogeneity of too much splitting and the homogeneity of too much lumping.

In the realm of exchange values, this means that the natural world of singular things must be arranged into several manageable value classes – that is, different things must be selected and made cognitively similar when put together within each category and dissimilar when put into different categories. This is the basis for a well-known economic phenomenon – that of several spheres of exchange values, which operate more or less independently of one another. The phenomenon is found in every society, though Westerners are most apt to perceive it in uncommercialized and unmonetized economies. The nature and structure of these spheres of exchange varies among societies because, as we can expect with Durkheim and Mauss (1963; original publication 1903), the cultural systems of classification reflect the structure and the cultural resources of the societies in question. And beyond that, as we may expect with Dumont (1972), there's also some tendency to impose a hierarchy upon the categories.

Spheres of exchange

A concrete example of an economy with clearly distinct spheres of exchange will help the discussion. In what is a classic analysis of a "multi-centric economy," Bohannan (1959) describes three such spheres of exchange as they operated before the colonial period among the Tiv of central Nigeria: (a) the sphere of subsistence items – yams, cereals, condiments, chickens, goats, utensils, tools, and the like; (b) the sphere of prestige items – mainly cattle, slaves, ritual offices, special cloth, medicines, and brass rods; and (c) the sphere of rights-in-people, which included rights in wives, wards, and offspring.

The three spheres represent three separate universes of exchange values, that is, three commodity spheres. Items within each were exchangeable, and each was ruled by its own kind of morality. Moreover, there was a moral hierarchy among the spheres: the subsistence sphere, with its untrammeled market morality, was the lowest, and the rights-in-people sphere, related to the world of kin and kin-group relations, was the highest. In the Tiv case (in contrast to that of many other similar systems), it was possible to move – even if in a rather cumbersome manner – between the spheres. Brass rods provided the link. In exceptional circumstances, people relinquished, unwillingly, rods for subsistence items; and, at the other end, one could also initiate with rods some transactions in the rights-in-people sphere. The Tiv considered it satisfying and morally appropriate to convert "upward," from subsistence to prestige and from prestige to rights-in-people, whereas converting "downward" was shameful and done only under extreme duress.

The problem of value and value equivalence has always been a philosophical conundrum in economics. It involves the mysterious process by which things that are patently unlike are somehow made to be alike with respect to value, making yams, for example, somehow comparable to and exchangeable with a mortar or a pot. In the terms we have been using here, this involves taking the patently singular and inserting it into a uniform category of value with other patently singular things. For all the difficulties that the labor theory of value presents, it at least suggests that while yams and pots can conceivably be compared by the labor required to produce them (even while allowing for the different investment in training that the labor represents in each case), no such common standard is available in comparing yams to ritual offices or pots to wives and offspring. Hence, the immense difficulty, indeed impossibility, of lumping all such disparate items into a single commodity sphere. This difficulty provides the natural basis for the cultural construction of separate spheres of exchange. The culture takes on the less sweeping task of making value-equivalence by creating several discrete commodity spheres – in the Tiv case, palpable items of subsistence created by physical labor, as opposed to the prestige items of social maneuvering, as opposed to the more intimate domain of the rights and obligations of kinship.

The drive to commoditization

From this perspective, a multi-centric economy such as that of the Tiv is not an exotically complicated rendering of a straightforward exchange system. It is rather the opposite – a feat of simplification of what is naturally an unmanageable mass of singular items. But why only three spheres and not, say, a dozen? The commoditization seems to be pushed to the limits permitted by the Tiv exchange technology, which lacked a common denominator of value more convenient than brass rods. One perceives in this a drive inherent in every exchange system toward optimum commoditization – the drive to extend the fundamentally seductive idea of exchange to as many items as the existing exchange technology will comfortably allow. Hence the universal acceptance of money whenever it has been introduced into non-monetized societies and its inexorable conquest of the internal economy of these societies, regardless of initial rejection and of individual unhappiness about it – an unhappiness well illustrated by the modern Tiv. Hence also the uniform results of the introduction of money in a wide range of otherwise different societies: more extensive commoditization and the merger of the separate spheres of exchange. It is as if the internal logic of exchange itself pre-adapts all economies to seize upon the new opportunities that wide commoditization so obviously brings with it.

One may interpret Braudel's recent work (1983) in this light – as showing how the development in early modern Europe of a range of new institutions shaped what might be called a new exchange technology and how this, in turn, led to the explosion of commoditization that was at the root of capitalism. The extensive commoditization we associate with capitalism is thus not a feature of capitalism per se, but of the exchange technology that, historically, was associated with it and that set dramatically wider limits to maximum feasible commoditization. Modern state-ordered, noncapitalist economies certainly show no signs of being systematically exempt from this tendency, even though they may try to control it by political means. Indeed, given their endemic shortages and ubiquitous black markets, commoditization in them expands into novel areas, in which the consumer, in order to purchase goods and services, must first purchase access to the transaction.

Commoditization, then, is best looked upon as a process of becoming rather than as an all-or-none state of being. Its expansion takes place in two ways: (a) with respect to each thing, by making it exchangeable for more and more other things, and (b) with respect to the system as a whole, by making more and more different things more widely exchangeable.

Singularization: cultural and individual

The counterdrive to this potential onrush of commoditization is culture. In the sense that commoditization homogenizes value, while the essence of culture is discrimination, excessive commoditization is anticultural – as indeed so many have perceived it or sensed it to be. And if, as Durkheim (1915; original publication 1912) saw it, societies need to set apart a certain portion of their environment, marking it as "sacred," singularization is one means to this end. Culture ensures that some things remain unambigiously singular, it resists the commoditization of others; and it sometimes resingularizes what has been commoditized.

In every society, there are things that are publicly precluded from being commoditized. Some of the prohibitions are cultural and upheld collectively. In state societies, many of these prohibitions are the handwork of the state, with the usual intertwining between what serves the society at large, what serves the state, and what serves the specific groups in control. This applies to much of what one thinks of as the symbolic inventory of a society: public lands, monuments, state art collections, the paraphernalia of political power, royal residences, chiefly insignia, ritual objects, and so on. Power often asserts itself symbolically precisely by insisting on its right to singularize an object, or a set or class of objects. African chiefs and kings reserve to themselves the right to certain animals and animal products, such as the skins and teeth of spotted wild cats. The kings of Siam monopolized albino elephants. And British monarchs have kept their right to dead whales washed ashore. There may be some practical side to these royal pretensions, which ecological and cultural materialists will no doubt diligently discover. What these monopolies clearly do, however, is to expand the visible reach of sacred power by projecting it onto additional sacralized objects.

Such singularization is sometimes extended to things that are normally commodities – in effect, commodities are singularized by being pulled out of their usual commodity sphere. Thus, in the ritual paraphernalia of the British monarchy, we find a Star of India that, contrary to what would normally have happened, was prevented from becoming a commodity and eventually singularized into a "crown jewel." Similarly, the ritual paraphernalia of the kings of the Suku of Zaire included standard trade items from the past, such as eighteenth-century European ceramic drinking mugs brought by the Portuguese, carried by the Suku to their present area, and sacralized in the process.

Another way to singularize objects is through restricted commoditization, in which some things are confined to a very narrow sphere of exchange. The Tiv system illustrates the principle. The few items in the prestige sphere (slaves, cattle, ritual offices, a special cloth, and brass rods), though commodities by virtue of being exchangeable one for the other, were less commoditized than the far more numerous items of the subsistence sphere, ranging widely from yams to pots. A sphere consisting of but two kinds of items – as in the classic model of the Trobriand kula exchange sphere of arm bands and bracelets – represents an even greater degree of singularization. The Tiv exchange sphere of rights-in-person achieved a singular integrity by a different though related principle, that of the homogeneity of its components. The two upper Tiv spheres, it may be noted, were more singular, more special, and hence more sacred than the lowest sphere, containing the many objects of mundance subsistence. Thus the moral hierarchy of the Tiv exchange spheres corresponded to a gradient of singularity.

If sacralization can be achieved by singularity, singularity does not guarantee sacralization. Being a non-commodity does not by itself assure high regard, and many singular things (that is, non-exchangeable things) may be worth very little. Among the Aghem of western Cameroon, with exchange spheres not unlike those of the Tiv, one could detect yet another and lower sphere, one below that of marketable subsistence items. Once, when trying to find out the precolonial exchange value of various items, I asked about the barter value of manioc. The response was indignant scoffing at the very idea that such a lowly thing as manioc should have been exchangeable for anything: "One eats it, that's all. Or one gives it away if one wants to. Women may help out one another with it and other such food. But one doesn't *trade* it." Lest the outburst be misunderstood and sentimentalized, let me stress that the indignation was not about a suggested commercial corruption of a symbolically supercharged staple, on the order, say, of bread among Eastern European peasants. The

Aghem are and were a commercially minded people, with no disdain for trade. The scoffing was rather like what an Aghem would get from a Westerner whom he asked about the exchange value of a match he proffers to light a stranger's cigarette. Manioc was part of a class of singular things of so little worth as to have no publicly recognized exchange value. To be a non-commodity is to be "priceless" in the full possible sense of the term, ranging from the uniquely valuable to the uniquely worthless.

In addition to things being classified as more or less singular, there is also what might be called terminal commoditization, in which further exchange is precluded by fiat. In many societies, medicines are so treated: the medicine man makes and sells a medicine that is utterly singular since it is efficacious only for the intended patient. Terminal commoditization also marked the sale of indulgences in the Roman Catholic Church of half a millennium ago: the sinner could buy them but not resell them. In modern Western medicine, such terminal commoditization is achieved legally; it rests on the prohibition against reselling a prescribed drug and against selling any medicine without proper licensing. There are other examples of legal attempts to restrict recommoditization: paperbound books published in Great Britain often carry a bewildering note forbidding the buyer to resell it in any but the original covers; and in America, an equally mystifying label is attached to mattresses and cushions, forbidding their resale.

Other factors besides legal or cultural fiat may create terminal commodities. Most consumer goods are, after all, destined to be terminal – or so, at least, it is hoped by the manufacturer. The expectation is easily enough fulfilled with such things as canned peas, though even here external circumstances can intrude; in times of war shortages, all sorts of normally consumable goods begin to serve as a store of wealth and, instead of being consumed, circulate endlessly in the market. With durable goods, a second-hand market normally develops, and the idea that it does may be fostered by the sellers. There is an area of our economy in which the selling strategy rests on stressing that the commoditization of goods bought for consumption need not be terminal: thus, the promise that oriental carpets, though bought for use, are a "good investment," or that certain expensive cars have a "high resale value."

The existence of terminal commoditization raises a point that is central to the analysis of slavery, where the fact that a person has been bought does not in itself tell us anything about the uses to which the person may then be put (Kopytoff 1982:223ff). Some purchased people ended up in the mines, on plantations, or on galleys; others became Grand Viziers or Imperial Roman Admirals. In the same way, the fact that an object is bought or exchanged says nothing about its subsequent status and whether it will remain a commodity or not. But unless formally decommoditized, commoditized things remain potential commodities – they continue to have an exchange value, even if they have been effectively withdrawn from their exchange sphere and deactivated, so to speak, as commodities. This deactivation leaves them open not only to the various kinds of singularization I have mentioned so far, but also to individual, as opposed to collective, redefinitions.

In the Bamenda area of western Cameroon, people prized large decorated calabashes that came over the border from Nigeria. The conduit for them was the Aku, a pastoral group whose women used them extensively and normally were willing to sell them. I had acquired several in this way. Yet one day I failed completely to convince an Aku woman to sell me a standard calabash to which she had added some minor decorations of her own. Her friends told her that she was being silly, arguing that for the money she could get a far better and prettier calabash. But she would not budge, no more than does that ever-newsworthy man in our society – part hero, part fool – who refuses to sell his house for a million dollars and forces the skyscraper to be built around it. And there is also the opposite phenomenon: the ideological commoditizer, advocating, say, the sale of public lands as a way of balancing the budget, or, as I have seen in Africa, calling for the sale of some piece of chiefly paraphernalia in order to provide a tin roof for the schoolhouse.

What these mundane examples show is that, in any society, the individual is often caught between the cultural structure of commoditization and his own personal attempts to bring a value order to the universe of things. Some of this clash between culture and individual is inevitable, at least at the cognitive level. The world of things lends itself to an endless number of classifications, rooted in natural features and cultural and idiosyncratic perceptions. The individual mind can play with them all, constructing innumerable classes, different universes of common value, and changing spheres of exchange. Culture, by contrast, cannot be so exuberant, least so in the economy, where its classifications must provide unambiguous guidance to pragmatic and coordinated action. But if the clash is inevitable, the social structures within which it takes place vary, giving it different intensities. In a society like the precolonial Tiv or Aghem, the culture and the economy were in relative harmony; the economy followed the cultural classifications, and these catered successfully to the individual cognitive need for discrimination. By contrast, in a commercialized, monetized, and highly commoditized society, the value-homogenizing drive of the exchange system has an enormous momentum, producing results that both culture and individual cognition often oppose, but in inconsistent and even contradictory ways.

Complex societies

I said above that the exchange spheres are, to us, more visible in non-commercial, non-monetized societies like the Tiv than in commercial, monetized ones like our own. Partly this is a matter of noticing the exotic and taking the familiar for granted. But it is more than that.

Certainly, in our society, some discrete spheres of exchange exist and are nearly unanimously accepted and approved. Thus, we are adamant about keeping separate the spheres of material objects and persons (a matter I shall elaborate on later). We also exchange dinners and keep that sphere discrete. We blandly accept the existence of an exchange sphere of political or academic favors, but would be as shocked at the idea of monetizing this sphere as the Tiv were at first at the idea of monetizing their marriage transactions. Like the Tiv, who carefully moved from the sphere of mundane pots to that of prestigeful titles by using the mediation of brass rods, so do our financiers cautiously navigate between exchange spheres in such matters as gift-giving to universities. A straight money donation in general funds, if it is of any size, is suspect because it looks too much like purchasing influence, and such donations, when made, are normally anonymous or posthumous. A money donation in installments would be particularly suspect, implying the donor's power to withhold the next check. But converting a large donation into a building moves the money into a nearly decommoditized sphere, freezes the gift into visible irrevocability, and shields the donor from suspicion of continuous undue influence on the university. Putting the donor's name on the building thus honors not simply the donor but also the university, which declares in doing so that it is free of any lingering obligations to the specific donor. The values underlying such transactions are, on the whole, societywide, or at least are held by the groups who wield cultural hegemony in our society and define much of what we are apt to call our public culture. "Everyone" is against commoditizing what has been publicly marked as singular and made sacred: public parks, national landmarks, the Lincoln Memorial, George Washington's false teeth at Mount Vernon.

Other singularizing values are held by more restricted groups. We have explicit exchange spheres recognized only by segments of society, such as professional and occupational groups, which subscribe to a common cultural code and a specially focused morality. Such groups constitute the networks of mechanical solidarity that tie together the parts of the organic structure of the wider society, the latter being ruled in most of its activities by commodity principles. Let me lead into my discussion by looking at an activity in one such group: the collection of African art among American Africanists.

In the simpler days of thirty or more years ago, African art picked up randomly in the course of fieldwork was placed entirely in a closed sphere with a sacred cast. The objects collected were greatly singularized; they were held to have for their collector a personal sentimental value, or a purely aesthetic one, or a scientific one, the last supported by the collector's supposed knowledge of the object's cultural context. It was not considered entirely proper to acquire an art object from African market traders or, worse, from European traders in Africa, or worse still, from dealers in Europe or America. Such an object, acquired at second hand, had little scientific value, and it was vaguely contaminated by having circulated in a monetized commodity-sphere – a contamination that was not entirely removed by keeping it thereafter in the same category as the objects "legitimately" acquired in the field. The exchange sphere to which African art objects belonged was extremely homogeneous in content. It was permissible to exchange them for other African (or other "primitive art") objects. One could also give them as gifts. Students returning from the field usually brought one or two as gifts to their supervisors, thus inserting them into another circumscribed sphere, that of academic patron-client relationships. The morality governing the sphere did not allow for them to be sold, except at cost to a museum. Nevertheless, as among the Tiv, for whom it was permissible though shameful to sell a brass rod for food, so here extreme need justified "liquidation" on the commercial art market, but it had to be done with appropriate discretion and it was certainly seen as converting "downward."

As Douglas and Isherwood (1980) show, the public culture in complex societies does provide broadly discriminating value markings of goods and services. That is, the public culture offers discriminating classifications here no less than it does in small-scale societies. But these must constantly compete with classifications by individuals and by small networks, whose members also belong to other networks expounding yet other value systems. The discriminating criteria that each individual or network can bring to the task of classification are extremely varied. Not only is every individual's or network's version of exchange spheres idiosyncratic and different from those of others, but it also shifts contextually and biographically as the originators' perspectives, affiliations and interests shift. The result is a debate not only between people and groups, but within each person as well. To be sure, the seeds for such debates also exist in societies like the precolonial Tiv, but there the culture and the economy joined hands to provide an approved model of classification. In a commercialized, heterogenous, and liberal society, the public culture defers most of the time to pluralism and relativism and provides no firm guidance, while the only lesson the economy can teach is that of the freedom and dynamism that ever-wider commoditization clearly brings with it.

The results can be partly glimpsed in what has happened to African art collecting over the past quarter century. The rules have been loosened in some of the same ways that monetization, according to Bohannan, loosened the rules among the Tiv – namely, by merging the previously distinct exchange spheres. There are, for example, no strictures now on buying an African art object at an auction in America, let alone from an African trader in Africa. Monetization in itself has become less contaminating as it has become more seductive, for no one can remain unaware that these objects are what every newspaper and magazine calls "collectibles." But the most noticeable change has been, quite simply, to make the rules less clear and more open to individual interpretations and to idiosyncratic systems of values. Where before the professional culture decreed that the value of these objects was sentimental when it was not scientific, now sentimental value is conferred as a matter of individual choice, perhaps more sincerely but also less widely. At the same time, puritans have arisen, thundering about the immorality of any kind of circulation of these objects and calling for their complete singularization and sacralization within the closed boundaries of the society that produced them. In brief, the rules of the professional culture have become less tight and the rules of propriety have become more idiosyncratic. The widespread rejection, since the 1960's, of the very idea of cultural restraints has, here as elsewhere, opened the door to a great variety of definitions by individuals and small groups.

What I am arguing here is that the crucial difference between complex and small-scale societies does not lie simply in the extensive commoditization in the former. There have been, we must not forget, small-scale societies in which commoditization (helped by indigenous money) was very extensive, such as the Yurok of northern California (Kroeber 1925) or the Kapauku of western New Guinea (Pospisil 1963). The peculiarity of complex societies is that their publicly recognized commoditization operates side by side with innumerable schemes of valuation and singularization devised by individuals, social categories, and groups, and these schemes stand in unresolvable conflict with public commoditization as well as with one another.

The dynamics of informal singularization in complex societies

There is clearly a yearning for singularization in complex societies. Much of it is satisfied individually, by private singularization, often on principles as mundane as the one that governs the fate of heirlooms and old slippers alike – the longevity of the relation assimilates them in some sense to the person and makes parting from them unthinkable.

Sometimes the yearning assumes the proportions of a collective hunger, apparent in the widespread response to ever-new kinds of singularizations. Old beer cans, matchbooks, and comic books suddenly become worthy of being collected, moved from the sphere of the singularly worthless to that of the expensive singular. And there is a continuing appeal in stamp collecting – where, one may note, the stamps are preferably cancelled ones so there is no doubt about their worthlessness in the circle of commodities for which they were originally intended. As among individuals, much of the collective singularization is achieved by reference to the passage of time. Cars as commodities lose value as they age, but at about the age of thirty they begin to move into the category of antiques and rise in value with every receding year. Old furniture, of course, does the same at a more sedate pace – the period that begins to usher in sacralization is approximately equal to the span of time separating one from one's grandparents' generation (in the past, with less mobility and more stylistic continuity, more time was required). There is also the modern and appropriately unhistorical adaptation of the antiquing process so perceptively analyzed by Thompson (1979) – the instant singularization of objects in the trash-pile-to-living-room decor of the upwardly mobile young professionals, bored with the homogeneous Scandinavian aridity preferred by the previous generation of their class.

As with African art, however, these are all processes within small groups and social networks. What to me is an heirloom is, of course, a commodity to the jeweler, and the fact that I am not divorced from the jeweler's culture is apparent in my willingness to price my priceless heirloom (and invariably overestimate its commodity value). To the jeweler, I am confusing two different systems of values: that of the marketplace and that of the closed sphere of personally singularized things, both of which happen to converge on the object at hand. Many of the new "collectibles" of the beer can variety are similarly caught in this paradox: as one makes them more singular and worthy of being collected, one makes them valuable; and if they are valuable, they acquire a price and become a commodity and their singularity is to that extent undermined. This interpenetration within the same object of commodity principles and singularization principles is played upon by firms specializing in manufacturing what might be called "future collectibles," such as leather-bound editions of Emerson, bas-relief renditions of Norman Rockwell's paintings on sculptured plates, or silver medals commemorating unmemorable events. The appeal to greed in their advertising is complex: buy this plate now while it is still a commodity, because later it will become a singular "collectible" whose very singularity will make it into a higher-priced commodity. I can think of no analogy to such possibilities among the Tiv exchange spheres.

Singularization of objects by groups within the society poses a special problem. Because it is done by groups, it bears the stamp of collective approval, channels the individual drive for singularization, and takes on the weight of cultural sacredness. Thus, a community of a few city blocks can suddenly be mobilized by a common outrage at the proposed removal and sale of scrap metal of the rusting Victorian fountain in the neighborhood. Such public conflicts are often more than mere matters of style. Behind the extraordinarily vehement assertions of aesthetic values may stand conflicts of culture, class, and ethnic identity, and the struggle over the power of what one might label the "public institutions of singularization."[1] In liberal societies, these institutions are higher nongovernmental agencies or only quasi–governmental ones – historical commissions, panels deciding on public monuments, neighborhood organizations concerned with "beautification," and so on; who controls them and how says much about who controls the society's presentation of itself to itself.

A few years ago, there was a public controversy in Philadelphia about a proposal to install a statue of the cinematic boxing hero Rocky on the Parkway in front of the Art Museum – an institution that happens simultaneously to serve as a public monument to the local social establishment and to satisfy the artistic needs of the professional intelligentsia. The statue came directly from the movie set of "Rocky," the success story of an Italian-American boxing champion from South Philadelphia. To the "ethnic" working-class sector of the Philadelphia population, the statue was a singular object of ethnic, class, and regional pride – in brief, a worthy public monument. To the groups whose social identities were vested in the museum, it was a piece of junk, deserving instant recommoditization as scrap metal. Here, the issues of singularization and commoditization were directly linked into disparate and morally charged systems. But the opponents of the statue were in a position to clothe their argument in the garb of public aesthetics, a field in which they held cultural hegemony. The statue was not installed at the Art Museum but in South Philadelphia, next to a stadium.

Most of the conflict, however, between commoditization and singularization in complex societies takes place within individuals, leading to what appear to be anomalies in cognition, inconsistencies in values, and uncertainties in action. People in these societies all maintain some private vision of a hierarchy of exchange spheres, but the justification for this hierarchy is not, as it was among the Tiv, integrally tied to the exchange structure itself; rather, the justification must be imported from outside the system of exchange, from such autonomous and usually parochial systems as that of aesthetics, or morality, or religion, or specialized professional concerns. When we feel that selling a Rembrandt or an heirloom is trading downward, the explanation for our attitude is that things called "art" or "historical objects" are superior to the world of commerce. This is the reason why the high value of the singular in complex societies becomes so easily embroiled in snobbery. The high value does not visibly reside in the exchange system itself – as it traditionally did among the Tiv, when, for example, the superiority in prestige (rather than mere exchange) of brass rods over pots was palpably confirmed by the ability of the brass rods to bring in ritual cloth or slaves. In a complex society, the absence of such visible confirmation of prestige, of what exactly is an "upward" conversion, makes it necessary to attribute high but nonmonetary value to aesthetic, stylistic, ethnic, class, or genealogical esoterica.

When things participate simultaneously in cognitively distinct yet effectively intermeshed exchange spheres, one is constantly confronted with seeming paradoxes of value. A Picasso, though possessing a monetary value, is priceless in another, higher scheme. Hence, we feel uneasy, even offended, when a newspaper declares the Picasso to be worth $690,000, for one should not be pricing the priceless. But in a pluralistic society, the "objective" pricelessness of the Picasso can only be unambiguously confirmed to us by its immense market price. Yet, the pricelessness still makes the Picasso in some sense more valuable than the pile of dollars it can fetch – as will be duly pointed out by the newspapers if the Picasso is stolen. Singularity, in brief, is confirmed not by the object's structural position in an exchange system, but by intermittent forays into the commodity sphere, quickly followed by reentries into the closed sphere of singular "art." But the two worlds cannot be kept separate for very long; for one thing, museums must insure their holdings. So museums and art dealers will name prices, be accused of the sin of transforming art into a commodity, and, in response, defend themselves by blaming each other for creating and maintaining a commodity market. It would, however, be missing the point of this analysis to conclude that the talk about singular art is merely an ideological camouflage for an interest in merchandising. What is culturally significant here is precisely that there is an inner compulsion to defend oneself, to others and to oneself, against the charge of "merchandising" art.

The only time when the commodity status of a thing is beyond question is the moment of actual exchange. Most of the time, when the commodity is effectively out of the commodity sphere, its status is inevitably ambiguous and open to the push and pull of events and desires, as it is shuffled about in the flux of social life. This is the time when it is exposed to the well-nigh-infinite variety of attempts to singularize it. Thus, singularizations of various kinds, many of them fleeting, are a constant accompaniment of commoditization, all the more so when it becomes excessive. There is a kind of singularizing black market here that is the mirror-image of, and as inevitable as, the more familiar commoditizing black market that accompanies regulated singularizing economies. Thus, even things that unambiguously carry an exchange value – formally speaking, therefore, commodities – do absorb the other kind of worth, one that is non-monetary and goes beyond exchange worth. We may take this to be the missing non-economic side of what Marx called commodity fetishism. For Marx, the worth of commodities is determined by the social relations of their production; but the existence of the exchange system makes the production process remote and misperceived, and it "masks" the commodity's true worth (as, say, in the case of diamonds). This allows the commodity to be socially endowed with a fetishlike "power" that is unrelated to its true worth. Our analysis suggests, however, that some of that power is attributed to commodities after they are produced, and this by way of an autonomous cognitive and cultural process of singularization.

Two Western exchange spheres: people vs. objects

I have so far emphasized the sweeping nature of commoditization in Western society as representative of an ideal type of highly commercialized and monetized society. But the West is also a unique cultural entity, with a historically conditioned set of predispositions to see the world in certain ways.

One of these predispositions I have referred to before: that of conceptually separating people from things, and of seeing people as the natural preserve for individuation (that is singularization) and things as the natural preserve for commoditization. The separation, though intellectually rooted in classical antiquity and Christianity, becomes culturally salient with the onset of European modernity. Its most glaring denial lay, of course, in the practice of slavery. Yet its cultural significance can be gauged precisely by the fact that slavery did present an intellectual and moral problem in the West (see Davis 1966, 1975), but almost nowhere else. Whatever the complex reasons, the conceptual distinction between the universe of people and the universe of objects had become culturally axiomatic in the West by the mid-twentieth century. It is therefore not surprising that the cultural clash over abortion should be more fierce in the twentieth century than it ever was in the nineteenth, and that this clash should be phrased by both sides in terms of the precise location of the line that divides persons from things and the point at which "personhood" begins. For both anti-abortion and pro-abortion forces agree on one point: that "things" but not "persons" can be aborted. Hence the occasional court battles when pro-abortionists seek court injunctions against anti-abortionists' attempts to ritualize the disposal of aborted fetuses, since ritual disposal presumes personhood. In terms of underlying conceptions, both sides here stand together in striking cultural contrast to the Japanese. The latter have few misgivings about abortion but acknowledge the personhood of aborted children, giving them the special status of *misogo*, lost souls, and commemorating them by special shrines (see Miura 1984).

There is, therefore, a perennial moral concern in Western thought, whatever the ideological position of the thinker, about the commoditization of human attributes such as labor, intellect, or creativity, or, more recently, human organs, female reproductive capacity, and ova. The moral load in these matters comes partly from the long debates on slavery and the victory of abolition. Hence the tendency to resort to slavery as the readiest metaphor when commoditization threatens to invade the human sphere, slavery being the extreme case in which the totality of a person is seen as having been commoditized. The moral indictments of capitalism by both Marx and Pope Leo XIII derived their force from the notion that human labor should not be a mere commodity – hence the rhetorical power of such terms as "wage slavery." The conceptual unease of conjoining person and commodity renders, in most modern Western liberal societies, the adoption of a baby illegal if it involves monetary compensation to the natural parent – something that most societies have seen as satisfying the obvious demands of equity. In the modern West, however, adoption through compensation is viewed as child-selling and therefore akin to slavery because of the implicit commoditization of the child, regardless of how loving the adoptive parents may be. Thus, the law specifically punishes such compensation in Britain, in most Canadian provinces, and in almost all states in the United States.

The hallmark of commoditization is exchange. But exchange opens the way to trafficking, and trafficking in human attributes carries with it a special opprobrium. For example, we do not – we cannot at this point – object to the commoditization and sale of labor (by its nature, a terminal commodity). But we do object to the trafficking in labor that a complete commoditization of labor would imply. We have abolished indentured labor, and the courts have struck down the commoditization of the contracts of athletes and actors. The cultural argument against a team's or a film studio's "selling" a ballplayer or an actor to another employer is cast in the idiom of slavery. The transfer of a contract forces the worker to work for someone whom he had not chosen himself, hence forces him to work involuntarily. We see here a significant cultural detail in the Western commoditization of labor – the commoditization must be controlled by the laborer himself. By contrast, contractual obligations to pay, as in promissory notes or installment buying, and rent contracts are legally negotiable; they can be and are regularly sold and resold. By the same cultural logic, the idea of nearly confiscatory taxation is far less shocking to us than even a modest amount of corvée labor. As with trafficking in labor, we find the direct commoditization of sexual services (also a terminal commodity) by the immediate supplier less objectionable than the trafficking in them by pimps. And so also we find the imminent possibility of terminal sales of human ova somewhat more morally acceptable than the idea of a commercial traffic in them.

The question remains, however: how secure are the Western cultural ramparts that defend the human sphere against commoditization, especially in a secularized society that finds it increasingly difficult to appeal to any transcendental sanctions for cultural discrimination and classification? I have suggested that economies are inherently responsive to the pressures of commoditization and that they tend to commoditize as widely as the exchange technology allows. What then, we may ask, are the effects, on the divide between the human and the commodity spheres, of the developing technology of transfer of human attributes? I am speaking here of recent medical advances in the transfer of organs and ova and the development of surrogate motherhood. The realm of human reproduction is one in which the difference between persons and things is particularly difficult to define, defying all attempts at drawing a simple line where there is a natural continuum.

The idea of direct surrogate motherhood – in which a woman simply bears a child for the future legal mother – required, of course, a legal more than a technical innovation. The idea had taken hold at the same time that technical advances in coping with female infertility had begun to raise the hopes of childless couples but without, in fact, helping many of them. It also came in response to the shrinkage in the supply of babies for adoption that occurred in the 1960's with the pill and the 1970's with the wider legalization of abortions. More recently, the picture has been complicated by the development of technical means for the actual transplantation of ova, opening the possibility of trading in the physical means of reproduction. The popular objections to surrogate motherhood are usually phrased in the idiom of the impropriety of commoditization. In the words of a Canadian provincial minister of social services, expressing his opposition: "You can't buy a baby in Ontario." It is, however, more acceptable, at least to some, when the surrogate mother announces that she receives not "payment" but "compensation" of ten thousand dollars – "because of the inconvenience to my family and the risk involved." And the agency arranging for surrogate child production makes a point of declaring "We are not in the rent-a-womb business." In the meantime, while ethicists and theologians argue, the cost of securing a surrogate mother has now risen to around twenty-five thousand dollars (Scott 1984).

There is, of course, a precedent for the commoditization of physical human attributes: the supply of blood in American medical practice depends overwhelmingly on a straightforward commodity market in blood – in contrast, for example, to most European countries, which have deliberately rejected the commodity approach (Cooper and Culyer 1968). At present, advances in organ transplants and the inadequate supply of organs raises the same question of public policy that was confronted in the past in the case of blood: what are the best ways of ensuring an adequate supply? In the meantime, advertisements have begun to appear offering to buy kidneys for transplantation.

How to deal with ova is only beginning to be discussed. Culturally, the situation is perceived as being more complex than in the case of sperm, which has been commoditized for some time without a great deal of discussion. Is this because the ovum is seen as the basic core of the future human being? Or because women are expected to feel maternal toward the ova as potential babies and should not sell them, whereas men are not expected to have paternal feelings about their sperm?[2] (Many societies describe the generation of life as the union of two elements; Westerners, however, choose the scientific metaphor in which one speaks of the fertilization *of* the ovum *by* the sperm, so that the ovum becomes a homunculus being activated into life.) The inevitable development into routine procedures of the transplantation of ova and the freezing of ova for storage will represent an expansion of the possibilities of the exchange technology for human attributes, including the possibility of trafficking in them. The question is whether this will increase the permeability of the boundary between the world of things and that of people, or whether the boundary will be displaced by recourse to new definitions but itself remain as rigid as before.

Conclusion: kinds of biographies

Although the singular and the commodity are opposites, no thing ever quite reaches the ultimate commodity end of the continuum between them. There are no perfect commodities. On the other hand, the exchange function of every economy appears to have a built-in force that drives the exchange system toward the greatest degree of commoditization that the exchange technology permits. The counterforces are culture and the individual, with their drive to discriminate, classify, compare, and sacralize. This means a two-front battle for culture as for the individual – one against commoditization as a homogenizer of exchange values, the other against the utter singularization of things as they are in nature.

In small-scale uncommercialized societies, the drive to commoditization was usually contained by the inadequacies of the technology of exchange, notably, the absence of a well-developed monetary system. This left room for a cultural categorization of the exchange value of things, usually in the form of closed exchange spheres, and it satisfied individual cognitive needs for classification. The collective cultural classification thus constrained the innate exuberance to which purely idiosyncratic and private classifications are prone.

In large-scale, commercialized, and monetized societies, the existence of a sophisticated exchange technology fully opens the economy to swamping by commoditization. In all contemporary industrial societies, whatever their ideologies, commoditization and monetization tend to invade almost every aspect of existence, be it openly or by way of a black market. New technological advances (for example, in medicine) also open previously closed areas to the possibilities of exchange and these areas tend to become quickly commoditized. The flattening of values that follows commoditization and the inability of the collective culture of a modern society to cope with this flatness frustrate the individual on the one hand, and, on the other, leave ample room for a multitude of classifications by individuals and small groups. These classifications, however, remain private and, except in the case of culturally hegemonic groups, without public support.

Thus, the economies of complex and highly monetized societies exhibit a two-sided valuating system: on one side is the homogenous area of commodities, on the other, the extremely variegated area of private valuation. Further complications arise from the constant referring of private valuation to the only reliable public valuation that exists – which is in the commodity area. It is inevitable that if worth is given a price, the going market price will become the measure of worth. The result is a complex intertwining of the commodity exchange sphere with the plethora of private classifications, leading to anomalies and contradictions and to conflicts both in the cognition of individuals and in the interaction of individuals and groups. By contrast, the structure of the economies of small-scale societies in the past resulted in a relative consonance of economic, cultural, and private valuations. These differences lead to quite different biographical profiles of things.

A caveat is required at this point. While in this discussion I have dwelt on the gross contrast between two ideal and polar types of economies, the most interesting empirical cases to be studied, with ultimately the highest theoretical returns, are the cases in between. It is from these cases that we can learn how the forces of commoditization and singularization are intertwined in ways far more subtle than our ideal model can show, how one breaks the rules by moving between spheres that are supposed to be insulated from each other, how one converts what is formally unconvertible, how one masks these actions and with whose connivance, and, not least, how the spheres are reorganized and things reshuffled between them in the course of a society's history. Equally interesting would be the cases where the different systems of commoditization of different societies interact. For example, Curtin (1984) has shown the importance, for the history of world trade, of trade diasporas; in these, traders, constituting a distinct *quasi*-cultural group, provided the channels for the movement of goods between disparate societies. The usefulness of such trading groups in mediating between the different exchange systems is manifest. By cushioning the direct impact of world trade, this mediation spares the societies involved from seeing their particular ideas of commoditization challenged, sheltering their baroque exchange systems in the comfort of their cultural parochialism. This, perhaps, would explain the striking viability, historically, of parochial economic systems in the midst of worldwide networks of trade. And it might also explain what has long been a puzzle in economic anthropology – namely, the limited spread, until the twentieth century, of "all-purpose" currency, a spread far more limited than diffusion theory or commonsense utilitarianism would have suggested. Having said all this, let me nevertheless return to the gross contrast between the "complex, commercialized" and the "small-scale" societies, the implications of which I have pursued throughout this paper.

One can draw an analogy between the way societies construct individuals and the way they construct things. In small-scale societies, a person's social identities are relatively stable and changes in them are normally conditioned more by cultural rules than by biographical idiosyncracies. The drama in an ordinary person's biography stems from what happens within the given status. It lies in the conflicts between the egoistic self and the unambiguous demands of given social identities, or in conflicts arising from interaction between actors with defined roles within a clearly structured social system. The excitement in the biographies is of the picaresque variety. At the same time, the individual who does not fit the given niches is either singularized into a special identity – which is sacred or dangerous, and often both – or is simply cast out. Things in these small-scale societies are similarly modeled. Their status in the clearly structured system of exchange values and exchange spheres is unambiguous. An eventful biography of a thing is for the most part one of events within the given sphere. Any thing that does not fit the categories is clearly anomalous and it is taken out of normal circulation, to be either sacralized or isolated or cast out. What one glimpses through the biographies of both people and things in these societies is, above all, the social system and the collective understandings on which it rests.

In complex societies, by contrast, a person's social identities are not only numerous but often conflicting, and there is no clear hierarchy of loyalties that makes one identity dominant over the others. Here, the drama of personal biographies has become more and more the drama of identities – of their clashes, of the impossibility of choosing between them, of the absence of signals from the culture and the society at large to help in the choice. The drama, in brief, lies in the uncertainty of identity – a theme increasingly dominant in modern Western literature where it is pushing aside dramas of social structure (even in the eminently structural cases dealt with in writings on women and "minorities"). The biography of things in complex societies reveals a similar pattern. In the homogenized world of commodities, an eventful biography of a thing becomes the story of the various singularizations of it, of classifications and reclassifications in an uncertain world of categories whose importance shifts with every minor change in context. As with persons, the drama here lies in the uncertainties of valuation and of identity.

All this suggests an emendation to the profound Durkheimian notion that a society orders the world of things on the pattern of the structure that prevails in the social world of its people. What also happens, I would suggest, is that societies constrain both these worlds simultaneously and in the same way, constructing objects as they construct people.

Notes

I owe thanks to Arjun Appadurai and Barbara Klamon Kopytoff for discussions that led to the writing of this paper, and to Jean Adelman, Sandra Barnes, Muriel Bell, Gyan Prakash, Colin Renfrew, and Barbara Herrnstein Smith for comments and suggestions that helped shape its final version.

1. I wish to thank Barbara Herrnstein Smith for drawing my attention to the importance of such institutions in the processes I am describing.
2. I am grateful to Muriel Bell for this suggestion.

References

Bohannan, Paul. 1959. The Impact of Money on an African Subsistence Economy. *Journal of Economic History* 19:491–503.

Braudel, Fernand. 1983. *The Roots of Modern Capitalism*. New York.

Cooper, Michael H., and Anthony J. Culyer. 1968. *The Price of Blood: An Economic Study of the Charitable and Commercial Principles*. London.

Curtin, Philip D. 1984. *Cross-Cultural Trade in World History*. Cambridge.

Davis, David Brion. 1966. *The Problem of Slavery in Western Culture*. Ithaca, N.Y.

1975. *The Problem of Slavery in the Age of Revolution: 1770–1823*. Ithaca, N.Y.

Douglas, Mary, and Baron Isherwood. 1980. *The World of Goods: Towards an Anthropology of Consumption*. London.

Dumont, Louis. 1972. *Homo Hierarchicus*. London.

Durkheim, Emile and Marcel Mauss. 1963. *Primitive Classification*. Trans. Rodney Needham. London. (Orig. French ed., 1903).

Durkheim, Emile. 1915. *The Elementary Forms of Religious Life*. London. (Orig. French ed., 1912).

Ekeh, Peter P. 1974. *Social Exchange Theory*. London.

Homans, George. 1961. *Social Behavior: Its Elementary Forms.* New York.
Kapferer, Bruce, ed. 1976. *Transactions and Meaning*. Philadelphia.
Kopytoff, Igor, and Suzanne Miers. 1977. African "slavery" as an institution of marginality. In S. Miers and I. Kopytoff, eds., *Slavery in Africa: Historical and Anthropological Perspectives*, 3–81. Madison, Wis.
Kopytoff, Igor. 1982. Slavery. *Annual Review of Anthropology*, 11:207–30.
Kroeber, A. L. 1925. The Yurok. *Handbook of the Indians of California*. (Bureau of American Ethnology Bulletin 78).
Langness, L. L. 1965. *The Life History in Anthropological Science*. New York.
Meillasoux, C. 1975. Introduction. In Meillasoux, ed., *L'esclavage en Afrique précoloniale*. Paris.
Miura, Domyo. 1984. *The Forgotten Child*. Trans. Jim Cuthbert. Henley-on-Thames.
Patterson, Orlando. 1982. *Slavery and Social Death: A Comparative Study*. Cambridge, Mass.
Pospisil, Leopold. 1963. *Kapauku Papuan Economy*. (Yale Publications in Anthropology No. 61). New Haven, Conn.
Rivers, W. H. R. 1910. The Genealogical Method Anthropological Inquiry. *Sociological Review* 3:1–12.
Scott, Sarah. 1984. The Baby Business. *The Gazette*, B–1, 4. Montreal, April 24.
Thompson, Michael. 1979. *Rubbish Theory: The Creation and Destruction of Value*. New York.
Vaughan, James H. 1977. Mafakur: A limbic institution of the Marghi (Nigeria). In S. Miers and I. Kopytoff, eds., *Slavery in Africa: Historical and Anthropological Perspectives*, 85–102. Madison, Wis.

Part IV
Processes: Spheres of Exchange

[22]

Some Principles of Exchange and Investment among the Tiv[1]

PAUL BOHANNAN
Oxford University

TIV are a pagan people numbering over 800,000 who live in the middle Benue Valley of northern Nigeria. The basis of their economy is subsistence agriculture, supplemented by an effective network of markets particularly in the southern and central portions of their country. Tiv pride themselves on their farming abilities and their subsistence wealth.

Today, however, their ideas of economic exchange and their traditional methods of investment and economic aggrandizement are being undermined by a new economic system which demands different actions, motives and ideas. This article deals with: (I) Tiv ideas of exchange as expressed in their language, (II) some traditional modes of investment and exchange, based on a ranked hierarchy of spheres or categories of exchangeable commodities, and (III) the impact of Western economy on such aspects of subsistence, exchange and investment which Tiv consider in terms of these spheres or categories.

I

Distribution of goods among Tiv falls into two spheres: a "market," on the one hand, and gifts, on the other.

The several words best translated "gift" apply—besides the cases which we in the West would recognize as "gift"—to exchange over a long period of time between persons or groups in a more or less permanent relationship. The gift may be a factor designed to strengthen the relationship, or even to create it. There are several Tiv words for "gift," the examination of which would require another article the length of this one. For our purposes, it is primary that any of these "gift" words implies a relationship between the two parties concerned which is of a permanence and warmth not known in a "market," and hence—though "gifts" should be reciprocal over a long period of time—it is bad form overtly to count and compute and haggle over gifts.

A "market" is a transaction which in itself calls up no long-term personal relationship, and which is therefore to be exploited to as great a degree as possible. In fact, the presence of a previous relationship makes a "good market" impossible: people do not like to sell to kinsmen since it is bad form to demand as high a price from a kinsman as one might from a stranger. Market behavior and kinship behavior are incompatible in a single relationship, and the individual must give way to one or the other.

The word "market" (*kasoa*) has several meanings in Tiv. It refers primarily to any transaction which is differentiated from gift exchange (and, as we shall see, from exchange marriage). It is also a meeting of people at a regular place and time for the primary purpose of exchanging food and other items. One's "market" is also an aspect of one's luck (*ikôl*)—some people have "good market

[luck]" and some have "bad market [luck]." Therefore, one's market can be affected by one's ritual condition, for fetishes (*akombo*)—not to mention witches (*mbatsav*)—can spoil a man's market (*vihi or kasoa*); indeed, curses and broken promises can also affect a person's market.

Everything, including women, which is exchanged has an exchange value or equivalent (*ishe*), whereas no gift has an exchange value. In a market situation *ishe* means vaguely "exchange equivalent"—one might even sometimes translate it "price"—though Tiv seldom ask or quote equivalents in their own trading. Rather, they effect bargains, usually without recourse to this word. An expensive item is a "thing of great value" or "thing of high equivalent" (*kwagh u kehe ishe*), and to haggle is to dispute the value or equivalent (*kperen ishe*). The general term both for economic trading and for exchange marriage can be translated roughly as "trading value" (*yamen ishe*).

In every market transaction, there is a man who sells (*te*) and a man who buys (*yam*). These words must be carefully examined for they do not exactly parallel their English equivalents. *Te* means to spread something out on the ground to the public view, as in a market place. By extension, it means "to sell"—there is no other way to say "to sell," and no other verb to designate that half of an exchange in which one releases or gets rid of an article. *Yam*, on the other hand, means "trade" in the widest sense, but refers primarily to that half of the exchange in which one takes or gains an article. It can, therefore, often be translated by the English word "buy." Its difference, however, can be seen in sentences such as "I bought money with it" (*m yam inyaregh a mi*—more accurately translated "I realized money on it," and still more accurately but less literally, "In this exchange what I received was money"). Activities of traders are called *yamen a yam;* exchange marriage is often called "woman trading" (*kwase yamen*) or, more politely, "value trading" (*ishe yamen*).

Although Tiv have a word which means approximately the same as the English word "exchange" (*musan*), which can sometimes be used to differentiate barter from money transactions, this word is not ordinarily used of trade or commerce.

II

Within the bounds of these words and basic concepts, Tiv image and communicate their ideas of economic transactions and investments. It is important to realize, however, that the ideas themselves may never be articulated as principles or as logical systems. The systematization may be, as in this case, the work of the ethnographer. Yet, this systematization is—or at least is consistent with—the Tiv covert ideology in the matter; its empirical validity is demonstrated when, in terms of it, the ethnographer can both sensibly discuss the ideas and images with Tiv in their language, and communicate them in another language to his colinguals and colleagues.

It is in these terms that we can say that in Tiv ideology it is neither usual nor desirable to exchange a commodity for just any other commodity. Rather, there are several different categories of interchangeable commodities and items, each of which is felt to be more or less exclusive. It seems to be necessary to distinguish three such categories.

The most apparent category of exchangeable items among Tiv consists primarily of foodstuffs (*yiagh*). All locally produced foodstuffs (imported, particularly European, food is not *yiagh*) are said by Tiv to be of a single economic kind, and immediately interchangeable. To trade pepper for locust-bean sauce or yams for guinea corn is a common transaction or "market" among Tiv. The quantities to be exchanged are never prescribed,[2] as they are in some societies—the bargain which any individual may drive within the sphere of foodstuffs is a reflection of the market aspect of his luck. If I, selling pepper, can get locust beans of a quality and quantity whose value I myself consider to be greater than the value of the pepper I gave for them, my market is good; if I get less, my market is bad—or, more commonly, the market of the other person is better than mine. The obvious advantage of such a line of reasoning is that, in really successful transactions, everybody's market is good.

Included within this same category are chickens and goats, as well as household utensils (mortars, grindstones, calabashes, baskets and pots) and some tools (particularly those used in agricultural pursuits), and also raw materials for producing any items in the category. For a woman to sell yams to buy a pot, for her to make a pot and sell it to buy yams—these are considered to be normal buying and selling (*yamen a yam*).

The second important category is that which includes slaves, cattle, that type of large white cloth known as *tugudu*, and metal bars. One is still entitled to use the present tense in this case, for ideologically the category still exists in spite of the fact that brass rods are today very rare, and that slavery has been legally abolished. Tiv still quote prices of slaves in cows and brass rods, and of cattle in brass rods and *tugudu* cloths. Akiga, in a hitherto untranslated part of his book, tells us that,

> You could buy one iron bar (*sokpo*) for a *tugudu* cloth. In those days five *tugudu* cloths were equivalent to a bull! A cow was worth ten *tugudu*. One brass rod (*bashi*) was worth about the same as one *tugudu* cloth; thus five brass rods were worth a bull.

Other Tiv would disagree about the actual values of these various commodities.[3] The value of the brass rod is said by all to have declined considerably just before the arrival of Europeans in Tivland. None, however, would disagree with Akiga's grouping of commodities.

This second category is associated with prestige (*shagba*) in the same way that the first category is associated with subsistence. Although slaves and brass rods, at least, had some economic value beyond their value as prestige-conferring property, this latter was their main use.

The supreme and unique category of exchange values contains only one item: rights in human beings other than slaves, and particularly rights in women. Even twenty-five years after official abolition of exchange marriage, it is this category of exchange in which Tiv are emotionally most entangled

(L. and P. Bohannan 1953: 69–71). All exchanges within this category are exchanges of rights in human beings, usually dependent women and children, so that the category may be called the category of dependent persons, and many of its values are expressed in terms of kinship and marriage.

This plan or scheme leaves out several important items of Tiv material culture: particularly weapons, specialists' tools like divining apparatus, etc., which do not, generally speaking, enter into exchange situations. Since I have no record of hearing these items discussed in a situation of exchange, I have no basis for assigning them to one category or another—indeed, I doubt that Tiv would do so. My purpose in reporting these categories is not the pedantic one of putting every commodity into one or the other; rather, the categories represent the fundamentals of Tiv notions of exchange and investment.

Further, several items which we consider as exchangeable wealth, and as bases for investment, are not included by Tiv in this system of thought. Services and labor, for example, are by and large reciprocal and form part of the age-set, kinship and domestic group structures and moralities. Tiv consider it rude and improper to discuss services in terms of "exchange" but insist rather that such matters be viewed as individual acts of generosity or as kinship or age-set obligations. They recognize the reciprocity, of course, but do not themselves cast it into terms which we would consider "economic." Land, which many peoples—including, perhaps, ourselves—consider to be the ultimate wealth, is not exchangeable among Tiv, not even for other land. Land is, to Tiv, the spatial aspect of social organization; land rights are conditions of agnation. It is impossible for a Tiv to invest in land, since his basic right in land is a right to sufficient land, and only secondarily a right to specific lands. No Tiv can control more land than he can use. (Both land rights and labor are discussed at some length in Bohannan 1954.) Therefore, it should be noted, we are dealing with Tiv exchange and investment, but Tiv notions cover only a part of the range to which the English words "exchange" and "investment" refer.

It is instructive of Tiv modes of thought about these three main categories of exchangeable items to note the manner in which individual items can be "removed" from the categories, or made incapable of further exchange. Individual items are removed from the category of subsistence by expenditure, including sacrifice to fetishes. Although yams have an exchange value as well as a utilitarian value, once eaten they no longer have either. Household equipment breaks or is worn out. All items which are removed from this sphere of exchangeable goods are removed either by being used up or by being sacrificed (and subsequently used up).

Removing individual items from the second category—that centering around prestige—is more complex, and its very complexity makes possible some of the characteristics of Tiv economy. Some individual items—cloth—can be removed by expenditure; other individual items—slaves—can be removed by death of human beings. Most of the items, however, are removed by an act which increases the prestige of the owner of the item by diminishing its utility or exchangeability. Thus, brass rods can be converted into jewelry, thereby increasing the prestige of ownership but diminishing the range of utility; cows can be butchered on festive occasions (cattle are never sacrificed for religious purposes among Tiv), thereby increasing the prestige of the owner but diminishing the utility of the commodity and nullifying its exchangeability.

Individual items are removed from the third category—that of rights in dependent persons—by death of the human beings, and by death alone.

The three chief categories of exchangeable items among Tiv, while considered of equal practical importance, are nevertheless arranged in a hierarchy on the basis of moral values. The category of prestige is superior to (but no more important than) the category of subsistence; great prestige assumes adequate or ample subsistence means. The category of dependent persons is superior to (but no more important than) the categories both of prestige and of subsistence. A large number of dependent persons, demonstrating success in attracting, getting, and keeping dependents, assumes adequate or ample prestige and subsistence goods. But, conversely, many dependents give one prestige and enable one to produce ample and generous amounts of subsistence wealth.

The moral basis of the hierarchy is evident in the fact that the ethics of kinship are more compelling than the ethics of mere prestige (and always take precedence—ideally one must always sacrifice prestige or hope of gain to aid a kinsman); the ethics of prestige are more compelling than the mores of markets and exchange of subsistence wealth—a man forgoes gain in subsistence wealth for the sake of prestige or to fulfill kinship obligations.

The hierarchal nature of the values involved in the three main categories of exchangeable goods provides a basis for investment and economic endeavor in Tiv society. The drive toward success leads most Tiv, to the greatest possible extent, to convert food into prestige items; to convert prestige items into dependents—wives and children. Tiv say that it is good (*do kwagh*) to trade food for brass rods, but that it is bad (*vihi kwagh*) to trade brass rods for food; that it is good to trade your cows or brass rods for a wife, but very bad to trade your marriage ward for cows or brass rods. Seen from the individual's point of view, it is profitable and possible to invest one's wealth only if one converts it into a higher category: to convert subsistence wealth into prestige wealth and both into women is the aim of the economic endeavor of individual Tiv.

That Tiv do conceptualize exchange articles as belonging to different categories, and that they rank the categories on a moral basis, gives rise to the fact that two different kinds of exchanges may be recognized: exchanges of items contained within a single category, and exchanges of items belonging to different categories. For Tiv, these two different types of exchange are marked by separate and distinct moral attitudes.

Exchanges within a category—particularly that of subsistence, the only one intact today—excite no moral judgments beyond comments regarding the "market" luck of one or both of the parties to the exchange. Exchanges between categories, however, excite a completely different sort of moral reaction: the man who exchanges lower category goods for higher category goods does not brag about his market luck but about his skill in investment, his personal magnetism, and his "strong heart." The man who exchanges high category goods for lower rationalizes his action in terms of high-valued motivation (most often the needs of his kinsmen).

To maintain this distinction between the two types of exchanges which Tiv mark by different behavior and different values, I shall use separate words. I shall call those exchanges of items within a single category "conveyances" and those exchanges of items from one category to another "conversions." (Steiner [1954] uses "translations" for what I have called conversions.) For purposes of analysis, I shall maintain the dichotomy between the two words representing types of exchanges more rigidly than would any Tiv between the two types of moral behavior in the normal course of living. Roughly, conveyances are—to Tiv—morally neutral; conversions have a strong moral quality in their rationalization.

The two institutions most intimately connected with conveyance are markets and marriage, particularly exchange marriage. Both these are special subjects and must be dealt with separately. The remainder of this section is concerned with conversion.

Conversion, unlike conveyance, is not mere exchange of equivalent goods. Because there is a definite moral dimension to conversion, it forms a strong source of motivation to individual action. It is in the light of such motivation that we must evaluate the fact that a very high percentage of autobiographies collected from Tiv contain variants of this story: "When I was a very small child, my kinsman gave me a baby chicken. I tended it carefully and when it grew up it laid eggs and hatched out more chickens; I exchanged these chickens for a young nanny goat, who bore kids, which I put out with various kinsmen until I could exchange them for a cow. The cow bore calves, and eventually I was able to sell the calves and procure a wife." Every successful man considers such a story one of the most important sequences of his biography; it proves that he has been successful.

Tiv say that it was often possible in the old days to buy brass rods for food, but usually only if the owner of the brass rods were short of food or required an unusually large amount to give a feast, making too heavy a drain on his wives' food supplies. They also say that no honorable man would exchange slaves for food—there were other means of getting food, especially along the extended web of kinship. Although all Tiv with whom I discussed the matter denied emphatically that Tiv would ever sell a kinsman, wife or ward to get food (there are other reasons for which such sales were made), Akiga—in an untranslated section of his book—mentions a famine which was so severe that, as a last resort, men sold their daughters to foreigners in exchange for food so that they could keep their sons alive.

Another conversion found among Tiv is marriage by bride wealth (which may be of several types, usually all lumped together and called ***kem kwase***). Although some forms of marriage by bride wealth were in the past actually delayed exchanges (and today can be seen as substitutes for exchanges [L. and P. Bohannan 1953:71–73]), to "receive a woman" (***ngoho kwase***)—to get wife or marriage ward without giving one in exchange—is every man's goal. A wife is traditionally acquired by being granted a sister or cousin (any woman in one's marriage-ward sharing group—the *ingôl* group of Akiga 1939 and Abraham 1940) to exchange for a wife, either directly or by means of bride wealth. A wife whom one acquires in any other way is not the concern of one's marriage-ward sharing group because the woman or other property exchanged for her did not belong to the marriage-ward group. The daughters of such a wife are not divided among the members of a man's marriage-ward group, but only among his sons. Such a wife is not only indicative of a man's ability and success financially and personally, but rights in her are the only form of property which is not ethically subject to the demands of his agnates.

Wives may sometimes be acquired by means of much more elaborate conversions. We discovered one case (in the course of a witchcraft moot) in which a man two generations ago had traded a slave for a cow, which he in turn traded for a marriage-ward to exchange for a wife; the distribution, as marriage-wards, of the daughters of this marriage (among his sons rather than his marriage-ward group) was called into question. Sometimes Tiv acquire foreign wives for cattle, from tribes whose custom it is to marry with cattle; the daughters of such women are considered to be Tiv, and can be exchanged in regular Tiv fashion—they do not go into the "pool" of wards in the marriage-ward group unless a man's agnates force him by threats of witchcraft to share his "property" with them.

There are many social sanctions for conversion of one's wealth to higher categories: Tiv are very scornful of a man who is merely rich in subsistence goods (or, today, in money); they say that if he has not converted his goods the reasons must be personal inadequacy. Tiv also say that jealous kinsmen of a rich man will bewitch him and his people by means of certain fetishes in order to make him expend his wealth in sacrifices to "repair" the fetishes. Once the conversion is made, demands of kinsmen are no longer effective—at least, they must take a new form.

A man who persists in a policy of converting his wealth into higher categories instead of letting it be dispersed by his dependents and kinsmen is said to have a "strong heart" (*taver shima*). He is both feared and respected: because he is strong enough to resist the excessive demands of his kinsmen, but still fulfills his kinship obligations generously, he is feared as a man of special, potentially evil, talents (*tsav*).

III

Tiv notions of exchange and investment are among the hardest hit of all their ideas by impact of Western ideology and by colonial economy and social organization because these ideas are immediately and obviously in conflict with Western ideas and practice. Today, Tiv are concerned because their categories of exchangeable items cannot be maintained. There are three main reasons for this fact: (1) two of the categories today have no overt validity, (2) many new commodities have been introduced which do not belong to any category, and (3) money has provided a common denominator among the categories which was previously lacking.

A moment's consideration makes it obvious that the category of prestige goods, centering mainly about cattle, slaves and brass rods, has ceased to exist in material terms, although the category is maintained ideally. Slave dealing was prohibited from the first effective European control (about 1910); brass rods are no longer generally available because the Administration regarded them primarily as currency and "replaced" them with pounds, shillings and pence. Perhaps of even greater moment was the fact that in 1927 the highest exchange category, that of rights in women, was dealt a crippling blow by Administrative abolition of exchange marriage and substitution of marriage by bride wealth (payable in money) as the legal form. The category of subsistence items is the only one that today can still be found in anything like its original form.

European and African traders have introduced many new commodities to Tivland, both of Nigerian and European manufacture, and have increased many fold the quantity of some other commodities which were formerly present in small amounts or small numbers. These goods, particularly European goods, were introduced concurrently with money, and they are considered part of the money complex. They do not enter into any formerly existing category, but form their own category only very imperfectly. Thus, there are today many more commodities than ever before which do not fit precisely into traditionally structured exchange situations.

Finally, and perhaps more important, is the introduction of currency, the very nature of which is to standardize the exchangeability value of every item to a common scale. The introduction of currency was not only to be expected with the extension of Western economic ventures, it was hurried by the Administration in its desire to collect tax in a convenient and readily transportable form. A money tax, payable by all adult males, was imposed throughout Tivland by the end of the first World War. Imposition of this tax coincided with the initiation of large-scale growing of beniseed (*sesamum indicum*) as a cash crop. Beniseed, although long known to Tiv, is today often called by the word for "tax" or "tribute" (*kpandegh*).

Even though it is possible to consider brass rods as "currency" in the old system, because they were a commodity whose exchange value was more far-reaching than that of any other commodity and because they belonged to the intermediary category, the introduction of coinage was not a simple "substitution" of one form of currency for another as was thought at the time to be the case. Brass rods were, it is true, the main medium of conversion in the old days: brass rods could be and sometimes were used to buy food, they could be and often were used to get a wife. But the penetrability of brass rods into the other categories of exchange, while more pronounced than that of any other commodity, did have limitations. Brass rods never provided a standard gauge against which the exchangeability value of all commodities was reckoned, as is the case with the coinage issued by the West African Currency Board.

Today all conversions and most conveyances are made in terms of money.

Yet Tiv constantly express their distrust of money. They compare the monetary system to the subsistence system at great length, always to the disfavor of the former. Money does not (they say) reproduce itself or bear seed. You spend (*vihi*, literally "spoil") money and it's gone—a man can't spend a field, and though he sacrifices a goat, it has already borne kids. Money, they feel, is the root of much of their trouble.

Tiv, both desiring and distrusting money as they do, have attempted at least in some contexts to relegate it to a fourth and lowest category of exchangeable goods. The logical end of such a classification, however, would be either that money is exchanged only for money, or that it is exchanged only for those European goods which were introduced more or less concurrently with it. This is precisely the view that many Tiv elders expound. It is a view, however, which cannot be maintained in the present situation in Tivland.

Concurrently with the introduction of money, pacification of the countryside and introduction of cash crops, a further factor arose: men's trading developed very rapidly. Men's trade, like women's, tends to be based on subsistence goods, but unlike women's, on goods which must be procured and traded over long distances: smoked fish from the Benue and Katsina Ala Rivers, camwood and kolas from Ogoja Province, and items such as cotton which are grown in some parts of Tivland and not in others. Today men up to the age of forty may carry their goods as much as 150 miles to market where it commands the highest price. This trade is usually carried out in terms of money, by semiprofessional traders. These men start with money and end with money; their purpose is to increase their money. Tiv consider this legitimate enterprise.

Tiv also say that women's trade is legitimate and sensible: a woman may sell one type of food to buy another, or sell food to buy a waist cloth for herself or small gifts and latter-day necessities for her children. All Tiv say that the fact that these transactions are carried out in money is beside the point: the woman has not made a conversion, for she has sold expendable subsistence goods and bought expendable subsistence goods.

The difficulty arises when the semiprofessional traders begin trading in the foodstuffs which were formerly the province solely of women. These men may invest sums of their capital in food for resale; in fact, these young semiprofessional traders are the most active buyers and sellers of grain at Tiv markets today, although women also speculate in grain and in yams to a smaller extent. A young trader buys grain in small quantities—often in two- and three-penny lots—from women who are selling it in the market. He collects this grain, may hold it for a while and almost certainly will transport it to another market for sale either to another middleman or to the Hausa or Ibo lorry drivers who visit the larger markets to buy food for export to the overpopulated areas of the Eastern Provinces or the new urban areas in Tivland.

Both the trade carried on by women and that carried on by these ambitious young professional traders are considered admirable by Tiv. The trader is not granted so favorable a position in Tiv society as he is in some other West African societies, and mere monetary or subsistence wealth is not sufficient in itself to afford great prestige. Trade of women stays within the category of subsistence (if one considers the end in view and discounts the presence of money, as Tiv do in the situation), while the trade of the professionals stays within the monetary category.

Yet Tiv see truckload after truckload of foodstuffs driven away from their large markets every fifth day. They say that food is less plentiful today than it was in the past, though more land is being farmed. Tiv elders deplore this situation and know what is happening, but they do not know just where to fix the blame. In attempts to do something about it, they sometimes announce that no women are to sell any food at all. But when their wives disobey them, men do not really feel that they were wrong to have done so. Tiv sometimes discriminate against non-Tiv traders in attempts to stop export of food, but their actions are seldom upheld by the courts to which the outsiders scurry, and in any case Tiv themselves are occupied in the export of food. In their condemnation of the situation which is depriving them of their food faster than they are able to increase production, Tiv elders always curse money itself. It is money which, as the instrument for selling one's life subsistence, is responsible for the worsened situation—money and the Europeans who brought it.

Yet they cannot fix the blame or stop the situation. When women sell to middlemen, Tiv class this exchange in the category of subsistence exchange. When middlemen sell to other middlemen or exporters, it falls within the ethics of money trade. That the two spheres have overlapped they find mysterious and frustrating, and in the nature of money. Yet, so long as a woman does not sell too much food, there is no feeling that she has done wrong; so long as a man buys a commodity with money and sells it for money, he has done nothing blameworthy.

Of even greater concern to Tiv is the influence money has had on marriage institutions, by affecting the interchange of rights in women. In response to what appeared superficially to be popular demand, the Administration (encouraged by the Missions and with the apparent concurrence of the tribal councils) abolished exchange marriage and substituted for it a form of marriage by bride wealth. It is the writer's opinion that both Tiv and Administration today believe this action to have been precipitate and ill-advised. Today every woman's guardian, in accepting money as bride wealth, feels that he is converting down. Although attempts are made to spend money which is received in bride wealth to acquire brides for one's self and one's sons, it is in the nature of money, Tiv insist, that this is most difficult to accomplish. The good man still spends his bride wealth receipts for brides—but good men are not so numerous as would be desirable. Tiv deplore the fact that they are required to "sell" (*te*) their daughters and "buy" (*yam*, but more euphemistically *kem*, to accumulate) wives. It smacks, they tell the investigator in low tones, of slavery. There is no dignity in it since the possibility of converting a bride-wealth marriage into an exchange marriage has been removed.

The fact that Tiv, in the face of the introduction of a money economy, have retained the motivations commensurate with their old ideology of investment based on a scheme of the discreteness of several categories of exchangeable items, hierarchically arranged, has created several difficulties and inconsistencies. It is considered admirable to invest one's wealth in wives and children—the least expendable form of wealth traditionally known to Tiv, and that form most productive of further wealth.

But Tiv have come upon a simple paradox: today it is easy to sell subsistence goods for money to buy prestige articles and women, thereby aggrandizing oneself at a rapid rate. The food so sold is exported, decreasing the amount of subsistence goods available for consumption. On the other hand, the number of women is limited. The result is that bride wealth gets higher—the price of women becomes inflated. Under these conditions, as Tiv attempt to become more and more wealthy in people, they are merely selling more and more of their foodstuffs and subsistence goods, leaving less and less for their own consumption.

Indigenous Tiv ideas of the sort we would call economic not only formed a basis for their intellectual ordering of their economic exchanges, but also supply motivation for their personal economic striving. These ideas are inconsistent with a monetary economy on the fringe of industrial society. Tiv, to whom these are not "economic ideas" but a "natural" ordering of phenomena and behavior, tend to see the difficulty as being with the monetary economy. The ethnographer can only look on and attempt to understand the ideas and motivations, knowing that the discrepancy between ideas and the actual situation will become greater until one is smashed and then adapted to suit the other—and he knows also that the conclusion is foregone.

NOTES

[1] Twenty-six months' research was carried out between July 1949 and January 1953 among the Tiv, under the auspices of the Social Science Research Council and the Wenner-Gren Foundation for Anthropological Research, with supplementary grants from the Colonial Social Science Research Council and the Government of Nigeria, to all of which bodies grateful acknowledgment is made.

[2] This fact may be a function of the time observations were made, which was a time of inflation in Tivland as elsewhere.

[3] I believe Akiga to be giving examples of a category rather than quoting prices here. But the price stability may have been generally recognized in the pre-money days of stable exchange to which Akiga refers.

REFERENCES CITED

Abraham, R. C.
1940 The Tiv people. 2nd ed. London, Crown Agents.

Akiga
1939 Akiga's story. Translated by Rupert East. London, Oxford University Press. For International African Institute.

Bohannan, Paul
1954 Tiv farm and settlement. London, Her Majesty's Stationery Office. In press.

Bohannan, Laura and Paul
1953 The Tiv of central Nigeria. London, International African Institute.

Steiner, Franz
1954 Notes on comparative economics. British Journal of Sociology. Forthcoming.

[23]

Fredrik Barth

Economic Spheres in Darfur [1]

This paper contains a concrete account of the main structure of the Mountain Fur economy. It also pursues an argument of greater generality concerning the use of the concept of spheres in the analysis of an economic system. Concretely, I try to show in what sense the flow of goods and services is patterned in discrete spheres, and to demonstrate the nature of the unity within, and barriers between, the spheres. I point to the discrepancies of evaluation that are made possible by the existence of barriers between spheres, and to the activities of entrepreneurs in relation to these barriers. To give the material, I also have to give a sketch of some important institutional complexes that constitute especially significant factors in determining the structure of the economy. Basic to the whole analysis is the view that the demarcation of spheres must be made with respect to the total pattern of circulation of value in an economic system, and not merely with reference to the criterion of direct exchangeability.

PHYSICAL BACKGROUND

Jebel Marra is a mountain massif located about 13° N. and 24° E., close to the centre of the African continent. The area is relatively self-contained, and is isolated by deserts to the North and East, arid and sparsely populated plains to the West, and the Bahr el Arab to the South. From a plain of about 2,000 to 3,000 ft in altitude the mountain rises to nearly 10,000 ft and creates an environment rather different from the surrounding savannah belt of the Sudan: despite a dry season from October till May there are perennial streams and stands of large forest. The mountain, particularly on its lower slopes, supports a dense population of Fur-speaking hoe agriculturalists, living in hamlets or villages of up to about 500 habitants (for general background, see Lampen, 1950; Lebon & Robertson, 1961).

Fredrik Barth

SUBSISTENCE

The crops cultivated on the Jebel Marra form two agricultural complexes: summer rainland crops, and winter crops on irrigated land. The predominant staple is bullrush millet (*dukhn*) grown on dry terraces and completely dependent on summer rains. Millet fields are prepared and hoed during May-June, the seed is sown as the rains start, and repeated weeding is required until harvest-time in September. The fertility of the soil is prolonged by periodic fallow periods, but extended use leads to impoverishment and final indefinite abandonment to bush.

In rocky fields, and inside the compounds, tomatoes are also grown in the summer, following their introduction by Egyptian troops some hundred years ago. Occasionally, wheat is also cultivated on the dry terraces in the summer, as a final crop before the fields are laid fallow. Low terraces by streams, on the other hand, are artificially irrigated and used for the cultivation of onion, garlic, and wheat in the dry winter season. Whatever manure is available is used on these fields; and they are not normally ever left fallow. In the summer, special crops of chillies, herbs, and potatoes are grown in these fields without irrigation. Scattered among the compounds are also a fair number of cotton bushes. To an increasing extent, irrigated lands are also being developed as orchards, containing limes, lemons, oranges, mangoes, papayas, guava, and bananas.

Of domestic animals, the most important is the donkey, on which the population depends for practically all heavier transport. Pigeons are kept by most families; goats are kept in small numbers for meat, with a negligible yield of milk. Cattle are kept by some, mainly for re-sale; they are not locally bred or milked. Swarming termites, locusts, wild figs, edible grasses, honey, etc. are collected and contribute significantly to subsistence.

INSTITUTIONAL FORMS

Besides this geographical and ecological basis for the Fur economy, there are also some basic institutions in Fur culture which may be regarded as primary, and from which forms in the economy may be derived. These relate to the size and composition of households, the forms of ownership of land, values concerning labour and reciprocal obligations, and the organization of weekly markets.

(*a*) First, the units of management need to be identified – the unit which organizes production and consumption and holds a separate 'purse'. In this respect, Fur society is extreme and simple, in that every individual has his own farm plots, his own grain stores, and his separate budget. Domestic units are not primary economic units; though marriage implies certain reciprocal obligations and services, it does not imply a joint household.

Husband and wife each cultivate separate fields and store their produce in separate, adjoining grain bins in their joint hut. Neither spouse is allowed to take grain from the other's store, nor are they obliged to give any foodstuffs to each other. The economic obligations in a marriage mainly concern services: the wife must provide the husband with female labour, especially for cooking and brewing beer (from the millet he supplies from his stores); the husband in return provides the wife and her issue with clothing – predominantly, and formerly almost exclusively, spun and woven by the man himself. Some spouses elect to work one or several fields jointly, and most do assist each other somewhat in cultivation; but this does not alter their basic independence as units of economic management.

Children are fed by their mother from her stores. Boys remain with their mother till the age of 8-10 years; then they leave their home village to live as wandering scholars, attending the schools of Koranic teachers (*Fakki*) and supporting themselves by begging. After three, four, or five years they pass a religious examination with the last teacher they have been attending, and return to their village, where they start cultivating fields of their own. Until marriage, they depend on a mother or a sister for the female labour of cooking and brewing. The father, and other close relatives, are obliged to assist the boy in providing a bride-price; but he alone is responsible for his own needs. Daughters, on the other hand, remain at home until marriage and, until that time, may either work together with their mother or cultivate separate fields but pool their produce.

Fredrik Barth

In other words, economic activities are characteristically pursued by single individuals, though in a matrix of obligations, mainly of providing labour, to persons in specified kinship positions.

(*b*) This means that every person must obtain individual access to the basic means of production: land. The rights over land are institutionalized as follows:

Territorial rights are associated with descent groups of a non-unilineal kind – large blocks of kinsmen, with an endogamous tendency, often spoken of as patrilineal in form but in fact of a much looser structure allowing membership 'through our grandmothers'. This looseness in structure is possible only because the groups are non-corporate – their joint rights are vested in a title-holder, who represents the kin group in question and is responsible for its joint estate.

His responsibility consists in essence in allocating usufruct rights to fields. Such rights are given to individuals and are usually retained by them until use of the land is discontinued – i.e. the usufruct rights do not lapse when fields are left fallow in a systematic rotational pattern, only when they are abandoned. However, inside a community, it is regarded as every individual's right to obtain the land necessary for subsistence. When need arises, and when there is no unused land available, usufruct rights may be revoked and some land taken from those who have plenty and given to those who are in need. The title-holder is the person with the power to revoke such rights and redistribute the land of his descent group. Because the argument from relative need is accepted, he will be obliged to allocate fields alike to members and non-members of the 'owning' group; and the distribution of plots shows little correlation with the distribution of the users' descent-group rights.

The rights of the cultivator as *user* as distinct from *owner* are expressed in the symbolic prestation of one pot of beer to the title-holder after each harvest – a custom that is not consistently practised but is universally regarded as correct and proper. No rent in kind or services, or other obligations, are required from the cultivator.

The more shifting nature of cultivation on the unirrigated

lands assures a fair circulation of usufruct rights in the population. There is some tendency for children to take over the dry farms cultivated by their parents, especially for daughters to succeed on the death of their mother; but there does not seem to be any question of the lineal transfer of usufruct rights over several generations. In the case of the irrigated lands, however, no periods of disuse intervene, and usufruct rights come up for redistribution only on the death of the cultivator. The argument of need is used to justify a reallocation of rights to small onion plots, but most of the irrigated land tends to remain in the same hands, and there is an increasing tendency, with the growth of irrigation agriculture, for title-holders to monopolize this resource (see below, p. 170).

None the less, the main picture remains that land, as the main productive resource, is made available to all without any significant rent or other counter-prestation.

(*c*) With every individual so characteristically constituting a separate unit of management for economic purposes, the predominant pattern of labour tends to be one where every person uses his or her own time to work for the direct satisfaction of his own needs. By Mountain Fur conventions, it is furthermore shameful to work for wages in the local community, though a few men have experience as migrant labour elsewhere. None the less, there are institutionalized opportunities for both symmetrical and asymmetrical transactions involving labour, and there are some kinship and neighbourhood obligations which commit fractions of a person's time and effort.

The Fur institution that facilitates labour exchanges is the beer party. This takes several forms, exemplified by informal reciprocal help, work parties with many participants, and house-building parties. In the simplest form, two or more friends may decide to work together for company, in which case they jointly cultivate each other's field in turn, he whose field is being cultivated providing a pot of beer for their joint consumption. Larger work parties may be arranged in a similar way, but without the obligation of reciprocity: a man will announce his intention a few days in advance, have a large amount of beer prepared, and ask his friends and neighbours to come to the work party. Besides those who are invited, any person who wishes may join the party and drink beer in return for working. In these cases, the beer must be plentiful and is supposed to compensate for the work being expended; when the beer is finished, the work party disperses. Finally, house-building has a communal and reciprocal character; a day is announced for the work – first one for the women, who plaster the hut walls, then for the men, who build the roof and thatch it. On the appointed day, kinsmen and neighbours who have been invited are obliged to come, bringing with them the materials that are needed in the building. Large amounts of beer must again be provided by the host, and other persons may join in the work, in which case they pay a 'fine' of 2 piastres (about fivepence) for not having brought building materials.

Close kin of the house-builders, especially brothers and sisters, also assist by supplying one or several pots of beer at such occasions, as well as by working themselves and egging on the other guests to work well. A person's freedom to allocate his own labour is thus restricted by some commitments; and his opportunities for disposing of it on the Fur labour-for-beer labour market are restricted by the number of occasions offered by work parties in the local or adjoining villages. These are, however, very frequent in the larger communities; and with the above reservations one may say that essentially, a person's time is his own, to use for labour in his own fields or to exchange for beer on a local, relatively open, labour market. The reciprocities that limit a person's freedom on this market derive from obligations of mutual sociability, i.e. they are associated with the 'party' and not the 'work' aspect of the work party. Labour is seen as adequately compensated for in beer, and there is no restriction that each person's input of work and of beer into the system should be equivalent. This fact, together with the considerable degree of freedom allowed persons in choosing partners and occasions for transactions, means that we are dealing with a *market* for the exchange of labour and beer. The fact that persons also enjoy the 'party' aspect of the work party does not affect this argument.

(*d*) Fourthly, the Fur have a well-organized system of market-places, which facilitates a great number of economic exchanges. The medium of exchange used at these markets is, and has for a long time been, money issued in the Nile valley. Previously, cloth may have served as a medium of exchange.

Each market-place is active one day, or in a few cases two days, a week. They are spaced at a distance of 15 to 20 km from each other on the perimeter of the mountain, so that every community is within walking distance of at least one market-place, enabling people to attend the market and return home the same day. Particularly in the slack agricultural seasons, markets are visited by large numbers of people, amounting to several hundred through much of the day.

Villagers bring all varieties of agricultural produce to the market-place, though millet, being very bulky and heavy in proportion to its value, is rarely marketed. Most producers bring only small quantities, since they sell only to obtain cash for specific purchases, though some, anticipating a good price or because of acute need, may also bring larger quantities to sell in bulk. Occasionally, cattle or goats are also brought for sale by their owners. Craftsmen, who form a small, discrete population of male smiths and female potters, also bring their products for sale, and the smith sets up a small anvil for incidental repairs. Finally, travelling pedlars, most of them Arabs but some Fur, set up shops in booths or on mats from which they sell imported industrial consumer goods, particularly cloth, utensils, sugar, etc.

Numerous middlemen appear and mediate the flow of trade while seeking profit, either by speculating in rising prices through the day, or by accumulating products in bulk for transport and re-sale at communication entrepots 50 to 100 km away. Each will specialize in one or two products – garlic, onions, dried tomatoes, or wheat – buying from the individual producers and accumulating for re-sale on the spot, or for transport. Middlemen also buy the livestock, slaughter and partition it, and sell it in small portions to local consumers. Some sales of fresh vegetables, fruits, and other garden produce also take place directly from producer to individual consumer.

Some women also brew beer and bring it for sale in the market-place. Though there is no dearth of buyers, especially as the afternoon wears on, the sale of beer is regarded as immoral and the women who do so are looked upon as immodest. This may be both because the making of beer is an intimate female service appropriate only in a close, domestic context, and because beer, as in a work party, is a festive idiom of cooperation and companionship and not appropriate as an object of commercial bargaining.

In the market-place, then, individual villagers are able to exchange their agricultural products for tools and utensils, cloth, and a variety of other consumer goods which they do not themselves produce. They do so by freely switching between the statuses of buyer and seller, and must deal with factors of supply and demand and with fluctuating prices measured in a monetary currency.

ECONOMIC SPHERES

The facts presented so far invite the use of a concept of economic spheres. They suggest the existence of two discrete spheres of exchange in the Mountain Fur economy: one that embraces a large variety of material items, including also a monetary medium, and is associated with the market-place facilities; and another that exists for the exchange of labour and beer. The two spheres are separated by the sanction of moral reprobation on conversions from labour to cash and from beer to cash. They thus would seem to fit well the definition of spheres given in Bohannan and Dalton (1965, p. 8), i.e. they each constitute a set of freely exchangeable material items and services. They also would seem to exhibit the feature of hierarchical ranking: conversions in the one direction are frowned upon; i.e. the sphere containing labour and beer would be regarded as the higher, that associated with the monetary medium the lower.

However, such a model is inconsistent with some of the empirical material. Thus some highly prestigious items of wealth, such as swords, are obtained in the cash sphere. Furthermore, the bridewealth for a wife is composed predominantly of cash and items from the cash sphere, and this would indicate a high rather than a low rating for the cash sphere.

Nor can one argue that these are the effects of breakdown associated with the introduction of money. Cash had been used in the Fur area long before colonial times, and the system described here is in this sense a traditional and relatively stable one in which cash is an integral part. If a concept of spheres is to be useful for the analysis of this system, the hierarchical assumption is best dismissed.

What is more, it is difficult to relate the labour-beer sphere significantly to the cash sphere by any patterned channels of conversion. On a more fundamental level, I would argue that a separation of spheres based on the criterion of exchangeability alone gives an unnecessarily inadequate representation of the structure of the economy. The concept of spheres has much greater analytic utility if it relates to all forms of circulation and transformation of value, whether by exchange, production, inheritance, or other means.

I shall therefore try to depict all the standard choices of alternative allocations of resources open to the units of management in the Fur economy, and to delimit the significant spheres with respect to the total pattern of circulation or flow of value. The units of management are single individuals, whose basic problem is to transform their own efforts into a range of items that satisfies their own consumption profile. The institutional forms I have described above may be regarded as the main facilities or means at their disposal to achieve this transformation; and the description of the economy is simplified by the fact that persons have approximately equal access to these facilities.[2] It is further simplified by the fact that, as members of a relatively homogeneous society, their habits and appetites are similar, except for the male-female differences which mainly reflect reciprocal obligations in marriage.

An attempt to aggregate the allocations of the whole population of management units, giving a picture of the *village* economy, is therefore unusually simple in this case. In the cash sphere, as long as there is no shortage of land, the village economy can be represented as the *sum* of decisions of management units, since these units do not seriously compete for resources and their activities do not have any great impact on market prices. Aggregating the decisions in the millet-beer-labour sphere is more difficult, since any transformation by a management unit of its beer into labour presupposes the

Fredrik Barth

presence of persons willing to exchange their labour for beer. The simplest procedure is to assume a certain supply of labour and beer and to see how the allocation decision of one member unit might affect the availability of these forms of value on the market, and possibly also affect the relative 'price' of each as measured in terms of the other. Some of these problems are taken up below in the section on management and stratification (pp. 165-166) and in connection with new uses of labour and possible responses to this (pp. 167 ff.).

The pattern of standard alternative choices for a Fur management unit can thus be represented as in the diagram. With the reservations noted above, this may simultaneously be regarded as a model of the village economy as a whole. The remainder of this paper is essentially an exposition of this diagram followed by a discussion of its implications.

THE PATTERN OF STANDARD ALTERNATIVE CHOICES FOR A FUR MANAGEMENT UNIT

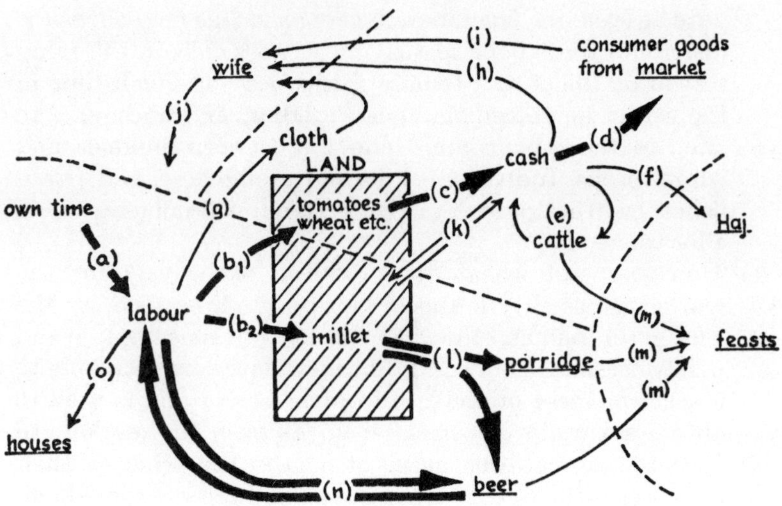

PATTERNS AND ALTERNATIVES OF ALLOCATION

(*a*) The input into the economic system is the person's own time, used as labour. All self-supporting persons in the society must and do have the basic skills necessary to cultivate the main varieties of crops, and to trade.

(*b*) To start production, a person next needs access to land. This is obtained either from a parent or close relative with plenty, or from one of the title-holders in the village. Every individual needs to obtain plots of several kinds, suitable for different crops and uses. A configuration of sizes and types of farm implies an allocation of labour to alternative products: millet, and some onions, for basic subsistence, and readily marketable crops such as tomatoes, wheat, garlic, onions for cash needs. The balance struck between these two categories of products depends on the person's obligations: women, especially those with small children, concentrate more of their effort on millet, while men, especially those with plural wives, have greater need for cash to meet the obligations of clothing their families, and to save towards bridewealth for themselves or their sons.

In the course of the year, every person will need to cultivate at least one farm in each category. One may choose to distribute the labour so that most work falls in the rainy season on millet and tomato farms, leaving much time in the winter for threshing, house-building, and trading, or to allocate the labour more equally between summer and winter crops. Individual skills and preferences, and established usufruct rights to irrigated land, will influence these allocations.

(*c*) Tomatoes and wheat are produced exclusively for the market, since they are used hardly at all as food by the Fur; garlic, onions, etc. are partly for own consumption and partly for sale. The weekly market-places are available to transform these products into cash. Cash again is used to obtain a variety of consumer goods from the market. In

(*d*) 1964 the annual cash needs of men in the prime of their lives was estimated by informants, and reported for themselves, to be about £8; that of women only £1, £2, or £3. The rate of consumption in the cash sector has, however, been increasing rapidly over the last years.

Also purchased for cash are tools – a relatively minor expense; donkeys, of which every man wishes to own one,

and young cattle. These last are bought from Baggara Arabs when they are about two years old, for about £6.
(*e*) They are then kept for some years, tended by the children of the owner, till they are ready for sale as meat on the market at the age of 5 or 6 years, when they bring about £11 or £12. No breeding or milking takes place, but the manure that accumulates where the animals are stabled at night is valued and used in the irrigated fields.

Livestock thus constitute a possible field of investment, if one has the children to tend them. Otherwise, the possibilities for investment of cash in productive enterprises are extremely restricted. Cash savings are useful as a store of wealth to secure against crop failure or sickness in the future; and amounts up to several hundred pounds are accumulated by some. But for most people who dare not use such savings for speculation and trade on the market, they remain inactive wealth, buried in a pot under the floor of the hut, and are not used as capital. A few villagers chose, usually fairly late in life, to use such savings to perform the
(*f*) *Haj* pilgrimage to Mecca. The returned Haji tends to take little part in village affairs, and so this conversion of wealth to rank has limited consequences in the Fur system.

(*g*) Men may somewhat reduce their cash expenditures by weaving cloth for their families rather than buying it. Cotton for such thread may be bought, or produced by the man himself. He spins it by hand while walking or sitting idle, and weaves it on a horizontal loom which, though nominally it may be owned by someone, is in fact used communally by all.

(*h*) A major cash expense is that of bridewealth, involving various traditional prestations to the wife and to her bilateral kinsmen totalling about £35 in value. This expense is borne by the groom and his father. Most of it is given in purchasable objects (donkeys, cattle, swords, cloth) or their cash equivalents. Two lengths of cloth must, however, be produced by the groom himself and given to the bride's parents. For the rest of their married life, the husband is further obliged to provide his wife, and small children, with
(*i*) basic necessities from the market.

Economic Spheres in Darfur

(*j*) In return, the wife must provide female services of sex, cooking, and brewing of beer.

(*k*) The other main kind of crop is millet. Some people find that they, in their initial allocation of labour (*b*), have struck an inadequate balance between production of cash crops and of millet. This can be corrected in the market-place: not infrequently, people run short of millet and have to buy some before the next harvest; while a few find that they have an excess which it is more convenient to store as cash than as grain. Much of the Marra mountain seems to be rather too high to offer optimal conditions for millet, and there is doubtless an overall import from lower-lying, surplus-producing areas.

(*l*) Millet is used for porridge and beer. Independent estimates in connection with sample budgets indicate that on an average about one-fifth of the total grain production goes into beer – more in the case of men, somewhat less in the case of women.

(*m*) Most of the porridge is consumed directly. On special occasions, however, connected with funerals and memorials for senior deceased relatives, or the life-crises of junior relatives, feasts are given at which porridge is also served to invited and uninvited visitors. At most feasts, beer is also given, and occasionally cattle are slaughtered. Such feasts bring honour to the person who gives them; but as they are given in the name of another person and are not formalized in grades or titles, it would be inappropriate to regard them as 'feasts of merit' in any real sense; and their effects on the political influence of the feast-giver seem to be minimal.

Beer-making is a rather complicated procedure which stretches over several days, and the product does not keep for long; so most households are unable regularly to have beer available for home consumption. Most of the beer produced thus enters the circuit of feasts and work parties,

(*n*) especially as a reciprocal in exchange for labour, as discussed above. Besides being used to mobilize labour in millet cultivation, where the large, uniform fields invite the use of communal labour, such beer-for-labour exchanges (*o*) are used in house-building. Indeed, a final marriage obligation, after a period of successful marriage, is the building of a hut by each spouse for his or her parallel-sex parent-in-law, using only labour mobilized by beer in a kinship/friendship network, and associated with special festive customs, dances, and songs.

POSSIBILITIES FOR GROWTH

The diagram thus depicts all the main forms of goods and services in the Mountain Fur economy, how they are produced and how they can be exchanged for each other – i.e. it depicts the flow of value through the system. The whole system is seen from the point of view of an ordinary villager, not a craftsman or a market-place speculator; and it presupposes the ecological and institutional facts outlined in the first part of the paper.

From the point of view of each individual unit of management, the central purpose of economic activities must be to direct the flow of his own assets in these various channels in such a way as (i) to achieve maximal increase in them while (ii) obtaining a balanced distribution of value on the various consumption items of market goods, porridge, beer, housing, *Haj*, and feasts. The balance in question is determined by each person's consumption profile.

Some general characteristics of the economy stand out very clearly in this diagram; most clearly, the limited possibilities for cumulative growth. Such growth possibilities depend on a recognized channel for reinvestment and will show up in the diagram as possible *circles* of flow, permitting what might most vividly be described as *spirals* of growth (Barth, 1963, p. 11). Only three such circles are present: (1) labour-cash-crops-cash-wife-labour, (2) cash-cattle-cash, and (3) labour-millet-beer-labour. The first of these circles is apparent rather than real; and all have built-in brakes which prevent them from serving as true spirals of growth.

As for the labour-cash-wife-labour circle, this is controlled by a number of factors such as the availability of marriageable women, the acceptance of the marriage offer by the woman and her kinspeople, and the ultimate limit of four legal wives. Of more immediate relevance, however, is the fact that the labour obtained from a wife is not of the same kind as that invested in work on the cash crops. A woman's labour obligations to her husband concern the special female services only; as a cultivator she is independent, and the cash crops which she cultivates are her own, not her husband's. Though spouses often work together in the field, this is on a reciprocal basis. Thus, plural marriages will not only deplete a man's savings, but also increase his cash expenses without providing him with any source of labour, from wives or from children, which he can use in the production of cash crops. There is thus no opportunity for cumulative increase of assets in this circle.

The cash-cattle-cash circle, on the other hand, offers a genuine circle for investment and increase provided that (otherwise essentially unusable) juvenile labour is available in the domestic unit. However, the erratic supply of young cattle constitutes a brake on systematic investment: there are no markets to facilitate trade in such animals, and the supply depends entirely on the whim of the Arab nomads, who offer the beasts for sale individually through random contacts and only in response to unforeseen and urgent cash needs. In a complete census of one mountain Fur community of 212 adult householders, one person owned 5 cattle, the rest fewer, and most of them none. Though restricted in this way, profits in this particular spiral are none the less frequently cited by villagers as the source of accumulated savings.

The labour-millet-beer-labour circle is the most clearly marked one in the economy. But it also has characteristic built-in brakes. General notions of reciprocity are not effective, as noted previously; but there is a tendency for labour efficiency to correlate negatively with the size of the task: the larger the field, the more beer and the more people are present, and the more quickly does the whole occasion degenerate into a pure drinking party. The host tries to control this tendency by bringing out his beer a little at a time; but if he is too careful people will leave the site in protest.

Furthermore, the circle is essentially a closed one: millet is not treated by the Mountain Fur as a cash crop, and so wealth once in this circle remains within it, and a person's incentive to try systematically to accumulate in a spiral is limited by his view of his possible consumption needs or appetites for porridge, beer, and thatched huts.

SPHERES AND BARRIERS

The items labour, millet, porridge, beer, and houses are thus closely interconnected, and most nearly constitute a sphere in terms of exchangeability. By also considering other regular modes of circulation, especially that of a production in which the factor of land is freely available, the interconnectedness of these items is more adequately depicted. It should be noted that all items are *not* freely exchangeable for each other, e.g. labour cannot be obtained in exchange for millet. But through the brewing of beer, labour is mobilized in direct proportion to the millet invested and there are no significant restrictions on the volume or timing of this transformation – i.e. it is present in the system as a constantly available possible allocation of the resources in question. It thus seems most meaningful to classify these items together as constituting a single economic sphere, and to demarcate such spheres by criteria of freedom of allocation and the facility with which each item or form can be transformed into any other.

The concept of spheres, then, serves to summarize the major structural features of a flow pattern. In this case, most items fall by such criteria clearly in either of two main spheres, that of labour, beer, etc. and that associated with cash. In addition, the diagram depicts conversions to *Haj* and feasts, in a sphere related to rank and influence that has no clear feedback into the economic system, and also some conversions into a sphere of kinship and affinal ties, represented here by wives as the only item with a significant, though limited, feedback on the labour side of the economic system.

The barriers between spheres, in this view, are barriers to ready transformation, i.e. all the factors that impede the flow of value and restrict people's freedom to allocate their resources, and reverse these allocations. Thus the allocation of cash to the purchase of a ticket to Mecca is a conversion to another sphere, since this amount of value can never be transformed back into cash. An allocation of labour to millet cultivation is likewise an allocation of resources to a non-cash sphere; because of the items in this sphere millet is for reasons of price and competition not a marketable cash crop, porridge has no buyers, the sale of beer is regarded as immoral, and the labour obtained for beer cannot be sold and has traditionally been used only in millet cultivation and house-building. Houses, finally, are not sold, because of the difficulty of finding buyers.[3] The barriers that prevent or restrict flow between spheres are thus compounded of a variety of factors, only some of them of a moral or socially sanctioned nature.

MANAGEMENT AND STRATIFICATION

Successful management consists in allocating labour wisely to the two main spheres, and steering one's assets through the channels of each sphere in such a way as to maximize increase. In the cash sphere, this involves agricultural skills and an adequate programming of labour input in terms of the changing requirements of hoeing, watering, guarding, and harvesting – and, in the case of tomatoes, also of drying the crop. Besides, relative gains or losses result from the choice of different alternative crops in different years, as a result of fluctuations in weather conditions and market prices. In general, cultivators seemed to feel that weather fluctuations were unpredictable; and many also seemed to choose their crops on a conventional or habitual basis, without reference to prognoses of changing prices. A steady rise in the price obtained for tomatoes over the last years none the less has resulted in a very considerable increase in the quantity of tomatoes cultivated.

Finally, the time of marketing affects the price obtained. Thus the price of onions sinks, when the new crop comes in, to less than half of the peak price that obtains in early winter. Persons with cash resources to cover current expenditure are thus able to postpone their crop sales and reap the greater profits.

The linear character of the flow channel in the cash sphere does not give much scope for management finesse, and only in the small cash-cattle-cash circle can careful saving and investment produce bonuses of any importance. Not so in the millet-beer-labour sphere, however: systematic management of millet cultivation and beer-labour mobilization is the corner-stone on which the prosperity of most villagers is based.

Let us first look at the direct relation between labour input and production. The millet-growing season extends over approximately 70 days; including the preparatory period of terrace-mending and hoeing, and the considerable concluding labour of threshing and winnowing, nearly six months are probably needed to produce a final harvest of reasonable size.

Villagers estimated that a woman with no cash-cropping commitment in the summer season should be able to produce at least 100 *mīd* (1,000 lb), by her own labour. As a daily rate this would correspond to more than 1/2 *mīd* (5 lb), per working-day.

Alternatively, much of the labour may be done with the aid of work parties. At such parties, the hosts generally estimate that a large – about 30 litre – pot of beer provides enough beer for six men for one day. By the brewing techniques generally used in the Marra mountain, millet produces about six times its own volume in finished beer. One *mīd* (corresponding to about 5 litres) of grain thus makes about 30 litres of beer. The daily consumption of beer per man in a work party is thus approximately 5 litres, corresponding to 1·7 lb millet.

Given an adequate store of millet, a person can thus mobilize labour at a cost of some 1·7 lb millet/day/man and apply it to a task that produces an average of some 5 lb millet, or three times the cost, per work-day. A reasonably skilful management in this flow circle thus secures a person an adequate supply of millet from a relatively small labour input. The person who cannot husband his resources, and whose thirst or hunger tempts him to join work parties so as quickly and directly to transform his labour into beer, will constantly be on the losing end of the deal. In Mountain Fur villages, the population thus has a tendency to fall into two strata: a majority of moderately prosperous persons, and a fraction who, because of disease, age, or bad management, have inadequate grain stores, and who supplement their food resources by frequent participation in work parties, thus serving as a labour reserve for the more prosperous villagers.

Economic Spheres in Darfur

DISCREPANCIES OF EVALUATION

I have argued elsewhere (Barth, 1966) that the barriers which separate spheres and limit the amount and occasions of flow between them will allow considerable discrepancies of evaluation to persist as between items located in different spheres. Such discrepancies may be discovered when barriers break down and new patterns of circulation are made possible, in which cases an increased flow may force people radically to revise their evaluations (see p. 170 below, on the value of land). Alternatively, these discrepancies may be demonstrated where it is possible to construct some common denominator, or coefficient, for comparing evaluations in one sphere with those of another. In the present case, such a common denominator may be constructed on the basis of the market price of millet – an 'imperfection' in the separation of the two major spheres, brought about mainly by the activities of travelling merchants who bring millet in from the adjoining ecological zone, but also occasionally by the sale of millet raised by the Mountain Fur themselves.

The price of millet in 1964 ranged from 4 to 6 piastres, i.e. around an average of 1 shilling per *mīd* (10 lb) of grain. We thus get the equations:

10 lb millet = 1 shilling = 30 litres of beer = 6 man days,
or 1 man day = 5 litres of beer = 2d. worth of millet.

This evaluation of what a man-day of labour is worth in beer may be compared to that obtaining in the cash sphere. The Sudan Forestry Department, and some other public bodies, make relatively unsuccessful attempts to recruit local labour in Jebel Marra. Their basic wage offer has been about 10 piastres = 2 shillings a day, or 12 times the value of the millet which a man demands for participation in a work party. Yet it has proved very difficult, especially in the initial years of recruiting in any one village or locality, to entice people to take work. Privately, I found that an arrangement for having fresh water brought to my hut, at the rate of about 1d. per 12 litre pot, was impossible to maintain because the women in the neighbourhood were dissatisfied with the rate of pay – the equivalent of half a day's 'millet pay' for 20 minutes' work. Admittedly, in these equations

I have ignored the value of the labour of brewing – as indeed I suspect that the Fur themselves, particularly the men, would do if they were to attempt the comparison. But this additional factor is far from sufficient to make good the discrepancies. Likewise, one might argue that the Fur idea that it is shameful to work for a wage should be represented as an additional cost for a man entering a wage contract, and that this constitutes the balancing factor. The empirical facts would, however, rather suggest that these costs are not so very great, since once the Fur are given enough opportunities to work for wages so that they discover the advantages of these wage rates, they eagerly accept the contracts, as in some of the Jebel Marra foothills areas. No matter how one chooses to represent it, there does seem to be a very great discrepancy between the values placed on beer and labour, and those placed on money.

INNOVATING ACTIVITY

So far I have discussed the economic activity of persons within the traditional framework of alternative allocations. But to the extent that the individual units of management really attempt to maximize their assets, they will assert a constant pressure on this framework, and will seek ways of utilizing new opportunities where they are apparent and not blocked by unreasonable risk factors or supervening social sanctions.

The most general change that is taking place along these lines in the Jebel Marra is a progressive increase in the range of crops cultivated, and a certain change in the whole agricultural regime because of the increasing importance of tree crops. This development has been initiated by some modest agricultural experimental stations, but is sustained without any supporting agricultural extension work. The development of orchards is leading to derivative changes in the views on land-ownership and tenure rights. Finally, in a few localities one can also find some truly entrepreneurial undertakings where new strategies of management and channels of conversion are being exploited. The forms which these changes take are to a marked degree determined by the economic system outlined above, and give further perspective on its structure.

Economic Spheres in Darfur

Orchard development

The development of orchards requires irrigated land – i.e. the tree crop is an alternative to the irrigated winter cash crops. Such a tree crop takes four years before it gives a significant product; however, in the intervening period the fields may also be used to raise an irrigated onion crop, so no significant loss of current production is suffered during the transition. The fruits are marketable for cash – limes, lemons, oranges, and mangoes particularly for export; papaya, guava, and bananas mainly for local consumption. The ease of production, and the relatively low value of the fruit in the case of limes and lemons, make them less attractive under present circumstances, whereas some varieties of oranges have been spectacularly profitable.

The labour to establish an orchard comes in addition to that normally required, since other cash crops must be cultivated to cover current expenses until the trees start producing. The development of an orchard thus requires an extra input of labour; and this has generally been done by the innovators with the aid of work parties, utilizing surplus millet for beer. A precedent is thus established for the use of beer-mobilized labour in the cash-crop sphere. So long as a person's millet resources are large enough to provide simultaneously for the other current uses, there are no sanctions against such an allocation; but it requires careful management, i.e. a successful large production of millet by beer work parties in the year preceding the orchard development. Perhaps for this reason, only the quite successful and prosperous have embarked on this production beyond the occasional planting of single trees. In the localities of fieldwork, the first orchards were planted in a village adjoining the foothills zone in 1956, in a high mountain village not till 1962. The mature orchards give large incomes with little input of labour, individual properties producing £20 to £30 worth of fruit annually.

Land rights

This change in agricultural regime has created some uneasiness with regard to land-ownership and usufruct rights. The principle of individual ownership to (wild) trees is established and recognized. The trees which a person plants will according to this

Fredrik Barth

principle be his, no matter who owns the land on which they grow. However, an orchard on irrigated land becomes so dense that it shades other crops and monopolizes that land. A person who obtains usufruct rights to irrigated land to which he has no title can thus, by planting an orchard, render it useless to all others for an indefinite period. Some men who held titles to land on behalf of their descent group were, in 1964, quite concerned over this, and pressed for the general acceptance of a rule forbidding the planting of orchards on borrowed land. Some few of them, on the other hand, had been quick enough to evict other users in time to secure ample areas for their private orchard developments.

Others, who had no such titular rights, wished to obtain the exclusive access to irrigated land that would make the long-term investment of orchard development a safe proposition. In the most sophisticated areas, a few sales and purchases of land had taken place by 1964, tentatively establishing truly private ownership to land. Both parties to such transactions were quite uneasy about the deal, the sellers because they were alienating rights which they held in trust for larger kin groups (and only those who belonged to nearly extinct, or emigrated, kin groups were willing to consider sale at all), the buyers because they felt that the price was excessive.

Indeed, the prices demanded are an extreme illustration of the discrepancies of evaluation that can obtain where the items, in this case land and cash, have not been in circulation in the same economic sphere. I recorded those few transactions of this kind that had taken place in one community. The first sale took place in 1961, when a field was sold for £17. The buyer planted orange trees, and proceeded to cultivate onions in the three transitional years. For these onion crops he obtained £27, £22, and £25, respectively. He expected his first proper yield of oranges to bring a larger income. He was personally no longer in doubt that the transaction had been to his advantage; but he failed by this argument to convince his friend to purchase a field for £30 which had regularly been giving an onion crop worth more than £15 annually. The man in question was willing to offer £25, but would not go higher – not because he did not have the money, but because he felt that, surely, no piece of land could be worth that much. One must assume that an increasing number of such transactions will progressively lead to a general revision of relative evaluations.

Entrepreneurial activity

On purely logical grounds I have argued elsewhere (Barth, 1966) that entrepreneurs will direct their activity pre-eminently towards those points in an economic system where the discrepancies of evaluation are greatest, and will attempt to construct bridging transactions which can exploit these discrepancies. The social factors which produce a reluctance to sell land serve as a general impediment on entrepreneurial activity in this field; besides, the profits connected with such transactions are long-term. But the disparities of evaluation between the cash and the millet-labour-beer spheres offer opportunities which have recently been discovered and exploited by a few entrepreneurs. The problem, when an entrepreneurial adventure consists in breaking through the barrier between spheres, is that of re-conversion of assets without loss – i.e. that of locating channels that allow a circle of reinvestment and growth (see above, p. 162, and Barth, 1963, p. 11).

Returning to the diagram the possibility of such a circle is apparent in the combination of channels (*k*) – (*l*) – (*n*) – (b_1) – (*c*). Concretely, what happened, apparently for the first time in 1961, was that an Arab merchant who regularly visited the market-places on the northern fringe of the Marra mountain, asked for permission to spend the rainy season in a village, and asked for an area of land on which to cultivate a tomato crop. He brought in his wife and settled her in a hut, and he bought a large amount of millet in the lowlands to the north-east, where the price is very low, which he transported in on his donkeys and camels. From the millet, his wife made beer; this beer he used to call work parties, applying the labour to the tomato cultivation. Without any significant labour input of his own, he thus produced a large tomato crop, which he dried and transported to el Fasher for sale after the end of the rainy season. On an investment of £5 worth of millet, he obtained a return of more than £100 for his tomatoes.

In 1962 and 1963, more merchants, and some local people,

adopted the same strategy with results nearly as spectacular. The precedent of orchard labour showed the way in which assets in the beer-labour circle could be converted to the cash sphere by being used in the production of cash crops – a conversion that takes advantage of the disparity in the beer versus cash evaluations of labour. The re-conversion of assets from the cash to the non-cash sphere through the purchase of millet again takes advantage of a favourable disparity of evaluations, and is particularly simple for a trader with access to lowland markets.

The profits on trade and transport of the products also enters into the enterprise of the merchant given above. The case of one of the first local men to attempt the scheme is therefore of special interest. On the local market, he purchased:

50 *mīd* of millet at 6 piastres per *mīd* – 500 lb millet:	£3	0	0
Also, for the main work party feast, 1 goat for 40 piastres:	0	8	0
Total labour costs:	£3	8	0

He had all the labour in the tomato field performed by work parties. The value of the tomato crop, ready for sale within about 5 months, was £38 – profits based entirely on production and conversions within the local economic system.

Again, one must assume that this situation is unstable: a re-evaluation as between spheres may be precipitated by this flow of value across the boundary, whereby evaluations in the two spheres are brought more closely in line. Alternatively, the critical conversions may be blocked: by a refusal to give land for cultivation to the entrepreneurs, or by the discontinuation of the beer-for-labour exchanges on anything but a reciprocal basis. There is some evidence for a trend in each of these directions, but as of 1964 no effective reaction blocked these enterprises. However, the increase in wage-labour opportunities which will probably take place will no doubt also affect this situation by making it more difficult to mobilize labour for beer on a non-reciprocal basis.

Economic Spheres in Darfur

CONCLUDING REMARK

In each major section of this description of the Mountain Fur economic system I have sought to make explicit the analytical steps that I have taken, and to give the argument a general form. It should therefore be unnecessary to formulate any extensive conclusion. One general feature of this analysis might however be noted. By discussing alternative allocations in terms of 'flow', and describing the concrete factors and barriers that channel this flow, one performs an analysis that is particularly useful for the study of change, and for short-range prediction. The model is, in this respect, amenable to developments and manipulations which a more strict structural representation would not allow. This increases its adequacy for the description of what is in fact taking place in the Jebel Marra area, and should also enhance its interest to economists.

NOTES

1. Based on a field visit of slightly over three months in 1964, during a year's contract with Unesco as visiting professor at the University of Khartoum. Incidental field expenses were covered by a University of Khartoum Ford Foundation research grant; an interpreter and various other help in the field were supplied by the Jebel Marra Project of the U.N. Special Fund. I wish to thank these institutions, and the authorities and persons with which I was in contact in the Sudan, for their cooperation and help.
2. In this, I disregard the members of the craftsman caste, whose numbers are very small and whose style of life differs considerably from that of Village Fur.
3. In some cases of inheritance, when none of the heirs wishes to use the house, empty houses are indeed offered on the market and bring anywhere from 6 shillings to £2. The difficulty then is to find a buyer, since those in need of a house can call on friends and relatives to contribute towards the construction of an entirely new house, at a chosen site, through expending less than about 5 shillings-worth of their own millet on beer.

REFERENCES

BARTH, F. 1963. The Role of the Entrepreneur in Social Change in Northern Norway. *Acta Universitas Bergensis. Series Humaniorum Litterarum* No. 3. Bergen; Oslo: Norwegian Universities Press.

—— 1966. Models of Social Organization. *Royal Anthropological Institute*, Occasional Papers, No. 23. [173]

BOHANNAN, P. & DALTON, A. G. 1965. *Markets in Africa.* New York: Doubleday.

LAMPEN, G. D. 1950. History of Darfur. *Sudan Notes and Records* **31** (2).

LEBON, J. H. G. & ROBERTSON, V. C. 1961. The Jebel Marra, Darfur, and its Region. *Geographical Journal* **127** (1). [174]

Part V
Processes: Markets

[24]

PRATIK: HAITIAN PERSONAL ECONOMIC RELATIONSHIPS[1]

Sidney W. Mintz

THE MOST VISIBLE features of Haiti's internal exhange economy are its market places. In 1954 there were 294 officially recognized and controlled market places in the Republic (Moral, 1959, p. 74). These are the intersection points in the trade network by which the bulk of Haiti's marketed agricultural product and its imports reach their consumers. Retail stores are much less important than the market places, even in the large towns; in the countryside such stores are of little significance in economic life. In the capital, Port-au-Prince, and in large provincial centers such as Cap Haïtien and Les Cayes, storage depots and import houses are tied in with market place trade; but retail stores have limited importance outside the capital.

Trade is carried on by thousands of intermediaries, most of them women. In a population believed to total 3,400,000, Moral's estimates (1959, p. 84) suggest somewhat more than 50,000 female and 15,000 male traders. These figures are very probably too low; omitted are the large numbers of children under fourteen years engaged in petty trade, and the numerous part-time unlicensed intermediaries who slip in and out of trade.

Through the market places, producers and consumers are united in exchange, but few transactions involve only producer and consumer, since intermediaries successfully interpose themselves. Such intermediaries render many different services, including bulking, transport, minor processing and packing, storage, breaking bulk, moneylending, and the provision of short-term credit. They hold their places in the distributive process by offering these services at prices their customers are willing to pay; were they redundant, their customers would circumvent them.[2]

The competition for the privilege of serving as an intermediary is stern, since the Haitian economy has a large supply of labor in all sectors. Accordingly, each market woman seeks to protect her stake within the arena of exchange by various means. A paramount feature of the struggle to secure and to profit from the right to render service is the institutionalized personal economic relationship referred to in Haiti as *pratik*.[3] It is toward an examination of this relationship that the present paper is directed.

Moral writes:

> L'attrait de l'argent est si fort dans les compagnes et la circulation monétaire si réduite que le "capitaliste" influent du bourg rural mène la spéculation pratiquement à sa guise grâce à une "clientele" étendue dont la fidélité est maintenue soit par le jeu compliqué des avances, des engagements et des dettes, soit par le respect qu'impose la réussité, soit encore par la tradition de la "pratique."

And he continues:

> C'est le mot-clé du petit commerce rural. Il désigne à la fois le vendeur et l'acheteur. Il traduit surtout la confiance réciproque et la force de l'engagement oral dans une société où le document écrit est une rareté (1959, p. 70).

That *pratik* means both buyer and seller emphasizes the reciprocal nature of the relationships. Métraux (1951, p. 121) points out that in Haiti "The women who buy and sell are on friendly terms, calling each other *bèl mè* (stepmother), *ma komè* (gossip) [i. e., "godsib" or ritual coparent] and *matelòt* (concubine of the same man)." In the *pratik* relationship, the participants are equals for purposes of trade.

A comparable terminology occurs in Jamaica, according to Katzin:

> The term "customer" is used by Jamaicans as a generic term applied to anyone with whom one has regular business dealings. Higglers call both those who sell to them and those who buy from them "my customers." One town higgler said: "The house buyers who buy from us are our customers, but country people call us customer and we call them customer. We are really the customer because we do the buying, but I don't know what we would call them, so we still call them 'customer' (1959, p. 19)."

In Haiti, one "has *pratik*" (*gê pratik*) and "makes *pratik*" (*fè pratik*). The degree of intimacy and mutual benefit varies, but since the relationships are intended to stabilize and maintain one's role in distributive activity, they are always built up over time and have economic value for the participants. As such, *pratik* ties add to the regularity and patterning of internal marketing activity.

In an economy typified by unscientific agriculture and poor agricultural technology, inadequate processing and preservation media, primitive transport and communications facilities, feeble and dispersed demand, and very numerous small-scale producers and intermediaries, each with limited means, distribution is likely to have a markedly irregular character. This unevenness is magnified when seasonal variation in the supply of various goods, and in income, is often sharp. All of these conditions are characteristic of the Haitian economy. There is further some movement of individuals in and out of the distributive system with changes in season, status, and fortune. Under such circumstances, *pratik* relationships stabilize sequences of dyadic economic transactions. Taken together, they afford greater order to the distributive system as a whole.

The personal element in economic activity is of course not limited to economies of the Haitian sort. But certain features of such economies affect the ways that the relationships are worked out. Haiti is famous for its relatively plentiful supply of labor, its relatively scarce supply of capital, its agrarian and nonindustrial character, and its low productivity. On all of these counts it is the least developed economy in the Caribbean area, with the lowest per capita income, and probably the lowest standard of living for the whole of Latin America.

Haiti is rural as well as agrarian. Moral demonstrates that the calculation that 12.6 per cent of the Haitian population is urban is arbitrary in the extreme; at most only approximately 8 per cent of the people live under even remotely "urban" conditions (1959, pp. 29-30). Country towns are above all political administrative centers. To some extent they also serve as regional entrepots for agricultural produce moving out of the surrounding region, and for finished goods moving into it (Mintz, 1960). Contact between the regional administrative centers and their countrysides, and between the various regions and the capital, rests to a considerable degree upon the distributive mechanisms of the internal market system. The sorts of information carried by market women and truckers in the course of their work include marketing intelligence, affecting the rate at which produce flows toward demand areas and helping to stabilize prices to some extent. The communication of a remote unsatisfied demand may even affect tendencies in production. In this sense intermediaries help to bring distant areas into firmer contact with the cities and with other regions by their activities. The distances covered in search of profit are staggering; to walk thirty miles in a day to acquire or dispose of stock is not unusual, and some women walk nearly twice that to attend particular market places. Such trips open regions and increase the likelihood that roads, trucks, and development activity will follow.

The nature of rural production in Haiti is such that relatively little agricultural land is held in large properties. Instead there are long-standing patterns of divided and subdivided small plots, worked by their owners, sharecropped, mortgaged, leased, rented, and held by customary tenure or by squatting. Agricultural production rests on a heterogeneous tenure situation, and is pursued on holdings which are prevailingly small. Farming itself is marked by crop diversification even on very small plots, by intercropping, and by successive harvests, up to four in a single year for some crops.

The rationale for maintaining highly diversified farms need not be considered here, but its relation to the distributive pattern is of interest. Rapid and efficient bulking of agricultural products for resale in cities or in other regions occurs readily only where production is quite specialized, or where many individual cultivators in a single subregion have very similar farm situations. Grapefruit from the north plain, onions from St. Raphaël, millet from Fond-des-Nègres, and rice from the Artibonite illustrate this sort of bulking to some extent. But even in these instances, the intermediaries may buy in relatively small quantities, limited by their available capital and media of transport, and their calculations of demand. Normally, the acquisition of stock by intermediaries for resale is a long, time-consuming procedure, involving personal dealings with a large number of individual producers or with other intermediaries.

Consumption both of finished goods and of agricultural produce exhibits certain parallels to production. The peasants customarily sell much of what they produce, and buy much of what they consume, but both sales and purchases are on a small scale. Whether it be millet, rice, cornmeal, root crops, greens, salt, spices, cloth, kerosene, cooking oils, soap, matches, or anything else, small sums are expended for small quantities. Such buying habits are analogous with the practice of selling off produce irregularly and in small quantities. These transactional habits are a function of the seasonal nature of the agriculture, its diversified character, the chronic shortages of cash, and the lack of adequate means of storage. They may also be conditioned by a cultural preference for small-scale and irregular expenditure of cash assets for consumption. Expectably, the distributive mechanisms which tie production and consumption together reflect their character.

Intermediaries are the living links between these two aspects of the economy. On the one hand they bulk produce when buying it up, on the other, they break bulk in resale. They render additional and incidental services, as noted, at the same time. The presence of an oversupply of individuals always ready to provide such services sharpens the competition between intermediaries, and keeps the costs of these services to the economy as a whole at a minimum. The constant search by large numbers of distributors both for supplies to be bought up for resale, and for loci of demand, helps to keep supply and demand in a more balanced relationship–as reflected in price changes–than would be the case were the number of distributors artificially reduced (Bauer, 1954; Mintz, 1957). It also serves to enhance the importance of the *pratik* relationships which are the major concern here.

A *pratik* may be either one who sells to a distributive intermediary or one who buys from a distributive intermediary. Since some products pass through the hands of more than a single intermediary, *pratik* relationships may tie together producer and middleman, or middleman and middleman, or middleman and consumer. For products which are bulked by an intermediary near the source of supply, and broken in bulk for resale by a retailer, the bulking intermediary may have *pratik* relationships with numerous small-scale producers on the one hand, and with several retailers on the other. Moreover, just as the producers may have *pratik* relationships with more than one bulking intermediary, so the retailers may have *pratik* relationships with numbers of consumers. Hence these ties from webs or networks of economic association.

The rationale behind the establishment of *pratik* is clearly economic in nature. This is confirmed by the results of scores of interviews with Haitian professional market women. Every such woman interviewed stated that she had *pratik;* and all of them made clear that the purpose of forming *pratik* ties is to secure and solidify the channels of trade. In general, the means for creating and maintaining *pratik* is by the granting of economic concessions. But obviously such concessions cannot be granted unilaterally, or they serve no economic purpose for one of the participants. Concessions (in the form of price, quantity, credit, or otherwise) are made by intermediaries both to producers and to consumers, and to yet other intermediaries. The reciprocal reward for these concessions takes the form of more assured pathways to supply and demand. In effect, the intermediary will be seen to be trading some portion of her potential profit in a theoretically random market situation, in return for some measure of assurance that she will be able both to acquire stock and then to dispose of it.

This point deserves some stress if only to clarify the wholly rational economic motives which lie behind *pratik* relationships. These ties are by no means uneconomic, noneconomic, or economically irrational; quite the contrary, in fact, since their existence demonstrates the Haitian market woman's clear recognition of the general character of the economy. Except in the instances of granting credit and lending money, and often, even then, the guarantees that a *pratik* relationship will persist and continue to be mutually beneficial are personal and customary, not legal and contractual. But dishonesty on the part of a *pratik* will end the tie, and women who behave unethically in such relationships soon threaten their own stakes in the distributive process.

No market woman interviewed denied having *pratik* relationships with those who "buy from her hand"; some, however, fail to have these ties with those from whom they buy, if those others are producers. Intermediaries who buy from producers do not uniformly make *pratik* of them. Retailers—intermediaries who sell to consumers—are like intermediaries between intermediaries, having bilateral relationships. But on the consumer side, the nature of the *pratik* arrangement will differ.

Commonly the *pratik* is defined as a "good customer."[4] When an intermediary has *pratik* among producers from whom she buys, she may theoretically buy at a higher price, accept a smaller quantity for the same price, or advance a loan against a future crop. No one indicated that she bought less of a given product for the same price. The intermediary as buyer is acquiring stock, and wishes to do so to the limit of her capital. She may pay a little more in order to improve her access to more stock in the future. But she will not buy less from a single seller than her capital makes possible at one time, if this means having to seek out another seller of the same produce.

At the other end of the chain, the retailer who has *pratik* with her consumer customers is readier to make small concessions in price—giving a little more for the same amount of money—than to give the same amount of stock for less money. Where perishable goods are concerned, the retailer when bargaining will increase quantity rather than lower price as a matter of practice, even when not dealing with *pratik* who buy from her.

Perishability and like considerations (such as fragility, short harvests, and high unit costs) enter into the shaping of *pratik* relationships in other ways. The intermediary buying from her producer *pratik* is unlikely to offer to buy at higher than the going price if the product rots easily, as in the case of onions or tomatoes. The producer-seller is going to sell off to the first buyer who comes along and offers the going price. He cannot hold stock of this sort, even for short periods, given his lack of storage and refrigeration facilities. Correspondingly, the buying intermediary wins no future assurance of supply by offering more than the going price precisely because the producer-seller is unable to hold stock for her.

But in the case of relatively more durable stock—unhusked millet or dried corn for instance—the producer-seller may be in a position to retain his supply in anticipation of a price rise. With substantially imperishable stock, particularly rice, this is even more the case. In such instances, and where the buyer-intermediary regularly acquires stock from the producer, she may be willing to pay slightly more per unit of purchase when she buys. Her concessions increase her chances of acquiring stock when goods are scarce and resale profits potentially high.

Generally speaking, relationships with producers based on price concessions develop when such producers have relatively large stocks of imperishable goods. Peasants in this situation are able to "hold back" on two counts: better storage facilities, and more capital available for necessities. Less well-fixed producers, even of imperishable stocks, are more likely to have to sell off to any buyers, much as if their produce were subject to rapid spoilage.

In the case of items which spoil readily, the most common basis for *pratik* with the producer is by loans against a future crop. Such loans are made either to large-scale or small-scale producers of imperishables (with large-scale producers also winning concessions in price); but loans, to the exclusion of price concessions, predominate in transactions with producers of perishables.

Loans to producers are made in several ways. In the Saint Raphaël region of the north, loans are made to producers of onions, which are subject to rather rapid spoilage, and to producers of rice and tobacco, both relatively durable. These loans are paid off in kind rather than in cash. Creditors are entitled to claim their stock at the very start of the harvest, at which time market prices are high. It appears to be the usual practice to estimate the price-to-be of the product and to lend money on these terms. Though some intermediaries claim that they have lost money on crop loans, the opening market prices for rice in the fall and onions in the spring make this unlikely. In the case of tobacco, however, marketing difficulties and the complaints some informants made indicate that they did lose money—some said they would advance no more money for tobacco crops, and this will probably affect the next year's tobacco crop.

Loans are usually advanced on the basis of acreage, or rather, on the estimated yield of a given acreage. The intermediary advances cash against the expected number of barrels of rice, or bags of onions, or bundles of tobacco to be harvested. She will either have some knowledge of the subject herself or depend on her husband or some trusted male friend in making such judgments. These estimates, though, are only a means for putting a reasonable ceiling on the loan, and do not affect the terms. Often the intermediary "buys" the total crop by making a flat cash payment before harvest, and claiming the entire harvest as it ripens.

Since it is likely that the producer who borrows from an intermediary will be turning over his product at harvest at a selling price below what he could get in the open market, it is relevant why peasants make such arrangements. The need for cash in the planting season is sometimes severe, while cash loans or credit are difficult to secure by other means. Loans made by intermediaries, though generally sealed by an informal contract, are generally small. The peasant does not normally put up his land or other real property as collateral, which he would be expected to do if he borrowed from a townsman or from a wealthy farmer. The intermediary who lends him money is probably resident in his community, and though she may handle more cash than he, their class position is not likely to be different. The *pratik* relationship itself is the basis for the loan even though the loan is contractual, and it is a relationship requiring some mutual trust and regard. When the budgets I collected are analyzed, it should be possible to specify the average earnings intermediaries in one community can make by investing their cash in this way. The lending intermediary in these cases takes two risks: one, of crop failure, and the other, of a market glut. Surely she does her best to protect herself in lending her capital to producers.

At the other end of the chain of intermediaries—that is, as between retailer and consumer—the character of *pratik* is different, both in kind and in scale. The retailer of vegetable produce in Port-au-Prince, for instance, whether itinerant house-to-house seller or stallkeeper in the large city markets, tries to acquire a group of steady customers. These customers are made and held by price and quantity concessions, but particularly by concessions in quantity. The "extra"—*dègi* or *tiyô* in Créole—is part of many transactions. All grains and legumes, for instance, are sold in units of tin cans of various sizes (Mintz, 1961) normally heaped to spilling; the "extra" given in these instances is in excess of the heaped tin. In food measured by the lot or pile, the giving of an extra portion is sometimes more subtle. The Haitian squash (Créole: *militô)*, the avocado, sweet potatoes, and many other perishable foods and some other items are sold in small piles. One will see a few such piles spread at the feet of a seller, and the differences between these piles are slight indeed, and difficult to measure. If the item in question varies much in size or quality, each pile will contain an assortment, and the piles are carefully prepared so that this will be so. "Extra" to *pratik* is then given by selecting the better items to make a pile, or by adding one or two additional units for the same price.[5]

On a given day at a particular time in any market, the going price for unit stock of this sort rapidly comes to be relatively uniform. The same is true for dried legumes such as rice, millet, corn and cornmeal, red and black beans, pigeon peas, and so on. Unless there is considerable variation in quality or condition, this uniformity of price will prevail. Prices for particular items take shape in a fashion surprisingly reminiscent of the textbook examples. The seller knows at what price a particular item sold on the previous market day; she also knows at what price she has risked buying. She sets her opening price in line with her expectations. If demand is steady and uncomplaining, she will raise her price but she rarely has to do this, since the asking price usually adjusts downward by small concessions until it becomes stabilized. If demand is slack (and customers voluble in their disdain), and other sellers are doing business at a lower price, she will reluctantly but quickly come down. What is worth remarking is the speed with which these adjustments are made, not over time or uniformly in different market settings, but for a given and particular situation. If there are a dozen sellers of cornmeal or red beans in a given market at ten o'clock in the morning—by which time the market has been in progress and prices have been finding their levels for several hours—it will be difficult to find a single seller whose price varies as much as a penny a unit for the stock in question. Exceptions occur, however, if the stock is very scanty and the demand high; if there are big variations in quality; or if sellers with very small stocks have the need to sell off very rapidly.

The implications of price uniformity for the *pratik* phenomenon are interesting. Each of the retailers of a certain product in the market may be expected to have *pratik;* they make these *pratik* and hold them essentially by giving more for less. But they remain in constant competition with other sellers of the same product, in terms of their asking price. Market women do not advertise their *pratik*. The *pratik* buyer comes to his or her *pratik* seller and inquires after the price of a certain good. The price quoted does not vary from that quoted to any other prospective buyer. But when the sale is consummated, the *pratik* buyer gets the product at a lower price—or else, and more typically, gets a greater quantity for the same price. Since this occurs only with *pratik*, it should not be thought that the intermediary is lowering the going price of her stock on the open market. The going price rises and falls in relation to supply and demand (Mintz, 1959, p. 24); price concessions of the sort described here are additional to general supply-demand based changes, or they may be thought of as occurring within the field of these wider changes.

The upshot of this is that two sorts of competition, very different from each other, are occurring in the same setting. The first sort, and more important, is the competition of the open market, revealed by the emerging uniformity of the asking price at any one time for a given product in a single market. The second sort is the competition for *pratik*, proceeding behind the screen of apparent price uniformity. Not all buying *pratik* are granted the same measure of concession, nor even necessarily the same kind of concession. Intermediaries admit both to having buying *pratik* and to concealing the details of their *pratik* relationships from their competitors; these relationships are pervasive at the same time that they are partly hidden.

It remains to discuss *pratik* relationships between intermediaries. These are various in nature, but only one category will be treated, namely, relationships between wholesalers and retailers of agricultural products. Many agricultural items, such as dried grains, legumes, and fresh fruits and vegetables, are bulked by intermediaries who buy from numerous small producers and wholesale to retailers who break bulk in selling to consumers. Such a series includes a minimum of four participants: producer, bulker, retailer, and consumer. It is to the center of this series that attention is now directed.

Credit extension and concessions in quantity are the major means of tying retailer *pratik* to the wholesaler. Price reductions are also employed. Retailer *pratik* are to be found mainly in the capital, in and around the big markets, and in the provincial cities. Since the bulking intermediaries carry relatively large stocks, they will make *pratik* with numbers of retailers. Though the quantities of any one item carried by a bulking intermediary and those purchased by any single retailer vary enormously, the relative scale can be suggested. An onion bulker from the north will usually carry from about seven to about twenty sacks of onions to the capital to wholesale. These sacks hold approximately fifteen to sixteen No. 10 canfuls of onions when filled to bursting. A Port-au-Prince retailer may purchase one sack, or two, or even six, for resale by the pound or canful. The bulking intermediary will buy onions from the producer at, say, U.S. $7.00 the sack, and resell at U.S. $9.00, if the market is very brisk. For her trade at large, she will reduce the quantity of onions in each sack by one or two canfuls, and thus put together enough onions for an extra sack. When reselling her onions at the U.S. $9.00 rate, she may provide her *pratik* with one of two kinds of advantage: reduce the price per sack, or refill the sacks to their original overflowing. She may also be willing to sell to some of her established *pratik* on credit, giving them a week or ten days to sell off and repay her in the form of cash. Sometimes these credit arrangements include a carrying charge or interest. A bulking intermediary with many retailer *pratik* may be able to dispose of half or more of her stock through her *pratik*. Since onions are speculative, yielding good profits sometimes but glutting the markets at certain periods, *pratik* with retailers is decidedly advantageous to the bulking intermediary.

Pratik relationships seem to have a characteristic way of taking shape. A bulking intermediary will call over a would-be buyer unfamiliar to her and invite her to buy. After some talk, if the seller likes the buyer's manner, she will make a very reasonable selling offer. As the sale is consummated, she will ask the buyer if she buys regularly on that day and at that place. If the answer is a friendly affirmative, she will say meaningly: "Wait for me. I always come on this day. I come from such-and-such a town. I come here with the truck called so-and-so. I keep my stock here, at the depot of Madame X." With more talk, an understanding begins to emerge. Each woman will carefully watch the other's behavior on subsequent occasions, until there is genuine mutual trust. When vaunting the solidarity of a *pratik*, an intermediary will say: "When I go to Port-au-Prince, my *pratik* never lets me sleep in the depot—I sleep in her house." Or: "When X promises to buy eggs for me, she hides them from the other women, and will not consider their offers."[6] A buying *pratik* who knows her selling *pratik* is coming will wait at the proper place and time, refusing to buy stock from others that she is sure her *pratik* is carrying.

To the extent that her stock is committed in such arrangements, a selling *pratik* will refuse to sell to others until she has met her *pratik* buyer. One may be led to believe that the selling behavior of intermediaries is random or whimsical, and that they may refuse to make certain sales because of some irrational streak. It should be clear, however, that personalized economic relationships, while they modify somewhat the nature of the distributive process, arise precisely because intermediaries understand the basic character of the Haitian economy so well.[7]

A final point may be considered here. In the brief discussion of Haitian agriculture undertaken earlier, nothing was said of the economic and social arrangements by which work is done. Considerable emphasis is put on cooperative work groups by those writing on Haitian rural economy (Métraux, 1951). But I think that in the Haitian countryside there is great economic individualism in agriculture, and in fact relatively little institutionalized cooperation. If this is true in agriculture, it appears to be even truer of marketing. Combines of intermediaries do not exist, and intermediaries do not at present form such combinations in order to bulk produce on a larger scale, reduce overhead, purchase trucks, fix prices, or otherwise act collectively in their own group interest. Intermediary activity has a highly fragmented individualistic character. But the *pratik* custom plays an integrating role. It is built up out of series or chains of dyadic relationships which persist through time, and are founded on mutual trust for mutual advantage. It may be that some observers of Haitian rural society have not noticed the variety of integrating social forms serving various ends. Ties of the *pratik* kind may be most common in those societies in which more extended formal social devices have never existed or have fallen into disuse. The *kôbit* and *kòvé* work societies of old have nearly disappeared from Haitian agriculture, to be replaced by day labor in most cases. But overmuch notice is still taken of these disappearing work groups since they have somehow caught the imagination of observers and visiting planners. *Pratik* relationships, partly because they occur mainly within the distributive system rather than wholly within production, partly because they seem socially narrow, fragile, and trivial alongside the work societies, have received little or no attention. It is at least worth considering whether cooperative economic activity in a country such as Haiti might not be realized more directly by careful prior analysis of dyadic relationships, than by the marshaling of nostalgic suppositions about an institution now nearly vanished from the scene.

Yale University

NOTES

1. The writer is grateful to the Guggenheim Foundation and to the Social Science Research Council for grants which made the research for this paper possible.

2. Bauer, 1954, has made the point eloquently for West Africa. Whether the interme-

diary's rate of profit is "unreasonable" does not appear to be a moral question but an economic one.

3. Créole words are transcribed in the Laubach orthography, on which see Hall, 1953. Créole words are italicized, and distinguished from French words by their orthography. The accent aigu over "e" is as in French. Over "o," the accent grave forms the equivalent of the French open "o." The "ou" is as in French, the "ch" as in English "sh," and the "j" as in French "z." The circumflex indicates nasalization.

4. From Fr. "pratique." A typical definition of *pratik* is the following. "It means that you are selling. I come to buy from you each day. I need credit; you sell to me [on credit]; the money is 'content' that you sell to me. I always buy from your hand; I pay you well. That means 'pratik'."

5. The same procedure is reported from Jamaica. Katzin writes (1959, p. 87): "Some sellers favor their regular customers in other ways. To give 'brawta' or 'make-up' is the practice, all along the line from rural producer to retail buyer. This is identical with the British and American practice of giving something additional in a transaction."

6. In this instance as in several described by Katzin for Jamaica, the economic rationality of such behavior is clearly demonstrated. Such examples make clear that the old woman on her way to market who refuses to sell her stock to a passing stranger at a very favorable price is not in fact behaving irrationally; quite the contrary. Nor does her unwillingness to sell demonstrate that her real purpose in going to market is merely to gossip with her neighbors, a charge which even local city people are fond of leveling at every opportunity. Careful examination of the Haitian situation throws light on James' claim (1942, p. 771) that "The markets which are held throughout rural Haiti, many of them in the open country, are attended primarily for social pleasure, not for buying and selling."

7. This understanding is often misunderstood to be a lack of commercial sophistication. James writes (1942, p. 771): "The average rural Haitian is not a person of great ambition, nor one who takes naturally to the complexities of commercial life."

BIBLIOGRAPHY

Bauer, Peter T.
1954 West African Trade. Cambridge, Cambridge University Press.

Hall, Robert A., Jr.
1953 Haitian Creole. American Anthropological Association Memoir No. 74, April-June, 1953. Menasha, Wisconsin.

Herskovits, Melville J.
1937 Life in a Haitian Valley. New York, Knopf.

James, Preston E.
1942 Latin America. New York, Odyssey Press.

Katzin, Margaret F.
1959 Higglers of Jamaica. Ph.D. Thesis, Northwestern University.

Métraux, Alfred, *et al.*
1951 Making a Living in the Marbial Valley (Haiti). Paris, UNESCO Educational Clearing House, Occasional Papers in Education, No. 10.

Mintz, Sidney W.
1957 Aspects of the Internal Distribution System in a Caribbean Peasant Economy. Human Organization, XV, No. 2, 18-23.
1959 Internal Market Systems as Mechanisms of Social Articulation, *in* Proceedings of [62]
the American Ethnological Society edited by Verne F. Ray. Seattle, University of Washington Press.
1960 A Tentative Typology of Eight Haitian Market Places, Revista de Ciencias Sociales, IV, No. 2, 15-57.
1961 Standards of Value and Units of Measure in the Fond-des-Nègres Market Place, Haiti, Journal of the Royal Anthropological Institute, XCI (in press).

Moral, Paul
1959 L'Economie Haitienne. Port-au-Prince, Haiti, Imprimerie de l'Etat. [63]

[25]

THE MARKET WHEEL: SYMBOLIC ASPECTS OF AN INDIAN TRIBAL MARKET

ALFRED GELL
London School of Economics & Political Science

A weekly market in Bastar District, Madhya Pradesh, India, is analysed from the point of view of its symbolic significance as a map of social relations in the area. The groups present in Bastar interact in the market more regularly than they do in any other context. The market plan shows their hierarchical relationships clearly, and this message is underscored by the hierarchical values attached to the goods transacted. It is argued that this symbolic interaction perpetuates an ideological representation of Tribal/Hindu relations which confers certain practical advantages on the Tribals at the expense of their being made symbolically peripheral.

Dhorai is the name of a market village located deep in the hinterland of North Bastar district, Madhya Pradesh (central India).[1] On non-market days Dhorai is a sleepy, tree-shaded hamlet straddling an unsealed road which winds its way through the forest. Occasionally its rural peace is shattered by the roar of a passing truck laden with massive logs of teak (timber production being the major industry in the region) or loud blasts from the horn of the local bus; but these interruptions are not frequent. Social life in Dhorai revolves around two primitive tea-shops with a clientèle of low-ranking employees of the State Forest service, whose misfortune it has been to be stationed in such a distant and insignificant spot. Dhorai boasts a tumbledown school, which doubles as a post-office, an imposing Forest Rest House (usually empty), a few substantial homesteads belonging to Hindus, a penumbra of rather less substantial huts inhabited by tribal Muria Gonds,[2] and not much else.

Dhorai on non-market days—every day except Friday, that is—hardly exists at all; but Dhorai on a market day might be a totally different place. Parked trucks jam the road, in charge of their drivers, burly Sikhs from the north, or dark, polysyllabic Telegus from Hyderabad. The lowly Forest Guards bustle about in smart, newly-pressed uniforms, while the more important officials of the Forest service, down for the day, oversee operations from the verandah of the Forest Rest House. They disburse payments to the tribal labourers, and check through the mounds of documentation which are the bane of a forest officer's life. In their quasi-military khaki they look like the officers of an occupying colonial power, whose successors they have indeed become.

While the officials hold court in the Rest House, files of Tribals continue to pour in from all directions, laden with the produce of the forest, of their fields and of their own manufacture. They are joined by Hindu vegetable sellers, and

Man (N.S.) **17**, 470–91

by specialised craftsmen, potters, weavers and blacksmiths. The general impression is one of richness and confusion, compounded by the fact that a religious ceremony, as well as a market, is in process. In front of the temple of the State Goddess, which faces onto the marketplace, the untouchable oboeist and drummer are performing, and a long-haired ascetic insults his back with chains. The whole world, it seems, is at the market, men and their Divinities alike.

The marketplace is a roughly quadrangular patch of ground, about 100 yards square, at the centre of which there grows a magnificent banyan tree. The thatched market stalls are arranged in a concentric pattern, and are divided by narrow streets or defiles, along which customers manoeuvre themselves as best they can in the crush, trying to avoid treading on the goods of less established traders, who make use of every nook and cranny between the permanent stalls to display their wares.

Beggary and poverty are not to be seen at the Dhorai market: the young are all dressed smartly, and their elders contrive to convey, at the very least, an impression of respectable solidity. The dressiness, the showiness of the market scene—the oiled hair, the ornaments, the brilliant-hued saris, the immaculate shirts and turbans—is not, indeed, an aspect of the market to be ignored: for it reveals, as clearly as anything, the fact that the market is a ceremonial as well as a commercial occasion. Participants adopt modes of heightened and stereotyped role-playing, appropriate for a ceremonial occasion, and the obligatory 'dressing up' is an aspect of this. Indeed, on closer examination, it is possible to perceive in the design of the market occasion an enactment of the social order in the widest sense, as it impinges on the people in the locality. For distinctiveness is at a premium, and the market provides an occasion *par excellence* for the differentiation of groups and for the articulation of inter-group relations, in ways not possible in the context of the daily routine of village life where these diverse groups come into contact only spasmodically. The market gives tangible expression to principles of social structure which transcend the village context. It locates the villagers in a holistic system of sociological categories, and binds them to this system by means of market relations. The intention of this article is thus to explore the Dhorai market from the point of view of its symbolic importance as an indigenous model of social relations.

The study of markets

'Markets which meet periodically in India have been neglected by geographers' writes Harriss (1976; cf. Bromley 1974), and despite some additions (Wanmali 1976; 1977; Agrawal 1978) this remains true. The anthropological literature on rural markets in India is no less sparse, though the monographs by S. Sinha *et al.* (1961) and D. Sinha (1968) are interesting exceptions. This neglect is curious, especially in the light of the copiousness of 'market' studies carried out in India's congener-societies in the developing world, a genre inspired by the example of *Trade and market in the early empires* (Polanyi *et al.* 1957) and culminating in such major syntheses as Bohannan and Dalton's *Markets in*

Africa (1962) and Skinner's *Marketing and social structure in rural China* (1964–65). In many non-industrialised societies markets are arguably central in the understanding of the social system as a whole. But this view would be completely heterodox in the Indian context, and for perfectly good reasons, no doubt, stemming from the self-sufficient nature of the traditional village economy and the prevalence of the jajmani system (Mandelbaum 1970). Nonetheless, periodic marketing systems are a common feature of rural India and are worthy of more attention from sociological observers than they have received. The question is, what *kind* of attention should they attract? Hitherto, they have been mainly the concern of economic geographers, interested in locational questions, periodicities, catchment areas and administrative problems (Wanmali 1976) and with problems of the general efficiency of rural marketing arrangements as means of distributing food cheaply and fairly (Harriss 1976). My concerns are quite different, which does not of course imply that I mean to deprecate the geographers' approach to applied social research. What follows can best be described as a 'thick description' of a rural market, undertaken in order to demonstrate the structural parallels which exist between the microcosmic system of the local market and the macrocosmic system of North Bastar society. The method is the one adopted in Geertz's famous account of the Balinese cockfight (1975; cf. Geertz *et al.* 1979).

Following Geertz, I take the market at Dhorai as an enacted 'text', whose meaning can be construed by providing the appropriate specification of context. My argument is that, for the participants, the market gives concrete representation of the ground-plan of their society, its hierarchical organisation and the scheme of values which sustains it. The market is a secular event, but it is also part of the ritual of social relations. Critics of this 'interpretative' approach may consider that it leaves untouched crucial questions having to do with 'why' things are as they are in Dhorai market and in Bastar society generally, and I am willing to concede this. However, it is heuristically practical to maintain a methodological separation between problems of cultural interpretation on the one hand and problems of causal/historical explanation on the other. It is all the more likely that I might arouse unfulfilled expectations with respect to the latter class of problems, in that my topic is the market, and 'market' studies have most frequently been undertaken with causal/historical analytical goals in mind; were I describing a festival or a *rite de passage* my interpretative intention would be more understandable, though still, no doubt, objectionable to certain points of view. The present choice of problem-definition is dictated not as a consequence of a theoretical prejudice against causal analysis,[3] but arises from data at my disposal which seem sufficiently suggestive to warrant analysis within a narrowly structural framework. My theme happens to be the market, but this article is not intended as a contribution to the theory of markets, nor more generally to exchange relations. I am more preoccupied with the elucidation of a secular ceremonial, following the proposal made by Leach in a famous passage in which he advises anthropologists to make themselves aware of the 'ritual' component in normal everyday actions (Leach 1954: 13). Dhorai market has a significant ceremonial component in that it provides a *mapping*, in space, time and in the form of market interactions, for the gamut of social relations found in the wider society in the region of North Bastar where Dhorai market is located. This 'mapping' is quite overt in the spatial layout of the market, and here I am extending the range of spatial representations of social relations already exemplified in such familiar instances as the layout of the village of Omarakana in the Trobriands (Lévi-Strauss 1964) or the arrangement of the negotiating table at the 1971 Paris peace talks over Vietnam (Douglas 1973).

This approach is familiar enough and only the context, perhaps, is novel. But in the Indian ethnographic milieu it would be strikingly aberrant were I not centrally concerned with the symbolic representation of hierarchy in social relations, since the inegalitarian premiss is so rooted in India, even in 'tribal' Bastar. Here I am perhaps entering an uncharted area, in that previous discussions of hierarchy in India have not taken into account the hierarchical aspect of market relations. I would acknowledge the impetus provided by the work of Carol Smith (1975; 1976) towards the germination of the ideas presented here. Smith has summarised her arguments in the following terms:

> Regional central-place organisation in Guatemala acts as a 'negative' or deviation-amplifying feedback loop between the irregular organisation of many local central-place systems, the ethnic divisions of the region, uneven rural development and underdevelopment and political inequality in the region (1976: 293).

While it should be apparent that Smith is dealing with questions of the most ambitious causal/explanatory kind, whereas I am not, the causal processes of hierarchy-accentuation *via* marketing organisation adverted to by Smith can be accompanied by processes of symbolic reinforcement of hierarchical relations of the kind I do discuss. This seems to be particularly a feature of those parts of India most distant from major centres of power, where state administration and Brahminical ritual dominance are weakly developed. Work on tribal Bihar (Sinha *et al.* 1961; Sinha 1968) supports this view: markets are most sociologically salient in areas which are 'backwaters' according to the historico-geographic regional typology of Schwartzberg (1967). I must defer, to a later occasion, the provision of the kind of regional geographical economic analysis provided by Smith, which leaves as an open question the applicability of her Guatemalan model to the very different circumstances, and very different cultural premisses, of North Bastar. But there seems to be scope for suggesting some degree of convergence between the microcosmic perspective adopted here (the world as seen from Dhorai) and the macrocosmic perspective so elegantly presented in Smith's work.

Social categories

If we are to see the Dhorai market as, in some sense, a 'map' of social relations, it is necessary to enumerate the major categories of people to be found in the market area. I propose to list these groups, simply for the sake of quick exposition, but must forestall a reasonable objection to this admittedly rather old-fashioned procedure. It may be felt that to list separate 'groups' in this way is to obscure the very point that I am seeking to demonstrate, namely, that the market reflects patterns of intergroup relations in the wider social field, since by simply enumerating groups as separate entities I leave unclarified the nature of the inter-group relationships supposedly reflected in the market arena; I would, by implication, be imputing to the market itself causal priority in the structuring of inter-group relations inasmuch as it is in the market alone that such inter-relationships can be concretely shown to exist. It would be more appropriate, such a critic might insist, to depict the different groups as organically related *outside* the market context – in a manner well known from the vast bulk of studies of multi-caste village societies in India – before turning to the market place where such a given disposition of relationships between socially and ritually ranked and economically differentiated groups could be seen as 'reflected' rather than as in any sense primarily constituted or established. This objection is perfectly in order, and it is not indeed my intention to argue that the market has causal priority in bringing about the pattern of existing inter-group relations. However, the objection loses a great deal of its force as a result of certain considerations peculiar to low-density, dispersed-settlement societies, such as characterise the Dhorai hinterland. It is simply a fact that there is very little sustained daily interaction between the major groups here discussed, a situation quite unlike that normally encountered in densely-packed, nucleated, multi-caste villages where a complex web of inter-caste relations is daily mobilised and continuously elaborated. If communal relations in the Indian village are usually, in Srinivas's famous phrase, 'back to back', it would be truer to say of the villages in the Dhorai area that they are out of sight, out of mind. But this is not to say that these inter-group relations are not clearly articulated, though they are expressed, outside the market context, by the absence, rather than the presence, of association. For this reason it is not misleading to give an initial account of 'groups' in the Dhorai area in the form of a listing of discrete social categories, rather than in the form of an account of dynamic interactions between them.

Gonds. The majority of people in the area served by the Dhorai market are *Adivasis* or Tribals. Around Dhorai the tribal population consists of Muria Gonds (the largest single group in North Bastar) and to the west, in the mountainous and unadministered Abujhmar region, the Hill Muria, another Gond group speaking a slightly different dialect. Gonds live in mainly single-caste communities, to which may be attached enclaves or colonies of 'caste' Hindus of various kinds. Purely Hindu settlements cluster around the lines of communications—roads, rivers and market centres—while the hinterland is predominantly tribal (Elwin 1947; Grigson 1936; Agarwal 1968).

The dispersed pattern of settlement seen in Gond villages—houses being scattered widely through the village territory—contrasts strongly with the much more nucleated pattern seen in Hindu settlements. The Muria Gond are settled agriculturalists, growing paddy on fields surrounded by water-retaining dykes but not otherwise irrigated. The main annual paddy crop is followed, weather permitting, by a cash crop (oil-seeds, pulses). Muria also derive cash from labouring for the Forest Department—work concentrated in the slack agricultural season—and from collecting such forest products as tamarind, teak-seeds and silk-cocoons.

Around Dhorai, if not always elsewhere, Muria tribal society is essentially intact, its institutions including the famous youth-dormitory (*ghotul*) still fully viable, and it would have appeared to have reached a stable *modus vivendi* with the Hindu presence, and with the government and its agencies. The older system of forest swiddening is closely controlled, where it is not banned altogether, but in exchange the Tribals receive protection for their land rights from the government, plus a permanent availability of a modest cash income from labouring for the Departments of Forests and Public Works, as well as from the sale of forest products, for which there is always a ready market.

Maraars. The most numerous non-tribal group in the Dhorai region are the Maraars. They claim to have migrated from the Kanker—Chhattisgarh district where they were market-gardeners and purveyors of flowers (*maraar* is said to be a corruption of *mali*, Hindi for 'Gardener'). Maraars are skilled agriculturalists and vegetable growers. Their settlements abound in the proximity of rivers, on whose banks they practise irrigated horticulture at a level of intensiveness far in advance of the Gonds.

Since the type of low-lying river-land used by the Maraars for irrigated cultivation and the use they make of it hardly overlap with the more extensive pattern of agriculture seen among tribal Muria, it would not be too far-fetched to see Maraar-Muria relations in terms of occupancy of separate and non-competing ecological niches. This is not altogether true, since Maraars also have paddy land of the ordinary kind, and cultivate more land on share-cropping arrangements from Muria landlords from whom they are prevented by law from buying land outright. It would be true to say, though, that the two groups do not see themselves as economically competing, and they are related by ritual ties which stress the primacy of the Tribals' ownership of the earth.

The Maraars are specialist agriculturalists with a strongly market orientation. They claim high ritual rank (as providers of flowers) 'like Brahmins' they say—and as there are no Brahmins for miles about to say them nay, they go uncontradicted. They are distinguished from the tribal population not only in their observance of Hindu dietary taboos and such, but also linguistically, in that they rarely speak any Gondi (the Dravidian tribal language). They speak instead an Indo-European regional *lingua-franca*, Halbi, and Chhattisgarhi Hindi.

Other Hindu groups. The most numerous non-tribal group in the mountainous area to the west of Dhorai are the Halba, descendants of the Maharashtrian soldiery of the kingdoms of Bastar and Chanda. They have lived among the tribal population for so long that they are classified as Tribals in the census. They are not numerous in the Dhorai area. A more significant group, though not a numerous one, are the Rawits or herdsmen. Most Muria villages contain a family or two of Rawits, migrants from the north who claim kinship to the important northern caste group of herdsmen known as Ahirs. Rawits, though maintaining their Hindu identity (not eating beef, wearing the sacred thread like the Maraars) are in effect a service caste to the Muria Gonds, whose cattle they look after and whose clients they are. They mostly cultivate land of their own as well, but are rarely well provided for in this respect. They milk the cows and sell milk in the market. Finally, mention should be made of the Kallar or distillers. This small Hindu caste was enabled to enrich itself during the period, up to the mid-sixties, when it held a legal monopoly of the trade in distilled liquor. Distillers rank high in the caste hierarchy, and own considerable amounts of land, from which they now derive their livelihood, as the sale of liquor has been officially banned.

Outcasts. Untouchability in its more extreme forms is not encountered in the region, but certain beef-eating, non-tribal caste groups have low social status. Of these the largest is the Ganda or weaver caste. Gandas are mostly poor, landless or nearly landless labourers. They are also musicians, and to a certain extent practitioners of their caste occupation of weaving. Gandas sell their cloths, which are expensive but exceptionally hard-wearing if somewhat old fashioned, in the market. Blacksmiths (Kachchi) are another low-ranking occupational caste. They are a sub-caste of Gonds, rather than Hindus, and produce mainly agricultural implements in the villages, from iron smelted from local ores. Bronze-workers (Ghassia) form a separate group. Ghassia are Hindus, and specialise mainly in the production of temple images, ritual drinking-vessels, trumpets, bells and so on. Ghassias are also occupationally specialised as assistants to jewellers-cum-moneylenders, for whom they perform debt-collecting and strong-arm-man functions. Kumhars (potters) are low-ranking and generally very poor; they carry on their occupational specialisations and sell their wares at the market.

Outsiders. The previously mentioned groups are all traditional occupants of the area, whose arrival in the region predates the turn of the century at the latest. But there are many much more recent and less assimilated caste Hindus in the area, particularly among the market traders. The caste status of these outsiders is for the most part irrelevant, especially if they are transient government employees. Their status depends on their importance in terms of the local government and Forest Department bureaucracy. But sometimes an outsider's caste status is significant (for example, a forest officer who is a knowledgeable Brahmin will be consulted on matters appertaining to astrology). This is particularly so in connexion with a key individual in the Dhorai market, the main jeweller, whose stall is the very hub around which the market revolves. This man comes, like most jewellers in the area, from Rajasthan. He carries with him a distinct air of northern, aristocratic culture, and he claims himself to be a Rajput. Most market traders of manufactured goods are Hindi-speakers from metropolitan areas, culturally quite distinct from the local Hindu groups. I return to the significance of this point later on.

Having discussed the major groups of people assembled at the market, I will now provide a brief sketch of the pattern of market relations they enter into. There are five main kinds of goods transacted:

(1) Imported manufactured items originating outside Bastar (which has no manufacturing industry), including jewellery (silver and gold) machine cloth, beads, trinkets, and more mundane items such as lamps, brass pots, knives, plates.

(2) Non-locally-produced food, notably salt, rice, pulse, turmeric, dried chillies, refined sugar, flour (and other consumables such as *bidi* cigarettes, perfumed hair oil, 'Himalayan Snow' face-cream, talc).

(3) Locally produced food, fresh vegetables such as tomatoes, *muli*, onions, and luxury foods such as *gur* (locally made sugar) and parched rice, to which should be added locally cured tobacco.

(4) Local manufactured (craft) items such as bamboo baskets and grain-bins, sleeping mats of woven rushes, the complete range of earthenware pots, locally made ironware, axes, knives, arrowheads, and local khadi cloth.

(5) Forest products and cash crops collected in bulk at the market and despatched to metropolitan centres, mainly tamarind, oil-seeds, silk-cocoons, leaves for use as wrapping, and teak-seeds.

Corresponding to these major categories of goods are market roles which can be listed as follows:

(1) Stallholders. These are without exception Hindus, not from the immediate locality, trading goods in categories 1 and 2. They can be subdivided into (a) jeweller/moneylender; (b) trinket sellers; (c) machine-cloth sellers; (d) hardware/drygoods (manufactured items and imported foods); (e) teashops (local Hindus).

(2) Open market produce traders. These consist of local Hindus (Maraars) and tribal Muria Gonds. They are divided into (a) parched rice/*gur* sellers (Chhota Dongar Maraars); (b) fresh vegetable sellers (other Maraars); (c) tobacco sellers (Maraar men and one tribal); (d) tribal vegetable sellers; (e) milk sellers (Rawits).

(3) Open market non-produce traders. These include (a) traders in baskets/mats/bamboo-work (Tribals from the Abujhmar); (b) potters; (c) blacksmiths; (d) weavers.

(4) Middlemen. Hindus who buy up tribal forest products and cash crops, paying with salt or money.

To this list we can add the three major categories of customers, who tend to be in the market for rather different things: (a) non-local Hindus (e.g. forest officers, officials); (b) local Hindus; (c) tribals; and the non-customer roles Policeman (Kotwal), Beggar (Hindu Sadhu) and spectator.

The following matrix diagram (fig. 1) summarises the pattern of transactions between the major categories of participants in the market. The structure of market relations shown in fig. 1 reposes ultimately on the purchasing power of the Tribals, who are the main customers for all categories of goods. The Tribals' cash is derived from the exploitation of their relatively rich resource base. Wealth derived from the sale of cash crops, forest products and from wages also circulates inside the village, where there is a thriving cash economy. The intra-village economy is rather different in character from the marketplace

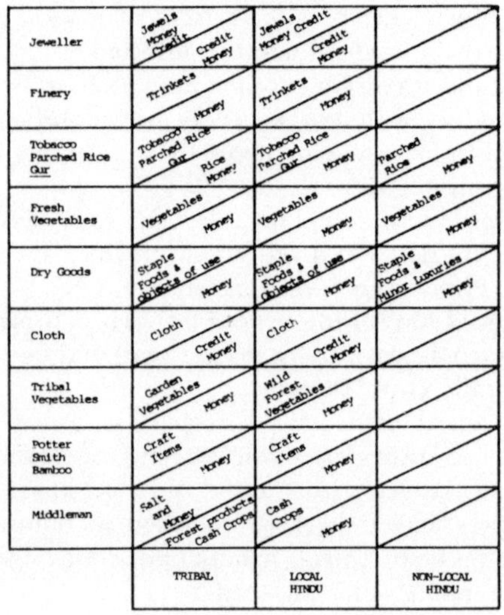

FIGURE 1. Transactions between categories of participants at market.

economy, since it is largely bound up with the buying and selling of livestock, both as draught-animals and for slaughter at ceremonies and feasts. The sale of livestock plays no part in the market at all. The intra-village economy is the arena for competition between tribal men of power and influence (*sian*) who finance feasts and marriages, which involve copious expenditures and long-term debtor-creditor relations. As I describe below, institutionalised credit is absent from the general run of marketplace relations, and is confined to the intra-village context. There are, in effect, two distinct frameworks for economic relationships, the village, and the market, with somewhat different economic ground rules in each case. The 'village' economy is embedded, 'personalistic', geared to the struggle for *internal* prestige between individuals who are equals in terms of the value system of the wider society, while the 'market' economy is hierarchical, anonymous, and geared to the values implicit in the state, the widest framework of social relations.

Time and space

The Dhorai market is primarily an institution of 'vertical integration' (in the sense of Mintz 1959). It integrates three levels of North Bastar society: (i) the village, (ii) the market area and (iii) the district as a whole, including its articulation to metropolitan centres. Market relations, seen from this point of view, are relations of encompassing and encompassed, macrocosm and microcosm. The ranking of market places by size and distance from a centre, first established as a theoretical scheme by Losch (1954) and Christaller (1964) and since that time extensively studied by geographers (Berry 1965; Smith 1976), is significant not merely to students of locational problems *per se*, but also to any kind of sociological analysis of communities which takes regional factors into account. The view of the world that members of a particular community maintain is determined by the nature of the access that they have to it, and this in turn is crucially modified by the hierarchialisation intrinsic to any regional system of communication, transport, exchange and distribution. It is outside the scope of this article to discuss market hierarchy theory in detail (cf. Smith 1977; Skinner 1964–5). Here it is sufficient to identify three levels only: *viz.* '*tehsil*' markets (the highest level of weekly markets), 'intermediate' markets which provide a full range of goods and marketing services in areas, away from district towns, not served by permanent bazaar areas, and finally, 'minor' markets which provide less than the full range of market facilities.

In the hierarchical order of the market system of Bastar as a whole, the Dhorai market occupies an intermediate place; it is superordinate in relation to the village economy, definitive in relation to the Dhorai-market-area economy, and subordinate in relation to the *tehsil* economy. People in the Dhorai market area are of course aware of the existence of other market centres, of various hierarchical orders, beyond the Dhorai market itself, and from time to time—especially when the market in question is combined with ceremonies connected with the Goddess cult—they participate in these markets. In other words, it is through the regional articulation of the market system, that people in the Dhorai market area conceptualise the structure of what can be called, in general terms, the state.

The market system of co-ordinates structure time (cf. Bohannan 1967). The week, of seven days, is the cycle between successive markets in any one market area, and the days of the week are distinguished, and hierarchialised, according to the markets which occur on given days at given places. The fundamental rhythm of the market-day cycle is established at Jagdalpur, the state and previously royal capital, over 150 km away. The Jagdalpur market is held on Sundays, which becomes, so to speak, the highest ranking day. However, Bastar district (whose total area is greater than that of Kerala) is much too large to function as a single market system, so each *tehsil* has its own Sunday market, in imitation of the one at Jagdalpur, at the *tehsil* headquarters. Dhorai is in Narayanpur *tehsil*, so Sunday is Narayanpur market day, a day consecrated to the centre and the state. Time and space coincide in expressing political hierarchy. Ranked beneath the Sunday markets, are the second order market centres such as Dhorai. The market traders of a *tehsil* concentrate in the *tehsil* headquarters on Sunday, and visit other, smaller market centres on other days. Monday, Tuesday and Wednesday are not market days (Tuesday is ruled out as the Hindu unlucky day,[4] and Monday and Wednesday are devoted to rest and replenishing stocks) leaving Thursday, Friday and Saturday as second-order market days. Second order markets are arranged along routes of communication fanning out from the *tehsil* headquarters, as shown in the hypothetical model in fig. 2.

Pharasgaon and Chhota Dongar markets are thus third order markets (fig. 3). The spatiotemporal hierarchy of market centres articulates between village-level society and the state: the *tehsil*-wide market system of Narayanpur recapitulates the organisation of the state (centering on Jagdalpur and divided into subordinate *tehsils*) while the pattern obtaining within the *tehsil* as a whole is itself recapitulated, on a microcosmic scale, by the order of events within a

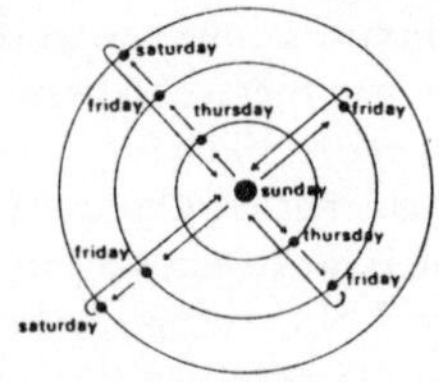

FIGURE 2. Model of time co-ordinates.

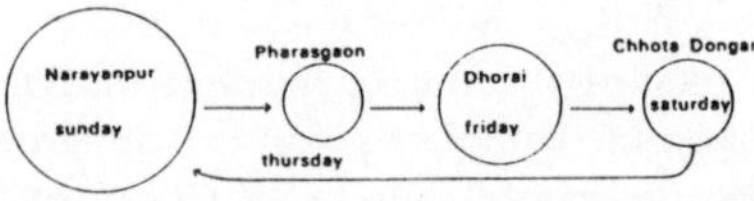

Size of circles expresses the relative importance of each market.

FIGURE 3. Spatio-temporal hierarchy of four market centres.

single second-order or third-order market area; thus, returning to fig. 2 we can see that *tehsil*-wide market organisation consists of an alternation of market concentration and dispersion (systole/diastole) which is mirrored within the single market area—the Dhorai market area let us say—by the concentration of people in the market (on market day) and their dispersion back to the villages on non-market days. In other words, Dhorai (and the other second-order centres) are to Narayanpur, as the component villages of the Dhorai Market area are to Dhorai; and as Dhorai is to Narayanpur, so Narayanpur is to Jagdalpur.

Markets are symbols of the social order because they are its product. Along with battles, ceremonies and political assemblies, they fall into the class of necessarily rather than contingently public occasions. They demand the renunciation of individual autonomy for the sake of ends (the exchange of goods and information) which can only be achieved collectively. Because of their logistic, co-ordinating, functions markets exert a profound influence over concepts of time and space in peasant societies and peasant states. The rhythm of market systole and diastole, emanating from Jagdalpur, is indeed nothing less than the pulse of the state itself.

The market place: equality and inequality

I turn now to the implications of fig. 4 which shows the layout of the Dhorai marketplace. The Dhorai marketplace is nothing less than a compendium of social relations in the Dhorai market area. These can be classified as relations between co-ordinate groups of approximately equal social rank, and relations between groups of different rank. These relations are expressed in two ways: (1) in the traditional layout which regulates where each group sits and transacts its business in the marketplace, and (2) by means of an implied hierarchy of *goods*, which ranks any kind of goods in the market as higher/lower/equivalent in relation to others, and accords them a more central or more peripheral place as the case may be.

In abstract terms the market can be imagined as a wheel; at the hub of the wheel is the central banyan tree, where sits the 'Rajput' jeweller, and on the outermost rim of the wheel are the basket-makers, potters and smiths. On the basis of this analogy, we can define two axes of market relations (1) the 'radial' axis along which participants are assymetrically related as more/less central and along which different kinds of goods are arranged as more/less prestigious; and (2) the 'circumferential' axis along which participants are linked by relations that are symmetric, equal and competitive, and along which goods of equivalent symbolic value are ranged. Let us examine these propositions in more detail.

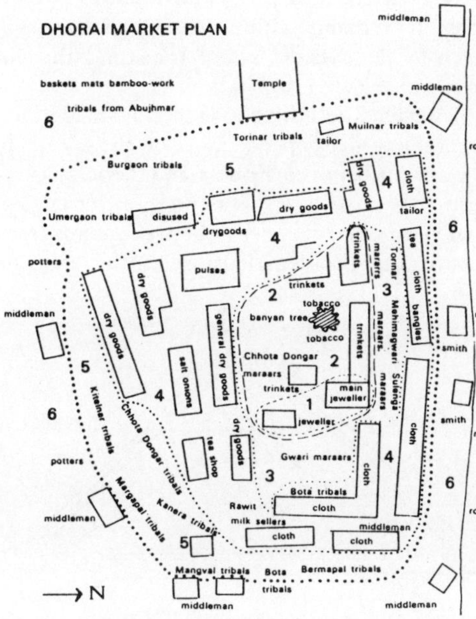

FIGURE 4. Dhorai market plan.

The market map is divisible into five concentric zones. The central zone is occupied by the jeweller, the richest, most sophisticated and best educated trader in the market. The stock he carries, only a portion of the stock-in-trade of his family, jewellers with a permanent shop in Jagdalpur, must be worth something in the region of 20,000 rupees,[5] and he has large sums of cash as well. He mainly sells relatively inexpensive trinkets in silver (such as hair-clips at 25 rupees each) but every so often he sells a more valuable object, such as the heavy silver neck ornaments favoured by tribal women (700–1000 rupees), and more rarely a gold necklace, prices for which range up to 5,000 rupees depending on the number of gold beads used. Just for comparison, land is sold between Tribals (non-Tribals not being permitted to acquire land from Tribals) at little more than 500 rupees a hectare, and a team of ploughing cattle is worth about 350 rupees. These gold necklaces can be worn by either sex but are most often worn by wealthy and influential tribal men.

The main jeweller's stock-in-trade are the symbols of rank and prestige in tribal society: and he himself is the most prestigious market trader on both cultural and economic grounds. Surrounded by his Ghassiya henchmen, he dominates the centre of the market, overseeing what may be, at times, quite enormous transactions by local standards. But at the same time he is a familiar and perfectly accessible, indeed genial, man: when more important transactions do not claim his attention he will occupy himself in extolling the virtues of his cheaper hairclips for the benefit of vacillating tribal girls with every appearance of complacency. And this is an important point, for in the market the jeweller is the symbolic exponent of ideas of pre-eminent value—power, superiority—but, like all symbols, he remains within the ordinary, everyday world, while the values he *represents* lie outside it and transcend the villagers' ordinary experience.

Facing the main jeweller's stall there is a second, smaller, jeweller, also from Rajasthan. This second jeweller depends more on the sale of cheaper items, and is intermediate in position between Zone 1 and Zone 2.

Zone 2 is interesting because it is so seemingly heterogeneous. On the basis of the hypothesis of symbolic equivalence between items transacted in a given zone of market space, our problem is to determine the implications of the following structure:

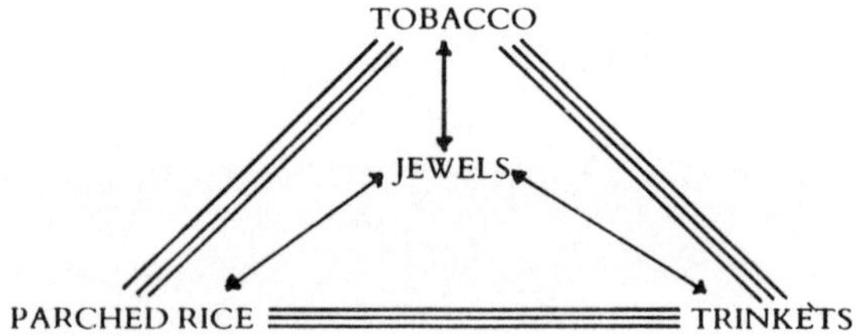

We may note, first of all, that all these goods are luxuries, but that only jewellery is a luxury which is also a permanent store of value. Trinkets are low-grade, perishable jewels: but what makes parched rice/*gur* and tobacco different from the general run of 'consumables' sold in Zone 3? The key seems to be the fact that they are processed or refined. Parched rice and *gur* are the local high-status luxury foods, and are produced by the local 'aristocratic' group—the Chhota Dongar Maraars, the wealthiest, most ancient, and the largest landowners among local Hindus. Women from this group are the main local traders and they dominate the trade in luxury food. Their traditional role in the market as 'adders of value' is interestingly brought out in the convention by which they exchange parched rice with Tribals for its equivalent *volume* in dehusked paddy. Thus Tribals, who are prevented by a taboo from selling paddy for money, will barter one pound, say, of paddy for the parched rice equivalent of perhaps half that amount, since in the processing of parched rice the grains swell up considerably. The Tribal has not offended the rice by 'selling' it: he (or more likely she) has 'valorised' it in the interchange with a high-status group. Similar considerations apply to *gur* and tobacco, both of which have been elaborately processed. Zone 2, then, is shared by luxuries: down-graded jewellery and up-graded consumables. Sociologically speaking, it is the zone of the locally dominant Hindus.

Zone 3 is also a 'Maraar' zone of vegetable sellers, mostly from Maraar communities which are offshoots from the ancient Chhota Dongar settlement, or more recent immigrants from elsewhere in Bastar. Maraars cultivate vegetables in irrigated gardens, specialising in items which cannot be produced, or not in quantity or not of such good quality, in the Tribals' own gardens. These vegetables (such as onions, chillies, tomatoes, *muli*, squashes, aubergines), are semi-luxury items, appreciated by Tribals as additions to their basic diet of rice, pulses and millet. It is noteworthy that the Maraar traders in zones 2 and 3 (mostly women, except for tobacco sellers who are all male) while they do not avail themselves of stalls, do always carry to market a stool to sit on, so as not to sit on the ground in the fashion of the Tribals. On the other hand no Tribal would presume to make use of a stool, so the Maraars are not only figuratively but actually 'higher' than the Tribals.

Zone 4 consists of the stalls of Hindu traders in non-luxury items. One half of this zone is comprised by the street of cloth sellers who deal in cheap machine-made sarees, blankets and such, the other half by the stalls of the dry-goods merchants. Cloth is not a luxury item, and the sale of cloth is not a prestige occupation as is the sale of jewellery or luxury foods. Cloth sellers behave in an unrestrained, vociferous, bumptious manner, quite different from the civilised standards of other Hindu traders. The dry-goods stalls also mainly sell non-luxury items, viz. small utilitarian objects or staple foods. They do carry some luxury items such as *bidi* cigarettes or biscuits, but these are not such as to appeal much to the Tribals, and are mainly sold to local Hindus, for whom they are not perhaps luxuries anyway. One form of local produce is sold in the fourth zone, namely milk. Milk is not a luxury food, and is indeed generally disliked as a food by the Tribals, so that the Rawit traders' output is purchased exclusively by Hindus. The intermediate status of the Rawits—lower than Maraars but higher than Tribals—is clearly expressed in the confinement of Rawits to zone 4.

The fifth zone consists of tribal sellers of vegetables. Here we find the mass of tribal women selling small quantities of vegetables in season, seated on the ground in lengthy rows, each according to their villages of origin. Tribal men also sit in these areas, sometimes selling, sometimes merely sitting. Men are more mobile though, and spend much of the time in more exclusive huddles off in the bushes at some distance, conducting meetings relating to intervillage affairs and drinking.

The sixth zone, finally, includes the low-ranking sellers of non-prestige craft items: smiths, basket makers from the Abujhmar and potters. Also located in this zone are the middlemen who buy up forest produce as it is brought into the market by Tribals. These middlemen (*seth*) are not really 'in' the market at all (they are there to buy rather than sell) and I discuss them separately.

The zonal arrangement of market space provides—with certain exceptions—a clear articulation of hierarchical relations, and serves very much as a ground plan of intergroup relations, both within the single market area and beyond it.[6] There is nothing immediately problematic about the hierarchy of people expressed therein ('Rajput' in the middle, the Maraars, local caste Hindus, then Tribal, then Abujhmaria low-ranking Gonds and polluting castes); what is perhaps more subtle is the way in which this hierarchy of people is correlated with a hierarchy of goods. Here the opposition seems to be between jewellery and luxuries versus consumer goods and craft items of a utilitarian nature.

The two axes mentioned earlier—the radial and the circumferential—may also be said to define two axes of economic choice for participants (buyers) in the market. Choices within a zone (circumferential choices) are selections made, on the basis of value-for-money, between objects whose symbolic value is equal, while choices between zones (radial choices) are of a more fundamental kind, between different types of value. The zones are hierarchically ranked in that implicitly a buyer of an item in a higher order zone (1 or 2 say) must already have a sufficiency of the gamut of utilitarian goods sold in lower order zones (2, 4, 5), or in other words higher order zones *encompass* lower order zones, just as according to Dumont (1966), Brahminical religious values encompass secular-political and economic values in the caste system generally. The full rigours of caste ideology are attenuated in Bastar society, where, in contrast to the typical Indian pattern, it is *only the state* which is hierarchically organised. Villages are virtually single-caste and politically egalitarian. Lacking grass-roots expression, the concept of hierarchy becomes attached to the market, and is communicated via the symbolic oppositions between goods of various orders. Higher-order goods communicate messages which mediate between individuals—themselves confined to the village/subsistence sphere—and the higher reaches of society. Here we encounter a profound paradox in tribal consciousness. The paraphernalia of 'tribal' body ornamentation, the heavy silver bangles, the golden earrings and necklaces, the mirrors, the bells, the pompoms, the whole panoply of exotic finery, is wholly manufactured by Hindus, largely outside Bastar, to supply the tribal market—since Hindus themselves have mostly abandoned these particular ornaments. These symbols which so strongly bespeak 'tribal culture'—particularly to the metropolitan Hindu—mean precisely 'Hindu' in the estimations of the Tribals who adopt them. They are glittering fragments of the Hindu world, for which the Tribals readily surrender their spare cash, as would an orthodox Hindu to secure a Brahmin's blessing.

The radial axis of market space, and the sequence of choices which lie along the radial axis, relates the world of subsistence production, the domestic unit, the fragmented village, to the unifying core of the state and to the symbols of value which emanate from the state. But what of the circumferential axis? In the market people are 'put in their place' in a sense rather stronger than is usually implied by that idiom and this applies equally to circumferential relations. These relations are symmetrical and competitive, as opposed to hierarchical (encompassing/encompassed by), and competition does not lie between unequal groups. In effect, circumferential relations in the outer zones are territorial and segmentary. It is an unspoken, but almost universally observed rule that sellers and spectators from a given locality will be seated together, and that their customary position will reflect the disposition of their village of origin *vis-à-vis* other villages in the area. Thus Tribals from Torinar (Taragaon, due west of Dhorai) sit on the western side, the Mehima-Gwari people (whose village is slightly north) to their left, and the Burgaon people (slightly south) to their right (see fig. 5). Maraars sit more centrally (reflecting their different position in the state hierarchy) but within their zone they, likewise, occupy positions which correspond to the geographical disposition of the settlements they come from.

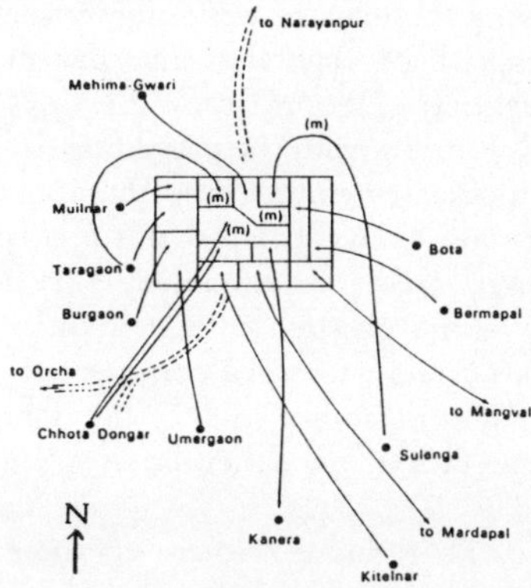

FIGURE 5. Diagram showing the relation between market space and the territorial arrangement of villages.

If one takes a tour round the periphery of the market place one is, in effect, traversing a small-scale model of a spatial/territorial relation in the Dhorai market area. One can readily see the significance of this for the hypothesis that the market provides a cognitive model of society at large. The next section, which is concerned with symbolic aspects of interaction in the marketplace, says a little more about the content of these circumferential relations.

Interaction in the market

The market is a paradigm of social relations; interaction in the marketplace is coloured by factors external to the marketplace, so that a Tribal interacting with a market trader does not see him simply as the purveyor of some good that he has in mind to buy, but as a representative of a category, relatively ranked in accordance with a sociological scheme of values. It is necessary to distinguish this categorical aspect of market relations (the replacement of the purely economic relation buyer/seller with the sociologically determined relation Tribal/Hindu) from the economic personalism often found in peasant markets elsewhere (cf. Davis 1973). Relations of a *personal* nature are precisely what these categorical relations rule out. One looks in vain for any analogue to Haitian *pratik* or similar kinds of clientèle-formation through the institutionalised extension of credit by traders in the Dhorai market. It would be going too far, though, to deny that credit is ever extended, by any class of trader in the market, towards individuals whose places of origin and degree of wealth happen to be known to the trader. The concept of extending credit (*laga arihana*) is familiar enough from the intra-village economy, and Tribals are not too shy to ask for credit if they consider they have some chance of obtaining it. But it remains the case that the great majority of transactions in all categories are for cash, with the possible exception of purchases from cloth-sellers. More importantly, price levels are set on the assumption of immediate cash payment: traders do not quote asking prices which are implicitly assumed to contain the costs they incur in carrying their customers' long term debts, carried over from week to week, as the price of clientage. The dearth of higgling-haggling, which so sharply differentiates Dhorai from others described in the ethnography of markets, derives, I think, from the prevailing notion that an asking price is an 'objective' price associated uniquely with the goods transacted, to the exclusion of factors deriving from the nature of the social relationship between buyer and seller. Where credit is extended, this is not indicative of a 'personalistic' element in the economic relation between the parties to the transaction, but reflects a straightforward commercial judgement, on the part of the seller, of the purchaser's ability to clear the debt in the reasonably near future. There is no expectation, on either side, of a continuing or exclusive relationship thereafter.

In spite of the absence of bargaining, either over the price asked for goods, or the quantities offered at a given price, in the general run of market transactions (again with the exception of purchases from cloth-sellers) it remains the case that there is an obvious advantage to the trader in increasing sales by offering marginally more attractive terms than competitors. Customers' goodwill is not won through leniency in the bargaining process or offers of attractive credit terms, since these mechanisms remain undeveloped, but is nonetheless sought through a device which is much more in tune with the anonymous and hierarchical ethos characteristic of this particular market. This is the device of *pura kiana* ('completing'), which, characteristically, places the buyer in the position of the recipient of the trader's *largesse*. This is seen particularly in the practice of the Maraar sellers of foodstuffs, who will invariably—but only when the sale has been agreed on—add a 'sweetener', in the form of an extra handful of rice or a couple of additional tomatoes, to the amount paid for. The buyer usually remonstrates at the inadequacy of this extra quantity, and may be successful in extracting a little bit more. This could be mistaken for bargaining over the quantity of goods offered at a fixed price, but it is important to stress that the sale is in no way dependent on the size of the 'extra' amount, having been concluded before anything additional is offered. What is bought and sold is a straightforward commodity, paid for at a given price; what is given as 'extra' is a *gift*, supplicated for as traditional *largesse*, which reinforces hierarchical relations between social categories.

Category relations laid down in the market are the co-ordinates of social distance: where transactions mutually involve persons who belong to different orders, this distance is not lessened as a consequence—on the contrary it finds tangible expression. When a Tribal seeks to buy something from (say) a dry goods merchant, there is a notable absence of sustained interaction; the Tribal indicates his wishes (often by pointing to or holding the object); the merchant, as curtly as possible, states a price. If the Tribal considers the amount excessive he puts the item back and takes himself off, and if he is satisfied he pays cash on the nail. None but the minimum of words are exchanged, eye contact is restricted, and no extraneous social signals pass between buyer and seller.

Radial relations are *ipso facto* relations between socially distant persons; the reverse is true of circumferential relations. The circumferential axis of market interaction corresponds to the major channel of inter-village communication and is intensely sociable. In particular it is at the marketplace that marriages are arranged and meetings which have to do with intra-village affairs (performances of ritual, apprehension of runaway couples, negotiations about brideprice and the return thereof in the case of divorce and so on) are conducted. Individuals seeking spouses visit the marketplace, so that a man who says 'I got my wife at the market' does not mean that she was purchased, but simply that he sought her out there. For Tribals, most of whom in any given week have little enough to sell and no inclination (if they have the money) to buy, the most important aspect of the market is its circumferential aspect. This gives rise to a great deal of what can only be called pseudo-marketing, particularly by tribal women whose strongly engrained work ethic prevents them from simply attending for pleasure and social enjoyment. A tribal women, desirous of visiting the market for purely 'social' reasons, will nevertheless provide herself with a 'stock-in-trade' (and hence an excuse) in the form of, say, a handful of microscopic and mostly rotten tomatoes, and will proceed to 'sell' this unsaleable item for the entire morning. In this way she manages to see her neighbours, friends and relatives, opportunities for social contacts outside the immediate family or hamlet being uncommon at other times because of the dispersed pattern of settlement in tribal villages.

One can therefore generalise by saying that interactions on the radial axis are characterised by distance and anonymity, while interactions on the circumferential axis are personal and specific. Social distance on the circumferential axis corresponds to segmentary and territorial oppositions, while on the radial axis it corresponds to category oppositions between ranked groups. However, there are certain anomalies, which may be discussed at this point.

The middlemen who station themselves around the paths leading into the marketplace, but outside the main area, are an exception to the normal rules first in that they are Hindus, but are peripheral, and secondly in that they solicit trade directly, sometimes using what appears to be physical coercion (grasping a tribal woman's basket of tamarind and attempting to prevent her going to another buyer); they often speak Gondi, and have Gonds as assistants. The aggressive, vociferous means they employ is deceptive to the extent that tribals are not genuinely coerced into selling forest products to a buyer not of their choice, and investigations did not turn up any significant differences in the prices being offered by different middlemen. Their profits are proportional to the volume of trade, and each is in competition with his colleagues to maximise volume short of actually offering an increased price over the consensual one, which does not fluctuate over a short-term period. They are consequently obliged to concentrate on building up a clientèle of regular suppliers, by developing social relationships with Tribals. Each one has a stall which adjoins one particular path leading to the market, and they concentrate on forming relationships with people from particular villages which lie along that path. They employ as assistants men drawn from the selected village or villages, who in turn influence the choice of middleman for their co-villagers. Their stall becomes a kind of meeting place where tribals like to relax and exchange gossip. They also advance money to individuals known to them, against future contributions of produce (not for interest, which is illegal). In short, they really operate in terms of the 'village' credit/debt economy—the personalised, embedded economy, in contradistinction to the anonymous 'market' economy. Hence their peripheral position, and the lack of social distance between them and their clientèle, confirms, rather than upsets, our general hypothesis.

A second slightly exceptional group are the cloth sellers. Bargaining is not normally a feature of interactions between socially differentiated participants in the market, but this is not so where the cloth sellers are concerned. Tribals do usually contest the asking price for cloth, and cloth sellers engage in patter routines to try to convince passers-by that their prices really are rock bottom. Cloth sellers extend credit to individuals known to them, but do not depend on a regular clientèle. The explanation for the rather more egalitarian interaction between cloth sellers and Tribals may be due to a conceptual identification between them and weavers (Gandas) who have low social status. It would of course be normal to haggle with a Ganda the price of a handloom cloth (Gandas visit the market but do not sit in any special place, wandering around the periphery hawking their wares).

Concluding remarks

The present account is intentionally limited in scope; it would be necessary to conduct more extensive researches into markets in Bastar, and in other parts of India, to explore the full ramifications of the relationships between village society, the market, hierarchy and the state. I hope that I have said enough at least to justify the idea that the Dhorai market provides, for those who come within its ambit, a ground plan of group relations, and in the hierarchy of goods, a scheme of values through which village dwellers encounter, on the level of *praxis*, superior values emanating from the state. All of which is only to say that the market has an ideological significance, very much as a ceremony, the performance of a religious rite, or the installation of an office holder has significance. The problem that I wish to raise, by way of a conclusion, is one common to all such value-laden performances: viz. the issue of truth versus mystification. We have become accustomed not only to tease out the implicit meanings of ceremonies but also to subject them to criticism, finding in them labyrinths of semantic manipulation, the net effect of which is to represent reality under such a guise as favours the interests of certain elements in the social whole, to the detriment of others. If it is true that the market occasion is ideologically significant, as I have claimed, is it also true that it is manipulative in this sense, depicting the forms of social reality so as to favour sectional interests, by mystifying the real basis of social relations?

There is one good reason why one might hesitate to draw this conclusion. The Dhorai market is not overtly a ceremony at all, but a straightforwardly instrumental institution, geared to the economic needs of people in the area. There is no element of make-believe, no communicative intent, behind the purchase of a packet of nails for eight annas, then, or the myriad of other, equally matter-of-fact transactions which collectively make up the market. The market cannot distort reality because it *is* reality. The money medium of the market accurately reflects relative economic strengths and weaknesses (in a way that the credit/debt economy within the village may not). Markets are information exchanges, but they differ from ceremonies in that the information exchanged is verifiable and overwhelmingly true—the market price of tomatoes is only in dispute until a sale is made; once made, the price is indisputable—while symbolic statements made in the course of a ceremony are always, and only, *claims*, for which no validation can ever be finally found.

There is thus no element of mystification in the instrumental aspect of the market as an exchange of (price, demand) information and goods. But at another level I believe that the Dhorai market is profoundly mystifying, yet not in a way which benefits a dominant sectional interest only, but in a way which reinforces the position of the very group who come off worse in the symbolic exchange, namely the Tribals. I have indicated the extent to which the market defines Tribals as peripheral and low, by contrast to Hindus, who are central and high. Moreover, the pattern of tribal purchases, their focus on obsolete jewels, trinkets, finery and traditional luxury foods (as opposed to the Hindu trend towards symbols of modernity such as biscuits and filter-tipped cigarettes) categorises them as childish and weak, easily seduced by baubles.[7] In other words, tribal market participation, both in terms of the spatial organisation of the market and the image projected by their evaluations of goods, perpetuates and reinforces the stereotype of cultural backwardness and political inferiority. This stereotype, however, has historically had certain advantages, and conceals a rather different reality. The tribal population of Bastar traditionally enjoyed the patronage of the state, without much interference in the course of their daily lives. The Rajah of Bastar was in effect a Divine King, the living embodiment of the State Goddess, and the duties of the tribal population in regard to him were of a ritual nature. Subsequently, as a result of various convulsions in the state, which cannot be discussed here, the Tribals of this part of Bastar, if not elsewhere, have developed a rather similar relationship with the government and its agencies. Legislation which protects tribal interests is enforced, and the continuation of the internal autonomy of tribal villages is permitted. The Tribals' basic motivation is the continuation of a hedonistic lifestyle to which they are deeply attached, but the price paid for it is the continuous exchange of myths—the myth of tribal primitiveness, Hindu patronage—with the Hindu population. Intelligent tribal men have firm views on the threat to themselves posed by any attempt by Tribals to infiltrate the Hindu-dominated power structure. It is because the interests of Tribals are protected by the aura of myth which surrounds them that the exchange of these myths, which one can see taking place very clearly in the marketplace, assumes such importance. But they are only myths: the resource base on which tribal society rests is a rich one by Indian standards, and it has not passed into the hands of outsiders. The effect of the market is to establish a stereotype of Tribals, and tribal-Hindu relations, in which Tribals retain actual control of their resource base, at the expense of becoming symbolically peripheral to Hindu society, wards of the state. For Hindus it is the establishment of symbolic hegemony, for Tribals, real security.

NOTES

The fieldwork reported on here was conducted in 1977–8 and was supported by the department of Prehistory and Anthropology, School of General Studies, Australian National University, to which I am very grateful. I was accompanied in the field by Simeran Gell who played a large part in collecting the data for this study. This article was first presented at the 1979 meeting of the Australian Anthropological Society at Sydney University.

[1] Data relating to Dhorai market as it was in the late fifties are to be found in Jay 1968.

[2] The terms 'Tribal' and 'Adivasi' are standardly used to cover Scheduled Tribes as listed in the Indian Constitution and enumerated in the Census. It is not to be supposed, however, that these terms have definite sociological meaning.

[3] I propose to turn to such matters in the future; in collaboration with Dr C. Gregory and with the support of the S.S.R.C. and the International Centre for the study of Economic and Related Disciplines (I.C.E.R.D.) the author is engaged on a detailed survey of marketing in N. Bastar.

[4] Wanmali (1977) states that in Singhbhum, Bihar, Tuesday was, in 1926, the most popular market day. Tuesday has since been displaced by Friday (now the most popular) and by Wednesday, Thursday and Monday as well. The reasons for changes such as these remain a matter for further investigation.

[5] The rupee was valued at Rs. 14 to the £ Sterling at the time of fieldwork in 1977.

[6] If it is true, as I have argued, that the hierarchy of groups in the Dhorai market area is encoded in the hierarchy of goods offered in the marketplace, it naturally becomes a question as to how this hierarchy of goods is sustained in the process of exchange, i.e. the way in which prices both reflect the symbolic aura of different kinds of goods, and at the same time operate so as to perpetuate the relative economic positions of the groups who bring each category of goods into the market. The question of price setting is too considerable to be dealt with here, and could only be elucidated in the context of a full-scale regional economic survey, a project the author and his collaborators have on hand at present.

[7] My colleague, Dr J. Parry, points out that amassing quantities of jewellery and gold ornaments is an objective shared by virtually all sections of Indian society, for reasons which have little enough to do with 'backwardness' in the sense implied here. While I accept this qualification, I think there is a distinction between the Muria estimation of jewellery as high-status conferring by virtue of its symbolic associations with the admired metropolitan ideal (mediated by the high-status trader) *versus* the more sophisticated attitude which sees jewellery as a convenient way of storing capital in a form which is both safe and ostentatious.

REFERENCES

Agarwal, P. 1968. *Human geography of Bastar district*. Allahabad: Gogra.

Agrawal, B. 1978. Economic networks and cultural integration in Madhya Pradesh. *Man in India*, **58**.

Berry, B. 196 . *Geography of market centres and retail distribution*. Englewood Cliffs: Prentice Hall.

Bohannan, P. & G. Dalton 1962. *Markets in Africa*. Evanston: Northwestern Univ. Press.

——— 1967. Concepts of time among the Tiv of Nigeria in *Myth and cosmos* (ed.) J. Middleton. New York: Natural History Press.

Bromley, R. 1974. *Periodic markets, daily markets and fairs*. Melbourne: Monash University, Dept. of Geography.
Christaller, W. 1974. *Central places in south Germany*. Englewood Cliffs: Prentice Hall.
Davis, W. 1973. *Social relations in a Philippine market*. Berkeley: Univ. of California Press.
Douglas, M. 1973. *Rules and meanings*. Harmondsworth: Penguin.
Dumont, L. 1970. *Homo hierarchicus*. London: Weidenfeld and Nicolson.
Elwin, V. 1947. *The Muria and their Ghotul*. London: Oxford Univ. Press.
Geertz, C. 1975. *The interpretation of culture*. London:
———, H. Geertz & L. Rosen 1979. *Meaning and order in Moroccan society*. Cambridge: Univ. Press.
Grigson, W. 1938. *The Maria Gonds of Bastar*. Oxford: Univ. Press.
Harriss, B. 1976. Social specificity in rural weekly markets—the case of Tamil Nadu. *Mainz. geogr. Stud.* **10**.
Jay, E. 1968. *A tribal village of central India*. Calcutta: Anthropological Survey of India.
Leach, E. 1954. *Political systems of Highland Burma*. London: Athlone Press.
Lévi-Strauss, C. 1964. *Structural anthropology*. New York: Basic Books.
Losch, A. 1954. *Economics of location*. New Haven: Yale Univ. Press.
Mandelbaum, D. 1970. *Society in India*. Berkeley: University of California Press.
Mintz, S. 1959. Internal market systems as mechanisms of social articulation. In *Social mobility and communication* (ed.) V. F. Ray. Seattle: American Anthropological Association.
Polanyi, K., C. Arensberg & H. Pearson 1957. *Trade and market in the early empires*. Glencoe: The Free Press.
Schwartzberg, J. 1967. Prolegomena to a study of Asian regions and regionalism. In *regions and regionalism in south Asia* (ed.) R. I. Crane. Duke University Program in Comparative Studies in South Asia Mimeo No. **4**.
Sinha, D. 1968. *Cultural change in an intertribal market*. Bombay: Asia Publishing House.
Sinha, S., B. Dasgupta & H. Banerjee 1961. Agriculture Crafts and Weekly markets of South Manbhum. *Bull. anthrop. Surv. India* **10**.
Skinner, G. W. 1964–5. Marketing and Social Structure in Rural China. *J. Asian Stud.* **24**.
Smith, C. 1976. *Regional analysis*. New York: Academic Press.
——— 1975. Examining stratification systems through peasant marketing arrangements. *Man* (N.S.) **10**.
Wanmali, S. 1976. Market centres and the distribution of consumer goods in Rural India. *Mainz. geogr. Stud.* **10**.
——— 1977. Periodic markets in south Bihar. *Management Lab. Stud.* **3**.

Part VI
Processes: Consumption

[26]
SEPARATE ECONOMIC SPHERES IN ETHNOGRAPHY

Economic Spheres

Ethnography can show clearly how patterns of frequency in social activities separate high- and low-status activities in tribal society and confer high and low value upon the objects used. Above all, tribal examples give clear demonstrations of how luxuries tend to be used as weapons of exclusion. At this stage everything in the argument seems to support the economists' puritanical bias in favor of necessities and against luxuries. Some moral reinstatement of nonnecessities must await a later stage in the argument.

Anthropologists have long been intrigued by what appear to be discrete, bounded economic spheres in small islands or isolated tribes. Elizabeth Hoyt's *Primitive Trade* [1] first drew systematic attention to these spheres. She drew many illustrations from the accounts of early travelers who needed different kinds of shell currency for different classes of transactions, even in the same village. As documentation increased, these discrete economic spheres with their nonnegotiable currencies were found to be not merely separate but also ranked, so that one sphere was more prestigious than another. Subsequently, the swelling reports of new examples have made the subject of discrete, ranked spheres of exchange in primitive economics a favorite problem of anthropologists,[2] and the whirl of complications has led one to declare that this is a problem fit to baffle economic analysis.[3] Elizabeth Hoyt, who originally noted the difficulties of travelers who could only use their stock of cornelian beads for one type of transaction, explained it by recourse to hypotheses about primitive psychology. Kroeber's well-described account of the Yurok will serve to sketch an explanation based upon technology and frequency of consumption events. Among the Yurok, separate bands of incompatible periodicities in the allocation of responsibility correspond to graded ranks. This tribe of Algonkin fishers and hunters numbered about 2,500 in the 1920s. They lived in village clusters along the lower Klamath River and along the Pacific shore in northern California. They had a culture as commercial in outlook as any modern industrial society today. Kroeber said of them:

> Money is prized and establishes influence everywhere in California. It certainly counts for more in private and public life among the average Californian people than among the tribes of the plains. . . . But whatever its influence in southern or middle California, that influence is multiplied among the Yurok. Blood money, bride-purchase, compensation to the year's mourners before a dance can be held, are institutions known to almost every group described in the present work. The north-westerners alone have measured the precise value of everyman's life or wife or grief. Every injury, each privilege or wrong or trespass, is calculated and compensated. Without exactly adjusted payment, cessation of a feud is impossible except through utter extirpation of one party, marriage is not marriage but a public disgrace for generations, [and] the ceremony necessary for the pres-

ervation of the order of the world is not held. The consequence is that the Yurok concerns his life above all else with property. When he has leisure, he thinks of money; if in need, he calls upon it. He schemes constantly for opportunity to lodge a claim or to evade an obligation. No resource is too mean or too devious for him to essay in this pursuit.

If such endeavours are to be realized, there are needed an accurately computable scheme of economic valuation and an elaborate and precise code of rights. The north-western has both. A few simple and basic principles are projected into the most intricate subtleties; and there is no contingency which they do not cover.[4]

Property and rights pertain to the realm of the individual, and the Yurok recognizes no public claim and the existence of no community. His world is wholly an aggregation of individuals. There being no society as such, there is no social organization. Government being wanting, there is no authority, and without authority there can be no chief. The men so-called are individuals whose wealth, and their ability to retain and employ it, have gathered around them a collection of kinsmen, followers, and semidependents to whom they dispense assistance and protection. The power of life and death is in the hands of the rich men; for the poor man the only chance of collecting debts owed to him is to have the backing of a rich man, and the latter backs him but at the price of allegiance. The blood money to be paid on killing a rich man was 50 percent higher than that for a poor man. The charge for marrying a rich man's daughter and the damages for adultery with a rich man's wife were always higher than for poor families.

As to art and culture, Kroeber says, there was practically none here, compared with the other tribes around (who took money a little less seriously). Of masks, altars, and sacred apparatus, there were none. "The tangible paraphernalia of public ceremony are objects that possess a high property value —wealth that impresses, but nevertheless profane and negotiable wealth. The dances are displays of this wealth as much as they are song and step."[5]

Implications for Social Policy

There can be no question of the ethnographer being mistaken about his tribe. Kroeber knew the Californian Indian cultures like the back of his hand. His description of just where the Yurok are like and unlike their neighbors to the north and south is brief and authoritative.

In such a small society, with the five largest towns together containing just over 600 persons, and most groups of villages being able to muster only 200, we have unfettered individualism and enormous discriminations of wealth. The example would be well chosen to counter an objection that, unlike ourselves, primitive peoples always live corporate lives, submitting individual desires to the needs of the community. Their household consumption was streamed in two directions. One was the ordinary household demand for the usual services, food, fishing tackle, hunting gear, medical services, and housing. Fishing sites might also be included here. All these things had a known price in shell money, but apart from medical treatment and fishing sites, they rarely were bought for cash, but instead were obtained on claims of kinship and neighborhood. They might be counted as those consumption goods in frequent use that everyone regarded as necessary. Since the other stream involved high risks, almost gambling, it was just as well that subsistence was separated and treated as an independent sphere. The second stream consisted of treasures valued in and substitutable for shell money: obsidian blades, rare pelts and colored feathers for dancing paraphernalia on public occasions, and boats. The shell money, in lengths of about 27 inches, were avidly sought after and passionately accumulated. With shell money each man contested with every other man his right to a place in society, to avenge insults, to marry his daughters to respected citizens, and to have his own little following of dependents. This was the political sphere,[6] attracting all the most important marking services. At prodigious dance displays, the rich man would decorate himself in these white deerskins and woodpecker scalps and show off his obsidian blades. No man could enter the political arena if his subsistence was not assumed. But subsistence alone would be unthinkable for a man without this second stream of wealth for transacting politically with other men. So for every Yurok man his welfare could be separated into two distinct parts, one domestic and one political, each with its distinctive periodicities and its relevant group of goods. Within the group of domestic goods there was substitutability, and complementarity; likewise within the group of political goods, but the two groups could be treated as practically independent. A good run of salmon or a bad year for berries made no difference to the demand for shells and for goods within the set relevant to the exchange of shells.

TABLE 7-1

Yurok Household Consumption

Irregular Feasts, Fines, and Fees	Sphere of Political Goods Substitutable for Each Other at Standard Exchange Rates	Shells Obsidian Blades Deer Pelts Woodpecker Feathers Boats	Low-Frequency, High Rank Activities Involving Large Units
Daily Needs	Sphere of Domestic Goods and Services Freely Exchangeable for Each Other	House Fishing Sites and Game Areas Gear Fishing Hunting Food Fish Game Vegetable Products	High-Frequency, Low Rank Activities Involving Small Units

This diagram shows a jump in value for the Yurok as between the two sets of goods. The domestic goods in high-frequency use posed no problem of distribution. No one went short of food unless there was a general shortage. A man in heavy debt might be forced to sell a fishing site, but this would be because of insolvency only less grave than the case in which he might have to sell himself—both unusual situations resulting from a general lack of support and credit-worthiness. Demand pressed heavily on the low-frequency political goods, the means of giving and getting valued marking services. At the top of the society were the leaders, the richest men. No one in his right mind would give up political treasure for domestic goods since the rate of return on loaning the former or otherwise laying it out was immensely greater than what could be expected from domestic goods. Collaboration among close kinsmen reigned in domestic goods, and competition among rivals in political goods, as Cora Dubois explains for a parallel case. Thus the discrete economic spheres here described pose no mystery. They can easily be interpreted by economic analysis. But the special interest of this case is the clear illustration of the principles set out in the last chapter. Based upon periodicities in consumption use, exactly as we would expect, there appears a strong separation between two classes of goods, such that rates of substitution between any pairs in one group are insulated from changes in quantities of any goods in the other group.

Scale of Consumption

The example can be used to make an advance in the argument. Whereas a connection has been indicated between high status of goods and low frequency of use and vice versa, and whereas there were obviously difficulties in making an analysis of all the relevant patterns of periodicity, the Yurok example suggests that the concept of scale of consumption activities would be a convenient shorthand for compressing these several related characteristics. Low-frequency, high-ranking activities involving large social units and necessarily putting those engaged in them into contact with the centers of power and influence can well be called a large-scale consumption pattern and can be assumed to be very advantageous for getting and controlling information. High-frequency, low-ranking activities involving small social units constitute a small-scale consumption pattern, disadvantageous for getting and controlling information. We have argued that assumptions of rationality lead us to expect the individual to aim at the large-scale type of consumption pattern, and the Yurok exemplify such striving. Theoretically they were an egalitarian society. They had no chiefs, no aristocrats. Anyone could enter the lists and everyone did. This does not mean that wealth was distributed evenly. An accelerator principle ensured that any initial advantage would lead to an increased scale of operations, and thus worked cumulatively to the further advantage of the lucky beneficiary. Thomas Mayer illustrates the point from the case of two pianists. Whatever the distribution of native ability, he says, the distribution of earnings will be more positively skewed than the distribution of abilities because the latter are reinforced by differences in the scale of operation. The abler of two pianists will have a higher income for two multiplicative reasons, first because people are willing to pay more for a ticket, and second because he will play in a larger hall.[7] Likewise among the Yurok the rich man got richer and the poor man poorer because the rich man had more followers, and more followers entitled him to demand higher rates of pay for his services, making him richer and therefore able to attract more followers. The Yurok rich man did not need to set up barriers restricting admission to the ranks of privilege. Everyone could compete, and the rules of the competition itself, like the market principle, secured further comparative advantages for those who started out well endowed.

IMPLICATIONS FOR SOCIAL POLICY

Refusal to Transact

Other examples of discrete spheres of exchange in tribal society show how they can be formed as monopolistic barriers controlling admission.

The Tiv of the lower Benue river, Nigeria, are alleged to have had three such separate spheres before European money wrecked their system.[8] The top-ranking one contained only rights over women. Access to it was so closely restricted that any suspicion of trying to buy a wife with material wealth would be scandalous. The Tiv "elders," influential men, not so very old but heads of lineages, transacted with one another, using rights over women for forging a network of alliances and making sure that anyone admitted as a son-in-law showed the right disposition and entrepreneurial talent. The next high-ranking sphere included metal rods, bales of cloth, guns, and slaves, all to be obtained by war or trade. Active young men acquired these goods and presumably paid them into the equivalent of the lineage treasury, getting thereby a good reputation among their seniors and the backing needful for marriage alliance. Or they may have used them to exert direct influence in the market and become "elders" themselves.[9] The lowest-ranking sphere was again the domestic one. There, chickens, hoes, baskets, pots, and grain could be exchanged for one another.

In this case again, though women worked in the domestic sphere, their men were responsible for them and used rights over them for advancing their interests. Men alone worked the prestige sphere. The domestic sphere was high frequency, low status in its normal activities, and the other was low frequency, high status. And as in the case of the Yurok, by energy and vigilance in the prestige sphere, a man acquired wives as well as politically useful alliances. So the problem allegedly posed by a barrier of nonconvertibility between the spheres, which has so much exercised anthropologists, disappears. The only

Separate Economic Spheres in Ethnography

TABLE 7-2
Tiv Household Transactions

a.	Marriage Alliance – Rights Over Women		
b.	Prestige Goods		
		Metal Cloth Guns Slaves Cattle	Low-Frequency Transactions Involving Large Social Units, High Rank
c.	Domestic Goods		
		Baskets Pots Hoes Grain Chickens	High-Frequency Transactions Involving Small Units, Low Rank

economic sense it would make for a Tiv man to agree to exchange precious guns or slaves for umpteen hundred baskets of chickens or grain would be if he planned on going into the chicken or grain business, but there was no profit to be gained that way. In such an imperfect market it was clearly more profitable to invest directly in prestige goods rather than in low-ranking chickens or grain. Keeping their sights on marriageable girls was better economic sense, as Trollope would have been the first to agree. Ultimately, the two big discontinuities arise from monopolistic barriers to entry. The elders had everything to gain by keeping tight control of the marriageable women, and they rightly refused to be tempted out of their corner by material considerations. Their political advantages meant that they were in control of the information system and had every incentive to stay there. Two things kept their privileges secure: one, their refusal to transact rights over women with outsiders; the other, their use of control over women for drawing the wealth in the second economic sphere into their control as representatives of the lineage. This is our own interpretation of the Tiv material, as Bohannan does not link this analysis of economic and political behavior (land rights, market control, and warfare) so closely to lineage control of women, which had been considerably disrupted by the time of his fieldwork. This synthesis is suggested by parallel researches among the Lele.[10]

One way to maintain a social boundary is to demand an enormous fee for admission. Another is to set the normal rate for settling of internal transactions so high that only the very rich can afford to join the game. The Yurok system was something like that, since a man needed great wealth in shells and rare valuables to enter the dance societies. A third way is simply to decline to transact with outsiders. Refusal to transact is such a common, if not worldwide, strategy of exclusion that we have been able to base a cross-cultural meaning for the notion of consumption. Consumption has been here defined as that area of social relations in which transactions are made freely, by the free election of the partners, constrained by nothing but their perception of their own intentions, beyond the law and beyond commerce. The Tiv put the transfer of women in marriage beyond commerce. They affected to despise neighboring tribes who accepted marriage payments for their daughters. In truth these other tribes also put marriage beyond commerce and did not reckon that by accepting the equivalent of a dowry from their son-in-law's family they were in any way selling brides. Their marriage transactions were no doubt just as restricted and they kept as firm a hold on admission to the status of relative in-law. But by their total refusal to transact women for goods, the Tiv could keep the whole intricate lineage structure in gerontocratic hands, and it may be that in the precolonial period only the disturbance of major wars gave the up-and-coming young warrior a chance to jump ahead of his generation into the ranks of elderhood and control. Bohannan suggests that the advent of European money, with its power to permeate all transactions, brought

Separate Economic Spheres in Ethnography

the collapse of the social system. But in the case of the Lele, the old men effectively resisted the infiltrations of money. If they had not refused to accept Belgian francs for marriage payments, always insisting on settlement in kind, they would have lost control of the marriageable girls, for the young men could earn francs and they could not. Their intransigence even produced a double exchange rate against the franc and a 10 percent discount for settlement in kind for all debts.[11]

Restricted Circulation

Now there appears nothing inexplicable, mysterious, or contrary to traditional economic theory about restricted economic spheres. The energy to protect boundaries from unwanted arbitrage is stoked by the sense of how much is at risk–personal survival in a competitive scene or collective survival in a whole system of values and traditions. Restricted circulation is not likely to flourish except as an element of the total system of work and reward.

At first sight the craze of the rich women traders of the Hausa Quarter of Ibadan for highly colored imported pots seems an irrational desire, a quirk of consumer tastes. And so it was, in respect of the colored pots themselves; the women's fancy could have lit on anything else: the choice of a material thing for a form of currency can well be fairly arbitrary. Their insatiable buying of more and more pots is fully explicable if the collection of pots, divisible, standardized, durable, storable, and portable, is interpreted as the currency for a restricted sphere of exchange.

In a chapter entitled "Trade from Behind the Purdah," Abner Cohen explains that the Moslem Hausa of Ibadan normally kept their womenfolk secluded.[12] One who wished for a private career as a prostitute had freedom to walk where she liked, but paradoxically this did not give her the opportunity to amass wealth that the respectable matrons enjoyed. The Hausa Quarter was in the 1960s a flourishing trade center, thronging with bachelors and strangers, all needing to be fed. The married woman could enter a profitable catering industry, cooking and selling food. For this she needed labor and capital. Her own daughters and the daughters of kinsfolk and even the children of foreigners fostered by her would run her errands and do her work and she would be expected eventually to help them to make suitable marriages. For capital she had three sources, an initial gift made at marriage, savings from the household money allotted by her husband, and the profits of trade. She would run a business with practically no overhead expenses, since her husband paid the rent and fed and clothed her. If she could develop a steady clientele, she could amass a great deal of wealth. But the social structure that ordained her seclusion ordained at the same time that there would be no way of investing her wealth in other forms of business, for catering was the only thing that did not compete with men. So it was understandable that a special consumption pattern should develop, shared only by married women traders, and, further, that this should become the public testing of each other's business success and credit-worthiness. Women could own houses and could hoard cash and jewelry,

But the particular craze among nearly all the housewives in recent years has been to sink all their profits in acquiring ever increasing numbers of Czechoslovak-made brightly coloured enamel bowls. Within the world of Sabo housewives, these bowls have become the most important status symbol and women are ranked in status according to the number of bowls they possess. Some housewives in the Quarter have managed to accumulate hundreds of them, which they meticulously arrange in ceiling-high columns in their small, dark rooms. A business landlord invited my wife to visit his two wives, but these asked him to fix the time of the proposed visit at a date which would give them nearly two weeks' grace during which they could wash and rearrange their treasured bowls. Space is scarce

Separate Economic Spheres in Ethnography

in Sabo, and husbands are greatly annoyed by the mountains of bowls. A current sardonic complaint among married men of the Quarter is that, because of the bowls, a man cannot nowadays find space in his wife's room for even his morning prayers.

A housewife thus accumulates bowls and when her own daughters or her foster-daughters get married she gives them part of her treasure, usually in proportion to the length of time the daughter has served her.[13]

It all sounds crazy, irrational, puppet consumption if ever there was any. But the ethnographer does not fall into the trap of treating utility as quite independent of earning ability. "A housewife will attract and retain more marriageable girls from her kin the more bowls she accumulates. The older a woman is, the more settled as a housewife she becomes and the more girls she attracts to her service." The connection between consumption and production is crystal clear.

Control over the Economy

In these cases and in many more that can be cited, the refusal to transact or the refusal to accept payment except in particular currencies does more than protect a privilege. The boundary being protected in effect encircles the whole structure of the economy, production, and consumption. Control of the whole social system, no less, may be at stake. When this point is fully appreciated, the theory of consumption can be detrivialized and reintegrated into the analysis of the whole economy.

Individual luxuries, acquired by themselves, signal nothing in particular. But a consistent array, understood by the other consumers, at least signals credit-worthiness. If it is not one interlocking series of objects, it will be another.

Among the rich pot-collecting women traders of Sabo, credit-worthiness was easily traced to its financial nexus in their system of production. But in the theory of consumption that best suits anthropological materials, the track is usually more roundabout. It is characterized by a more diffuse respectability, a sense of occasion, the signs of ability to discriminate finely and to know the social scene from top to bottom that brings in marking services and identifies the superconsumer who cannot be left out of any major celebration. This kind of social creditworthiness is perfectly well known and needs no underlining. But a few implications are more hidden. The Sabo ladies were frankly commercial in their dominant interests: enforced seclusion from the rest of society narrowed their scope, and correspondingly their choice of luxuries was confined. For freer individuals the main characteristic of a luxury is that it forms part of a widely varied range of goods. The one-luxury man is a poor man. As a man gets richer his most income-responsive buying habits diversify, and one should consider the total structure of his luxuries if one is to understand their nature. One of the many advantages of being relatively rich is that when a drop in income enforces economy, there is a whole series of goods which are only weakly interdependent on each other and which each can be considered for cuts. Economists normally assume that this diversity arises because the possibility of getting enjoyment out of increasing units of any one good declines with the quantity available of that good. But I will argue that it has an information aspect. The ladies of Sabo were insatiable where their collection of pots was concerned. They could not have too many. If they had a richer social life, plausibly they would have wanted other things as well as pots to show their visitors and to give as wedding presents.

There are two points to be made concerning luxuries as consumption goods in an information system. One is that in a highly diverse society, the demand for luxuries has to be correspondingly diversified: each item sends its signal, but each also represents a special field of social relations with its appropriate consumption activity. As far as information goes the rich individual has more finely attuned reception and signaling by the goods he can use. Their very diversity is an important fact about luxuries, each the latest word in style and comfort in a highly specialized activity. The second is, paradoxically, their tendency to be standardized, as any public person going out to dinner on public ceremonial events will testify: the same hors d'oeuvres, the same pheasant and salmon according to season, the same vegetables and desserts followed by the same small sips of concentrated hot and cold liquids. It is as if the current formula for high-ranking occasions cannot be tampered with at risk of giving wrong signals.[14]

What is the point about this tendency to standardize? It seems likely that it would not arise except where close comparisons of value are required. At the fringes of a market system, where turnover is slower, where knowledge is incomplete, and big profits riskier, discrepancies in standards can pass. But where the competition is hottest, standardization emerges. The Sabo women have standardized on Czechoslovakian enamel pots, a field they can master completely. In the Trobriands, exchange of Kula objects is closely standardized: only two kinds of item are acceptable, red shell beads and white shell armbands. The items are known individually and their relative value can be established since everyone in the circle is a connoisseur.[15] Among the Yurok, as we saw, only certain classes of goods count as equivalents, and their rate of substitution is precisely known. When the tendency to standardize values is strong, some crucial form of social control is being exerted: it is a sign that we are near the hot center of a competitive system where small differences matter a lot.

The ethnography of distant tribes may lull the reader into complacency. But that would be a pity. If production and consumption are shown as part of a circular process, the accusing finger that points at production must point just as truly at consumption behavior. A myriad of self-interested refusals to transact (whether by not joining wedding feasts or beer-

Implications for Social Policy

drinking) could undo the effects of redistributive legislation as it affects wealth holding and consequent advancement. For consumption, insofar as it depends on the principle of strictly judged reciprocity, is like a market from whose ranks the less efficient members can be driven down successively to less exacting and less rewarding echelons.

[146]

Notes

1. Hoyt, Elizabeth E. *Primitive Trade: Its Psychology and Economics.* London: Kegan Paul, Trench Trubner, 1926.

2. Firth, Raymond, ed. *Themes in Economic Anthropology* (A.S.A. Monograph no. 6), pp. 18–20. London: Tavistock, 1967; Barth, Fredrik. "Economic Spheres in Darfur," in *Themes in Economic Anthropology,* edited by Firth, pp. 149–173.

3. Sahlins, M. *Stone-Age Economics,* pp. 299–301. London: Tavistock, 1974.

4. Kroeber, A. L. *Handbook of the Indians of California* (Bulletin 78). Washington, D.C.: Smithsonian, Bureau of American Ethnology, 1925.

5. Kroeber. *Handbook of the Indians of California,* p. 4.

6. Dubois, Cora. "The Wealth Concept as an Integrative Factor in Tolowa-Tututni Culture." In *Essays in Anthropology Presented to A. L. Kroeber,* pp. 49–65. University of California Press, 1936.

7. Mayer, Thomas. "Investment in Human Capital and Personal Income Distribution." *Journal of Political Economy* 66:283, 1958.

8. Bohannan, P. "Some Principles of Exchange and Investment Among the Tiv." *American Anthropologist* 57:60–70, 1955.

9. Bohannan, Paul, and Bohannan, Laura. *Tiv Economy.* Northwestern University Press, Evanston, Ill.: 1968.

10. Douglas, Mary. *The Lele of the Kasai.* Oxford: Oxford University Press, 1963.

11. Douglas, Mary. "Raffia Cloth Distribution in the Lele Economy." *Africa* 28:109–122, 1958.

12. Cohen, Abner. *Custom and Politics in Urban Africa: A Study of Hausa Migrants in Yoruba Towns,* pp. 59, 66–68. University of California Press, Berkeley, Ca: 1969.

13. Cohen, *Custom and Politics in Urban Africa,* pp. 67–68.

14. Leymore, V. *Hidden Myth: Structure and Symbolism in Advertising,* pp. 125–127. London: Heinemann, 1975.

15. Malinowski, B. *The Argonauts of the Western Pacific.* London: Routledge and Kegan Paul, 1922.

[213]

[27]

contesting the margins of modernity: women, migration, and consumption in Thailand

MARY BETH MILLS—*Colby College*

A friend who had been working in Bangkok came back to visit [our village]. She wore beautiful clothes. When she saw me, her greeting was, "Oh ho! How did you get so run-down looking? Want to come work with me?" . . . [That night] I lay thinking, "I ought to go give it a try." I dreamed that I would go [to the city], work really hard, and save money to help my family. I lay unable to stop thinking about this until I slept. I got up early in the morning and at once rushed to find my friend. I was so happy that I could go with her. I got my clothes ready and said good-bye to my brothers, sisters, father and mother [Khem, Bangkok textile worker, age 21]

In this brief passage a young Thai labor migrant gives an account of how she left home to begin urban employment at the age of 16.[1] Central to this narrative is the moral impetus of a daughter's obligation—"I would work really hard and save money to help my family"—that anchors Khem's story in the affective world of village kin and agricultural poverty. But this projection of virtue and self-sacrifice is paralleled by an alternate vision, that of the confident returning migrant with her "beautiful clothes" and teasing disdain for the sorry existence of her rural friend. Khem's thoughts, which propel her rapid departure, are animated as much by the idea of urban sophistication and accumulation as by her concern for the household economy.

Khem's narrative, which places kinship-based morality alongside desires for autonomy and commodified display, highlights widespread themes within rural-urban migration in contemporary Thailand. In these few sentences Khem constructs two potential selves: the "good daughter" who is motivated by emotional ties and a deep sense of responsibility to rural family, and the "modern woman" whose independence and mobility are tied to her experience with urban society. For Khem and thousands of other young women working in Bangkok, both these self-images are desirable and both play a key role in their decisions to migrate to the city; but they are also potentially at odds with each other. Each rests on a different set of priorities: saving money to assist family at home, or spending it to acquire the commodity markers of urban status and modern style. Consequently, rural-urban migration involves much more than a shift in physical location. As young Thai women move into Bangkok employment they engage in a process of self-construction, laying claim to, negotiating, and at times contesting these different aspects of gender identity.

It is important to note that these efforts at self-construction do not necessarily involve an explicit, self-conscious choice between clear and distinct identities. Rather the experiences of

Rural women who move to Bangkok for employment confront significant social and economic constraints as low-wage, low-status migrant labor; yet experiences of exploitation in the workplace are widely mediated by aspirations for and participation in new patterns of commodity consumption. In this article, I examine these consumption practices as important sites of cultural struggle in which young women seek to construct new identities and contest their marginalization within the wider society, albeit with conflicting and often ambivalent results. [consumption, discourses of modernity, rural-urban migration, gender, identity, Thailand]

American Ethnologist 24(1):37–61.

young Thai migrants illustrate what Henrietta Moore has identified as the necessity of theorizing the "internally differentiated subject" (1994:58). In this sense the lived experience of individual identity—including that of gender identity—is an ongoing process of negotiation and contestation between and within available "subject positions" (such as "good daughter" or "modern woman" in the case at hand). These subject positions are themselves constituted by the multiple discourses that exist in any society. The hegemonic effects of these discourses may limit what individuals perceive as the subject positions available to them; nevertheless, people continually select between and maneuver within these potential selves or self-images in the course of everyday life (Moore 1994:58–60).

Khem is but one among hundreds of thousands of rural women whose labor in Bangkok manufacturing and service jobs has sustained Thailand's drive toward the ranks of Asia's celebrated "newly industrializing countries" (Bell 1992; Girling 1981:178–79).[2] Village households practicing small cash and subsistence crop production have played an essential part in the rapid expansion of Thailand's urban industrial economy. They provide a highly flexible pool of labor through out-migration while, at the same time, the continuing economic ties between workers and their village homes bear part of the cost of maintaining and reproducing this labor force, thereby allowing urban employers to pay lower wages and offer fewer benefits (Porpora and Lim 1987).[3] Indeed, women like Khem—unmarried and in their late teens and early twenties—now constitute the preferred workforce of many Bangkok employers. Few, if any, communities in rural Thailand, and especially in the economically disadvantaged Northeast (Isan), remain untouched by this youthful outflow. In towns and villages throughout the region it is a virtual cliché to observe that "there is no one left [in the villages] but the old people and little children." It is by no means true that all young people leave the countryside for urban employment; the high rates at which they are leaving, however, often make it more meaningful to ask any rural household, not whether adolescent children will go to Bangkok, but when.

At one level, this exodus represents yet another example of how an expanding global economy of "flexible accumulation" has targeted young, rural women as an easily controlled and relatively inexpensive workforce (Harvey 1989:153–155). Similar patterns in contemporary experiences of industrialization have been identified around the world and constitute the central focus of a growing literature on the gendered dynamics of late 20th-century capitalism and what is commonly called the New International Division of Labor. These developments are linked to underlying patriarchal assumptions within international capital: young women without the responsibilities of a family are expected to have a limited commitment to wage employment—working for a few months or years before marriage—and consequently can be expected to put up with low pay, limited benefits, and job insecurity. Their youth and gender also suggest a workforce already schooled in obedience to (parental) authority, hard work, and the patience and dexterity required for such domestic chores as weaving and sewing. Women's character and skills are seen by employers to be particularly well-suited for the fine detail and endless repetition of textile and electronics manufacturing, industries that have dominated the shift to globally dispersed production sites.[4]

In Thailand young men are also important participants in these migration circuits, but I focus my attention here on the experiences of women for several reasons. Contemporary labor migration by rural men, while involving them in new activities and social relations associated with proletarian labor, still parallels historical patterns of male mobility in the form of adventuring travel *(pay thiaw)*, or as practiced by itinerant Buddhist monks, cattle sellers, and other traveling salesmen (Kirsch 1966). City-bound migration by men is also consistent with long-standing cultural ideals concerning the acquisition of status and social influence through contact with institutions of power and knowledge located in urban centers (O'Connor 1987, 1995), activities that have long been more accessible for men. Women's geographic mobility, by contrast, has been conventionally much more restricted, especially before marriage; yet over the past two decades women (particularly young unmarried women) have begun moving into Bangkok at rates that generally equal those of their male counterparts and at times have exceeded the latter by as much as two to one (NSO 1983, 1992; Wilson 1983:58; see also Aphichat et al. 1979). While I do not wish to argue that urban employment has had no transformative effects on Thai men or on cultural constructions of masculinity, the greater historical and ideological disjunctures surrounding women's mobility reveal in sharper detail some of the structural and ideological tensions at work in contemporary Thai society.

Knowing that young women in Thailand and elsewhere appeal to employers as a presumably quiescent and inexpensive labor force tells us little about why women themselves take up wage work, nor does it tell us how they construct their experiences of it. In Thailand, as in many other parts of the world, explanations of labor migration have usually pointed to the effects of economic disparities between urban and rural sectors.[5] The concentration of capital investment in cities along with widespread conditions of indebtedness, cash dependency, and scarce sources of credit in rural areas foster patterns of labor out-migration from peasant communities all over the world. In such contexts the deployment of sons' or unmarried daughters' labor can be one option available to peasant households seeking to increase their cash income. But current thinking about households as sites of conflict, competing interests, and contested authority (e.g., Wolf 1992) makes it increasingly difficult to accept interpretations of women's employment and migration that presume the functional, strategizing unity of the household. Models that restrict analysis to household economic strategies and the pressures of rural poverty fail to account for the varied dynamics of migration decisions and practices in actual situations. As Diane Wolf's recent comparison of Javanese and Taiwanese workers has shown, parents' ability to direct the labor and control the wages of daughters is an empirical question, the answer to which may vary widely both between and within specific cultural settings (1992:174–178).

In Thailand young women like Khem almost always take credit for the decision to leave the village and find urban work, sometimes with the active support of their parents, sometimes against their will. The economic returns to rural households from daughters' employment are not always clear; parents with whom I spoke often complained about infrequent or inadequate wage remittances. Furthermore, women's out-migration is not limited to the more impoverished segments of a community but involves families across social strata; young women who leave for Bangkok come from poor, middle-range, and even quite prosperous peasant households. It is thus essential to examine the entry of young rural women into urban labor as a product of complex motivations. As Khem's words reveal, labor mobility is embedded in social and cultural tensions within households and within the individual herself. Female labor mobility reflects not just dominant ideals of filial obligation (to "save money to help my family") but equally powerful perceptions of status lost to already mobile peers and desires for "beautiful clothes" and other commodified signifiers of urban glamour and sophistication. The movement of young women into Bangkok has as much to do with aspirations for particular kinds of personhood as with specific material goals.

Cynthia Enloe makes the obvious but often overlooked point that young women around the globe enter and stay in new types of employment—despite low wages, harsh labor discipline, and unhealthy working conditions—not solely for the money earned but also to achieve more complex social goals: "Without women's own needs, values, and worries, the global assembly line would grind to a halt" (Enloe 1989:16–17). As local arenas of social and cultural production increasingly intersect with global processes of capitalist expansion and commodification, the "needs, values, and worries" of Thai women revolve not only around familiar meanings of family and community but also newly imagined (and imaginable) needs and possibilities, often conveyed through technologies of mass communication. In this article I explore how the "needs, values, and worries" that promote the movement of rural Thai women into wage employment are informed not only by local gender and household relations but, no less significantly, by dominant cultural discourses about Thai modernity and progress. Attention to these complex motivations as they converge and collide in the course of migration can in turn illuminate women's diverse and often ambivalent responses to the urban sojourn. In particular I focus on newly industrialized workers' engagement in novel patterns of commodity consumption. The conflicting and often ambivalent dimensions of labor migrants' choices as consumers reveal some of the ways their experiences both promote and constrain the construction of new ideas about themselves and about the world around them.

commodities and consumption as social practice

Over the last two decades scholars have begun to document women's new and varied experiences of proletarianization in societies around the world. Some of the most exciting research has explored the ways in which encounters with capitalist labor discipline, while often constraining women's choices, may also open up avenues for contestation and resistance. The latter may range from expressions of discontent couched in precapitalist idioms—such as spirit possession in Malay electronics factories (Ong 1987)—to explicitly class-based confrontations, including cases of organized labor protest—such as those among groups of textile workers in South Korea and Mexico (Ogle 1990:80–86; Tirado 1994) and Free Trade Zone employees in the Philippines (Roha 1994:90–91). In addition, experiences of wage labor at different times and places have provided some women room to maneuver within and potentially rework household divisions of labor and authority (see, for example, Benería and Roldán 1987; Lamphere 1987; Safa 1995; Wolf 1992). My goal here is not to dispute these important findings but rather to suggest that in addition to the impact of encounters with new relations of production, it can also be useful to examine the role of new experiences of consumption in these processes of social transformation. The general absence of sustained attention to consumption as social practice in this wider literature on women's global entry into industrial labor is due, at least in part, to the lingering sense that commodity consumption by working-class actors, however necessary for the daily reproduction of their labor power, entails a kind of complicity in their exploitation, for they are consuming the products of their own alienated labor for the profit of capital. Consequently, the pursuit of commodities as markers of symbolic value or social status appears as a particularly insidious form of false consciousness in the face of capitalist hegemony.[6]

Among Thai migrant workers, participation in Bangkok's mass-market commodity culture is one of the most salient aspects of their time in the city. In part this reveals the power of new technologies of representation—television and other forms of mass media—over the popular imagination in Thailand; these now pervasive forms of cultural production invest accumulation and display of commodities with dominant meanings about "progress" and the desirability of modern styles and attitudes. Women's rural-urban labor migration is closely tied to the production of these imagined possibilities in the dominant Thai culture.[7] In effect, their geographic mobility is informed by what Moore has called "fantasies of identity," that is, "ideas about the kind of person one would like to be and the sort of person one would like to be seen to be by others" (1994:66).[8] For young Thai women, the imagined possibilities of migration and urban employment are intricately bound up in desires for enhanced personal autonomy and status.

The prospect of working in Bangkok conveys a level of independence largely unavailable to women within the village setting and certainly not to unmarried daughters subordinate to parents and other elders. Thai women enjoy a high degree of autonomy as economic actors and household decision makers—at least in comparison to women in more rigidly patriarchal cultures in other parts of Asia—but these conditions are concomitant with marriage and motherhood.[9] Although women's authority may increase with age and the responsibilities of raising a family, this is small consolation to the adolescent whose peers are all working in Bangkok. Her friends bring back cash and other gifts on their visits home and tell tales about urban life that invoke images of glamour and style she might otherwise only see on television. But if these cultural constructions of urban modernity—what rural youth refer to as "up-to-date" *(than samay)*—help to shape migration aspirations, they do not always fit with the lived realities of Bangkok.

The potential exists for the production of new meanings and practices in the resulting disjunctures between dominant meanings and lived experience, and between imagined possibilities and limited opportunities. William Roseberry (1989:45) argues that the recognition of such breaks between dominant cultural meanings and lived experiences provide subordinate groups with crucial openings to contest hegemonic forms and generate alternative understandings.[10] But if tensions between dominant discourses and lived realities may lead to a critical or oppositional consciousness, they are just as likely to result in more fragmentary, limited, or ambivalent responses. In a recent literature review, Aihwa Ong (1991) argues that attempts to assess women's reactions to new forms of wage-labor in terms of classical models of proletarian resistance cannot always encompass the conflicting tensions and frequent ambivalence that characterize new encounters with capitalist wage-labor relations. A clear understanding of these relations requires attention to localized patterns of "cultural struggle," the varied ways that people receive, negotiate, and potentially rework dominant "cultural meaning, values, and goals" in the context of women's new employment (Ong 1991:281).[11] In this article I examine the consumption aspirations and practices of Thai migrants as precisely such a field of cultural struggle.

The recent emergence of consumption as a focus of ethnographic research is itself a highly contested field of inquiry. By approaching consumption as a form of social practice, I follow Daniel Miller (1995) in arguing for a contextual and contingent analysis, a middle ground between assumptions that commodities are "fetishistic vehicles of false consciousness," their presence evidence only of hegemonic domination, and overly "romanticized" views in which commodity consumption by subaltern groups is read as evidence of "everyday resistance" (Miller 1995: 271–272; see also Orlove and Rutz 1989).[12] For women working in Bangkok, commodity consumption—both of material goods and of commodified images and events—presents an arena within which they may confront and attempt to rework the tensions and contradictions that underlie their status as urban wage laborers; the result, however, is not necessarily the production of openly critical or oppositional beliefs and practices. This is not to deny that workers' encounters with capitalist labor relations are a significant aspect of the migration process; as I point out in a later section, the exploitation and discipline of wage work pose serious constraints throughout women's urban employment. Nevertheless, their experiences as workers do not provide the only or even the most compelling framework through which many migrant women assess their time in the city. Rather it is in new forms of urban consumption as much as on the job—although these fields of action cannot be wholly separated from each other—that the tensions and contradictions of the migration process are most keenly felt. Viewing migrants as consumers, rather than solely as producers, reveals more complex dimensions of women's urban employment and highlights a powerful avenue by which labor migrants may pursue new forms of autonomy and agency and the construction of socially satisfying and valued identities.

migration and discourses of modernity

When young migrants like Khem speak of their decision to go to Bangkok, their stories almost always invoke the gendered imagery of "good daughters" and "modern women." In the former image, women's labor migration invokes obligations of respect and gratitude owed by all children to their parents; from this perspective migration to Bangkok is an important means for youth to acknowledge their debts to parents by earning money to send home. This is especially significant for young women who, unlike their brothers, cannot serve as Buddhist monks to earn religious merit for their parents. Spending a few months as a monk remains among the most important obligations a son has to his mother and father, one that can often take precedence over economic contributions. Daughters, however, are raised to express their gratitude and loyalty by attending to the day-to-day needs of household members. They are expected to be more industrious and responsible than their brothers in such matters. According to Nid, whose Bangkok wages as a maid in a tourist guesthouse paid for the care of a seriously ill father, young men in the village only "play and run around." They may spend days, weeks, or months sleeping in the temple or at a friend's house, she claimed; they do not see what the family needs or lacks. "Men don't see, they don't pay attention. But women are responsible, they see what's missing; they know when there's not enough rice. Women have to look after the family." Urban wages present an opportunity for young rural women to fulfill these expectations in a form that is both concrete and highly valued by family at home.

Just as powerful in shaping migration decisions is an explicit desire to be "up-to-date" (than samay) and to participate in Thai modernity. Let me be clear that here the term "modernity" refers not to an objective social reality but to a powerful field of popular discourse and cultural production. In Thailand, as around the world, ideas about modernity are closely linked to an increasingly global capitalist political economy that manifests itself in different forms and provokes varied responses across time and space. The result is what Michael Watts (Pred and Watts 1992:18) identifies as the "production of . . . new, local modernities" out of the historical experiences and the cultural and symbolic resources available to people in specific settings. In contemporary Thailand, discourses of modernity permeate much of everyday life. People at all levels of Thai society are familiar with and frequently employ a language of "being modern" *(khwaam pen than samay,* literally "being up-to-date"), "new times" *(samay may)* and "progress" *(khwaam charoen)* to discuss and at times criticize perceptions and experiences of social and cultural change.[13] For example, the urban elite, scholars, and policy makers frequently debate whether national political and economic development has meant too much modernity—that is, at the expense of what are claimed to be traditional values. To rural producers the images of urban wealth and commodified progress that pervade Thai popular culture pose models of consumption and social status that, however difficult to achieve, are impossible to ignore. In particular, the ownership and display of new technologies and consumer commodities are increasingly valued as symbols of modern success and social status throughout Thailand.

Most rural youths, then, see the move to Bangkok at least in part as an opportunity to be at the center of contemporary Thai society—to "open their ears and eyes" *(poet huu poet taa)*—and to earn the cash necessary to purchase the commodity emblems of a than samay identity.[14] Young rural women confront these seductive attributes of "modern," than samay, selfhood in a strikingly gendered form: throughout Thailand images of the beautiful than samay woman—on billboards, television advertisements, serial dramas, and in many other formats—set powerful standards for defining this status. Moreover, city life provides a multitude of settings and social institutions—from beauty parlors and shopping malls to movie theaters and nightclubs—where migrants can observe and pursue these standards of modern womanhood.

Bangkok is the center for the production and dissemination of meanings and symbols of Thai progress (khwaam charoen) and than samay styles. The spread of communications technology throughout the country—most notably television and radio, a development in which the remittances of migrant workers have played no small part—has made Bangkok styles and standards a presence even in remote communities. In turn these sights and sounds of the modern Thai nation present rural audiences with images that equate personal fulfillment with urban-based identities and commodity consumption. Moreover, the availability of mass consumer products in commercial markets throughout the country provides tangible means for appropriating these symbols of up-to-date selfhood—only, of course, if one has access to sufficient cash income. Migration for urban employment not only offers village youth the opportunity to earn the money they need but also allows young women and men to participate in this culture of modernity at its most dynamic core, the Bangkok Metropolis. Let us examine a television commercial:

> Two young women in their early twenties face each other across a café table in downtown Bangkok, casually sipping coffee and laughing at each other's stories. A soundtrack of lively pop music renders their conversation inaudible. These are carefree and sophisticated women and their clothing bears witness to this—one wears a sleeveless, front-buttoning chemise, the other a loose, draping blouse with dangling decorative strings; both sport fashionable earrings and blue jeans. Also the venue, an air-conditioned café, and their beverage, hot coffee, are distinctive signs of urbanity and at least middle-class wealth. A young, strikingly handsome man passes their table but the two women do not return his interested glance—although they are clearly aware of it. The next moment the two women have left the café and are dashing boldly across the mad traffic of a Bangkok road, laughing and holding hands as close friends do. The fast rhythm of the musical soundtrack seems to match the dynamic pace of the women's motion—long hair flowing out behind them, stylish leather shoulder bags bumping against their denimed hips. Now the view cuts to a changing room lined with lockers where the two women are breathlessly beginning to disrobe; neither has sought the privacy of a separate cubicle or the more common technique of changing under a sarong wrap. Suddenly the pop-rock soundtrack changes to the sedate, classical sounds of the *khim* (a Chinese cembalo—a low, flat, stringed musical instrument played by striking the strings with two delicate felt-covered mallets). Simultaneously, the visual image switches to the khim players: they are the same two women, but now clad in demure though no less stylish skirts and long-sleeved blouses. They sit formally on the floor behind their instruments at slightly oblique angles to each other; they are playing in what appears to be a spacious, modern performance hall. The two smile knowingly at each other as the logo and picture of a scented deodorant fades in on the lower half of the viewer's screen.

In the slick, sophisticated packaging of Thailand's media, whether television commercials and movies or printed posters and magazines, women and women's bodies provide a predominant source of visual imagery. Feminine beauty has become one of the most powerful symbols for representing Thai progress and modernity. In advertising and the entertainment media, the beautiful woman is celebrated and promoted as an example of "up-to-date" style and independence. The fashionably dressed, stylishly coifed, carefully made-up "modern woman" *(phuu ying than samay)* parades her beauty at work and leisure in the city setting. Although the than samay woman may be identified with the urban context, and especially with Bangkok, national television and the print media as well as villagers' own encounters with educated, middle-class women of district and provincial towns have made images of modern femininity increasingly familiar to the entire population.

Than samay beauty is not defined primarily through conventional images of maidenly modesty and interpersonal restraint—ideal standards of behavior for unmarried women in the countryside—although, as in the final scene to the deodorant commercial, these qualities may be invoked to establish the essential "good girl" characteristics of a modern woman. Instead the modern woman is identified, on the one hand, by her sophisticated use of fashion and other market commodities of bodily display, and, on the other, by the ease with which she negotiates the diverse scenes and dynamic pace of urban life. Like the young women laughing over their coffee or dashing across a busy street, the than samay woman's beauty is linked to her active, mobile participation in urban society.

Part of what draws young rural women into the city is an unspoken but powerful suggestion that there they can be at once beautiful, modern, and mobile. With an urban income they can enhance their own beauty and modernity; they can participate in the adventure, excitement, and independence of modern city life. Indeed, one of the most valued benefits for migrants is that urban employment allows them to work indoors, away from the skin-darkening effects of the sun. White skin is a crucial marker of physical beauty in both urban and rural Thai aesthetic systems. Older villagers often describe women and men moving into Bangkok as "going to get [white] skin" *(pay aw phiw)*. While some offer these comments as a disparagement of youthful vanity, migrants on return visits are frequently complimented on their pale skin. At the same time that they acquire such signs of modern attractiveness, young migrants also hope that by sending money back to parents and siblings they can maintain their standing within the home community as good women and daughters.

Than samay beauty and urban consumer lifestyles present seductive models for how young women might retain and enhance their youthful beauty while exercising their own independence and mobility. Nevertheless, aspects of than samay womanhood contrast sharply with household-based values of maidenly modesty, virginal beauty, and constraints on female spatial mobility. The portrayal of women and women's bodies in the dominant urban-centered culture, linking beauty with modernity and active sexuality, flirts dangerously with equally powerful ideas about beauty predicated upon women's sexual propriety and modesty. The deodorant commercial is a case in point. The loose abandon with which the two women begin to disrobe carries a strong suggestion of sexual freedom: nudity is associated with sexual experience or availability, just as physical modesty is equated with virginity. Highly sexualized images of women's bodies, already familiar to villagers from television, movies, and other media, are reinforced in urban settings by the proliferation of commercial enterprises—shopping malls, salons, nightclubs, discos, massage parlors, and go-go bars—many of which link the celebration of modern female beauty to the actual sale of women's sexual services (Van Esterik 1988). This association of commercial sex work with popular and contemporary images of femininity points to a darker side of modern Thai womanhood. The prostitute stands as a reminder of the disreputable consequences that being too modern and too up-to-date may entail for the unwary.[15]

Migration decisions, then, involve a fragile convergence between young women's sense of duty and her desire for adventure. Working in the city offers women the chance—before marriage and motherhood—to pursue a level of personal autonomy unavailable to them in the village, while at the same time allowing them to uphold their obligations to their families.[16] In Bangkok lies the possibility to be both a modern woman and a good daughter. Once they have arrived in the city, however, the realities of low wages, minimal benefits, and often harsh working and living conditions mean that daughterly responsibilities and the pursuit of than samay ideals of autonomy and material display frequently come into conflict.

being up-to-date: migrants and commodity consumption

The young women that I knew both in Bangkok and in rural communities found these images of than samay identity compelling and the prospect of remaining at home dull by comparison. When describing their experiences before coming to the city, many migrants alluded to feelings of boredom: "in the village there's nothing to do." The Bangkok they see on nightly television broadcasts and hear about from friends is, by contrast, a place of boundless novelty and excitement. As one young textile worker explained, "I had to go see for myself." Perhaps more important, Bangkok is also where they can earn the money needed to actively enjoy the style and amenities of a modern identity. Thip, a textile worker who left her village home at age 19, wanted to work in Bangkok because "at home there was no money and nothing to do. I wanted to have lots of money, money to send home and to buy things for myself as well."

Urban wages, or more particularly what those wages can buy, provide the primary vehicle for most migrants' aspirations to modernity; in some ways, however, young women's desires to be up-to-date can be addressed through the work experience itself, especially when they find employment in Bangkok's booming manufacturing sector. In contrast to the undesirable and decidedly old-fashioned associations of peasant production (hard, heavy, largely unmechanized work performed outdoors), urban factories in themselves carry an attractive aura of participation in than samay society (lighter—even if highly repetitive tasks—that involve impressive new technologies and are performed indoors, away from the sun and rain). Migrants express pride in the acquisition of technical skills such as the ability to run complex textile machinery. Other aspects of the work process—such as special uniforms, or, most common in larger factories, management-sponsored sports competitions, beauty contests, or annual banquets—can be invested with a positive sense of than samay style. The employer-sponsored "Sports Days" that I attended at two Bangkok textile factories were good examples. While each aimed, in not very subtle ways, to promote worker identification—pitting groups from different production departments or different factories owned by the same parent company against each other—the events also incorporated a wide array of commodities and other emblems of modernity. Players donned new shirts, hats, and other items printed in special team colors and marked with company insignia; in one case those who wished to participate in the day's activities were required to purchase these items out of their own wages. At the same time workers sitting on the sidelines participated in animated chants and cheers modeled on the cheering songs of university and college students, an arena of than samay prestige and status with which many migrants would otherwise have little contact. A sound system providing loud music, microphones for announcers and cheerleaders, and trophies or prizes for the winners of each contest added to an overall atmosphere of excitement and modern style.[17] But if factories can project an image of "up-to-date" agency and status to employees, this image is not always easy for employees to sustain, especially as migrants struggle to cope with low wages and limited benefits. Employees in large manufacturing companies generally earn the legal minimum (just under U.S.$4.00 per day in 1990), but even after many years of service wages rarely rise much above this.[18] Many women in Bangkok earn even less. In the late 1980s 50 or 60 baht per day (U.S.$2.00–2.50) was not an uncommon wage for workers on temporary or probationary contracts, an arrangement that until the passage of legislation in 1990 could be prolonged for months and sometimes years. Earning lower than minimum wages was frequent among the women I interviewed, especially those working in small garment factories or piece-rate sweat shops; less than minimum wages was the rule for those employed in streetside restaurants or as domestic servants.[19] Even when an employer paid the legal minimum, many women reported that their already low wages could be further depressed by fines for lateness, failure to make production quotas, or minor infractions of shop-floor regulations.

Wage limitations are often compounded by women's encounters with the rigid time-discipline of urban work. Small shops that subcontract for larger companies, especially common in Bangkok's large garment industry, usually pay employees on a piece-rate basis and frequently operate 12 hours or more each day, especially when an order is due. Larger manufacturing enterprises have standard eight-hour shifts; overtime, however, can be frequent and may involve anywhere from two to eight additional hours of work.[20] Moreover, the largest factories tend to operate in three shifts around the clock. Shifts rotate once a week, forcing workers into a new cycle of sleep and eating every seven days. Even without the strains of overtime, this constant upheaval in daily routines frequently results in health problems such as disrupted menstruation, headaches and insomnia, and intestinal problems and ulcers, not to mention some of the more immediate physical threats to which women may be exposed in the workplace—toxic chemicals and gases, accidents caused by improperly maintained machinery or worker fatigue, respiratory infections from poorly ventilated work sites, and so on.

While acknowledging the hardships of long hours and often unpleasant, if not unsafe, working conditions, many of the migrants I interviewed appreciated their relative freedom after working hours. Company dormitories or rented rooms in the slums are often crowded, hot, and dirty, yet they still offer the chance to escape from direct supervision on the shop floor. It is here, at the end of the shift and outside the factory gates, that migrants are best able to explore and absorb images of sophisticated urban lifestyles by watching television and popular movies or going to department stores, entertainment parks, and similar sites of modernity. For many young women, these ventures into urban consumer culture are valued aspects of their time in the city and it is the opportunity to engage in these new consumption practices as much as concerns over difficulties on the job that preoccupy them on a day-to-day basis.

The young women to whom I spoke were often reluctant to reveal exactly how much they spent in the city, especially on nonessential items; yet any visit to the rooms of young workers reveals the importance given to commodity purchases and display. Ut and Tiw's small lodging is a case in point. From May to November of 1990, I regularly visited the two sisters at their rented room, one of four tiny partitions on the second floor of an old wooden house. It measured about two and one-half meters across and four meters long. One corner was walled off as a tiny bath and toilet area and another was used as a makeshift kitchen with a few pots and dishes, an electric rice cooker, and a small gas ring. The rest of the room was furnished with a few blankets and cushions along with Ut and Tiw's prize possessions. An electric fan sat in one corner, usually idle unless the sisters were entertaining visitors. On a set of shelves by one wall a small tape deck stood next to a row of cassettes. These included recordings by well-known Thai performers of popular "folk" style vocal music,[21] as well as recent albums by Thai pop-rock groups. A half-dozen small photo albums and a camera occupied another shelf, while yet another held a haphazard collection of cosmetics—a bottle or two of deodorant, powder, and lotion—along with combs, brushes, small novelty items, hair clips, and ribbons. Not long after I first began to visit Ut and Tiw, I arrived one week to discover that a small color television had been added to their belongings, the culmination of nearly three years' effort. The sisters had saved the 7500 baht (U.S.$300) purchase price out of their wages and by taking on occasional piece-rate assembly work given out by Tiw's company for those wanting to earn extra money on their own time.[22]

In addition to acquiring particular mass-market commodities, participation in new commodified patterns of sociality is equally attractive to many rural-urban migrants. At home a young women is enmeshed in an intense web of social relations with parents and siblings, neighbors, and friends, all of whom can observe, comment upon, and potentially influence her behavior. As factory workers in the city, migrants enjoy the most immediate and intimate social interaction almost exclusively with friends and coworkers, the majority being of similar age and background. The expectations and interests of their peers play an important role in shaping the consumption behavior of many migrants.

Working side-by-side, sharing a rented room or living in the common quarters of factory dormitories, young women find themselves in an intense world of peer-oriented companionship, far removed from the authority of parents and elders that frame and intersect such ties in the village setting. Friendly pressures to participate in common activities—such as shared meals and outings—place steady demands on the cash earnings of young workers. Many of the young women that I knew in Bangkok described themselves as "great spenders" *(chay ngoen keng,* literally, "good at using money"). Money, they said, is hard to keep, not because of large or flamboyant purchases but because of the everyday demands of urban existence, including the desire to hang out and have fun with friends. In my experience these interactions rarely took the form of competitive consumption in the form of having better or more expensive items than others, or treating friends to meals or snacks. Instead, the factory workers I knew were quite scrupulous in their attempts to even out expenses, to pay their own share of meals eaten at streetside restaurants, to repay small debts (such as money borrowed during a trip to the market) to coworkers, and so forth. The egalitarian emphasis of these interactions nevertheless supports a constant focus on consumption: whether gatherings revolve around purchased meals,[23] trips to local markets, or, more rarely, spending a day off at one of the city's commercial amusement parks (such as "Happyland" or the part-zoo, part-rock concert venue, "The Crocodile Farm"). Participating in peer group activities also requires investing in certain kinds of commodity display such as urban styles of clothing, especially those including one or more pairs of blue jeans.

These peer group "outings" (pay thiaw) in search of fun and entertainment are, for many migrants, among the most satisfying experiences of life in Bangkok. Given migrants' limited leisure hours and low wages, a thiaw is usually brief—an afternoon's trip to the market, a shopping mall, or a park; but it may also be a much longer excursion, perhaps over a holiday weekend, to the beach or more commonly to a friend's home in a distant and unfamiliar province. Such outings offer a dramatic break from the tedium and exhaustion of factory shifts. They also offer the best chances for most migrants to approximate dominant images of a modern lifestyle by their own actions. Women dress carefully for these events, usually in blue jeans and colorful blouses or tee-shirts. Other commodities like cameras can also be in high demand, especially on longer trips.[24]

Even a small thiaw involves the mobilization of such commodity symbols of than samay self-presentation. One Sunday afternoon (the day most factory workers have free) I was visiting Ut and several other women from her village who all worked at the same Bangkok textile factory. We had gathered in Ut's rented room but soon decided to go visit some young men from the same village who were living in a one-room flat about 30 minutes away by bus. In preparation, two of the women had to go back to their dormitory rooms to change out of the casual shorts they were wearing; I stayed with Ut and her friend, Noi, who had suggested the outing. While we waited, Noi looked over Ut's small collection of cosmetics and began to try on two different colors of lipstick. When she turned back to us, Ut had finished changing into a pair of black stretch slacks. Noi scolded her: "Don't you want to wear something more up-to-date [than samay]? You look like a country hick *[duu baan nohk loey]."* Ut quickly changed into a pair of blue jeans, even though they were not quite dry from the morning's laundry.

urban dilemmas: confronting ambivalence and marginality

While the acquisition and display of commodities in these ways provide crucial demonstrations of than samay identity and status among migrant peers, within the broader urban setting these claims receive little recognition. Amid Bangkok's exploding consumerism, migrants' consumption patterns—restricted as they are by low wages and limited leisure time—offer only a weak approximation of up-to-date urban living. There are always more and newer commodities to acquire, more places to see, more outings to take. Wearing jeans and cosmetics, and taking trips to the Crocodile Farm or an air-conditioned department store are pleasant and attractively than samay activities. Surrounded by the city's hypermodernity and intense commercialization, however, rural women's access to and control over the extensive cultural repertoire of "being up-to-date" is partial at best.

It is not surprising, then, that the women I knew in Bangkok almost universally expressed ambivalence about their experiences in the city. And their unease tended to increase over time. In the words of one woman with nearly 20 years of migration experience: "Bangkok is a city of heaven and a city of hell." Many migrants acknowledged the "heavenly" aspects of urban life: the city is a place of "progress" (khwaam charoen) where people and society are "up-to-date" (than samay). Living there has taught them a great deal; it has "opened the ears, opened the eyes." They appreciate the many comforts and conveniences of city life: easy access to running water, electricity, transportation, markets, and entertainment. And central to these advantages is the fact that "in the city there's money, in the village there's none." Just as recognizable, however, is Bangkok's "hellish" side: the pollution, noise, and congestion; crowded living spaces in which, nevertheless, it is very easy to feel alone and isolated; insecure, unhealthy, and often oppressive working conditions. Among the women I knew, whether they had worked in Bangkok for six months or 16 years, enthusiasm for the than samay qualities of city living was always tempered by unease about its alien and alienating aspects. In some cases these tensions lead to an explicit critique of their circumstances, sometimes in the form of active participation in trade unions and labor protest (Mills 1994); but labor organizing remains a difficult and often risky venture. Only a tiny minority of migrant workers even have access to independent union institutions. The vast majority of migrants in Bangkok responds to the ambivalence engendered by urban experiences with less radical actions, neither outright resistance nor passive acquiescence, but what might better be described as "coping strategies" (see Lamphere 1987:30). A major focus of these strategies is the maintenance of connections with rural kin and community.

Throughout my fieldwork, suggestions to migrant women that their urban sojourns had turned them into city people brought sharp denials, usually accompanied by a strong affirmation of a rural identity. In the words of Daeng, a 20-year-old textile operative:

> People in the city and people in the village aren't the same. City people, Bangkok people, you can't trust them, they only think of themselves. In the city people don't know each other. I've lived in this room for many months now and I still don't know the neighbors. In the village I know everyone. We grow up together, we're all relatives and friends together. I know where they come from, their background. I can trust them.

Ties to rural family and community remain crucial to most migrant women, no matter how long their stay in Bangkok.[25] Almost without exception women speak of plans to return to live in their villages; periodic visits home are eagerly planned and awaited.

The continuing strength of this identification with rural family and community—what informs the "good daughter" imagery of Khem's and other migrants' stories—is at least partly rooted in pragmatic assessments of their longer term insecurity as urban laborers. Migrants' experiences with urban employment policies contribute significantly to these concerns. Few factories, they say, will hire women over the age of 25, and some restrict new hiring to women of 21 or younger. Women who stay in the city after their mid-twenties are very careful not to lose their current employment lest they find themselves choosing between a premature return home or poorly paid informal sector work such as domestic service or subcontracted sweatshop labor. Similar fears underlie a widespread reluctance among migrant women to marry and start a family in the city. Workers know well that urban employers tend to prefer not only youthful but also unmarried, unencumbered employees. A married woman or a woman with children is at a significant disadvantage in the labor market. Aware of their marginal position within the urban labor market, rural women realize that a return to the village household remains their most reliable source of economic security after marriage. Poor married women in Bangkok are often relegated to a secondary labor market of insecure, low-paying jobs such as scavenging, small-scale cottage industries, and vending (Thorbek 1987:61, 72–75). The insecurity and hardship of such a future was widely acknowledged by the migrants I met.

These concerns are only strengthened by women's own perceptions that men in the city are often unreliable providers. "Men are not responsible"; "men like to have lots of wives"; "men drink, gamble, and spend their money on their friends"—these were all commonly expressed opinions. Many of the migrants with whom I spoke felt that if a woman settled in the city there was a good chance that she would have to support herself and her children on her own. Almost universally women told me that men in the city were more likely to run after other women and not contribute to the household budget. And most can point to a friend or acquaintance whose city romance has left her in difficult straits. On one occasion, I went with several textile workers to visit a former coworker who had been abandoned by her husband. We spent an hour or two helping her assemble small plastic holders for artificial flowers; with this work she earned a small piece-rate wage—amounting to less than 30 baht (U.S.$1.20) per day—to support herself and her infant son. On the return trip, my companions were quick to point out the cautionary effects of their friend's situation. Said one, "You see, Mary, marriage only means problems for women. A good man, one to trust, is hard to find. You've got to be careful." Although abuse and neglect occur in village families, most women believed both that it was less frequent and that the consequences for women were less severe because of their access to the moral and economic support of relatives and neighbors.[26] In the city a young woman may be free from familial supervision but she is also no longer within easy reach of familial assistance. Some women I know responded to these circumstances by deciding—usually after working in Bangkok until their late twenties or older—that they would prefer not to marry at all, but most women were not willing to forego the pleasures—and sacrifices—of having a family of their own. Yet when they did marry, these women said, it would be to men of rural background, preferably from their own village or region, with whom they would then return to live in the country. And, with few exceptions, those migrants of my acquaintance who later married did exactly that.

But this generalized perception of long-term vulnerability in the city does not mean that the prospect of a return home is without problems. If the idea of settling in the city is fraught with difficulty, going home to a future of rice farming and motherhood raises a different set of concerns. These are linked to migrants' ongoing aspirations for than samay forms of success and autonomy. The wages they can earn in Bangkok, limited though they may be, provide a steady and individualized source of cash income, unlike the more irregular, often unpredictable, and collective earnings that characterize household agricultural production. A former textile worker in her mid-twenties, having returned home to prepare for her marriage to a local man, was quick to identify the unfortunate consequences that this move would have. She was happy with her prospective husband, but their union would put an end to her time in Bangkok; from then on she would be "only a mother and housewife." Her sense of loss was shared by many young women as they contemplated leaving urban work for the burdens of raising their own family.

One response among migrant women is to plan for a return home but to do so in a way that will preserve some of their hard-won than samay status and autonomy. A common ambition is to open a small shop or food vending enterprise. Others who are able to marshal their resources and energy during their limited leisure hours choose to invest in further education or vocational training. Maew, an employee in a leather bag factory, decided at age 19 to reduce drastically both her expenditures in the city and her remittances home in order to pay for a high school education. When I met her she had been taking adult education classes every Sunday for the previous two years; she expected to complete her diploma in another two or three years. She was also saving money in a bank account, so that when she left Bangkok to go home she would be able to continue her education at the provincial teachers' college. Lek, a textile worker from the same village as Maew, saved her wages until she could pay the 7000 baht (U.S.$280) tuition at a Bangkok beauty school. On her days off from the factory she attended classes and practiced the skills of hairdressing and cosmetic application. Although Lek did not think that she could make a living in this way in her village, she thought she might be able to find a job in a hairdressing shop in a nearby town.

Lek and Maew were somewhat unusual in their ability to marshal their resources for such specific long-term goals. For Maew this decision resulted in an ongoing conflict with family members in the village—particularly with her mother, who regularly requested that Maew contribute money to the rural household and periodically threatened to travel to Bangkok (and did so on at least one occasion) to get the money from Maew in person. Most of the rural-urban migrants that I knew either had less concrete plans for their future or were unable or unwilling to ignore parental expectations so consistently. Nevertheless, they too hoped to be more than just "rice and upland crop farmers" *(chaaw naa chaaw ray)* when they left the city. Achieving this goal is difficult—and even Maew and Lek wondered whether their educational investments would really pay off in the end. Moreover, young women who plan and work toward a successful return to the village may find that circumstances intervene. A sudden illness, an accident on the job, factory layoffs, a family crisis, or, as in the following example, the competing demands and expectations of parents—such events can quickly force a woman into an agonizing decision.

This was Noi's predicament during her sixth year of urban employment when—in part for reasons of kin ties with the prospective in-laws—her parents pressured her into becoming engaged to a man she did not want to marry. Immediately after the engagement was formalized Noi fled back to Bangkok and refused to see or talk to her parents or fiancé when they followed her. Spending time with sympathetic friends, Noi took to drinking herself into a stupor at regular intervals. She was eventually able to break off the match, but only after several months of anguish and self-destructive behavior. As she said at the time, she felt trapped and did not know what to do: "How can I live with someone I don't like? If I don't like him now, I'm not going to like him later." Significantly Noi argued that her fiancé had "never even been to Bangkok." In other words, he would appreciate neither the kind of experiences she had enjoyed there nor the person she had become as a result.[27]

Not all women encounter the conflicting cultural and economic expectations of rural-urban migration in the same fashion as Noi. They nonetheless confront a similar dilemma during their time in the city. Attempts to pursue than samay aspirations are fundamentally at odds with young women's obligations to rural kin. Whatever the purpose of their urban expenditures—personal items, daily needs, entertainment with friends, education, or vocational training—every baht spent in Bangkok is, at least in theory, one baht less for the family at home. New patterns of commodity consumption, while necessary for the pursuit of a than samay sense of self, confront migrants both with their own marginal status within the dominant, commodified culture of Bangkok and with their potential (or actual) failure to maintain the ideal image of a "good daughter." Although, among the women I interviewed, the economic hardships of rural households were rarely the primary motivating factor in their migration decisions, all recognized the moral force of family obligations. Women who described themselves as "good spenders" (chay ngoen keng) often did so in the context of explaining their irregular remittances to village kin.[28] The amount and frequency of migrants' contributions to rural households varied widely among the women I interviewed; women commonly reported contributions totaling anywhere from 30–80 percent of monthly income, but these initial claims were usually revealed later on to represent much more occasional remittances. There were very few women who would admit to never having sent money, but most agreed that they would rather wait and save a particular sum (often 2,000 or 3,000 baht, U.S.$80–$120) over several months; they could then take this money home on a visit instead of sending back smaller but more frequent contributions.[29]

In part this pattern allowed the women to exercise greater control over the use of their earnings by saving for particular consumption projects, the most common being the purchase of materials to use in building their parents a new house. These goals are often supported by rural kin but they can also be frustrated by periodic demands for increased or immediate contributions. Some of these requests tend to come at regular intervals: calls for help with harvest or transplanting expenses, or with younger siblings' school costs at the beginning of term—for uniforms, books, high school tuition, and so forth. At other times migrants will be called upon to help out in a household emergency, particularly when a sudden or severe illness strikes. Although young women may complain among themselves that people in the village think only about money, most migrants do their best to comply with requests from home. But sometimes daughters find themselves in the position of censoring the consumption demands of their own parents. For example, when Lan's mother asked for a color television to replace the black-and-white set that Lan and a sister (also working in the city) had bought a few years before, Lan responded with some exasperation, "I'm saving now for the cost of building her a new house. [My sister and I] bought the supporting posts last year. Mother will have to wait for the television."

Such feelings are aggravated by a perceived—and often actual—difference between men's and women's respective consumption behavior. Both in the city and the village, Thai men are allowed more discretionary use of their personal income. Parents and kin usually expect young men to bear considerable expense for entertainment: cigarettes, alcohol, gambling, and women. While parents generally view a certain amount of personal expenditure as unavoidable for migrant daughters, it should not be of the same type or on the same scale as that demanded by young men's urban consumption practices. According to some women in the city, daughters who fail to send home money are liable to far greater criticism from parents and other villagers than are delinquent sons. Several spoke of migrant brothers who had "never" or only infrequently sent home their city earnings; their parents "never said anything about it."

If the demands of urban consumption styles jeopardize the fragile balance of migrants' desires to be both "modern women" and "good daughters," there are moments when migrants can confront these tensions and rework them to their own benefit. Here the importance of maintaining ties to rural kin can be seen as not only a matter of migrants' pragmatic concerns for the future but also because through trips home—which include bringing money, wearing new clothes, and being accompanied by new friends—migrants can resolve, however briefly, the disjunctures of urban life and project a solid identity of both than samay success and filial respect and gratitude. This is a crucial aspect of one of the most popular activities in which rural-urban migrants engage: the organization of, and participation in, elaborate ceremonial trips to make ritual donations to village temples. Although framed within the merit-making language of popular religious discourse, the enthusiasm with which migrants participate in these events often has less to do with the desire to add to their store of karmic merit (although such goals are by no means irrelevant) than with the opportunities that these trips provide to resolve, if only temporarily, some of the tensions encountered during the course of their urban experiences. Specifically, these merit-making trips are occasions when migrants' than samay consumption practices parallel and even support their commitment to their village homes.

On these occasions several people, usually from the same village, plan an excursion, rent a bus, and recruit friends in the city to come along. Passengers pay a fare for the bus trip and contribute to a merit fund that will be offered to the community temple. These trips are organized around significant temple ceremonies: an ordination, commonly held at the beginning of the Buddhist Lenten season; a *thoht kathin,* the ritual presentation of new robes to monks at the end of this season; or, most often, a *thoht phaa paa* ("offering of forest robes") that may be held at almost any time of year. All involve rituals during which, in addition to the presentation of robes and other items to resident monks, significant offerings can be made to the host temple. In this way a donation of several thousand baht may be collected, usually for a particular purpose such as the construction of new temple buildings.

But organizing a merit-making trip, as the women I knew quickly pointed out, means much work. A successful trip, one that raises a substantial amount of money, depends on recruiting many participants. Migrants from the same village, including both women and men, must coordinate the project among themselves—not an easy task when they may live and work in opposite ends of Bangkok and seldom have access to private telephone lines. A rented bus must be reserved for the occasion, invitations to participants and envelopes for their contributions printed, and donors solicited. This last task is often the most troublesome. One worker in a large cotton factory complained that every year so many ceremonies took place that she was reluctant to ask her friends to contribute to yet another one. "If you ask them they try to give something but it may only be ten baht (U.S.$0.40). And finding people to be *kamakaan* (committee members) is really hard." This latter category is largely an honorary position; the incumbent's name is printed on official invitations and any other documents acknowledging key participants. In return for this honor, however, the committee member is expected to contribute a significant sum of money, usually at least 100 baht (about U.S.$4.00)—the equivalent of a day's pay or more for most migrant workers. Kamakaan should also attend the ceremony in person, although this is not considered essential. If the trip's organizers cannot recruit enough people to be kamakaan, the chances of collecting a respectable donation are seriously reduced. Should this happen, I was told, the organizers would lose face at home for bringing in a disappointing amount. For example, when Ut and her friends—all from the same Northeastern village—were approached in the fall of 1990 by their community's leaders to help organize a thoht phaa paa from Bangkok, they were less than enthusiastic. The village was planning to build a new temple *saalaa* (meeting hall), the full cost of which was expected to be close to several hundred thousand baht (U.S.$10,000). Although the thoht phaa paa was not expected to raise anywhere near the full amount, the women were clearly reluctant to take on the task: "We just did one last year," several told me, "and already they want another one!" They were not sure it would be worth all the time and effort.

It is clear from such comments that these ceremonial trips do not in fact erase the tensions that arise in the course of migration experiences; in the actual performance of these events, however, migrants enact the close convergence of ongoing ties to kin and community with their claims to than samay autonomy and urban success. On the several merit-making trips I attended, a large passenger bus, packed with people and decorated on one side with a long banner proclaiming the destination and ceremonial objective of its purpose, left Bangkok in the evening; this usually took place on a Saturday at the end of the afternoon factory shift. We traveled all night, arriving at the host community by the middle of the morning or earlier. Each time, the journey began in an atmosphere of celebration and revelry that continued throughout the night, fueled in part by a steady flow of alcohol (consumed mostly but not exclusively by men), along with soft drinks and other treats purchased by passengers in anticipation of the evening's festivities. Those who tried to rest their heads against seat backs and windows in the hope of catching a little sleep were loudly serenaded by their more energetic companions, usually with the aid of a microphone hooked into the bus's internal sound system and backed by drums and cymbals brought along by the celebrants. Sometime during the night the organizers of the trip passed through the bus collecting envelopes they had distributed earlier and that passengers had filled with cash contributions. The amounts would later be recorded along with participants' names for the final offering at the temple.

The ceremony itself took place soon after reaching the host community. On one thoht phaa paa to a village in the Northeastern province of Khon Kaen, we arrived in time to complete the phaa paa presentation before the daily offering of the monks' late morning meal, the food for which had been prepared in large quantities by villagers so that everyone attending could eat once the monks had consumed their share. The presentation of money for the temple was the focus of the ritual but it also included offerings of commodity items for the personal use of resident monks: robes, bath and laundry soap, toilet paper, packaged drinks, and drink mixes such as Ovaltine. These were presented in elaborate cellophane wrapped bundles, a format that has been standardized by urban stores specializing in such ready-to-go merit packages. The ceremony ended with speeches by community leaders and the most senior organizers of the thoht phaa paa, and with ritual chants and blessings led by the temple monks. Meanwhile the final amount of money donated had been tallied and was announced for everyone to hear. The largest contributors were awarded special recognition in the form of gifts of cloth and pillows.

When the ritual itself was finished the merit makers could finally relax. Migrants visited with family and introduced the friends who had accompanied them from Bangkok. Fresh from the successful display of devotion to temple and community concerns, they could enjoy their status, however temporary, as good daughters and sons whose successful sojourns as modern wage workers in the nation's capital had made their contributions to the prosperity of the village temple possible—and by extension of the community as a whole. The congratulatory atmosphere continued well into the evening with a performance by a folk-opera *(moh lam)* troupe hired by the host community for the occasion. The next morning it was time to get back on the bus and return to the city. This trip had been planned to coincide with a national long-weekend holiday, making it possible to stay away for an extra night. (The merit makers usually return to Bangkok on the same day, having spent only a few hours in the host village, in order not to risk missing a day's work.) On most merit trips the return journey is a chance for yet more excitement; organizers choose a route that will include at least one (and sometimes several) sightseeing attractions. These may include famous temples, caves, waterfalls, national parks, dams, or archaeological ruins. Organizers frequently play up the attractions of these natural and architectural sites when recruiting their friends to participate in a merit-making trip. Returning from the thoht phaa paa ceremony in Khon Kaen, for example, we detoured nearly two hours to visit the site of a major hydroelectric power dam. Cameras clicked; souvenirs and samples of local delicacies were purchased. The passengers became modern tourists for a few whirlwind hours before the bus turned toward Bangkok once again.

Young people working in Bangkok acknowledge the religious merit that participants earn on these excursions but often accord more emphasis to their entertainment value. This combination of spiritual and worldly purposes in merit-making ceremonies is central to the power of these ritual events to help defuse ongoing conflicts, at least temporarily, between migrants' aspirations for achievement within the dominant culture of urban modernity and their continuing attachments to village family and community. Thoht phaa paa and other ceremonial trips provide an opportunity to display success and to show off urban friends to people back home, as well as to renew and affirm solidarity with the rural community and its moral focus, the temple. It is one of the few moments when fulfilling one's filial obligations as a good village native and the pursuit of than samay identity appear to coincide.

Moreover, the migrants achieve this balance by acting in the most prestigious arena of the Thai social and moral order: Buddhist merit making. Offerings of money, robes, and other items earns spiritual merit for all participants and especially the organizers. In addition, the money raised by a thoht phaa paa is often earmarked for new temple construction or renovation, widely viewed as among the most meritorious acts to which a person can contribute. The value of earning merit in this way is acknowledged by organizers and participants alike, even as they appreciate the opportunities for worldly entertainment that the trips offer. In addition, merit-making trips require—and demonstrate for all to see—a level of organizational skill and material sacrifice that would not usually be expected of young people who remain in the village, where they are considered dependents in their parents' households. Rural youth make merit by attending temple festivals and other ritual events, just as they have in past, but the responsibility and control over material resources that migrants demonstrate in the course of these merit-making trips are qualities normally exercised by their parents and grandparents (see Tambiah 1970; also Lefferts n.d.). Religious duties and daily support for the monks are tasks supervised and organized by community elders. Young women and men living in rural communities may help with preparations for major rituals, give food offerings to monks, and attend temple ceremonies, but they are not usually involved in the organization and planning of these events.[30] Young people in Bangkok who organize thoht phaa paa or other ceremonies and make sizable contributions out of their own pocket are thus engaging in activities that, in the village setting, are quite unusual for people of their age and social status.

Furthermore, the number of participants from outside the home village and the substantial monetary offerings are not features common of most village ceremonies. Many aspects of these excursions from Bangkok—the long distance traveled, the participants from many different parts of the country, the drama, and (at least potentially) the large sums of money donated—are strongly reminiscent of the prestigious ritual offerings that wealthy patrons and ambitious politicians sponsor, usually at famous temples in Bangkok and provincial towns. Although none of my informants made this connection explicitly, it seems likely that part of the attraction of merit-making trips for young villagers lies in this vicarious association with the elaborate style of merit offerings practiced by the powerful and wealthy, groups to whom migrants and their families must defer in everyday life.

In a variety of ways, migrants' sense of self as up-to-date or modern is denied or marginalized within the dominant Bangkok culture; moreover, by pursuing styles and standards of urban commodity consumption, women can quickly diminish their ability to make the economic contributions that are expected of them by people at home and that the women themselves acknowledge as their responsibility. Viewed from one perspective, the merit-making trips discussed above might simply demonstrate the extent to which hegemonic discourses of modernity increasingly permeate the understandings and practices of subordinate groups in Thailand, but this would only be a partial reading. By organizing and participating in ceremonial offerings, young rural women are able to affirm their connections with kin and community while also demonstrating their claims to personal autonomy and material success before an appreciative audience—perhaps the only such audience available to them. Seen within the broader context of women's migration experiences of and participation in urban employment and consumerism, merit-making trips emerge as an important cultural arena in which migrant workers find room to maneuver despite the structural and ideological constraints they face in everyday life. Merit-making trips allow village youths to assert some of the social authority and prestige that they had hoped to gain through migration to Bangkok but that is denied to all such proletarian wage-earners. By mobilizing the signs and symbols of a than samay identity within the conventions of these Buddhist rituals, young migrants contest—if only in veiled and temporary fashion—their material and ideological marginalization within the dominant, urban society.

conclusion

In this article I have focused on what can be learned about women's experiences as labor migrants in Thailand through their consumption practices. Commodity consumption is a central goal in migration decisions and an important feature of the urban sojourn. Migrants' consumption is not simply a reflection of material interests or economic need but is also a cultural process, engaging powerful if often conflicting cultural discourses about family relations, gender roles, and Thai constructions of modernity. Urban consumption practices are constitutive of young migrants' sense of themselves as modern women, but the latter is sharply constrained both by women's lived experiences of Bangkok employment and by cultural expectations and personal desires linked to rural kin and community. As a result, market commodities and commodified forms of social practice serve as important vehicles for the construction and contestation of identity. Attention to workers' commodity consumption points not only to some of the cultural conflicts involved in labor migration but also to an important arena wherein women can mobilize dominant symbols and meanings to serve their own interests and to stretch, if only temporarily, the limits of their subordination within the wider society.

This highlights the importance of examining the specific and culturally contingent motivations—or, to return to Enloe's phrase, "needs, values, and worries"—that help to shape local participation in and lived experiences of new relations of production and authority. As the dramatic rates of women's entry into proletarian labor gains ever more attention worldwide, it is important to ask, at different places and times, how women's own desires and concerns may complement or conflict with the expectations and interests of both capitalist employers and workers' families and home communities. The answers can point not only to the kinds of tension that neophyte wage laborers will probably confront but also to the spaces that may exist for negotiating and reworking their new circumstances. While my argument relates most specifically to the experiences of young Thai women involved in rural-urban labor migration, it holds broader implications for the study of newly proletarianized groups both in Thailand and more generally within the contemporary global economy. At the very least, sustained attention to the processes and meanings of consumption practices broadens the framework of analysis and may permit more complete and complex understandings of contemporary cultural and economic transformation in different situations and societies around the world. In the analysis of local encounters with capitalism, it is important to see how new structural relations are actively received and even appropriated by people on the ground. As Orlove and Rutz have argued, attention to the complex agency underlying consumption practices, beliefs, and motivations can help avoid reductionist views of social and cultural transformation and may provide a richer and more complete understanding of local experiences of change (1989:6, 14–15). In different parts of the world, popular confrontations and resistance to wage labor and commodity markets exist alongside the rapid—and even enthusiastic—incorporation of capitalist forms and relations into daily life. Examining specific consumption patterns may illuminate how and why local responses to global processes vary. It thereby becomes clear that "consumption . . . can powerfully affirm certain social orders and can be a key arena of contestation and change of others . . . consumption is thus linked to the constitution and transformation of hegemony" (Orlove and Rutz 1989:39).

In contemporary Thailand, the gap between hegemonic cultural constructions of urban modernity and lived experiences of city life sets up a fundamental tension in the daily lives of rural-urban migrants. Young women moving into Bangkok confront seductive images of consumption-oriented lifestyles, yet their ability to achieve these desired than samay standards are constrained by their low-wage, low-status employment. Rural-urban mobility brings young women into the heart of Thai modernity, but working and living in Bangkok merely confirms their marginalization, not only as subordinate employees but also—what is just as important to many migrants—within the urban consumer culture. These encounters with new forms of domination and hegemonic representations, and the gaps between dominant meanings and lived experience that they must face as a result, offer fertile ground for migrants' "cultural struggles" (Ong 1991). In the course of moving between rural and urban settings, young Thai women must negotiate not only shifts in space but also shifting identities and social relations. Women's labor and women's bodies constitute crucial factors of economic production. They are also evocative symbolic resources in present-day Thailand. Women's labor, a cheap and highly flexible labor force mobilized through rural-urban migration, has been a key component in Thailand's recent economic boom. But while the Thai media celebrate national progress and modernity, including the symbolic deployment of women's mobile and commodified bodies, young migrants encounter these images as seductive but largely unattainable, potential selves. In this context, rural-urban mobility must be recognized as more than a strategy for economic survival or accumulation; it is also a vehicle through which migrants struggle over what it means to be modern in contemporary Thai society and attempt to reconcile these aspirations and images with equally compelling concerns for, and moral commitments to, rural kin and community.

In the midst of these structural and ideological contradictions, it is little wonder that women should experience the movement into urban employment in highly ambivalent ways. Nevertheless, this ambivalence cannot be taken as passivity or as a failure to recognize the inequities they encounter. Throughout their time in the city, young women make very real efforts to maintain a sense of meaning and purpose despite the many difficulties they face. Young women in Bangkok are often torn between duty and affection for rural kin on the one hand and personal desires for autonomy and urban adventure on the other. The choices they make, however, are shaped not only by the structural disparities of the contemporary Thai and global political economy but also by the cultural resources that are available to them—resources through which they seek to understand who they are and who they wish to become.

notes

Acknowledgments. This article is based on research conducted with the permission of the National Research Council of Thailand in 1987–88 and 1989–90, and supported at different stages by National Science Foundation and the Social Sciences and Humanities Research Council of Canada doctoral fellowships, and Social Science Research Council and Fulbright-Hays doctoral dissertation research grants. A brief follow-up visit in 1993 was aided by grants from the Social Science Division and the International Studies program at Colby College. Final revisions were made while on a postdoctoral fellowship at the Program in Agrarian Studies at Yale University. I am grateful to Michael Herzfeld and three anonymous *AE* reviewers; their close and critical readings of the manuscript were immensely valuable. The comments of friends and colleagues have helped me to sharpen my analysis: Arun Agrawal, Jenny and Paul Alexander, Catherine Besteman, Christine Bowditch, Donna Goldstein, Jill Gordon, David Nugent, Pauline Peters, Jesse Ribot, and K. Sivaramakhrishnan. The content of the article, however, is my own responsibility. I am indebted to Leedom Lefferts, Aihwa Ong, Herbert Phillips, Akin Rabhibhatana, Penny Van Esterik, Juree Vichit-Vadakan, and Michael Watts for their encouragement and guidance at earlier stages of the research. My deepest thanks and respect are owed to the many women and men in Bangkok and in the northeast of Thailand whose gifts of time and friendship made this work possible.

1. Khem is a pseudonym, as are the names of all informants cited in the text. Her statement is translated from a short autobiographical narrative that she wrote during the time I was interviewing her in 1987–88. Parts of it have been published in the monthly newsletter of Friends of Women, a Thai women's rights organization. See Friends of Women 1988.

2. Thailand's National Statistical Office (NSO 1992:38) reported that between 1990 and 1992 more than 272,000 women and 281,000 men moved from rural to urban areas, while 1,149,000 people (of whom 41% were women) moved in the opposite direction. The excess of urban-rural over rural-urban moves in this report reflects the timing of the survey (i.e., conducted from September to November, the months leading into the main rice harvest of the year). Given the difficulty of counting the variety of temporary and circulating moves that characterize most rural-urban mobility in Thailand, these figures probably underestimate the full extent of population movement.

3. Thus, for example, men and women working in Bangkok may receive supplements of rice, other foods, and even cash from rural households; children born to urban workers are frequently sent home to be raised by grandparents or other kin in the countryside; and rural households provide care and support to migrant members in cases of illness, unemployment, or other crises they may encounter while working in the city.

4. For a recent review of the literature on this topic, see Ong 1991. Useful case studies from Asia to Africa to Latin America and the Caribbean include Benerí and Feldman 1992, Fernandez-Kelly 1982, Kung 1983, Nash and Fernandez-Kelly 1983, Ong 1987, Safa 1995.

5. There is an extensive literature on rural-urban labor migration in Thailand. For the most part this research has focused on demographic and economic policy-oriented questions of identifying population flows (and determining whether they can or cannot be redirected away from Bangkok), patterns of urban assimilation, or the economic impact of remittances on rural households (see, for example, Aphichat et al. 1979; Fuller et al. 1983; Goldstein and Goldstein 1986; Lightfoot et al. 1983; Parnwell 1986; Pawadee 1984; Porpora and Lim 1987). Relatively little of this work has taken an anthropological perspective, although notable exceptions include Anchalee 1981; Juree 1983; Muecke 1984, 1992; and Textor 1961. For a more extensive review of this literature see Mills 1993:234–244.

6. For a more general discussion of the place—or dearth until recently—of consumption studies in anthropology as a whole, see also Miller 1995.

7. This phenomenon is not unique to Thailand; similar effects operate in societies around the world. Arjun Appadurai, in particular, has identified the rise of such "global cultural processes" with a transformation of the social imagination:

> [T]he imagination has become an organized field of social practices, a form of work (both in the sense of labor and a culturally organized practice) and a form of negotiation between sites of agency ("individuals") and globally defined fields of possibility. . . . The imagination is now central to all forms of agency, is itself a social fact, and is the key component of the new global order. [Appadurai 1990:5]

While any claims for the human imagination as a fundamentally new component in social creativity can easily be overdrawn, the new and increasingly global technologies of mass communication have certainly had important and wide-reaching effects on how people think about themselves and the world around them. For a useful application of these ideas see Steven Kemper's (1993) reading of Appadurai in relation to the social production of a national(ist) imagination in Sri Lanka through the practice of new forms of mass consumption such as lotteries.

8. Moore argues that such "fantasies of identity," because they are "linked to fantasies of power and agency in the world" (1994:66), play a significant role in the way individuals confront and potentially transform existing social discourses about appropriate roles and (gendered) identities.

9. The extent to which Thai women do in fact enjoy a high social status has been the subject of considerable debate. See, for example, Keyes 1984; Kirsch 1982, 1985; Van Esterik 1982.

10. Roseberry's work is informed by the seminal insights of Raymond Williams (1977), specifically Williams's concept of "structures of feeling" arising from the interplay between dominant cultural constructions and alternative understandings (i.e., "residual" or historically rooted and traditional meanings, and "emergent" or new and innovative ideas) that exist within and can potentially challenge hegemonic cultural formations (Williams 1977:121–135).

11. Such an analysis need not apply only to women's newly industrialized labor but can also illuminate experiences of cultural disjuncture and contests over dominant meanings more generally. See, for example, Mills 1995 and Rouse 1992.

12. These concerns about the study of consumption echo recent calls for more complex and nuanced approaches to the analysis of hegemony and resistance in anthropology as a whole. See Ortner 1995 for one of the most current contributions on this subject.

13. An interest in the constitution of Thai modernity is also an underlying theme in academic debates, especially those on the social, political, and economic transformations involved in the construction of the modern Thai nation-state. For early "modernization" studies see, for example, Jacobs 1971 and Riggs 1966; for more recent anthropological and historical analyses, see Keyes 1989 and Thongchai 1994.

14. Similarly, Juree Vichit-Vadakan (Juree 1983) observed that young people migrating to Bangkok did so for economic purposes but also, and just as importantly, for the experience of modern, urban comforts and excitement; this, she argued, is a factor working against policy attempts to redirect migration toward less developed (and less glamourous) regional centers.

15. Prostitution is not new in Thailand. The country's present-day sex industry, however, is connected to the more respectable marketing of modern female beauty in many ways—not only by a shared imagery of the commodified female body. For instance, popular beauty contests are commonly believed to be arenas for recruiting high-class escort and call girl services. Indeed recent research indicates that some women in the sex industry enter and continue their work at least partly because of its particular opportunities for economic autonomy, including modern display and accumulation (e.g., Lyttleton 1994:267). Although the strength of such considerations for women in commercial sex work vary widely (Lyttleton 1994:272–276), the linkages between prostitution and notions of modern womanhood remain problematic for migrants in other occupations and within the wider society. For the industrial laborers with whom I have worked the stigma associated with prostitution still carries considerable force. No migrants I met who were not themselves sex workers viewed sex work as a desirable option. Awareness of AIDS remains relatively limited among most migrants; as public education campaigns increasingly identify the disease with prostitution, however, common assessments of the risks involved in sex work are not likely to decline. For analyses of the cultural contradictions that frame the experiences of some women sex workers in Thailand, see Lyttleton 1994 and Muecke 1992.

16. Urban employment and the separation from parental and community supervision that this entails suggest a degree of personal autonomy for young women that is potentially greater even than what they can hope to experience later in life as mothers, and without the burdens and sacrifices that motherhood entails. Although the relative status of women in Thai Buddhist culture has been the focus of some debate, few would deny that motherhood has historically been an important—if not the primary—basis for women's status and decision-making authority within rural households (see Keyes 1984; Kirsch 1985; Van Esterik 1982). Labor migration offers young unmarried women a degree of independence and physical mobility to which few can aspire should they remain in their parents' home. Muecke (1984) found similar patterns at work among Northern Thai women involved in construction labor; she argued that cash earnings were replacing maternity as their main source of social value.

17. It is important to note that workers' enjoyment of "up-to-date" styles and events associated with the workplace makes these potentially useful to management as strategies for structuring worker morale, an informal means of labor control. But these events can occasionally have rather different effects. The distribution of uniforms and hosting competitions and banquets may be represented by management as a gift or act of patronage toward employees, but the same acts can be perceived as rights or benefits owed and therefore become points for contestation. For example, in 1987 I met one young woman who had participated in a confrontation with her employer because she wanted the factory to institute a system of uniforms. In another example, one male worker was moved to consider union membership after he was reprimanded and fined for wearing a company soccer team shirt on the shop floor.

18. Bangkok minimum wage rose to 110 baht (U.S.$4.40) as of 1994; somewhat lower rates apply in some other regions of the country.

19. In some cases legal loopholes may support the payment of lower wages; in others, wage laws are simply ignored. The inequities of urban employment are exacerbated by the fact that many of the jobs women find in Bangkok, such as those available in small-scale sweatshop operations and domestic service, receive limited protection under Thai labor laws. Even so, industrial jobs are among the best paid employment available to rural women. Servants' wages are generally the lowest, even when free room and board are counted. A 1980 survey of northeastern women working in Bangkok found that domestic servants earned a mean monthly income, including payments in kind, of 800 baht or U.S.$32 while those with factory jobs averaged 1,200 baht (U.S.$48) per month (Pawadee 1982:103). While similar survey data on income in the late 1980s and early 1990s is unavailable, anecdotal reports by migrants indicate that domestic service remains very poorly paid. The greatest earning potential for migrants is often in the sex trade, although this

also depends upon highly variable working conditions, from relatively autonomous enterprise to virtual slave labor (see Truong 1990:185–188).

20. Many migrant women actively seek overtime. Given low base wages, overtime hours are often the only way to earn enough to cover their living expenses while also saving money to send home or purchase valued commodity items.

21. These conventional "child of the fields" *(luuk thung)* and ethnic Lao-Northeast Thai *(moh lam)* singing styles have become major genres of popular entertainment in Thailand's highly commercialized media industries.

22. In addition to occasional industrial homework of this sort, some migrant workers attempt to earn extra income through small-scale sales activities—for example, purchasing goods (e.g., jeans or tee-shirts) at Bangkok wholesale markets for resale to friends and coworkers or becoming agents for pyramid sales outfits (e.g., Avon, Amway), which are increasingly common in urban Thailand. Relatively few of the women I interviewed engaged in these practices, preferring whenever possible to work overtime at their regular factory job. Nevertheless, the fact that these retail enterprises are seen as viable options for some migrants indicates the extent to which ongoing, if small-scale, commodity purchases are an important part of the everyday setting for urban workers.

23. Food is a basic consumption need and not all meals involve peer-based sociality. The extent to which migrants engage in these meals—often featuring special regional cuisines, seasonal fruits, ready-made sweets and soft drinks consumed either in local food shops or purchased in the market and taken back to be served in workers' lodgings—is striking. They do so even when living in factory dormitories where all or part of their daily meals are provided by the employer. In part this may reflect on the quality of food provided and the often limited cafeteria hours, but group outings to markets and restaurants are also important and enjoyable social occasions.

24. Of course not all leisure time is spent on such outings. Many migrants spend much of their time off doing laundry and other chores and generally resting. Resting, however, often includes visiting with friends, chatting or watching television, and perhaps sharing a meal, activities that incorporate aspects of more elaborate consumption-oriented thiaws.

25. This finding parallels that of Anchalee Singhanetra-Renard (1981) with respect to out-migration from a northern Thai community. She observed that villagers did not measure the strength of continuing community membership by the distance or time period of a move but by the degree to which mobile individuals maintained their economic and social ties through visits, remittances, and ceremonial donations.

26. Their perceptions parallel Suzanne Thorbek's analysis of women's lives in a Bangkok slum. She points out that urban women's economic vulnerability is rooted in the transformation of the household division of labor by gender. While rural income and daily reproduction are generated in large part through cooperative household activities, urban income is earned outside the household through wage work. Men have greater access to such employment than do married women, especially when the latter cannot leave the home for long periods because of childcare responsibilities or for fear of theft (Thorbek 1987:61).

27. When I returned to Thailand for a brief visit in 1993, I found that Noi was married and pregnant with her first child. She was still living in Bangkok but was going to return to her home village "to become a *mae baan* [housewife]" a few weeks before her delivery. Her husband, however, was not the fiancé of three years earlier; Noi had successfully avoided that match by remaining in Bangkok without returning home for over a year, until the young man and his family gave up and withdrew their offer. Instead she had married another man from her village, a successful overseas contract laborer. They lived together for about a year and then he made plans to go on a new work contract to Taiwan. Noi confided that he was not her romantic ideal but that she liked him well enough. "And anyway," she said, "it's better to marry the one who loves you [rather than the one you love]." Moreover his own past travels made him sympathetic to Noi's urban experiences, while his absence abroad would now give her considerable day-to-day autonomy in his absence.

28. Interestingly, very few migrant women I met participated in "share games," a kind of informal credit circle. These are prevalent in many parts of urban Thailand and are an important mechanism for saving among industrial workers in other parts of the region (e.g., Wolf 1992:188–189). Several women mentioned fear of being cheated if the share game organizer could not keep control of the participants. Migrants were most likely to accumulate savings in the form of gold jewelry or bank accounts.

29. In fact, few of the migrants I knew made regular monthly remittances to village families. Those who did were usually working to support a child left at home in the care of grandparents.

30. Rural youths often look forward to Buddhist ceremonies and festivals, although, as for many migrants, this is frequently less from religious devotion than because these occasions have historically been opportunities for young people to mingle more or less freely and perhaps meet lovers or potential suitors.

references cited

Anchalee Singhanetra-Renard

1981 Mobility in North Thailand: A View from "Within." *In* Population Mobility and Development: Southeast Asia and the Pacific. Gavin W. Jones and Hazel V. Richter, eds. Pp. 137–166. Canberra: Australian National University.

Aphichat Chamratrithirong, Krittaya Archavanitkul, and Uraiwan Kanungsukkasem
1979 Recent Migrants in Bangkok Metropolis: A Follow-up Study of Migrants, Adjustment, Assimilation and Integration. Bangkok: Institute for Population and Social Research, Mahidol University.
Appadurai, Arjun
1990 Disjuncture and Difference in the Global Cultural Economy. Public Culture 2(2):1–24.
Bell, Peter F.
1992 Gender and Industrialization in Thailand. Paper presented at the 44th Annual Meeting of the Association of Asian Studies, Washington, DC. April 2–5.
Benería, Lourdes, and Shelley Feldman, eds.
1992 Unequal Burden: Economic Crisis, Persistent Poverty, and Women's Work. Boulder, CO: Westview Press.
Benería, Lourdes, and Martha Roldán
1987 The Crossroads of Class and Gender: Industrial Homework, Subcontracting, and Household Dynamics in Mexico City. Chicago: University of Chicago Press.
Enloe, Cynthia
1989 Bananas, Beaches and Bases: Making Feminist Sense of International Politics. Berkeley: University of California Press.
Fernandez-Kelly, Maria Patricia
1982 For We Are Sold, I and My People: Women and Industry in Mexico's Frontier. Albany: State University of New York Press.
Friends of Women
1988 *chotmaay khaaw phúan ying*. (Friends of Women Newsletter). Bangkok, Friends of Women Group. February.
Fuller, Theodore, Peerasit Kamnuansilpa, Paul Lightfoot, and Sawaeng Rathanamongkolmas
1983 Migration and Development in Modern Thailand. Bangkok: Social Science Association of Thailand.
Girling, John L. S.
1981 Thailand: Society and Politics. Ithaca, NY: Cornell University Press.
Goldstein, Sidney, and Alice Goldstein
1986 Migration in Thailand: A Twenty-Five Year Review. Honolulu: East-West Population Institute. Papers of the East-West Population Institute, 100.
Harvey, David
1989 The Condition of Postmodernity. Oxford: Blackwell.
Jacobs, Norman
1971 Modernization without Development: Thailand as an Asian Case Study. New York: Praeger.
Juree Vichit-Vadakan
1983 Small Towns and Regional Urban Centers: Reflections on Diverting Bangkok-Bound Migration. Thai Journal of Development Administration 23:79–99.
Kemper, Steven
1993 The Nation Consumed: Buying and Believing in Sri Lanka. Public Culture 5:377–393.
Keyes, Charles F.
1984 Mother or Mistress but Never a Monk: Buddhist Notions of Female Gender in Rural Thailand. American Ethnologist 11:223–241.
1989 Thailand: Buddhist Kingdom as Modern Nation-State. Boulder, CO: Westview Press.
Kirsch, A. Thomas
1966 Development and Mobility among the Phu Thai of Northeast Thailand. Asian Survey 6:370–378.
1982 Buddhism, Sex-Roles and the Thai Economy. *In* Women of Southeast Asia. Penny VanEsterik, ed. Pp. 16–41. DeKalb: Northern Illinois University, Center for Southeast Asian Studies.
1985 Text and Context: Buddhist Sex Roles/Culture of Gender Revisted. American Ethnologist 12:302–320.
Kung, Lydia
1983 Factory Women in Taiwan. Ann Arbor: University of Michigan Press.
Lamphere, Louise
1987 From Working Daughters to Working Mothers: Immigrant Women in a New England Industrial Community. Ithaca, NY: Cornell University Press.
Lefferts, H. Leedom
n.d. Women, Men and Merit: The Household in Rural Thai Buddhism. Unpublished paper. Department of Anthropology, Drew University, Madison NJ.
Lightfoot, Paul, Theodore Fuller, and Peerasit Kamnuansilpa
1983 Circulation and Interpersonal Networks Linking Rural and Urban Areas: The Case of Roi-et, Northeastern Thailand. Honolulu, HI: East-West Population Institute, East-West Center.
Lyttleton, Chris
1994 The Good People of Isan: Commercial Sex in Northeast Thailand. The Austrailian Journal of Anthropology 5:257–279.
Miller, Daniel
1995 Consumption Studies as the Transformation of Anthropology. *In* Acknowledging Consumption: A Review of New Studies. Daniel Miller, ed. Pp. 264–295. London and New York: Routledge.

Mills, Mary Beth (Elizabeth)
1993 "We Are Not Like Our Mothers": Migrants, Modernity, and Identity in Northeast Thailand. Ph.D. dissertation, University of California, Berkeley, University Microfilms.
1994 Nimble Fingers or Raised Fists?: Rural Thai Women in the Labor Movement. Paper presented to the 95th Annual Meeting of the American Anthropological Association, December, Atlanta, GA.
1995 Attack of the Widow Ghosts: Gender, Death, and Modernity in Northeast Thailand. *In* Bewitching Women, Pious Men: Gender and Body Politics in Southeast Asia. Aihwa Ong and Michael Peletz, eds. Pp. 244–273. Berkeley: University of California Press.
Moore, Henrietta L.
1994 A Passion for Difference: Essays in Anthropology and Gender. Bloomington and Indianapolis: Indiana University Press.
Muecke, Marjorie
1984 Make Money Not Babies: Changing Status Markers of Northern Thai Women. Asian Survey 24:459–470.
1992 Mother Sold Food, Daughter Sells Her Body: The Cultural Continuity of Prostitution. Social Science and Medicine 35:891–901.
Nash, June, and Maria Patricia Fernandez-Kelly, eds.
1983 Women, Men, and the International Division of Labor. Albany: State University of New York Press.
NSO (National Statistical Office)
1983 The Survey of Migration in Bangkok Metropolis, Nonthaburi, Pathum Thani and Sumut Prakan: 1983. Bangkok: National Statistical Office, Office of the Prime Minister.
1992 Report of the 1992 Migration Survey. Bangkok: National Statistical Office, Office of the Prime Minister.
O'Connor, Richard A.
1987 Mechanical and Organic Solidarity in Bangkok. Contributions to Southeast Asian Ethnography 6:13–26.
1995 Indigenous Urbanism: Class, City and Society in Southeast Asia. Journal of Southeast Asian Studies 26:30–45.
Ogle, George E.
1990 South Korea: Dissent within the Economic Miracle. London and Atlantic Highlands, NJ: Zed Books.
Ong, Aihwa
1987 Spirits of Resistance and Capitalist Discipline: Factory Women in Malaysia. Albany: State University of New York Press.
1991 The Gender and Labor Politics of Postmodernity. Annual Review of Anthropology 20:279–309.
Orlove, Benjamin S., and Henry J. Rutz
1989 Thinking about Consumption: A Social Economy Approach. *In* The Social Economy of Consumption. Monographs in Economic Anthropology, 6. Henry J. Rutz and Benjamin S. Orlove, eds. Pp. 1–57. Lanham, MD: Society for Economic Anthropology and University Press of America.
Ortner, Sherry B.
1995 Resistance and the Problem of Ethnographic Refusal. Comparative Studies in Society and History 37(1):173–193.
Parnwell, Mike
1986 Migration and the Development of Agriculture: A Case Study of Northeast Thailand. Hull, UK: University of Hull, Center for Southeast Asian Studies. Occasional Paper, 12.
Pawadee Tongudai
1982 Women, Migration and Employment: A Study of Migrant Workers in Bangkok. Ph.D. dissertation, New York University.
1984 Women Migrants in Bangkok: An Economic Analysis of Their Employment and Earnings. *In* Women in the Urban and Industrial Workforce: Southeast and East Asia. Gavin W. Jones, ed. Pp. 305–323. Canberra: Australian National University.
Porpora, Douglas, and Lim Mah Hui
1987 The Political Economic Factors of Migration to Bangkok. Journal of Contemporary Asia 17:76–89.
Pred, Allan, and Michael John Watts
1992 Reworking Modernity: Capitalisms and Symbolic Discontent. New Brunswick, NJ: Rutgers University Press.
Riggs, Fred
1966 Thailand: The Modernization of a Bureaucratic Polity. Honolulu, HI: East-West Center Press.
Roseberry, William
1989 Anthropologies and Histories: Essays in Culture, History, and Political Economy. New Brunswick, NJ and London: Rutgers University Press.
Roha, Kumudhini
1994 The Conditions and Organisational Activities of Women in Free Trade Zones: Malaysia, Philippines and Sri Lanka, 1970–1990. *In* Dignity and Daily Bread: New Forms of Economic Organising among Poor Women in the Third World and the First. Sheila Rowbotham and Swasti Mitter, eds. Pp. 73–99. New York and London: Routledge.

Rouse, Roger
1992 Making Sense of Settlement: Class Transformation, Cultural Struggle, and Transnationalism among Mexican Migrants in the United States. *In* Towards a Transnational Perspective on Migration: Race, Class, Ethnicity, and Nationalism Reconsidered. Nina Glick Schiller, Linda Basch, and Cristina Blanc-Szanton, eds. 645:25–52. New York: Annals of the New York Academy of Sciences.
Safa, Helen I.
1995 The Myth of the Male Breadwinner: Women and Industrialization in the Caribbean. Boulder, CO: Westview Press.
Tambiah, Stanley J.
1970 Buddhism and the Spirit Cults in North-East Thailand. Cambridge: Cambridge University Press.
Textor, Robert B.
1961 From Peasant to Pedicab Driver: A Social Study of Northeastern Thai Farmers Who Periodically Migrated to Bangkok and Became Pedicab Drivers. New Haven, CT: Yale University Southeast Asia Studies, Cultural Report No. 9.
Thongchai Winichakul
1994 Siam Mapped: A History of the Geo-Body of a Nation. Honolulu, HI: University of Hawaii Press.
Thorbek, Susanne
1987 Voices From the City: Women of Bangkok. London: Zed Press.
Tirado, Silvia
1994 Weaving Dreams, Constructing Realities: The Nineteenth of September National Union of Garment Workers in Mexico. *In* Dignity and Daily Bread: New Forms of Economic Organising among Poor Women in the Third World and the First. Sheila Rowbotham and Swasti Mitter, eds. Pp. 100–113. London and New York: Routledge.
Truong, Thanh-Dam
1990 Sex, Money and Morality: Prostitution and Tourism in Southeast Asia. London: Zed Books.
Van Esterik, Penny
1982 Laywomen in Theravada Buddhism. *In* Women of Southeast Asia. Penny Van Esterik, ed. Pp. 55–78. DeKalb: Center for Southeast Asian Studies, Northern Illinois University.
1988 Gender and Development in Thailand: Deconstructing Display. Toronto: York University, Department of Anthropology, Thai Studies Project.
Williams, Raymond
1977 Marxism and Literature. Oxford: Oxford University Press.
Wilson, Constance M.
1983 Thailand: A Handbook of Historical Statistics. Boston: G.K. Hall.
Wolf, Diane Lauren
1992 Factory Daughters: Gender, Household Dynamics, and Rural Industrialization in Java. Berkeley: University of California Press.

submitted February 16, 1995
revised version submitted October 25, 1995
accepted January 22, 1996

Name Index

The International Library of Critical Writings in Economics

1. Multinational Corporations
   Mark Casson

2. The Economics of Innovation
   Christopher Freeman

3. Entrepreneurship
   Mark Casson

4. International Investment
   Peter J. Buckley

5. Game Theory in Economics
   Ariel Rubinstein

6. The History of Economic Thought
   Mark Blaug

7. Monetary Theory
   Thomas Mayer

8. Joint Production of Commodities
   Neri Salvadori and Jan Steedman

9. Industrial Organization
   Oliver E. Williamson

10. Growth Theory (Volumes I, II and III)
    R.Becker and E. Burmeister

11. Microeconomics: Theoretical and Applied (Volumes I, II and III)
    Robert E. Kuenne

12. The Economics of Health (Volumes I and II)
    A.J. Culyer

13. Recent Developments in Macroeconomics (Volumes I, II and III)
    Edmund S. Phelps

14. Urban and Regional Economics
    Paul C. Cheshire and Alan W. Evans

15. Modern Public Finance (Volumes I and II)
    A.B. Atkinson

16. Exchange Rate Economics (Volumes I and II)
    Ronald MacDonald and Mark P. Taylor

17. The Economic Value of Education: Studies in the Economics of Education
Mark Blaug

18. Development Economics (Volumes I, II, III and IV)
Deepak Lal

19. The New Classical Macroeconomics (Volumes I, II and Ill)
Kevin D. Hoover

20. The Economics of the Environment
Wallace E. Oates

21. Post Keynesian Theory of Growth and Distribution
Carlo Panico and Neri Salvadori

22. Dynamic Labor Demand and Adjustment Costs
Giorgio Galeazzi and Daniel S. Hamermesh

23. The Philosophy and Methodology of Economics (Volumes I, II and III)
Bruce J. Caldwell

24. Public Choice Theory (Volumes I, II and III)
Charles K. Rowley

25. Evolutionary Economics
Ulrich Witt

26. Economics and Psychology
Shlomo Maital and Sharone L. Maital

27. Social Choice Theory (Volumes I, II and Ill)
Charles K. Rowley

28. Non-Linear Dynamics in Economic Theory
Marc Jarsulic

29. Recent Developments in Experimental Economics (Volumes I and II)
John D. Hey and Graham Loomes

30. Monopoly and Competition Policy (Volumes I and II)
F.M. Scherer

31. The Economics of Technical Change
Edwin Mansfield and Elizabeth Mansfield

32. The Economics of Exhaustible Resources
Geoffrey Heal

33. The Economics of Institutions
Geoffrey M. Hodgson

34. The Economics of Transport (Volumes I and II)
Herbert Mohring

35. Implicit Contract Theory
Sherwin Rosen

36. Foundations of Analytical Marxism (Volumes I and II)
John E. Roemer

37. The Economics of Product Differentiation (Volumes I and II)
Jacques-François Thisse and George Norman

38. Economic Growth in Theory and Practice: A Kaldorian Perspective
John E. King

39. Markets and Socialism
Alec Nove and Ian D. Thatcher

40. Recent Developments in the Economics of Education
Elchanan Cohn and Geraint Johnes

41. The Theory of Inflation
Michael Parkin

42. The Economics of Location (Volumes I, II and III)
Melvin L. Greenhut and George Norman

43. Financial Intermediaries
Mervyn K. Lewis

44. The Political Economy of Privatization and Deregulation
Elizabeth E. Bailey and Janet Rothenberg Pack

45. Gender and Economics
Jane Humphries

46. Macroeconomics and Imperfect Competition
Jean-Pascal Bénassy

47. Labor Economics (Volumes I, II, III and IV)
Orley C. Ashenfelter and Kevin F. Hallock

48. The Economics of Altruism
Stefano Zamagni

49. The Economic Analysis of Rent Seeking
Robert D. Tollison and Roger D. Congleton

50. Economics and Biology
Geoffrey M. Hodgson

51. The Economics of Ageing
John Creedy

52. Fiscal and Monetary Policy (Volumes I and II)
Thomas Mayer and Steven M. Sheffrin

53. The Economics of Information (Volumes I and II)
David K. Levine and Steven A. Lippman

54. Transaction Cost Economics (Volumes I and II)
Oliver E. Williamson and Scott E. Masten

55. Agricultural Economics
George H. Peters

56. International Debt (Volumes I and II)
Graham Bird and P. Nicholas Snowden

57. Economics and Discrimination (Volumes I and II)
William A. Darity, Jr

58. Business Cycle Theory
Finn E. Kydland

59. International Trade (Volumes I and II)
J. Peter Neary

60. The Money Supply in the Economic Process
Marco Musella and Carlo Panico

61. Small Firms and Economic Growth (Volumes I and II)
Zoltan J. Acs

62. Producer Cooperatives and Labor-Managed Systems (Volumes I and II)
David L. Prychitko and Jaroslav Vanek

63. Ethics and Economics (Volumes I and II)
Alan P. Hamlin

64. The Economics of the Family
Nancy Folbre

65. The Economics of Training (Volumes I and II)
Orley C. Ashenfelter and Robert J. LaLonde

66. Chaos Theory in Economics: Methods, Models and Evidence
W. Davis Dechert

67. General Equilibrium Theory (Volumes I, II and III)
Gérard Debreu

68. Economic Growth: Theory and Evidence (Volumes I and II)
Gene M. Grossman

69. Long Wave Theory
Christopher Freeman

70. The Economics of Communication and Information
Donald M. Lamberton

71. The Foundations of Public Finance (Volumes I and II)
Peter Jackson

72. The Theory of the Firm
Mark Casson

73. The Economics of Uncertainty (Volumes I and II)
John D. Hey

74. The Economics of Global Warming
Tom Tietenberg

75. The Development of Ecological Economics
Robert Costanza, Charles Perrings and Cutler Cleveland

76. Economic Growth in the Long Run: A History of Empirical Evidence (Volumes I, II and III)
Bart van Ark

77. The Economics of Productivity (Volumes I and II)
Edward N. Wolff

78. The Economics of Population: Key Modern Writings (Volumes I and II)
Julian L. Simon

79. Political Business Cycles
Bruno S. Frey

80. Cultural Economics: The Arts, the Heritage and the Media Industries (Volumes I and II)
Ruth Towse

81. Law and Economics (Volumes I, II and III)
Richard A. Posner and Francesco Parisi

82. Independent Central Banks and Economic Performance
Sylvester Eijffinger

83. Culture, Social Norms and Economics (Volumes I and II)
Mark Casson

84. Industrial Policy and Competitive Advantage (Volumes I, II and III)
David B. Audretsch

85. The Economics of Housing (Volumes I and II)
John M. Quigley

86. Economic Demography (Volumes I and II)
T. Paul Schultz

87. Trade and the Environment: Economic, Legal and Policy Perspectives
Alan M. Rugman and John J. Kirton with Julie A. Soloway

88. The Economics of Fiscal Federalism and Local Finance
Wallace E. Oates

89. Price Theory and its Applications
Bernard Saffran and F.M. Scherer

90. Women in the Labor Market (Volumes I and II)
Marianne A. Ferber

91. Market Process Theories (Volumes I and II)
Peter Boettke and David Prychitko

92. Input–Output Analysis (Volumes I, II and III)
Heinz Kurz, Erik Dietzenbacher and Christian Lager

93. Mathematical Economics (Volumes I, II and III)
Graciela Chichilnisky

94. The Foundations of Regulatory Economics (Volumes I, II and III)
Robert B. Ekelund, Jr.

95. The Economics of Marketing
Martin Carter, Mark Casson and Vivek Suneja

96. Service Industries in the Global Economy (Volumes I and II)
J.R. Bryson and P.W. Daniels

97. Economic Justice (Volumes I and II)
Giorgio Brosio and Harold M. Hochman

98. Foreign Exchange Intervention: Objectives and Effectiveness
Sylvester C.W. Eijffinger

99. Economic Anthropology
Stephen Gudeman

100. Consumer Theory
Kelvin Lancaster

101. The Economics of Famine
Jean Drèze

102. Microeconomic Theories of Imperfect Competition
Jean J. Gabszewicz and Jacques-François Thisse

103. The Economics of Executive Compensation (Volumes I and II)
Kevin F. Hallock and Kevin J. Murphy

104. The Foundations of Long Wave Theory
Francisco Louçã and Jan Reijnders

Future titles will include:

Recent Developments in Game Theory
Eric S. Maskin

The Economics of Unemployment
P.N. Junankar

The Economics of Energy
Paul Stevens

The Economics of Science and Innovation
Paula E. Stephan and David B. Audretsch

International Finance
Robert Z. Aliber

Welfare Economics
William J. Baumol and Janusz A. Ordover

The Economics of Crime
Isaac Ehrlich

The Economics of Integration
Willem Molle

The Rhetoric of Economics
Deirdre McCloskey

The Economics of Defence
Keith Hartley and Nicholas Hooper

The Economics of Business Policy
John Kay

The Economics of Increasing Returns
Geoffrey Heal

The Balance of Payments
Michael J. Artis

Cost-Benefit Analysis
Arnold Harberger and Glenn P. Jenkins

Privatization in Developing and Transitional Economies
Colin Kirkpatrick and Paul Cook

The Economics of Intellectual Property
Ruth Towse

The Economics of Tourism
Clem Tisdell

The Economics of Organization and Bureaucracy
Peter Jackson

The Economics of Commodity Markets
David Greenaway and Wyn Morgan

Realism and Economics: Studies in Ontology
Tony Lawson

The Economics of the Welfare State
Nicholas Barr

Path Dependence
Paul David

Alternative Theories of the Firm
Richard Langlois, Paul Robertson and Tony F. Yu

The Economics of the Mass Media
Glenn Withers

The Economics of Budget Deficits
Charles Rowley

Economic Forecasting
Terence C. Mills

The Economic Theory of Auctions
Paul Klemperer

Corporate Governance
Kevin Keasey, Steve Thompson and Mike Wright

Welfare Measurement
John Creedy

The Economics of Regional Policy
Harvey W. Armstrong and Jim Taylor

Forms of Capitalism: Comparative Institutional Analyses
Ugo Pagano and Ernesto Screpanti